Investment in Women's Human Capital

Investment in Women's Human Capital

Edited by T. Paul Schultz

The University of Chicago Press
Chicago and London

T. Paul Schultz is the Malcolm K. Brachman Professor of Economics and Demography and director of the Economic Growth Center at Yale University.

The University of Chicago Press, Chicago 60637
The University of Chicago Press, Ltd., London

© 1995 by The University of Chicago
All rights reserved. Published 1995
Printed in the United States of America

04 03 02 01 00 99 98 97 96 95   5 4 3 2 1

ISBN (cloth): 0-226-74087-0
ISBN (paper): 0-226-74088-9

Chapters 1, 5, 6, 7, 9, 10, 11 are copyright © 1993 by the Board of Regents of the University of Wisconsin System, and are reprinted with permission from *The Journal of Human Resources* 28, no. 4 (Fall 1993).

Library of Congress Cataloging–in–Publication Data

Investment in women's human capital / edited by T. Paul Schultz.
    p.   cm.
    Includes bibliographical references and index.
    ISBN 0-226-74087-0. — ISBN 0-226-74088-9 (pbk.)
    1. Human capital—Developing countries. 2. Sex discrimination in education—Developing countries. 3. Women—Employment—Developing countries. 4. Sex discrimination in employment—Developing countries. I. Schultz, T. Paul.
HD4904.7.I58   1995
331.4—dc20   94-40577
                                                                                                          CIP

⊗ The paper used in this publication meets the minimum requirements of the American National Standard for Information Sciences—Permanence of Paper for Printed Library Materials, ANSI Z39.48-1984.

Contents

Introduction
T. Paul Schultz   1

I. Overview and Experience of High-Income Countries

1. Investments in the Schooling and Health of
   Women and Men: Quantities and Returns
   T. Paul Schultz   15

2. Obstacles to Advancement of
   Women during Development
   Ester Boserup   51

3. The U-Shaped Female Labor Force
   Function in Economic Development
   and Economic History
   Claudia Goldin   61

4. Public Policies and Women's Labor
   Force Participation: A Comparison of
   Sweden, West Germany and the Netherlands
   Siv Gustafsson   91

II. Labor Markets, Uncertainty, and Family Behavior

5. Women, Insurance Capital, and Economic
   Development in Rural India
   Mark R. Rosenzweig   115

6. Information, Learning, and Wage Rates in
   Low-Income Rural Areas
   Andrew D. Foster and Mark R. Rosenzweig   138

III. Health

7. Gender and Life-Cycle Differentials in the
    Patterns and Determinants of Adult Health
    *John Strauss, Paul J. Gertler, Omar Rahman,
    and Kristin Fox*   171

8. Quality of Medical Care and Choice
    of Medical Treatment in Kenya:
    An Empirical Analysis
    *Germano Mwabu, Martha Ainsworth, and
    Andrew Nyamete*   214

IV. Education

9. Daughters, Education, and Family
    Budgets: Taiwan Experiences
    William L. Parish and Robert J. Willis   239

10. Gender Differences in the Returns to
    Schooling and in School Enrollment
    Rates in Indonesia
    Anil B. Deolalikar   273

11. Educational Investments and Returns for
    Women and Men in Côte d'Ivoire
    Wim P. M. Vijverberg   304

V. Household Structure and Labor
    Markets in Brazil

12. Poverty among Female-Headed
    Households in Brazil
    *Ricardo Barros, Louise Fox,
    and Rosane Mendonça*   345

13. Gender Differences in Brazilian Labor Markets
    *Ricardo Barros, Lauro Ramos,
    and Eleonora Santos*   380

    References   425

    Index   451

Introduction

T. Paul Schultz

Many recent studies of education, nutrition, health, labor mobility, and training have sought to measure the contribution of these forms of human capital to the productivity of workers and to modern economic growth. The base of knowledge in this field is qualified, because returns to investments in human capital are only realized over a generation, while few social experiments are designed to assess without bias how policy interventions work through the actions of the family and individuals. Nonetheless, microeconomists and other social and biological scientists have examined the economic and physical functioning of individual workers with different characteristics, while macroeconomists have analyzed aggregate output, measured inputs, and the economic growth experience of nation states. A consensus has been forged that periods of sustained growth in total factor productivity are critically dependent on improvements in a population's nutrition, health, education, and mobility.

How are these human capital investments allocated between women and men in families and in societies? Numerous books have been written on the status of women, without agreement on how status should be measured. Gender inequalities in wages, education, nutrition, and health are widely deplored, but they are less often empirically analyzed to understand what institutions and conditions create and change them, and what they imply for how well a society uses its productive resources. Analyses of sex differences in human capital have not been common, despite the growing importance of human capital investments and the concreteness of these indicators of individual well-being and economic and social status.

The objective of this book is to collect empirical analyses of who receives human capital—nutrition, health care, education, mobility, training—and what explains this allocation of intergenerational investment between males and females. The primary, but not exclusive, concern is with low-income countries where these gender inequalities tend to be relatively larger. Are the magnitudes of these investments broadly congruent with labor market private returns on these investments? If we found this congruence, would it suggest that these investments are efficiently governed by market signals? How can analyses deal with the many confounding factors that cloud the simple evidence but provide a more realistic set of institutional assumptions, rigidities, heterogeneity in preferences, interpersonal conflicts of interest, and externalities? How does the family deal with risk-pooling strategies in the nuclear unit and in the extended and intergenerational units, and how does that affect women as a vehicle for family human capital?

1

What imperfections or asymmetries in information affect the achievement of efficient investments in human capital? A major transition for the economy with implications for the sexual division of labor is the shift of work from the family to firms and thus to wage labor markets. As wage labor—in casual day markets and under longer-term employment contracts—replaces family- and self-employment, how are the returns to human capital affected for men and women? If it is sometimes difficult for social scientists to identify the connection between childhood investments and adult productivity, or to interpret the correlation between a mother's education and the likelihood of her children's survival, could these linkages themselves be changing with economic development and with the arrival of new technologies in the world? Is family financing of these various types of human capital investment forward-looking and well informed, or is it based on out-of-date experiences? The agenda of research to answer such questions is extensive, and research priorities are in a state of flux. While the conceptual framework for studying human capital is well established, its empirical implementation beyond education and training to health, nutrition, mobility, and birth control remains at an explorative stage.

Three decades ago, new economic models of family behavior brought coherence and gave direction to a generation of research on the formation of human capital and its effect on household consumption and production (T. W. Schultz 1961, 1974; Mincer 1963; Becker 1964, 1965, 1981). But these unified models of the family did not prescribe how intrahousehold distribution issues would be resolved. Nor was there clear agreement on how the composition of family consumption affected the well-being of various family members. Perhaps this inability to bring quantitative tools to bear on intrahousehold allocation explains why economists have not until recently contributed more to the study of gender inequalities in the family. These questions may be more fruitfully explored using a bargaining model of family behavior that recognizes the possibility of conflicting interests of family members and the incomplete pooling of individual resources within the family (McElroy and Horney 1981; Schultz 1990b; Thomas 1990).

Because human capital is both a significant and growing share of the wealth of nations and a personal asset that should enhance individual control over consumption, it appears a useful indicator of intrahousehold resource allocation. These productive stocks of nutritional status, health, schooling, training, and mobility are good predictors of an individual's lifetime economic productivity and purchasing power. As disparities in personal lifetime consumption opportunities across families diminished in more advanced economies in the first half of this century, inequalities in consumption opportunities within the family have become more salient, even though they too may have diminished. Are these gender gaps due to the different specialized activities performed by men and women in the family and in society? Despite the possibility that biology may be one factor affecting how these intergroup investment differences arise and are maintained, men's and women's human capital appears to bring us closer to this dimension of socioeconomic egalitarianism than do alternative available measures of consumption, family composition (e.g., female-headed households), participation in the labor force, civil and marital rights, and treatment by the state through taxes and transfers.

Several quantitative measures of human capital have become widely accepted, although many additional ones are debated (cf. Strauss et al. and Barros, Fox, and Mendonça in this book). Nutritional status is represented by anthropometric indicators correlated with mortality and morbidity that have the advantage of being continuous and do not ask respondents to subjectively categorize their health status. They are undoubtedly noisy measures of the outcome of the human capital investment process we seek to understand, and consequently they may require special statistical precautions and techniques. *Height* as an adult is thought to be largely formed by early childhood and hence represents a summary measure of stunting, or the balance between childhood nutritional intakes, including those experienced in the uterus, and the burden that disease and physical activity impose on nutritional intakes before they can contribute to body growth and physical development (Falkner and Tanner 1986; Fogel 1993). A second indicator of nutritional status describes more nearly the current balance of food intake and activity and infection demands, given stature or height. A common indicator for this current nutritional status of the adult is the *body-mass-index* (i.e., weight divided by height squared) (Fogel 1991). Education has traditionally been measured within and across societies by *years of schooling completed,* but may be refined to reflect days enrolled per year attended, repetition rates, and where possible the resource intensity of schools. Although migration has been studied by demographers and economists for many years, it is perhaps the least adequately measured indicator of investment for male-female comparisons because the family generally shares a residence and hence moves together, although these moves do not necessarily enhance equally the productive opportunities of men and women in the family (Mincer 1978).

The papers collected here are an unrepresentative sampling of a large and diverse literature on women, human resources, and development. There are conflicting paradigms guiding various groups of scholars concerned with the basic gender issues that motivate many of the studies. One tradition explores how social institutions and culture prevent women from accomplishing as much as men, in part by denying women the same access as men to acquisition of human capital and undervaluing their contribution to welfare because the family and the labor market are often male dominated. Scholars from this tradition are understandably worried that if gender issues are approached within the neoclassical paradigm that views the unified family as behaving economically efficiently, subject to its constrained endowments and market opportunities, important institutional and cultural aspects of these problems will be overlooked or misinterpreted. The second tradition is that of empirical microeconomics that analyzes statistically gender differentials in human capital in order to understand their origins and consequences. Quantification of such regularities in behavior and outcomes may discriminate between alternative models of family decision rules and thereby help societies to increase the Pareto efficiency of resource allocations and to evaluate means available to redistribute resources among members of the family. Although the institutional and cultural constraints emerge most clearly in the papers by Boserup, Goldin, and Gustafsson, the distinctive feature of this collection is that most authors share some elements of the neoclassical paradigm, and do not expect it to conceal what the data have to tell us about empirical regularities. Differential treatment of women and men may occur in the labor market given their innate endowments and acquired human capital, but differential treatment may also occur at an earlier stage in the family, in terms of acquiring human capital.

Even at this basic level of using the human capital and labor economics framework to decompose the differences in productive capacity between men and women, it is possible that different productive traits are valued differently in different sectors of the economy, and heterogeneous individuals choose their sector to fetch the highest wage for their traits (Heckman and Sedlacek 1985). In this scheme there is no single measure of the productivity of a worker's trait in the economy, as typically assumed for convenience in the neoclassical labor market framework. The problem of valuing the traits of women workers engaged in home production may be distorted, therefore, if we rely on their wage opportunities in the labor market. But this approach of the Roy model has not been used often because of its identification and data requirements.

There are major limitations to our conceptual frameworks and quantitative techniques for understanding social and family allocation rules. Nonetheless, these tools have the promise of being helpful in examining data that contain both the human capital outcomes and the conditions that give rise to these outcomes in different cultures and institutional settings. Most of the studies collected here are empirical and statistical, not dogmatic or rhetorical. The contribution of this volume is to suggest the need for concerted analysis with a common conceptual framework. These new directions may reinvigorate the old field of gender studies.

Originally these papers were discussed at a meeting at the Rockefeller Foundation's Bellagio Conference Center in Italy in May 1992. The Rockefeller Foundation not only provided this splendid setting for the conference, they also supported the conference and the preparation of this book through their grant to the Economic Growth Center of Yale University for training and research on the family in low-income countries. It is a pleasure to acknowledge debts both to the Foundation and to the guidance of Joyce Lewinger Moock who has added much to the planning and implementation of the conference. In addition to the authors of the papers included here, who responded solicitously to rounds of comments and discussions, I wish to thank the other participants: Bina Agarwal, Angus Deaton, Katherine Namuddu, Diana Sawyer, Burt Singer, Jim Smith, Barbara Torrey, and Duncan Thomas, who brought diverse viewpoints and different perspectives to the conference discussions. Mark Rosenzweig and John Strauss helped me with editorial guidance, and M. Ann Judd assisted in copyediting the manuscript. Charles Manski, editor of the *Journal of Human Resources,* encouraged me to include a few of these papers in a symposium issue of that journal, despite the international perspective of the conference, and the journal's managing editor, Jan Levine Thal, gave me much valued advice. Most important to the progress of this project has been the nurturing family investment of my wife, Judy.

The first paper is an introduction to the topic of the book; it outlines the empirical regularities of increasing schooling and decreasing mortality of women compared to men. Where these developments are more advanced, economic growth in this century has been more rapid. On the surface, these trends suggest a relative redistribution of investments from males to females. Family resources are being allocated to forms of consumption—nutrition, health, and education—that are thought of here as human capital because they augment the productivity of adult labor and raise future earnings. The share of national income attributed to labor is simultaneously increasing. Thus, the redistribution of family resources is not necessarily leaving men less productive, but it is eroding the relative advantage men hold over women and hence reducing a longstanding source of personal inequality in the world.

A redistribution of wealth of this scale does not occur without many institutional changes, political frictions, lobbying, and renegotiations of vested interests, both within the family and in other social institutions, such as government bureaucracies. Even in the United States (Goldin 1990) and other high-income countries (Mincer 1985), the complexity of the process is not yet comprehensively understood. Ester Boserup (1970) set forth a variety of frameworks within which the status of women was explicitly linked to our study of developments occurring in low-income countries. As women have reallocated their time between home and labor force, between children and market careers, adaptation has taken many forms, differing across cultures. Societies in South and West Asia and North Africa are not investing in women to the same degree as those in Latin America and Southeast and East Asia, but change is cumulating. Sub-Saharan Africa encompasses especially diverse patterns of sex differences in educational attainment. Starting from very low levels of income, high child mortality, and high fertility, there is evidence that African women are slowly increasing their share of education in the current generation. This trend has not been reversed, to my knowledge, despite this continent's recent decades of intermittent recessions and government retrenchments.

Ester Boserup is generally credited with starting the field of Women and Development with her comprehensive and provocative book *Women's Role in Economic Development* (1970). Her essay here examines some of the limitations of industrialization and development for the advancement of women. She is skilled in pointing out the gaps in our knowledge, where commonly accepted generalizations fail to fit the facts, where institutions and culture resist as well as facilitate the changes that help women share more equally in the productive gains of development. The same institution that provides women with some degree of autonomy and opportunity to acquire skills and govern the transmission of those skills to girls can also slow the progress of women as the economic and technological environment changes. Family enterprises are initially a productive outlet for a woman's energy as well as a power base. These enterprises can also later become a deterrent to her advancement by placing her outside the modernizing sectors of the economy where her labor productivity increases only slowly and her output must compete with decreasing-cost, manufactured substitutes. Industrialization gradually eliminates family enterprise from many sectors and replaces family training with school systems that distance women from critical investments in human capital skills.

Boserup cogently argues that social institutions that encourage age and sex segregation in work have wide ramifications for women's economic opportunities, whether or not this process is described as discriminatory against females. The consequences of economic development on the family and women's roles in society, we are reminded by Boserup, are much broader than most of our economic models would suggest, and these issues therefore continue to benefit from multi-disciplinary research.

The history of women's advance in obtaining education and vocational skills and employing these productive talents in the home and labor force starts with the experience of the countries that have industrialized first, in Western Europe, areas of European settlement, and Japan. Claudia Goldin's study, *Understanding the Gender Gap* (1990), is already the classic study of that history of American women. Her essay for this volume builds on her knowledge of the U.S. historical materials and relates to international differences across countries. Comparing the rate of labor force participation by women across countries today, ordered by the country's level of GDP per capita, Goldin documents the U-shaped curve others have noted but not explained, where female participation initially falls at early stages in development and then rises as development exceeds some threshold. Goldin develops several hypotheses for this puzzling reversal in the direction of this basic relationship as development proceeds (Durand 1975). Why should the income effect predominate over the own-wage-substitution effect withdrawing women from the labor force at early stages in development, whereas the own-wage-substitution effect predominates over the income effect in industrially advanced countries thus increasing the fraction of women engaged in labor force activity (Mincer 1985)?

There is further evidence in support of Goldin's puzzle from studies within developing countries. The relative size of the own-wage-substitution effect and the (absolute value of) husband-income effect changes across more and less developed sectors of low-income countries. In Colombia, for example, the positive own-wage-substitution elasticity is absolutely larger than the negative husband-wage elasticity in the urban half of the population in 1973, whereas the reverse is true in the rural half of the population (Schultz 1981, table 7.7). It is the changing balance of own-wage and husband-wage elasticities that accounts for the gradual decline in the initially low rates of women's participation in rural areas of Colombia from 1951 to 1974, while urban rates begin to rise, particularly among the young, better-educated women. After 1974 the growing urban share of the population in Colombia contributes to the rapid increase in countrywide rates of female labor force participation

Is this dichotomy between the rural and urban populations due to the absence of nonmanual work available to women in rural Colombia and the stigma thus associated with wives accepting manual work outside of the home, versus the greater availability of nonmanual work for women in urban Colombia, in activities such as domestic service and clerical jobs? Or is this changing relative magnitude of own-wage and husband-wage effects simply a function of the higher wage levels in urban than in rural areas? Or are these sectoral differences in female labor supply parameters a reflection of a cultural gap in which rural families are more traditional and patriarchal, and urban families are less so? Does economic theory of labor supply require that the underlying income and substitution parameters be constant across income levels or should future studies explicitly allow for their variability? Goldin's portrayal of the stigma husbands feel when their wives engage in manual work outside of the home provides a vivid explanation for these empirical regularities. To discriminate among these several hypotheses will require unusual data and flexible econometric specifications of women's labor supply behavior. Women in a low-wage, traditional setting must be confronted by nonmanual job opportunities outside their home. How female labor force participation responds, in particular for married versus single women, in such a setting might help to test the competing hypotheses developed in Goldin's study.

The state can influence the achievements of women in education and in labor market productivity by its design of the personal income tax system and by how the costs of children are publicly subsidized. Siv Gustafsson contrasts the experience of three European societies in these areas of public finance: Sweden, (West) Germany, and the Netherlands. The tax system, by progressively taxing the individual regardless of marital status, can be a powerful factor encouraging women to participate in the labor force. In addition, public child care systems and parental leave benefits can sharply reduce the cost of childbearing while ameliorating the traditional conflicts for women between family and career.

Gustafsson first reports how the simple Mincerian (1985) model of female labor supply accounts for a substantial share of the cross-sectional, individual variation in these three European countries. But she expresses her doubts that the same model has the capacity to explain why these countries differ. The tax treatment of married women helps to explain the greater participation of Swedish women than German women but does not account for the low level of participation in the Netherlands. Subsidized child care may also partly explain the higher Swedish levels of female participation, for these institutions are much less widespread in the other countries. Nonetheless, she notes that even if state policies can account for country-level differences in women's participation in the labor force, the deeper question remains why barriers to women's participation were retained in some countries in the form of marriage bars and tax and transfer policies, whereas they were eliminated much earlier in others. In sum, she restates a general limitation of social science research evaluating public policies. When public policy varies across populations allowing the researcher to relate the policy to behavioral outcomes, how can one know if the policy can be treated as an exogenous explanatory variable in our models, or if it represents a latent variable for differences in national preferences or revealed demands.

Intrahousehold financial transfers have been confirmed by a variety of studies to be important means for consumption-smoothing in poor, traditional, agricultural societies, such as in India. Mark Rosenzweig's contribution extends this research to include marriages of sons and daughters and their migration as they affect intrahousehold transfers and loans that occur in response to income variation. Technological change, by undermining the capacity of the family to assess risk and monitor behavior, weakens the advantages of such traditional marriage-based risk pooling. Although technological change does not affect the traditionally low preference of Indian couples for daughters compared with sons, both household wealth and the education of mothers relative to fathers (heads) appear to increase preferences for daughters relative to sons in Rosenzweig's sample.

The study by Andrew Foster and Mark Rosenzweig addresses the perennial problem of how to interpret group differences in wage rates that cannot be explained by observable skills (for example, human capital) or job characteristics (for example, amenities). Are unexplained gender gaps in wages, education, or nutrition due to discrimination, allocative inefficiency, or unobserved abilities? Agricultural wage rates are paid to some workers by time worked and to others by piece rate or a share of physical output. Information on both forms of payment for the same workers engaged in similar activities allows the authors to model, with measurement error, how much of the gap in hourly time wages between men and women is due to statistical (group) discrimination, and how much is due to endowment differences in observables, and to unobservables or individual heterogeneity. They then explore, with data from India and the Philippines, the conditions of male and female workers, such as tenure in the labor market, that might explain why women are disadvantaged relative to men. They present evidence that employers may be more uncertain about the productivity of workers who have less tenure in the local labor market. The resulting statistical discrimination against women could help to explain why women acquire less human capital than do men. The informational inefficiency of traditional casual labor markets in low-income countries could, according to their interpretation of the evidence, lower the private returns to some forms of difficult-to-observe human capital of women relative to men.

There has been relatively little research on the morbidity of adult men and women in low-income countries. This is in part because there is no consensus on how to measure adult health, how to represent the cumulative process producing that health, or how to assess its economic and psychological consequences. Childhood and adult investments in health-related inputs combine over time with work activities, and possibly reproduction, to shape differences in the health of men and women. Many possible explanations for sex differentials, including biology, can be hypothesized. With few even stylized facts, it is difficult to begin to discriminate among plausible hypotheses, or to develop a satisfactory theoretical framework for more sharply focused analyses of gender differences in adult health.

As the epidemiological transition progresses in the world and infectious and parasitic diseases are controlled that contribute to most child mortality, low-income countries need to formulate their priorities to improve adult health. Without reliable registration of deaths or survey methods to assess the low incidence of adult mortality, the challenge is to develop gender- and age-neutral indicators of adult health and then begin to explore their relationship to adult productivity and well-being in the low-income world.

The essay by John Strauss, Paul Gertler, Omar Rahman, and Kristin Fox compares indicators of adult health of men and women in four countries: Malaysia, Jamaica, Bangladesh, and the United States. The authors present evidence that activity limitations increase with age and tend to occur more frequently for women than for men. They also observe that the health advantage enjoyed by more educated women and men diminishes among the elderly. The sex differences, however, do not decline with age and may, in fact, widen. If these self-reported health indicators can be reliably measured and then related to significant welfare consequences, these questions on activity limitations should soon be routinely incorporated into household surveys in low-income countries. The biological or behavioral causes for the gender gap in adult health that this study reports remain a challenge for researchers to elucidate and to relate to the higher male than female mortality rates observed in the same populations.

One of Boserup's (1970) insights was that government programs often provide males with greater access to public services than females, and thereby reduce the earnings opportunities of women compared with men in developing countries. The example she discussed was agricultural extension services that were staffed largely by men and were oriented toward serving male farmers, often in their development of cash crops where labor productivity was greatest. This occurred, she observed, even in countries where the majority of workers in agriculture were women, such as in sub-Saharan Africa. This distorted pattern of providing public services is often cited in the women and development literature today. But it is hard to find carefully constructed empirical evidence for such a gender bias in access to public services, although it could be widespread and might explain in part why the investment in women's human capital lags so far behind men's. Consequently, the next study explores the demand for public and private health care to suggest how representative survey data might be used to measure whether men and women do indeed have differential access to public sector services, holding constant for the characteristics of the individual and the public service. I would hope to see in the future similarly structured studies measure the gender bias in use of agricultural extension services, subsidized credit, schooling and adult literacy services, and a wide variety of health care services. Analyses of the demand for public services may be particularly valuable in South and West Asia and North Africa where women appear to be at a particular disadvantage in the marketplace for public goods and services.

Much research on health in low-income countries has been directed to understanding the determinants of health care utilization. This follows from the need of administrators to know who has access to health care. More specifically, will charging user fees for public health services depress the demand for these forms of health care, perhaps disproportionately among the poor, and thereby worsen a population's health? The offsetting attraction of user fees is that they would relax the severe financial constraint on the public sector and allow it to provide higher quality services, as, for example, by increasing clinic inventories of essential drugs. A puzzling finding from this literature is that prices have small effects on consumer demand, once people are ill. It is speculated that this finding is due to inadequate controls for the quality of medical care that are expected to be positively correlated with price.

The paper by Germano Mwabu, Martha Ainsworth, and Andrew Nyamete applies the multinomial logit framework to analyze health care choices made in rural Kenya. They improve on existing studies by including better measures of the quality of care provided by government, private, and missionary clinics. They show evidence that higher prices shift consumers among providers, as well as increase the number who rely on self-treatment or traditional healers. They also distinguish carefully how the demand for medical care of men and women differ and find evidence that women are more responsive to time and monetary costs of medical care than are men, but use it more frequently.

Three papers then address different issues related to how schooling investment decisions for males and females are determined in three countries: Taiwan, Indonesia, and Côte d'Ivoire. William Parish and Robert Willis analyze the educational outcomes for sons and daughters of Taiwanese families. They want to understand how birth order and sex affect educational attainment of siblings, and how the timing of the marriage process may affect the educational opportunities of children, presumably daughters. They describe three models to guide their examination of the data; these models emphasize patriarchal order, conditional altruism, and current credit constraints. Children of either sex benefit from being born at a later calendar time or later birth order. The marriage of an older sister benefits the remaining family, whereas the employment of an older sister less clearly benefits the family, probably because she retains part of her earnings. But the converse implication of the patriarchal model is not confirmed, for the income and educational prospects of daughters are not hurt by brothers. Secular growth of personal income in Taiwan has been rapid, and this fact alone implies educational advantages for those born later within a family. The authors interpret this secular trend as consistent with their credit constraint hypothesis.

Anil Deolalikar examines two related outcomes in Indonesia: the wage returns to schooling of males and females, and the school enrollment rates of boys and girls. The former favors females, while the latter favors males. Why does the labor market scarcity of an educated female worker not induce families to invest more equally in the schooling of daughters and sons? The large surveys of Indonesia allow the author to document many empirical regularities in wage rates, but all reported specifications confirm that the wage premium for additional schooling, beyond the primary level, is relatively larger for women than for men. Indonesian women are acquiring secondary and tertiary education in greater numbers, perhaps in response to the noted wage returns, but the gap in enrollments remains substantial and is not explained by the other features of the households examined in the paper.

In contrast to Indonesia, where educational levels are relatively advanced and women's participation in the wage labor force is extensive, the youth of Côte d'Ivoire rarely reach the secondary school level, and few women work for wages in the labor force. Wim Vijverberg explores returns to educational investment for men and women in this environment of Côte d'Ivoire. He incorporates into his evaluation of these schooling returns two other decisions that potentially affect the productive opportunities available to more educated workers and that might bias uncorrected schooling returns: the migration from rural to urban regions and the participation in wage and nonfarm self-employment. The corrected rates of return are high for both men and women, but relatively favor women. Nonetheless, male wages exceed those of females. His methodology should be replicated in other populations to learn how much of the returns from education are earned through migration and choice of job type.

The last two chapters of the book deal with the case of Brazil. In the study by Ricardo Barros, Louise Fox, and Rosane Mendonça, the authors seek to understand the causes and consequences of the increasing prevalence of female-headed households, in particular as it may affect the welfare of children. Three issues are addressed in their analysis of 1984 data for three major metropolitan areas of Brazil: Recife, São Paulo, and Porto Alegre. First, they consider two types of female-headed households, one with children and another without. The latter group without children is presumably largely elderly women, often widowed or divorced, and their relatives; whereas the former are younger women with their own children but without fathers present in the household. Only the female-headed households with minor children are overrepresented in poverty. Second, they decompose the variance in poverty for female-headed households and find that the lower level of earnings of women compared to men explains most of the excess poverty of female-headed households. In other words, the women in female-headed households are working to the same degree as men in male-headed households, and these patterns hold for both female-headed households with and without children. Third, they trace out the welfare consequences on children in terms of decreased enrollment in school and increased participation in the labor force. These consequences on child schooling and work behavior are linked to the poverty of their household, regardless of whether they reside in a female- or male-headed household. One might conclude that until the gap between female and male wages closes in Brazil, female-headed households are likely to remain poorer than average, and the next generation of children, who are increasingly reared in these households, will be relatively deprived of educational opportunities.

The second paper by Ricardo Barros, Lauro Ramos, and Eleanora Santos examines the origins of gender differences in wages in metropolitan Brazil. The sample is men and women aged 25 to 50 living in urban areas and working in nonagricultural occupations from 1981 to 1989. By repeated decompositions of their sample to explain the level and distribution of the female-male wage gap, they show that the distribution of workers by age, education, and region does not explain the gap, nor has the gap changed appreciably over the last decade. Education, age, and region can be viewed as productive characteristics of the worker and potentially exogenous, if the self-selection of migration is ignored. They then consider the occupation and type of job (formal, informal, and public wage earners, self-employed, or employer) of the worker. These two job choice variables, in contrast, describe a matching of the worker and job, and hence are not standard human capital endowment or investment variables that can be readily included as exogenous arguments in a wage function. Somewhat surprisingly, men's greater employment in better-paying occupations, at the level of aggregation (seven) considered here, does not explain the gender wage gap in Brazil. However, if women were distributed across the job-type classes as men were, the overall gender gap would be reduced by 13 percent.

These varied studies resolve a few questions in a specific context and pose many new ones for general research. They represent a research frontier for which replication and sensitivity testing across alternative models and estimation strategies may be particularly useful since our knowledge of the productivity of men and women, from which we can infer human capital stocks, is very limited for those parts of the world where women have received the least education and live the shortest lives. In these same societies, the percentage of women who work

I   Overview and Experience of High-Income Countries

1 Investments in the Schooling and Health of Women and Men
Quantities and Returns

T. Paul Schultz

T. Paul Schultz is a professor of economics at Yale University. The author appreciates the comments on an earlier version of this chapter from J. Heckman, B. Herz, T. W. Schultz, D. Thomas, B. Torrey, and R. Willis.

I. Introduction

This paper surveys the evidence on recent trends in the growth of human capital investments in women. The fraction of national income allocated to human capital formation in both high- and low-income countries has grown decisively in this century, and if height is interpreted as an indicator of health investments in reduced disease and improved nutrition, increases in height can be traced back several centuries in portions of Western Europe (Fogel 1990). The share of these human capital investments that raise women's productivity has risen in this century in most countries, but the forces behind this widespread development are poorly understood. The consequences of this fundamental redirection of social resources are only beginning to emerge from the disparate lines of research reflected in this book.

One economic explanation for this development is that the private rates of return to investments in women's human capital have increased relative to the private returns on alternative investments, including those in men's human capital. Societies may also want more investments in women, because of the greater social returns (external benefits) accruing from women's human capital compared to men's. Independent of these private and social economic returns, as parents become wealthier, they may attach greater value to equalizing their investments in their daughters and sons. Some evidence for the "relative returns" and "personal income" hypotheses is discussed below.

In order to test the relative returns hypothesis with regard to human capital, the private and social productive returns to education, health, etc., must be esti-

mated for all women and men, some of whom cannot report the monetary equivalent to their labor productivity. Those who make up the majority of the world's
population do not work for a wage; their labor productivity is therefore difficult
to measure apart from factor payments due other family workers and non labor
inputs, such as land (Schultz 1990a). In the 1960s when Becker first sought to
estimate how college education enhanced the productivity of persons, he implicitly assumed that these returns to college accrued to individuals only to the extent
that they worked in the market labor force (Becker 1964). Yet because time in
school is treated as a full-time investment cost valued at the market wage rate,
application of Becker's methodology biases downward educational returns calculated for women and other groups who do not participate full-time in the labor
force after completing their education. Many studies in the last three decades
have shown that education also increases the productivity of individuals in nonmarket activities (Michael 1982, Haveman and Wolfe 1984). The direction of the
bias in calculating women's returns is clear, but no satisfactory approach has
been developed for aggregating the variety of often nontraded home outputs and
nonwage production, along with wage production, to shed light on an average
economic returns to schooling for the entire population, regardless of how they
allocate their productive time (see Jorgenson et al. 1987).

The challenge is to estimate a single rate of return parameter that will summarize the economic pay off to one form of human capital investment for the entire
population, when labor productivity is confidently observed for only wage earners. This problem is related to that posed by Heckman (1979) for dealing with
sample selection bias. The assumptions underlying Heckman's formulation of the
sample selection model are currently being refined, reevaluated, and in some
cases, relaxed, as in the case of nonparametric methods. Alternative plausible
specifications of these models will need to be considered, and confidence in the
empirical results from these models will hinge on their robustness to apparently
minor variations in specification. The critical economic issue here is the choice
of a defensible exclusion restriction to identify the role of sample selection in
the joint estimation of the private return to human capital. A simple basis for
identification will be proposed and implemented on several national population
samples at the conclusion to this paper. This statistical approach is gaining widespread acceptance, but deserves a critical evaluation, and even when based on
persuasive identification restrictions, it may or may not affect comparisons of
female and male returns from country to country and from one time period to
the next.

The health and nutritional investments received by males and females are more
difficult to assess than are educational investments. Sex-differentials in mortality
and causes of death may be modified by changing occupational risks and health
investments, broadly conceived. Adult height and weight indicate the net nutritional balance of individuals, given their exposure to disease, access to health
care, and self-selected forms of activity. Because males and females may biologi-
cally differ in their vulnerability to certain of these health conditions, sex differences in health outcomes may reflect both sex-specific genetic endowments and
intra- and inter-family allocations of nutrition, health care, and work. Changes in
reproduction and breastfeeding practices may also relieve women of certain

health risks and expose them to new ones, as responses to environmental changes.

This paper is organized as follows. Section II presents patterns in school investments in men and women across regions and across birth cohorts within countries. Section III reviews gender differences in mortality and nutritional status. Section IV describes how market failure could be responsible for families investing less than the socially efficient amount in girls than boys, while Section V sets forth the problems of measuring without bias these private and social returns. Section VI illustrates the social externalities associated with educating men and women. Empirical patterns across countries in estimated returns to schooling are then summarized in Section VII. Sample-selection corrected private returns to schooling are estimated in Sections VIII and IX. A concluding section poses questions for further research.

II. Measures of the Investment in Schooling of Women and Men

The average number of years of schooling completed by men and women in various age groups can be derived from some population censuses, but these estimates of stocks of education in the population are available from only a few low-income countries over time. School enrollment rates by sex are published in the *UNESCO Statistical Yearbook* for most countries annually over the last several decades. A single measure of the flow of investment in education for a cohort is the "expected years of school enrollment" (Schultz 1987). It is constructed by multiplying the gross enrollment rates at each school level (or age), by the number of years of study at that level (or age bracket), and summing over levels. There are, of course, many limitations to this single synthetic measure of educational investment in a cohort: (1) it ignores repetition of grades and partial attendance; (2) it is not adjusted for length of school hours and school year; (3) it neglects quality of the schooling which might be related to school resource per student; and (4) it combines different levels of education indiscriminately, whereas each year of schooling increases the value of the child's time in the next level of education as does the child's aging itself. All of these factors may contribute to overstating the value of education acquired at earlier years compared to later years, and to overstating the value of the same level of education in lower compared to higher income countries. This crude physical measure of expected *years* of enrollment will be subsequently refined with data on public expenditures per student year by school level.[1]

---

1. For example, in Thailand in 1975 this measure suggests that women could expect to be enrolled for about seven years if they experienced the age specific enrollment rates prevailing in 1975 from age 7 on (in other words, .81 × 7 years + .23 × 5 years + .027 × 5 years = 6.96 years). A ratio of this summary measure of schooling investment for women relative to men in Thailand in 1975 is .91. But this female/male ratio of enrollment rates declines from nearly parity at the primary school level to .82 at the secondary level to .68 at the post secondary school level. Clearly, this synthetic measure of per child investment in schooling is not adjusted for the repetition rates, and should therefore be viewed as years of exposure to schooling rather than years completed as typically measured in censuses to approximate a stock of human capital.

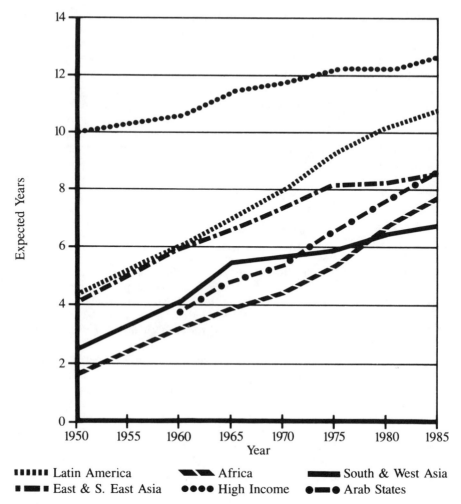

Figure 1
Expected Years of Enrollment, by Region, 1950–85

Data notes on Figures 1 and 2:

The expected years of enrollment are based on the gross enrollment rates for three age (or school level) groups multiplied by the number of years in the age (school level) group. For example in the *1984 Statistical Yearbook of UNESCO*, Table 2.11 provides the age-specific enrollment rates for designated regions. In this case the three age-specific enrollment rates are each for six year brackets (ages 6–11, 12–17, and 18–23), and thus are each multiplied by six and summed for a measure of "expected years of enrollment." To obtain disaggregated estimates for South and West Asia and East and Southeast Asia, enrollment rates for individual countries were aggregated, by school level, and weighted by the population in the age groups conventionally attending that school level. Table 3.2 provides the primary,

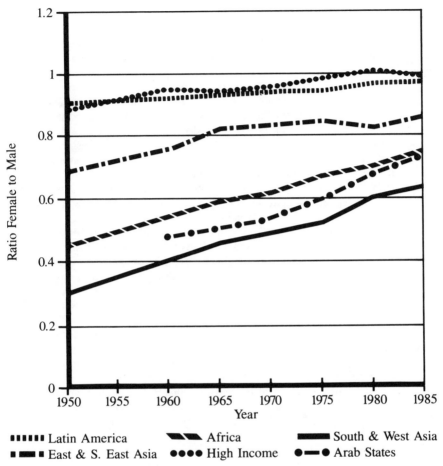

Figure 2
Female to Male Expected Years of Enrollment by Region, 1950–85

secondary, and tertiary enrollment rates, whereas the conventional duration of each nation's school system's levels is reported in Table 3.1 in the UNESCO Yearbook. In the earlier years, some countries do not report enrollment rates in Asia, such as North Korea and Afghanistan. These countries do not represent a significant share of the Asian regions reported here, and for simplicity enrollment rates are assumed not to have changed in these countries from 1950 to the first year for which figures are reported, usually 1960, whereas UN population estimates by age are available for all countries to weight the enrollment rates. The figures for China are more unstable, and probably are subject to more error, despite the fact that they are derived from time series on enrollments that are consolidated into standard Chinese yearbooks on education. But these estimates for China are not necessarily the same as those implicitly used by UNESCO.

Expected years of school enrollment is converging between low- and high-income countries, as evident from Figure 1 where the gap is shown to have closed from about seven years in 1950 to five years in 1985. Figure 2 also shows that women today are receiving nearly as many years of "enrollment" as men in industrially advanced, high-income countries. Latin America and to a lesser extent South East and East Asia are relatively similar to the high-income countries. At the other extreme are most of the countries of South and West Asia and North and sub-Saharan Africa in which women receive about two-fifths to three-fourths the number of years of schooling as men do. This pattern for Latin America, Africa, and high-income countries is based on UNESCO regional estimates representing all countries of these regions. I have computed my own estimates separately for the subregions of Asia from individual country enrollment figures because of the noted differences in levels and trends between the subregions of Asia. In every region distinguished in Figure 2, however, the ratio of female-to-male expected years of enrollment increases from 1950 to 1985.

From the alternative source of data on educational attainment, population censuses, years of schooling completed are shown in Figure 3 by age for seven selected countries. The ratio of female-to-male educational attainment is then plotted in Figure 4. At older ages (in other words, earlier birth cohorts), the relative gap between men and women in educational attainment is substantially larger, with the exception of the United States (see Goldin 1992). School attainment and enrollment data, which typically come from independent statistical sources, imply similar estimates of years of educational investment for recent birth cohorts within this group of countries. The more widely available school system data on enrollments, thus, do not appear to be a misleading indicator of the years of the education that cohorts eventually complete who are currently matriculating in the system. But enrollment rates describe only current investment flows and do not describe directly the stocks of human capital available to the economy or labor force at any particular point in time. It is often difficult to estimate low-income countries' enrollment rates before about 1960. For this reason, estimation of educational attainment among older cohorts from historic enrollment trends is uncertain but probably not too misleading for the entire labor force because of its youthfulness (World Bank 1992). From both sources of data women's years of schooling are more nearly equal to that of men's in countries with higher per capita income, and over time within countries; women are making relative gains in those countries that achieved more rapid economic growth in the period 1960–80 (Schultz 1989b).[2]

---

2. Another interpretation is that the higher levels of investment in women's schooling contribute to greater social product and income. In this case, ignoring nonlabor inputs, one might fit an aggregate production function by regressing the logarithm of GNP (ln y) per adult (potential workers over age 15) on the expected years of male (S_m) and female (S_f) school enrollments (lagged a decade to better correspond with the stock of schooling in the labor force). These regressions for 65 countries for which all three levels of enrollment rates are available back to 1960 yield the following estimates for 1970 and 1980:

(1) For 1970 ln y = 5.02 + .098S_m + .169S_f R^2 = .85
                (35.2) (2.02)   (4.18)

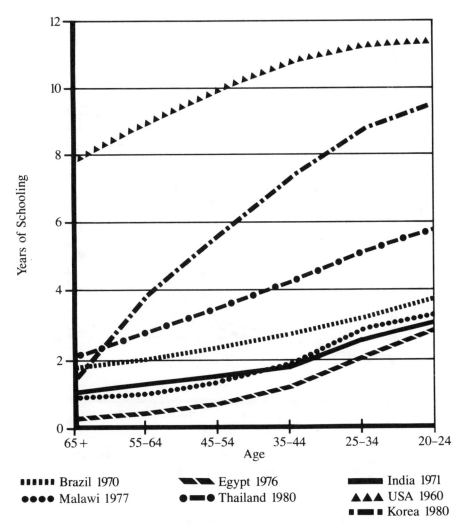

Figure 3
Years of Schooling Completed, by Age, for Selected Countries

(1)   For 1980 ln y = 4.63 + .110S_m + .182S_f R^2 = .78
              (21.6) (1.45)   (2.81)

where absolute values of the t ratios are reported in parentheses beneath the OLS coefficients. For details on the composition of the sample and sources of data, see Schultz (1987, 1989b). This cross-sectional evidence of production suggests that the "return" on female schooling is substantially higher than that on male schooling. Identifying the aggregate production function parameters from the parameters of household demand functions is not currently feasible. Only these partial correlations between schooling and income are available, that require more structure than is commonly provided in either the literature on aggregate growth models with human capital inputs or private or social demand models for schooling.

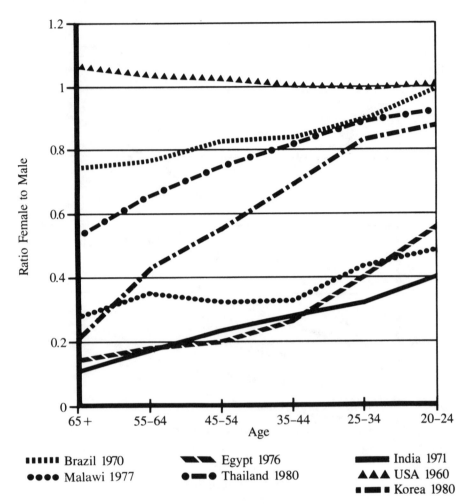

Figure 4
Female to Male Years of Schooling Completed by Age, from Selected Countries

Public expenditures on education are reported for at least five years in 47 countries in real local currency units. These expenditures are converted according to 1969–71 foreign exchange rates into 1970 dollars. Averages of these expenditures per student in these countries are reported in Table 1 for 140 country-year observations, included at five-year intervals. These estimates should be treated with caution because this small sample of countries may not be representative of the regions I have grouped them into or of the world as a whole.

Expenditures per student increase across regions with increasing income, with the exception of South and West Asia which spends more per student than does Latin America and South East and East Asia. This anomaly can be traced to the

higher relative cost of teachers in the South and West Asian region (Schultz 1987). In each country, however, public expenditures per student increase markedly at the secondary and higher educational levels compared to those at the primary level, particularly in low-income countries, and especially in Africa and South Asia (Psacharopoulos and Woodhall 1985).

Although public expenditures on education cannot be disaggregated into those spent on educating boys and girls, the expected years of enrollment, which are available by sex, can be weighted in these 47 countries for differences in average (boys and girls combined) public expenditure per student at the three levels of schooling. This adjustment incorporates the tendency for the fraction of female students to decline at higher levels in the school system, and for public subsidies per student to increase at these higher levels. Any differences in expenditures on male and female students within a given schooling level is neglected by this procedure, and particularly at higher levels of education it may be important, such as between teacher colleges for women and technical universities for men. No data could be found for most countries on the costs of educational subsystems and their sex composition.

In most countries, relatively few youth attend school beyond the secondary level. Nonetheless, the inclusion of the higher level of education increases by 26 percent the total public outlays on education in this sample. Because women receive an especially small fraction of these opportunities for higher education in many countries, the ratio of female-to-male public expenditures on education is .76 for the full sample (in other words, the world), though women receive 91 percent as many years of education as do men. In Africa, the female-to-male ratio of years of enrollment is .73, while the ratio of public school expenditures is only .50. Even in Latin America, East Asia, and the high income countries, where the ratio of enrollments approaches parity, the ratio of expenditure on women relative to men declines to .83, .86, and .93, respectively. In the South and West Asia region the ratio of female-to-male enrollments start at .59 and declines further in terms of public expenditures to .52. In sum, there is today a noted division in the developing world between those countries that are approaching parity in educational expenditures on women and men (>.83) and those that are not (<.52). Are these regional divisions closing over time and are women's human capital investments catching up to men's, in terms of education?

Rates of growth over time in the level and gender composition of school enrollments and public expenditures on education can also be calculated for the same sample of 47 countries. These annual percentage growth rates are reported in Table 2. Expenditures have increased twice as rapidly as enrollments in the world. The exception to this pattern is Africa where enrollments increased nearly as rapidly as expenditures. African school systems have reduced their costs per enrolled student. This has been accomplished through a reduction in the relative cost of teachers associated in part with replacing expatriates with natives, and reducing the relative wages of teachers as the available native supply of potential teachers increased (Schultz 1987). Salaries of teachers accounted for 90 percent of public expenditures on education in low-income countries in 1981—as they did in the last half of the nineteenth century in the United States (World Bank 1981, Fuchs 1968). The capacity of an educational system to reduce the cost of

Table 2

Annual Growth Rates in Percent of Expected Years of School Enrollments and Public Expenditures per School Aged Child, from 1960s and 1970s: Averages for a Sample of Countries

Region (Number of Countries Observed[a])	Expected Enrollment per Child[b] (Years) (1)	Public Expenditure per Child[c] (1970 $) (2)	Ratio of Female-to-Male	
			Years Enrolled (3)	Public Expenditures (4)
World				
(47)	2.0	5.4	0.74	0.85
Africa				
(13)	3.3	3.7	1.6	0.70
Latin America				
(8)	2.3	5.2	0.07	1.2
East and Southeast Asia				
(6)	1.1	3.3	0.81	1.8
West and South Asia				
(5)	2.8	7.7	1.5	0.45
High income countries				
(15)	0.95	7.2	0.10	0.52

Notes: See Table 1.

teachers—the dominant input to education—can contribute importantly to the rate of expansion in enrollments, and alleviate the requirements for public education resources during the early stages of expansion of the national school system. There are dynamic external economies of scale in education, because increases in output contribute to reducing the cost of the main input of schools, teachers. Expansion of the school system is often implicated in the compression of wages, contributing to a reduction in the returns to education (Knight and Sabot 1987, Lam and Levison 1991, Almeida and Barros 1991, Londoño 1990).

Every region in Table 2 shows a tendency for the ratio of female-to-male enrollments and the ratio of female-to-male school expenditures to increase. The increase varies substantially across regions, however, as does the gap to be closed between human capital investments in men and women. The slowest rate of increase to female-to-male expenditures on schooling is in South and West Asia, .45 percent per year, and this slow advance is based on the initially low level of the female-male expenditure ratio of .52 (Table 1). Thus, the low-income region that currently invests the least in the education of women compared to men, is closing this gap in expenditures more slowly than other regions, or falling further behind. Why are these regional differences so substantial and persistent?

There are two plausible reasons parents in low-income countries do not invest more in the schooling of their children: the low returns on schooling and their own low income. Parents may see the expected private rate of return to schooling of their children as low relative to their alternative investment opportunities. Even when expected returns are competitive, parents may not invest an efficient amount in the education of their children because of their aversion to the associated risks or because of credit constraints that limit their ability to borrow funds to invest in the future productivity of their children. Both risk aversion and credit constraints are likely to be more important among the poor who have fewer opportunity to diversify such risks in their portfolio or offer other collateral for borrowing to finance investment in education.

Education can also be viewed by parents partly as a normal consumption good for which their demand increases with their income, holding constant the return (or inverse of the net price) of education. Parents may be called "altruistic" if they derive utility from increasing their children's future consumption by educating them. From either perspective, parent income moderates the effect of risk aversion and credit constraints on the demand for the investment good, or parent income increases the demand for education as a consumption good. Clearly, it is difficult to distinguish between these alternative explanations for there being a relationship between parent income and child education. From either viewpoint, parent demand for schooling is expected to increase with their income and decrease with the price, even though schooling is considered mainly as an investment good, at least by economists.

Based on cross-country comparisons from 1950 to 1980, school enrollment rates increase with national income per adult and decrease with the relative cost of teacher salaries. The estimated positive income and negative price elasticities of school enrollments are both larger in absolute value for female enrollment rates than for male enrollment rates (Schultz 1987). Larger responses of female than male enrollment rates to income and prices are also observed within countries over time during the 1960s and 1970s (Schultz 1989b). Per capita income increases and the relative price of teachers decreases with economic development, and according to these estimates both changes reduce the relative and absolute gap between enrollments of women and men. Family level studies have also found that the household income elasticity of the school enrollment rate of daughters exceeds that of sons, and distance from residence to school is a greater deterrent to enrollment for girls than boys (Lavy 1992, Tansel 1993, Deolalikar 1993).

Public expenditures on education are not commonly disaggregated by sex of student. It is not possible, therefore, to estimate how public sector expenditures on female and male schooling respond distinctly to income and prices, but the income elasticity of total public expenditures on schooling clearly exceeds one, and not surprisingly. The income elasticity is higher at higher levels of education, when estimated from cross-sectional or time series variation at the national level (Schultz 1987, 1989b).

A question that has not been pursued, to my knowledge, is whether gender differences in educational investments across countries and within countries over time are a response to gender differences in private returns or social returns to schooling in those countries. If enrollments do not respond positively to returns, then are we to conclude that the distribution of schooling is misallocated as an investment? Does the allocation of human capital between the sexes affect the differentials in returns to schooling and lead men and women with comparable skills to perform different tasks in the economy? This set of issues is clearly difficult to pursue and not attempted here.

III. Women's and Men's Health and Nutritional Status

Much less is known about nutritional inputs and health-related care that are invested in men and women than about the gender allocation of educational investments. Biological relationships are postulated between human nutritional inputs, physical growth, metabolic requirements for body mainte-nance, and finally an energy "excess" that can be allocated to productive and leisure activities. The efficiency of this energy conversion system, however, is affected by exposure to disease, and the immune system itself makes require-ments on nutrition inputs to fight infections and parasites. Given the complexity of these processes and the long lags between inputs and outcomes, research on nutrition has sought indicators of the net (or final) outcome (for example, height) rather than trying to quantify all of the inputs and production functions that underlie human growth and health status. Moreover, as long as health and nutri-tion inputs are themselves allocated within families and societies in response to unobserved (by researcher) healthiness of individuals, direct estimates of health technology, or the effects of inputs on health outcomes, can be quite misleading. This heterogeneity bias will be present even if all inputs are accounted for and functional forms of the health production process are known (Rosenzweig and Schultz 1983).

Most analyses of health technology have focused on the least ambiguous (and most final) outcome, mortality. Anthropometric indicators of health, such as birthweight, height for age, body-mass-index (defined as weight divided by height squared), and skinfold thickness, are justified as readily measured proxies of cumulative health status by the strength of their correlations with age-specific mortality (Fogel 1990). There is, however, a view that too much emphasis has been given to mortality, and conversely that measures of morbidity, such as limitations on physical functioning, should be consulted to assess the health of the living. For this view to carry weight different health investments and behavior must be effective in modifying morbidity compared with mortality, and gender differences, in particular, in these two measures of health are certainly not always congruent (see Strauss et al. 1993).

Under the conditions prevailing today, females appear to live longer than males, given apparently equivalent diet and medical care. In the industrially advanced countries of Europe, European settlements, and Japan, females at birth are today expected to live four to eight years longer than do males (United Nations 1982). The mortality advantage of women seems to be a recent development, however. Before the twentieth century, male mortality appears to have been infrequently higher than female mortality, and sometimes lower (Preston 1976b, Fogel 1986, Pope 1992). Some countries in South and West Asia continue to report more males than females in their population, such as India, Pakistan, Bangladesh, or

Nepal, and this can be attributed to the higher mortality rate among females than males from birth until at least the end of childbearing or age 45 (for example, Visaria n.d.). In general, where the overall level of mortality is lower and life expectancy at birth is longer, the relative mortality advantage of women compared to men is larger (Stolnitz 1956, Preston 1976b).

Three hypotheses for this change in sex differences in mortality are that (1) the causes of death have changed, probably due to the introduction of medical treatments for infectious and parasitic diseases, or (2) the diet and/or medical care of females compared to males improved, or (3) differences in occupations have changed and the health risks associated with these roles differ, with the new outcome favoring women. Data on cause-of-death are not particularly reliable historically, and are often of uncertain quality even today in many low income countries. Most cause-of-death rates by sex indicate more frequent male than female deaths within most cause-specific categories, with a few notable exceptions. However, the shift in the cause of death composition of deaths with rising incomes does not, according to Preston (1976b), explain the increasing female advantage in survival over males in the twentieth century. Only a small part of this change, for example, can be explained by the decline in fertility and reduced risk of immediate maternal mortality.

Confronted by this puzzle, Preston disaggregated age-standardized death differentials between males and females into 13 causes of death. He finds that the increase in male relative to female mortality associated across countries with rising average income is explained mostly by cardiovascular disease, neoplasms, TB, and influenza/pneumonia/bronchitis. Family and social allocations of health investments may play some role in some of these sex differences in mortality by cause, but the evolving exposure of men and women through occupational roles determined by technological change and urbanization, as well as possible biological differences in their vulnerability to specific diseases, cannot be ruled out as the originating factor for these patterns. For example, diarrheal diseases and other infectious and parasitic diseases that are a major cause of high mortality at low-income levels, and which might be expected to respond noticeably to intrahousehold resource allocations of food and care, are not quantitatively important in the changes in the gender balance of mortality that occur with development (Preston 1976b).

If the decomposition of death rates by cause does not generate any salient hypotheses for why female mortality declines more than male mortality in this century and with development, several characteristics of the environment of the individual do. Problems of multicollinearity among explanatory variables at the national unit of observation limit the confidence we can attach to such estimated relationships, but they are a useful source of hypotheses that may be refined at the micro level. Agricultural populations have higher female relative to male mortality and higher overall death rates. Cardiovascular and neoplasm deaths and those related to respiratory diseases become relatively more important in urban areas and take a disproportionate toll of males (Preston 1976b).

Preston then considers another variable that is more difficult to interpret, because it is a product of two functionally dissimilar variables: the grams of animal protein consumed per capita and the female-male ratio of primary school enroll-ments. This hybrid variable, holding constant for metropolitanization and agricul-tural employment share, is associated with greater male relative to female mortal-ity, through its correlation with deaths due to cardiovascular disease, to violence other than automobiles, and because of declining fertility to maternal mortality. Other than this single study by Preston (1976b) and Preston and Weed (1976), there are few multivariate explanations for the recent marked changes or variation in the sex balance of mortality. All that is known, then, is that with metropolitaniza-tion and a shift of employment out of agriculture, mortality declines more rapidly for females than for males.[3] It is possible that this is related to increasing returns to health investments in women in urban areas where women have increased their schooling and entered the labor force as their wage opportunities have im-proved relative to those of men. Alternatively, other changes in the rural/urban composition of endemic diseases and the greater availability of public and private health services in urban locations may have favored the health of urban women independently of their economic productivity.

Adequacy of diet contributes to adult height and the age pattern of growth and timing of sexual maturation, but is presumably also affected by diseases and behavior (Falkner and Tanner 1986, vol. 3). Historical analyses of the level and change in height in Western European populations in recent centuries has docu-mented substantial growth in stature in "man" (Tanner 1981, Fogel 1986), but relatively little attention has been paid to measuring male-female differences in height or analyzing the origins of changes in these sex differences, if any.[4] Some

---

3. Preston (1976b, Table 6.10) reports relationships between the difference in age standardized male and female mortality and country characteristics based on data drawn from the 1960s. Although I did not compile the cause-specific mortality rates examined by Preston, the aggregate mortality levels for males and females were consulted to ascertain whether the gender differences in overall mortality (measured by the sex difference in life expectancy at birth) continue to be related in the 1980s to the same variables found to be important by Preston, and whether changes within countries also confirmed the causal relevance of the same variables in explaining changes occurring over time. In the case of the share of agricultural employment (measured among males, to reduce the cultural variations across countries in whether women are counted as being active in agriculture), there continues to be greater female than male mortality in populations more dependent on agriculture, and the relationship is also evident in changes over time and is particularly strong among children less than five years of age (Schultz 1994b). Urbanization performs as an alternative proxy for agriculture, but the two variables are highly correlated and thus cannot always be used together as explanatory variables. Education of women relative to men reduces female mortality relative to male in the 1980s (and in the 1960s) and in the change relationship from the 1960s to the 1980s. One relationship that Preston noted, but is absent in the 1980s or in the time series changes, is the proportion of the population in large cities (over a million), after holding constant for agricultural share. The interaction of animal fat in the diet and gender differences in school-ing that Preston considered performs more poorly in predicting overall gender differences in mortality in 1980 than the two variables considered separately. If the ratio of female to male education is summa-rized, more plausibly, by the entire span of schooling (in other words, expected years enrolled), and is not to be limited, as in Preston's study, to Level 1 (primary), the explanation of female/male longevity is substantially more significant.

4. Most comparisons that document the growth in stature over decades or centuries within a population are derived from administrative records of the military, and thus pertain only to males. By the 19th century, school studies of physical growth of male and female children had become common, but they

have argued that females, compared to males, "are more readily thrown off their growth pathway by environmental adversities, such as malnutrition and disease, and that they respond more dramatically to environmental improvement" (Bielicki 1986, p. 298), but the evidence is weak. Sexual dimorphism in regard to human growth may not, however, all be biological (in other words, genetic) in origin, but rather it could be a response to cultural and economic factors filtered through household allocations (van Wieringen 1986, Waldron 1983b, 1986). How surpluses and shortfalls in food supplies are shared in the family and society is affected by the roles men and women undertake and the physical claims that these work activities place on their dietary intakes (see Pitt et al. 1990).

Few studies separately assess how the height of men and women varies with economic conditions and how their height affects mortality, morbidity, or economic functioning.[5] There is little evidence that adult height has increased relatively more for females than for males in the nineteenth and twentieth centuries in West European populations, although the adolescent spurt of growth may have shifted to a younger age by a greater amount for girls than boys (Bielicki 1986).[6] There is also evidence that height increased more rapidly in urban than in surrounding rural areas in several European populations, but sex differentials in these gains or how they contributed to improved adult health or economic functioning is not discussed.

In sum, there has been a dramatic, but largely unexplained, advance in female longevity relative to male in the twentieth century that is evident in most countries, with the exception of certain countries in South Asia. This development is associated with the shift of populations from dependence on agriculture to working in urban areas. Height, due to dietary gains and control of disease, has been increasing for as long as two hundred years in some Western European populations. New studies are needed to assess the conditions under which gains in stature differ for women and men with distinct consequences for their economic functioning and welfare. Have health inputs for women increased relative to men from families or from society at large? The gains in longevity and stature have not yet been analyzed in conjunction with women's schooling and labor force participation, inside and outside of the family, to assess whether these factors account for the increasing productivity of females relative to males. These changes are a major source of decreasing inequality within and between countries in this century (Rosenzweig and Schultz 1982, Schultz 1990a).

were most useful in confirming changes in the timing of the adolescent growth spurt and the onset of puberty. They are much less useful for documenting change in the adult height for men and women over time. Relatively few males and far fewer females were still in educational systems by age 18. This well-educated population is not likely to be representative of the entire population (Tanner 1981; Falkner and Tanner 1986).

5. The association between height and mortality of male and female slaves in Trinidad during the 19th Century was founded by John (1984) to be significant only for male adults, whereas child mortality is several times more responsive to height fluctuations in the population than adults. Friedman (1984), on the contrary found significantly higher survival rates for both males and females who were taller, controlling for origins, occupation and other factors. See also summary by Fogel (1986).

6. See endnote 4.

IV. Individual and Social Returns to Education: Conceptual Distinctions

Returns to education are calculated from information on the benefits and costs, and can be reckoned from three perspectives: that of the individual student, the student's parents, or the society. The private individual's future after-tax gains in productivity associated with schooling are offset by private opportunity (time) costs lost to the family and direct private costs. Individuals are assumed to maximize their lifetime wealth by investing first in forms of human and physical capital that earn them the highest internal private rates of return.

In reckoning education's costs from the perspective of the society, public sector subsidies to education are included with the private costs of education. In addition, there may be social benefits from the educated individual's increased future productivity and altered behavior that are not captured by the individual.[7] More educated workers may also modify their labor supply to taxable activities. Taxable labor supply tends to increase with the education of women, but the wives of more educated men supply fewer hours of labor in taxed activities. Moreover, men's market or wage labor supply tends to be relatively unresponsive to increases in their education (Schultz 1981).

Education of women influences their health, longevity, and welfare and that of their children, and perhaps other members of their family (see, for example, Cochrane et al. 1980, Schultz and Tansel 1992, Strauss et al. 1993). It also influences family size as well. If these effects embody social as well as private benefits, they are externalities of women's education that should be taken into account in setting public sector priorities. Indeed, public subsidies are already provided to improve child health, nutrition, and schooling, and through family planning programs, to help couples avoid unwanted births. In the literature on educational returns, however, social externalities are in practice neglected, because their quantification is controversial and there is no agreement on how to value them equivalently to the opportunity costs and market production gains of education. Most estimates of social returns to education therefore simply adjust the private individual returns downward by adding into the computation the public subsidies for education (Psacharopoulos and Woodhall 1985). Despite the measurement difficulties, the difference between social and private returns is the relevant criterion for allocating public resources (including education) among competing programs to maximize social welfare. If private resources were initially allocated efficiently to activities generating the highest individual returns, social subsidies should supplement private resources only in those activities where social returns exceed private returns.

Between the individual and the society there exists a fuzzier intermediate level of aggregation, the family, or more specifically, parents who have some interests

---

7. The increased taxes that the more educated individual pays back to the state can be viewed as an externality, if the added taxes contribute to a reduction in tax rates that reduce the distortionary burden imposed on resource allocation. The returns to human capital can be effectively taxed only when educated persons hold jobs where their productivity is readily monitored by the state, such as in wage employment.

in and responsibility for their children. Educational decisions for children are undoubtedly influenced by the willingness of parents to sacrifice their current consumption for the schooling of their offspring. How are the motivations of parents to be characterized? One view of the family is that it provides a context for people to transfer resources over time.[8] The inability to internalize in the family all of the individual-private returns to human capital investments in children because credit markets facing parents are imperfect could explain the common practice of public subsidies for education, as well as special interventions to help investors in human capital, such as need-based scholarships and student loans.

In their investments in and transfers to children, parents need not treat all of their children as equal. The private returns to schooling for different children may differ. The family must then consider whether to be guided only by efficiency, in other words maximizing total private returns, or whether to also assign a value to equality in consumption oportunities among offspring.[9]

With these distinctions in mind, the educational investments in men and women can now be considered as a potential instance of market failure. Three factors might motivate parents to invest systematically more in the health or education of boys than of girls (Gertler and Alderman 1989). First, private individual returns to education for women may be lower than for men, possibly because the technologically derived demands for female labor do not assign as large a relative premium to educated female labor as to educated male labor. This line of reasoning presumes that the labor of males and females is technically different in the sense that they are imperfect substitutes for each other in some activities. These female and male market returns to more educated workers are estimated later in this paper to assess whether they commonly diverge from equality.

Second, remittances to parents may be smaller from daughters than sons. Third, for reasons unrelated to the individual private returns or to rates of remittances, parents may derive more satisfaction from the economic success of their sons than of their daughters. If the second and third sources of intrafamily gender differences in human capital investment are important, parental allocations of

---

8. A child implicitly borrows from her or his parents to invest in schooling and is thereby obliged to support parents in the future when parent productivity may be lower. Repayment could take alternative forms, such as supporting younger siblings through their schooling, marriage or borrowing requirements (see Parish and Willis 1993). Thus, the family may smooth consumption as would a credit market, because of the distinct life cycle phases of investment, production, and consumption that individuals experience. Even when financial markets and government social insurance schemes provide for old age support without relying on children, the young may still be credit-constrained, and their educational investments may depend in part on the altruistic behavior of their parents. Extreme forms of "dynastic altruism" that assign equal weight to own and offspring consumption may be unrealistic. A gap between the parent-private return to investment in the schooling of their children and the child's individual-private return could arise from credit market constraints, and would suggest arrangements outside of the family are needed to allow children to invest optimally in their own education.

9. This consideration of equity might lead parents to invest more than the efficient amount in the children whose educational investments yield lower returns, or parents might consider transferring to these children nonhuman capital assets from which competitive returns would presumably be earned (Becker and Tomes 1979). There is, however, little evidence that this pattern of portfolio balancing behavior is empirically common even within rich families.

these human capital investments will not be productively efficient. Subsidized loans for female education could, under these conditions, promote a socially more efficient pattern of investment that would maximize economic growth. Social external returns to women's schooling provide a further rationale to subsidize female education more than male education.

V. Measurement of Returns to Schooling and Health: Model Specification

There are three limitations in our capacity to measure the economic returns to education. Comparative studies of worker productivity cannot, in most cases, be based on experimentally controlled variation in human capital investment across people. Thus, those who acquire more education than others may differ in many ways that could influence their productivity, whether or not they are educated (Griliches 1977). Controls for ability and other characteristics of the worker may reduce omitted variable bias in estimates of the returns to education, but the introduction of these controls into the wage function also increase errors in the measurement of schooling with the consequence of adding a downward bias to the estimated returns to education (Griliches 1977, Lam and Schoeni 1993). Evidence that additional controls for ability alter appreciably male-female comparisons of the private individual's returns to education has not been advanced, and I expect whatever bias is present will be similar for both sexes.

Second, labor productivity of the individual is inferred readily only if the worker is paid wages; it is substantially more complex to measure the product of an individual who is self-employed or works without a wage in a family enterprise. Moreover, studies of self-employed men and women in a variety of countries, including Thailand, Colombia, and Israel, have not detected major differences in the monetary returns to schooling associated with working in wage and nonwage sectors (Chiswick 1979, Fields and Schultz 1982, Ben Porath 1986) and Thomas and Strauss (1992) report similar evidence for urban Brazil. Again, this problem is difficult to resolve entirely, but whatever biases it may exert on estimates of the returns to education, they have not yet been shown to differ systematically for men and women.

Third, many individuals at the time of a survey are not in the labor force. Rates of return to education can typically only be estimated for those who are "self-selected" into the labor force, and often only for those in the wage labor force. Are these estimates applicable to the average or representative person for whom schooling investment decisions are intended to be applicable? This statistical problem of "sample-selection" is common to much of nonexperimental social science (Heckman 1979, 1987); statistical methods are required to explain first the reason some people are "selected" into the wage labor force and this information is then used to eliminate potential bias in the estimation of the private returns to schooling arising from unobserved factors that affect the marginal productivity of labor, in other words, wage rate, and also affect the probability that the person is a wage earner.[10] Because the proportion of women working in the labor force is substantially smaller than the proportion of men in most countries (Schultz 1990a), this source of sample selection could be a more serious source of bias in estimating educational returns for women than for men. Estimates of selection corrected returns may be sensitive to the choice of assumptions underlying the statistical approach. There is, however, some theoretical basis for the statistical identification of the sample selection model subsequently proposed for estimating wage functions.

Productive benefits from health and nutrition can be estimated by including health characteristics of the worker in the wage function, just as currently schooling and post-school experience are included (Mincer 1974). If earnings are used partly to improve health or nutrition, then the impact of nutrition and health on wage rates must be estimated by simultaneous equation methods to disentangle only one direction in the causal system. Parameter bias due to errors in the measurement of health and nutritional status may be an even more serious problem than in the case of schooling, biasing down the directly estimated (in other words, OLS) effects of health and nutrition on productivity. To estimate the effect of health or nutrition on wages without bias from errors in measurement and simultaneity requires generally the specification of a valid instrumental variable or an exclusion restriction. Food prices and health/programs are candidates for exclusion from the wage functions, and these variables are then assumed to influence the household's demand for nutrition and health inputs and consequent labor productivity. Prices and programs thereby affect labor productivity only through their predicted impact on nutritional status and health but do not shift community labor supply which would affect wage levels. The wage is measured in real terms, deflated for the local price level, but this requires that the relative prices of food items do not affect labor supply. This approach was proposed by Strauss (1986) in a study of family farm labor productivity as a function of predicted caloric availability in Sierra Leone, and employed to analyze height and weight by Deolalikar (1988) in India, Sahn and Alderman (1988) in Sri Lanka, Bouis and Haddad (1990) in the Philippines, and to analyze adult disability days by Schultz and Tansel (1992) in Côte d'Ivoire and Ghana. These estimates of the benefits of calories, height, and a reduction in morbidity have not yet been combined with the costs of investments required to improve these nutritional and health statuses, as will eventually be necessary to derive private or social rates of return to investments in health that are commensurable to those for schooling. There is insufficient evidence as yet to assess whether private productive returns to health and nutrition differ for men and women. A study of the intra-household allocation of nutrition, time, and productivity in Bangladesh provides a broader family context in which to analyze these interdependent decisions (Pitt et al. 1990).[11]

---

10. The exclusion restriction that secures identification depends on the researcher knowing some information that influences the probability of sample selection, but does not affect the market wage offer. Functional form assumptions regarding the selection equation, for example, normal errors in a probit equation, can provide formal identification, but not a particularly strong theoretical or empirical basis for identification. See later discussion in sections 9 and 10.

11. But education and health are themselves interdependent. The connections between education and health are not yet clearly documented, in part because mortality or morbidity rates are not often available

VI. Productivity in the Home and Social Externalities

Because of the difficulty of measuring and valuing nonmarket production, economists focus on the marketable component of income of families and individuals. In principle, personal and national income should include the market value of home-produced and -consumed goods, such as the production and preparation of food and fuel, the fetching of water, and maintenance of housing, for which there are sometimes market-priced equivalents. But in practice, the complexity of imputing a value to goods one produces and then consumes leads to their frequent omission. Moreover, untradable home-production activities, such as child-rearing, are ignored entirely, although they are economically valued outputs of society. By omitting these nonmarket components of personal income, economists understate sources of income that are of relatively greater importance to poor families. Within families these conventions of economic measurement understate women's economic contribution relative to men's.

The distinctive role of women in managing consumption of and investment in children within the family is a major reason for social intervention to increase women's capabilities and control over resources. Improving the productivity of women through investments in their human capital directly advances economic development and the growth of measured output. Human and nonhuman capital controlled by women appears to channel associated new streams of income and resources toward particular ends: consumption and investment in food, medical care, and schooling of children (Schultz 1989a, Thomas 1991).[12]

The effects of male and female human capital on fertility have been frequently studied (Schultz 1994b). In most societies, fertility is lower among women who are better educated and can therefore expect to be offered a higher wage. Education thus increases a woman's potential income, but also increases what she must

---

for analysis by educational attainment. Recent research has linked mother's education to the survival of her children in low income countries (Cochrane et al. 1980), whereas other studies have suggested that nutrition and health of children can affect their school achievement (Moock and Leslie 1986). Height is believed to be largely determined by nutritional status of the individual before reaching age four (Fogel 1990). Height can then be viewed as an indicator of long-run nutritional status that is essentially fixed in early childhood and may therefore be assumed exogenous in an adult's wage function in the same way that education is. Weight or a body-mass-index or current caloric intake or acute illness, on the other hand, is more reasonably viewed as simultaneously determined with current productivity and income. Calorie consumption as an indicator of short run nutritional status can be estimated as a determinant of productivity by instrumental variable methods but may only be a quantitatively important determinant of labor productivity and wages at very low levels of income or calorie intake (Strauss 1986). See also Thomas and Strauss (1992).

12. Increases in a mother's schooling decreases mortality of her children. This pattern is widely replicated in surveys from countries in every region of the world. An added year of mother's education is associated with a 5 to 10 percent reduction in child mortality (Cochrane et al. 1980). Levels of mortality tend to be higher in rural than in urban populations of low-income countries, but the proportionate reduction in child mortality associated with an additional year of mother's schooling is about the same magnitude in both urban and rural areas of the same country. Although father's education in years is also correlated with lower child mortality, it has a smaller coefficient than mother's education. The correlation between women's schooling and lower child mortality across low income countries is also robust to the inclusion of income per adult, men schooling, caloric consumption and other factors (Schultz 1994b).

give up in order to bear and rear an additional child. The latter "price effect" on fertility invariably outweighs the former "income effect" in empirical studies, and fertility tends to decline as women's market wage opportunities rise. Increases in the labor productivity and wage rates of men, on the other hand, do not appear to deter larger families and are often associated with higher levels of fertility, consistently so in low-income agricultural societies. As a consequence, a redistribution in the balance of education from men to women, if the number of places in school were fixed, should have the unambiguous effect of reducing fertility and slowing population growth.

Although male education is not held constant, the tabulation of fertility in Table 3 by woman's education in the 38 countries where the World Fertility Surveys (WFS) were conducted during the 1970s illustrates the widely observed pattern. In all of the regions distinguished, women at age 40–49 with seven or more years of schooling have 1.6 to 2.9 fewer births over their lifetime, on average, than women with no schooling (Column 1). The measure of recent total fertility rates, based on reproductive rates in the five years before the survey, report a larger educational differential, 2.0 to 3.6 fewer births for this more educated group of women (Column 2). The difference between children ever born at age 40 to 49 (Column 1) and "desired" fertility (Column 3) (across all ages) is a rough indicator of the recent change in the latent demand for birth control among women in the childbearing ages. This measure of latent demand for greater birth control than was used in the past by women aged 40–49 is concentrated in Asia and Latin America within the least educated strata of women. Education of women is thus associated with a reduction in fertility and in a reduction in unwanted fertility.[13]

VII. The Levels of Returns to Investment in Schooling: Stylized Facts

As noted earlier, estimates of the returns to human capital have their limitations, but the accumulating evidence from studies in many countries, based on a wide variety of working assumptions and sources of data, imply that private and social returns to primary and secondary education are substantial, ranging between 5 and 40 percent per year. One survey of empirical studies in African, Asian, and Latin American countries concluded that the average social returns to investment in primary, secondary and higher education were 27, 16, and 13 percent per year, respectively (Psacharopoulos and Woodhall 1985, p. 58). The returns to education within a level of schooling tend to be lower in high-

13. The less-educated are most likely to benefit from a family planning information campaign and by subsidized birth control and the supply of associated services. However, it may be noted that these data from the 1970s do not yet reveal much latent demand to restrict traditional fertility levels among African women, either among those with high or low educational levels, perhaps because of the high overall levels of child mortality in Africa (Okojie 1991). The Demographic Health Surveys from the late 1980s are documenting regions in Africa where demands are beginning to change, but these surveys lack economic information to facilitate analyses of the economic determinants of fertility or the independent effects of health and family planning programs.

Table 3

*Children Ever Born, Recent Total Fertility Rate, and Desired Fertility:
Averages for Countries with World Fertility Surveys in 1970s,
by Region and Education of Woman*

Regions (Number of Countries Observed) Years of Schooling Completed by Women	Children Ever Born[a] (1)	Total Fertility Rate[b] (2)	Desired Family Size[c] (3)
Africa (8 to 10)			
0 years	6.4	7.0	6.9
1–3	6.5	7.2	6.4
4–6	6.1	6.2	5.9
7 or more	4.8	5.0	5.0
Difference (0–7+)	−1.6	−2.0	−1.9
Latin America (13)			
0 years	7.1	6.8	4.8
1–3	6.8	6.2	4.7
4–6	6.0	4.8	4.2
7 or more	4.2	3.2	3.7
Difference (0–7+)	−2.9	−3.6	−1.1
Asia and Oceania (9 to 13)			
0 years	6.7	7.0	5.4
1–3	6.7	6.4	4.3
4–6	6.4	5.8	4.2
7 or more	4.9	3.9	4.0
Difference (0–7+)	−1.8	−3.1	−1.4

a. Women aged 40–49 years.
b. The average number of children that would be born alive to a woman during her lifetime, if during her childbearing years she were to bear children at each age in accord with the estimated age-specific birth rates in the five years before the survey.
c. Means are adjusted for the effects of age differences between educational groups. National age composition used to compare means.
Source: Summary of data collected in 38 World Fertility Surveys around 1975. United Nations (1987, Tables 112 and 115).

income countries than in low-income countries, but the relationship is not always monotonic. Middle income countries often appear to have higher returns to secondary and higher education than do the lowest income countries (Jain 1991).

In a growing number of countries it is possible to follow over time wage differentials by education, and thereby estimate a time series on the returns to education in a particular country. The majority of such studies confirm that private returns tend to decrease over time, although perturbed from a smooth path by business and trade cycles (Schultz 1988, Psacharopoulos 1989, Jain 1991). The slope of the education-earnings profile associated with the private returns to schooling is decreasing over the long run and is an important factor reducing income inequality in some Latin American countries, Kenya, and Korea in the 1980s (Almeida and Barros 1991, Londoño 1990, Knight and Sabot 1987, Choi 1991). Secondary schooling has become a bottleneck in some countries where enrollments have not stayed up with labor market demands, and the private returns are consequently substantially higher at the secondary level than at the primary level (Schultz 1988). Within countries, the general rule is for the social rate of return to decline at higher levels of education, noticeably at the university level, where public subsidies are often relatively large. This is particularly evident in Africa (Psacharopoulous and Woodhall 1985).

As already noted, the majority of studies of returns to education are limited to wage earners. To estimate the returns to education among self-employed workers more data and different analytical methods are required. In agriculture, the education of the family (male) head is associated with significantly higher farm profit, but returns to the education of other family workers, such as women, are generally ignored in these studies (for example, see Jamison and Lau 1982).

Analogous private returns on physical capital investments in factories, equipment, inventories, and infrastructure are generally lower than estimates of the private returns to primary and secondary education. The market increase in investment in education in low-income countries in the last 50 years can be interpreted, on the basis of these micro-economic studies, as a monetarily justified investment of individuals and governments compared to the returns on alternative nonhuman forms of private and social investment (Schultz 1988).

VIII. Gender Differences in Returns to Schooling and Measurement Bias

The primary problem emphasized here with extending the empirical analysis to gender differences in returns to schooling is the need to incorporate the nonmarket returns to education for women. Because nonmarket output cannot be comprehensively evaluated in monetary terms, it is unavoidable that quantitative analyses deal only with the wage rates of wage earners. There is no a priori reason to expect the sample selection bias in this case to understate or overstate the true return to education evident in accepted market wage offers for all women or all men, or to affect differentially this bias between women and men. The direction and origins of such a bias is an open issue in need of more empirical research. The composition of output and employment (Fuchs 1968), the capital intensity of production (Griliches 1969), the rate of technical change (Schultz 1975) and perhaps measures of sex segregation in employment by industry and occupation (Boserup 1970) might all plausibly modify which males and females are selected to be wage earners and thus bias estimates of schooling returns.[14]

---

14. Most research on the sorting of students by ability and its effects on estimated wage returns to schooling has analyzed these relationships for males, and then mostly in the United States. It is possible that the investments of families in the schooling of daughters is more (or less) responsive to the ability

It may be useful to consider several hypothetical sources of sample selection that illustrate how bias in estimating returns to schooling might arise. In the first case, assume that virtually all women with higher education work for wages, but that only half of those who have only a secondary education work for wages. Suppose further that the half of the secondary educated persons who work for wages are not a representative sample of this population, but for some unobserved reason they are more (less) productive workers. The difference between the wages received by wage earners with only a secondary education and those with a higher education will, in this case, understate (overstate) the productivity gain an average person could expect to receive by studying to obtain a higher education.

To correct for sample selection bias in estimating the returns to education, some specific variable must be known that affects the probability that a person works for wages, but this variable cannot affect the worker's productivity as a wage earner or her market wage offer.[15] I will assume that this identifying variable is the individual's ownership of land and other assets which yield nonearned income; this asset or income steam is expected to raise the individual's shadow value of time in nonwage activities, and thereby reduce the likelihood that the individual will be a wage earner. But this asset or nonearned income variable is assumed not to influence what an employer would offer her as a market wage.[16]

---

of the girls than in the case of boys (see Parish and Willis 1993). Alternative hypotheses regarding the family's objectives in educating sons and daughters will need to be rigorously formulated and tested. We may expect then to be able to reject in some settings the simplified wealth-maximizing model of the family that is assumed to treat boys and girls as identical.

15. The probability of participating as a wage earner can then be estimated as a probit model jointly with the wage equation for the censored sample of wage earners. Maximum likelihood methods, where the covariance (rho) between the errors in the two equations is estimated, is the standard means of estimation, although the two-stage method (if the standard errors are adjusted) is also consistent although less efficient than the joint procedure (Heckman 1987).

16. The sample selection correction can be statistically identified from the nonlinearity of the probit wage earner selection equation with its normally distributed error (Heckman 1987). However, in most economic contexts it is desirable to have a stronger basis for identifying the model than only a relatively arbitrary assumption as to functional form. Exclusion restrictions based on a theoretical framework are the preferred estimation strategy. However, asset income may not in all contexts be independent of the wage rate, if for example the assets represent accumulated savings that are a positive function of past wages, or if asset income encourages more investment (consumption) in unobserved health and nutritional inputs that augment labor productivity. Land may also have relatively little value for self employment in some parts of the world, and land per household may be allocated in some regions of Africa by the community in proportion to the number of unskilled workers in the household, and not be a good indicator of wealth per person or per adult, e.g. in Côte d'Ivoire or Uganda.

The return coefficient on education in the wage function could be biased by multiple sources of sample selection. For example, suppose the multiple choices that determine sample selection involve different processes of, say, migration from rural to urban labor markets, working in the paid labor force, and working as a wage earner. This chain of decisions appears to be often sensitive to the educational attainment of the individual (Schultz 1988). If unobserved factors related to wages and schooling are associated differentially with the probabilities of each choice in the chain occurring, the procedure to correct for selection bias requires the covariance between the errors in each choice process and the wage function to the estimated. Vijverberg (1993) proposes such an approach in his paper on Côte d'Ivoire and Thomas and Strauss (1992) implement a similar scheme in their analysis of urban Brazil.

A second source of selection bias might arise in a modern welfare state that could be most pronounced among the least educated. Suppose, for example, that persons in this low education group who decide not to engage in wage employment are the least productive workers. This alternative pattern of selection could be reinforced either by public assistance programs that provide workers with welfare support if they do not accept a wage job or by minimum-wage legislation that discourages employers from hiring workers whose productivity is below the minimum wage floor. This form of sample selection bias might become important when unemployment, welfare, and disability insurance benefits are set at relatively generous levels, or where legislation sets the minimum wage high enough to reduct the number of job offers for less productive workers (Schultz 1990a). In this case, the wage earner sample of the lowest education group is only the most productive members of the group. The estimation sample of wage earners becomes more representative of the entire population as a group's level of education increases. According to this second hypothetical source of sample selection bias, standard estimates of private wage returns to relatively low levels of education would be biased downward. Identification of the selection equation might be possible in this case, if welfare legislation or its implementation differed randomly across regions of the sample and induced variations in the wage labor force participation rate.

Some recent studies of wage structures of males in the United States are consistent with this second hypothesized source of sample selection bias, but they have not been extended to a comparison of the wages of men and women. At the lowest tail of the distribution of educational attainment in the United States, in each birth-cohort by state of birth, there is a threshold below which the returns to education for men appear to fall off markedly, to approximately zero. Card and Krueger (1992) estimate this threshold as occurring at the two percentile level, whereas other empirical studies often omit the lowest educational group, with less than eight years of education, to smooth patterns in the tails of the population distribution (Murphy and Welch 1990). If the minimum wage floors applied to male and female workers are the same and welfare support programs are more generous for women relative to the distribution of their wage opportunities than for men, one might expect the downward bias in estimated returns to schooling caused by this source of sample selection to extend further up the distribution of educational attainments for women than for men.

IX. Selection-Corrected Private Wage Returns to Schooling

Several empirical examples are presented in this section to illustrate how private returns to schooling at the primary, secondary, and higher education levels can vary for women and men. These returns are first calculated as conventionally reported by ordinary least squares (OLS) for wage earners. Then these estimates are corrected for sample selection bias where property income and assets, such as land ownership, are used to identify the selection correction procedure. Notes to each Table describe other included variables and estimation methods.

Thailand has grown rapidly for the last several decades. Women have historically played a major role in the market economy, both in traditional agricultural pursuits and in more modern labor force activities. Thailand instituted universal primary education in the 1930s, and by the 1970s nearly all boys and girls completed primary school. The difference in education received by men and women remains substantial at the secondary school level but has narrowed recently at the university level. Private returns to schooling are estimated in Table 4 from the two most recent rounds of the Socio Economic Survey (SES) collected in 1985–86 and 1988–89. Estimates of returns to schooling based on similar assumptions from earlier rounds of this survey in 1975–76 and 1980–81 are reported elsewhere (Schultz 1989a). By 1988–89 the selection-corrected returns to schooling in Thailand do not differ substantially from the direct OLS estimates for either women or men. By comparison, in 1985–86 (and in earlier surveys) primary schooling returns are higher when sample selection is taken into account, whereas secondary schooling returns are lower, again for both men and women. After secondary school, the correction for sample selection increases the returns for women and decreases them for men until the most recent survey in 1988–89. Corrected returns are generally highest from women at the secondary level, whereas they peak at the primary level for males. At the primary school level men have slightly higher returns than do women, 17 versus 13 percent, whereas women receive higher corrected returns at the secondary school level, 25 versus seven percent in 1985–86 and still markedly higher returns than men in 1988–89, 20 versus 12 percent.

Wage ratios associated with each year of primary schooling, corrected for sample selection, have been of a similar magnitude for men and women in Thailand as have enrollment rates. But where women have received only two-thirds of the years of secondary education compared with men, their wage returns have been consistently higher than men, though falling gradually in recent years, from 31 percent in 1975–76 to 20 percent in 1988–89. Only about one-tenth of the Thai survey population has any higher education, but by 1988–89 the SES reports women with 85 percent as many years of higher education as men, whereas in 1975 they had only about half as many years. Women's returns to higher education greatly exceeded men's returns until 1988/89, when this pattern reversed. Under conditions of rapid economic growth in Thailand, returns to schooling for men and women appear to be of a similar magnitude, with the exception of secondary school where the supply of educated Thai females relative to male is lowest and returns to women have greatly exceeded men's for the last 15 years.

Table 5 reports estimates from the Living Standards Measurement Surveys of private returns to schooling from Côte d'Ivoire in 1985, 1986, and 1987 and Ghana in 1987–88 and 1988–89 (Ainsworth and Muñoz 1986). Economic growth until the late 1970s was sustained and rapid in Côte d'Ivoire, whereas economic output per capita declined in Ghana over the 1970s. Over the previous 25 years, national income per capita grew by 70 percent in Ghana, whereas it more than quadrupled in Côte d'Ivoire (World Bank 1991a).

Private returns are uniformly higher for *Côte d'Ivoire* than for *Ghana*. The

Table 4
Estimates of Private Wage Return to Schooling in Thailand, in 1985 and 1988, by Sex, Without and With Statistical Correction for Sample Selection Bias[a]

Year-Unit of Earnings (Sample of Wage Earners/ Population)	Without Correction (OLS) By School Level			With Correction (ML) By School Level		
	Primary	Secondary	Higher	Primary	Secondary	Higher
1985–86—Monthly Earnings						
Female	8.2	31.0	9.5	13.0	25.0	18.0
(2,709–8,606)	(4.75)[b]	(18.7)	(4.31)	(7.00)[c]	(9.84)	(5.45)
Male	14.0	18.0	12.0	17.0	6.8	7.8
(4,199–7,685)	(9.40)	(14.4)	(6.81)	(11.3)	(5.34)	(4.61)
1988–89—Monthly Earnings						
Female	13.5	20.8	9.0	13.8	19.8	8.2
(2,222–8,924)	(8.53)	(16.5)	(5.79)	(9.24)	(10.2)	(3.14)
Male	15.6	12.9	11.8	15.5	12.4	11.3
(3,362–7,733)	(13.8)	(15.2)	(10.4)	(14.3)	(12.7)	(7.31)

a. The coefficients reported are those on the variable years of education completed at each school level, in a logarithmic monthly wage function, which also includes experience (for example, age-schooling-7), experience squared, and several regional dummy variables (Bangkok, municipal, sanitary district (in other words, suburban), and Northeast region). The estimation sample is restricted to wage and salary earners between the ages of 25 and 54. The Ordinary Least Squares (OLS) estimates of the education coefficients are reported in the first three columns, whereas the second set of three columns report the Maximum Likelihood (ML) estimates of the joint probit model for participation as a wage or salary worker and the log wage function. The probability of participation as a wage or salary earner is assumed to be affected by hectares of irrigated and dry land owned and nonearned income. These identifying variables are assumed to be exogenous to the wage function, and do not affect the wage offered to the individual. See Schultz (1989a) for a further discussion of model specification and full ML estimates and parallel estimates for 1980–81 and 1975–76 based on the same Socio Economic Survey in these earlier years.
b. The absolute value of the t statistic is reported in parentheses beneath each OLS regression coefficient on years of education.
c. The absolute value of the asymptotic t statistic is reported in parentheses beneath each ML coefficient estimate on years of education.

Table 5
Estimates of Private Wage Return to Schooling in Côte d'Ivoire and Ghana by Sex, Without and With Statistical Correction for Sample-Selection Bias[a]

Country, Year, and Sample (Sample of Wage Earners/ Population)	Without Correction (OLS) By School Level			With Correction (ML) By School Level		
	Primary	Middle	Secondary	Primary	Middle	Secondary
Côte d'Ivoire 1985–87						
Female (376–9,099)	10.9	24.3	22.4	7.8	20.9	20.2
	(4.08)	(7.45)	(9.95)	(1.26)	(2.71)	(4.22)
Male (1,452–7,832)	14.0	27.4	22.4	11.6	24.1	20.0
	(11.5)	(15.3)	(18.0)	(7.03)	(10.3)	(11.5)
Ghana 1987–88, 1988–89						
Female (454–6,067)	−1.0	14.5	10.4	−1.2	14.2	10.1
	(.34)	(3.95)	(8.30)	(.31)	(2.97)	(2.07)
Male (1,471–5,605)	−1.3	7.0	11.8	−1.3	7.9	12.3
	(.72)	(3.15)	(15.1)	(.78)	(2.73)	(9.27)

a. The coefficients reported are those on the variable years of education completed at each school level, in a logarithmic hourly wage function, which also includes experience (age-schooling-7), experience squared, and several regional dummy variables (capital city, north, central, south, and other urban). The estimation sample is restricted to wage and salary earners between the ages of 15 and 65. The Ordinary Least Squares estimates of the education coefficients are reported in the first three columns, whereas the second set of three columns report the Maximum Likelihood (ML) estimates of the joint probit model for participation as a wage or salary worker and the log wage function. The probability of participation as a wage or salary worker is assumed to be affected by various forms of financial and business assets including land. These identifying variables are assumed not to be exogenous to the wage function, and do not affect the wage rate offered to the individual. See Schultz and Tansel (1992) for further discussion of the Living Standards Measurement Surveys on which these estimates are based and a complete reporting of parallel ML estimations with the inclusion of adult health disability variables.

b. The absolute value of the *t* statistic is reported in parentheses beneath each OLS regression coefficient on years of education.

c. The absolute value of the asymptotic *t* statistic is reported in parentheses beneath each ML coefficient estimate on years of education.

correction for sample selection in Côte d'Ivoire, where only 18 percent of men and 5 percent of women age 15 to 65 are wage earners, lowers marginally the estimated private returns to schooling. Although women have obtained only half as many years of schooling as men, the private returns are similar for men and women. In Thailand, the labor of more educated men and women does not appear to be a perfect substitute for each other, and the gender balance of labor supplies by education level seems to have influenced returns at the secondary level. The evidence from Côte d'Ivoire, on the other hand, is consistent with the interpretation that male and female educated labor are reasonable substitutes for each other in this economy. Other investigations of wage determinants in Côte d'Ivoire also find few indications of gender differentials between observationally similar workers (Van der Gaag and Vijverberg 1987, Vijverberg 1993).

Ghana began the 1960s with more widespread education than Côte d'Ivoire, but Ghanaian women also receive only half the number of years of education as do men. There are relatively few students who exit the school system before completing nine years, but for those few who do, there have been no private returns to show for the first six years of primary schooling in Ghana, for either sex. At the middle level, where women have obtained 61 percent as many years of schooling as men, the relative wage gain for more educated women is almost twice as large as for men, 14 versus 8 percent, respectively. These higher private returns for women than for men are not evident at the secondary school level and beyond, where women have obtained only 40 percent as many years of schooling as men. Many college graduates in Ghana migrated abroad during the 1970s and 1980s in search of jobs, and may make the observed sample that stayed at home unrepresentative of all those who received educations at the secondary and higher levels.

The *United States* is examined in Table 6, as an example of a high-income country where wage earners are a large fraction of the labor force, and education is more equally distributed between men and women (Schultz 1994a). The state level duration of unemployment benefits and the value of AFDC benefits in cash and food stamps for a mother and child are added to the individual's property income as identifiers of the wage earner sample selection model. Not surprisingly, the sample selection procedure indicates that the nonrandom selection of wage earners is a less important source of parameter bias in the United States than in Thailand or Ghana. But there is, nonetheless, a tendency, when sample selection bias is corrected, for women's private returns to increase more than do men's returns, and they exceed men's returns both among blacks and whites. Only at the higher education level do U.S. women have a smaller number of years of schooling than men. One interpretation of this pattern is that the derived demand of firms for workers with a college education in the U.S. economy treats men and women as imperfect substitutes. Contrary to our hypothetical example, correcting for sample selection bias does not raise the low returns to the lowest levels of schooling in the U.S. labor market, although the unemployment and welfare benefits have the theoretically expected effect of reducing wage participation, as does nonearned income, assets and land in the previously reported three studies.

There are relatively few studies of the returns to schooling for men and women

Table 6

Estimates of Private Wage Returns to Schooling in the United States in 1980, by Sex, without and with Statistical Correction for Sample-Selection Bias[a]

Sex (Sample of Wage Earners/Population)	Without Correction (OLS) By School Level			With Correction (ML) By School Level		
	Primary	Middle	Secondary	Primary	Middle	Secondary
White females	.18	5.1	10.4	.11	5.6	10.6
(5,909–9,752)	(.11)[b]	(5.72)	(21.5)	(.09)[c]	(1.66)	(13.9)
White males	3.3	7.1	7.0	3.3	7.6	7.0
(7,430–9,334)	(2.66)	(9.13)	(17.2)	(3.02)	(5.22)	(16.8)
Black females	-2.2	9.6	9.8	-2.4	11.2	10.6
(5,213–9,075)	(1.20)	(8.71)	(12.9)	(1.35)	(4.46)	(7.47)
Black males	1.5	7.4	7.0	1.3	7.9	7.2
(5,334–7,762)	(1.10)	(7.15)	(8.56)	(1.02)	(2.63)	(6.21)

a. The coefficients reported are those on the variable years of education completed at each school level, in a logarithmic hourly wage function, which also includes experience (age-schooling-7), experience squared, urban (in other words, SMSA) resident dummy, and hispanic origin. The estimation sample is restricted to wage and salary earners between the ages of 15 and 64, reporting weeks worked and usual hours worked per week in 1979, so that an hourly wage could be defined as annual earnings divided by the product of weeks worked and usual hours worked last year. The sample includes all blacks and one in ten white persons from the 1 in 1,000 public use sample A of the U.S. Census of Population. The Ordinary Least Squares (OLS) estimates of the education coefficients are reported in the first three columns, whereas the second set of three columns report the Maximum Likelihood (ML) estimates of the joint probit model for participation as a wage or salary worker and the log wage function. The probability of participation as a wage or salary worker is assumed to be affected by individual's receipt of income in 1979 from dividends, interest, and rentals (in linear and quadratic form), and the duration of unemployment benefits in the state of residence, and the maximum AFDC cash and food stamp benefit level paid to a single mother and one child in the state of residence. These identifying variables are assumed to be exogenous to the wage function and do not affect the wage an individual is offered. See Schultz (1994a) for a more extensive discussion of the specification of the model and the full ML estimates.

b. The absolute value of the t statistic is reported in parentheses beneath each OLS regression coefficient on years of education.

c. The absolute value of the asymptotic t statistic is reported in parentheses beneath each ML coefficient estimate on years of education.

that have corrected estimates for sample selection, but the number is growing rapidly. The findings from several other studies are summarized in Table 7 and others are presented in papers at this conference (for example, Deolalikar 1993; Vijverberg 1993; Thomas and Strauss 1992). Because men and women in Latin America receive similar levels of education (Figure 1), I do not expect gender differences in returns to schooling would be particularly sensitive to sample selection bias in this low-income region. The 1985 estimates of male and female returns to schooling for Peru, for example, were not greatly affected by sample selection correction based on land and wealth variables, although women's returns at the secondary level exceed noticeably those to men (Khandker 1989). The first six studies in Table 7 for Latin American countries are reported, therefore, with the expectation that they are not seriously distorted by their neglect of the sample selection problem. No evidence emerges from these studies that individual private rates of return to schooling among wage earners are systematically lower for women than for men in Latin America. Indeed, they tend to be somewhat higher, on average.

Estimates of the returns to women's schooling are more difficult to infer in regions where women have not yet received more than a primary level of schooling and where women are an especially small part of the wage labor force. These conditions hold in most of rural South and West Asia and much of rural Africa. Analysis in these regions could be particularly valuable for understanding why parents in these regions tend to invest more in the schooling of their sons than their daughters.

To estimate with more confidence the returns to schooling, it is necessary that our models account for the individual's allocation of time, particularly to wage employment. This knowledge of how to model wage participation decisions motivates the identification of these sample-selection corrections. Understanding how resources are pooled and labor market behavior is coordinated within the family may be critical to this process. The appropriate theory of family labor supply is therefore important to estimating without bias wage functions. More comparative research is needed to assess whether variations in the specification of models of labor supply behavior, such as by treating it as a cooperative bargaining process (for example, Schultz 1990b, Thomas 1990), alter importantly the parameter estimates of the private returns to schooling of women and men. This matter promises to be more important in low-income than in high-income countries, but there are as yet too few studies of even high-income countries on which to base any generalizations.

X. Issues for Further Study

Schooling for women may be justified in terms of efficiency (high individual private market returns), social externalities (for example, reduced child mortality and fertility), intergenerational redistribution (for example, better health and education of children and a slower growth in population), and equity (an increase in the productive capability of poorer individuals relative to richer individuals). This paper has concluded by estimating for several countries the private

Table 7

Estimates of Private Wage Return to Schooling of Women and Men from Selected Studies in 1970s and 1980s

Country, City, or Regional Coverage and School Level	Year	Women	Men
Argentina Buenos Aires	1980	6.6%	9.3%
Bolivia La Paz	1980	11.0	9.8
Brazil Sao Paulo	1971	6.3	5.4
Colombia National	1973	18.0	18.0
Paraguay Asuncion	1979	8.0	11.0
Peru National	1974	14.0	14.0
India Madras	1981	14.9*	15.8*
Thailand National	1980–81	20.1*	11.3*
Côte d'Ivoire Urban Secondary School	1985	28.7*	17.0*
Peru National Secondary School	1985	14.6*	8.8*
Indonesia National General High School	1986	9.6**	6.2**

Sources: For Peru, see Khandker (1989), for India, see Malathy (1989), for others, see sources in T. Paul Schultz (1989a).

*Sample Selection correction based on land or nonearned income included in the selection equation but not in the wage function.

**Fixed effect for family included which, however, does not correct for problems associated with only selected families having both a male and female earning wages.

a. The coefficients reported are those on the variable years of education completed (on school level if indicated), in a logarithmic wage function, which also includes experience (for example, age-schooling-7), experience squared, and regional and rural/urban dummy variables if a national sample. Samples tend to be at least 1,000 and often much larger including all wage and salary workers between the ages of 25 and 64. The coefficients on the education variable are all statistically significant at conventional levels. In several cases age is used in place of experience.

efficiency of women's and men's schooling, while observing that health and nutritional investments may be equally important and involve similar issues. Aspects of social externalities and intergenerational redistribution are difficult to quantitatively assess but social returns that can be measured favor social subsidies for investments in women. Others have discussed the justification for making transfers to women on the grounds of equity (for example, Tinker 1990).

During this century, human capital investment in women has increased relative to that made in men, at least as measured by either years of schooling or years of longevity.[17] These shifts in the gender composition of human capital formation have occurred at about the same time that women have entered in increasing numbers into the market labor force, particularly in employment outside of the family for wages (Schultz 1990a). The coincidence of these trends in female labor force participation and their schooling support the conjecture that women realize more returns to their education through their work in the market labor force.

Most studies of labor force participation of women confirm that women with more education supply more of their time to market work, and more specifically to wage employment, holding constant male education or wages and nonhuman wealth. This is true in each of the four countries analyzed in this paper, and is notable in many studies of Latin America in recent decades (ECIEL 1982). The release of time from childbearing and childrearing activities is also associated with women leaving home for market employment in the higher income countries (Mincer 1985). Which comes first, the market labor force commitment, the decline in fertility, or the educational attainment of women? Education is often treated as being determined first, based on an individual's expected returns to education and on parents endowments, both educational and financial, that allow parents to promote their children's schooling. By this reasoning, fertility and specialization between home and market labor force skills are modified by prior educational attainment. To disentangle with greater rigor this lifecycle causal chain (or system) a suitable source of variation in schooling is needed that is independent of the child's (or parent's) preferences for adult careers of childbearing or market employment. This source of variation in education may then be used to identify the effect of education on individual productivity and behavior. It should then be possible to infer how variation in women's education affects their wage opportunities as well as their fertility and labor force behavior and other choices involving migration and sector of employment (see Vijverberg 1993, Thomas and Strauss 1992).

---

17. Most indicators of adult health status or morbidity are based on self-evaluations of a survey population and are criticized as being excessively subjective. Consequently, comparisons of the health status of men and women across cultures based on these indicators are controversial (Schultz and Tansel 1992). Height and Body-Mass-Index appear to predict mortality and the onset by middle age of chronic diseases (Fogel 1990, Costa 1993), but these anthropometric indicators of adult health have not yet been systematically collected for women, as well as for men, to assess how sex differences in these indicators vary across groups in a society, across populations at different stages in the development process, or over time within a population. More research is therefore required on the consequences of adult health for females and males separately. It is conjectured that because the declines in mortality have been generally more favorable for females than for males, other objective indicators of health will confirm a similar pattern. The empirical basis for this presumption is currently limited.

The returns to education and health investments may interact and partially account for the shifting emphasis toward women's human capital. Medical knowledge appears to have contributed little to the decline in mortality before the twentieth century (McKeown and Record 1962, Preston and Haines 1991), and yet the creation and spread of public health and medical technologies are believed to be important factors in the demographic transition in this century. Have these new technologies given educated persons a new survival advantage. And in the case of women, the health advantage has been effectively extended to their children. If this is a relatively recent phenomenon, then it might help explain the shift of resources toward women's education, even when women in low-income countries are still primarily engaged in household production tasks within the family. Increased nutrition and health status of populations may also reinforce the rising productivity of more educated workers. Were this true, the contribution of education to labor productivity as estimated in wage functions could overstate the returns to schooling because of the failure to hold constant nutritional status. Thomas and Strauss (1992) support this hypothesis in urban Brazil.

Studies of human capital have emphasized the heterogeneity of labor as a productive factor, and the substantial share of that heterogeneity that is a produced means of production, created by the secularly rising investment of families and society in the nutrition, health and schooling of people. How are we to explain that a widening circle of countries, indeed those that have been more successful in stimulating modern economic growth, are also tending to invest an increasing share of their human capital in women? With all the limitations of current data and statistical methods, this paper has reported for several countries estimates of private market returns to schooling that are of a similar magnitude for men and women. In some, but not all, countries educated male and female labor appear to be imperfect substitutes, and their relative supplies are inversely associated with the returns they receive on their skills. Specifically, when women have received a small fraction of the secondary or higher education in a society, women with these more scarce skills tend to receive a larger relative wage premium than do men. Although the relative wage returns to schooling for women and men may be of a similar magnitude, as in the United States, this does not imply, as we all know, that the *level* of women's wages is equal to men's. Private returns are approximated by the *ratio* of the wage of the more educated worker to that of a worker with less education (of the same sex), divided by the years a student must forego employment to acquire this extra education (Mincer 1974). Both the wage gains and opportunity costs of schooling are generally lower for women than for men, but roughly in the same proportion, implying comparable internal private rates of return.

Future research should estimate the effects of relative supplies of sex-specific educated labor on the level of and differentials in wages, holding constant for the effect of the composition of aggregate demand on these wage structures. That objective is beyond the scope of this paper, for it will require consistent compilation of microdata across many countries and perhaps within them over time. But no evidence has emerged in this study that supports the view that educating more women, even if it involved educating fewer men, would lower potential aggregate output.

2 Obstacles to Advancement of Women During Development

Ester Boserup

Ester Boserup is a former member of the Advisory Committee on Development of the EEC, the Governing Board of the United Nations International Research and Training Institute for the Advancement of Women, and the United Nations Committee on Development Planning. She has also held administrative and research positions with the Danish government. Boserup is the author of *Conditions of Agricultural Growth, Population, and Technological Change,* and *Woman's Role in Economic Development.*

I. Introduction

Economic development is a process of technological change. It influences people's production and consumption, health and length of life, education and professional training. It moves them from the countryside to large agglomerations and from work in family farms and other family enterprises to work in giant industries and large bureaucratic establishments.

By changing the way of life, economic development also influences people's opinions and attitudes, but often with a considerable time lag. Traditional opinions and customary behavior are most often opinions and behavior that were rational at an earlier stage of development, but survive after technological and economic change have made them irrational and counterproductive. Many of the handicaps from which women in developing (and developed) countries suffer are due to the survival of irrational and counterproductive beliefs and attitudes. These beliefs and attitudes are neglected by economists if they make the assumption that rational behavior is the rule under all circumstances.

Outdated ideas and attitudes are often kept alive because they serve the interest of some large and influential group in the population, and men's interest in preserving the traditional ranking order between the sexes should not be underestimated in any analysis of women's position; it should not be overestimated either. Some men are more "altruistic" than others, and many women are eager enough to defend traditional attitudes, when they serve the interest of the group to which

51

they belong. Moreover, very often women themselves want to preserve traditions and attitudes that are contrary to their own interest.

Traditional attitudes affect women's positions in the family, in the labor market, and in public life. The effects of the changes caused by economic development in all three spheres interact and produce a complicated pattern, which will be described in the following sections. The second and third sections deal with the change in women's positions, resulting respectively from increasing commercial production in family farms and other family enterprises and from the growth of modern industries and private and public services. The last two sections focus on the erosion of family authority as a result of development and on psychological obstacles to improvement in the position of women during development.

II. Division of Labor in Family Production

The countries that are classified as "developing" by the United Nations are at widely different levels of economic development. The least developed among them have low rates of urbanization, and most of the inhabitants in rural areas are predominantly subsistence producers with extremely low money incomes. In contrast, many other developing countries have high rates of urbanization and have incomes per capita that deviate little from those in some high income countries and are sometimes higher.

In rural areas where production is partly or predominantly for consumption in the family, there is a division of labor by sex and age. Some tasks are performed by men, who teach the necessary skills to young men and boys; other tasks are performed by women, who pass their skills, both agricultural and domestic, to younger women and girls. This division of labor between the sexes is rational, because everybody needs half as much training and gets twice as much work experience as would be the case if everybody were to learn and perform all the tasks that are needed for subsistence production of goods and services.

Owing to the sex and age specialization of work, the housewife in most traditional subsistence families has much authority. She can dispose of the labor power of the young female family members: children, unmarried daughters and sisters, younger wives in polygamic marriages, and daughters-in-law. She can use these persons as unpaid family labor power in both domestic and other work. Similarly, her husband disposes of the labor power of younger male family members. But here the equality between the sexes ceases because in nearly all traditional subsistence families the wife is subordinate to her husband, who can dispose of her labor power and other activities (Tinker 1990; Law and the Status of Women 1977; Ngondo 1988).

In the course of economic development, more and more rural families combine production and sale of one or more products or services with subsistence production of food, services, and some nonagricultural products. Such a combination of subsistence production and production for sale is the predominant way of life for most rural families in nearly all developing countries. In addition, in urban areas of developing countries, large numbers of families combine production and sale of one or more nonagricultural products and services with subsistence production of some food items and services. In Boserup (1970) this type of production was labeled "the bazaar and service sector," but subsequently the term "informal sector" has become generally accepted in the development literature.

If families in the informal sector specialize in the production of goods or services that are usually produced for subsistence by male family members in that community, men manage, and men and boys work in these family enterprises. However, if the goods and services produced for sale are traditionally produced for subsistence by female family members, the small enterprises in the informal sector usually have an entirely female staff, managed by the housewife (or one of the wives in a polygamic marriage) using her daughters and other female family members as unpaid family labor. In family farms with commercial production of some products, women often produce and sell those products traditionally produced by women in that area. Sometimes women also sell the men's products. In other words, both the usual age hierarchy and the economic advantage of sex specialization of labor are preserved when subsistence production is replaced or augmented by informal sector activities. Young family members of both sexes are becoming trained in the necessary skills by older family members of the same sex.

In much of Africa, Asia, and Latin America, a large share of the family enterprises in the informal sector are operated by married women, divorcées and widows with or without help from daughters and other women and girls (Arispe 1977; Bohman 1984; Tinker 1987). But in most of South Asia and in the Arab world, nearly all family enterprises are operated by men with male assistance. If women produce for sale, in addition to their subsistence production and domestic duties, it is usually home production in the family dwelling, leaving the products to be sold by children or male family members. In these regions, trade, including market trade, is a male occupation.

However, the female family enterprises belonging to married women suffer from serious handicaps because their female manager is not autonomous. In many developing countries, the husband has legal right to dispose of his wife's labor and earnings, and only men can inherit. However, even in countries without legal discrimination between men and women, the wife may be powerless in relation to her husband or other male family members because custom is stronger than the law, at least in rural areas. Therefore, female enterprises suffer from serious handicaps compared to male-headed ones.

First, the husband may forbid his wife to engage in any independent production of goods or services for sale and may require that she use all her time on domestic work and care of husband and children.

Second, the husband may only permit his wife to do home work in the family dwelling, with other family members selling her products in the market. In regions where women are limited to home work and domestic duties, the oversupply of female-produced home products often makes the hourly earnings from home production derisory.

Third, the husband may not prohibit his wife from engaging in money-earning activities, but he may require that, in addition to subsistence production and domestic duties, she give so much assistance to his money-earning activities that she is, in reality, prevented from money-earning work on her own account.

Fourth, the husband may permit, and perhaps insist, that his wife undertake a money-earning activity, but he may also insist that the share of her income handed over to him, or used for family consumption, be so large that nothing or too little is left for the necessary expenditures in her business.

In many developing countries a large share of the households are headed by women. In many of these the female family head is a widow, divorcée, or woman abandoned by her husband; in others the husband is a migrant worker or is living with another formal or informal wife. It is often assumed that these households do not suffer from the handicaps enumerated above, but if a migrant worker leaves his wife behind, he usually leaves some other male family member, a father, brother, or other relative, in control of his wife. Also, widows and divorcées living alone or with children are often under the control of a male family member (Lloyd and Brandon 1991).

Moreover, not only the woman's husband or other male family members, but also other male co-villagers may insist on male priority in the use of resources. In many parts if the world, women are growing crops or gathering fodder for their animals on common land belonging to their village and are selling the products in the market. This important source of money earnings for female villagers is reduced or disappears when population increases, and expanding male market production, leading to the increased privatization of land, reduces the area of common land. Even in areas where women are allowed to own and inherit land, they rarely benefit from the privatization of land, either by legal action or by land grabbing. If they have no husband present to defend their interests, increasing land shortages may put them out of business (Carney and Watts 1991; Chipande 1988).

III. From Age Hierarchy to Skill Hierarchy

The traditional age distribution of work disappears when large-scale modern industries and modern services invade a labor market that was hitherto dominated by family enterprises. Technological change devalues traditional skills taught by parents to children and youth and replaces them with modern skills and knowledge. The modern sector does not rely on a labor force with family training, with young as assistants to older workers. It has a much more elaborate division of labor than the traditional one by sex and age. Above the unskilled workers are layers of supervisors and people with specialized skills. These specialized skills are not family skills, but are learned in schools, high-level educational establishments, or professional training courses, outside or within the enterprises.

In other words, the age hierarchy is replaced by a skill hierarchy. The place in the job hierarchy and the level of wages and salaries for both young and old members of the staff depend on the level of skills they have acquired, either before becoming employed or by formal on-the-job training during employment. In developing countries with rapidly increasing levels of education and training, younger workers will usually be more skilled than older ones, and the age hierarchy is reversed. To the extent that modern industries and services are manned not by foreigners but by nationals in high-level jobs, incumbents will be young people from families that are rich or powerful enough to have provided them with a high level of education and training. With the rapid spread of high school education, people with only a primary education will at best be able to obtain low-level jobs in the modern sector, and illiterates will more and more be confined to work in the agricultural and informal sectors.

The skill hierarchy in modern industries and services is a serious handicap to female workers, because they are recruited to unskilled, routine work. Modern industries in developing countries usually recruit only young unmarried women, most of whom withdraw voluntarily, or are fired, when they marry or have children. Since they are likely to stay on the job for only a short time, neither their employers nor their parents have sufficient motivation to provide them with industrial skills.

The young girls benefit from earning wages instead of being unpaid family workers, but their wages are considerably below those of unskilled male workers, so the industries are motivated to employ them. But because they have worked in industry instead of learning traditional skills from their mothers, they are handicapped if they later become dependent on earning money incomes after they have become barred from industrial employment. So, while industrial employment provides men with modern skills and good permanent incomes, the effect of industrial employment of women is to deprive them of traditional skills, except for domestic ones, without providing them with any modern skills. Add to this the fact that, with economic development and increasing urbanization, many of the domestic skills that were needed for subsistence production become superfluous because more and more products and services are purchased or delivered by public establishments.

Also, the rapidly growing modern services offer some jobs for women in most developing countries. These are primarily low-level jobs in modern offices and shops. Some of these jobs require secondary education, and some require degrees from technical schools or universities, for example, many positions in health or education services. However, since parents can never know beforehand how long a time even professionally trained daughters will stay in the labor market, they have more motivation for educating and training sons than daughters at all levels of the educational ladder. Therefore, these jobs are filled mainly by daughters from relatively wealthy families that can afford to educate not only their sons, but also their daughters. Some of these families may educate their daughters as a means to obtain a more favorable marriage, or for family prestige.

This small elite of professionally trained women has lower wages and many fewer career opportunities than do male colleagues with similar education and skills. However, they earn much higher money incomes than both other women and the majority of men. In other words, development creates a large gap in incomes not only between men, but also between women from better-off and from low-income families. On the top of the ladder is a small elite of women with academic and middle-level professional training; below them are the young female workers in modern industries, especially multinational ones; below them are women who are money earners in the informal sector and agriculture; and, finally, at the bottom are female domestic servants and unpaid family workers in the informal, domestic, and agricultural sectors. But, of course, many of the latter may benefit from relatively large money incomes earned by their male family members.

It is often assumed that when modern industry and services are introduced into a country the modern sector rapidly outcompetes traditional family enterprises so men and women in urban areas have a choice only between the modern sector and unemployment. However, to a large extent modern enterprises and small family enterprises cater to different types of customers. The upper and middle classes, and some of the workers in the modern sector, can afford to use factory-made products and modern service establishments, but low-paid workers, people in the informal sector, small farmers, and agricultural workers use the much cheaper products and services delivered by enterprises in the informal sector. Therefore, cheap products made in the informal sector by female family enterprises, for example, food cooked at home and sold in the streets, and many other homemade products offered for sale in the streets, open-air markets, and bazaars, do directly compete with the much more expensive products and services produced by modern establishments. The latter are mainly replacing imported manufactures and services, which also cater to better-off customers. This implies that, even at relatively advanced stages of development, women, especially married and older women, have much more economic security if they belong to a community with a tradition for female family enterprises than if they belong to one with female seclusion, or semiseclusion.

IV. Changes in Women's Position in the Family

In recent decades the large-scale transfer of modern technologies from high-income countries to developing ones together with the rapid spread of modern education and means of mass communication have resulted in important changes both in the economy and in family organization. With the rapid growth of urbanization in most developing countries in recent decades, a much larger share of the youth are growing up in metropoles and other urban areas, and not only urban but also rural life has changed rapidly. Market production has substituted for, or added to, subsistence production; transportation, communications, and other economic and social services have appeared or improved, including rural schools and health services. The major changes in the lives of young women resulting from this process of modernization are more access to jobs in large-scale industries and modern services, much more literacy and higher education and much more familiarity with conditions in the outer world, and much better access to health services and family planning with resulting declines in maternal and child mortality.

The jobs offered to young women in large-scale industries, offices, and shops follow the usual pattern in the old industrialized countries: young women are recruited to the lowest jobs, are paid lower wages than male colleagues with similar qualifications, and are often gotten rid of when they marry or grow older. However, their low status on the job does not prevent the new job opportunities from resulting in important improvements in the position of young women. Although many of them remain under the authority of older family members, to whom they must deliver their earnings, the fact that they are earning money improves their status in the family. Parents are more motivated to provide education and professional training to their daughters when there are possibilities for wage or salary incomes later. Young girls improve their status vis-à-vis parents, brothers, and marriage partners by becoming economically self-reliant, or cash contributors to the family economy. Employed daughters can better resist the parents' choice of unwanted marriage partners. Moreover, both the women themselves and their parents become interested in later marriages, either so more money can be earned before losing the job or so it would be possible to finish an education, which in turn could give access to a better-paid and more permanent job.

For the older generations of women, there has been much less change, and it has often been negative. The large majority of these older women are housewives, farmers' wives, market women, or women who have worked in or managed other family enterprises and still do so. The increase in female education levels and the increase in the employment of unmarried daughters in modern industries and services have added to the work burden of the housewife because she gets less help from her daughters for child care and other work in the household and in her family enterprise.

In countries where female education has spread very rapidly, a large share of the female school leavers have illiterate mothers; and illiterate mothers and mothers-in-law often have daughters and daughters-in-law who are educated. If these daughters and daughters-in-law also have jobs with more prestige and higher incomes than the older women, the status hierarchy among female family members has been upset. Mothers have little authority over their daughters: they lose help from their daughters not only while they are at school or in their job, but also because they have become less obedient. If their daughters deliver part or all of their wages as a contribution to the family economy, they may be unwilling to work as unpaid family labor in their spare time. For older, illiterate women, modernization results in a serious loss of prestige and power within the family hierarchy.

Moreover, it is mainly young women who benefit from the rapid spread of communications, both those that require literacy and those, like radio, video, TV, and meetings, that although in principle are accessible to illiterates and barely literates, reach younger women more frequently than older women. Because of the improvements in communication and their frequent contacts in schools and workplaces, younger women have become much better informed about the lifestyle of women outside their own narrow circle. Even in the least-developed countries, a female elite of professional and other educated women has been influenced by the recent, radical changes in women's position in industrialized countries and by the efforts of the United Nations and Human Rights Organizations to improve the position of women in developing countries. Many factors combine, therefore, to create a large gap in attitudes between young women and the older generations of women, who often have more to lose than to gain from modernization.

V. Legal Change and the Status of Women

Not only the authority of older women, but also that of older men, is undermined by the progress in education and communications and the changes in the labor market. Young sons with a better education, and perhaps a higher income than their fathers, are unlikely to be obedient to the family head, whether the sons stay at home or live elsewhere. Not only in the labor market, but also within the family, skills and income levels are replacing age as marks of distinction and authority. In addition, economic development makes it difficult for the family head to control other family members, either because they spend part of their time in schools and enterprises located away from the family home, or because the family head himself gets work that keeps him away from the household most of the time.

Government attitudes to societal change are important and vary strongly from country to country. Some governments in developing countries attempt to modernize the country on Western lines, so they have passed or are passing legislation that limits the power of the family head over the other members of the family, especially the daughters. Examples of such legislation are: compulsory school attendance laws for girls combined with school curricula that do not support, but deviate from, traditional ideologies and beliefs; laws that permit and support family planning; legislation that raises the marriage age for girls; laws that forbid marriage payments or forced marriages; and laws that modernize divorce procedures and women's access to economic support from the husband, to inheritance, and to the ownership and free disposal of property.

Other governments promote industrialization and other technological modernization, but do what they can to prevent economic development from changing the traditional position of women. The Iranian half-way solution allows university attendance and employment of young women, but makes such activities punishable without the chador. This is an extreme example of a policy that aims at economic development without cultural change.

Much modernizing legislation in favor of women remains on paper only because of a lack of popular support not only from men but also from women, especially older women. India is one among many examples. The Indian government has supported most of the legislative changes in favor of women that were mentioned above. India was one of the first countries to support family planning and has encouraged both government employment and other employment of women. Nevertheless, in India fertility decline is slow, female employment and school attendance of girls are low and are rising less rapidly than in most other developing countries, while intrafamilial inequalities in health and mortality are exceptionally large (Schultz 1989a).

From ancient times, Indian culture has stressed the inferiority of women and their role as modest and submissive servants to men, even more than most other cultures. Even today, most mothers in India, especially in the northern states (Boserup 1970), accept this picture of the ideal wife and teach the virtue of differential treatment of the sexes to their boys and girls from an early age. Early indoctrination of children is very resistant to change by later educational efforts and experiences (Boggild 1983), and small boys and girls get the lesson both orally and by observing family discrimination in the distribution of, for example, food, work, access to school education. Hanna Papanek has called Indian culture "a culture of female sacrifice" (Papanek 1990).

The family socialization of Indian women, a behavior that Amartya Sen has called "hard exploitation of Indian women" (Sen 1990), is accepted without protest by most women. Therefore, Indian men have little reason to fear that a significant share of the women will contest their privileges in spite of the liberal legislation and secret ballots in parliamentary elections. Algerian women seem to be less submissive, since it was recently decided to allow the head of household to cast his wife's vote only if he could produce a written permission signed by her.

It may seem a paradox that it is precisely in India, as well as some other Asian countries with strong discrimination against women and adherence to separate roles in the family and in the society at large, that female prime ministers and presidents have been acceptable. But it is in reality a proof of the strength of the traditions in these stratified societies that men are prepared to accept female rulers before economic development has reached a very high level. All the female Asian prime ministers and presidents succeeded their husbands or fathers in office after these men were killed or died a natural death. These women do not rule in their personal capacity, but as representatives of their families, whose power and income opportunities they help to preserve. Also, many male rulers in developing countries act as representatives of their families and place family members in top jobs or as successors, treating public property as their family fortune. Similar to queens, female members of high caste, or other high-status families, are considered superior to male members of families with lower status. Therefore, they may be acceptable in traditional, stratified societies as successors to male relatives.

In contrast to India, social stratification in most African societies is less pronounced and sometimes of recent origin. Married women who only do domestic work for their own family are rare, and female participation in agricultural work and family enterprises is very large, as mentioned earlier. So women in Africa are better able to support themselves and children than are most Indian women. Therefore, a woman's bargaining position in relation to that of her husband is less influenced by fear of divorce, which may often weaken a man's bargaining position more than that of his wife because of the large contribution African women make to household expenditures and to the husband's income-earning activities (Bassett 1991).

Because of their frequent participation in market trade and other labor market activities, African women have much more contact with others, both males and females, than the typical Indian woman. They become much more aware of the changing world, inside as well as outside their own country. Modern forms of communication, radio, films, television, and video, transmit information about other parts of the world with larger opportunities for women, not only to the female elite, but to large numbers of women, even illiterates and barely literates. Conservative Indians are worried about the importation by satellite of Western ideas and ideals (Imhasly 1991), but such imports have long been much more widespread in Africa than in India, facilitated by the familiarity of a considerable share of Africans with one of the European languages.

Similar to India, family socialization of African children stresses male superiority and female subordination to men, but men's control of their wives is based more on wife-beating and threats of it than on cultural indoctrination. Treatment of female children is much better in Africa than is typical in India: there is no sex differential in mortality, and the increase in school attendance for girls has been very rapid, partly because the larger female participation in money-earning activities provides more economic motivation for parents to educate their daughters.

Moreover, the rate of increase in urbanization in most of Africa has been much more rapid than the increase in urbanization that occurred in India in the period after independence. Many metropolitan towns have had explosive growth of population and employment, not so much in industry as in modern private and public services and in the informal sector. Traditional patterns of marriage and relations between the sexes have not been unaffected by this development (Antoine and Nanitelamie 1990; Caldwell et al. 1991; Lututtala 1991; Meekers 1988; Pilon 1988). The rapidity of the breakdown of formal marital relations and traditional lifestyles in some African metropolis resembles recent changes in European cities more than is the case in the much more conservative Indian cities.

Another contrast between Africa and India concerns the legal position of women. It was mentioned earlier that women's contributions to both agricultural production and female-headed family enterprises were severely handicapped by the legal discrimination between men and women in nearly all African countries. Because of their legal disabilities, African women are less able than men to adjust their economic behavior to the changes in technology and institutions that accompany (and are conditions for) economic development. But because African women are more self-reliant and contribute more to the family economy, while their husbands have no legal obligation to do so, and because they are less psychologically attached to their marriage and husband than Indian women are, African women would probably react to an improvement in their bargaining position due to legal reforms by becoming less obedient to their husbands and more likely to break up their marriage. Therefore, nearly all African men are emphatically opposed to legal modernization, which would increase women's bargaining power. Legal reforms should not be considered an inefficient means of improving women's conditions simply because they have had little effect in some countries.

VI. Conclusion

There are several factors that make it possible for men to control their wives and other female members: women's economic dependence on male relatives, legal discrimination, wife-beating, and psychological indoctrination. The degree to which one or the other is used varies from community to community. Therefore, a purely economic theory of the position of women in development is as misleading as one that neglects the micro- or macroeconomic factors, or both. Multidisciplinary cooperation is indispensable in this field of research.

Access to money-earning activities, education, family planning, and improved health are very important means to improve women's position, but the other features discussed above must also be studied in order to explain why the generally agreed upon measures are likely to be efficient in some communities, but not in others.

3 The U-Shaped Female Labor Force Function in Economic Development and Economic History

Claudia Goldin

Claudia Goldin is professor of economics at Harvard University. She has previously held positions at the University of Pennsylvania, Princeton University, and the University of Wisconsin. She is author or editor of several books, including *Understanding the Gender Gap: An Economic History of American Women, The Regulated Economy,* and *Strategic Factors in Nineteenth Century American Economic History.* The author thanks Robert Barro for the use of his educational attainment data, and Anne Hill for generously sharing her personal data files. Boris Simkovich and Linda Tuch served as very able research assistants on this project. The Brookings Institution provided funding for both the author's leave and the research assistance of Linda Tuch. Lawrence Katz and T. Paul Schultz provided valuable criticism and insights.

"It is open to men to debate whether economic progress is good for men or not, but for women to debate the desirability of economic growth is to debate whether women should have the chance to cease to be beasts of burden, and to join the human race."
    W. Arthur Lewis, *The Theory of Economic Growth* (1955)

Gender equality and economic development share a synchronous existence. Gender equality is a spur to economic development, particularly where the well-being of children is concerned, and economic development, as the headnote graphically suggests, fosters gender equality.

It is the relationship from economic development to greater gender equality that is explored here. I examine the roles played by education and the emergence of a white-collar sector in fostering the paid employment of married women. The movement of women from the home to the workplace promotes various types of gender equality both in society at large and in the home, although the process has been protracted in a number of countries. Women's changing status across

61

economic development can be studied in the histories of developed economies and through a cross section of the world's economies. The historical case used here is the United States over the past century, and the cross section is a data set of more than one hundred countries.

Across the process of economic development the adult women's labor force participation rate is U-shaped. When incomes are extremely low and when certain types of agriculture dominate (for example, poultry, dairy, rice, cotton, peanuts; generally not grains, livestock, tree crops, sugarcane), women are in the labor force to a great extent. They are sometimes paid laborers but more often are unpaid workers on family farms and in household businesses, often doing home workshop production. As incomes rise in most societies, often because of an expansion of the market or the introduction of new technology, women's labor force participation rates fall. Women's work is often implicitly bought by the family, and women then retreat into the home, although their hours of work may not materially change. The decline in female labor force participation rates owes, in part, to an income effect, but it may be reinforced by a reduction in the relative price of home-produced goods and by a decrease in the demand for women's labor in agriculture. Even when women's relative wage rises, married women may be barred from manufacturing employment by social custom or by employer preference.

But as female education improves and as the value of women's time in the market increases still further, relative to the price of goods, they move back into the paid labor force, as reflected in the move along the rising portion of the U-shaped curve. The process suggests an initially strong income effect combined with a small own-substitution effect.[1] At some point the substitution effect increases while the income effect may decline. During the falling portion of the U the income effect dominates, but during the rising portion of the U the substitution effect dominates. I will address how the substitution effect comes to dominate and what relationship exists between the income and the substitution effects.

The notion that economic development enhances gender equality is not, I know, shared by all (see, for example, Norris 1992 for a model of immiseration). Nor is it universally agreed that a movement toward gender equality, as expressed, for example, in greater female schooling, causally enhances economic development. But I believe both notions are valid for the vast majority of countries and economies at least in certain ranges of economic development. In many cases the reason for the controversy regarding the first line of causality—running from economic development to greater gender equality—concerns the U-shaped relationship between economic development and female labor force participation. Movements along the declining portion of the U may lead to the immiseration of women. But those along the rising portion generally do not.

Central to understanding the relationship between the economic status of women and economic development is isolating the factors that cause the U-shaped

---

1. By an income effect I mean the change of hours of work of an individual with respect to a change in family income. The own-substitution effect is the change in hours of work of an individual with respect to a change in their wage, holding income constant. I will refer to the own-substitution effect simply as the substitution effect. By the substitution effect I will mean the compensated wage effect.

function to change direction and rise with economic development, rather than fall. A further issue is what meaning increased labor force participation outside the home has in the lives of the world's women. Factors will vary from country to country, but there is considerable evidence that as women's work moves out from the home and family, even if such work was previously market oriented, women gain freedoms in the polity, in the society, and in their own households.[2] The relationship is far from perfect, and in some cases political freedoms actually occurred decades before economic change was apparent. But the relationship does appear to exist. There is also the issue of decision making in the household. We know little about how resources are divided within the home, particularly among households in the richer nations of the world. We do know, however, that when women have the capacity for economic independence, they generally make more decisions within the household and control more resources (see, for example, Thomas 1990).

The first issue to address is the general U-shaped relationship between economic development and women's labor force participation. An uncomplicated graphical model of household and market production guides the discussion of the factors accounting for the U shape. Data on about a hundred countries are examined to establish the relationship between women's labor force participation and economic development, and among female education, the clerical sector, and economic development in cross section. The historical record for the United States since 1890 provides evidence concerning the transition to the upward portion on the U. Finally, I return to the large cross section of countries to explore the relationship between economic history and economic development in terms of women's economic role and status.

I. Economic Development and the U-Shaped Female Participation Rate Function

A. The U in Cross Section

Several students of economic development have made reference to a U-shaped relationship between women's labor force participation rate and economic development (for example, Durand 1975 and Psacharopoulos and Tzannatos 1989; see Schultz 1991, however, on the distinction between wage and nonwage labor). The association between the two can be seen in Figure 1, which graphs the participation rate of women 45 to 59 years old against (log) per capita GDP (1985 $), where all variables are for c. 1980.[3] Per capita GDP may not be the best variable to proxy economic development, and the relationship is also graphed in

---

2. Miller (1982) is a fine study of the effects of women's employment in India on reducing female seclusion and segregation.

3. All countries with available data except those in the Middle East and those centrally planned are shown. The centrally planned economies are: Bulgaria, China, Czechoslovakia, Cuba, Hungary, Romania, the USSR, East Germany, and Yugoslavia, although data for some of these countries were not available. Also excluded are countries for which the labor force data differ substantially from those relating to employment status. The results do not materially change if all available countries are included.

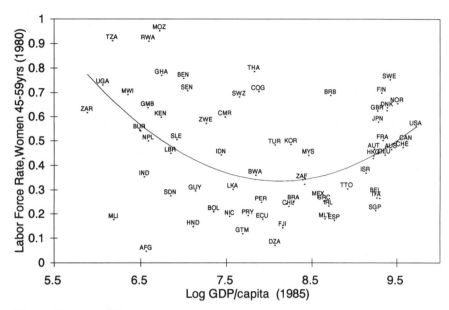

Figure 1

Labor Force Participation Rates for Women 45 to 59-Years-Old (c. 1980) and the Log of GDP/Capita (1985, 1985 $)

Sources: Labor force participation rates: United Nations (1992); GDP/capita in 1985: Summers and Heston (1991).

Notes: See Appendix 1 for the country codes; dots are given for countries that would have overlapped with others. The centrally planned countries and those of the Middle East (except Israel) are omitted from the diagram. Also omitted are twenty countries for which the WISTAT (United Nations 1992) labor force data differ substantially from those given for employment status; see text. The regression line is a quadratic in the log of GDP/capita.

Figure 2 using the number of years schooling of the male population over 25 years old, also for c. 1980. Each graph contains the regression line from a simple quadratic equation.[4]

I should acknowledge at the outset that the data come from the work of many other researchers. The education data are from Barro and Lee (1993), the GDP/capita (1985 $) data are from Summers and Heston (1991), and the female labor force participation rates are from the extensive United Nations WISTAT collection (United Nations 1992), as are additional data, used below, on sectoral or occupational shares.[5] It should also be noted that the definition of employment

---

4. Even though certain religions are important in determining female labor force participation rates across countries in a regression of the participation rate on a quadratic in per capita GDP, the percentage Muslim is not once the countries of the Middle East have been excluded.

5. The economically active population data on which the labor force numbers are based comes from International Labour Office (1986) according to the WISTAT reference manual. Justifications for using the Barro and Lee data in preference to those of the World Bank can be found in Barro and Lee (1993).

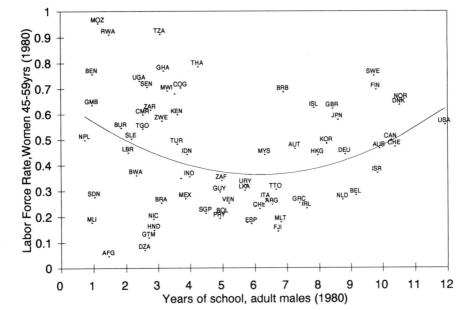

Figure 2

Labor Force Participation Rates for Women 45 to 59-Years-Old and Years of School for the Adult (> 25 years) Male Population, Both c. 1980

Sources: Labor force participation rates c. 1980: United Nations (1992); years of school for the adult (> 25 years) male population in 1980: Barro and Lee (1993).

Note: See Appendix 1 for the country codes; dots are given for countries that would have overlapped with others. The centrally planned countries and those of the Middle East (except Israel) are omitted from the diagram. France has also been excluded because of definitional problems in measuring total years of education. Also omitted are 20 countries for which the WISTAT (United Nations 1992) labor force data differ substantially from those given for employment status; see text. The regression line is a quadratic in years of school.

varies across the countries, but it generally includes unpaid family farm workers, those in family businesses, and own-account traders.[6]

---

6. I have explored differences between the labor force data in WISTAT (which are from International Labour Office 1986) and those (also from WISTAT) from various country sources that are subdivided by employment status (wage labor, self-employed, unpaid family worker). There are several countries in which the differences are very large. In some cases the labor force numbers are greater, and in others those by employment status are. Bangladesh, the Central African Republic, the Dominican Republic, El Salvador, Guinea-Bissau, Jamaica, Jordan, Lesotho, Niger, and Pakistan all have differences exceeding 30 percent in absolute value. There are eight other countries in which the differences exceed 20 percent in absolute value but are below 30 percent. Another twenty have differences that exceed 10 percent but are below 20 percent. These countries have been excluded from both Figures 1 and 2. In only a few cases can I figure out the precise reason for the discrepancy (e.g., differences in dates, exclusion of unpaid family workers). I should note that only the labor force data are given by sex and age, and that is the reason for preferring them.

The general contours of the diagrams are not decidedly different when one of the younger age groups—25 to 44 years old—is graphed.[7] The lower-aged group, however, contains many unmarried women, particularly at the younger ages, and women whose fertility decisions also impact their labor force decisions. The older age group is preferred for various reasons, although it, too, presents problems. The older group will contain widows and abandoned women, and thus will not fully reflect the determinants of female labor force participation I would like to isolate. There is yet an additional problem presented by the older age group. I would like to see if educational advances and structural change in the economy are later reflected in the female participation rates. But these changes would first impact young, single women. For the employment decisions of the older age group to reveal changes in schooling levels would mean that the educational advances would have had to occur some twenty to thirty years before. Many of the countries of the world, even those in the poorer category, have witnessed substantial advances in education (see the essays in King and Hill 1993, for example). But these advances have been somewhat recent in origin for the developing world.

One final point about the participation rate data concerns the differentiation among the labor force by employment status and by sector. Various researchers have noted inconsistencies in the definition of the labor force across the world's countries and have emphasized the need to separate employment into wage, unpaid family, and self-employed workers (see, for example, Schultz 1990a, 1991). Most of the countries reporting labor force data in WISTAT include all three sectors, although there are some inconsistencies (see notes to Figures 1 and 2). Schultz (1991) reports that the U cannot be observed for any one sector. Employment in unpaid family work and among the self-employed decreases with economic development, and the percentage in wage labor is fairly constant until much later stages of economic development, when it rises. Thus the U is traced out by changes in the sectoral composition of the labor force.[8]

Few regions of the world have incomes and educational attainment that span a very wide range. The U-shaped function in Figures 1 and 2 is generally traced out by the regions, rather than by the countries within them. Beginning at the upper left of each of the graphs and stretching somewhat down the function are

---

7. The WISTAT data contain only three age groups in the 20 to 59 year range—20 to 24, 25 to 44, and 45 to 59 years. There are also data by marital status and age, but many countries are not covered in sufficient detail.

The relationship between the labor force participation rates of the 25 to 44-year-old group and those of the 45 to 59-year-old group is quite tight. For all countries in the sample (not excluding those of the Mideast, for example) the relationship is: lfpr 25–44 = 0.095 + 0.927 lfpr 45–59, corrected R^2 = 0.854 (N = 164 countries).

8. See Hill (1983), for example, for an analysis of the determinants of female labor supply in Japan (c. 1975) which takes into consideration the choice of wage employment, family employment, and nonemployment. The determinants between wage and family employment are very different. Whereas the wage and income effects on wage employment have the usual signs, those on family employment have signs that are difficult to interpret and suggest that some determinants have not been adequately controlled for in the analysis. Duraisamy (1993) analyzes the determinants of wife's employment in wage labor and self-employment in urban south India and finds more neoclassical results in both employments. There is, however, a greater negative effect of assets on wage employment than on self-employment.

East, Middle, and West Africa. Below them and somewhat to their left are North Africa and South Asia. Just to the right of and somewhat below East, Middle, and West Africa are South Africa and South East Asia. These seven poorer regions comprise most of the downward portion of the graph. At the bottom and into the beginning of the rising portion are South America and Central America. The upward bend starts with southern Europe, somewhat above it is East Asia, then western Europe, northern Europe, North America, and parts of the Pacific. There are outliers in various regions, but most groupings are fairly tight. The outliers include countries in the Caribbean, whose female labor force participation rates are higher than predicted by the regression line, possibly because women often work as servants for foreigners and tourists.

The downward portion of the U has been interpreted in several complementary ways. When incomes are very low, women often work with other household members on family farms, in home workshop production, and as own-account workers. As incomes rise, various parallel changes occur that affect women's labor force participation. Economic development generally shifts the locus of production from the family farm and business to the factory, firm, and other places of wage labor. These shifts often occur because of increased relative productivity outside family enterprises. Rather than working for the family, there is now the option of wage labor in agriculture and manufacturing at increased remuneration. But a general increase in income could serve to decrease women's paid work and unpaid labor in family enterprises through a simple income effect. Much depends on the existence of a social norm or stigma against married women's working at manual labor in agriculture, industry, construction, and transportation. Boserup, for example, maintains that factory work is almost universally abhorred by married women in many parts of the developing world (1970, p. 115), and there is considerable evidence that this social norm is widely held.[9] There is also the much-debated issue of how new technologies in agriculture impact women's work. It is often claimed that various technologies, while increasing income, also displace female workers through a reduction in female-specific tasks and an increase in machinery operated by men. Both an income and a complex demand effect are implied.[10]

As development proceeds, education levels increase, particularly for the males in the population. Only much later, in many countries, do they increase for

9. Hein (1986) reports that in Mauritius "the general tendency among single [women] workers is to leave factory employment around the time of their marriage, even before they are pregnant or have any children to look after" (p. 288). The timing of these withdrawals is precisely what I have found for the United States from 1890 to 1940 (Goldin 1989, 1990). As in other countries, Hein notes that "husbands' opposition to their wives' working, particularly in a factory, is a crucial factor in these withdrawals" (p. 288). Mauritius is at the bottom of the U in Figure 2.

10. The impact of the Green Revolution is a good example. Mukhopadhyay (1991), for instance, demonstrates that in West Bengal, India, the introduction of high-yield varieties increased income, decreased female labor force participation, and increased fertility. The direct income effect is only one part of the reason for the decrease in women's participation in agriculture. The other part has to do with changed demands for sex-specific agricultural duties. Weeding, a female occupation, was reduced considerably with the introduction of weedicides, but the use of machinery, a male occupation, was increased with Green Revolution technology. One may question the impact of the technological changes in the absence of income changes.

women. Incomes, therefore, will continue to rise, but women's relative productivity might not for some time, all of which could serve to reduce women's labor force participation levels further.

The rise in the U comes at a considerably more advanced stage of economic development, and in most countries it surfaces only as female education levels have increased beyond elementary school. As women gain education at the secondary school level and can obtain positions in the white-collar sector, their labor force participation rates increase.

B. The U in Theory

The previous discussion contained an implicit framework to interpret changes in women's employment across the process of economic development. A simple version of the framework is diagrammed in Figure 3. There will be two variants of the framework. One is termed the nonstigma equilibria and the other the stigma equilibria. Although it is possible to obtain a U-shaped labor force function with economic development (e.g., increases in per capita income) in the nonstigma case, the quantitative and narrative evidence appears more consistent with the stigma case. I begin with the nonstigma case. The difference between the two is that, in the stigmatized equilibrium, families compare the difference in their utility when the wife is working in the manufacturing sector and when she is not with their loss in utility from the stigma imposed by her labor. The stigma is "all or none" (that is, it does not depend on the number of hours worked for the firm). Therefore whether or not the stigma-equilibrium is binding depends solely on the utility comparison.

The model contains one good (G) that can be produced by the family or by a manufacturing concern (the firm).[11] Women (meaning wives) can work for the manufacturing concern as operatives (manual, blue-collar workers) or, if they are sufficiently educated, as white-collar workers. Other family members work either at home production or outside the home for the manufacturing concern. There are three uses of the time of women: production of G by the family, production of G by the firm, and child care (C).[12] Total time in hours (per unit time, say, a year) is given by T. Production of G within the family is governed by a production possibilities frontier (PPF) given here by gaT. Increased income from other family members lifts the production possibilities frontier upward by ΔG. The initial level of other family income is normalized to 0. Decisions regarding the woman's time allocation are made by the woman who also considers the impact of her work on the social status of her family. Her utility function is given by $U = U(G,C) - \delta S$, where S is the utility value of the stigma and δ is a 0 or 1 indicator variable.[13] It is 1 if the wife produces G in the (manual or blue-collar) wage sector, even if for only a few hours a week.

I consider three periods. In the first there is no firm employment. In the second

---

11. The model borrows from that in Gronau (1977).
12. There is no pure leisure time. The G produced by the firm and the G produced by the home are perfect substitutes, as in clothing made by machine in a factory or in a home workshop.
13. The stigma (S) is treated as a positive number and is, therefore, subtracted from the utility level.

Goods (G)

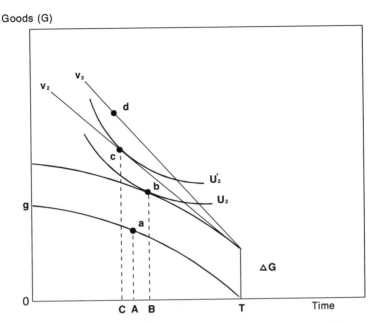

Figure 3
A Model of Household and Market Production with a Nonstigma and a Stigma Equilibrium

period a firm offers a wage and income for families rises because other family members work for the firm. Women have the option of working for the firm as operatives. In the third period wages for women rise further, because women's education advances and they are offered jobs in the white-collar sector of the firm. I will assume that there is a relationship between labor force participation and the number of hours the representative woman (wife) works and that hours worked are total hours spent in the production of G, independent of their source.[14]

Figure 3 depicts a time allocation choice for a representative woman (wife) who chooses point a and works AT hours in home production of G and $0A$ hours at child care in period 1. With increased income of ΔG, but no change in her productivity, the woman moves to point b and reduces her time in the home production of G to BT. This change reflects the operation of the pure income effect. But the appearance of the firm also means that the woman is offered a wage to work outside the home. Assume that the wage, relative to the price of G, exceeds the slope of the PPF at b and that it is given by line v_2. With line v_2 a nonstigma or unfettered equilibrium has the property that the woman would

---

14. The model could easily be extended to the case in which there is wage work in home production before wage work that takes place at the firm. The relationship between female labor force participation and hours of work is discussed, for example, in Goldin (1989).

choose either to work for the firm and do child care or just do child care alone. With a wage given by line v_2, there will be no home production of G.[15]

Thus in period 2 if the increase in family income comes first, the woman would reduce her time in G production by AB (that is, by choosing point b). If the change in her wage occurs together with the rise in family income, she could increase her total hours in G production (say, by CA) over that in period 1 (that is, by choosing point c).[16] Note, however, that at point a the wife spends AT hours producing G in the home, but at point c she spends CT hours producing G in the firm. The nonstigma equilibrium holds open the possibility of a U-shaped labor force function, but not necessarily if economic development increases family income and women's wages at the same time.[17]

In period 3 the woman's wage increases somewhat more, as given by line v_3, through an increase in her education and her employment in the white-collar sector of the firm. The change in labor supply is now determined by the usual (uncompensated) wage effect. For the sake of completeness, assume that the woman chooses point d.[18]

A norm that stigmatizes families, particularly husbands, for having their wives work at wage labor in manufacturing (or other manual jobs) will alter the equilibrium, particularly the change from period 1 to 2 and from 2 to 3. The equilibrium in period 1 is unchanged, but the response to the increase in the wage with the appearance of the firm in period 2 could be.

Each family has a value S giving the utility that would be lost from the social stigma of having a wife work for wages as a manufacturing operative or manual laborer. The stigma is not a function of the number of hours at work but is "all or none." The wife can do no better than point c, given the option of working along v_2. She can do no better than point b in the absence of that option. The question, then, is simply whether $(U_2' - U_2) >/< S$. If the utility value of the stigma is greater than the gain from being at point c compared with point b, the family will choose to remain at point b. The utility the family loses from having the wife work in the manufacturing sector is more than offset by the gain in utility from an expanded choice set. The probability the stigma will be binding is likely to be greater the lower the family income and will be greater the lower the woman's wage.[19]

---

15. The wage is always expressed relative to the price of G. With a wage somewhat less than that given by v_2, there would be some household production of G. None of this affects the results but makes the diagram cleaner.

16. Of course, the exact positions of points b and c are indeterminate. If child care and goods are both normal goods (that is, if the income effects of both are positive), point b must lie to the northeast of point a. By the same logic, point c would lie to the northeast of a point on U_2 (not drawn on the diagram) that is at the tangent of U_2 at a slope given by v_2. I have drawn point c so that the substitution effect outweighs the income effect of the increase in the wage. That is, there is an increase in time spent at work with an increase in relative wage. But the income effect of an increase in wages could outweigh the substitution effect and time spent at work could decrease (that is, point c could be to the northeast of point b).

17. As noted before, point c can lie to the northeast of point b.

18. Once again, I am assuming that the substitution effect of a change in the woman's wage swamps the income effect of the same.

19. It will be greater the higher is the wage increase, for the simple reason that a higher wage increases

The social stigma against wives working in paid manual labor outside the home is apparently widespread and strong. It almost always attaches to the work of women in male-intensive industries (e.g., mining, iron, and steel), but also exists in female-intensive (e.g., clothing, textiles) and mixed industries (e.g., food processing). The prohibition is so ubiquitous that it seems likely to be connected with many of the most basic norms in society—those that bind the family together as a productive unit. The stigma is a simple message. Only a husband who is lazy, indolent, and entirely negligent of his family would allow his wife to do such labor. This stigma does not appear to attach to widows and to female children doing the same work. The shame, therefore, attaches to the husband and serves to enforce a powerful social norm that obliges men to provide for their families. For various reasons, discussed below, the stigma does not generally attach to women working in the white-collar sector.

If the stigma equilibrium is binding, the woman will choose point b in period 2, but she will select point d when offered a white-collar job. Thus the movement across the three periods is from a to b to d, tracing out a U-shaped labor force participation function.[20] Note that when the stigma effect is binding on at least some families, the econometrician will incorrectly measure the true, underlying wage effect. It will be measured as 0 between periods 1 and 2, and will be considerably larger than the true underlying wage effect between periods 2 and 3.[21] The response to a change in wages is first underestimated and then overestimated by the family's fettered equilibrium. As more families make the move from a point like b to a point like d, the measured wage effect will decrease. Therefore, the econometrician will observe first a negligible wage effect, then a very large one, and then one of some moderate (and more accurate) proportion.[22] The same

---

the change in potential utility from working outside the home. It will be greater the higher is family income if marginal utility of income decreases with income.

20. Additions to the model will reinforce the U-shape. For example, if the movement from home production to firm production involves a fixed cost, the line v_2 will be lowered a fixed amount, equal to the fixed costs of going to work, getting another family member to take care of the children, and so on. The choice set is now constrained to be some combination of the PPF and the line v_2 shifted down.

Another addition concerns the efficiency of household production when the firm competes with it. The model is constructed so that there is no change in the efficiency of home production and no change in the price of the home-produced good relative to the firm-produced good (as might exist if there were differences in quality). One possibility is that as some households reduce their production of the good, the fixed costs of marketing it increase. If the goods were collected by agents, the price received for it could decrease as the market became geographically thinner. Indeed, the market could become so thin that production is driven to zero.

21. Note that the wages of women will be correctly measured because women also include non-wives, who do not experience the stigma, and because some wives will not face a binding stigma-equilibrium. The econometrician will measure the correct wage increase for women from period 1 (not shown) to v_2 in period 2 because wages will be recorded for some women. But families in which S is low will have wives who shift from point b to point c, whereas in families having a high S wives will remain at point b. By the "true wage effect" I mean the response from point b to c, that is in the absence of the stigma. The more families with a high value of S, the lower will be the measured wage effect. If S went to zero for all families (perhaps because the job were no longer manual labor but was, instead, an office position), all wives would move from b to c, and the true wage effect would equal the measured wage effect. When S is high enough, the measured wage effect (from period 1 to 2) will be zero but will be equal to the true wage effect (from period 2 to 3) when wages (in office work) rise to v_3.

22. I say "more accurate" in terms of the nonstigma equilibrium.

effects can be produced by a model with fixed costs. As the wage rises, the fixed cost effect of entering work outside the home binds fewer families.

The income effect is also biased. At higher levels of income there is a greater probability of having the stigma effect bind.[23] Thus if the only wage work for women is in the manufacturing sector, their participation will decrease more as income increases. Some of the decrease will be due to a decrease in home production (as in the movement from a to b). But some will be because more and more families reach the point where $(U_2' - U_2) < S$.

Thus, one explanation for the U-shaped function is that we initially observe the impact of an income effect when women's educational levels have not yet advanced and when their only employment opportunities outside home production are manual labor jobs in manufacturing and agriculture, for which there is often a social stigma. Women's labor force participation will fall as incomes rise and even as their own wage rises. Only when women are enabled to enter jobs in nonmanual work through their increased education will their labor force participation rate rise again.

C. Evidence on the Rising Portion of the U-Shaped Function

The downward portion of the U has been explained by several related changes, only some of which are directly captured in the framework just outlined. Women's labor force participation decreases with economic development because their household production declines as economic development progresses while their wage labor does not immediately increase. A simple income effect may be operating. Household-produced goods may become unprofitable to make and sell relative to factory production. Similarly, changes in agricultural technology may reduce the demand for women workers.[24] A central issue is why women do not follow production into the factory. Their reluctance can be explained by the existence of a stigma or by any fixed expense of entering the paid labor market outside the home, such as travel costs.

Understanding why the female labor force function begins to rise is the next topic and leads to an exploration of the relationships among economic development, female education, and white-collar employment. The first issue to address is when female schooling levels increase.

At relatively low incomes and low male schooling levels, the ratio of male to female education is extremely high. As resource constraints are reduced, both

---

23. Although this need not hold, it is likely to hold for some range of income.
24. One way of incorporating the possibility that home or agricultural production methods change, but that women are excluded from the new technology, is to consider the fact that the old technology can still be used but that the price of the output decreases relative to the value of time in using the new technology. That is, the value of G is reduced relative to family income.

There is also the possibility that as fewer families produce in home workshops, the costs of marketing and distributing the goods and inputs increases. When families are engaged in piece-rate production, for example, the greater the density of such families, the lower the costs of distributing the inputs and collecting the finished pieces. As fewer families are involved in piece-rate production, the per unit costs will rise. This change can be incorporated into the model by lowering the PPF, viewed here as net production (actual production minus the costs of distribution and marketing).

male education and female education rise, but female education rates rise faster and begin to converge on those of males. The sources of reduced resource constraints can be found at the household and governmental levels.

Figure 4 shows the relationship between the ratio of male to female secondary schooling gross enrollment rates and years of education among the male adult population. With increased male education, the ratio of male to female gross enrollment in secondary school declines, rapidly becoming 1 and often less.[25] Increased income, as reflected in the increase in education levels for the male adult population, at some point leads families to endow their girls with relatively more education and also aids in the extension of publicly provided education.

Increased income fuels schooling and expands the supply of educated workers to the white-collar sector. Figure 5 shows the positive association between white-collar employment and GDP/capita.[26] But increased GDP/capita is also an indicator that the economy has undergone a structural transformation that decreases the agricultural sector and increases the services sector. Both demand and supply effects work in tandem to increase the share of the labor force in white-collar employment. At higher income levels the demand for educated workers is greater and with greater incomes the supply of educated workers expands.

But increased GDP/capita alone, or its general correlate years of schooling for the adult male population, is insufficient to raise the fraction of all employed women who are clerical workers or to raise the proportion of all clerical workers who are women. Figure 6 graphs the relationship between the ratio of female to male clerical workers and the log difference between adult male and female years of education (see also the discussion of this relationship in Boserup 1970, chapter 8). A line has been drawn at the 15 percent difference mark in terms of male and female educational levels and at equality in their employment in the clerical sector.

Most of the countries to the southwest of the crossing point have very low levels of both female and male education. They have few women relative to men in clerical work despite equality of education. Those countries to the northeast, and there are only three, have a high ratio of women in clerical work although their educational levels are less equal. Two of these countries are Singapore and Hong Kong. All the rest of the countries lie along what appears to be a hyperbola, with the very highest ratios of women to men in the clerical sector found for those countries with the most equality of education between the sexes (note that several countries, including the United States, having a sex ratio in the clerical sector above 3 have been omitted from the graph). As long as males receive considerably more education than do females, the ratio of women to men in the clerical sector is low.

But the relationship graphed in Figure 6 might be caused by the fact that women's education levels are low, not just relative to men's, when the difference in the education is highest. Their absence as clerical workers, then, would stem

---

25. Many of the countries that lie below the line of equality of education between males and females—that is, have greater secondary schooling rates for females than for males—are in Latin America.

26. The percentage of the total labor force in the clerical or office work sector could also have been used. About one-third of all white-collar workers are clerical workers.

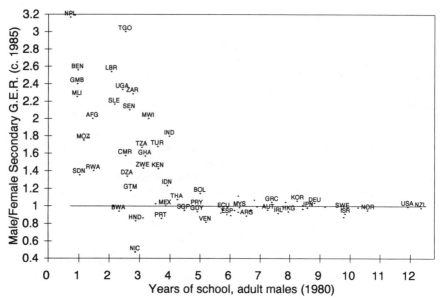

Figure 4

Ratio of Male to Female Secondary School Gross Enrollment Rates and Years of School for the Adult (> 25 years) Male Population, 1980s

Sources: Male and female secondary gross enrollment rates: United Nations (1990); years of school for the adult (> 25 years) male population in 1980: Barro and Lee (1993).

Notes: Years of school for the adult male population is for c. 1980. The latest year of gross enrollment rates from the source was used. It is generally between 1985 and 1988. See Appendix 1 for the country codes; dots are given for countries that would have overlapped with others. The centrally planned countries and those of the Middle East (except Israel) are omitted from the diagram.

from their lack of education in absolute terms. In a regression context we can hold both constant and observe that the ratio of the male to female educational attainment matters, to some degree, even when the percentage of women in the adult population who attended any secondary school is included (see Table 1). The ratio of female to male clerical workers rises with female secondary schooling and falls as the ratio of male to female total years of education for the adult population rises. As Boserup observes, competition from men serves to force women out of clerical employment.

Both effects—increased education and increased white-collar employment—impact the labor force participation of women, particularly those who are married and older. The social stigma against a wife's working generally does not exist for occupations in office work and sales, even when it is very strong in manual labor.[27] Thus increased education of women, particularly at the secondary school

---

27. Boserup (1970) quotes from an ILO report on Uganda that "The idea of being employed by an outsider except in a post requiring education is distasteful both to her [the woman] and to her family

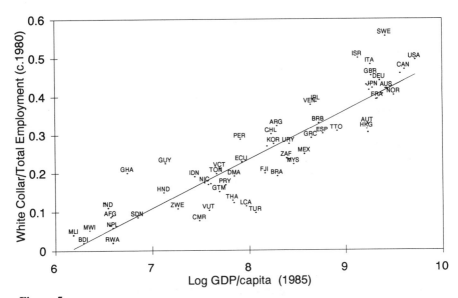

Figure 5

Fraction of Total Employment in White-Collar Occupations (c. 1980) and the Log of GDP/Capita (1985, 1985 $)

Sources: Occupational distribution: United Nations (1992); GDP/capita: Summers and Heston (1991).

Notes: White-collar occupations include those in the professional, managerial, clerical, and sales categories. The percentage in white-collar occupations is for c. 1980 unless data were unavailable in which case the latest date was used (often in the mid-1980s) or, if that were unavailable, the c. 1970 figure was used. About 25 cases did not have data for c. 1980. See Appendix 1 for the country codes; dots are given for countries that would have overlapped with others. The centrally planned countries and those of the Middle East (except Israel) are omitted from the diagram.

level, will increase the female share of office and sales employment. The increase will be almost immediate, since these women often take such positions directly after their school years. But the impact on the labor force participation of married women could take several decades more. The young women whose educational levels increase and who become office workers upon graduation will marry, have children, exit from the labor force, and then return to the work force later in their lives. Thus part of the rising portion of the U-shaped function may trace out the increase in women's secondary schooling and their employment in the clerical and sales sectors of the various economies.

Strong evidence for the theory just proposed is difficult to muster in large

and husband" (p. 116). In her discussion of India and Pakistan she notes that "public opinion makes a sharp distinction between work in home industries and 'literate work' which are regarded as respectable occupations, and factory work which is not regarded as respectable for women" (p. 115).

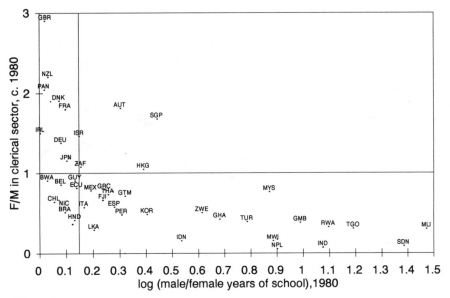

Figure 6

The Ratio of Female to Male Employment in the Clerical Sector and the Log Difference between Total Years of School for the Male and Female Adult Populations (> 25 years), c. 1980.

Sources: Occupational distribution: United Nations (1992); years of school for the adult (> 25 years) male population: Barro and Lee (1993).

Notes: The percentage in clerical occupations is for c. 1980 unless data were unavailable in which case the latest date was used (often in the mid-1980s) or, if that were unavailable, the c. 1970 figure was used. About 25 cases did not have data for c. 1980.

Five countries (AUS, CAN, FIN, NOR. USA) with ratios of female to male employment in the clerical sector >3, one (AFG) with a log difference between male and female years of education >1.5, and two countries (ARG, URY) with negative log differences have been excluded from the graph for reasons of clarity. See Appendix 1 for the country codes; dots are given for countries that would have overlapped with others. The centrally planned countries and those of the Middle East (except Israel) are omitted from the diagram.

measure because the data available are not appropriate to it. The theory is one of generational change, but the data sets are generally cross-sectional or have limited historical information for the countries. For one suggestive regression, see Table 2. The labor force participation rate of women 45 to 59 years old decreases with increases in the white-collar fraction of all employed men, a likely consequence of an income effect. It decreases with increases in the percentage of the female labor force in the clerical sector when female education is below about 7 years, but it rises with the proportion of female workers in the clerical sector when female education levels are above 7 years, that is, at the secondary school level. It also rises with female schooling, although not significantly. It is most

Table 1

Dependent Variable: (Female/Male) Clerical Workers

Log (male/female years of education)	−0.375	(1.84)
Percent females with secondary education	0.0315	(6.23)
Constant	0.523	(3.03)

adjusted R^2 = 0.47; number of observations = 83
Ordinary least squares estimation; t-statistics in parentheses

Sources: Occupational distribution and labor force participation rates c. 1980: United Nations (1992); years of school for the adult (> 25 years) female and male populations in 1980: Barro and Lee (1993).

Table 2

Dependent Variable: Female Labor Force Participation Rate of 45- to 59-Year-Olds

Percent male labor force in white-collar sector	−0.793	(2.16)
Percent of female labor force in clerical sector (%FCLER)	−1.25	(2.16)
Years of schooling of adult women (FSCHL)	0.0153	(0.83)
%FCLER × FSCHL	0.168	(2.25)
Constant	0.514	(8.59)

adjusted R^2 = 0.18; number of observations = 82
Ordinary least squares estimation; t-statistics in parentheses

Sources: Occupational distribution and labor force participation rates c. 1980: United Nations (1992); years of school for the adult (> 25 years) female population in 1980: Barro and Lee (1993).

important that the female labor force participation rate rises with female schooling in relation to the proportion of the female labor force in the clerical sector. The interaction between female schooling and the proportion of the female labor force in the clerical sector is the most telling result. Neither in isolation is sufficient.[28]

The rising portion of the U-shaped function has suggested to many that the (negative) income effect eventually becomes swamped by the (positive) substitution effect. I have suggested that this effect is either caused by or reinforced by the existence of a fettered equilibrium. The fettered equilibrium can be driven by a stigma regarding woman's work in the manufacturing sector or by fixed costs of working outside the home.

---

28. When the same equation is estimated for the 25- to 44-year-old group slightly different results are found. Years of schooling for adult women has a greater impact, but the percentage in the clerical sector has a smaller and less statistically significant impact. The interaction effect is also smaller.

One may wonder why the social norm against married women's working in manual labor generally does not exist for white-collar labor. The social stigma against a wife's working in the white-collar sector may be low because highly educated women across many cultures are given license to work for pay. The women thus employed are often teachers and nurses, but are also in a variety of white-collar occupations such as sales and office work. If higher-class women are given the privilege of working for pay in these sectors, then, the argument goes, lower-income women can as well. The point is that when a woman takes a job in manual labor she is signaling that her husband is neglectful and thus the norm— one protecting the family—can take effect. No educated, higher-income man would allow his wife to work in the manufacturing sector; thus the wife in such families must come from a lower-income household. But the signal is mixed when a woman takes a white-collar job. She could be an educated woman married to a hard-working man, or she could be an educated woman married to a slothful man.[29] The norm cannot take effect.

I am suggesting that one reason for the existence of the U-shaped female labor force participation rate function is the relationship between female education and economic development. At low levels of development, education increases for males far more than for females. Incomes rise and the income effect on female labor supply serves to lower female participation. A norm against women's working in manufacturing serves to reinforce the income effect, because the higher is income the greater the probability of a binding stigma effect. As incomes rise even more, educational resources are freed and females receive more education. As women take jobs in the white-collar sector the stigma effect is eliminated, and the substitution effect increases. With greater education for women and a larger white-collar sector, the income effect falls because more families no longer face the stigma effect of manufacturing work. The U is thereby traced out.

II. The Origins of Married Women's Labor Force Participation in the United States

A. *The U-Shaped Female Participation Rate Function in U.S. Economic History*

The labor force constructs that lie behind the various data in Figures 1 and 2 are vaguely consistent from country to country but not ideal. The constructs that are readily available to trace one country through its history are often far worse. In the United States, for instance, the modern concept of the labor force was first embodied in the 1940 census. The concept previously used was that of "gainful employment," for which having an occupation was equivalent to being in the labor force. Most adult men listed an occupation, but the vast majority of adult women did not.

---

29. Boserup (1990b, p. 141) suggests that as white-collar work expands for women in developing countries many will marry men with lower levels of education than they. Thus blue-collar workers will have wives who are white-collar workers. But as long as the wives of white-collar workers are themselves employed in white-collar work, such work cannot be stigmatized in the same way that blue-collar work is for married women.

Without careful archival research our knowledge of women's employment in the past would be woefully lacking. In 1890, for example, less than 3 percent of all married, white women gave the census taker an occupation (see Table 3).[30] But we now know that a far greater percentage worked for pay or produced for the market sector in their own homes, on the family farm, or in the family business. Still others worked intermittently or for few hours a week and never reported their occupation to the census taker. Given the social stigma against their working, it is not surprising that the reported labor force participation of married women was extremely low when women's work was primarily in domestic service and manufacturing.

The historical record on women's work in the United States is now sufficiently complete that a U-shaped functional relationship can be found there as well. Rather than a participation rate of 2.5 percent for all married, white women, an adjusted figure is probably just under 15 percent in 1890. The adjustments add in a fraction of boardinghouse keepers, unpaid family farm workers, and uncounted female workers in manufacturing.[31]

The more inclusive measure of the participation rate of married, white women probably exceeded 15 percent earlier in the nineteenth century, and it may have been considerably higher. We now know, for example, that urban women in the late eighteenth and early nineteenth centuries took part in their husbands' trades when the businesses were operated in the family's domicile (Goldin 1986b) and that women contributed to market production on farms in a myriad of ways. Thus it is likely that married women's labor force participation rate first fell before beginning its steady climb upward sometime in the twentieth century.

By 1940, when the procedures used by the census established the labor force construct, the labor force participation rate of all married, white women was just 12.5 percent. The adjusted estimate for 1890 is a bit below 15 percent. Thus even though we do not know the precise dimensions of the U-shaped function for U.S. history, it seems clear that it existed. I believe that the bottom was reached sometime in the 1920s.

It is not surprising that most of the discussion of women's labor force participation in U.S. history has ignored the falling portion of the U, for it became apparent only as researchers scoured sources other than the U.S. federal population census. It also became more obvious as scholars looked to the development literature for guidance on studying the histories of industrialized countries (Durand 1975). Their reasoning was quite simple. If all countries taken together trace out a U-shaped function, then each country's history probably did.

The rising portion of the U has dominated the literature on female labor force participation in the United States and other developed economies. Beginning at

---

30. The percentage of married African-American women who listed an occupation was considerably higher. Almost all of them were domestic servants or agricultural laborers.

31. For comparability with the labor force construct of modern estimates only a fraction are included to get an hours-adjusted measure. See Goldin (1990, Appendix to Chapter 2).

One could also question whether the data from certain developing countries accurately count women whose labor is often hidden from view even though they are involved in market-oriented production. Many of the censuses on which the ILO data are based do try to count these workers, but, as was pointed out in an earlier section, there are inconsistencies across countries.

Table 3

Married Women's Labor Force Participation Rates: The United States, 1890 to 1980

Year	White, All Ages	White, 25–34 Years	White, 45–54 Years
1890	2.5 [12.9][a]	2.6	2.3
1900	3.2	3.1	2.6
1910[b]	n.a.	n.a.	n.a.
1920	6.5	7.7	4.9[c]
1930	9.8	11.5	7.8
1940	12.5	16.7	10.1
1950	20.7	21.0	22.2
1960	29.8	26.7	38.6
1970	38.5	36.2	46.7
1980	49.3	56.0	53.4

Source: Goldin (1990), tables 2.1, 2.2, and 2.9.

a. The figure in brackets is a revised estimate that includes various omitted categories, such as boardinghouse keepers and unpaid family farm laborers (both adjusted by hours of work), and manufacturing workers not included in the population census. It is likely that this figure is still an underestimate of a female labor force datum that would be consistent with that in 1940, when the construct changed from one of "gainful employment."

b. Published data for the 1910 census are inconsistent with prior and subsequent data because of a change in the labor force question that led considerably more women on farms to list an occupation.

c. Includes married, white women aged 55–64.

least with Mincer's (1962) pioneering article on the female labor force, the central question for economists has been how women's labor force participation could increase in the face of rising incomes given the negative impact of the income effect. The answer, supplied by Mincer, is that the substitution effect was strongly positive and that it swamped the income effect (see, for example, the articles in Layard and Mincer 1985 for a confirmation of the relationship across a variety of developed economies).[32]

We now know that the histories of women's employment in many developed economies trace out the same type of U-shaped function apparent across a variety of the world's countries at any point in time, such as those in Figures 1 and 2. If the substitution effect strongly outweighs the income effect along the rising portion of the U, what happens at the other side of the U and what causes the function to change directions and turn upward? The existence of a U-shaped

32. Most of the studies I cite estimate the income effect primarily from data on the income of the husband, not from data on wealth. Thus there is an implicit constraint on the compensated cross-substitution effect of a change of the husband's wage on the wife's time allocation. It is assumed to be zero.

function raises the distinct possibility that measured income and substitution effects may not be constant across the process of economic development.

The reasons why the function changes direction can be sought in whatever factors cause the substitution effect to increase and eventually outweigh the income effect. As noted previously, the estimated income effect may decrease over time as the substitution effect increases. By reinforcing each other, changes in both the income and substitution effects could have contributed to the upward portion of the U. There is also the possibility that relative prices (including wages) change across the process of economic development or that certain fixed costs, for example, of travel to factory work, decrease. Although these are possibilities, the record for the United States, at least, suggests that the primary change is found in the parameters of the income and substitution effects.

B. Secondary Schooling and Female Labor Supply

The increase in the substitution effect, and the probable decline in the income effect, occurred in the United States some time after the increase in secondary schooling for both male and female youths.[33] Secondary school enrollments and graduation rates advanced at remarkable rates in the first several decades of the twentieth century. The graduation rate in the non-South regions of the United States rose from less than 10 percent of the 17-year-old population in 1910 to about 50 percent by about 1937 (see Figure 7). Thus the median 17-year-old in the non-South United States in 1937 was a high school graduate, even though just twenty-seven years before fewer than one in ten 17-year-olds would have received a high school diploma.[34] It should also be pointed out that the graduation rates in Figure 7 have been drawn to the late 1950s to highlight the fact that the growth of high schools during the 1920 to 1937 period was extraordinary. Virtually all of the increase during the half-century depicted occurred in that seventeen-year period.

Female youths were 1.5 times more likely to graduate secondary school than were male youths in the 1910s and 1.25 times more likely in the 1920s. In fact, in every year and in every region in the United States, young women were more likely to enroll, attend, and graduate from secondary school than were young men.

Many of the world's countries have undergone a similar transformation of their secondary schools during the past thirty years. That occurring in the southern portion of the Western Hemisphere comes the closest to what occurred in the

---

33. Secondary schooling in the context of United States history is grades 9 through 12. The secondary schooling data for the cross section of countries include 7 through 12, or generally ages 12 through 17 rather than 14 through 17.

34. It should be noted that these data are not yet corrected for various undercounts in both public and private graduation data. It is unlikely that these adjustments will increase the 1910 figure to more than 15 percent. That for 1937 is likely to be virtually unaffected. Also, the data on private school graduation do not exist for all years after 1933. The entire function should be about 10 percent higher after that date. These and other corrections will be made in my future work on the history of secondary schools (for a preliminary work, see Goldin 1994). Only the data for the non-South are used here because the South lagged in education in various ways.

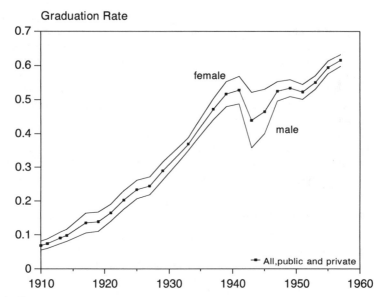

Figure 7

Male, Female, and Total High School Graduation Rates in the United States (Non-South Regions), 1910 to 1960

Source: U.S. Commissioner of Education (various years); see Goldin (1994).

Notes: Graduation rates are computed by dividing the number of graduates in a given year by the number of seventeen-year olds. Graduation rates include public and private schools to 1933. After 1933 the number in public schools is multiplied by 1.1. The figures do not yet correct for underreporting in the U.S. Commissioner of Education reports. They also do not yet include graduation from the preparatory departments of colleges and universities. Graduation from high school almost always meant completion of grade 12.

United States during the 1920 to 1937 period, although the levels are a bit lower. Mexico in 1960, for example, had a secondary enrollment rate of 8 percent, but by 1987 it was 53 percent; that in Colombia rose from 11 to 56 percent in the same interval. Almost all the countries of South America, Central America, and the Caribbean had secondary enrollment rates in 1960 in the 10 to 20 percent range (with the exceptions of Argentina, Jamaica, Panama, and Uruguay which were considerably higher, and Haiti which was far lower), but by 1987 most Latin American countries had secondary enrollment rates in the 40 to 60 percent range.[35] Because these rates also include the lower secondary grades whereas

35. These data have been provided by Anne Hill and form the basis of Hill and King (1993). Data in Schultz (1988, Table A-2) are similar and show that Latin American countries had an increase in secondary enrollment rates from 14 to 44 percent from 1960 to 1980. See also Bustillo (1993) who reports somewhat higher rates than Hill and King (1993), although the end date is 1987, somewhat later than in Hill and King.

those for the United States generally include only grades 9 to 12, comparability is imperfect. But it is likely that a comparable enrollment rate for the non-South United States in 1910 was about 40 percent and that it was 87 percent by 1937.[36]

Another important area of similarity between U.S. educational history and recent trends in Latin America concerns gender differences. Latin America is the only part of the developing world in which girls are educated in secondary schools to the same degree or greater than boys. It is extremely interesting that the labor force participation rates of women in many Latin American countries are at the bottom of the U in Figures 1 and 2, raising the distinct possibility, explored in the final section, that Latin America will soon see large increases in female labor force participation very similar to those experienced in the United States in the post–World War II period.

The equality of education by sex in the United States at the primary and secondary school levels—indeed the superiority of female education—almost throughout its history is unique in the world's educational history. The only other countries that come close to such equality of treatment are those that have been affected by U.S. occupation and, as just noted, much of Latin America but only for the past several decades. Part of the reason for gender neutrality in educational attainment in the United States is the universal public funding of primary and secondary schooling in the United States. But girls were taking advantage of this free schooling at decidedly higher rates than were boys.

The reason girls attended secondary school for longer periods than did boys, and attained high school diplomas at far greater rates, was because such schooling had more obvious and higher returns for them. The alternative to secondary school for a young woman was a manufacturing job. Secondary schooling, on the other hand, offered her the option of an office job. At the turn of this century many office jobs—typists, stenographers, secretaries—earned very high wage premia. But by the 1920s the wage premium paid to female clerical workers had fallen with the large influx of teenagers from high schools and other students from a variety of business and commercial schools. By the 1920s, the average female office worker earned about thirty percent more than her counterpart in manufacturing, and that premium probably remained in place until the 1940s (Goldin 1984, p. 14). It should be noted, however, that the private internal rate of return to education is not so easily calculated. Had these individuals worked for the remainder of their lives, the return would merely be the premium divided by the number of additional years of school needed to move from the manufacturing to the clerical job. But women in the 1920s and 1930s did not work for very long after they married, even when they made the transition to white-collar employment.

Manufacturing jobs were not demeaned just because they paid less than did those in offices, because many industrial jobs paid relatively well by the 1920s. Office jobs were decidedly preferred because they were "nice" jobs, and they

---

36. The enrollment rate of 14 to 17-year-olds was about 20 percent in 1910 and 80 percent in 1937 in the non-South United States. Virtually all 12 to 14-year-olds were in school in the non-South even in 1910. I assume that there were half as many 12 and 13-year-olds as 14 to 17-year-olds and that all of the 12 and 13-year-olds were in school to obtain the numbers given. If the proportion of 12 and 13-year-olds in school were 80 percent in 1910, the 1910 figure would become 33 percent.

were the jobs that "nice" girls took. They were cleaner, neater, generally shorter in hours, and they commanded considerably more respect. That young women gave these factors considerable thought is found in the contemporary literature on vocations. "The ambition of the school girl to 'work in an office' in preference to work in a factory has often been commented on by vocational counsellors and others in touch with girls who are seeking their first jobs" (Breckinridge 1933, p. 181).

A few years of high school catapulted a young woman from a life of drudgery and disrespect into a world of comfort and courtesy, or so it seemed to her. The young man, however, did not often see high school as having so positive an impact. The rather dead-end clerical and sales positions opened to young women were not the road to success for the young man. Machinists, electricians, and other tradesmen could enter their craft with far less than a high school diploma and little apparent loss. Thus the apparent private return for young women was actually higher than for young men, even though the latter remained employed for a considerably longer fraction of their lives.

Another change for young women in the 1920s was their ability to remain in white-collar employment after they married. Only in textile-mill towns and other cities with light industry were married, white women employed to any extent outside the home in the pre-1940s period. Employment changes of the 1920s were apparent to many commentators and were expressed, for example, in the famous ethnographic study of the Lynds. "When one speaks of married women's working in Middletown one is talking almost exclusively of Middletown's working class and the lowest rungs of the business class. Among these last . . . there is discernible a tendency for a young wife to retain a clerical job until her husband begins to get established. At the other extreme of the business class, there are one or two young wives of men so wealthy that there can be no question locally of their 'having to work,' and thus no reflection on their husbands' ability to 'provide' " (quoted in Goldin 1990, p. 134). As more women became educated, the social stigma of a wife's working declined.

The notion that the substitution effect rose over time and that the income effect declined in absolute value is not just a theoretical idea or mere rationalization of the time series movement. Rather, there are a host of cross section studies from 1900 to the 1960s that, taken together, exhibit such changes (see Goldin 1990, table 5.2). The studies suggest that the substitution effect was at a high point for women in the United States in the 1950s and 1960s, whereas the income effect may have continued to decline from the early twentieth century down to the present.

Thus Mincer's study, as well as other influential analyses of female labor supply, may have been executed at the peak of the own-substitution effect in the United States (see Bowen and Finegan 1969 for another important early study). Of more significance for the total impact of an increase in women's real wages, it may reflect a historic peak in the difference between the own-substitution effect and the total-income elasticity (the income effect × (the wife's full-time income/ family total income)). Also historically high during the 1950s and 1960s was the difference between the wage elasticity and the income elasticity. It is this difference that moves us along the upward sloping portion of the U-shaped function as incomes rise, as long as wages rise equally (or greater) for women than men. The stability in the gender gap in wages during that period is evidence that they rose at approximately equal rates.

C. The Rise of Women's White-Collar Employment

I have alluded to the impact secondary schooling had on the occupations of young women in the 1920s and 1930s but have not yet demonstrated that their work was fundamentally altered during the period. Also left to be established is the notion that participation in these jobs early in their lives altered their predisposition to paid employment later, a somewhat more slender thread in the empirical analysis. Although the discussion emphasizes the clerical group, many in the sales and professional sectors, particularly teachers and nurses, could also be included.

The clerical sector is emphasized because office work required nothing more than some secondary schooling, and its rise led to the first large shift in female employment away from operative positions in manufacturing. It was also a sector that grew enormously in absolute terms and in terms of its female composition during a brief period in American history that coincided with the expansion of publicly provided secondary schooling.

In 1890 about 15 percent of all office workers were female and just 4 percent of all employed women in that sector were married (see Table 4). By 1910, 36 percent of all office workers were female, and in 1920 the figure had risen to 48 percent. Thus by the 1920s office work in the United States had become feminized. The share of women in the total employment of the clerical sector remained at about 50 percent from 1920 to 1940. But the share of employed female clerical workers who were married reached 26 percent by 1940 and then climbed to 42 percent by 1950 when 62 percent of all clerical workers were women. Whereas only 4 percent of all non-farm-employed women were in the clerical sector in 1890, more than 20 percent were thus employed by 1920.

Table 4
Female Clerical Employment in the United States, 1890 to 1950

Year	Percent in Clerical Sector of All Female Workers	Percent Female of All Clerical Sector Employment	Percent Married of Female Clerical Workers
1890	3.9	14.6	4.1
1900	6.3	24.0	3.7
1910	11.0	36.2	n.a.
1920	21.7	47.7	9.2
1930	22.7	51.5	18.7
1940	22.3	51.5	26.1
1950	27.6	62.1	41.5

Source: Goldin (1984), table 1.

The point is that office work became mainly a female domain in the 1920s, although at the time it was the bastion of single, not married, women. Married women, however, increased their numbers in this sector at a greater rate than they did in the nation's employment as a whole. Although clerical work was a field dominated by relatively young women in 1930, it had the same proportion of married women as did the female labor force as a whole by 1950.

The rapid increase in the number of young female clerical workers in the two decades after 1910 was fueled by the phenomenal increase in secondary school enrollments and graduation rates, as shown in Figure 7. These workers were primarily unmarried women, some of whom continued working in offices and in sales positions for short periods after they married. But some married women in the 1920s and many in the 1930s were faced with bars against their employment in office work. Marriage bars—the stated policies of firms not to hire married women in certain positions and to fire single women who married while in their employ—existed in the 1920s in some firms, but they became far more widespread during the Great Depression (see Goldin 1991).[37] Thus the longer-run and full impact of the increase in white-collar employment in the 1910 to 1930 period had to wait for the 1940s and 1950s when marriage bars were generally dissolved and when the women of these cohorts were in their forties.

The evidence on the impact of early work experiences on later labor market participation is slim for the period under consideration. One data set, however, has been found that contains information on women from a wide variety of backgrounds, interviewed in 1939 about their past work and educational histories (Goldin 1989, Table 3). The data suggest that women who had worked in manufacturing early in their employment histories were less likely to be labor market participants later in their lives. Their participation rates were 10 percentage points lower than were those of the other women whose first jobs were in sales, clerical, professional, and other service employments. Because the base labor force participation for this group was 25 percent, the impact of first employment in manufacturing was substantial.

The data set is insufficiently rich to separate the impacts of income effects, substitution effects, and changing taste for work. There is, however, confirmation that whatever the locus of reasons, a change in the employment of young women from manufacturing to white-collar work—even lower-paid white-collar work in offices and stores—can increase labor force participation later in their lives.

The key point I am making is that the rise of office work in the 1920s and 1930s was an important component of the increase in married women's labor force participation in the 1950s. The explosion of married women's labor force partici-

---

37. The ILO has documented that these policies were widespread in the teaching field across a variety of countries (see Goldin 1991). It is interesting that firms and school districts instituted these marriage bars in white-collar employment since the societal norm against married women working in these fields was considerably less than in manufacturing and manual labor. The husband was made to feel the stigma of his wife's working in blue-collar employment, but society imposed a rule against her working in white-collar employment.

pation in the 1940s and 1950s was primarily experienced by women older than 40 years (see Table 3). Although there were important increases at the younger ages during those decades, the participation rates of married women under 40 years were to soar later, from the end of the 1960s to the 1980s.

Although I have thus far emphasized only the white-collar occupations that required just a high school education or diploma, the rise of high schools in the early twentieth century also fueled the increase in college, normal school, and nursing school enrollment in the post-1940s. In the college graduating class of 1957, for example, more than 60 percent of the women became teachers, social workers, nurses, and librarians in their first few months after graduation (Goldin 1990). The vast majority of these women would exit the labor force with the birth of their children and would remain out for varying lengths of time. But their intention in getting their degrees and in their early employment was to establish an opportunity for future participation. The next cohort of women would enter the labor force after school with the full intention of remaining in it with only small breaks for childbearing and rearing.

A decisive shift had been made in married women's labor force participation. No longer would young women exit from the labor force upon marriage not to reenter unless family income was extremely low or when they became widowed or were abandoned. Women now planned their education and labor force investments with a considerably longer time horizon for their employment. All of these changes find their origins in the rise of secondary schooling in the first few decades of this century and in the rise of white-collar employment of women.

III. Economic Development and Economic History:
Concluding Remarks

The path the world's developing countries are currently taking will never trace out that which the United States took to the present. The United States, for example, was never as poor on a per capita basis as are the poorest countries today, and it never had as high a percentage Muslim, Hindu, or Catholic as many of the world's countries, to mention but two differences that affect comparisons in the status of women. But there are many similarities in the role of education in spurring change for women.

In the early twentieth century the United States underwent changes in education not unlike those currently underway in Latin America. In both cases, secondary schooling advanced sharply in a brief period of time, and the levels for girls and boys were very similar. Many of the countries in Latin America currently occupy the base of the labor force U-shaped functions of Figures 1 and 2. In all but the Caribbean, female labor force participation rates (for those 25 to 44 years) are in the 20 to 40 percent range.[38] The percentage of female workers who are

---

38. Note that I have switched to a younger age group because the interest here is in seeing the impact of increasing education on the jobs and labor force participation of younger women. The data I have currently available do not divide the occupational data by age.

employed in the clerical sector is in the 10 to 20 percent range, approximately what it was in the United States in the 1920s.[39] The percentage of all clerical sector employment that was female is in the 30 to 40 percent range, once again approximately equal to what it was in the United States in the 1920s.

Although I do not know from the aggregate data which women are occupying these white-collar positions, I suspect it is disproportionately younger women, as it was, until the 1950s, in the United States. It is likely, therefore, that many women in Latin America are ripe for the transition to the upward sloping portion of the U and that married women's labor force participation rates will rise substantially in the next decade or so even if income levels do as well.

The newly industrialized countries of Asia present a mixed picture. In some, for example, Singapore and Hong Kong, educational change has been rapid and women are quickly moving into white-collar occupations. But in others in which educational advances are also great, for example, Korea, women are poorly represented in the clerical trades. This is also the case in the Philippines in which incomes are lower than in the three countries just mentioned but schooling levels are quite high.[40] According to the framework proposed, married women's labor force participation rates will, in the future, advance less in Korea and the Philippines than in Singapore and Hong Kong, and women's status in various ways will progress differentially between the two groups.

In sum, I have demonstrated that the labor force participation of women is generally U-shaped over the course of economic development. The reasons for the downward portion of the U are probably found in a combination of an initially strong income effect and a weak substitution effect, and a change in the locus of production from the home to the factory. It was the rising portion of the U that concerned most of this essay. Why the function changes direction holds the key to why women enter the labor force at higher stages of economic development and why their social, political, and legal status generally improves with economic progress. The reasons were sought in the change in the education of females relative to males as educational resource constraints are relaxed, and in women's ability to obtain jobs in the white-collar sector after school completion. Their increased education and their ability to work in more prestigious occupations both increases the substitution effect and decreases the income effect. As the substitution effect begins to swamp the income effect, the upward portion of the U is traced out, and women's labor force participation enters the modern era.

---

39. See Table 4 for the United States data. I have excluded female farm laborers from the United States calculation but have not for Latin America. Thus the percentage would be higher in Latin America than the 10 to 20 percent given, and more like the United States in the 1920s when it was slightly higher than 20 percent.

40. The percentage of all female workers who are clerical workers was 19 percent in Hong Kong and 26 percent in Singapore in 1980, but only 8 percent in Korea and 5 percent in the Philippines. The proportion of all clerical workers who are women was 51 percent in Hong Kong and 63 percent in Singapore, but 33 percent in Korea and 42 percent in the Philippines. Hong Kong and Korea also had female labor force participation rates for the 25- to 44-year-old group that exceeded those for the 45- to 59-year-old group of women, whereas in Korea the older group's participation rate is higher.

Appendix 1

World Bank Three-Letter Country Codes

All countries, with known codes, are listed even if the countries are excluded from the analysis for various reasons.

AFG	Afghanistan	SLV	El Salvador
AGO	Angola	ETH	Ethiopia
ALB	Albania	FJI	Fiji
DZA	Algeria	FIN	Finland
ATG	Antigua and Barbuda	FRA	France
ARG	Argentina	GAB	Gabon
AUS	Australia	GMB	Gambia
AUT	Austria	DEU	Germany, Federal Republic of
BHS	Bahamas	GHA	Ghana
BHR	Bahrain	GRC	Greece
BGD	Bangladesh	GRD	Grenada
BRB	Barbados	GTM	Guatemala
BEL	Belgium	GNB	Guinea-Bissau
BLZ	Belize	GIN	Guinea
BEN	Benin	GUY	Guyana
BTN	Bhutan	HTI	Haiti
BOL	Bolivia	HND	Honduras
BWA	Botswana	HKG	Hong Kong
BRA	Brazil	HUN	Hungary
BRU	Brunei Darussalam	ISL	Iceland
BGR	Bulgaria	IND	India
HVO	Burkina Faso	IDN	Indonesia
BDI	Burundi	IRN	Iran
CMR	Cameroon	IRQ	Iraq
CAN	Canada	IRL	Ireland
CPV	Cape Verde	ISR	Israel
CAF	Central African Republic	ITA	Italy
TCD	Chad	JAM	Jamaica
CHL	Chile	JPN	Japan
CHN	China	JOR	Jordan
COL	Colombia	KEN	Kenya
COM	Comoros	KOR	Korea, Republic of
COG	Congo	KWT	Kuwait
CRI	Costa Rica	LBN	Lebanon
CIV	Côte d'Ivoire	LSO	Lesotho
CUB	Cuba	LBR	Liberia
CYP	Cyprus	LBY	Libyan Arab Jamahiriya
CSK	Czechoslovakia	LUX	Luxembourg
DNK	Denmark	MDG	Madagascar
DMA	Dominica	MWI	Malawi
DOM	Dominican Republic	MYS	Malaysia
ECU	Ecuador	MDV	Maldives
EGY	Egypt	MLI	Mali

MLT	Malta	SLB	Solomon Islands
MRT	Mauritania	SOM	Somalia
MUS	Mauritius	ZAF	South Africa
MEX	Mexico	ESP	Spain
MAR	Morocco	LKA	Sri Lanka
MOZ	Mozambique	LCA	St. Lucia
BUR	Myanmar	VCT	St. Vincent/Grenadines
NPL	Nepal	SDN	Sudan
ANT	Netherlands Antilles	SUR	Suriname
NLD	Netherlands	SWZ	Swaziland
NZL	New Zealand	SWE	Sweden
NIC	Nicaragua	CHE	Switzerland
NER	Niger	SYR	Syria
NGA	Nigeria	THA	Thailand
NOR	Norway	TGO	Togo
OMN	Oman	TON	Tonga
PAK	Pakistan	TTO	Trinidad and Tobago
PAN	Panama	TUN	Tunisia
PNG	Papua New Guinea	TUR	Turkey
PRY	Paraguay	UGA	Uganda
PER	Peru	ARE	United Arab Emirates
PHL	Philippines	TZA	United Republic of Tanzania
POL	Poland	GBR	United Kingdom
PRT	Portugal	USA	United States
PRI	Puerto Rico	URY	Uruguay
QAT	Qatar	VUT	Vanuatu
ROM	Romania	VEN	Venezuela
RWA	Rwanda	YEM	Yemen
SAU	Saudi Arabia	YUG	Yugoslavia
SEN	Senegal	ZAR	Zaire
SYC	Seychelles	ZMB	Zambia
SLE	Sierra Leone	ZWE	Zimbabwe
SGP	Singapore		

4 Public Policies and Women's Labor Force Participation
A Comparison of Sweden, Germany, and the Netherlands

Siv Gustafsson

Siv Gustafsson is professor of economics in the faculty of economics and econometrics at the University of Amsterdam. Gustafsson has written extensively on women's labor force participation and child care in Sweden, the Netherlands, and Germany.

I. Introduction

It has been argued that schooling for women may be justified in terms of high individual private market returns, social externalities related to reduced child mortality and fertility, redistribution of resources to improve the health and education of children, and equity (Schultz, chapter 1). The shift in the gender composition of human capital toward women has occurred at about the same time as women have entered more frequently into the market labor force. Given all these aspects of female education, governments ought to be interested in increasing investments in female human capital. This chapter attempts to evaluate differences in policies and their effects on women's propensity to participate in the labor market for three Western European countries.

In 1983 Jacob Mincer and Richard Layard organized a conference on "Trends in Women's Work, Education and Family Building" involving research from scholars covering twelve different countries (Layard and Mincer 1985). The common conceptual framework adopted for all papers was based on theories that have become known as "economics of the family."[1] An important implication of these theories is that fertility and married women's labor supply are jointly determined by the wife's price of time, other sources of household income, and relative prices. The marginal value or the price of a wife's time tends to be the same in all uses of time: market work, producing child's well-being, and producing

---

1. Important references for this field are Schultz (1974), Becker (1981), and Cigno (1991).

91

other sources of her standard of living (Willis 1973). Generally we can expect a decrease in time spent child rearing and an increase in time supplied to market work as market wages increase. A negative correlation between fertility and women's labor force participation, therefore, is anticipated, but it is not a causal relationship. For some developing countries where population growth is too rapid, a decline in fertility is a desired outcome of development. For some Western European countries, as will be shown in this chapter, it is rather the other way around with the public concerned over fertility rates that are too low.

The "Wages and Incomes" model of demand for married women's labor supply performs remarkably well in most of the country studies in Layard and Mincer (1985). However, if the model performs well within countries, would one then not expect that the countries with the lowest labor force participation of married women would be the countries with the highest fertility rates? Is the standard economic model of married women's labor supply applicable when it comes to explaining differences between countries? In this chapter I will try to answer these questions by analyzing differences among Sweden, the former West Germany,[2] and the Netherlands.

All the country studies in the Layard and Mincer volume used wife's before-tax wage to explain her probability of labor force participation. Differences in income taxation have potentially important effects since *individual taxation* of husband's and wife's incomes implies a favorable treatment of the secondary worker's earnings, whereas *joint taxation* penalizes the earnings of a secondary worker by taxing them at the joint higher marginal tax rate. In this chapter the effect of differences in the tax treatment of spouses among the three countries are evaluated for their effect on married women's labor supply. Of the three countries, Sweden has had a tax system that greatly favors the secondary wage earner, and Germany one that imposes the largest penalty on secondary earnings. I present results from a microsimulation of effects of the tax system on women's labor supply.

The effects of day care subsidies on mothers' labor supply are also evaluated for Sweden. In the Netherlands, hardly any day care exists, while in Sweden there is an extensive program for providing subsidized day care in order to accommodate mothers' working hours. Full-day, out-of-home care for children in Germany is also rarely available. In addition to individual taxation of earnings and subsidized child care, other programs, such as paid parental leaves and six-hour work day for a parent with a young child, have also contributed to the growth of female labor force participation in Sweden.

II. Conceptual Framework

Following Willis (1973), Gustafsson and Willis (1990), and Gustafsson and Stafford (1992), we analyze the labor supply and fertility decisions within a joint framework. In order to focus on the effects of differences in policies

2. In this paper Germany means the Federal Republic of Germany or the former West Germany. The data from 1984 apply to the FRG.

in a simple context we abstract from the sequential and stochastic nature of the family's economic and demographic life cycle. We assume that each couple has perfect and costless control over their fertility and possesses perfect foresight concerning all relevant economic variables so that the lifetime plan adopted ex ante at marriage coincides with ex post observations of their completed fertility. The model is to be used to predict how a representative couple would behave in terms of fertility and wife's labor force participation.

We assume, following Becker (1965), that the family combines time supplied by family members with goods and services purchased in the market to produce within the household the more "basic" commodities, which are the true objects of utility. Examples of basic commodities are good health, meals, and satisfaction from children. We assume that the family attempts to maximize a utility function over commodities subject to its limited capacity to produce these commodities. The utility function of the decision maker, for simplicity assumed to be the woman, is the following:

(1) $U = U(C,S)$

where C is the total satisfaction that parents derive from their children and S is a composite good consisting of all other components in the standard of living that parents value. The two commodities, child satisfaction C, and adult standard of living S, are produced with inputs of time and market goods according to the following household production functions:

(2) $C = f(t_c, x_c)$

and

$S = g(t_s, x_s)$

here t_c, t_s = total time input into child services or adult satisfaction measured in equivalent units of wife's time, and x_c, x_t = total goods input measured in equivalent units of market goods. We assume that only wife's time is productive in child satisfaction, and treat husband's time as exogenously devoted to full-time work. A further important assumption is that "children's well-being" production is more time intensive than "standard of living" production, in other words, $t_c/x_c > t_s/x_s$. The level of utility the family can achieve is limited by its capacity to produce C and S. This capacity is limited by the family's lifetime supplies of goods and time. The children do not contribute market earnings to family income. The structure of relative market prices remains fixed so that the Hick's composite commodity theorem may be used to justify treating goods inputs as an aggregate good x with a price index p. Under these assumptions, the family's input of purchased goods is limited by its lifetime money income (or money wealth), which in turn is equal to the family's nonlabor wealth, and the lifetime market earnings of the husband and wife. The husband is assumed to work full time in the labor market during marriage. His lifetime earnings and the family's nonlabor wealth together will be called the husband's lifetime income or wealth, A, and will be treated as an exogenous variable.

We also assume, following Gronau (1977), that intermediate goods cannot only be purchased in the market but can also be produced in the household by the wife according to the household production function:

(3) $x_h = x_h(t_h)$ $x_h' > 0$
                        $x_h'' < 0$

where x_h is goods produced by the wife in the household, and t_h is time spent by the wife in the household in such activities. It is rational for the wife to first produce goods with expensive market alternatives. Only with a considerable supply of hours of household work will she produce goods that have fairly inexpensive market alternatives.

Therefore, labor's marginal product in household production, evaluated by prices of market alternatives, is decreasing in time spent in housework. We can think of x_h as another income component, namely, the shadow income that results in money savings to the household because of the services not bought because the wife does the work, in other words, laundry, cooking, baking, cleaning. Thus, $x_c = q_c + (1 - r)x_h$, and $x_s = q_s + rx_h$, where r is the share of home-produced goods going into the composite, other goods.

Total time available, T, can be divided among child-rearing time, t_c, time for adult standard of living, t_s, market work, h, and time spent producing intermediate goods, t_h. The time constraint is:

(4) $T = t_c + t_s + h + t_h.$

Income can be spent on c-goods, q_c, or s-goods, q_s. The budget constraint therefore is:

(5) $A + hw = p_1q_c = p_2q_s,$

where A is nonlabor income, including husband's earnings, w is the wage rate after taxes, and p_1 and p_2 are the prices of c-goods and s-goods, respectively.

In the following the effect of separate as opposed to joint taxation as well as the effect of child care subsidies are illustrated by making use of the model.

A. Individual as Opposed to Joint Taxation

In Figure 1 the effects of changing from a joint taxation system to an individual taxation system are shown. The choice in this model is between spending resources of time and goods on the adult standard of living, S, and on child services, C. This choice is depicted in the output space, Figure 1B. The resources of time and money available to the decision-making woman, on the other hand, are depicted in Figure 1A, the input space. The input space depicts the familiar budget sets in a classical labor supply model where utility is maximized over income and leisure subject to the budget constraint. The linkage between the price of time of the wife, w, and the shadow price of children is given by the Stolper-Samuelson theorem (see Willis 1973).[3] Child services, C, can be thought

---

3. The reason we are allowed to draw the unobserved opportunity set in the output space on the basis of considerations about what happens in the input space is given by the famous Stolper-Samuelson Theorem, which states that there is a one-to-one monotonic correspondence between factor and com-

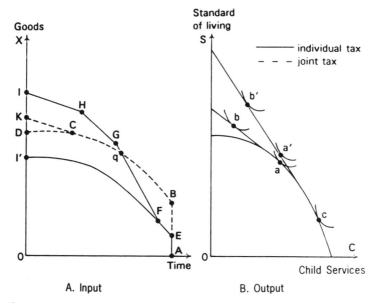

Figure 1
Effects on Labor Supply and Demand for Children by a Change From Joint to Separate Taxation

of as the product of number of children, N, times the quality per child, Q, in other words, $C = Q \times N$. If quality is assumed by parents to be equal for each child, then C is also an index of the demand for children.

The budget set in the case of joint taxation is given by the curve $ABCD$ in Figure 1A, where AB is the exogenously given nonlabor income including husband's earnings, A. The wife has the opportunity to extend the endowment of goods by working in the household BCD. She can also extend the goods endowment by working in the market (BCK), and her market earnings will then be taxed at the marginal tax rate of her full-time working husband.

If the tax system changes to individual taxation the husband loses his right to deduct double basic allowances in the case that his wife is a housewife. This corresponds to a decrease in nonlabor income from point B to point E in Figure 1A. On the other hand, the wife's income is taxed at a low rate if she works short hours, which in Figure 1A corresponds to an increase in her hourly wage after tax. The budget line $AEFGHI$ that results due to changing to individual taxation assumes three marginal tax brackets FG, GH, and HI. The last tax bracket is

modity prices in a two-factor (time and goods), two-commodity (child and adult standard of living) general equilibrium system if the following conditions are met: (1) the commodity production functions and linearly homogenous, (2) the factor intensities of the two commodities differ, and (3) the sign of the factor intensity ordering is invariant over all possible values of the factor price ratio. For a textbook proof of the Stolper-Samuelson Theorem, see Layard and Walters (1978).

reached by full-time workers and has been drawn parallel to the tax bracket that the wife would otherwise encounter in the joint taxation case.

The outcome of the time use depends on her choices between C and S in output space (Figure 1B). Three possibilities have been depicted in Figure 1B, with varying degrees of "child-oriented" preferences. In the most child-oriented preferences case there is no effect on demand for children, case c; in the middle case, aa', there is an increased demand for "standard of living" and no change in demand for children; and in the least child-oriented preferences case, bb', the demand both for adult standard of living and for children increases. In this model we can have a positive correlation between female labor force participation and fertility as shown by the change from b to b', which runs contrary to the generally observed negative correlation.

B. Day Care Subsidies

Let us now, following Gustafsson and Stafford (1992), modify the budget constraint into:

(6) $A + h (w - k) = p_1 q_c + p_2 q_s$

to allow for the fact that a working mother has to pay an hourly child care cost of the amount k. In Figure 2A the curve $AEFPI'$ reproduces the home production without market opportunities of Figure 1 and the curve $EFGHI$ the opportunity set given individual taxation of Figure 1. If the mother has to pay the full day care cost without subsidy her opportunity set may well decrease to $AEPL$, and there is likely to be a substantial decrease in labor supply in comparison to a case where no day care costs have to be paid. Day care subsidies can counteract this effect bringing the opportunity set closer to the no day care cost set, for example, to $AEFM$.

In the output space, a child-related subsidy extends in Figure 2B the opportunity set disproportionately in favor of children, although part of the money freed from the subsidy can be used for increasing the adult standard of living. Child care subsidies are thus likely to induce market work, thereby increasing the goods endowment, which can be used alternatively in C- and S-production. However, if none of the subsidy is used for C-production the effect is zero because in order to enjoy a child care subsidy you have to have a child who uses a space in the child care center. Child care subsidies are, therefore, pronatalist. Compare the shift from C to C' in Figure 2B.

III. Trends in Female Labor Force Participation and Fertility

Table 1 summarizes a few cross-sectional characteristics of the three countries. Swedes marry about three years later (30.4 median for men and 27.7 for women) than do the other two nationalities. Swedes are less likely to

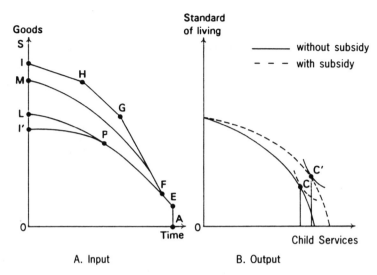

Figure 2
Effects of a Child-Care Subsidy on Labor Supply and Child Services

marry and more likely to divorce than are persons in the other two countries. In spite of the low rate of marriage and the high rate of divorce, Swedish women have more children than women in the other two countries. Swedes, both men and women, are more likely to have jobs than are Germans or Dutch, and, in particular, Swedish women participate in the labor force to a much larger extent than do women in the other two countries. The biggest differences are among mothers of preschool children of which 85 percent of Swedish mothers, 35 percent of German mothers, and only 26 percent of Dutch mothers participate in the labor force. The Dutch women have the smallest attachment to the labor market. The difference between the Netherlands and the other two countries is quite pronounced in hours of work. One-third of the Dutch women who do have a job work fewer than 20 hours per week and only 40.5 percent work full time. Among German women who have a job, two-thirds work full time, whereas a large share of Swedish women work between 20 and 35 hours per week. German women who work part time are more likely to choose much shorter hours than half-time. This may be explained by the German tax system, which allows a small amount of earnings from the secondary worker to be taxed less, without regard to husband's earnings, whereas thereafter the rule is joint taxation (see Gustafsson 1992). Swedish parental leave legislation allows a parent to shorten the work day to a six-hour day until the youngest child is eight years old. A large majority of Swedish mothers of young children take advantage of this opportunity and work 30 hours per week.

The female to male wage ratio is considerably larger in Sweden (.90 for blue-collar workers and .74 for white-collar workers) as compared to ratios in Germany

Table 1

Women's Demographic and Labor Market Characteristics in Germany, Sweden, and the Netherlands in 1987 or Latest Available Year

Characteristic	Germany	Sweden	Netherlands
Women's age at first marriage (median)	24.9	27.7	24.8
Men's age at first marriage (median)	27.5	30.4	27.0
Marriages per 1,000 population	6.3	4.9	6.0
Divorces per 1,000 population	9.7	11.4	8.1
Total fertility rate	1.34	1.96	1.5
Percent of labor force participation of women aged 15 to 64	54.1	81.1	50.0
Percent of labor force participation of women with preschool children[a]	34.6	84.6	26.0
Percent of labor force participation of men aged 15 to 64	82.3	85.7	80.0
Blue-collar female to male wage ratio	.734	.899	.746
White-collar female to male wage ratio	.641	.740	.631
Percent women who work fewer than 20 hours	18.9	6.1	32.8
Percent women who work more than 20 but fewer than 35 hours	13.5	37.2	26.7
Percent women who work full time 35 hours or more	67.6	56.7	40.5

Source: Gustafsson and Bruyn-Hundt (1991).
a. Sweden, children aged 0–6; Germany, children aged 0–5; the Netherlands, children aged 0–4. The year refers to 1985.

and the Netherlands (.63–.64 for white-collar workers and .73–.74 for blue-collar workers).[4]

Table 2 shows the trends in labor force participation in the three countries. All three countries show decreasing labor force participation rates among men and increasing labor force participation rates for women. The decreasing labor force participation of men is primarily among the youngest age groups, because of extended education, and the oldest age groups, because of earlier retirement. The decrease in male labor force participation has been more pronounced in Germany and the Netherlands than is the case in Sweden. The recent history shows that Dutch women, starting from a very low level, have increased their labor force participation at a rapid rate, but they have still not reached the level that Swedish

4. Data presented by Barros, Ramos, and Santos (chapter 13) indicate that the female to male wage ratio in Brazil is only .54, which according to standard economic analysis would, other things being equal, contribute to a relatively low labor force participation rate of women, but it is nonetheless increasing rapidly.

Table 2

Percent Labor Force Participation in Germany, Sweden, and the Netherlands

| | Germany (FRG) Age 15–64[a] | | Sweden Age 16–64 | | Netherlands Age 15–64 | | Mothers | | |
| | | | | | | | Germany[b] (Age of child: 0–5) | Sweden (Age of child: 0–6) | Netherlands (Age of child: 0–4) |
Year	Men	Women	Men	Women	Men	Women			
1963	91.9	46.9	89.9	54.5					
1964	90.4	46.9	89.6	54.0					
1965	90.2	46.9	89.3	53.8					
1966	90.6	46.7	89.0	55.1					
1967	89.3	45.6	88.1	54.9					
1968	89.6	45.9	88.0	56.4					
1969	89.2	46.0	87.5	57.6					
1970	88.5	46.2	87.0	59.3				47.5	
1971	88.1	46.5	86.9	60.9	85.1	30.0		50.1	
1972	87.4	47.5	86.6	62.0			32.5	52.1	
1973	86.6	48.2	86.8	62.7			33.9	52.2	
1974	85.8	48.1	87.5	65.2			33.6	55.3	
1975	86.0	48.2	88.3	67.9	83.9	34.0	32.9	58.8	14.6
1976	85.0	48.3	88.6	69.1			32.9	61.2	
1977	84.6	48.9	88.0	70.6	82.3	33.3	33.6	64.4	14.9
1978	84.5	49.0	87.6	72.1			33.4	67.2	
1979	84.5	49.7	87.8	73.8	78.4	34.5	33.8	70.3	17.9
1980	81.4	50.2	87.7	75.1			35.1	73.7	
1981	83.5	50.6	86.6	76.3	78.1	38.8	35.6	79.6	20.9
1982	83.0	51.0	86.3	76.9			35.7	79.6	
1983	82.0	50.7	86.0	77.6	77.9	41.4		81.3	24.6
1984	81.4	51.7	85.6	78.2				82.2	
1985	81.9	52.7	86.0	79.2	76.7	42.5	34.2	84.2	26.0
1986	82.0	53.4	85.9	80.0			34.4	84.6	
1987	82.3	54.1	86.7	81.1	80.0	50.0	34.6		
1988	82.5	55.0	86.2	81.1	80.0	52.0			
1989					81.0	52.0			

Sources: *Sweden:* AKU Årsmedetal, (Labor Force Surveys) yearly. *The Netherlands:* CBS: Arbeidskrachtentelling (1985), Enquete beroepsbevolking (1987). *Germany:* a. Statistische Jahrbücher, diverse Jahrgänge; b. Statistisches Bundesamt, Bevölkerung und Erwerbstätigkeit, Reihe 3, Haushalte und Familien.

women had already obtained by 1963. The labor force participation rate of German women has shown the smallest rate of increase, but the growth of the rate accelerates after 1983. If broken down by age and marital status, there has been a decrease of labor force participation among young German women because of increasing schooling which conceals an increase of labor force participation among prime age married women (Franz 1985).

Figure 3 shows total fertility rates for the Netherlands, Sweden, and Germany from 1940 to 1990. Sweden was below the average of EEC countries for the entire period until 1983, with the exception that the peak after World War II came earlier in Sweden than in the EEC countries. The Netherlands, on the other hand, had far higher fertility than the average of EEC countries until 1970, with a peak after World War II reaching 4 children per woman. The fall in German fertility started a bit later than the fall in Swedish fertility, but then accelerated, so that in 1984 Germany had the lowest fertility in the world, on the order of 1.3. Swedish fertility since 1983 has increased sharply and reached the level of 2.1 in 1990.[5]

Figure 4 plots labor force participation of women against the total fertility rate for 21 OECD countries. The traditional patterns of a high fertility rate and a low rate of female labor force participation is exhibited by Ireland. The study of Sundström and Stafford (1992) also collected information on whether there is individual or joint taxation, the share of public consumption, the length of parental or maternity leaves, and whether the country has a significant supply of day care for children. They found that the size of leave benefits has a positive effect on women's participation rates if there are long leaves. Short leaves reduce labor force participation. Public consumption as a share of GNP has a positive effect.[6] This variable probably has both a demand side effect on services that women produce and is an indicator of the availability of services to substitute for women's work at home.

IV. The "Wages and Incomes" Model of Married Women's Labor Supply

In a number of studies (Smith 1980; Killingsworth and Heckman 1986) and particularly for Sweden (Gustafsson and Jacobsson 1985), the Netherlands (Hartog and Theeuwes 1985), and Germany (Franz 1985), female labor supply has been estimated according to the following model.

Assume that a person participates ($h_i > 0$) if the market wage (w_i) exceeds the shadow wage (w_i^*) at zero hours, the market wage being determined by human capital variables and labor market characteristics (Z_i) and the shadow wage by variables that affect the value of nonmarket time in home production and leisure (X_i). We wish to estimate

(7) $pr(h_i > 0) = pr(w_i > w_i^*),$

---

5. Data for figure 3 were supplied by Hettie Pott-Buter (1993), who presents a seven-country comparison of total fertility rates between 1900 and 1990.
6. The regression reported was the following:

$$FLFPR = 60.57 - 14.23\,TFR + 1.11\text{ individual tax} + 1.40\,PUBCONS - 1.43\text{ Leave ben}$$
$$(3.74) \quad (1.45) \qquad (0.27) \qquad\qquad (2.25) \qquad\qquad (2.77)$$

$$+ .0309\text{ (leave ben)}^2 + 18.7\,DAYC.$$
$$(2.97) \qquad\qquad (3.48)$$

Adjusted $R^2 = 0.565$; t-ratios are shown in parentheses beneath each OLS coefficient.

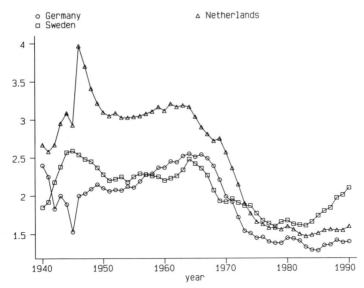

Figure 3
Total Fertility Rates for Sweden, the Netherlands, and Germany, 1940–1990
Source: Pott-Buter (1993).

where

(8) $w_i = Z_i\gamma + \varepsilon_i$,

(9) $w_i^* = X_i\beta + e_i$.

The market wage is not observed for all persons who do not participate in paid work in the sample. Therefore, the first step in the estimation procedure is to estimate a "Mincer earnings function" (Mincer 1974) which is a log-linear wage regression with education and years of post-schooling experience as the most important explanatory variables. The wage regression may be corrected for sample selection bias according to the Heckman (1980) procedure where λ (inverse of the Mills ratio) is identified by an exclusion restriction. The wage equation is then estimated:

(10) $\ln w_i = Z_i\gamma + \mu\lambda + v$,

and the wage for each individual predicted according to:

(11) $\hat{w}_i = exp\,(Z_i\gamma)$

Predicted wages are used for nonworkers and observed wages for workers in the estimation of the labor force participation equation:

(12) $P_i = \alpha_0 + \alpha_1 w_i + \alpha_2 A_i + \alpha_3 C_i + u_i$,

where P is a dummy variable equal to 1 if the person participates in the labor market and zero if the person does not participate in the labor market. The most

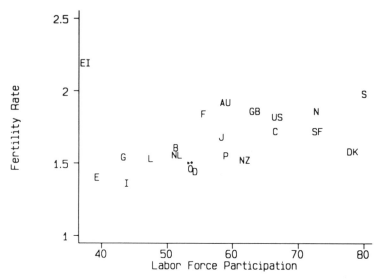

Figure 4

Female Labor-Force Participation and Fertility in Sweden and Twenty Other OECD Countries

Source: Sundström and Stafford (1991).

AU	Austria	F	France	NL	Netherlands
B	Belgium	G	Greece	NZ	New Zealand
C	Canada	GB	Great Britain	Ö	Austria
D	Germany	I	Italy	P	Portugal
DK	Denmark	J	Japan	S	Sweden
E	Spain	L	Luxembourg	SF	Finland
EI	Ireland	N	Norway	US	United States

important explanatory variables are the women's wage (w), husband's income (A), and the number of children and their ages C; where C_i is a vector of variables and α_3 is a vector of the corresponding parameters to estimate. However, the household demand (Becker 1965) approach suggests that a woman's number of children or fertility is jointly and simultaneously determined with a woman's past and current labor force participation. Consequently, conditioning on the observed number of children is likely to bias the estimates of the women's participation response to her wages and husband's income (Schultz 1980). Only if children are treated as endogenous and the suitably expanded model indicates a basis for statistically identifying the effect of "children" on a woman's labor supply can the full model be estimated satisfactorily. It is common, however, to include the "children" variable as though it is exogenous, presumably to approximate short-run behavioral patterns taking current children as given. In practice, however, a better basis for predicting long-term economic responses in female labor force behavior may be to use estimates of a reduced-form model of women's labor supply from which the "children" variable is excluded. The labor force participation equation (12) is estimated either by the logit technique in which case the probability of labor force participation (lfp) is:

$$(13) \quad Pr(lfp_i) = \frac{\exp(\hat{P}_i)}{1 + \exp(\hat{P}_i)}$$

or by the probit technique:

$$(14) \quad Pr(lfp) = 1 - F(-\hat{P}_i) = F(\hat{P}_i),$$

where F is the cumulative normal distribution (Maddala 1983, p. 22).

Hartog and Theeuwes (1985) estimate the model described above by (14) on cross-section data in the Netherlands for 1979. At that time labor force participation of married women in the Netherlands, excluding self-employed and employed in husband's business, was 22.1 percent. They then predict backwards for the years 1947, 1960, and 1971 using aggregate data for the previous years. Their aggregate variables were: (1) number of children aged 0–4 per married woman 15–44; (2) number of children aged 5–14 per married woman 15–44; (3) the logarithm of the female wage rate in 1979 guilders; (4) the logarithm of the male wage rate in 1979 guilders; and (5) the nonlabor income per household in 1979 guilders. With this simple procedure they predict female labor force participation to be .7 percent in 1947 (observed 2.3), 1.5 percent in 1960 (observed 4.2), and 11.4 percent in 1971 (observed 12.2). A criticism of their analysis is that they use fertility as one of their predictors when there are strong arguments for treating fertility and labor force participation as jointly determined.

Hartog and Theeuwes (1985, p. 235) draw the following conclusions from their study:

> The rate of participation in the labor force by married women is lower in the Netherlands than in similar industrialized countries. However, since the end of the Second World War the participation rate increased from almost zero to almost one-fourth in less than 35 years. Using estimation results obtained with a probit model on a 1979 nationwide cross-section, this paper tries to reconstruct the postwar growth in the participation rate. It is found in particular that the increase in the real wage for female workers contributes substantially to the explanation of the observed long-run change. Given the relatively high own-wage elasticity, one would also expect Dutch wives to catch up in the future with the level of participation observed in neighboring countries.

Gustafsson and Jacobsson (1985) estimate their model on Swedish microdata separately for 1967, 1973, and 1980. Labor force participation is then predicted for all three years using estimates for all three years. The best predictions are obtained using the 1967 estimates to predict forward for 1973 and 1980. Predicted values were for 1967: 59.3 percent (observed 58.3), for 1973: 73.5 percent (observed 72.8), and for 1980: 87.0 percent (observed 83.5). Predicting backwards using estimates for 1980 performs much less well in the sense that it overpredicts the 1967 female labor force participation to be 71.6 percent in comparison to the observed figure of 58.3 percent. The authors conclude (Gustafsson and Jacobsson 1985, p. S256):

Labor force participation of married women increased from 49.1 percent to 83.5 percent during the past 2 decades. By cross-section estimates on micro data of the probability of labor force participation in 1967, 1973, and 1980 and by using these estimates for predicting changes in labor force participation, we have found that increases in own wage has been by far the most important explanatory factor. Women's real wages have increased relative to husband's after-tax earnings both as an effect of the introduction of compulsory individual taxation in 1971 and as an effect of dramatically decreased sex differentials in pay partly associated with increased female education.

These two studies, compared in Table 3, imply that if only women's wages grow, their labor force participation will also grow. Franz's (1985) analysis of German women's labor force participation does not report such a prediction exercise. If the "Wages and Incomes" model performs well within a country, is it then simply a question of higher husband's income in the Netherlands and higher female wages in Sweden that explain the fact that women participate much less in the labor market in the Netherlands than in Sweden? It seems unlikely that this could be true. As Goldin (1990, p. 126) observes:

> The finding that just two variables can explain so much of the change in participation and hours of work frankly overturns the conventional wisdom that women entered the labor force as a result of a more complex set of factors—changes in social norms, declining barriers to their paid work, increasing work flexibility, smaller numbers of children, and the diffusion of labor-saving devices in the home, to mention a few of the most cited reasons. But according to these (Mincer 1962; Smith & Ward 1984) and other scholars, increased real earnings of female workers, not a shift in their labor supply function, was of primary importance in the secular increase in female labor force participation and in their hours of paid work. Increased participation within this framework resulted largely from a shift of the demand curve over a rather elastic and relatively stable supply function.

However, the remarkable success of the model has inspired me to analyze differences between Sweden and Germany within the same simple model and recompute wages and incomes to make them more comparable between the two countries. Doing this, one has to take taxes into account, because if one can argue that all individuals within a country are exposed to the same tax system when making comparisons between countries, individual taxation increases women's wages after tax and decreases husband's income after tax in comparison to joint taxation (see section II above).

A. Income Taxes and Wives' Net Earnings

In this section the "Wages and Incomes" model will be extended by taking income taxes into account.[7] Sweden has completely individual taxation, Germany

---

7. In Gustafsson (1992) Swedish and German income taxes are compared and the "Wages and Income" model is estimated using the German SEP data and the Swedish HUS-data for 1984. In Gustafsson and

Table 3
*Observed and Predicted Values of Labor Force Participation
of Married Women According to Hartog and Theeuwes (1985)
for the Netherlands and Gustafsson and Jacobsson (1985)
for Sweden*

	Netherlands		Sweden	
Year	Observed Value	Predicted Value	Observed Value	Predicted Value
1947	2.3	0.7		
1960	4.3	1.5		
1967[a]			58.2	59.3
1971[b]	11.4	12.2		
1973			72.8	73.5
1980			83.5	87.0

a. Estimates for 1967 used for forward prediction for Sweden.
b. Estimates for 1971 used for backwards prediction for the Netherlands.

has joint taxation, and the Netherlands has individual taxation with an element of joint taxation. Let us first define the net wage of the wife at her given hours of work according to each tax system as

(15) $w^j = (x_2^j - x_1^j)/h$ for $j = G,S,N$

where G is the German tax system, S is the Swedish tax system, and N is the tax system of the Netherlands, $x_2^j =$ income after tax for the two-earner couple, and $x_1^j =$ income after tax for the one-earner couple.

Income after tax for the two-earner couple according to the German tax system can be described as follows:

(16) $x_2^G = (y_f + y_m) - t^G(y_f + y_m - 2b^G),$

where y_f is the before-tax income of the secondary wage earner, y_m is the before-tax income of the primary wage earner, t^G is the joint tax rate of the German tax system, and b^G is the basic allowance per person.[8] The tax rate is progressive,

---

Bruyn-Hundt (1991) the tax systems of the three countries are compared, and incomes after tax simulated using microdata from the three countries.

8. More details about the German tax system are given in Gustafsson (1992). In the German tax system there are also social security payments paid partly by the employee. Those are separately deducted from each person's income. In Sweden social security is an employer-paid tax of 37 percent of the wage bill. The Netherlands has a system similar to Germany where part of social security payments are paid by the employee as an extra tax. Since 1990 the "Oort" tax reform lowered social security payments for the one-earner couple in comparison to the two-earner couple or a single person (Gustafsson and Bruyn-Hundt 1991).

$t_G = t_G(y)$; $t'_G > 0$. For the Swedish two-earner couple income after tax is described as follows:

$$(17) \quad x_2^S = y_f - t_f^S(y_f - b^S) + y_m - t_m^S(y_m - b^S),$$

where t_f^S, t_m^S are the tax rates of the Swedish tax system that apply at the particular incomes y_f and y_m, respectively. Since Swedish taxes are progressive, $t_f^S \neq t_m^S$ with the exception of $y_m = y_f$. The Dutch tax system resembles the Swedish tax system for the two-earner family but the German tax system for the one-earner family. Thus

$$(18) \quad x_2^N = y_f - t_f^N(y_f - b^N) + y_m - t_m^N(y_m - b^N), \text{ if } y_f > b^N.$$

Income after tax for the one-earner couples according to the respective tax systems can be written:

$$(19) \quad x_1^G = y_m - t^G(y_m - 2b^G),$$

$$(20) \quad x_1^S = y_m - t_m^S(y_m - b^S),$$

$$(21) \quad x_1^N = y_m - t_m^N(y_m - 2b^N),$$

where $t^G = t^G(y)$ because of progressivity will be smaller in (19) than in (16). In fact t^G is calculated so that a couple is taxed at the same tax rate as if their joint income was half that of a single person, the "splitting tariff." On the contrary, the Swedish $t_m^S(y_m)$ is the same in (17) as in (20) because no consideration is taken of the fact that two people have to live off the income in x_1^S. A single earner pays the same tax as the one-earner couple. In the Netherlands there is a tax rebate for the one-earner couple of $t_m^N b^N$ in (21) as compared to (18).

We can now define wife's contribution to family income before tax:

$$(22) \quad p_y = \frac{y_f}{y_m + y_f},$$

and wife's contribution to family income after tax as:

$$(23) \quad p_x^j = \frac{x_2^j - x_1^j}{x_2^j} \quad \text{for } j = G,S,N.$$

In Table 4 estimates of p_y and p_x^j are presented for the three countries. Swedish women contribute the most to family incomes because of their higher labor force participation rate and the higher female to male wage ratio compared to the other two countries. The differences in labor supply of women between Sweden and Germany are accentuated by the after-tax adjustment of wages. The individual taxation of Sweden taxes the lower income of the wives at a lower tax rate than the higher incomes of the mostly full-time working and better-paid husbands, whereas the German system taxes secondary earnings at the top marginal tax rate of the primary earner. Table 4 clearly shows that $p_x^G < p_y$ and $p_x^S > p_y$, whereas for the Netherlands we find the smallest difference comparing wife's contribution to family income before tax to that after tax.

Table 4

Wife's Contribution to Earned Family Income as a Proportion of Total Earned Family Income

	A. Before Tax (p_y)			B. After Tax		
	Germany	Sweden	Netherlands	Germany (p_x^G)	Sweden (p_x^S)	Netherlands (p_x^N)
All	.150	.288	.119	.124	.311	.116
Two-earner	.322	.376	.302	.310	.406	.295
Without children under age 13	.187	.306	.167	.154	.332	.163
With youngest child						
Age 0–2	.072	.246	.066	.060	.262	.065
Age 3–6	.103	.276	.087	.085	.297	.084
Age 7–12	.101	.280	.078	.083	.305	.078
According to education of wife						
Lower	.142	.270	.092	.117	.290	.090
Higher	.195	.336	.215	.159	.368	.209
n	1860	613	272			

Source: Author's computations based on HUS 84 for Sweden, SOEP 84 for Germany, and SWOKA 88 for the Netherlands. See Gustafsson and Bruyn-Hundt (1991) for details.

B. Education and Hours of Work

The level of income of parents may also affect how much schooling their children receive, and this income effect could differ for daughters and sons. In the three countries I survey, the decision of whether to continue in school is probably an individual decision of the young woman or man. Typically tuition fees are small or even nonexistent in these countries, and there are government loans or subsidies available to finance student living costs. In Sweden, moreover, student loans are not means-tested against parents' income. Social security pensions are also substantial, suggesting that parents would not invest in their children's schooling as their primary means of securing support in their old age. It can be argued, therefore, that a higher female labor force participation rate and a higher female to male wage ratio as observed in Sweden would encourage more equal investments in the schooling of men and women.

Comparisons for the three countries are presented in Table 5 based on the author's tabulations of microfiles. The proportion of wives who have college education in comparison to husbands is highest in Sweden followed by the Netherlands and is most dissimilar in Germany. Goldin (1992) describes women graduating from college in the 1950s in the U.S. as a group that went to college to find

Table 5

Education and Hours of Work of Wives and Husbands

	Germany		Sweden		Netherlands	
	Wives	Husbands	Wives	Husbands	Wives	Husbands
Proportion of wives and husbands by education						
Compulsory minimum	.718	.621	.620	.563	.643	.579
High school	.220	.233	.293	.315	.242	.231
College	.062	.146	.087	.122	.115	.190
Hours of work per week						
All couples	15.6	40.1	24.9	36.8	9.9	37.1
Dual-earner couples	30.2	42.6	30.8	42.9	23.9	41.4
Hours worked per week						
0	.482	.057	.196	.094	.584	.104
1–10	.084	.004	.056	.013	.157	.005
20–24	.0182	.016	.404	.063	.140	.040
35+	.252	.923	.343	.838	.119	.851
Proportion with college education participating in the labor force	.612	.912	.786	.962	.664	.904

Sources: Estimated by author from the following sources of microdata. *Sweden:* HUS-panel (1984); *Germany:* SOEP (1984); *Netherlands:* OSA (1988).

Notes: Couples are living together, legally married, and not legally married, between the ages of 20 and 59. Educational groups are defined as follows for Sweden and Germany: compulsory minimum is $S \leq 11$, high school is $12 \leq S \leq 15$, and college is 16+. For the Netherlands the groups are: compulsory includes the third year of "middle school" or students aged 15, high school includes the sixth year of "middle school" or students around age 18, and college includes all years of education beyond high school. For details see "Standaardonderwijsindeling" SOI (1978) part 2, Central Bureau of Statistics of the Netherlands.

a partner. College was more of a marriage market at that time, and few women could use their education and training in paid work. Do we see any of this in a Western country with a small percentage of female labor force participation such as the Netherlands, where 58 percent are outside the labor force? The last line shows that in Sweden almost 79 percent of women with academic training have paid jobs, in Germany 61 percent, and in the Netherlands 66 percent. In Germany and the Netherlands the higher the women's education the more likely she is to be in paid work, whereas in Sweden there is not much of a difference according to education. Academically trained women actually work less than average, because some of them are still studying; recall that we include women from age 20–59.

Goldin's observation for American college graduates of the 1950s does not appear to be true today even for the Netherlands which is a country with a relatively low female labor force participation rate.

In Sweden, women of female-headed households have the same earnings capacity as other women and work longer hours, though the female to male ratio of earnings capacity is considerably higher, which mitigates the consumption problem of living in a female-headed household in Sweden (Gustafsson 1994a). The behavior of women compared to men is more similar in Sweden than in the other two countries.

How do the differences in taxation affect women's labor force participation? Gustafsson (1992) estimated the determinants of participation using the "Wages and Incomes" model, taking taxes into account, based on the German "sozioökonomische Panel" for 1984 and the Swedish HUS-data for 1984. In this case the budget constraint (6) is changed into:

$$(24) \quad x_1^j + hw^j = p_1 q_c + p_2 q_s.$$

Although the tax system is exogenous to the labor supply decision the net wage is endogenous because of progressive taxes. The estimating equation for labor force participation (12) is now modified:

$$(25) \quad P_i = \alpha_0 + \alpha_1 w_i^j + \alpha_2 X_{1i}^j + \alpha_3 C_i + u_i,$$

where w^j is fixed at 10 hours or 40 hours alternatively and $j = G, S$, for Germany and Sweden, respectively, in the estimating equation. The logit specification model is assumed, as above.

For each individual woman, w^S, wage according to the Swedish tax system, and w^G, wage according to the German tax system, as well as X_1^S and X_1^G, family income after tax assuming that the wife does not earn any income, are computed. As shown in Figure 1B above $w^S > w^G$ and $X_1^S < X_1^G$. For each individual woman we predict labor force participation under the condition that w_i^S and X_{1i}^S are changed into w_i^G and X_{1i}^G for the Swedish sample:

$$(26) \quad \hat{P}_i = \alpha_0^S + \alpha_1^S w_i^G + \alpha_2^S X_{1i}^G + \alpha_3^S C_i + u_i,$$

and the other way around in the German sample:

$$(27) \quad \hat{P}_i = \alpha_0^G + \alpha_1^G w_i^S + \alpha_2^G X_{1i}^S + \alpha_3^G C_i + u_i.$$

The results in Table 6 show that Swedish wives would decrease labor force participation from 80.2 to 60.4 percent if confronted with German taxes, and German wives would increase their labor force participation from 50.3 to 60 percent if confronted with Swedish taxes.

These simulated results show that taxes are important. However, if we were to explain the difference in labor force participation between Germany and the Netherlands, the differences in the tax systems are not as marked. Germany taxes more secondary earnings than does the Netherlands, as is clear from Table 3 above, and yet labor force participation of German women is higher than that of Dutch women.

Table 6

Predicted Labor Force Participation for Swedish and German Wives if Confronted with the Other Country's Tax System

	Swedish Wives		German Wives	
	Participate at all hrs > 0	Participate full time hrs > 30	Participate at all hrs > 0	Participate full time hrs > 30
Mean net wage increase				
Swedish crowns	−6.32[a]	−2.32[b]	6.57[a]	3.23[b]
(standard dev.)[a]	(4.29)	(4.48)	(4.30)	(3.91)
Mean income increase				
1,000 Swedish crowns	20.04	20.04	−23.3	−23.3
(standard dev.)[b]	(16.8)	(16.8)	(17.8)	(17.8)
Actual outcome lfp	.802	.454	.503	.278
Predicted outcome due to change in tax system lfp	.604	.385	.600	.306

Note: See Gustafsson (1992) for details.
a. $w^S - w^G$ for Swedish wives, $w^G - w^S$ for German wives.
b. $x_1^S - X_1^G$ for Swedish wives, $X_1^G - X_1^S$ for German wives.

C. Day Care

From the discussion of Figure 2 above we concluded that child care subsidies are likely to increase mothers' labor supply by altering the opportunity set in the input space (Figure 2A) for mothers from *AEFPL* to *AEFM*. A day care subsidy changes the budget restriction (6) into:

$$(28) \quad X_1^i + h(w^j - k - s) = p_1 q_c + p_2 q_s,$$

where k is the hourly child care cost and s is the hourly child care subsidy. We can now extend the "Wages and Incomes" model by taking day care cost into account.

This has been done by Gustafsson and Stafford (1992) analyzing the labor force participation decision of Swedish mothers of preschool children. Because day care in Sweden in practice has been a community monopoly, whereas quality standards in terms of children per teacher, building space per child, and teacher's educational standards have been nationally determined, we have a situation of price differentiation for a standardized quality. The price parents pay to the community day care averages 10 percent of total cost, the remainder being covered by a national state subsidy averaging 47 percent, and the remainder from community budgets. Since our data set, the HUS 1984, has information on the community in which the family lives, we have information on the price of child care both for users and nonusers. However, demand for public day care has increased much faster than supply, creating a rationing problem. The labor force participation equation is extended, therefore, to include variables on the price paid by parents and whether the family lives in a community where spaces are rationed.

The estimation equation of labor force participation (25) now becomes:

(29) $P_i = \alpha_0 + \alpha_1 w_i^S + \alpha_2 X_{1i}^S + \alpha_3 C_i + \alpha_4 P_{pj} + \alpha_5 NR_j + \alpha_6 (P_p \times NR)_j + u_j$

for the ith woman and the jth community where P_p is price of public day care to parents; NR is a dummy variable equal to one if the community where the family lives is nonrationed. The coefficient α_6 is an estimation of the interaction effect of the price of public day care and living in a nonrationed community. This coefficient is of particular interest since it estimates the effect of child care prices on female labor force participation in a nonrationed community. We find a negative and significant estimate of α_6 implying a price elasticity in nonrationed communities of -2.7. Thus, child care subsidies seem indeed to stimulate female labor supply.

Maassen van den Brink (1994) estimates the effect of child care price on mothers' labor supply for the Netherlands. Although 41.5 percent of Dutch mothers of preschoolers make use of day care, only 27.4 percent are labor force participants (Maassen van den Brink 1991). Maassen van den Brink shows that the wage elasticity of labor supply is much higher than the elasticity of labor supply with respect to the price of child care, and she concludes, therefore, that day-care subsidies are an inefficient means of increasing female labor supply.

In Sweden, in 1988, among children aged 1 year, 41 percent had a space in the public subsidized day care system. This is in comparison with 53 percent of the two-year-olds, and 55 percent of the three-year-olds. Since Sweden allows parental leaves of 15 months to be shared between the father and the mother at their choice, 90.5 percent of the children less than one were cared for by a parent at home and only 4 percent were in the public day care system (Gustafsson 1994a). In the Netherlands only 1.3 percent of preschoolers have a space in subsidized child care (VNG 1991), although child care is becoming a "hot issue" in the Netherlands as more mothers are seeking paid employment and the central government has decided to devote some money to child care subsidies.

Another difference between Sweden and the Netherlands is that compulsory school starts when the child is four years old in the Netherlands, but in Sweden it starts when the child is seven years old. In Sweden a prerequisite to enroll your child in a subsidized day care system is that the parents have jobs or school work for at least 20 hours per week, although there are some children who get a space because they have special problems. The different requirements may explain why day care subsidies are effective in increasing female labor supply in Sweden but not in the Netherlands.

Sweden also has more generous paid parental leaves now amounting to 15 months of paid leave with a job security of 18 months (see Sundström 1991 for a description of these policies). The financing of paid parental leaves is also important. Gruber (1991) finds that mandatory health insurance benefits for maternity leave in the United States were fully shifted to the beneficiaries by lowering wages of women of childbearing ages by as much as 5 percent. To avoid lowering the net wage of women, paternal leaves may be financed through a general tax for the public health insurance system, rather than financed by the specific employer.

V. Concluding Remarks

In this paper I have argued that the standard "Wages and Incomes" model of female labor supply, although it has good explanatory power across individuals within a society, gives little insight into differences in female labor force participation across countries. In order to improve the model, programs that complement women's work or substitute for child care must be incorporated into the choice set, and the form of income taxation in each country must be taken account of. The "Wages and Incomes" model was extended to allow for differences in the tax system when comparing Sweden and Germany. The results showed that labor force participation by German women would have increased from 50 to 60 percent if the German women had been confronted by Swedish taxes, and it would have decreased for Swedish women from 80 to 60 percent if they had been confronted by German taxes. Including day care subsidies for Sweden suggests a negative and significant day care price elasticity on women's labor supply.

Programs of this type should be included in comparisons of female labor supply between countries. However, even if we could explain 100 percent of the differences across countries by explicitly modeling different programs that affect female labor supply, this does not explain why one country has policies that favor wives' labor force participation and another country has policies that penalize female labor force participation. To understand that, one has to study the history of women's work and the imposition and abolition of marriage bars (see Gustafsson 1994b). In a comparison of Sweden and the Netherlands, Swedish policies since the 1930s can be characterized as "Female Labor Supply Promotion and Pronatalism." In the Netherlands, at least until the 1960s, public policies were dominated by ideas of "Paternalism and the Holy Family," which led to idealizing the mother and supporting antifeminist legislation (Pott-Buter 1993), in the same way as has been shown to have occurred in the United States (Goldin 1990).

II   Labor Markets, Uncertainty, and Family Behavior

5 Women, Insurance Capital, and Economic Development in Rural India

Mark R. Rosenzweig

Mark R. Rosenzweig is a professor of economics at the University of Pennsylvania.

I. Introduction

In recent years attention has been directed to the question of how resources are distributed among family members within households, in particular to the distribution of resources between men and women and girls and boys. While the precise nature of decision-making within the household is not yet settled, empirical studies have focused on the intrahousehold distributional effects of differences in the capital embodied in or owned by the adult members of the household. And, as indicated in a number of studies, sex differences in human capital (schooling), work opportunities and asset ownership appear to be related to sex differences in the intrahousehold allocation of resources (for example, Thomas 1990, 1991; Rosenzweig and Schultz 1982; Schultz 1990b).

Another strand of literature has examined the relationships across households between family members (Lucas and Stark 1985; Cox 1987, 1990; Altonji et al. 1992; Rosenzweig and Wolpin 1993a). Work in this area based on data from India, in particular, suggests that kinship and marital ties are valuable forms of household human capital, with returns similar to those of insurance contracts that protect against the consequences of adverse events such as earnings losses and illness (Caldwell et al. 1986, Rosenzweig 1988, Rosenzweig and Stark 1989). This "insurance" capital differs among members of households, however, and these differences may also affect how household resources are allocated. In particular, these studies suggest that household ties created or reinforced by marriage facilitate risk sharing among spatially separated households.[1] In this context, in

---

1. The Indian survey data used in Rosenzweig (1988) reports the location of transaction partners for the surveyed households. In that sample of farm households in the semi-arid tropics, 59 percent of transfers, in value terms, originated from a nonvillage source. In contrast, fewer than 12 percent of all loans were

which almost all adult women in a household are migrants from other households (and villages), but men are lifetime residents in the household and village, the resident married women (and the nonresident daughters of the household head) but not the resident men embody insurance capital. The families of origin and destination of married women participate in mutual aid schemes.

The evidence from studies of intrahousehold resource allocations that point to the role of the contributions of household members as an important factor thus imply that the prevalence and significance of marriage-based risk pooling could have important implications for how resources are shared within households between men and women. The empirical findings on the importance of risk-sharing, however, come mainly from studies of a few villages in India. Such villages, moreover, are not typical of those of India in general in that they have experienced little technological development, have not been participants in the "green revolution." In traditional settings where weather is the principal source of earnings volatility, household mobility is low, and risk prospects are readily assessed, knowledge about risks and about households can have accumulated over many years. It is not surprising, therefore, to observe quite extensive and sophisticated risk-pooling mechanisms in such environments (Townsend 1989). It is thus not yet clear how prevalent and important a role marital ties play in risk pooling in general in India or, in particular, how economic development affects such arrangements and thus, perhaps, the sex-based distribution of human capital and resources within households. It is possible that radical changes in the technology of production, which among other effects obsolesce experience and change the nature of risks, may impair the ability of individuals to engage in risk-sharing arrangements. This may adversely affect the stability of family relationships and, in particular, the resource allocations to women.

In this paper I use panel data from a national probability sample of households in rural India, many of but not all of whom were exposed to the agricultural technical change associated with the "green revolution," to assess the importance of marital-based insurance arrangements for consumption-smoothing and the effects of agricultural technical change on the returns from this form of insurance capital, on loan-taking, on the stability of household structure and on mobility patterns. I also look at the implications of the risk-reducing roles of marital arrangements for technology adoption and how exposure to technical change affects sex preferences within households. In Section II, I set out the basic framework for studying the relationship between transfers, credit and household structure and marital ties and their relationships to technical change. In Section III, the data and statistical methodology for identifying the determinants of insurance-based transfers and loans are described and in Section IV, estimates are presented of the joint effects of marital ties, exposure to new agricultural technologies and the presence of local credit institutions on the responsiveness of interhousehold transfers and loan-taking to changes in household earnings. In Section V, the relationship between the adoption of new technologies and informal risk sharing

---

obtained from sources outside the home village. Rosenzweig and Stark (1989) report that in Malaysia 79 percent of the value of transfer inflows for "emergency support" and "consumption maintenance" traversed distances of 20 or more miles.

is further explored. Estimates of the effects of household structures conducive to risk-sharing on the probability of adopting the new (at the time of the study) high-yielding grain varieties and of the effects of technology change on household structure and stability are presented. Finally, in Section VI some evidence is presented on the effects of technological change on sex preference.

II. Risk Pooling and Consumption Smoothing

Assume that the earnings Π_{it} of farmer i at time t is given by

$$(1) \quad \Pi_{it} = \mu_i + u_t + \delta_{it},$$

where μ_i is a farmer-specific time-invariant component, u_t is a time-varying component that is common to all farmers, and δ_{it} is a farmer-specific time-varying shock to earnings. Consumption c_{it} by the farmer in any period may diverge from that period's earnings by the use of two consumption-smoothing mechanisms that depend on the cooperation of agents: lending or borrowing (credit use) b_{it} and transfers to or from other households τ_{it}. That is, in period t

$$(2) \quad c_{it} = \Pi_{it} + b_{it} + \tau_{it}.$$

If the farmer pools with each of n other households in the economy some fraction Γ_i of that part of his earnings that is time-varying ($\delta_{it} + e_t$), then his transfer income τ_{it} at time t is

$$(3) \quad \tau_{it} = (1/2)\Gamma_i \left(\sum_{j=1}^{n} \delta_{jt} - n\delta_{it} \right)$$

where j indexes all households participating in the risk-pooling scheme and $\Sigma_{j=1}^{n}$ $\Gamma < 1$. Thus, the extent to which transfers insure against fluctuations in earnings depends on the farmer's ability to contract with other parties, in particular those whose earnings shocks are not highly positively correlated with those of the farmer and who have knowledge about the farmer's circumstances or can trust the revelations made by the farmer about those circumstances. As discussed in Rosenzweig (1988) and Rosenzweig and Stark (1989), family members and marital arrangements play an important role in risk pooling. Altruism among and perhaps specific knowledge held by family members allow kin-related households to take advantage of the risk-pooling benefits of spatial separation without the high costs associated with moral hazard. In particular, in that framework exogamous marriages in rural India, in which daughters of the head of a household move out of the village to another (rural) household, reflect in part the desirability of forming alliances among spatially separated households with minimally correlated risk patterns in order to pool risk most efficiently.

If there are important risk-pooling benefits to marriage, then the "value" of the human capital of a married woman to a household is thus not simply her contribution to household earnings via work activities as conventionally measured (in the market and in the home) but is also the insurance premium associated with the household's improved ability to smooth consumption. The human capital of married women thus also includes a component—"insurance capital"—that is not so easily measured. To the extent that an incentive for the parents of a married woman to assist the household of their married daughter reflects parental concern about their daughter's welfare, then such arrangements also insure in part against their daughter's being mistreated in her husband's household. Similarly, unmarried daughters are also valuable in a context in which risk-sharing mechanisms are prevalent, as they represent potential insurance capital. Thus, to the extent that the intrahousehold allocation of resources reflects the value of any individual member's contributions or potential contributions to household welfare, more resources flow to both daughters and daughters-in-law the greater the value of the informal insurance arrangements associated with marital ties.

Informal insurance arrangements involving transfers across households would appear to be inherently fragile. One reason is that for arrangements undertaken by households that transfer resources from those experiencing negative earnings shocks from those with positive shocks, beliefs about each farmer's future willingness to participate in the income-pooling arrangement are critical (Foster 1988, Coate and Ravallion 1993). Each participant must believe that other participants will not renege on commitments in the future. These considerations suggest that economic development may importantly affect the ability and willingness of households to engage in these arrangements, with perhaps consequences for the allocation of resources between men and women in households.

There are three ways in which economic development, in particular increases in farm earnings brought about by agricultural technological change, may reduce the role of insurance-like transfers and thus the insurance premium attached to marriage. First, technological change may increase mobility, the likelihood that established households will not necessarily remain on the same land. As discussed in Rosenzweig and Wolpin (1985), technical change erodes the value of land-specific experience and thus loosens the ties binding family members to the family land. As shown by Coate and Ravallion, the prospects of increased mobility of any household participating in the income-pooling scheme increases the divergence between first-best and optimal-constrained transfer arrangements, as it increases the likelihood that the future benefits from such a scheme will not be forthcoming to all participants.

A second reason that technical change may reduce the insurance value of marital ties is that increases in earnings, given declining risk aversion and/or improved abilities to accumulate assets, reduce the demand for such insurance. Note that with forward-looking households, it is only necessary that one of the partners believe that earnings growth will in the future reduce the likelihood of future participation for the arrangements to be broken off in the current period. Thus, even farmers experiencing earnings growth but who wish to continue such arrangements may not be able to if their partners are less likely to do so.

While a farmer's ability or desire to participate in informal transfer arrangements would appear to be reduced by prospects of future earnings growth induced by agricultural technical change, his ability to borrow may increase. This is because the willingness of credit sources to provide credit depends on their perceptions and beliefs about the farmer's ability and willingness to repay a loan in the future. The farmer's future ability to repay is thus of paramount importance in determining the supply of borrowed funds, and the expectation of future earnings growth may increase the willingness of lenders to provide loans where there are expectations of continuing technical change.

Finally, all of the parameters in the risk-sharing decision rules reflect the bargaining parties' mutual assessment of risk and their knowledge of the technology of production. Changes in technology, at least initially, by changing risks and making risk assessment more difficult necessitate new arrangements. This may decrease the ability to risk pool and thus make farmers more reliant on alternative mechanisms to smooth consumption.

Thus, farmers who adopt new technologies may as a consequence be less protected ex ante against earnings fluctuations via risk pooling arrangements. This not only has implications for marital arrangements and inter and intra-household resource allocations but for technology adoption. In particular, if adoption reduces a farmer's risk protection arising from informal transfer schemes, then farmers who rely on such mechanisms to smooth consumption may be more reluctant to adopt new technologies. Note that the new technologies may in fact turn out to be less risky ex post than the old technology; it is the initial lack of common knowledge about such risks that makes farmers who initially adopt new technology less insurable.

III. Data and Estimation Procedure

The Additional Rural Income Survey (ARIS) of India, a national probability sample of approximately 5,000 Indian rural households surveyed by the National Council of Applied Economic Research (NCAER), is a very useful data set with which to examine the insurance value of marital ties and the effects of technological change on the use of transfers and credit to smooth consumption. This comprehensive survey, conducted in three rounds in the crop years 1968–69, 1969–70, and 1970–71, has five features that make it particularly relevant for a study of earnings insurance arrangements in rural settings. First, there is information on net transfers (cash and kind) and borrowing as well as on earnings from all activities. Second, because the data are longitudinal, it is not necessary to fully specify the time-invariant determinants of earnings. Identification of transitory earnings shocks and responses to them is thus facilitated. Moreover, many of the biases due to heterogeneity in (presumably time-invariant) risk preferences that jointly influence all choices of income-smoothing mechanisms, ex post and ex ante, such as household structure and marital arrangements, can be avoided. Third, because of the geographical scope and time-period of the survey there is variation in the exposure of households to agricultural technical change. In particular, the ARIS-NCAER survey was undertaken at a time when the green revolution in India was just getting underway in particular areas of the country. This makes it feasible to examine how risk pooling arrangements are affected by technology change. Fourth, because there is variation across villages in access to credit facilities, the importance of such institutions in facilitating consumption smoothing can thus be assessed.[2] Finally, because the data set identifies the geographical location of the sampled households, it is possible to merge the household data with information at the more aggregate level on the local agroclimatic environment so as to better characterize the natural risks presumably influencing farmer behavior.

Two files from the survey are used and combined. The first contains longitudinal earnings and income information, by type, on the 4,118 households successfully interviewed in all three survey rounds. The second contains more comprehensive information obtained from the last sample round on family structure and on asset holdings. The longitudinal file contains 3,328 households who were cultivators in at least one survey round and 2,536 households who were cultivators in all three crop years. Of these, 12.8 percent transferred income, in cash or kind, over the three-year period. Note that the proportion of households actually transferring income understates the extent to which the total population of households is engaged in risk-sharing schemes. This is because the transfers only occur when there are presumably significant shortfalls in "normal" earnings. It would not be expected that most households would, in any given short period, require indemnification of losses. Moreover, the average transfer inflow for those receiving transfers was 1,376 rupees and the average outflow was 1,918 rupees, which represent substantial proportions of total earnings. Average total household earnings in the sample, including earnings from all agricultural activities (net of paid out costs), salary income, and agricultural wage earnings, is 4,336 rupees.

Some 59 percent of the farmers borrowed money (net) over the three years; the average loan amount was 1,160 rupees. This figure overstates the extent to which loans serve to smooth consumption, however, as a substantial proportion of loans is used for financing variable production inputs and longer-term investments. Interestingly, only 27.6 percent of farmers repaid loans (net) over the same period; the average net repayment was 837 rupees.

Because of the relative scarcity of both transfers and loans in any given year, I estimate a discrete choice model from which the effects of marital ties and technology shifts on the probabilities of receiving loans and transfers can be obtained. In any given period, a farm household may be in four states—receiving a transfer, receiving a loan, receiving a loan and a transfer, and receiving neither a loan nor a transfer. Utility in each period is a function of consumption in that period, and the utility functions for each state, given (2), are thus, respectively: I. $U = U(\Pi_{it} + \tau_{it}, e_1)$, II. $U = U(\Pi_{it} + b_{it}, e_2)$, III. $U = U(\Pi_{it} + b_{it} + \tau_{it}, e_3)$, and IV. $U = U(\Pi_{it}, e_4)$, where the e_k are state-specific errors.

I assume that the risk pooling shares Γ_{it} in (3) are functions of family and household characteristics and the presence of new technologies, such that

(4) $\Gamma_{it} = X_{fi}\beta_{f1} + \beta_{f2}T_{it}$

---

2. The prior work on the determinants of interhousehold transfers in rural India (Behrman and Deolalikar 1987, Rosenzweig 1988) utilized a longitudinal data set from a survey of households in only six villages. Such data cannot be used to estimate how differences in access to credit institutions influence informal risk pooling.

where X_{fi} = vector of characteristics of farmer i and his potential household partners that facilitate interhousehold risk pooling and $T = 1$ if there are new technologies. Given the definition of the X_{ji}, all of the elements of β_{f1} are positive but the coefficient $\beta_{f2} < 0$ if technological change reduces informal risk pooling.

Following Rosenzweig (1988) and Rosenzweig and Stark (1989), I constructed three variables presumed to facilitate risk pooling among households and thus contained in X_{fi}. The first variable is the number of married women residing in the household. In most Indian households, sons remain in the household and import wives while daughters leave the household when they marry. To compute the total number of marital connections associated with a household it is thus also necessary to know the number of absent daughters. To obtain this, I subtracted the number of resident daughters of the head from the number of surviving daughters of the wife of the head, obtained from the household roster information and the fertility histories provided in the third round of the survey. I also computed using the same method the number of absent sons, some of whom may be household migrants. As in the prior studies, it would be expected that households containing higher numbers of married women and having greater numbers of absent sons and daughters would have higher interhousehold risk pooling shares Γ_{it}. To establish that it is marriages that are conducive to risk sharing and not simply household size and sex-composition, I also include in the vector X_{fi} the number of adult men and adult women residing in the household.

Technological change is represented by an indicator of whether the household is in a district containing the Intensive Agricultural District Program (IADP). This program was in set in place in 1961 in one district in every Indian state, with two districts in the state of Kerala, to encourage farmers to adopt modern production practices, provide advice on efficient use of new technologies, and help to assure adequate supplies of production inputs such as fertilizer and seeds. The districts were selected with a purpose; in particular, areas were chosen where it was assumed, based on crops grown and other geoclimatic conditions, that the new high-yielding seeds associated with the green revolution and that were becoming available at that time would be particularly successful. Thus the program not only encouraged farmers to adopt new technologies but also provided an early signal that technological change was going to take root.[3] Because of the stratified sampling scheme of the NCAER-ARIS survey, approximately 25 percent of sample farm households reside in IADP districts.

Loans are also assumed to be a function of household earnings and of technological change, with, however, the presence of the latter presumably increasing farmer's abilities to obtain loans when earnings are temporarily low because of the expectation that the farmer will have a greater ability to repay where earnings are expected to advance relatively rapidly. However, loans given in a period t will also depend negatively on the debt status of the household in that period, as greater debt impairs repayment. In contrast, transfers in the current period, to the extent that they represent the outcomes of an insurance scheme, should not

---

3. Estimates are presented below that, net of household characteristics, farmers in the IADP areas were more likely to have adopted the new seed varieties associated with the green revolution.

depend on whether a household has experienced bad earnings years in the past, and thus took on more debt, unless that affected the perceptions of the risk-pooling partners that the household would reneg on its future commitments to the scheme. Finally, as credit institutions may specialize in types of loans—for consumption-smoothing, for investment, and so on, the responsiveness of credit to earnings may differ across types of institutions. The data indicate the presence of three credit sources in the villages in which the households reside—money lender, cooperative bank, commercial bank.

To obtain estimates of the parameters of the state-specific lifetime utility functions, Equations (1), (3), and (4) are substituted into (2). I assume, as an approximation, a linear specification for the parameters characterizing each utility state inclusive of the error terms e_k. A major estimation problem, however, is the presence of the unmeasured time-persistent components of earnings μ^i in (1), inclusive of agroclimatic conditions such as soil quality, rainfall distributions, which may influence transfers, loans, household structure and marital arrangements, as well as the location of credit institutions and the IADP in different localities. Moreover, the unobserved household preferences (for risk-taking) affect household arrangements and may influence transfers and loans to the extent that these are known by the transaction partners. This would lead to biased estimates of the indirect utility parameters and thus of the roles of marital ties and technical change in affecting the income-smoothing role of transfers and loans.

To obtain estimates that are free of the biases due to the omitted unmeasured characteristics of the households and their environment, I assume that preferences (the e_k) follow a permanent-transitory scheme, with transitory components i.i.d. extreme value. Given this assumption, a multinomial fixed effects procedure (Gary Chamberlain 1980) yields consistent estimates of the parameters characterizing the utility states associated with the consumption-smoothing alternatives when there is heterogeneity in permanent preferences and in earnings that is known by the transaction partners (in-law households and credit institutions), as long as the latter do not know the purely transitory preferences of the households. The fixed-effects procedure thus avoids biases due to the endogeneity of both family arrangements and the geographical distribution of public and private institutions, as long as neither importantly responds to unmeasured *transitory* preference shocks.

The disadvantage of the fixed-effects procedure is that the influence of permanent attributes of households and their environment on the receipt of transfer income and loans are obviously not estimable. For example, the use of transfers to equalize wealth across family members living apart cannot be discerned. The estimates cannot be used therefore to discriminate between altruistic and exchange motivations for interhousehold private transfers (Cox and Jiminez 1989). The fixed effects estimates provide (unbiased) information only on the contributions of household and village characteristics to the responsiveness of transfers and loans to transitory earnings changes. A remaining estimation problem not eliminated by the use of the fixed-effects procedure is that the transitory earnings of the partner-households, which affect the transfers received by the sample households, in (3), are not observed. This is a feature of almost all data sets based on household surveys. The unavailability of partner-household earnings realizations only biases estimates to the extent, however, that the *transitory* earnings of the members of the risk-pooling scheme are correlated, and one objective of the scheme is to minimize this correlation. Indeed, Coate and Ravallion show that because the gains from income-pooling are smaller the higher the correlation in transitory earnings, the higher this correlation the more likely transfers will be reduced relative to those manifested from the first-best risk-sharing arrangement.[4]

IV. Estimates of the Contributions of Transfers and Borrowing to Income Smoothing

Table 1 reports descriptive statistics for the 3,328 households for which the requisite data were available for all variables. The fixed-effects multinomial logit estimates for the three states involving transfers, loans, or both are reported in Table 2, where the left-out utility state is that in which the household receives neither form of assistance. Estimates from two specifications are reported. The first specification omits the characteristics differentiating the transfer rates and loan-taking across households, while the second includes these characteristics.

The results in Table 2 obtained from the noninteractive specification indicate that, as expected, the log-odds of receiving only transfers, only loans or both relative to neither rise as earnings fall—both loans and transfers contribute to consumption-smoothing. The estimates obtained from the full specification, however, suggest that the log-odds for each category differ significantly across households, as the set of household and village-specific characteristics add significantly to the explanatory power of their respective equations. The relevant joint F-statistics associated with the hypothesis that the coefficients associated with *i*) the number of resident married women, the number of absent daughters and the migrant men are jointly statistically significant in the transfer (only) equation and *ii*) the credit institutions are jointly significant in the loan (only) equation are 3.55 for degrees of freedom 3 and 435 and 4.83 for degrees of freedom 3 and 3186, respectively.

I also tested the hypothesis that the presence of the lending institutions in the village affected the log-odds of receiving transfers without a loan, which would only be the case if the transfer "rules" were based on transitory incomes gross of loans for consumption purposes. The set of credit-institution coefficients was not statistically significant at even the .10-level of significance ($F(3, 435) = 2.03$). I also tested whether the log-odds of obtaining a loan but no transfer relative to

---

4. Another problem caused by the data is that no information is available on the time spent by family members in agricultural production. This means that agricultural earnings net of paid out costs will reflect in part the labor supply decisions of the household, and fluctuations in net own farm earnings will in part be due to the response of labor supply to income shocks. Wage earnings also reflect labor supply responses. However, experimentation with the use of wage earnings defined by multiplying time-invariant market labor supply (300 days) by the village-specific and year-specific wage (by sex), as in Rosenzweig (1988), indicated that this did not influence perceptibly the estimates reported.

Table 1

Descriptive Statistics: NCAER Farm Households, 1968–70

Variable	Mean	Standard Deviation
Annual income from agricultural operations (rupees)[a]	2,715	3,777
Coefficient of variation (3 years)[a]	55.9	42.6
Percentage ever receiving or providing transfers in 3 years[a]	13.0	—
Percentage ever receiving loan in 3 years[a]	56.4	—
Number of married women in household	1.43	1.02
Number of daughters of head outside household	0.78	1.20
Number of adult females in household	1.92	1.18
Number of sons of head outside household	0.70	1.20
Number of adult males in household	1.21	1.29
Bank in village	.577	.754
Money lender in village	.799	.401
Cooperative credit institution in village	.903	.296
Intensive agricultural district program (IADP)	.214	.410
Number of households[b]		3,328

a. Based on all three sample rounds. All other household and village-level variables from the third round.
b. Households engaged in cultivation in at least one survey round.

no assistance was a function of those household characteristics evidently conducive to obtaining assistance via transfers, namely the married daughter and daughter-in-law and absent sons variables. These variables did not add significantly to the loan (only) equation, suggesting that the credit institutions do not take into account the insurance provided by the informal transfer schemes.

The qualitative results for the transfer income and credit equations appear consistent with the hypotheses that marital arrangements facilitate income-smoothing via interhousehold transfers, as both the number of resident married women and the number of absent daughters significantly increase the responsiveness (strengthen the inverse relationship) between household earnings and the log-odds of receiving a transfer without a loan relative to receiving no assistance. Migrant sons also contribute, but the coefficient is half that of the daughter and daughter-in-law coefficients.

The estimates from the log-odds transfer (only) equation also appear to indicate that the effects on transfer responsiveness are no different for resident married women and absent daughters, as the coefficients for these two variables are not statistically different. However, this does not imply that adding a household to the risk pool by importing a woman via marriage has the same effect as adding a household by exporting a daughter. This is because the total number of women is also held fixed in the specification. The appropriate interpretation of the coefficient for the number of married women is that it represents the effect of *replacing* a single woman by a married woman, not just adding a married woman. The effect of the latter is the sum of the married women and total woman coefficients. The effect of exporting a daughter is the external daughter coefficient minus the effect of the total number of resident women.

The estimates from the loan-only equation indicate that the presence of a village money lender makes loans significantly more responsive to transitory earnings, while the presence of a commercial bank or credit cooperative does not. This result is consistent with direct loan source and loan "purpose" information in the NCAER-ARIS data, which indicate that money lenders are the principal source of loans for "consumption." The estimates also indicate that the log-odds of receiving a loan are significantly less for households with higher levels of debt, although debt does not appear to influence the log-odds of receiving a transfer. These latter results confirm the basic distinction between transfers, which are assumed to be the outcomes of an insurance scheme, and loans, which require repayment.

The estimates of the effects of being in an IADP area also differ across the transfer and loan log-odds equations in a way consistent with the distinction between credit and insurance. As hypothesized, transfers are significantly less responsive to earnings shocks in households located in IADP areas presumably experiencing and expecting to experience technical change. In contrast, loans in those areas are more responsive to earnings fluctuations and more helpful in smoothing income. Evidently the prospects of future earnings gains, which improve repayment prospects, affect access to loans in bad times, but the improvement in earnings prospects and the (hypothesized) effects of technical change on the stability and mobility of farm households reduces reliance on transfers.

Because of the multinomial logit structure, it is difficult to discern directly from the Table 2 parameter estimates the magnitudes of the effects of changes in the regressors, such as the number of marital ties or the introduction of technical change, on the probabilities of receiving transfers and loans. To do so requires that the regressor derivatives on the probabilities be computed. Because of the nonlinearity of the multinomial logit form, the evaluation of the effects of changes in the regressors on the state-specific probabilities requires that a particular sample point (or set of points) be chosen, as the relevant formula in this case is:

$$(10) \quad \frac{dP_{ki}}{dX_i} = \left(\hat{\gamma}_k P_{ki} - \sum_{m=1}^{4} \hat{\gamma}_m P_{mi} \right) P_{ki},$$

where P_{ki}, P_{mi} = probability of choice k or m for observation i; $\hat{\gamma}_k, \hat{\gamma}_m$ = estimated logit coefficient.

Table 3 presents results from experiments, based on (5), that compare the probabilities of receiving transfers and loans for alternative values of earnings shocks and types of marital ties and under a regime of technical change, as represented by IADP. The first row (1) of Table 3, the baseline, indicates the separate probabilities of receiving a transfer and a loan or neither based on the sample probability distributions for households located in non-IADP districts with sample average characteristics but with an earnings level that is the sample aver-

Table 2
Fixed-Effects Multinomial Logit Estimates: Determinants of Transfers and Loans In Farm Households

Variable ($\times 10^{-4}$)	Receipt of Transfer Only		Receipt of Loan Only		Receipt of Transfer and Loan	
	(1)	(2)	(1)	(2)	(1)	(2)
Transitory income	−.311 (1.35)[a]	−.750 (1.00)	−1.68 (10.8)	−1.40 (2.75)	−3.80 (2.25)	47.6 (1.68)
Debt	—	1.12 (1.29)	—	−20.7 (18.2)	—	−4.12 (1.17)
Income × married women in hh ($\times 10^{-4}$)	—	−1.22 (2.67)	—	—	—	−7.09 (1.18)
Income × daughters outside hh	—	−1.35 (2.81)	—	—	—	3.75 (1.02)
Income × total women in hh	—	.967 (1.95)	—	—	—	−4.07 (1.31)
Income × sons outside hh	—	−.676 (1.65)	—	—	—	−9.80 (1.71)

Income × total men in *hh*	—	.199 (0.74)	—	—	—	-.697 (0.15)
Income × IADP	—	2.81 (3.16)	—	-.938 (1.90)	—	-1.98 (0.21)
Income × money lender in village	—	—	—	-1.50 (2.78)	—	-24.3 (1.48)
Income × bank in village	—	—	—	.690 (1.82)	—	4.14 (0.43)
Income × coop in village	—	—	—	2.04 (2.53)	—	-15.3 (1.11)
Number of observations contributing to likelihood	446	446	3,186	3,186	63	63
Number of total observations	9,984	9,984	9,984	9,984	9,984	9,984
Number of households	3,328	3,328	3,328	3,328	3,328	3,328
Percentage of observations in total, dependent variable = 1	3.39	3.39	25.7	25.7	0.65	0.65

a. Asymptotic *t*-ratio in parentheses.

Table 3
Effects on Probabilities of Receiving Transfers and Loans of a One Standard-Deviation Decrease in Income, by Changing Family Structure and Environment

Household	Transfer		Loan		Neither	
	Probability	% change from baseline	Probability	% change from baseline	Probability	% change from baseline
(1) Baseline: income one sd below mean, mean household characteristics[a]	.028	0	.31	0	.672	0
(2) Income two sd's below mean, mean household characteristics[a]	.039	39.3	.35	12.9	.629	−6.4
(3) (2) with one daughter leaving (marrying)	.049	75.0	.34	9.7	.628	−6.5
(4) (2) with one son marrying (addition of married women)	.041	46.4	.35	12.9	.622	−7.4
(5) (2) with one son migrating	.045	60.7	.35	12.9	.625	−7.0
(6) (2) in IADP area	.031	10.7	.38	22.6	.605	−10.0

a. In non-IADP area.

age intertemporal standard deviation below mean earnings (1,518 in 1970 rupees). The next row (2) shows what happens to those probabilities as earnings decline by an additional standard deviation, again for a non-IADP household with average characteristics. The remaining rows then indicate the effects on the probabilities of: (3) marrying off a daughter (adding a nonresident daughter and reducing the number of resident females by one), (4) importing a daughter-in-law (adding a married female and a resident female), (5) exporting a son (reducing the number of adult males by one and adding a nonresident male), and (5) moving the household to an IADP district.

The experiment reported in row (2) indicates that the probability of receiving a transfer is more elastic to earnings than is the probability of receiving a loan—the additional one standard-deviation decrease in earnings increases the transfer probability by almost 40 percent, but the loan probability by only 13 percent. Because of the relatively low proportion of households actually receiving a transfer, however, in absolute terms the probability of receiving a loan rises by more, by four percentage points compared to the one percentage point rise for the transfer probability.

The experiments involving increasing marital ties and changing household structure based on the multinomial logit estimates that are reported in rows (3) through (5) indicate that the marriage of a daughter has the largest effect on the response of the transfer probability to a negative earnings shock—marrying off a daughter results in a 75 percent increase in the probability of receiving a transfer compared to the rise of 40 percent over the baseline probability for the average household in response to the negative earnings change. The results also indicate that the addition of a married woman to the household increases the probability of receiving a transfer by 46 percent while adding a migrant son increases the probability by 61 percent over the baseline. In contrast, the results in row (6) indicate that the effect of moving a household with the same structure and experiencing the same negative earnings shock to an IADP district would lower the probability of receiving a transfer by almost one percentage point, or by 21 percent.

The results in Table 3 also indicate that the response of the loan probability to the earnings shock is not sensitive to household structure or marital ties. However, a household with average characteristics in an IADP district with a two standard-deviation negative earnings shock has a probability of receiving a loan that is three percentage points higher than an otherwise identical household outside the IADP area. The increase in the probability of a loan is greater than the decrease in transfers in the first column of Table 3; the last column estimates indicate that households in the IADP areas are less likely to receive neither form of consumption assistance in response to the earnings shortfall compared to non-IADP households.

V. Risk Pooling and Technology Adoption

The results in Tables 2 and 3 suggested that farmers in areas characterized by the use of relatively new technologies, in the form of the green revolution high-yielding seed varieties, engaged in less risk pooling. This finding is consistent with the hypothesis that technical change makes the formation or persistence of risk-sharing arrangements more difficult, due to expectations of increased mobility among transfer partner households, higher probabilities that such households, even if intact, would have less need of such support in the future, and the difficulties of assessing the new risks associated with the new inputs and practices. In this section I test an implication of this hypothesis, that farmers better able to risk pool under traditional technologies will be less willing to take on the new risks entailed by adopting a new technology because such farmers have more to lose. In particular, I test whether households with a structure evidently more conducive to risk pooling are less likely to have adopted the high-yielding seed varieties (*HYV*). I also test whether in fact, among observationally identical households, those in IADP areas were more likely to be using *HYV* seeds.

Because information on family structure is only available from the last round of the survey (in 1970–71), the fixed effects procedure cannot be used to mitigate the effects of heterogeneity. In this case the problem is that unobserved permanent attributes of the family, for example, risk preferences, and of the agroclimatic environment may jointly influence technology adoption and family structure. Moreover, adoption of the new technology which increases earnings from agricultural production, may directly affect family structure if it is income elastic. To circumvent this simultaneity problem, I use instrumental variables, exploiting the ability to merge the ARIS data with area-specific time-series information on agroclimatic conditions.

In a dynamic framework, decisions in any period that have future consequences, such as the adoption of a new technology, depend on current state variables and any variables providing information about the future at time t. Farmers deciding whether to adopt a new technology in period t will be influenced by such state variables as their wealth and, presumably, family structure at time t, the cost and availability of credit and time-invariant agroclimatic endowments, including the characteristics of the distribution of risks, which influence expected returns. Given the state variables at time t, however, all realizations of earnings or the stochastic variables (for example, weather) prior to t will not influence the adoption decision at period t if such past realizations are not serially correlated and as long as it is relatively costless to change technologies.[5]

Information on (serially uncorrelated) weather outcomes prior to the 1970–71 crop year can thus be used to create identifying instruments for the farmer's wealth and family structure in 1970–71, the survey round with information on these state variables. District-level annual time series information on rainfall for the years 1961–82, along with five district-level agroclimatic endowment variables

---

5. Fixed effects autocorrelations based on the annual rainfall data were estimated in Rosenzweig and Wolpin (1993b). The Box-Pierce statistic applied to the residuals from the aggregate time-series data, based on lags of up to 20 years, indicated no autocorrelation. Costs of switching technologies do not appear to be high. Of those farmers using *hyv* in the first round of the survey (18.1 percent), 53.4 percent subsequently switched back to traditional varieties in at least one of the subsequent two periods. Of those using *HYV* in both the first and second rounds, 16.4 percent dropped *HYV* in the third round.

were extracted from a data file, described in Binswanger, Khandker, and Rosen-zweig (1993) and merged with the ARIS data. The five endowment variables are: the average length of the rainy season, the average number of months with excessive rain, the number of months with temperatures below 18 degrees celsius, the percentage of district land liable to flooding, and distance to an urban center. In addition, from the annual 22-year time series of rainfall from 1961 to 1982, the mean and coefficient of variation of rainfall was computed for each district. All of these variables could only be obtained for 80 of the 85 districts represented in the ARIS data set, so that some loss of observations is entailed in their use (districts in the states of Orissa and West Bengal are missing).

Table 4 reports the two-stage maximum-likelihood probit estimates, based on the method outlined in Smith and Blundell (1986), of the determinants of the adoption by farmers of the new green revolution technology in the crop year 1970–71. The farmer's total wealth in that year and the five household structure variables are treated as, and are confirmed to be, endogenous variables by the Hausman-Wu test statistic also reported in Table 4. The identifying instruments are the annual rainfall in each of the years 1961–69 interacted with the five agroclimatic variables. The estimates indicate that an increase in the number of married women in the household, for given number of adult women, decreases significantly the likelihood of using the new technologies as does an increase in the number of sons of the household head who reside outside the household. These two variables were significantly associated with higher rates of interhousehold risk pooling, as seen in Table 2. Only the nonresident daughters variable is not in conformity with the hypothesis that advantages in risk pooling make farmers reluctant to adopt new risks. However, the coefficient for this variable is not statistically significant and is quite small.

Of the other estimates, it is notable that wealthier farmers and those with more schooling are more likely to adopt *HYV*, while farmers in areas with more rainfall variability are less likely to be using the new seed varieties. This latter result suggests the returns from the new seeds are slightly more sensitive to rainfall and is consistent with the positive estimated effect of electrification on adoption, as electrification facilitates water control by irrigation systems using pumpsets. Finally, the availability of credit appears to hasten adoption, as the presence of a bank or a money lender in the village is significantly and positively associated with *HYV* adoption. This result is likely due to the complementarity between the new seed varieties and fertilizer, increasing the need for *production* credit among farmers adopting the new technology. The Intensive Agricultural District Program (IADP) was instituted specifically to enhance credit availability and provide assured supplies of fertilizer in anticipation of this. And the results in Table 4 suggest that the program did increase *HYV* adoption rates.

If the adoption of new technology renders the risk-pooling advantages of marital ties less strong, as suggested by the results in Table 2 through 4, it might be expected that the availability of the new technology would ultimately reduce the value and thus the presence of married women in households. Moreover, if new technologies reduce returns from land-specific experience, adult sons will be less likely to remain in the household. As daughters of the head traditionally leave

Table 4

Two-Stage Maximum-Likelihood Probit Estimates: Determinants of Adoption of High-Yielding Seed Varieties[a]

Variable	
IADP	.549
	(3.51)[c]
Rainfall *CV*	−2.90
	(3.15)
Mean rainfall ($\times 10^{-3}$)	−.214
	(1.66)
Bank in village	.1295
	(1.49)
Money lender in village	.329
	(2.65)
Small scale industry in village	.0760
	0.46
Village electrified	.373
	(2.73)
Wealth[b] ($\times 10^{-4}$)	.611
	(6.11)
Number of married women in household[b]	−3.14
	(3.76)
Sons residing outside household[b]	−1.92
	(5.44)
Daughters residing outside household[b]	.604
	(1.21)
Adult males in household[b]	2.14
	(2.53)
Adult females in household[b]	−3.22
	(2.22)
Schooling attainment of head	.313
	(3.70)
Age of head	−.0523
	(0.95)
Age squared ($\times 10^{-3}$)	.559
	(1.14)
Constant	10.9
	(4.65)
Number of farmers	1,330
Exogeneity test statistics ($\chi^2(6)$)	14.2

a. Exogenous variables also include six district-level agroclimatic variables. See text.
b. Endogenous variable. Identifying instruments = rainfall in each of prior ten years in district and adverse weather indicators in preceding two years in village.
c. Absolute values of asymptotic *t*-ratios corrected for use of predicted variables in parentheses.

the household, technological change should not affect significantly daughter mobility. It is the mobility of sons that represents a break from traditional patterns.

Table 5 presents reduced-form estimates of the effects of the IADP, net of the other village and district-level characteristics, on the number of resident married women and on the number of nonresident sons and daughters of the household head. The results indicate that in districts subject to the IADP, households had 20 percent less married women in residence and 16 percent more sons who had left the household.[6] As expected, however, IADP appears to have had no effect on the absence of daughters, who leave the home when marrying. Because the effect of IADP in reducing the number of resident married women is greater than the effect of IADP in increasing the absence of sons, the net effect of the subsidization of the new technology on potential intrafamily risk pooling is negative, as resident married women have a larger effect on risk pooling than do nonresident sons (Table 3).

VI. Technological Change and Sex Preferences in the Household

Is there any evidence in the data that in the new technology areas the within-household distributions between men and women are affected in ways consistent with the findings on risk-sharing and household stability? In particular, is the reduced value of insurance capital in IADP areas suggested by the prior results manifested in less resources going to women within households? The NCAER-ARIS data provides some indirect evidence. A woman from each sampled household was asked to provide the "ideal" number of girls and boys she would like to have. Approximately 28 percent of the women provided a response to this question.[7] Of the responses, the average of the difference between the preferred number of girls and boys reported by each woman was −.9, reflecting an overall preference for boys among this group.

To ascertain whether boy preference is exacerbated in IADP areas, I selected a subsample of the respondent women who were aged 30 and under, to avoid ex post rationalization bias—the actual sex ratio of births may influence sex preference, and this effect would be more intense among women who were close to the end of their childbearing.[8] I constructed as a measure of sex preference the

---

6. The erosion of any returns to experience specific to the household's land entailed by technological change may also directly weaken the incentives for sons to coreside with the household head (Rosenzweig and Wolpin 1985).
7. The households of the women answering this question were more likely to be in IADP areas and had a lower proportion of heads with formal schooling. The proportion of women with formal schooling was not statistically different between the two groups. I did not attempt to "correct for" the selectivity of the respondent sample in obtaining the estimates reported below.
8. In principal, the sex ratio of births could be "controlled." However, there is evidence in the data that the sex ratio at birth is not reported accurately and, moreover, also reflects sex preferences (there are far too few reported female live births, particularly as reported by women for pregnancies more than 10 years prior to the survey).

Table 5

Maximum Likelihood Tobit Estimates: Determinants of Household Structure[a]

Variable	Number of Married Women in Household[b]	Number of Sons Residing Outside Household	Number of Daughters Residing Outside Household
IADP	−.320	.214	.109
	(2.18)[c]	(1.36)	(0.83)
Bank in village	.0771	.106	−.157
	(0.43)	(0.54)	(0.96)
Money lender in village	−.167	.0127	.0886
	(1.27)	(0.10)	(0.74)
Small-scale industry in village	.247	−.143	−.150
	(1.28)	(0.69)	(0.87)
Village electrified	.294	−.0319	−.0982
	(2.47)	(2.46)	(0.91)
Age of head	−.0283	.0709	.112
	(1.15)	(2.46)	4.56
Age squared ($\times 10^{-3}$)	.747	−1.01	−1.11
	(3.12)	(3.53)	(4.57)
Schooling attainment of head	.134	.0463	.0157
	(4.24)	(1.29)	(0.53)
Sigma	1.58	1.94	1.65
	(30.6)	(40.6)	(44.4)
Number of farmers	1,545	1,545	1,545
−ln likelihood	1,663	2,519	2,563

a. Also includes as regressors: six district-level agroclimatic variables, mean and coefficient of variation of district rainfall, rainfall in each of prior ten years in district, and adverse weather indicators in the village in the three rounds of the survey.

b. Lower bound = 1.

c. Absolute values of asymptotic *t*-ratios in parentheses.

log of the ratio of the ideal number of girls to the ideal number of boys.[9] As determinants of this variable, I used the IADP indicator variable and household wealth, treated as endogenous, along with variables indicating whether the household head (male) and his wife had received any formal schooling, wife's age and infrastructural variables (small-scale industry, factories, electrification).

Care must be taken in interpreting the effects of the IADP variable on sex preferences. Because technical change increases incomes, as long as sex bias is income elastic, such change will affect preferences. Indeed, Rosenzweig and Schultz (1982) found evidence based on the same data that households with larger landholdings exhibited less favoritism to boys, as indicated by relatively lower

9. I placed the ideal number of boys in the denominator because some fraction of responding households indicated that the ideal number of girls was zero. Because of the overall preference for boys, the average value of the log ratio is thus negative.

Table 6

Two-Stage Least Squares Estimates: Effects of IADP and Wealth on Log Earnings and on the Log Ratio of the Reported "Ideal" Number of Girls to Boys

Variable	Log Earnings[a]	Log Ratio Girls/Boys[b]
IADP	.045	−.00039
	(1.31)	(0.01)
Wealth $(\times 10^{-4})^c$	.113	.0431
	(6.41)	(1.73)
Formal schooling, head	.288	−.140
	(8.49)	(1.89)
Formal schooling, wife	.319	.0994
	(6.93)	(1.06)
Number of observations	2,004	173

a. Specification also includes an indicator for whether the village was electrified, the head's age and its square, and an indicator of adverse weather in 1970–71 crop year in village.
b. Sample of women aged less than 30 years. Specification also includes an indicator for whether the village was electrified, contained a factory or any small-scale industry and the head's age and its square.
c. Endogenous variable. Identifying instruments include land owned, indicators of bad weather in the village in the prior two crop years, and annual district rainfall variables.

female child death rates. This evidence would suggest that, in the absence of any erosion of insurance capital embodied in women and girls, technological improvements and thus the IADP variable should be positively associated with the sex preference measure—relatively higher numbers of girls preferred. To see if this effect of IADP is also operating, I regressed the log of household earnings on IADP, including as well in the specification the (endogenous) wealth measure. If IADP areas have higher incomes, net of wealth and schooling, and if wealth reduces the bias toward boys, then IADP areas should be characterized by less sex bias unless this effect is offset by other factors, including the increased inability of households to engage in marriage-based risk pooling.

Table 6 reports the results from the estimation of the determinants of log earnings and of the sex preference measure. In the first column, it is seen that earnings are 4.5 percent higher in IADP areas, although the effect is not measured precisely. In this equation, as expected, (predicted) wealth and schooling, of both the head and wife, contribute positively to earnings. In the sex preference equation, it is also seen that preference for girls relative to boys is higher in households with greater wealth, confirming the hypothesis that boy preference is (negatively) income elastic. However, the expected increase in the relative preference for girls in the IADP areas (net of wealth effects) due to income effects is not observed; if any different, boy preference is actually higher, suggesting that the income effect associated with the influence of technical change on preferences is offset by other factors.

How good a measure of actual intrahousehold resource allocations is the reported difference in "ideal" numbers of children by sex? While it is not possible to answer this question directly in the absence of information on actual household resource allocations, it is interesting to note that the effects of the head and wife schooling variables display patterns that are consistent with the findings in the literature on actual intrahousehold distributions and outcomes (for example, Thomas 1991)—the schooling of the head is negatively related to relative girl preference while that of the wife is positively related to girl preference. Of course, these estimates cannot necessarily be interpreted as indicating the effects of exogenously increasing schooling levels of either men or women, as the schooling of men relative to women in any household may itself reflect sex bias, although the schooling of the parents was achieved prior to the initiation of the "green revolution."

VII. Conclusion

In societies in which incomplete markets are pervasive, the returns to human capital may be particularly difficult to measure. Yet such returns may have important consequences for the distribution of resources and overall welfare. In this paper I have used longitudinal data from a national probability sample of rural households in India to assess how the traditional migration of women across households via marriage, by contributing to consumption smoothing, augments the returns to women as human capital and how these returns from women as insurance capital are affected by economic development propelled by agricultural technical progress. The estimates confirmed earlier findings based on more geographically confined data from India that interhousehold financial transfers play a small but significant role in contributing to consumption-smoothing. Such transfers appear to be more responsive to a household's fluctuations in earnings than are loans, and this responsiveness is significantly augmented in households with more informal connections to other households that arise due to the marriages of sons, who stay in the parental household, and daughters who migrate.

The estimates also suggested that technical change, presumably because of its impact on the returns to experience, on earnings levels and on risk assessment, represents a threat to the traditional household and, in particular, to marriage-based risk pooling. The results also supported the conventional wisdom that traditional, extended-family households tend to resist the adoption of new technologies. This appears to be true not because such households are inherently conservative but because of real losses in their abilities to smooth consumption ex post via interhousehold transfers that accompany the adoption of a new technology.

The results thus suggest that the transformation of traditional agriculture through technological change extends beyond agricultural practices to the relationships among households and within households. Whether the evident reduction in the value of insurance capital embodied in women induced by technical change also spills over to the intrahousehold distribution of resources across men and women in India cannot be fully explored with the data used here. The results based on subjective information reflecting the valuation by mothers of children by sex suggest, however, that the income gains from economic development may not, at least in the short run, lead to a more equal distribution of resources between men and women, despite equality evidently being a normal good.

The impact of technical change in this study was inferred from cross-sectional differences across households stratified according to whether they were residing in areas identified, from the placement there of a government program, as particularly productive for the new green revolution grain varieties. While the evidence suggests that households in the program areas were more likely to adopt the new seeds, it is not possible to know whether the observed differences across the areas in the role of transfers in consumption-smoothing, in household structure and in incomes and sex preferences predated the new technologies. Preliminary evidence from a resurvey of the sample households twelve years after the first survey concluded suggests, however, that the intact households in the program areas in the first rounds of the survey were significantly more likely to have subsequently split than intact households in nonprogram areas.

6 Information, Learning, and Wage Rates in Low-Income Rural Areas

Andrew D. Foster
Mark R. Rosenzweig

Andrew D. Foster and Mark R. Rosenzweig are professors of economics at the University of Pennsylvania. This research was funded in part through NICHD grant HD28687. The authors would like to thank IFPRI for the Philippine and Pakistani data.

I. Introduction

Two principal issues in the study of labor markets in environments in which workers are heterogeneous concern how employers select workers for employment and how worker contributions are rewarded. An essential ingredient of the processes by which heterogeneous workers are matched to jobs and rewards are allocated to workers is the information available to employers about workers. Employers must be able to discriminate among workers in order to match optimally worker characteristics to particular tasks as well as to compensate them appropriately. Thus, the quality of information available in the labor market is an important factor in the efficiency of the market and, because it determines who among workers are rewarded well and less well, it can have a significant effect on the formation of human capital and the distribution of income.

While a number of theories of labor markets have focussed on labor market information problems, these have for the most part been concerned with moral hazard and the effort incentives for unmonitorable, but homogeneous, workers in jobs. Much less attention has been paid to the sorting of heterogeneous workers among employers and tasks in markets in which information about a worker's potential productivity is imperfectly known by employers. Moreover, the empirical evidence on the importance of employer ignorance and, in particular, its relevance to low-income countries and to the process of development has been given little attention. If there are important information problems in these labor markets, then an understanding of labor-market-related behaviors requires that attention be paid to the extent of information problems as well as variation in the extent of these problems across areas.

For example, investment in human capital is likely to be quite sensitive to rates of return to human capital which are themselves affected by the ability of employers to distinguish individuals with different levels of human capital and therefore productivity. Consequently, the extent of human capital investment that is undertaken in the context of a labor market in which employers have little ability to distinguish workers with different levels of productivity is likely to be quite different from that in a labor market where information is more complete. For example, if caloric allocations importantly affect worker productivity, but employers have little ability to distinguish between more and less productive workers, there will in general be underinvestment in calories on the part of workers relative to what is socially efficient. Moreover, if there are particular subgroups of the population for which information problems are more acute such as those with intermittent labor force attachment, then human capital investment is likely to be especially low for these individuals as a group.

In this essay, we attempt to establish whether information problems arising from the fact that employers are not fully knowledgeable about the potential contributions of workers who differ in their skills is an important component of causal labor markets in developing countries. We focus in particular on the casual labor markets that characterize most rural areas of low-income countries. We do this not only because these markets are so important in most of the world, but because, as we discuss, such markets permit more readily the empirical study of information barriers. Moreover, by understanding the contrast between the features of these markets and those characterizing developed countries, it is possible to assess the implications of information costs for development.

We begin by discussing possible sources of inefficiency in labor markets in the context of an efficiency-wage model incorporating adverse selection. We identify four possible sources of inefficiency: (1) misallocation of workers to tasks and sectors; (2) supervisory costs; (3) unemployment; and (4) the inability to fully capture returns to investment in human capital. We then turn to the related question of how, in the presence of imperfect information, employers use signals of worker productivity to discriminate among workers with different abilities. We then illustrate how wage inequality in the presence of signalling exhibits similarities to that arising from employers' preferences for or against workers on the basis of traits unrelated to their productivity.

We then discuss how the processes by which employers learn about differences in worker capabilities have important implications for the changes in wage inequality over the life-cycle of workers, and thus for how changes in the age structure and of worker mobility characterizing a labor market alter income inequality and labor market efficiency. Finally, we discuss one possible source of unobserved differences in worker productivity, differences in nutrient consumption. In particular, we consider the implications of unobserved differences in nutrient consumption for one of the more important theories of low-income labor markets, nutrition-wage theory, and the problems with the empirical evidence on this theory that have arisen due to the absence of attention to information problems.

In the second part of the paper, we employ data sets from three countries, India, the Philippines and Pakistan to test for information asymmetries in rural labor markets of low-income countries. First, we obtain a direct measure of the extent of heterogeneity in worker productivity. Our evidence indicates that there is substantial heterogeneity in workers' contributions to output, as measured by the inter-worker variability in piece-rate wages. While a substantial portion of individual worker skills are rewarded in time-rate wages, the evidence suggests that there is also considerable ignorance among employers about individual differences in worker abilities, with the degree of diffusion of information about worker abilities differing across the Indian and Philippines settings.

We then show that the data from the three countries exhibit a number of features that should be expected in labor markets in which information problems play an important role. We first show that the labor market in the Philippines exhibits adverse selection—evidently because employers are not fully able to identify the better workers, such workers tend to participate less in jobs paying time-rate wages, as implied by information theory. We also find evidence of statistical discrimination in both the Philippines and India: net of actual productivity men receive a higher wage than do women, but net of expected productivity men and women receive similar wages. While there is no evidence of taste discrimination on the part of employers with respect to women, we do find evidence of taste discrimination with respect to low caste individuals in the Indian sample.

We then show evidence of employer learning in both the Indian and Pakistan data sets. As workers' participation ("exposure") in the local labor market and, in particular, job tenure increases, differences between the time-rate wage received by an individual and his actual productivity appear to narrow. Finally, we provide evidence suggesting that one important source of these unobserved productivity differentials is, in fact, caloric consumption: although differentials in calorie consumption contribute to productivity differentials among workers, these are not rewarded in time-rate markets.

The empirical evidence presented in this paper is not meant to be conclusive about the effects of information barriers in low-income labor markets. They suggest, however, that further attention to these issues may have significant payoffs in terms of understanding the structure of labor markets and human capital investment in developing countries. We discuss some of these issues in the concluding section of the paper.

II. The Information Problem in Labor Markets

Many models of labor market processes assume that a fundamental problem in wage setting is that (i) employees are heterogeneous in their abilities or contributions to output and (ii) employers do not have full knowledge of each worker's productivity. If we let the productivity of worker i be μ_i, then a worker i's productivity as perceived by employers, μ_i^*, is based on a set of observed worker characteristics; in other words,

(1) $\mu_i^* = E(\mu_i | Z_{mi} \forall m \in M_E)$

where M_E is the set of characteristics that are observed by the employer, and

(2) $\mu_i = \mu_i^* + u_i$

where u_i is that component of actual productivity that is unknown to employers. There is imperfect information in the labor market if $var(u_i) > 0$. The importance of Equation (1) is that rewards paid to workers by employers will depend on μ_i^* and only on true productivity μ_i to the extent that these are correlated. The wedge between rewards paid to workers and their productivity represents an allocative cost to an economy and as well has implications for the distribution of earnings and for the types of contractual arrangements involving employees and employers that will exist. A theory of labor markets is incomplete without explicit assumptions about the limits on information about workers and about the processes by which employers' perceptions of worker productivity are formed; in other words, what observable worker characteristics enter into M_E and how the information varies with respect to contractual arrangements between employer and employee and with other features of an economic environment. In the discussion that follows we identify and discuss a number of different features of a labor market in which information problems play an important role.

A. Efficiency Costs of Information and Adverse Selection

One of the principal implications of the presence of incomplete information in the labor market is that an efficiency cost is introduced. In particular, inefficiency can arise from four sources: (1) misallocation of workers to tasks and sectors; (2) supervisory costs; (3) unemployment; and (4) the inability to fully capture returns to investment.

The first source of inefficiency, the misallocation of workers to tasks, arises from the fact that, in the absence of complete information, it may not be possible to allocate a worker to a task or sector of the economy in which he/she has comparative advantage. Consider, for example, a model in which a worker who works for a wage w_k to perform a task k receives a utility of $U(w_k - k)$, where k reflects the utility cost (in terms of consumption) of undertaking this task. If workers are paid on a piece-rate basis then it is easily seen that the most productive workers will allocate themselves to the high k tasks—they experience the same cost of doing these tasks as do less productive workers but they are better remunerated because they can earn more pay if they are paid on a piece-rate basis.

If workers are paid on a time-rate basis, however, and if employers cannot distinguish between more and less productive workers then it will no longer be the case that the most productive workers will be allocated to the high k tasks. Because there is no way of differentially rewarding more productive individuals for doing the high-wage task, the less productive workers will prefer the high k task whenever the more productive workers do. This inability to allocate workers to tasks in which they have comparative advantage results in a loss of efficiency.

Because it is argued that a piece-rate payment system will be fully efficient, even in the presence of employer uncertainty, it seems sensible to ask why time-rate wages might be paid under circumstances in which there is employer uncertainty about worker abilities. The answer is that there are costs associated with piece-rate employment that do not arise in the context of time-rate employment. In the context of casual labor markets in developing countries it has been shown that costs of monitoring output quantity and/or quality will be higher in piece-rate employment for technological and other reasons (Roumasset and Uy 1980). Foster and Rosenzweig (1991) show that, for low levels of employment, supervisory costs are higher when piece-rate employment is used than when time-rate wages are used. The cost of supervising piece-rate workers thus is both a barrier to the efficient allocation of workers by task, and when piece rate employment is used, a source of inefficiency. Of course, supervisory costs in the time-rate sector also represent a loss of efficiency that may result in part from problems of information.

The literature examining forms of payment in labor markets in developing countries also emphasizes the importance of supervisory costs as a contributor to the decision on the part of employers to pay workers on a piece versus a time-rate basis. In contrast to the studies of casual labor markets in developing countries, however, this literature gives substantial attention to the role of long-term employment as an alternative mechanism for dealing with unobserved variation in worker productivity (Goldin 1986a, Lazear 1986). Goldin (1986a), for example, uses a model in which male and female workers differ primarily in their attachment to the labor force to explain the fact that women in the United States in the late nineteenth century were frequently paid on a piece-rate basis while men who were doing similar jobs were paid on a time-rate basis. Consistent with the model, she finds that supervisory costs were lower for men when they were paid on a time-rate basis but lower for women when they were paid on a piece-rate basis.

The possibility that informational asymmetry can lead to equilibrium unemployment as well as an inefficient allocation of workers across sectors of the economy has been examined in detail by Weiss (1980). The source of the problem is that individuals in rural areas of developing countries face the opportunity to work in the time-rate labor market, in which unknown productive differentials cannot be compensated, as well as the opportunity to work on their own farm or on a piece-rate basis. Because time-rate wages will always underpay the most productive workers while the latter types of employment fully reward productivity differentials, the composition of workers willing to work for a particular time-rate employer will be affected by the level of wages that he pays. From an alternative perspective, the reservation wage for time-rate employment will be an increasing function of the level of productivity. Although the focus of the Weiss model is on understanding unemployment in developed countries, it is arguably a more appropriate characterization of labor markets in developing countries. Indeed, as Weiss points out "The positive correlation between acceptance wages and productivity is easily justified in the context of a less developed country where acceptance wages are determined by output in agriculture and handicrafts" (Weiss 1980, p. 29).

The simplest version of the Weiss model incorporates the assumption that productivity differentials are completely unobservable to the employer but are known to the employee. Under these circumstances we may let $q(w)$ denote the efficiency of the worker who is just indifferent between working for time-rates and working elsewhere. The assumption that more productive workers have higher reservation wages implies that $q'(w) > 0$. Because only workers with efficiency

$q \leq q(w)$ will be willing to work in the time-rate sector if they are offered a wage of w, the average efficiency of workers in the time-rate sector may be written:

$$(3) \quad Q(w) = \frac{\int_0^{q(w)} q\,dF(q)}{F(q(w))}$$

where $F(q)$ is the distribution function of worker efficiency in the labor market. It is easily seen that $Q'(w) > 0$: a higher wage draws more productive workers into the time-rate sector and thus raises the average productivity in that sector.

The empirical implication of wage rates affecting the distribution of workers, adverse selection, is that among groups of workers defined by characteristics known by the employer, those individual workers with higher productivity, as reflected by their piece-rate performance, will participate less in the time-rate market in circumstances in which they have an opportunity to work on a piece-rate basis. However, we are unaware of any empirical evidence demonstrating this phenomenon, despite its central role in this influential model.

Unemployment is one possible result of the adverse-selection equilibrium. Under asymmetric information, equilibrium in the labor market depends on supply and demand conditions at the wage which minimizes the cost per efficiency unit of labor ($w/Q(w)$), w^* where $w^*Q'(w^*) = Q(w^*)$. If labor demand exceeds supply at this wage then competition between firms will bid up the wage which then attracts more productive workers until the labor market equilibrates. If labor supply exceeds demand, however, then there will be queues in the time-rate labor market: there will be individuals in the labor market who strictly prefer work in the time-rate sector at the going wage to working in piece-rate. Employers will not employ these workers at a lower wage because to do so would raise the cost per efficiency unit of labor.

The adverse selection model also yields implications for the distribution of jobs across workers differing by observable characteristics such as sex or age that signal productivity. Specifically, suppose that potential employees can be divided into a number of different groups with similar observed characteristics but that there remains substantial heterogeneity in productivity within each group. As Weiss shows, equilibrium in this more complex labor market can be identified by first ranking each of the groups in terms of the minimum cost per efficiency unit of labor. Employers will then choose workers on the basis of their observed characteristics, selecting first that group with the lowest cost per efficiency unit. If labor supply in this group exceeds demand then members of this group will face job queues and members of other groups will be excluded entirely from the time-rate labor market. Otherwise other groups may be employed in inverse order of the minimum cost per efficiency unit of labor.

Under these circumstances, the allocation of workers to jobs will depend not on differences in average productivity but on the distribution of perceived productivity within each group. This has an important implication for discrimination. Let $c^*(\eta)$ denote the minimum cost per efficiency unit of labor arising in a group with an unobserved productivity distribution $F(q;\eta)$, where η parameterizes the distribution in such a way that $\eta' > \eta$ implies $F(q;\eta')$ second-order stochastically dominates $F(q;\eta)$ and F is differentiable with respect to η for all q. An application of the envelope theorem to the cost-minimization problem yields the following result:

$$(4) \quad \frac{dc^*(\eta)}{d\eta} > 0 \Leftrightarrow F(q(w^*)) \int_0^{q(w^*)} G(q;\eta)dq - G(q(w^*)) \int_0^{q(w^*)} F(q;\eta)dq > 0$$

where

$$G(q;\eta) = \frac{\partial F(q;\eta)}{\partial \eta}.$$

Thus a sufficient condition for a small mean-preserving increase in spread to raise the minimum cost per efficiency unit of labor is that $G(q(w^*);\eta) \le 0$.[1] Coupled with the fact that employer information will be more precise for individuals who are more active in the labor market as established above, this result describes the conditions under which individuals with less labor market experience as a group, for example women, will find it more difficult to find time-rate employment even if the lack of work experience has no effect on their actual productivity.

The implications of the Weiss model for efficiency stem largely from the question of whether groups that are excluded from the time-rate labor market have comparative advantage in that sector. If, for example, more productive individuals have comparative advantage in planting, but, for technological reasons, planting tends to be paid on a time-rate basis, there would be a gain in efficiency if productivity differentials were known and thus these workers could be allocated to the time-rate sector.

The final efficiency cost associated with informational asymmetries arises from the fact that investments in human capital may not be fully rewarded if the resulting productivity differentials cannot be perfectly measured. Not only does this mean that there will be underinvestment in human capital on average, but also that underinvestment will be largest for those groups for whom signals of productivity are the least accurate (Lundberg and Starz 1983).

The basis for this argument is that, in the presence of imperfect signals of productivity, employer expectations with regard to worker productivity may be thought of as a weighted average of the average productivity of a particular type of worker (for example, women) and an individual signal of productivity such as an assessment based on recent labor market experience. For groups with less experience with a particular employer (or group of employers) this latter signal will be less precise, and thus the individual signal will receive a lower weight than that in groups with more experience. Consequently, the returns to the individual for investing in human capital will be lower if that individual is from a

---

1. This latter condition will obtain if the efficiency wage is sufficiently high. If the efficiency wage is low then it is possible that a mean-preserving increase in spread will permit an employer to hire a more homogenous group of workers thus reducing the minimum cost per efficiency unit (see, for example, Weiss 1990, p. 32).

group with less (or less concentrated with respect to employers) exposure in the labor market.[2]

B. Taste and Statistical Discrimination

As is true in the adverse selection model, labor market information problems have implications for the interpretation and analysis of discrimination on the part of employers, particularly with regard to the important issue of distinguishing statistical and taste discrimination. Statistical discrimination is implied by Equation (1), and results from imperfect information held by employers and their efficient use of what is in their information set. The notion underlying the term taste discrimination is that employers have a preference for employing certain types of workers so that, net of *perceived* productivity μ_i^*, as given by (1), such workers will receive higher wages.

In the absence of taste discrimination a simple model with a competitive labor market yields the result that workers should be paid according to their expected productivity. In linear form, with or without some employer ignorance, but with taste discrimination, wages are paid according to

$$(5) \quad w_{ti} = \sum_{m \in M_D} a_m^* Z_{mi} + a_\mu^* \mu_i^*$$

where Z_{mi} represents the mth characteristic of individual i and M_D describes the set of characteristics of an individual subject to taste discrimination.

The fundamental problem with the empirical literature concerned with identifying whether or not the a_m^* are nonzero is the absence of information on μ_i^* or even knowledge of the set of worker characteristics M_E employers use to predict worker productivity. Most studies attempting to measure the effects of taste discrimination include, along with the variables over which employers may have preferences, a vector of characteristics, measured in the data that are hypothesized to be the set M_E that employers use to predict productivity. If employers know more than the researcher and the omitted component of μ_i^* is correlated with the hypothesized "taste" characteristics, Z_{mi} for m in M_D, then incorrect inferences result. If, for example, height is a determinant of productivity that is known to employers but height is not known by the researcher, then it may appear that men receive higher wages than women net of other observed characteristics.

The existence of imperfect knowledge on the part of employers means that even if the researcher can measure workers' productivities exactly (μ_i is known), identification of taste discrimination, a_m^*, is not possible without knowledge of the employer's information set (Z_{mi} for all m in M_E), because worker compensation depends only on that part of μ_i that can be predicted on the basis of the

---

2. This argument should be contrasted with the usual argument relating differences in human capital investment by sex to differences in labor-force attachment (see, for example, Mincer and Polachek 1974). The point of the present argument is that even if the social returns to human capital investment for men and women were the same (in other words, the gains in terms of productivity), in the presence of greater informational asymmetries for women, the private returns accruing to women in the form of wages would be lower.

characteristics known to the employer. Foster and Rosenzweig (1991) show that the coefficients arising from a regression of time-rate wages on actual productivity of the following form

$$(6) \quad w_{ti} = \sum_{m \in M_D} A_m Z_{mi} + a_\mu \mu_i$$

will not yield consistent estimates of the parameters of Equation (5) which can reveal taste discrimination.

Consider a population containing four types of individuals in equal proportions with different levels of productivity: productive (4) and unproductive (2) men and productive (3) and unproductive (1) women where the numbers in parentheses describe, for example, the number of baskets of corn that can be picked in an hour. Note that men are on average more productive than women but that more productive women can pick more in an hour than less productive men. Assume further that employers cannot distinguish between productive and unproductive individuals of the same sex, that monitoring costs preclude the use of piece-rate payments, and that labor is supplied inelastically by the four groups. Under these circumstances a nondiscriminating employer in a competitive labor market will pay individuals according to their expected productivity: all men will receive a wage of 3 and all women a wage of 2. Because all men receive a higher wage than all women a regression of wage on actual productivity and sex [equation (6)] will yield a coefficient of 1 on male and a coefficient of zero on productivity. Thus if problems of information were ignored, the incorrect conclusion might be drawn that women are subject to discrimination and that productivity differentials are totally unrewarded.

While estimation of such a regression can be misleading, it is nonetheless of some interest. Specifically, the regression does indicate that a man would have a higher wage than an equally productive woman. The result that efficient employers tend to pay higher wages to individuals who come from groups with above-average productivity is what is implied by statistical discrimination (see, for example, Aigner and Cain 1977). To distinguish this form of statistical discrimination from discrimination arising from the exercise of employer preferences that are orthogonal to perceived worker abilities is the principal objective in the empirical literature on discrimination in labor markets.

C. Life-Cycle Inequality in Earnings and Information Costs

A third implication of information problems in the labor market is that, to the extent that encounters between workers and employers persist over time, employers will exhibit learning with respect to persistent differences in worker productivity. This learning behavior has implications for the evolution of wages over time, that differ substantially from those arising in the now-conventional life-cycle model which emphasizes the roll of investments by workers and firms in human capital (Mincer 1974). In this latter framework, if labor markets are competitive and there are no differences in worker abilities but workers choose different life-cycle investment paths, earnings inequality first decreases on average with worker time in the labor market (work experience) and then increases until worker retirement.

In a world in which there are no human capital investments but there is a labor market information problem, however, the life-cycle trajectory of earnings inequality is quite different. It is a well-known result from basic probability theory that the variance of u_i^* will be larger the more information employers have about μ_i. That is, if e is measurement error that is uncorrelated with any of the elements in the information set and M_{E1} is a larger set than M_{E2}, then

(7) $E(\mu_i|Z_{mi} \forall m \in M_{E1}) = E(\mu_i|Z_{mi} \forall m \in M_{E2}) + e$

and

(8) $\text{var}(E(\mu_i|Z_{mi} \forall m \in M_{E1})) > \text{var}(E(\mu_i|Z_{mi} \forall m \in M_{E2}))$

If the labor market experience of workers leads not to increased worker skills but to the transmission of better information on workers' time-invariant abilities to employers, then the variance in worker earnings, based on employer expectations, will increase monotonically with worker experience, which in this case might be better named worker exposure. Intuitively, employers' priors on yet unobserved worker's ability will be relatively homogeneous and will converge to the true distribution of abilities, which are less homogeneous, with increased observations on workers.

With respect to the time path of earnings (wage rates) for individuals, in the Mincer world of homogeneous (preinvestment) abilities, earnings of all workers will either be flat or rise over the life-cycle. In a heterogeneous world without investments, however, some workers will experience declines in wages paid (those with below-average μ_i), while others (with above-average productivity) will experience wage increases as worker abilities are revealed. On average in the human capital model with no heterogeneity earnings rise with age; in the heterogeneous worker model with information problems, average wage rates are constant over the life cycle, or a major part of it. Moreover, in the Mincer-type model with no heterogeneity, lifetime earnings are the same for all workers while in the imperfect information model (i) higher-ability workers have greater lifetime earnings but (ii) because of information barriers, the differential between the lifetime earnings of low- and high-productivity workers is attenuated the greater and the more persistent is employer ignorance. The latter is true because initially (among workers with little exposure in the labor market) high-productivity workers are underpaid and low-productivity workers are overpaid. In the extreme, when employers know nothing and learn nothing about worker productivities, all wages are identical.

In a world in which there is both human capital investment and employer learning, the implications of information considerations with respect to life-cycle wage inequality hold within observable investment groups. Glaeser (1991), in a paper that directly tests some of the implications of information theory in labor markets, shows that residuals from wage regressions on worker schooling and potential work experience (age less schooling years less six) do increase with worker experience in the United States. In a more sophisticated analysis based on Bayesian models of learning with the same longitudinal data, he also shows that employer updates of workers' productivity shrink faster the longer a worker has been employed with a particular employer and not very much, given job tenure, with total labor market experience. Thus, in a developed economy like that of the United States, there appears to be employer-specific accumulation of knowledge about individual workers that is not readily transferrable, which may have implications for job mobility.

It is not clear how relevant findings on the role of information from developed countries are to the casual labor markets in low-income countries, where worker-employer attachment is rare, job tenure intermittent, and worker geographic mobility relatively low. Given the latter, worker exposure in the local labor market may be importantly related to worker time-rate compensation via general employer learning in such environments. Moreover, in casual labor markets, where work is mostly based on rudimentary, physical tasks, it is likely that learning by doing is of considerably less importance compared to developed countries, and may be less important than employer knowledge accumulation. This means that the implications of information theory for life-cycle wage-inequality in low-income countries may be more salient and interventions dealing with information problems in those contexts may have dramatic effects on the distribution of earnings.

Tests for employer learning may also be more clear in casual labor markets. This is so because in developed countries where human capital accumulation is important, worker abilities and worker investments may be correlated, which makes more difficult the identification of employer learning. In such a world, wages rise faster for the inherently more able workers. Thus, wage deviations from average wage growth rates increase for the more able and decrease for the less able. This mimics the patterns expected if employers learn about worker abilities and worker investments are either nonexistent or are orthogonal to ability.

The distinction between the two causes of the life-cycle growth in wage inequality is important because if the growth in wage inequality over the life-cycle of workers is due to employer learning, then that is evidence of information barriers and, perhaps, market failure. Such barriers may potentially be reduced with appropriate labor market policies, with possible overall efficiency benefits to an economy (although reductions in information costs, as noted, exacerbate life-time wage inequality). The life-cycle growth of wage dispersion as a result of complementarities between worker abilities and human capital investments, however, does not obviously require policy attention per se unless the cause of this correlation is due to failures in markets providing the resources for such investments.

D. Nutrition Efficiency-Wage Theory and Information

One of the most influential models of wage-setting in low-income countries, nutrition efficiency wage theory, makes a very strong assumption about employers' information set. This theory posits that there is not only a significant relationship between worker productivity (μ_i) and food consumption that is known to all employers but that employers know the food consumption of each individual worker and offer wages on a time-rate basis to workers on the basis of that knowledge. The theory is important because it provides an explanation for a "natural" floor on wage rates in low-income rural areas and has strong implications for the relationship between efficiency and inequality in such settings both within and across households. The wage minimum exists in this model because below some level of consumption an increase in the time-rate wage paid increases worker productivity by more than the wage increase. It therefore is not profitable for employers to hire low-consumption workers below some minimum wage. Because the least wealthy workers are likely to be those whose consumption at wages below this minimum would be inadequate and unprofitable, they are the ones most likely to be unemployed.

Even without the hypothesized nonlinearity in the relationship between worker productivity and consumption which sets a minimum wage, however, the model predicts that wages paid will be closely tied to consumption, with better-fed workers receiving higher wages in competitive labor markets and lower wages in monopsonistic markets (since such workers will be more efficient than less well-fed workers at the same wage). Thus, the operation of the labor market either exacerbates or reduces income-inequality, as opposed to conventional (but perfect markets) models in which wealth (and thus the ability to finance consumption) is independent of wage rates. Moreover, if consumption at the margin is differentially rewarded across jobs, then the distribution of foods within households will depend on the occupational distribution of household members (Pitt et al 1990).

The nutrition-based efficiency wage model has intuitive appeal because of its potential relevance to low-income countries where consumption levels are low and are more likely to be closely tied to income. The strong informational assumption of the model that the individual consumption of workers is part of employers' information set M_E is less appealing, however, and is critical to the model. If employers do not know who among job applicants has a higher level of consumption, then they have no basis for rationing jobs among particular workers, and wage rates paid on a time basis cannot be related to consumption. Despite this, only the assumption of the model concerning the productivity-consumption relationship has received appropriate empirical attention.

Strauss (1986), based on Sierra Leone data, and Deolalikar (1988), based on data from the semi-arid tropical region of India, tested whether the food consumption and/or nutritional status of workers affected their productivity by estimating farm-level production functions incorporating worker consumption. Both of these studies, in which the obvious simultaneous relationship between consumption and production was taken into account, found that increased calorie consumption did significantly affect productivity. Neither study, however, tested appropriately the second assumption of the model, that daily time-rate wages paid by employers were influenced by worker consumption. In the Strauss study, it was noted that wage rates, by sex, did not vary across workers. Deolalikar attempted to test directly whether calorie consumption affected wage rates. However, in that study he failed to distinguish between time-rate and piece-rate wages. The latter wage rates will always reflect worker productivity; if most of the wage rates paid are on a piece-rate basis then his finding of a positive relationship between worker consumption or health and wage rates may merely indicate (again) that consumption augments productivity but not anything about employers' knowledge of individual worker consumption. And in the environment in which the survey providing the data was undertaken, it is known, for example, that harvest operations, which employ the most people, are almost exclusively paid on a piece-rate basis (Walker and Ryan 1990). Indeed, if food consumption is only rewarded at harvest time, food consumption may exhibit seasonal patterns—higher levels of food consumption at harvest time, when incomes are also high—that mimic patterns indicative of credit constraints but are wholly the result of changes in payment regimes over the year.

The distinction between the effects of worker food consumption on time and on piece-rate wages provides evidence on the information set of employers. Strauss' observation that time-rate wages in his sample area of Sierra Leone were more or less uniform, despite heterogeneity in consumption levels and consumption-productivity effects, is suggestive of the importance of the information problem. Experimental evidence reported in Basta et al (1979) also illustrates the consequences of constraints on employers' abilities to discern consumption and the importance of distinguishing between payment methods—in that experiment, randomly selected anemic (identified by blood tests) plantation workers in Indonesia were given either an iron supplement or a placebo. The study found that relative to the workers given the placebo, the iron-supplement workers paid on a piece-rate basis received higher wages, while those paid on a time basis were not. Given that the supplement was random and temporary, it is not surprising that employers paying time-rate wages had little or no basis on which to discriminate among workers with respect to their iron consumption. In nonexperimental local labor markets, employers may have better information on workers that they can use to predict consumption over the long term. But there is of yet little evidence on whether employers in rural labor markets of low-income countries are in fact able to discern and reward workers using time-rate wages on the basis of their consumption, a necessary condition for the distributional implications of efficiency-wage theory based on nutritional considerations.

II. Data

Information on worker productivity is a key feature of data that are needed to learn about employers' perception of, and the allocation of rewards to, worker's performance and abilities. A common practice in agricultural labor markets is the use of piece-rate payment methods in at least some agricultural operations. Given common payments per piece across workers and farms, piece-rate wages should provide a good measure of workers' productivities. With data on piece-rate wages in environments in which the same workers are also paid per unit of time worked, with time-based wages, it is thus possible to assess directly the extent to which employers are cognizant of individual productivity differences across workers. Moreover, it is possible to examine the determinants of the accuracy and the biasedness of employer assessments of worker productivity differences by comparing the time-rate wages offered to workers to their productivity as measured by their piece-rate performance.

Of course, piece-rate wages per time-period may not be identical to wages paid purely on a time basis for the same worker in the same activity even if information on piece-rate wages is available to all employers because of the moral hazard problems associated with time-rates.[3] We would expect, however, that piece-rate performance is the best predictor of productivity under time-rate wages. Moreover, it is reasonable to assume that more able workers in a task, those earning higher piece-rate wages in the task, incur less disutility from work in that task and thus not only are more productive in that task compared to other workers but are less prone to shirk if there is lax supervision.[4]

We have selected two data sets to explore the issues of information asymmetries and employer biasedness that enable the comparison of piece-rate and time-rate wages for individual workers. The first is data from a stratified random panel of 448 households in Bukidnon in northern Mindanao, the Philippines, who were interviewed in four rounds at four month intervals in 1984–85 as part of a study carried out by Bouis and Haddad (1990) under the auspices of the International Food Policy Research Institute (IFPRI) on nutritional effects of export cropping. Among the relevant information (available in each round) are general household demographics, individual food-intakes of all individuals on a 24-hour recall basis, and own and off-farm labor activities and wages for all family members by type of activity, crop and payment method (piece-rate or time).

Three important characteristics of labor markets in the Bukidnon survey area make it particularly well-suited to the study of information problems in casual labor markets. First, due to evident scale-economies in supervision costs and differences in the scale of operations (land size) across employers, both piece and time-rate wage payment methods are used for the same operations in the same time period (Foster and Rosenzweig 1991). Second, due to a relative absence of seasonality, the same crop activities occur at different times of the year across different employers. Third, few workers work for the same employer for any length of time; they move from employer to employer as operations are finished. Thus, the labor market is almost exclusively a spot market, and most laborers are casual laborers. Most importantly, those employers employing workers on a piece-rate basis are not the same as those using time-rate wages; thus unbiased discrepancies between time-rate wages and piece-rate productivity measure the extent to which information on worker abilities is diffused across employers.[5]

3. See Foster and Rosenzweig (1992) for evidence that moral hazard is indeed a problem when workers are employed on a time-rate basis.

4. It is, of course, possible that the extent of shirking in the time-rate sector is not perfectly negatively correlated with productive capacity as measured in the piece-rate sector. For example, individuals who work in the labor market on an infrequent basis (such as those with large landholdings of their own) may be less concerned about the possibility of being caught shirking than those who work for wages on a more-or-less full-time basis. In the simplest case where the extent of shirking is uncorrelated with actual productivity as well as employer-observed characteristics, our procedure would lead to an overestimate of the extent of employer ignorance. If the extent of shirking is well-predicted by employer-observed characteristics, however, the bias could be of the opposite sign.

A second problem may be that productivity in the piece-rate sector may differ in some way from that in the time-rate sector. For example, some activities (such as weeding) may be especially suited to those with good manual dexterity whereas others (such as plowing) may be better suited to those who are relatively strong.

5. The possibility exists that piece-rate performance might differ across farms depending on the levels

The second principal data set we examine that provides information on piece and time-rate wages is from the Indian Village Level Studies (VLS) of the International Crops Research Institute for the Semi-Arid Tropics (ICRISAT). These data provide detailed information for up to ten years at approximately three-week intervals on all transactions and on labor supply and wage rates for all individuals residing in a sample of 40 households in each of ten villages in the semi-arid tropics of India. As in the Bukidnon survey area, almost all workers in the labor market are hired on a daily basis and work in the village in which they reside, and the survey data provide information on the basic demographic characteristics, work time and wage rates of all workers. In addition, there is information on the caste "rank" of all of the households based on a detailed classificatory study by a resident anthropologist (Walker and Ryan 1990). Thus it is possible with these data to study employer discrimination with respect to both the sex and caste of workers.

One important shortcoming of the ICRISAT survey, a feature it has in common with most other data sets, is that no direct information was elicited on the type of payment method used in the labor market. However, because for most of the Indian villages agricultural operations are highly seasonal (unlike in the Philippines case) and because there is information on the type of activity (agricultural operation), it is possible to infer payment method and thus to identify, for the same workers, piece and time-rate wages. This is because workers engaged in harvest operations in this setting are exclusively compensated on a piece-rate basis.

Another unfortunate limitation of the ICRISAT data is that the information on worker activity (harvest, planting, etc.) is only provided for household transactions that cannot be linked to individuals. To infer whether an individual worker's wage was paid on a piece-rate basis, it was thus necessary to use the information on the timing of the wage payment and the timing of agricultural operations, based on the transaction information. In three of the ten villages (Aurepalle, Rampura and Shirapur), harvest operations did not overlap significantly with other operations during certain periods of the year, due to the highly seasonal nature of this monsoon economy. Thus, we use the information from these villages only, in which piece-rate wages are the wages paid to workers in periods that are exclusively devoted to harvest operations. Thus, unlike in the Bukidnon, Philippines sample, it is necessary to assume for tests performed using the ICRISAT data that a worker's harvest productivity, measured by his/her harvest piece-rates, is a relevant measure of productivity in the other pre-harvest operations paid on a time-rate basis. The almost universal and exclusive use of piece-rate wages for the harvest operation means that many employers will be able to observe the piece-rate performance of a worker that they might hire at a different time in the year for time-rates, albeit for a different agricultural task. This could imply that information on individual worker productivities is better known in the

---

of complementary inputs. However, in the context of the survey area, farms do not differ very much in the capital equipment used in the relevant agricultural operations. This equipment includes knives (harvest), rakes etc. Farms do differ in the scale of operations, however.

Indian context compared to the Philippines setting in which payment regimes differ across employers.

An important advantage of the ICRISAT survey is that it has a significant longitudinal component. For two of the three villages from which piece-rate wage rates can most precisely be inferred, consistent time-series on individual wage rates and market participation are available over the years 1979–84 and for one village (Rampura) such information is available for the period 1980–84. The longitudinal nature of these data permits assessments of the role of worker labor market exposure in the village on employers' ability to discern accurately worker productivity. Finally, in one of the village areas (Shirapur), there is nearby a major governmental employment program that accounts for a significant share of the total wage employment of village residents. To the extent that this program offers a non-discriminatory (in the tastes sense) opportunity for all workers, we can assess its impact on wage differences caused by tastes discrimination by the village employers, if we find evidence of such discrimination.

III. Evidence

A. How Much Do Employers Know About Worker Productivity?

In this section we establish the information needed to measure the extent of employer uncertainty about worker productivity as well as to test for the presence of adverse selection in the labor market. The objective is to obtain an estimate of the variance in worker productivity, $\sigma^2(\mu)$ and then to decompose this variance into that component that is known $\sigma^2(\mu^*)$ and that component that is unknown $\sigma^2(u)$.

The first step involves estimation of $\sigma^2(\mu)$. Assuming that the piece-rate wage at any particular point is equal to actual productivity plus an error term which reflects measurement error and an idiosyncratic component of the piece-rate wage:[6]

(9) $w_{pi} = \mu_i + \varepsilon_{pi}$

and assuming that the error terms ε_{pi} are uncorrelated, it is easily seen that using two piece-rates for each individual, w_{p1} and w_{p2}, $\sigma^2(\mu) = \text{cov}(w_{p1}, w_{p2})$.

In order to estimate the component of productivity that is known by the employer we first compute the covariance of one piece-rate and one time-rate wage, w_{t1}, for each individual. Using Equations (2), (5), and (9) (assuming there is no taste discrimination in (5)) along with the fact that u_i is uncorrelated with μ^* and assuming that the measurement error in the piece-rate wage is uncorrelated with measurement error in the time-rate wage, it is easily seen that $a_\mu^* \sigma^2(\mu^*) = \text{cov}(w_{t1}, w_{pi})$. Thus if an estimate of a_μ^* can be obtained it will be possible to solve for $\sigma^2(\mu^*)$ and, since $\sigma^2(\mu) = \sigma^2(\mu^*) + \sigma^2(u)$, $\sigma^2(u)$ as well.

---

6. If piece-rate data include information on different tasks as in the case of the Philippines, then task controls may be estimated using a fixed-effects procedure and then a noisy productivity estimate, net of task, may be constructed. The rest of the procedure remains unchanged.

The principal problem that arises in an attempt to estimate a^* is that, as noted above, a regression of the time-rate wage on actual productivity μ will not yield a consistent estimate because μ is a noisy measure of that component of productivity that actually affects the wage, μ^*. The implication is that if one can identify variables that are correlated with μ^* but not with $u = \mu - \mu^*$ or time-rate wages net of predicted productivity then instrumental variables may be used to obtain consistent estimates of the parameters in Equation (5).

Instruments are readily available as long as there are researcher-known worker characteristics that (i) are correlated with productivity (ii) are known by the employer (iii) can be argued on a priori grounds to be not subject to taste discrimination. The reason for this is that, as argued above, an optimizing employer will form expectations of productivity based on any worker characteristics that he knows. Thus any characteristics that are known by the employer must be uncorrelated with the unknown component of productivity, u. Moreover, as long as these characteristics are correlated with productivity and not subject to taste discrimination they will be correlated with expected productivity but not with time-rate wages net of expected productivity.[7]

Estimates of a^* and λ_m for the Indian and Philippine samples are presented in Table 1, where the λ_m are coefficients associated with measurement equations

(10) $Z_{mi} = \lambda_m \mu_i^* + \varepsilon_{zmi}$

relating perceived productivity to a series of employer-known measures of worker productivity. In both cases, higher perceived productivity is associated with significantly higher time-rate wages[8] and a number of other factors including education, sex, village, and caste are associated with the employer-predicted productivity. It should be emphasized that there is nothing structural about these estimates: they simply reflect the covariance between these employer observed attributes and productivity. Thus, for example, the covariance between education and perceived productivity may result from the fact that sex is correlated with productivity and education is correlated with sex. Moreover, these correlations only reflect the sample of individuals who work in the labor market and thus are affected by selection into or out of the labor market.

It is apparent from these estimates that men in both labor markets are more productive than are women and that taller individuals (who are more likely to be men) are also more productive. Of greater interest are the estimates of the variance decomposition, given in the top two rows of Table 2. In both countries there is evidence of significant uncertainty about productivity differentials on the part

---

7. Instead of computing a series of separate covariances as suggested by the above discussion, we use an alternative approach to estimation which involves fitting the theoretical covariance matrix implied by the model and parameters to the data covariance matrix. There are several advantages to this approach. First, simultaneous estimation of the different components of the model leads to an increase in efficiency. Second, if errors are distributed as multivariate normals, then the approach is maximum likelihood and is therefore fully efficient. Third, standard errors can be computed for variance estimates thus making it possible to test hypotheses about the structure of information. These and other standard errors can be corrected so that they are robust to misspecification of the distribution generating the data.

8. The fact that the estimate of a_μ^* in the Philippines is higher than that in India is attributable to the fact that the productivity estimate in the Philippines is net of crop and task.

Table 1
ML-*Estimates of the Relationship Between Time-rate Wages,
Employer-Observed Worker Characteristics, and Perceived
Worker Productivity in India and the Philippines*

	India	Philippines
ln W_t	0.960	1.476
	(19.252)	(2.414)
Age	1.562	10.053
	(0.399)	(1.508)
Age-squared ($\times 10^{-2}$)	0.759	
	(0.175)	
Education	1.094	1.558
	(5.232)	(.734)
Male	1.453	1.582
	(19.897)	(2.500)
Height		0.197
		(2.122)
Shirapur village[a]	−0.287	
	(2.530)	
Aurepalle village[a]	0.307	
	(4.964)	
Low caste	−0.176	
	(2.434)	

a. Reference village is Rampura.
b. Absolute values of asymptotic t-ratios in parentheses.

Table 2
ML-*Estimates of Employer Knowledge of Worker Productivity
in India and the Philippines*

	India	Philippines
$\sigma^2(\mu^*)$	0.061	0.015
	(11.933)	(1.637)
$\sigma^2(u)$	0.008	0.032
	(3.282)	(2.007)
$\sigma^2(\mu^*)/(\sigma^2(\mu^*) + \sigma^2(u))$	0.884	0.319

a. Absolute values of asymptomatic t-ratios in parentheses.

of employers ($\sigma^2(u) > 0$), although the magnitude of the effect is quite different. Specifically, in the case of the Philippines only about 32 percent of the variance in productivity is known by employers while the corresponding figure in India is 88 percent.

That information appears to be more complete in the Indian context may be the result, as noted above, of the fact that fewer employers in the Philippines area employ the same workers under the two payment regimes compared to employers in India. Thus the Philippines farmers have less opportunity to observe workers on the basis of their piece-rate performance unlike almost all farmers in the ICRISAT villages. The relatively high degree of employer information among the Indian farmers may also indicate that harvest piece-rate productivity is a good predictor of productivity in other activities. However, because piece-rate productivity estimates in India were constructed by selecting wages from periods where harvesting predominated means that some of the piece-rate wages that are used may in fact be time-rate wages. If this is indeed the case then the estimate of the variance in true productivity (μ) in the Indian villages will be too low, but the estimated variance of the known component of productivity (μ^*) will be unaffected. This will lead to an overestimate of the proportion of productivity that is known.

Other possible reasons for the difference in the extent to which employers in the Indian and Philippines samples differ in their information may be related to the differential mobility of the workforce in the two areas. As noted above, the extent of employer ignorance will depend on the exposure of individuals in a particular labor market. Thus increased mobility will lead to greater unknown variance in productivity. Similarly, the size of the labor market may affect the extent of employer uncertainty: if villages are relatively isolated and individuals are unlikely to move from village to village to find employment, then information on even casual workers should be relatively complete. A complete investigation into the causes of differences in employer knowledge is beyond the scope of this essay, but is clearly a topic of importance for learning about remedies for information problems.

B. Is There Adverse Selection?

Having decomposed worker productivity into components corresponding to those known and unknown by employers, we can estimate the extent, if any, of adverse selection in the market by estimating the covariance of the share of labor force time spent in piece rate work (*PRS*) with that component of productivity that is *not* known by the employer. Specifically, $\sigma(w_{pi}, PRS) = \sigma(\mu, PRS)$ and $\sigma(w_{ti}, PRS) = a_\mu^* \sigma(\mu^*, PRS)$ and thus $\sigma(u, PRS) = \sigma(w_{pi}, PRS) - \sigma(w_{ti}, PRS)/a_\mu^*$. The test of adverse selection, however, can only be carried out using the Philippines data because, as noted, in the India sample villages piece-rate wage activities and time-rate activities do not occur at the same time of the year, while in the Philippines both types of payment methods exist contemporaneously. The estimated covariation between u and *PRS* in the Philippines data is .021 with an associated asymptotic t-ratio of 1.75, significant at the .08 level, suggesting that there is adverse selection in the Philippine labor market. This estimate and the variance estimate of u in Table 2 suggests that a 10 percent increase in the unobserved component of productivity in the Philippines leads to 6.6 percent increase in the share of market work time that a worker devotes to piece-rate activities.

C. Do Employers Discriminate Against Women and By Caste?

The ICRISAT villages and the Bukidnon survey area both exhibit patterns of time-rate wages by sex that are similar to many areas of the world. Table 3 reports the average wage rates of men and women in the two surveys, classified by payment method. The figures in the table indicate that in the ICRISAT sample, male daily time-rate wages are on average 62 percent higher than those of women; in the Philippines sample, male time-rate wage rates are 24 percent higher than female time-rate wages. These differentials by sex in time-rate wages are not very different from those in piece-rate wages in the two samples, however—the differential is 87 percent in favor of males in the Indian villages and is 20 percent in favor of males in the Philippines survey area. Strong differentials in work activities across men and women are also evident in the two areas. For example, 26 (24) percent of the days men spend in the wage labor market are devoted to plowing, the highest paid activity, in the Indian villages (Bukidnon), while only one (three) percent of women's labor market days are spent in plowing (Foster and Rosenzweig 1991). The wage patterns displayed in Table 3 are, however, less clear for differentials by caste in the India villages, with low-caste women's time-rate wages evidently lower than those of other women but low-caste men's wages higher.

To identify how much, if any, of the time-rate wage differentials by sex and caste exhibited in Table 3 reflect *individual* productivity differentials, employer's use of proxies for individual productivity, or employer prejudice, we first use the information on piece-rate and time-rate wages to carry out a test for the presence of *statistical* discrimination. This involves the equivalent of a regression of the time-rate wage on a series of employer-observed characteristics and actual productivity (μ_i) based on two observations for the same worker on his/her piece-rate wages (to eliminate measurement error). These estimates are presented in Table 4, where we have used variables that are plausibly observable by the employer and are available in the data. These include the worker's age, schooling, and sex for both samples, and height for the Philippines sample and caste and village for the India sample.

In the equations determining the existence of statistical discrimination, the presence of a positive coefficient for a particular characteristic implies that individuals with that characteristic will receive a higher wage than equally productive individuals without that characteristic. As noted above, this difference could arise because of either the presence of taste discrimination or statistical discrimination. The most striking feature of Table 4 is that men are paid a higher wage than women among workers with the same productivity, with this differential significant and of a similar magnitude in the Indian and Philippine villages. Thus there is either taste or statistical discrimination in favor of males. Our findings that both populations exhibited (i) significant employer ignorance (Table 2) and (ii) a covariance between perceived productivity and sex (Table 1) suggests that statis-

Table 3

Average Time and Piece-rate Wage Rates by Sex and Caste in the Three Indian ICRISAT Villages and by Sex in Bukidnon, Philippines

	ICRISAT Indian Villages (1984–85)[a]		Bukidnon, Philippines (1984–85)[c]	
	Time Wage	Piece-rate Wage[b]	Time Wage	Piece-rate Wage
Men	7.87	7.17	23.3	29.7
	(1.91)	(1.84)	(8.75)	(13.3)
Women	4.85	3.83	18.8	24.8
	(2.35)	(0.82)	(5.61)	(12.1)
Low-caste men	8.16	6.30	—	—
	(1.74)	(2.42)		
Low-caste women	3.60	3.91	—	—
	(0.61)	(0.71)		

a. Wage rates in rupees per day.
b. Based on harvest wage.
c. Wage rates in pesos per day in fourth round.

tical discrimination may play an important role. The estimates also indicate that among workers with the same productivity, low caste workers in India also receive a lower wage. Again, because caste was observed to be correlated with productivity this result may reflect statistical discrimination, although taste discrimination may also play a role.

Table 5 provides a clear resolution of these issues. In contrast to the equation whose estimates are reported in Table 4, the estimates reported in Table 5 control for *perceived* worker productivity rather than actual productivity. Thus, as indicated in Table 5, because sex does not affect the time-rate wage net of perceived productivity in either sample, we may conclude that the significant effects of sex observed in Table 4, and some of the wage differentials by sex exhibited in Table 3, are due to statistical discrimination but are not due to taste discrimination. A rather different picture emerges, however, with regard to the effects of caste: among workers whose productivity our estimates suggest is perceived by employers to be the same, low caste individuals evidently are paid a wage that is 6.8 percent lower than that paid to workers of higher castes. Thus at least some component of the caste differential in Table 4 appears to be due to taste discrimination, a result not very apparent in the gross time-rate differentials by caste in Table 3.

The presence of a government employment program in Shirapur provides an

Table 4
ML-*Estimates of Statistical Discrimination in India and the Philippines*

	India	Philippines
Age	0.579	0.424
	(3.387)	(1.552)
Age-squared	−0.474	
	(3.056)	
Education	−0.005	0.006
	(0.393)	(0.673)
Male	0.110	0.150
	(2.910)	(2.844)
Height		0.256
		(0.710)
Shirapur village	−0.046	
	(1.743)	
Aurepale village	0.014	
	(0.537)	
Low caste	−0.072	
	(3.986)	
μ	0.690	0.761
	(9.879)	(2.281)

a. Absolute values of asymptotic *t*-ratios in parentheses.

Table 5
ML-*Estimates of Taste Discrimination in India and the Philippines*

	India	India	Philippines
Male	0.030		−0.143
	(0.691)		(0.830)
Low caste	−0.068	−0.083	
	(3.655)	(4.131)	
Low caste × Shirapur		0.064	
		(1.384)	
μ^*	0.878	0.946	2.77
	(8.956)	(18.945)	(2.13)

a. Absolute values of asymptotic *t*-ratios in parentheses.

opportunity to examine the hypothesis that taste discrimination, which evidently exists in the study villages, can be reduced or eliminated through the provision of alternative employment. The second set of estimates from the Indian sample are from a specification that includes a dummy variable for Shirapur interacted with caste. Although the resulting interactive coefficient is only significant at the .15 level, the point estimate suggests that there is substantially less taste discrimination in this particular village. Indeed, while one can soundly reject the hypothesis that there is no taste discrimination in the other villages, one cannot reject this hypothesis in the case of Shirapur. Of course, there may be relevant characteristics other than the presence of the government program that lead to this difference in wages for low caste individuals across the three villages, but exploring this issue requires data with more environments. An investigation into the causes of differentials in the extent to which taste discrimination affects wages is clearly, however, an important topic.

D. Learning by Employers, Inequality, and Age

1. Time in the Local Labor Market

As noted, an important implication of information models of the labor market is that if the achievement of more accurate assessments of worker productivity depends positively on the number of employer observations of workers' performance then, in the absence of important investment effects, inequality in time-rate wages among heterogeneous workers rises as the workers age. The longitudinal character of the ICRISAT data and the ability to measure productivity with piece-rates enable a direct test of whether employers are better able to discern the productivity of daily wage workers who have participated longer in the wage labor market. That is, we can test whether there is general information, diffused among employers, that increases with the wage labor force experience of individual workers in a local labor market. That there is a general information effect of labor market experience is possible in the casual labor market because most of the workers are employed by farmers residing and farming in the same village (Rosenzweig 1988). Unlike in Glaeser (1991) we do not need to make assumptions about the homogeneity of workers across experience groups. We can assess directly whether the discrepancy between piece-rate (actual productivity) and time-rate wages (employers' perceptions of productivity) for any individual worker decreases with the labor force experience, or more appropriately, the labor market exposure of the worker.

The finding that employer ignorance of worker ability decreases with the worker's labor market exposure, as noted, would imply that the variance in the time-rate wages of a group of heterogeneous workers with respect to productivity would increase with the age of the workers to the extent that age and average cumulative labor market exposure are positively correlated even if their labor market experience did not augment productivity. Indeed, as noted, it is likely that in the agricultural environment characterizing the survey areas in both India and the Philippines, there is little scope for learning-by-doing among workers, as most operations are quite straightforward and mechanical in nature. There thus is likely to be little effect of worker experience on either time or piece-rate wage rates on average, a proposition we can test using the piece-rate productivity measure. Rather, some workers will experience a downward path of time-rate wages and others a rising time path, in both cases with the time-rate wages approaching their time-invariant piece-rate wage if there is learning by employers.

Because wage-work experience is clearly endogenously related to the market wage of the worker (for example, if more able workers invest more) and because the ICRISAT data only provides a segment of any worker's total wage employment history, corresponding to the 1979–84 or 1980–84 survey intervals, we again employed a two-stage estimation procedure. We first regressed the actual number of days a worker participated in the wage labor market over the sample period on his/her age and age squared, sex, and landholdings. We then used this predicted wage-market experience in regressions in which the dependent variables were (i) the piece-rate wage, (ii) the time-rate wage, and (iii) the absolute value of the difference between the log piece-rate and log time-rate for the worker, the measure of employer ignorance of worker productivity.

The two-stage least squares estimates of wage market experience on the three dependent variables are reported in Table 6, where we also include "controls" for worker sex and caste. These estimates indicate that neither piece-rate wages nor time-rates are influenced by worker market exposure; there appears to be no direct experience effects on productivity. However, consistent with the hypothesis that workers who have spent more time in the wage labor market are better-known by employers, increased exposure in the wage labor market does reduce employer ignorance. In particular, for each year (300 days) a worker is in the wage labor market, while working for different employers, the absolute value of the difference between his/her piece-rate and his/her time-rate wage declines by 6.5 percent. The estimates also imply that net of labor force exposure, there is no difference in employer uncertainty about productivity across men and women or across low-caste and other workers. However, because women on average spend less time in the local labor wage market than do men, the estimates imply that there will in general be more uncertainty about any given woman's productivity compared to any man with the same observable characteristics. Information theory suggests that employers would therefore find it more costly on average to hire women even if they were on average as productive as men, as noted above.

The results in Table 6 thus imply that in the casual labor markets of these Indian villages, wage inequality monotonically increases on average as the population ages without any significant skill augmentation by any (manual) workers. Unfortunately, there are too few observations either over time or in a given year to describe accurately the time-rate wage distribution by worker age. As noted, an additional reason why some workers are less known by employers, apart from their labor market participation rates and age, is that some workers arrive at different times in a local labor market. Newly arrived heterogeneous inmigrants should thus have lower variability in time-rate wages than life-time residents who are otherwise compositionally similar in terms of productivity, and the variance in wage rates should rise with length of residence, given age, for any group of heterogeneous workers. While there are few wage labor in-migrants in the ICRI-

Table 6

Two-Stage Least Squares Estimates: Effects of Cumulative Days in the Wage Labor Market by the Worker on Employer Ignorance of Worker Productivity, on (Log) Actual Worker-productivity, and on Worker (Log) Time-rate Wage—ICRISAT Villages

Worker Characteristics	Employer Ignorance[a]	Log Piece-Rate Wage	Log Time-Rate Wage
Cumulative days in market ($\times$ 10)$^{-3}$	−0.285 (2.27)[b]	0.217 (0.79)	0.000954 (0.04)
Male	−0.0107 (0.43)	0.534 (9.85)	0.484 (10.8)
Low-caste	−0.0348 (1.14)	−0.0378 (0.56)	−0.0681 (1.23)
Literate	−0.0392 (1.30)	0.0214 (0.33)	−0.0133 (0.25)

a. abs (log time-rate wage—log piece-rate wage).
b. Absolute value of asymptotic t-ratio in parentheses.
Number of observations = 114 (one randomly-chosen time-period per wage-worker). Specification also includes village dummy variables.

SAT villages who arrived at an age significantly above twenty,[9] another IFPRI data set, the Pakistan Food Security Survey, provides information on worker (time) wage rates in an area in which there is evidently significant in-migration. This IFPRI Pakistan survey was based on a stratified sample of 926 households in three major wheat-growing provinces of Pakistan—Punjab, Sind, and the Northwest Frontier Province—followed in twelve rounds over the period July 1986 through September 1989, with information on length of residence in the village for each sample individual collected in the fifth round. Unfortunately, no information on piece-rate payments was collected in the survey, so that it is not possible to compare true and employer-perceived productivity across workers classified by their years of settlement. However, we can examine wage variances by length of residence.

Table 7 provides the average and standard deviation in wage rates for male daily wage workers by the number of years the workers had resided in the village. These figures, consistent with learning by employers in the villages in which these workers currently reside, show a monotonic rise in the standard deviation in wage rates as the average length of residence of the workers increases from 0–5

9. The in-migrants are almost exclusively women who marry village residents (Rosenzweig and Stark 1989).

Table 7

*Relationship Between Years Settled in the Village and Wage
Dispersion: Male Wage Workers in IFPRI Pakistan
Rural Household Survey*

Years in Village	Wage Rate		Number of Workers	Test statistic (d.f.,d.f.)	
	Mean	Standard Deviation			
0–5	24.3	5.23	15	2.70	$(165,14)^c$
5–10	24.3	7.93	16	1.36	$(165,15)$
>10	26.2	9.25	166	—	
≤10	24.3	6.80	31	1.85	$(165,30)^c$

a. In 1988 rupees.
b. Test of difference in the wage standard deviation of row group with workers settled more than 10 years in village.
c. Significant difference at .02 critical value.

years to 5–10 years to greater than 10 years. While the average wage rate of workers residing more than 10 years in a village is 7.8 percent greater than the average wage of workers with less than or equal to 10 years of residence, this difference in mean wages is not statistically significant. The 36 percent differential in the standard deviation in the wage rates of these two groups of workers, however, is statistically significant—wage-inequality is smaller among new in-migrants compared with the resident population, as implied by imperfect information theory.

2. Job Tenure Effects

The results from the ICRISAT Indian and the IFPRI Pakistan data suggest that information about workers with little or no attachment to particular employers becomes diffused among employers in a geographically-limited labor market as the workers increase their participation in that market. The IFPRI Bukidnon data enable us to test whether the tenure of workers with specific employers also provides informational benefits. In that environment a proportion of the workers are "permanently" attached to employers. We can compare the variance in time-rate wage rates for these workers with the more prevalent temporary workers. If the continuity of employment with particular employers increases the speed at which worker productivity is discerned and appropriately rewarded, then permanent workers should be characterized by a higher time-rate variance given the same variance in productivity. While we cannot obtain enough piece-rate wage observations for the small group of permanent workers to assess whether the variance in actual productivity differs across workers classified by their attachment to employers, we can control for observable worker characteristics and type of work (agricultural task and crop) by estimating a regression of time-rate wages on these variables and comparing the residual variances.

Table 8 reports the gross variances and the residual variances of the time-rate wages of permanent and temporary workers. While the gross wage variances that do not control for differences in worker heterogeneity are no different across the two groups, the variances net of differences in observable worker characteristics and in types of work are, as expected, higher for the permanent workers, a difference that is statistically significant. Thus, there is support for the hypothesis that worker tenure is negatively related to employer ignorance, although it is possible that there are remaining differences in the variances of worker productivity across these type of workers that is not captured by age, sex, and work task.

E. Is Worker Calorie Consumption Known By Employers?

Although the preceding analysis has provided evidence that there are important differences in productivity across workers and that these differences are not readily known by employers, we have made little attempt to evaluate possible sources of these differences. As noted, the nutrition-wage literature suggests one possible source of variation in productivity: calorie consumption. This idea can be tested using the IFPRI Bukidnon data, which provides information on individual calorie consumption for all sample household members, including those who participated in the labor market as wage workers, in all survey rounds. To test whether employers are able to discern and thus reward (or exploit) worker consumption, we need first to establish that increased calorie intake augments actual productivity. Given that piece-rate wages reflect worker contributions to output, we can do this readily by ascertaining if calorie consumption and piece-rates are positively correlated. As is well-known, however, to establish that calorie intake causes productivity to increase, account must be taken of the possibility that higher wage rates may cause calorie consumption to increase (for example, Strauss 1986). To eliminate this simultaneity problem, we employ instrumental variables. We assume that (i) a worker's landholdings, as a proxy for wealth, affects his/her calorie consumption but does not, given consumption, directly affect wages, either because employers do not know worker land ownership or, more plausibly, it is irrelevant, given calorie intake, to productivity,[10] and (ii) the sample period (round) affects calorie consumption, because of seasonality in prices and imperfect-ability to smooth consumption, but not productivity, except through its influence on calories.

Table 9 reports in the first column the weighted, by total days of employment, two-stage least squares estimate of the effect of calorie consumption on harvest

---

10. We justify the use of land as an instrument under the null hypothesis that time-rate employers fully know (and reward) worker productivity. The specification is also appropriate under the alternative hypothesis that productivity differentials are not fully rewarded in the time-rate labor market; however, the interpretation of the resulting coefficient on calories in the time-rate wage equation depends on the extent to which land is known by employers. If land *is* known then the coefficient on calories represents the effect of a unit increase in *expected* calories on time-rate wages given other observed characteristics. If land is not known then this coefficient represents the effect of an *unobserved* (to the employer) increase in calories on time-rate wages.

Table 8

Tests of Equality of Time-rate Wage Variances for Permanent and Temporary Workers: IFPRI Bukidnon, Philippines Survey

	Worker-Type		
	Temporary	Permanent	P-value
Wages	7.673	7.398	0.323
Residuals[a]	5.942	7.145	0.007
Observations	240	133	

a. Residuals obtained from regression of time-rate wages on crop, task, age, age squared, sex and type of worker.

wage rates, where, as in most of the econometric studies, we do not distinguish between piece and time-rate wages. The estimates indicate a positive relationship, net of the sex of the worker, and his/her height and age. The first column estimate thus would lead researchers to conclude that there is support for the competitive version of nutrition-based efficiency wages. However, we chose the harvest wage because harvesting is characterized by the highest incidence of piece-rate wage payments (about 60 percent of total employment days) of all the agricultural operations in the Bukidnon area in order to get the most precise estimate of calorie consumption on productivity. The first column estimates may thus only reflect the productivity effects of calorie consumption and not necessarily employer's recognition of worker consumption as reflected in time-rate wages rewarded.

In the second column we report the estimates of calorie intake on piece-rate harvest wages. These indicate a significant positive productivity effect of increased calorie consumption. However, in the third column we see that there is no effect of calorie consumption on harvest wages when they are paid on a time basis. The estimated time-rate calorie effect is (in absolute value) less than one tenth that of the effect on the piece-rate wage, is not statistically significant and is not even the expected sign. Thus, when attention is paid to payment method, we see that there is no support for nutrition-based efficiency wage theory—employers do not appear to be able to differentiate workers according to their calorie consumption, even though it evidently affects workers' contribution to output.

In the last column of Table 9 we report a test of whether the effect of increased calorie consumption is greater on a worker's productivity, measured by the piece-rate wage, than on the worker's time-rate wages by regressing the difference between a worker's piece-rate and the time-rate wages received in a survey round on the worker's (predicted) calorie consumption in that round. This estimate confirms what is indicated by the estimates in columns two and three, that calorie intake augments productivity significantly more than time-rate wage rates. The

Table 9

Weighted Two-Stage Least Squares Estimates: Effects of Calorie Consumption on Log Wage, by Payment Method: IFPRI Bukidnon, Philippines Survey

Difference: Variables	All Harvest Wages	Harvest Piece-Rate	Harvest Time-Wage	Within-Round Piece-Time-Rate Wage
Calories consumed[a]	0.211	0.438	−0.0153	0.316
($\times 10^{-3}$)	(2.36)[b]	(3.13)	(0.22)	(2.59)
Age	0.0208	0.0153	0.0567	−0.074
	(0.82)	(0.43)	(2.02)	(1.38)
Age-squared ($\times 10^{-3}$)	−0.142	−0.216	−0.721	1.09
	(0.38)	(0.41)	(1.70)	(1.41)
Height	1.04	0.446	0.040	1.91
	(2.37)	(0.74)	(0.30)	(2.18)
Male	−0.366	−0.357	0.285	−0.628
	(2.37)	(2.66)	(0.61)	(3.59)
Constant	0.747	1.40	1.59	−1.72
	(0.90)	(1.21)	(2.22)	(1.15)
F(5,d.f.)	2.81	2.17	2.73	2.72
d.f.	322	286	108	188

a. Endogenous variable. Identifying instruments include land owned by worker round dummy variables.

b. Absolute value of asymptotic *t*-ratio in parentheses.

information set of employers thus does not appear to contain worker consumption; this constraint on information thus makes it impossible, at least in the Philippines context, for employer wage-setting to be nutrition-based even though it evidently would be advantageous for employers to take into account worker consumption.

These results also have implications for the intra-household distribution of calories. Indeed, in an analysis of calorie allocations using the Philippine data, Foster and Rosenzweig (1992) provide evidence that calorie consumption is more responsive to the amount of time an individual spends working in piece-rate than in time-rate activities in a particular period. If employers exhibit learning about worker productivity as suggested by the previous section, then an increase in calorie consumption in one period will lead to a more favorable assessment of a worker's productivity in future periods and thus an increase in wage. Thus, individuals with greater attachment to the labor force have more incentive to increase calorie consumption, even while working in the time-rate sector. Because of the signalling value associated with consumption by those with stronger labor force attachment, productivity differentials between men and women might emerge even if, given equal consumption, productivity would be equal.

IV. Conclusion

It has long been argued that employer's inability to completely discern worker productivity plays an important role in determining the structure of labor markets in rural areas of developing countries. Little evidence, however, has been advanced concerning the importance of this problem. In this paper we have used survey data from three developing countries, the Philippines, India, and Pakistan, to show that information asymmetries in developing country labor markets may be substantial and that these asymmetries importantly affect the distribution of wages across workers and over time for individual workers.

A key implication of these results is that models or analysis that ignore the role of information asymmetries in developing countries can provide misleading conclusions and therefore lead to the development of inappropriate policy. The most obvious example of this possibility is provided by the analysis of taste and statistical discrimination. Faced with the evidence that men receive higher wages than equally productive women one might be lead to conclude that discrimination is present. Because this discrimination might lead to an inefficient allocation of women's time or underinvestment in human capital, this evidence might lead one to justify a women's employment program on the grounds of efficiency as well as equity.

Recognition that the wage differences may be attributable in part to differences in expected productivity of men and women complicates the story considerably. First, if wage differentials result from statistical discrimination, and the government has no more information about differences in worker productivity than do village employers, then the employment program may not result in a more efficient allocation of women's time. Indeed, if as might be expected, the government has less complete information than that of village employers, then the efficiency costs associated with adverse selection may be compounded by the introduction of the program. Moreover, to the extent that employment of women in the outside labor market reduces their exposure to local employers, information problems may increase as a result of the new program.

Evidence that wage differentials are in part attributable to statistical discrimination does not, however, imply there is no scope for intervention. First, intervention may be justified on grounds of equity. Second, taste discrimination may nonetheless be present. As noted in the Indian data, the opportunities provided by the public works program in Shirapur may have reduced the impact of taste discrimination against low-caste workers. Third, interventions that increase the role of small-scale rural industry that may be self-owned or easily compensated on a piece-rate basis, may reduce the importance of information asymmetries.

Fourth, statistical discrimination arising from information asymmetries can lead to inefficient investment in human capital. Differences in expected productivity between two different groups can arise from differences in human capital investment that are themselves a result of information problems. For example, if as a result of lower attachment to the labor force, productivity differentials among women are less likely to be rewarded than those among men, women may underinvest in human capital, which, in turn, leads to greater male-female wage differentials. Under these circumstances, interventions that subsidize human capital or that reward forms of human capital that are readily measurable (such as formal schooling) may provide the best opportunity for gains in efficiency.

Finally, it is important to recognize that the relative importance of information imperfections as a source of wage differences between men and women is likely to change as an economy develops. In the early stages of development, increased mobility of workers may increase the importance of information problems. As development progresses, however, there are a number of countervailing forces which mitigate these effects. Of particular relevance are the increases in the importance of formal schooling and in the permanency of labor contracts. While it is likely that some of the insights gained in an analysis of casual labor markets will apply in the context of more complex labor markets, the nature of information problems as well as the specific implications of these problems for policy are likely to change.

III   Health

7 Gender and Life-Cycle Differentials in the Patterns and Determinants of Adult Health

John Strauss
Paul J. Gertler
Omar Rahman
Kristin Fox

John Strauss is a professor of economics at Michigan State University, Paul J. Gertler and Omar Rahman are researchers at the RAND Corporation, and Kristin Fox is a researcher in the Jamaican Ministry of Health. This research was partly funded by U.S. Bureau of the Census contract number 50-YABC-1-66007, U.S. National Institutes of Child Health and Human Development grant number P01-HD28372-01, and the Safe Motherhood Initiative of the World Bank. The authors are grateful to Barbara Torrey and Kevin Kinsella for initial encouragement; to Mark Rosenzweig and T. Paul Schultz for detailed comments on an earlier draft; to Michael Grossman, Mark McClellan, Henry Mosely, Guilherme Sedlacek, James P. Smith, Duncan Thomas, and participants of the Rockefeller Foundation Conference on Women's Human Capital and Development for helpful suggestions; to the Planning Institute of Jamaica for making the data available; and to Carol Edwards, Adnan Rahman, My Vuong, and Nga Vuong for excellent programming assistance.

I. Introduction

Adult health is becoming an issue of increasing importance in developing countries. Population structures are beginning to age in many Asian, Caribbean and Latin American countries as a result of large fertility declines and longer life expectancies (Kinsella 1988). The health status of adults is of great importance both because there are direct productivity losses (World Bank 1991b), potentially large indirect costs (Over et al., 1992) and because adult ill-health can place large demands on already stretched health systems. In particular treating

171

the health problems of older populations often requires a different health infrastructure than the currently child oriented health systems available in most developing countries. Indeed current health systems are often inadequately prepared to cope with health problems due to advancing age, including cancer, circulatory problems and dementia. Moreover, formal institutions such as social security, pensions and health insurance that financially support older people in times of poor health cover only a small portion of society (for example, Martin 1988 or Ju and Jones 1989). Yet despite the pressing policy relevance and in contrast to child health, surprisingly little research has been done on adult health in developing countries.[1]

This study begins to fill this gap by investigating the patterns and socioeconomic determinants of adult ill-health. We begin by comparing measures of adult ill-health in four countries: Bangladesh, Jamaica, Malaysia, and the United States. We find very robust gender differentials over the life-cycle. Specifically, despite greater longevity of women, they report significantly more problems with physical functioning and with general health across all ages. That this pattern is repeated across such different economic and cultural settings as the United States, Jamaica, Malaysia, and Bangladesh suggests that it is unlikely to be a reflection only of reporting bias.

Since one of the potential biases in the gender comparisons is mortality selection (if men have higher mortality, more men in poor health would have died than women in poor health), we recalculate the percentages in poor health by adding to that group the expected number (of men or women) who have died and would presumably have been in poor health. While the mortality adjustment does substantially cut the gender gaps, it does not eliminate them. A strong implication of this result is that current developing country policy emphasis on longevity and mortality, to the exclusion of quality of life (health status), is likely to lead to a misallocation of resources.[2]

This raises the question of why such a gap should exist; different hypotheses are discussed and investigated in a multivariate analysis using data from Jamaica. An explicit economic model is introduced, which along with the descriptive results, serves to motivate the multivariate analysis. Specifically, we investigate in detail, the socioeconomic determinants of various dimensions of ill-health in Jamaica, for adults spanning the life-cycle, from age 14 to death. To do this, we use a unique data set, the third round (November, 1989) of the Jamaican Survey of Living Conditions (SLC). This nationally representative survey combines detailed individual-level health data on adults of all ages with extensive individual and household socioeconomic information. This is in contrast with many household

---

1. Among the studies that do examine socioeconomic influences on illness are Wolfe and Behrman (1984). Pitt and Rosenzweig (1985), Behrman and Wolfe (1989), and Schultz and Tansel (1992). These papers estimate reduced form equations explaining whether or not adults experienced an illness (or the number of days ill), using individual, household and community-level covariates. Other studies have examined factors underlying incidence of specific diseases. For instance, Castro and Mokate (1988) and Fernandez and Sawyer (1988) both study the impact of socioeconomic variables on the incidence of malaria in Colombia and the Amazon region of Brazil, respectively.
2. For example, Feachem et al. (1992) in a review of adult health status and policy in developing countries focuses much of the book on mortality, in part because of data availability.

surveys, which collect at most limited information on health and often exclude the elderly (for example, labor force surveys).[3]

Jamaica is an interesting case study because its population structure is aging far more quickly than in most developing countries and because of the availability of a very good data set. Jamaica is estimated to have had 12 percent of its population older than 55 in 1988 (Kinsella 1988), a percentage projected to increase to 16.6 by 2020. This relatively large older population enables an examination of life-cycle differences in the various influences on adult health. To contrast, in 1980 only 5.6 percent of Malaysia's population was older than 60 (Andrews et al. 1986), while in 1988 in Bangladesh only 7.9 percent were over the age of 55 (Kinsella 1988). On the other hand 21 percent in the United States were over 55 years in 1989 (U.S. Bureau of the Census 1991).

Among the key results we find in the multivariate analyses is first: there are dramatic age/cohort differentials in health, and important differences between men and women. Many problems of physical functioning begin by age 40, but become pronounced at older ages. Women report more health problems than men across the life-cycle. Furthermore, these age-related gender differentials persist after controlling for education and location factors. Second, higher education lowers the probabilities of having problems with physical functioning and other dimensions of health. Third, we find evidence that it matters where one lives. Whether the availability and quality of health care underlies part of the community influence will be the subject of extensions to this work. Fourth, we find some evidence that long-run income (treated as endogenous) may affect the health of men, though there is some reason to doubt the adequacy of our income measure and our instruments. We also find some evidence of positive correlations between moderate measures of physical functioning and having had children, although we can't infer causality.

Finally, we find many fewer socioeconomic influences for older adults, particularly those over 70 years. A leveling of socioeconomic differences among older Jamaicans could imply that there exists less of a role for these factors; that nonbehavioral biological factors become more important. Part of this result could also be attributable to selective mortality of older adults in worse health (and with lower education and income); this is an important avenue for future research.

II. Adult Health and its Measurement

In contrast to child health and survival, very little is known about the patterns and effects of underlying socioeconomic factors on adult health in developing countries. Furthermore, much of what little discussion exists centers mostly around mortality. For instance in a recent World Bank volume morbidity is not addressed until chapter three (Feachem et al. 1992) and the chapter is entitled "Limited Data and Methodological Uncertainty." Even for adult mortal-

---

3. A few surveys of the elderly exist (for example, the WHO or ASEAN surveys; Andrews et al. 1986; Ju and Jones 1989). However they did not collect much information on the household in which the seniors reside and thus did not collect nonhealth and health information on younger adults.

ity, knowledge of its underlying determinants is scant as most of the literature is still concerned with ways to estimate levels from existing, imperfect data. A recent exception is a study by Rahman, Foster, and Menken (1992) using data from Bangladesh, which investigates the impacts of widowhood and marriage on survival.[4]

Many analysts shy away from other types of health data, such as on morbidity, because of potentially severe reporting biases when the information is self- or proxy-reported (see Hill and Mamdani 1989, for a good discussion of various morbidity and mortality measures, and their potential drawbacks). As one illustration of potential difficulties, Schultz and Tansel (1992), using the World Bank's Living Standards Surveys from Côte d'Ivoire and Ghana, find significantly positive effects of primary schooling on the number of days ill reported by adults.[5] Using the same data, Over et al. (1992) find that persons in households with higher per capita expenditure are more likely to report an illness. Self-reported measures of general health are also sharply criticized, as in the U.S. labor supply and retirement literature.[6]

Focusing only on mortality, however, gives only a very partial picture of adult health. Health arguably has multiple dimensions (Ware, Davies-Avery, and Brook 1980) and indeed the measures used in this study are supportive of that interpretation. Diseases which can have very acute symptoms, including death, may have very little long run consequences on survivors. For instance, in Bangladesh cholera and dysentery are leading causes of adult mortality, yet will have little long-run consequences on survivors. To rely only on mortality measures, then, will miss very important aspects of the health status of the living. As we argue in this paper there exist measures of adult health, which, though not without their problems, are quite useful.

In this study we compare adult health using both self-reported measures of general health and a variety of measures of physical functioning (so-called activity of daily living, ADL, measures). The general health measures are based on self-evaluations of health on an ordinal scale: typically ranging from excellent to good to fair to poor, with possibly more or less categories.[7] The measures of physical functioning derive from questions asking whether one's health limits (possibly with gradations as to the degree) specific activities, such as bending, walking uphill, "moderate" activities or "vigorous" activities.[8] A range of limitations are

---

4. Rahman et al. find marriage is correlated with high survival probabilities. Hu and Goldman (1990) find similar results across a wide range of industrialized countries. A potential statistical reason for this finding is selective mortality and marital sorting. A paper by Goldman (1993) explores whether similar correlations in Japanese data can be plausibly caused by selective mortality, finding that such biases are quite consistent with observed correlations.

5. When they stratify by wage earners, the effects become insignificant. However, it may be that these workers have a higher opportunity cost of time, which may make them less likely to allow a given illness to interfere with normal activities. This would result in a negative bias.

6. Recent studies include Bound (1991) and Stern (1989). Also see Anderson and Burkhauser (1984, 1985).

7. The Jamaican data have five categories, very good being the fifth; the Malaysian data have only three: good, fair, poor.

8. Examples of what is considered "moderate" or "vigorous" are provided to the respondent; for

covered, from less severe: such as limitations in performing vigorous activities; to more moderately severe: such as limitations in walking uphill or walking one mile; to the very severe: such as walking 100 yards, or at the extreme eating, bathing or using the toilet. This range of outcomes may reflect different dimensions of health limitations, so that combining these into a single index may not be a useful way to begin analyzing them.

Self-reported physical functioning and general health measures have been used widely in studying the health of the elderly in the United States.[9] ADL measures have been used in southeast Asia in a series of recent surveys by the World Health Organization (WHO) and the Association of Southeast Asian Nations (ASEAN).[10]

Considerable effort has gone into testing these self-reported measures for reliability and validity. Examples include testing done for the RAND health insurance study (Stewart, Ware, Brook, and Davies-Avery 1978; Ware, Davies-Avery, and Brook 1980), the RAND Medical Outcomes Study (Stewart, Hays, and Ware 1988) and WHO surveys in Korea, Malaysia, and the Philippines (Andrews et al. 1986) and the ASEAN surveys in Indonesia, Malaysia, the Philippines, and Singapore (Ju and Jones 1989). Reliability tests are usually of the test-retest variety, persons being revisited within a short time of the initial interview and asked the same battery of health questions. Experience in the United States and southeast Asia has shown that self-reported measures of physical functioning are reliable in this sense. Validation has been done in several ways: first internal consistency is examined between the various physical functioning measures and between these and self-reported measures of general health. It should be the case, for example, that persons reporting extreme difficulties in walking should be much less likely to report being in excellent general health. The RAND, WHO, and ASEAN studies all find high degrees of internal consistency. Correlations between physical functioning and socioeconomic measures, particularly education, are also examined to check for clear patterns of misreporting, such as often exhibited by illness measures. The RAND studies have demonstrated that in U.S. populations at least, fewer difficulties are reported in physical functioning by better-educated persons. In some cases it may be possible to develop measure more objective measures; for instance, people can be timed walking one mile.[11] A recent review by Guralnik et al. (1989) suggests using this approach when possible, however there is as yet limited experience, particularly in developing countries.[12]

---

example, in Jamaica examples of "vigorous" activities include running, lifting heavy objects, doing hard labor, or participating in strenuous sports.

9. Studies that have used ADL measures include the RAND health insurance study (for instance, Manning, Newhouse, and Ware 1982), the RAND medical outcomes study (Stewart, Hays, and Ware 1988) and various studies of Ken Manton and his colleagues (for example, Manton, Woodbury, and Stallard 1991).

10. See Andrews et al. (1986) and Ju and Jones (1989). To date analyses of the ASEAN data have focused on living arrangements and not on health (for example, Martin 1989a, 1989b).

11. At least for persons who are physically able to complete it.

12. For many measures, such as difficulty in eating or using the toilet, measurements by enumerators might raise even more questions of interpretation than self-reported measures.

III. Descriptive Results From Four Surveys

In this section we use comparable data from four countries to look for robust patterns in adult health status. Each of these surveys have collected both extensive health and socioeconomic data at the individual and household levels, unlike some of the earlier health surveys. Measures of physical functioning along with a general health measure were collected in each case. The RAND Health Insurance Experiment (HIE) was conducted in the United States from 1974 to 1982 in six sites.[13] While many measures of limitations on physical functioning were collected (see Ware, Davies-Avery, and Brook 1980), we use a subset that is comparable to those collected in Jamaica, Malaysia, and Bangladesh. The 1982 sample includes 5,244 persons, aged 14 to 65, of which 2,455 are males and 2,789 are females. While a few groups were excluded from the HIE, it is a reasonably representative sample of the population, excluding the oldest old.[14] The third round of the Jamaican Survey of Living Conditions (SLC) was collected by the Statistical and Planning Institutes of Jamaica, with assistance from the World Bank's Living Standards Measurement Studies division and RAND. This round has broad-based economic, demographic, and health information on 4,000 households. The health questionnaire contains information on a variety of health measures for adults, including measures of physical functioning and of general health. The sample is nationally representative. It includes 5,223 males and 5,350 females aged 14 and over. The Malaysian data come from the Senior Sample of the second Malaysian Family Life Survey (MFLS-2), fielded by RAND in 1988. MFLS-2 is representative of peninsula Malaysia; the Senior sample includes one person over 50 years (if one existed) randomly drawn from each survey household. Some 671 men and 686 women are covered. The Bangladesh sample comes from a pilot survey conducted by Omar Rahman in the Matlab surveillance area of the International Center for Diarrheal Disease Research (ICDDR-B). The survey canvassed 114 seniors: 60 females and 54 males aged 60 and older; drawn by a stratified (on age, land ownership, and marital status), random sample from a frame based on ICDDR-B's population census.

A. Data Validity

Although other studies have looked at the validity of measures of physical functioning, it is still useful to verify that these measures make sense in the data we use. Appendix Table 1 reports the cross-tabulation for one such indicator, walking uphill, against the general health measure, using the Jamaica SLC. The two health measures are highly correlated, moreover this pattern is repeated for the other ADL measures for the Jamaica data, as well as for the MFLS-2, HIE, and Bangladesh data.[15]

---

13. These were Seattle, Washington; Fitchburg, Massachusetts; Franklin County, Massachusetts; Dayton, Ohio; Charleston, South Carolina; and Georgetown County, South Carolina. See Manning et al. (1987) for more details.

14. Those excluded include persons older than 62 at their enrollment in the experiment and persons with very high incomes.

15. Details are available from the authors.

Systematic reporting bias often exists for morbidity measures. In particular, it is common to find that better-educated persons from higher income households report more illness. While we cannot test the existence of reporting bias we can examine whether such biases are so strong as to result in positive correlations with socioeconomic variables such as education. Appendix Tables 2A and 2B show for the Jamaican and Malaysian data that, controlling for age and gender, more education is associated with fewer reported problems. This pattern exists for the general health indicator as well as the physical activity limitations.[16,17] In the Jamaica sample there appears to be some evidence that education differentials disappear for the older old. Data for Malaysian seniors (those over 50) exhibit the same general pattern; more highly educated persons are less likely to report difficulties. Thus, these bivariate results suggest that the general health and physical functioning measures are not as plagued by systematic reporting problems as are measures of morbidity.

B. Gender and Age Patterns

Figure 1 exhibits the incidence of reported health problems for men and women 50 years or older in each of the four surveys.[18] All measures are included, both general health and measures of physical functioning.[19] The physical functioning measures are roughly ordered from less to more severe. Correspondingly, a much lower proportion of people report being limited by the more severe measures. This pattern suggests that to aggregate these measures into a single index will result in loss of information.

A strong and consistent pattern that appears in the data is that women report more problems and begin reporting them earlier than do men, despite their greater longevity.[20] In some cases the differences in proportions reporting problems is large; for example in the Jamaican SLC 52 percent of women 50 or older report difficulty in walking uphill, compared to 36 percent of men in the same age group.[21]

It may be that part of the difference in reported health results from age differences, particularly if women tend to be older because their adult mortality rates are lower. To check for that possibility we stratify by age group. Figure 2 shows the patterns in Jamaica for four physical functioning measures. It is apparent that

---

16. In these tables fair and poor health are grouped together as are being limited a lot and a little. In the regressions these aggregations are relaxed.

17. The Health Insurance Experiment data show the same patterns with education; see Stewart et al. (1978).

18. The ages underlying this figure are kept to 50 and older (except for Bangladesh, for which it is 60 and older) for comparability, as the four surveys include differing age groups.

19. A general health measure does not exist for Bangladesh. Rather, health was scored as "good" if a person had no problem with any of the 12 measures of physical functioning.

20. That adult mortality rates are higher for men than women is well known and can be seen from vital statistics data; for instance U.S. National Center for Health Statistics (1991) and the Statistical Institute of Jamaica (1990). Male mortality is not, however, greater for all adult age groups. Often female mortality is higher for young adult and child bearing years.

21. Tests based on analysis of variance indicate that these differences are generally significant at under the 5 percent level.

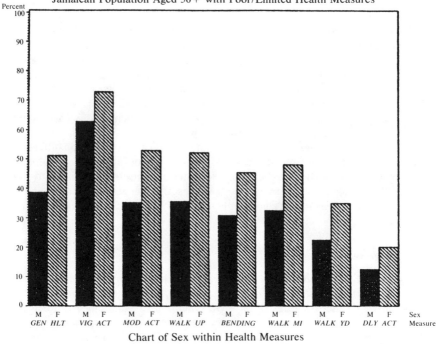

Jamaican Population Aged 50+ with Poor/Limited Health Measures

Chart of Sex within Health Measures

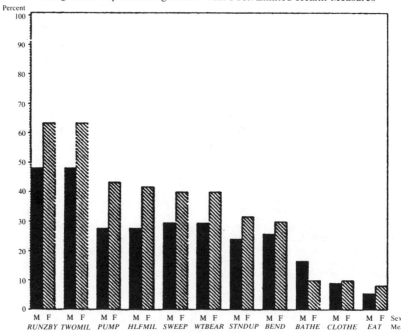

Bangladesh Population Aged 60+ with Poor/Limited Health Measures

Chart of Sex within Health Measures

Figure 1

Malaysian Population Aged 50+ with Poor/Limited Health Measures

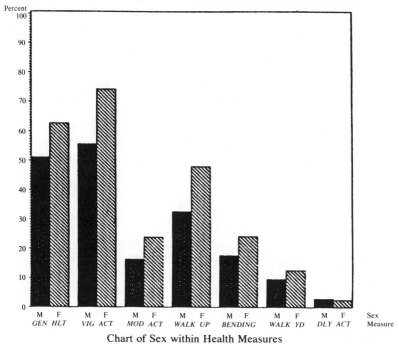

Chart of Sex within Health Measures

U.S. Population Aged 50+ with Poor/Limited Health Measures

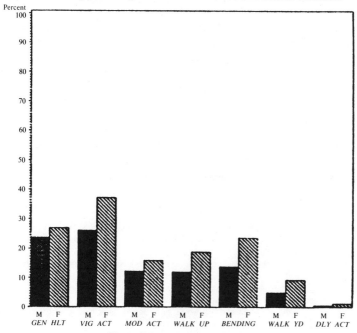

Chart of Sex within Health Measures

Figure 1 (*continued*)

gender differences within age groups persist.[22] Note that the ages at which the largest gaps appear are quite different for the different measures. For limitations on performing vigorous activities, for example, the gap exists across all age groups and is largest among persons aged 30–49. This pattern suggests a potential role of childbearing. For walking uphill the largest difference occurs among people in their 60s, while for having trouble eating, bathing, or using the toilet, gender differentials are largest among the older old, those older than 70. Thus there is some indication that gaps for the more severe measures occur later in life. This is not surprising given that small proportions of younger persons are afflicted by more severe problems of functioning and again is evidence that combining these measures hides much useful information.

Figure 2 shows age to be a critical factor in self-reports of different dimensions of ill-health, as one would expect. Nearly 15 percent of Jamaican males in their 30s and 40s report problems in engaging in vigorous activities. This escalates rapidly to nearly 45 percent between ages 50 and 59, reaching over 80 percent for men in their 70s.[23] For women in their 30s and 40s, 30 percent report problems in performing vigorous activities, which rises to 55 percent for those in their 50s and to almost 90 percent by the 70s. More severe limitations afflict fewer people and later in life, with some tendency for a jump in difficulties during one's 50s.[24]

C. Corrections for Differential Mortality

One possible explanation for these gender differences in health, especially for the older population, may be differential mortality by gender. Given that men are more likely to die, if the less healthy are dying first, then the proportion of those living who claim to be in fair or poor health will be understated compared to what would exist if those who died were still living. To attempt to gauge the importance of selective mortality, we assume that those who died would have been in fair or poor general health. This is an extreme assumption since mortality and reported general health are not likely to be perfectly correlated; the estimate should thus provide a lower bound for the gender differential.[25] We use auxiliary information on age and gender specific death rates, obtained from national vital statistics for the United States and Jamaica, from vital statistics from the International Center for Diarrheal Disease Research, Bangladesh (ICDDR-B), and from MFLS-1 and -2 for Malaysia, to estimate the number of persons in each age group who would have died.[26] This estimate is then added to the number in fair or poor health and new proportions are calculated.[27]

---

22. The same is true for the Malaysian and U.S. data, when broken down by age. Results are available from the authors.

23. Since the data are from a cross-section, cohort effects also play a role.

24. The age gradient is much less steep in the U.S. data, perhaps reflecting a health care system better geared towards care for an older population.

25. It would be heroic to assume that the dead would have reported problems with physical functioning, so we do not attempt to correct those figures.

26. In Jamaica accidents and violence are quite important as causes of death and accounting for it vastly increases the gender differentials in mortality (Statistical Institute of Jamaica 1990). Since there is no reason to suppose that persons dying a violent death would be in fair or poor health we use only the mortality differentials in deaths due to natural causes.

27. More specifically, we use the gender-specific probability of survival from age 15 to roughly the

Figure 3 presents these results for the general health measure in the Jamaican and Malaysian surveys.[28] Differential mortality does make a difference in the magnitude of the gender gaps, but only at older ages. For instance, in both Jamaica and Malaysia the corrections make little difference until age 60. The gender gap is narrowed for those in their 60s and roughly halved for those over 70. For the United States, the difference is eliminated for those over 50, consistent with other evidence cited by Wingard (1984). For Bangladesh, the gap is halved for those in their 70s. Thus it appears that correcting for differential mortality does make a difference to gender comparisons of poor health; however, such corrections do not eliminate the gaps, except perhaps among older age groups in some countries.[29]

D. Discussion

How can we explain the excess ill-health of adult women relative to men, particularly accounting for the excess mortality of adult men? A large literature has emerged on this in the United States.[30] On one level this literature explores differences in the types of diseases prevalent among men and women in the United States. Alternative biological and behavioral hypotheses to explain these patterns also have been offered.

In the United States, women suffer more from illnesses that are not life threatening, specifically acute and chronic nonfatal diseases.[31] Acute conditions that women in the United States suffer from more than men include infective/parasitic, respiratory, and digestive. Nonfatal chronic conditions that women suffer more from include varicose veins, constipation, gallbladder problems, arthritis, anemia, and chronic enteritis and colitis. Many of these conditions could well lead to reports of ill-health and of various problems of physical functioning. At least until very recently, men in the United States have higher rates of life-threatening chronic diseases such as coronary heart disease, arteriosclerosis, and emphysema. For Jamaica, unpublished Ministry of Health data from hospital records indicate that women suffer more from hypertension and diabetes, while men from coronary illnesses. Unfortunately good quality morbidity and cause of death data is scant in Malaysia and Bangladesh, so similar comparisons cannot be made.

Three broad groups of explanations have been offered to explain gender differentials in ill-health: biological, differences in behavior, and reporting differences.

---

midpoint age of each group to estimate the number of men and women who would have died from age 15 to the particular age-group. For the Malaysian data we use the fact that we have a panel covering the 12 year span, 1976 to 1988. We know the proportion of men and women 38 years or older in the 1976 sample, MFLS-1 (these people would have been 50 or older in 1988 and thus eligible to be in the Senior Sample) who died by 1988. We use these proportions to make the corrections for the MFLS-2 data.

28. An analogous figure using the U.S. and Bangladesh data is available from the authors.

29. It is tempting to speculate that the disappearance at older ages may be a function of the level of economic and health development. However, data from many more countries would be necessary to show this convincingly.

30. See, for example, Waldron (1983a). Verbrugge (1976, 1980, 1985, 1989) or Wingard (1984). Sindelar (1982) is one of the few economists who has analyzed this issue, focusing on medical care use.

31. This summary relies heavily on Verbrugge (1985).

Jamaican Population with Limitations to Vigorous Activities

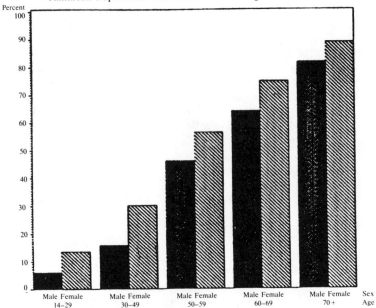

Chart of Sex within Age Categories

Jamaican Population with Limitations to Walking Uphill

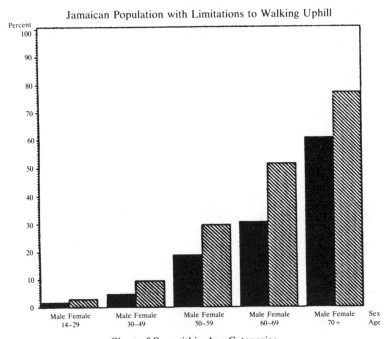

Chart of Sex within Age Categories

Figure 2

Jamaican Population with Limitations to Moderate Activities

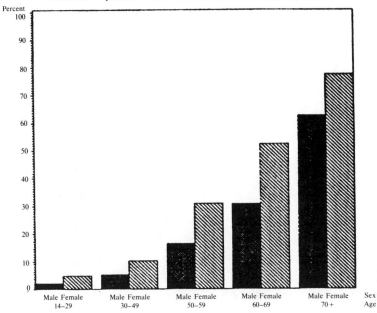

Chart of Sex Within Age Categories

Jamaican Population With Limitations to Daily Activities
Eating, Bathing or Using a Toilet

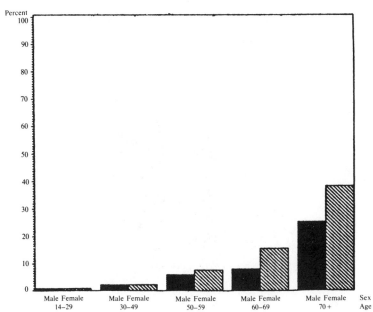

Chart of Sex within Age Categories

Figure 2 (*continued*)

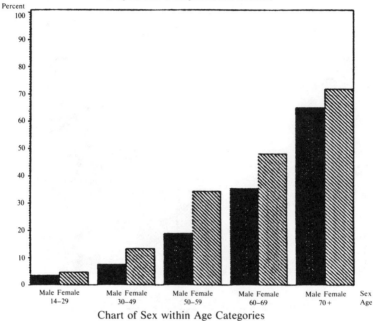

Jamaican Population With Fair–Poor General Health
(Population Unadjusted for Deaths)

Chart of Sex within Age Categories

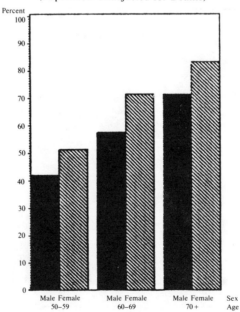

Malaysian Population With Fair–Poor General Health
(Population Unadjusted for Deaths)

Chart of Sex within Age Categories

Figure 3

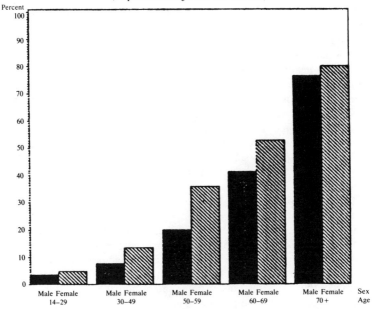

Jamaican Population With Fair–Poor General Health
(Population Adjusted for Deaths)

Chart of Sex within Age Categories

Malaysian Population With Fair–Poor General Health
(Population Adjusted for Deaths)

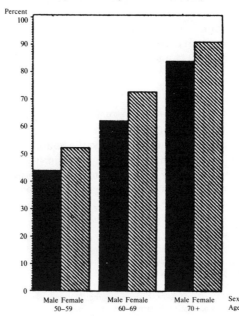

Chart of Sex within Age Categories

Figure 3 (*continued*)

Biological explanations center around genes and hormones. Prior to menopause, for instance, women may have less risk to certain cardiovascular diseases due to endogenous sex hormones (Verbrugge 1985).

Behavioral choices are thought to have a very important effect on the gender differential in health. Bearing children may have negative influences for women, particularly in areas with high fertility rates and poor health infrastructure. Women who have many closely-spaced children may suffer from maternal deple- tion, which could well affect physical functioning.[32] Different occupational and time allocation choices by gender may result in quite different physical and mental stresses, leading to different levels of health and physical functioning. Differing behaviors with respect to smoking and drinking is yet another example. Finally, there may be quite different access to medical care, resulting from both household choices and from health provider behavior. As a group, these behaviors are not likely to work favoring men or women exclusively; it is not clear which ones are most important and with what effect.[33]

Various hypotheses have been put forth explaining why there might be system- atic reporting bias (see Verbrugge 1985 for a summary). The fact that gender health differences exist in such a variety of economic, social and cultural settings as the United States, Jamaica, Malaysia, and Bangladesh would seem to counsel against accepting reporting bias as being the principal explanation. If this conclu- sion is accepted then it is important to explore potential reasons. We turn to this task with multivariate analysis of the Jamaican data.

IV. Analysis of the Jamaican SLC Data

Our aim is to investigate how age and socioeconomic factors affect adult health outcomes. We are particularly interested in how these influences may differ between genders and between younger and older adults.

A. Model and Empirical Specification

To better understand these influences, we outline and estimate a reduced form household production model of the outcomes, relating the outcomes to the under- lying constraints faced by the individuals and the households in which they reside. Because the health outcome measures are long-run, we relate them to long-run constraints. These constraints are at the individual, household, and community levels. Individual and household-level constraints include the person's age and sex, and education, which are related to life-cycle resources but may also have

---

32. The importance of maternal depletion is not well established (see, for example, Miller et al. 1992 or Pebley and DaVanzo 1988). To date studies have not controlled for the fact that child-spacing is a choice of women and families, thus endogenous in empirical models.

33. A paper by Verbrugge (1989) attempts to shed light on these questions using cross-sectional data from Detroit. The analysis, however, estimates a hybrid function, mixing elements of a health production function with elements of a reduced form. Also, simultaneity of variables subject to choice is not treated. In consequence, the results cannot be interpreted as Verbrugge would like.

independent effects. Constraints at the community level include the disease environment and the availability and quality of health care facilities. The constraints work their influences through more immediate factors such as health care utilization, which directly affect health outcomes. In some cases there may be a direct effect as well.

The model we develop follows Grossman (1972) in treating health as a stock of human capital. An individual's health stock at a point in time is determined by an initial genetic endowment, subsequent behavioral choices (such as levels of work activity and exercise, medical care choices, or smoking), and effects of the public health environment, such as contracting cancer from toxic waste. Over a period of time, the change in a person's health status is determined through a production function which transforms inputs, such as individual behaviors and the public health environment, into health:

(1) $H_t = H(H_{t-1}, X_{ht}, \hat{\mu}_{ft}, \hat{\mu}_{ct}, \varepsilon_t)$

where H_t is health at time t; X_h is a vector of health-related inputs including time allocated to different activities; $\hat{\mu}_f$ is a vector of individual and family characteristics such as age, gender or education of caregivers; $\hat{\mu}_c$ is a vector of community characteristics, such as environmental factors and availability and quality of health infrastructure; and ε is a term which covers unobserved individual endowments. The change in health over a period of time may also depend on the stock of health at the beginning of the period(s). For example a frail person's health may depreciate faster than that of someone who is robust.

In terms of the health variables available for this study, it is reasonable to suppose that health has several dimensions, which these measures are capturing. In the extreme, each measure may have its own production function. How to specify these biological production functions is not at all clear to us, in contrast to child growth or to certain childhood illnesses such as diarrhea, for which the biological processes are better known.[34] Even if we could specify the biology, to estimate the adult health production functions requires an enormous amount of data, which are certainly not available in the data we use, nor to our knowledge in other data sets. We consequently take the approach of estimating the reduced form determinants of these health outcomes.

To derive the reduced forms we make the standard economic assumption that households are making decisions rationally by maximizing their overall welfare as they define it; *given* their resources, the information available to them, their beliefs and the underlying health and sanitation environment. This assumption provides the mechanism by which those individual and household behaviors, the X_h's, which directly affect health are decided. The reduced form equations for health status are then derived from this behavior, taken together with the underlying health production, income, and time constraints.

Formally, we assume the household maximizes a weakly time-separable utility function and that the felicity function in each period, U_t, is a function of a vector

---

34. For instance, see the volumes by Falkner and Tanner (1986) and Waterlow (1988).

of consumption goods, X_{ct}, a vector of health stocks of each family member, H_t, and a vector of family members' leisure, l_t:

(2) $U_t = U(X_{ct}, H_t, l_t; \bar{\mu}_{ht})$

Preferences may also be affected by household characteristics, $\bar{\mu}_h$, such as education of various members.

The budget constraint relates current wealth as the present value of wealth left over from the previous period, the excess of income over expenditure, plus any net borrowing:

(3) $W_t = W_{t-1} + (1 + r)(Y_t - p_t X_t) + B$

where Y is household income, the sum of labor earnings and nonlabor income, p_t is a vector of prices, X the vector of goods purchased (both those in the utility function and purchased health inputs), r is a (time-invariant) real interest rate, and B is net borrowing (or, more generally, transfers). Labor earnings are, of course, the product of hours supplied and a wage rate, both of which may be affected by current health status; thus implying that income is endogenous.

The reduced form health equations can be derived as:

(4) $H_t = H'(\mu_f, \mu_c, W_0, H_0)$

where the subscript, $_0$, refers to the initial period (of adulthood). One important implication of the conceptualization is that measures of a health stock, such as indicators of physical limitations, are a function of *past* as well as of *current* values of the constraints. Indeed, because the model is dynamic *future* values of constraints, such as prices, matter as well.[35] For some of the conditioning variables, such as education, this does not present a problem, since adult education is usually time-invariant. For future time-varying variables, such as prices or expected prices, this means that we have omitted variables to the extent that the time-invariant covariates we use do not span the information set used to form expectations. However, it is not at all clear how this will affect either the age or education coefficients. A more serious potential source of bias derives from the common problem of missing measures of health and wealth at early adulthood.[36] To the extent that own education is correlated with both early adult health and initial family wealth, it will pick up those effects as well as its own effect on current resource availability and allocation.

B. Results: Ages Pooled

The multivariate analysis concentrates on the effects of individual and household covariates, controlling for community influences with parish-level dummy vari-

---

35. In a perfect foresight model all future values of time-varying constraints would affect current outcomes. If uncertainty is allowed, then the determinants of their expectations would enter the reduced forms.

36. Note that because lagged health affects current health and is unobserved, even reduced forms derived from constant marginal utility of wealth (or Frisch) functions (for example, MaCurdy 1981; Browning, Deaton, and Irish 1985) with preferences that are time-additive will be a function of past constraints.

ables plus a dummy for urban location. All analyses are stratified by gender, testing differences between coefficients. Five year age-cohort dummies are included in addition. For a subset of results, we also stratify on age: less than 50 years, between 50 and 69 and 70 or over; still including five year age-group dummies within these broader age classes. Ordered probits are estimated, separating the categories of having serious difficulties, limited difficulties, or no difficulties for the ADLs, and reporting poor, fair, and good (or better) health. Table 1 and Figure 4 report the main set of results for women and men, pooled across age groups. We focus on the effects of own education and also include tests of location dummies and of differences in sets of coefficients between men and women. Graphic representation offers an easy way to see the life-cycle/cohort gender differences; in Figure 4 we plot a subset of the simulated age-profiles for the probabilities of having health problems, using the ordered probit estimates.[37] We concentrate not only on the main effects, but also on whether there are differential effects across gender as a potential way of explaining the gender gaps in reported health.

1. Education Effects

Among the socioeconomic variables, own education turns out to be very important. A linear term in completed years of education significantly reduces the probability of reporting a problem for the general health measure as well as for six of the seven physical functioning measures, for both men and women.[38] Education is related to health measures of varying severity, even for the most severe measures. As will be seen below, once we stratify on age, these results are strengthened for prime-aged adults. Thus, as it does for child mortality and child health, education plays an important role in affecting health of adults.

To gain a sense of the magnitudes involved, we simulate the probabilities of having health problems for someone with six years (completion of primary school) and 11 years (secondary school completion). These are also reported in Table 1.[39] For men, the probability of being in poor health drops by 25 percent (from 14 to 10.4 percent) as education is increased from six to 11 years. The probabilities of experiencing difficulties with walking uphill decline from 10.8 to 9.1 percent, bending from 9.4 to 7.0 percent and eating, bathing, or using the toilet from 4.3 to 2.8 percent. For women, the magnitudes are similar; comparing completion of primary to secondary school results in a decline in the probability of having poor or fair general health from 20.7 to 16.9 percent. For problems with walking uphill, the decrease is from 18.7 to 16.2 percent; bending, from 15.0 to 12.6 percent; and for eating, bathing, and using the toilet, from 6.5 to 4.9 percent.

---

37. Specifically, we plot the expected probability of having a health problem (either with some or much difficulty) for the same age groups as we have dummies in the ordered probits. To do this, we hold constant for each person their nonage characteristics, vary their ages from 14–19 to over 75, and in each case calculate the resultant probability of having a problem. For each age group we then average probabilities over all individuals to arrive at the expected value.

38. A negative coefficient means the probability of reporting a problem is decreasing in that variable.

39. The simulations are done in the same way as the age simulations; see footnote 36.

Table 1
Education Influences on Female and Male Ill-Health: Age Pooled[a]

Limitations on	General Health		Vigorous Activities		Moderate Activities		Walking Uphill	
	Female	Male	Female	Male	Female	Male	Female	Male
Education (years)	−.038	−0.48	−.005	−.014	−.037	−.026	−.030	−.028
	(3.79)	(4.52)	(0.59)	(1.40)	(3.60)	(2.22)	(2.81)	(2.31)
Simulated probabilities								
Education = 6 years	.207	.140	.348	.224	.205	.112	.187	.108
Education = 11 years	.169	.104	.340	.211	.170	.095	.162	.091
χ^2 test statistics								
Location dummies (14 df)	168.0	116.8	412.3	216.5	129.3	67.4	67.2	49.1
Equality of male and female								
Education (1 df)		0.4		0.4		0.4		0.0
Location dummies (14 df)		17.2		53.2		33.8		20.8
Age dummies (12 df)		28.5		15.2		12.8		18.4

	Bending		Walking 1 Mile		Walking 100 yards		Eating, Bathing, Toiletry	
Education (years)	−.034	−.046	−.033	−.034	−.028	−.039	−.039	−.048
	(2.94)	(3.68)	(2.99)	(2.73)	(2.13)	(2.84)	(2.66)	(3.20)
Simulated probabilities								
Education = 6 years	.150	.094	.170	.098	.110	.068	.065	.043
Education = 11 years	.126	.070	.144	.079	.094	.051	.049	.028
χ^2 test statistics								
Location dummies (14 df)	50.4	48.9	31.6	29.3	50.0	44.2	36.6	24.2
Equality of male and female								
Education (1 df)		0.6		0.0		0.4		0.2
Location dummies (14 df)		22.9		23.4		14.6		14.9
Age dummies (12 df)		35.5		30.8		21.6		23.9

a. From ordered probits including parish, urban, and five-year age group dummies, Asymptotic normal z-statistics in parentheses.

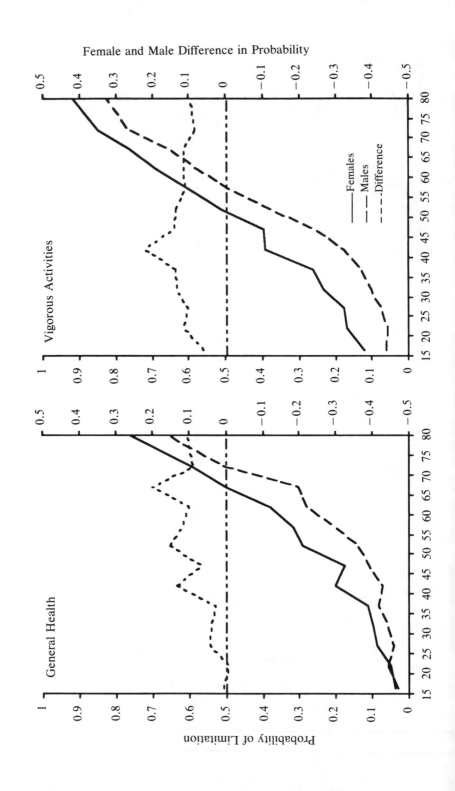

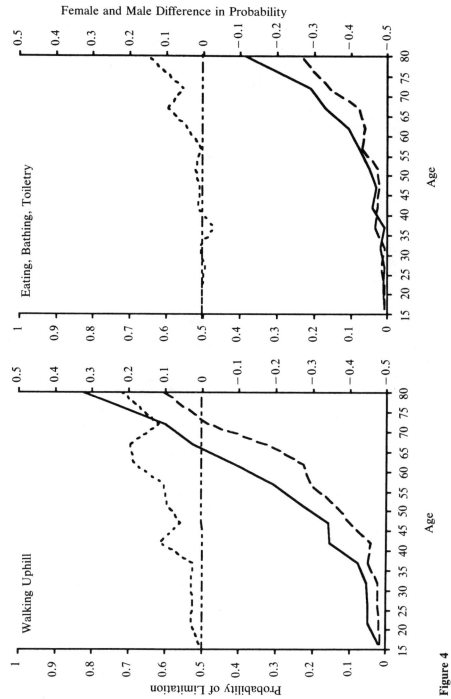

Figure 4
Simulated Probabilities of Health Limitations by Age

A linear specification is reported in Table 1. Nonlinearities in education were examined and found not to be important for women, based both on polynomials, dummy variables, and splines. For men, some evidence exists that the marginal effect of education declines at post primary levels. For instance, using dummy variables for completing exactly six years, completing seven or eight years (some middle school) or completing nine or more years (the end of middle school); we find for general health that completion of primary school has a coefficient of $-.28$ (asymptotic z-score of 3.35), while the coefficient on completing middle school or higher is only $-.32$ (z-score of 3.87). Not completing middle school actually provides no advantage over not completing primary school, which may reflect unobserved characteristics of those dropping out of middle school.[40] The same nonlinear pattern is found for bending, walking one mile, walking 100 yards, and for eating, bathing, or using the toilet.

As can be seen in Table 1, chi-square tests do not permit us to distinguish the effects of education between men and women. Furthermore, it can be seen from Appendix Table 3 that the distribution of education is quite similar among men and women in Jamaica. Thus differences in education or its effect cannot explain the gender differences in adult health in Jamaica.

2. Location Effects

The parish and urban dummy variables are significant at 5 percent or under for all the male and female equations. Conditional on parish of current residency, whether the person is living in an urban area has a positive effect on some of the ADLs for women, though generally not for men. The parish effects suggest that factors related to residency may be important. Obviously, several factors could be responsible and this is an area that bears further investigation. In particular it would be interesting to examine whether different levels of public and private health facility quality were partly responsible.

For the most mild problems of physical functioning, such as problems with vigorous or moderate activities, there is a differential effect of parish on men and women. However, for more moderate and severe measures, no significant differences of parish appear. These gender-specific effects of location on mild limitation measures could arise for several reasons, including differential access to health care or differential treatment by physicians. Of course, other infrastructure could also have effects which affect men and women heterogeneously.

3. Differences Over the Life-Cycle

In Figure 4 one can immediately see the enormous differences in reported problems by age net of education and location influences and that the gender differences vary by the severity of the problem.[41] Since the data are from a cross-

---

40. Strauss and Thomas (1991) find similar relationships of not completing education levels on wage outcomes in Brazil.

41. Data for the remaining functioning measures are available from the authors.

section, these patterns also reflect cohort differences.[42] In general, the age/cohort profiles for both men and women look convex; although the ages at which the profiles begin turning up varies with the problem. Thus as individuals age (or for older cohorts), their health deteriorates at an increasing rate.

For general health, women begin to report significantly greater problems by the time they are 25 to 29, both relative to the younger aged women and to men. The difference grows after that until age 65 or so, after which it declines some. For the less severe limitations on physical functioning, such as in performing vigorous activities, women report more difficulties than men throughout the age distribution, starting in their teens. Furthermore the age-cohort profile is steeper for women than men until roughly age 40, after which gender differences actually decline.

For more severe measures, the age-profiles don't begin rising until later ages, nor do gender differentials become large until later. Moderate activities displays a much flatter age/cohort profile until the late 30s for women and early 40s for men. After these points the profiles become quite steep, with the gender gap slowly rising until age 60, after which it flattens. A similar pattern emerges for problems in walking uphill. For the most severe measure, problems in eating, bathing, or using the toilet, the age/cohort profiles show very low probabilities at younger ages. Probabilities of having difficulties don't rise over 10 percent until age 60 for women and during the late 60s for men. Gender differentials don't appear until the late 50s, rising for older ages.

It is interesting that for general health and the less severe measures that the age gradients for women are steeper than for men beginning in the 20s. Note too, that there exist jumps for women in the probabilities of having difficulties with physical functioning in the late 30s and early 40s. This is most pronounced for general health and vigorous activities, but is apparent for walking uphill and even eating, bathing, and toiletry. The other ages at which there seem to be common jumps are the early 50s and, except for vigorous activities, the early 70s. Notice that men don't seem to exhibit common jumps in the late 30s. Both the jumps in gender differentials during the late 30s plus the emergence of differentials in the 20s suggests childbearing as being one of the underlying factors. The jumps at older ages suggest other factors are likely to be responsible as well.

4. Discussion

To sum up, there are several results that come out of the age-pooled health probits. First, higher education lowers the probabilities of reporting problems of ill-health for both men and women. Second, controlling for education, and area of residence, most of the differences between men and women in their reported

---

42. The economy in Jamaica was stagnant during the 1980s. Very little investment occurred in health infrastructure (Lewis 1988). In consequence at least during this period it can be argued that different cohorts faced similar health conditions. Furthermore, although the slope of the age-profiles may be biased upwards if more recent age cohorts did experience better health conditions, the *differences* across gender should be relatively free of bias provided different cohorts of men and women experienced similar differential conditions.

health status appears to be related to different life-cycle or cohort profiles. Jamaican women, like women in other countries, tend to report more non–life-threatening health problems and at earlier ages than do men. This could result from many factors, both biological and behavioral (such as childbearing); since we are estimating reduced forms it is not possible to distinguish between different factors. Third, where one lives does matter; which dimensions of location are important cannot be determined from the results in this paper.

C. Results: By Age Group

Log-likelihood ratio tests strongly reject equality of all slope coefficients by age group; we thus estimate the models stratified by age. Table 2 reports these statistics, plus the coefficients and asymptotic normal statistics from the by-age results, using the same specification as in Table 1.

Strong differences exist in the effect of education and other variables between younger and older ages. Education clearly discriminates between those with various health problems and those without for both men and women under 50 years. Indeed the magnitude of the coefficients rises considerably above the age-pooled results. For those aged 50 to 69, however, the estimated coefficients decline dramatically and are significant for only one measure of function for women and for one measure of function, plus general health for men. For persons older than 70, education is only significantly related to problems for the most severe functioning measure (eating, bathing, or using the toilet) and only for men.

The parish dummy variables again tend to be significant in the age-stratified results. For the more severe measures it is interesting that the χ^2 statistics are larger for the older age groups, implying that the parish dummies have more explanatory power for these groups.

One caveat to these age-stratified results needs to be made: if mortality is linked to factors which we aren't able to measure and if these same factors are linked to health status for survivors then our comparisons between age groups will be biased. In particular, it is plausible that if the less well-educated and lower income persons die earlier, the education coefficient will be biased toward zero.[43] Mortality selection is likely to be an issue only for the older part of the sample, as adult mortality rates are probably too low to have much of an effect for prime-aged adults; the results depicted in Figure 3 are consistent with this supposition. Unfortunately, the Jamaican SLC does not contain the data necessary to test the existence and strength of this potential effect. This is a potentially useful avenue for research with other data.

D. Additional Explanations: Expenditures, Partner, and Fertility Effects

In this section we take advantage of data available in the Jamaican SLC to augment our base specification. As discussed in section IVA, one would ideally want

---

43. Menchik (1993) shows strong permanent income differentials in mortality for men in the United States, using the National Longitudinal Survey. As noted below, we are not able to measure permanent income well in the Jamaica SLC.

to have information on initial wealth and health endowment. Although no measure of initial assets is available in the SLC, there is a measure which might be related to long-run income: per capita household expenditure (PCE). If households try to smooth consumption over time, this should be a measure of permanent income. Per capita household consumption has been successfully used in studies of child health (Thomas, Strauss, and Henriques 1990). Here we explore the use of PCE to explain adult health. Using PCE raises several issues, such as the likelihood that causation runs in both directions; since income, even permanent, may be a function of long-run health. We use an instrumental variables approach to address this issue (see Rivers and Vuong 1988, for an application to probit regressions), by including the residual from a regression predicting per capita expenditure (PCE), or its log. The instrument set includes, in addition to the other variables in the health equations, years of education, age, and age squared of the senior male and senior female in the household.[44,45]

We also allow the partner's characteristics to directly affect health by including his or her age, education, and whether he or she exists.[46,47] However, it is arguable that the existence of a partner is a reflection of the health of both partners, hence endogenous within our model. For this reason the base specification does not include partner characteristics. As will be seen below, our results are consistent with an interpretation of endogeneity.[48]

For per capita expenditure, partner and senior male and female characteristics there is an additional potential problem; the expenditure of the household in which the respondent currently resides (or characteristics of the current partner or current household senior male and female) may be only weakly related to expenditure (characteristics) over the bulk of the life-cycle. This is especially likely to be a problem for older adults who may have moved into their children's

44. In Jamaica, some 40 percent of adults live in households headed by women, hence using head of household and spouse would confound potential separate effects of men and women. Because there are cases in which a male or female household head has no partner, we also include dummies measuring the existence of a senior male or female.
45. Quadratics in education are not used because we have opted for linear term in education in the health probits. The first stage regressions explaining the log PCE have R^2s of around .3 for women and .35 for men. The identifying variables are significant; for instance, in the male regression the eight coefficients on existence of the senior male and female and their education, age, and age squared have an F-statistic of 73.4. These variables are also jointly significant in the female log PCE regression, although the F-statistic is much lower, 23.4.
46. In Jamaica partner and spouse are distinct. We use the characteristics of partners, which include spouses, and common law partners.
47. It would also be interesting to explore the effects of characteristics of the children, possibly including whether the parent is living with the child. In the Jamaican SLC data information is only available on children who are living in the household. As this may be a very select set of available children, we choose not to explore this dimension with these data.
48. It may be possible to use unobserved factor models as one way around the potential endogeneity of the spouse variables. We could take advantage of having data on multiple health variables by adding to the model a person-specific unobserved variable that belongs in each health equation, though with a different coefficient in each. By allowing the unobservable to depend upon the right-hand side covariates we could allow for covariation between the person-invariant unobserved factors that presumably are behind the potential correlation between spouse variables and own health (see Chamberlain 1984, Gertler 1988). In order to identify the parameters, however, we would have to assume that a subset of the health outcomes are indicators of the same underlying health variable, which we are loath to do.

Table 2
Education Influences on Female and Male Ill-Health: By Age Group[a]

Limitations on Age Group	General Health			Vigorous Activities			Moderate Activities			Walking Uphill		
	14–49	50–69	70+	14–49	50–69	70+	14–49	50–69	70+	14–49	50–69	70+
Females												
Education	−.051	−.031	−.002	−.008	−.003	.020	−.055	−.027	.004	−.055	−.009	.008
	(3.69)	(1.70)	(0.06)	(0.66)	(0.20)	(0.68)	(3.75)	(1.52)	(0.16)	(3.56)	(0.47)	(0.31)
χ^2 test statistics												
Location dummies (14 df)	69.1	70.1	31.1	265.3	75.2	37.6	107.4	22.6	19.5	31.3	45.9	25.6
Age-pooling (32 df)			34.4			71.9			69.1			60.8
Males												
Education	−.055	−.055	−.025	−.028	.005	−.045	−.062	−.002	−.022	−.067	−.009	.007
	(4.72)	(2.86)	(0.90)	(2.05)	(0.29)	(1.60)	(3.44)	(0.08)	(0.81)	(3.68)	(0.49)	(0.24)
χ^2 test statistics												
Location dummies (14 df)	45.8	77.8	37.8	154.8	66.0	34.0	58.3	20.3	24.4	27.8	30.5	24.5
Age-pooling (32 df)			52.7			94.3			53.0			63.1

	Bending			Walking One Mile			Walking 100 Yards			Eating, Bathing, Toiletry		
Females												
Education	−.050 (2.78)	−.044 (2.33)	.028 (1.08)	−.053 (3.22)	−.024 (1.30)	.005 (0.17)	−.055 (2.64)	−.022 (1.07)	.011 (0.41)	−.059 (2.43)	−.014 (0.59)	−.022 (0.80)
χ^2 test statistics												
Location dummies (14 df)	22.3	33.6	39.8	23.7	20.7	17.4	18.8	22.1	38.7	16.9	11.0	27.7
Age-pooling (32 df)			79.9			52.3			50.5			47.2
Males												
Education	−.082 (4.38)	−.042 (1.97)	−.005 (0.19)	−.078 (4.09)	−.016 (0.79)	.003 (0.12)	−.088 (4.27)	−.006 (0.24)	−.011 (0.37)	−.063 (2.77)	−.025 (0.92)	−.067 (2.10)
χ^2 test statistics												
Location dummies (14 df)	28.3	31.0	36.2	20.5	21.0	28.3	20.6	24.1	48.6	11.8	15.8	35.4
Age-pooling (32 df)			78.5			60.6			62.6			32.7

a. From ordered probits with parish, urban, and five-year age-group dummies.

households late in life; their children being on a different expenditure trajectory than they were.[49] To minimize this potential problem we estimate specifications with per capita expenditure (treated as endogenous) and partner characteristics on the sample of younger adults (14–49 years).

Tables 3A and 3B report for women and men the results for the baseline specifications for 14–49 year olds (specification 1), plus ones adding per capita expenditure and its residual from the first-stage regression (specification 2) and partner characteristics (specification 3).[50] The log of household per capita expenditure (logPCE) does not significantly affect health of women. For men, the expenditure variable is just significant at 5 percent for bending and walking 100 yards and at just above 5 percent for walking one mile.[51] Thus, for men some evidence exists that long-run income may be related to ill-health. In general the education coefficients don't decline, they even rise a little in some instances. Thus as is true for child health, the role of education seems to be largely independent of income for both men and women.

The residual term for log PCE is not significant,[52] suggesting that endogeneity of PCE may not be a problem. However when log PCE is treated as exogenous, it is significant for men for general health and six out of seven ADLs. Furthermore many of the coefficients are altered substantially, as well as the standard errors becoming lower.[53] It seems prudent not to rely on the exogenous PCE results, given the small number of identifying variables and thus the potential poor power of the Wu-Hausman test; the strong presumption that health problems, at least serious ones, do affect wages and perhaps labor supply; and the possibility that PCE is only weakly related to initial wealth or even life-cycle income. For women, log PCE is never close to significance, even when it is treated as exogenous.

When characteristics of the partner are added, they are jointly significant in the male equations, but generally not in the female equations. For males, evidently, having a female partner present in the household is associated with better reported health, an effect mitigated by advancing age of the partner.[54] Education of the partner does not have a significant impact on male adult health, although the direction is usually to improve it. Presence of a male partner has, if anything, a negative impact on female health, but one which as mentioned, is usually not jointly significant. These partner effects are quite similar in direction to the marriage premia found in labor market earnings in the United States and to the health premia found in adult mortality.[55] Just as in those other examples, it is not clear from these results whether the effect of a female partner being present is real

---

49. We are indebted to Jim Smith for this point.
50. Polynomials and splines in log PCE were experimented with, but were also not significant.
51. Since we had some evidence of nonlinearities in education for men, we also replaced the linear education term with a set of dummy variables, the expenditure results being essentially the same.
52. The significance of its parameter is a test of exogeneity of expenditure (see Rivers and Vuong 1988).
53. The coefficients are actually higher in the instrumental variables estimation, which is consistent with PCE being an error-ridden measure of life-cycle income or initial wealth, or with the instruments being correlated with unobserved health-related factors.
54. In results not reported, characteristics of the partner do not have significant effects for men 50 and older.
55. For instance, Korenman and Neumark (1991, 1992) and Hu and Goldman (1990).

or represents nonrandom selection together with positive assortative mating on health.[56]

Finally, for a subset of the female sample, we have complete fertility histories. Fertility histories were collected on one woman aged 14–45 per household, "randomly" chosen. Because of the potential importance of childbearing in explaining excess female health problems, we add this information to the baseline specification. Although childbearing decisions should be treated as endogenous within a life-cycle model for women, given data limitations we treat it as exogenous, trying to see if sensible correlations exist.

Unfortunately, the subsample of women having fertility histories is not exactly comparable to the general sample. The sample of women, aged 14–45, with fertility histories, is a subset of the 3,580 women aged 14–49 we analyze; 2,016 having complete data. Differences arise both because households with two or more women of childbearing age have different characteristics from households with only one such woman and possibly because women given the fertility histories were not chosen completely randomly. The subsample with fertility data tend to be younger than the women who were not respondents (partly since 46–49 year-olds are excluded), but also are more likely to be the head of household (25 versus 18.7 percent), have a partner living with them (38.7 versus 23.9 percent), have higher mean education (9.24 versus 8.91 years; 49 percent having some secondary school versus 41.5 percent), and be in households with higher log PCE (8.51 versus 8.36). Differences in health between the two samples are fairly small. Thus, less well-educated women, who are not heads of households and who have no male partners living with them are less likely to be included in the fertility sample.

With that caveat in mind, we turn to discussing the results, which are reported in Table 4. We do find some correlations between having had children and the less severe measures of physical functioning. The relationship, moreover, appears to be quite nonlinear. The number of children ever born has no measurable effect on any of our health outcomes. However, once we specify a dummy variable for having any children, we do see a significantly negative effect (at the 5 percent level) on the probability of having difficulties with vigorous activities. Furthermore, having a second or three or more children has no additional effect; it is the first child that is responsible for the partial correlation. While having a child has a positive partial correlation with problems in performing moderate activities, walking uphill, and bending, the coefficients are not significant. Having three or more children has a marginally significant (at the 10 percent level) partial correlation with walking uphill and likewise, there appears to be an effect (though not significant) of having two and three or more children on problems with bending. Note, however, that having had children makes no difference on reporting problems with more severe measures. Furthermore, it is correlated with women being more likely to report having good overall health. Why this should be is unclear; it may emanate in part from higher self-esteem associated with having children; it may also be that a few women in bad health have difficulty in bearing children.

---

56. For example, female partners may be present because they are in better health.

Table 3A
Education, Income, and Partner Influences on Female Ill-Health: 14–49 Year-Olds[a]

Limitations on Specification	General Health			Vigorous Activities			Moderate Activities			Walking Uphill		
	1	2	3	1	2	3	1	2	3	1	2	3
Own education (years)	-.051	-.051	-.046	-.008	-.024	-.014	-.055	-.063	-.056	-.055	-.073	-.053
	(3.69)	(2.54)	(3.21)	(0.66)	(1.54)	(1.12)	(3.75)	(3.19)	(3.68)	(3.56)	(3.46)	(3.31)
Log household per capita expenditure (PCE)		-.012			.249			.124			.286	
		(0.05)			(1.59)			(.057)			(1.19)	
Residual log PCE[b]		-.038			-.256			-.155			-.331	
		(0.05)			(1.58)			(0.69)			(1.33)	
(1) if partner in HH			.326			.198			.573			.536
			(1.13)			(0.82)			(1.93)			(1.72)
Partner education			-.026			.023			-.007			-.011
			(1.29)			(1.38)			(0.32)			(0.49)
Partner age			-.004			-.005			-.008			-.006
			(.070)			(1.10)			(1.42)			(1.10)
χ² for partner covs (3 df)			1.9			18.5			11.3			8.1

	Bending			Walking One Mile			Walking 100 Yards			Eating, Bathing, Toiletry		
Own education	−.050 (2.78)	−.056 (2.28)	−.045 (2.39)	−.053 (3.22)	−.066 (2.97)	−.054 (3.20)	−.055 (2.64)	−.072 (2.50)	−.063 (2.97)	−.059 (2.43)	−.056 (1.50)	−.064 (2.52)
Log household per capita expenditure (PCE)		.094 (0.32)			.229 (0.92)			.274 (0.79)			−.075 (0.16)	
Residual log PCE[b]			−.140 (0.96)			−.203 (0.78)			−.345 (0.96)			−.042 (0.09)
(1) if partner in HH			.389 (1.11)			.230 (0.69)			.031 (0.07)			.059 (0.12)
Partner education			−.022 (0.88)			.005 (0.23)			.036 (1.14)			.017 (0.45)
Partner age			−.001 (0.18)			−.003 (0.48)			−.004 (0.52)			−.005 (0.56)
χ^2 for partner covs (3 df)			4.3			4.1			3.5			0.6

a. Five year age-group and location dummies are also included.
b. From regression of log household per capita expenditure. Identifying instruments include education and age of the senior male and female in the household, plus quadratics in their ages.

Table 3B
Education, Income, and Partner Influences on Male Ill-Health: 14–49 Year-Olds[a]

Limitations on Specification	General Health			Vigorous Activities			Moderate Activities			Walking Uphill		
	1	2	3	1	2	3	1	2	3	1	2	3
Own education (years)	−.055 (4.72)	−.046 (2.71)	−.062 (4.08)	−.028 (2.05)	−.036 (2.31)	−.026 (1.76)	−.055 (3.75)	−.047 (2.24)	−.054 (2.84)	−.055 (3.56)	−.053 (2.46)	−.058 (3.03)
Log household per capita expenditure (PCE)		−.183 (1.17)			.128 (1.00)			−.309 (1.63)			−.307 (1.53)	
Residual log PCE[b]		.061 (0.36)			−.205 (1.50)			.160 (0.80)			.133 (0.63)	
(1) if partner in HH			−1.44 (3.00)			−.319 (0.98)			−.487 (1.16)			−.360 (0.85)
Partner education			.065 (1.98)			−.006 (0.26)			−.034 (1.13)			−.039 (1.28)
Partner age			.023 (2.62)			.013 (2.00)			.023 (2.67)			.020 (2.36)
χ^2 for partner covs (3 df)			11.0			4.9			9.6			8.3

	Bending			Walking One Mile			Walking 100 Yards			Eating, Bathing, Toiletry		
Own education (years)	−.050 (2.78)	−.062 (2.75)	−.073 (3.74)	−.053 (3.22)	−.059 (2.59)	−.070 (3.55)	−.055 (2.64)	−.068 (2.68)	−.089 (4.12)	−.059 (2.43)	−.057 (2.12)	−.068 (2.91)
Log household per capita expenditure (PCE)		−.460 (2.11)			−.417 (1.90)			−.508 (2.00)			−.142 (0.56)	
Residual log PCE[b]		.257 (1.12)			.250 (1.09)			.250 (0.94)			−.051 (0.19)	
(1) if partner in HH			−.690 (1.54)			−.557 (1.24)			−1.465 (2.38)			−1.852 (2.70)
Partner education			−.039 (1.21)			−.031 (0.97)			.013 (0.31)			.037 (0.83)
Partner age			.030 (3.30)			.024 (2.61)			.040 (3.51)			.043 (3.51)
χ^2 for partner covs 3 df			14.0			8.7			13.4			13.0

a. Five-year age-group and location dummies are also included.
b. From regression of log household per capita expenditure. Identifying instruments include education and age of the senior male and senior female in the household, plus quadratics in their ages.

Table 4

Correlations of Fertility With Female Ill-Health: 14–45 Year-Olds[a]

Health Measure	Number of Children			χ^2 test (3 df)
	1+, 1	2	3+	
General health	−.187			—
	(1.64)			
	−.169	−.154	−.223	3.0
	(1.22)	(1.07)	(1.70)	
Vigorous activities	.179			—
	(2.03)			
	.190	.142	.188	4.5
	(1.89)	(1.25)	(1.81)	
Moderate activities	.122			—
	(1.05)			
	.138	.125	.101	1.2
	(1.03)	(0.83)	(0.73)	
Walking uphill	.171			—
	(1.20)			
	.051	.199	.264	3.6
	(0.30)	(1.13)	(1.64)	
Bending	.174			—
	(0.98)			
	.067	.213	.266	2.2
	(0.31)	(0.96)	(1.30)	
Walking one mile	−.053			—
	(0.37)			
	−.065	−.045	−.047	0.2
	(0.38)	(0.25)	(0.29)	
Walking 100 yards	−.008			—
	(0.03)			
	−.077	.109	−.025	0.6
	(0.29)	(0.41)	(0.09)	
Eating, bathing, toiletry	−.251			—
	(1.11)			
	−.271	−.205	−.263	1.3
	(0.98)	(0.71)	(1.00)	

a. From ordered probits with reduced sample having fertility information. Years of education, age, and location dummies are also included. Asymptotic normal statistics in parentheses.

The difference in the fertility correlations is another demonstration that various health measures are not capturing identical dimensions. However, overall, it appears that while fertility may play a role in explaining the gender gap in physical functioning, it is probably small and then limited to less severe problems. One must be careful in making this claim too strongly from this evidence because we have not accounted for potential biases from fertility being endogenous, also we do not have enough data on health experiences during childbirth to carefully examine whether having had certain health problems may lead to later difficulties in physical functioning.[57]

V. Summary

This paper has attempted to cover several areas related to the determinants of adult health in developing countries. First, we argue that not enough attention has been paid to the underlying causes of adult health and not enough to nonmortality dimensions of health. Second, we argue that measures of physical functioning, together with a measure of general health form a useful, though not exhaustive, set of adult health measures. Using these measures, we add to the evidence that women report more problems of ill-health across all age categories and adjusted for mortality. Moreover, our evidence on a gender adult health differential cuts across both economic and cultural dimensions, casting doubt on systematic reporting bias as the cause.

We then use the Jamaican Survey of Living Conditions data to examine in more detail the underlying determinants of adult health. We find strong effects of own education. While some of the measured effect may represent the impact of endowed health or initial wealth, we find the effect is robust to inclusion of a measure of long-run income, per capita household expenditures. This robustness suggests a role for education apart from generating higher incomes, similar to results on the effects of parental education on child health. Presumably part of the education effect is transmitted by affecting health related behaviors, although we can not demonstrate how from our reduced form evidence on outcomes.

The education effects seem to dissipate as people age. That socioeconomic differentials decline with age is potentially important. It suggests that policies focusing on the health and health behaviors of prime-aged adults may be the most effective way to improve health of adults.

Further, these education effects are quite similar for men and women. This finding, together with the fact that the distribution of years of education is quite close for men and women in Jamaica, suggests that education is not an explanation for the observed gender differentials in reported health status.

We also find that location has a significant effect on health. This effect differs by gender for the more mild measures, a finding which could indicate an explanatory role for heterogeneous influence of health services (or other infrastructure)

---

57. Although data do exist on health problems, they are only for pregnancies during the past five years. A significant part of the already reduced sample would thus be excluded. Furthermore, such exclusion would raise nontrivial sample selection issues that would further complicate any interpretation.

on the health outcome of women and men. For instance, it could be that women have less access to health care than men. Such hypotheses need to be verified by disaggregating community factors.

Our most robust finding is a set of very strong life-cycle/cohort patterns, which do differ across the health measures used and by gender, even after controlling for socioeconomic status and community environment. For most of the measures, the gender gap seems to appear during an age window that varies by severity of the problem, although there seems to be some evidence that for many measures the gap begins during child-bearing years. Indeed, for the more mild measures, particularly problems in doing vigorous activities, there does seem to be direct correlations with having had a child. For severe problems, however, the gender differentials are largest at older ages and no correlation exists with childbearing. These life-cycle/cohort profiles seem to explain most of the reported gender gap in Jamaica; exactly what biological or behavioral factors they represent is not as yet clear.

Appendix Table 1

Cross-Tabulation of Problems Walking Uphill by General Health: Jamaican SLC, Men and Women

| Walking Uphill | General Health | | | | | |
	Excellent	Very Good	Good	Fair	Poor	Total
Limited a lot						
Frequency	13	17	59	147	351	587
Percent	0.12	0.16	0.56	1.40	3.34	5.58
Row percentage	2.21	2.90	10.05	25.04	59.80	
Column percentage	0.39	0.63	2.11	13.03	59.90	
Limited a little						
Frequency	26	107	257	379	147	916
Percent	0.25	1.02	2.44	3.60	1.40	8.71
Row percentage	2.84	11.68	28.06	41.38	16.05	
Column percentage	0.79	3.96	9.19	33.60	25.09	
Not limited						
Frequency	3,260	2,580	2,481	602	88	9011
Percent	31.01	24.54	23.60	5.73	0.84	85.70
Row percentage	36.18	28.63	27.53	6.68	0.98	
Column percentage	98.82	95.41	88.70	53.37	15.02	
Total	3,299	2,704	2,797	1,128	586	10,514
	31.38	25.72	26.60	10.73	5.57	100.00

Appendix Table 2A
Percent of Jamaicans with Poor/Fair and Limited Health Measures by Education Level and Age Group

	General Health		Moderate Activities		Bending, Kneeling, and Stooping	
	<9 years	> = 9 years	<9 years	> = 9 years	<9 years	> = 9 years
Females						
14–29	4.9	4.8	3.5	1.7	2.6	2.3
30–49	17.1	10.5	7.8	3.7	6.0	8.2
50–59	36.6	29.3	16.3	18.4	13.0	24.5
60–69	47.1	50.5	33.3	24.0	28.4	46.8
70+	70.7	76.0	64.3	55.1	58.0	69.9
Males						
14–29	5.0	3.2	7.1	4.6	1.0	1.8
30–49	10.8	5.5	12.1	9.3	2.5	3.5
50–59	21.5	15.7	32.9	28.0	9.5	14.7
60–69	38.3	28.0	53.5	48.5	18.0	41.8
70+	64.9	65.4	76.4	82.0	62.8	75.0

Appendix Table 2B

Percent of Malaysians (>50 years) with Poor and Limited Health Measures by Education Level

	Females		Males	
	<8 years	> = 8 years	<8 years	> = 8 years
General health	63.3	51.4	53.3	36.8
Vigorous activities	75.0	60.0	58.7	34.5
Moderate activities	24.4	14.3	17.8	6.9
Walking uphill	48.5	37.1	35.5	13.8
Bending	24.1	25.7	18.8	10.3
Walking 100 yards	12.9	5.7	10.6	3.5
Daily activities	2.6	0.0	3.3	1.2

Appendix Table 3
Jamaican SLC Variable Means and Standard Deviations

	Pooled Ages		14–49		50–69		70 Plus	
	Female	Male	Female	Male	Female	Male	Female	Male
Sample size	4,896	4,847	3,580	3,688	883	794	433	365
Health indicators								
General health								
% Poor	6.8	4.2	1.5	1.1	12.4	6.4	39.5	31.0
% Fair	12.7	8.9	6.5	3.9	28.0	20.3	32.1	34.0
% Good +	80.5	86.9	92.0	95.0	59.6	73.3	28.4	35.1
Vigorous activities								
% limited a lot	16.9	9.3	6.9	2.8	31.1	20.2	70.8	51.8
% limited a little	18.0	13.1	13.7	6.7	35.2	35.3	18.5	29.6
% not limited	65.1	77.5	79.4	90.5	33.7	44.5	10.6	18.6
Moderate activities								
% limited a lot	7.5	3.6	1.7	0.8	11.3	5.5	47.2	27.7
% limited a little	12.1	7.3	5.5	2.4	30.1	17.5	30.3	34.6
% not limited	80.4	89.1	92.8	96.8	58.6	76.9	22.5	37.6
Walking uphill								
% limited a lot	7.2	3.7	1.5	0.9	11.2	5.8	46.8	27.1
% limited a little	11.0	7.0	4.2	1.9	28.9	18.5	30.1	32.6
% not limited	81.8	89.4	94.4	97.2	59.8	75.7	23.1	40.3
Bending								
% limited a lot	5.7	3.0	1.0	0.8	7.6	3.8	40.0	23.8
% limited a little	9.0	6.1	2.3	1.5	25.1	14.0	31.3	34.8
% not limited	85.4	90.9	96.7	97.7	67.3	82.2	28.7	41.4

Appendix Table 3 (*continued*)

	Pooled Ages		14–49		50–69		70 Plus	
	Female	Male	Female	Male	Female	Male	Female	Male
Walk one mile								
% limited a lot	7.5	3.9	1.5	0.9	11.2	5.7	49.5	31.0
% limited a little	8.9	5.6	3.2	1.4	24.4	14.9	24.1	27.1
% not limited	83.6	90.5	95.3	97.7	64.4	79.5	26.4	41.9
Walk 100 yards								
% limited a lot	4.5	2.6	0.8	0.7	6.3	3.0	31.7	21.7
% limited a little	6.4	3.9	1.2	1.0	15.6	8.6	29.9	23.1
% not limited	89.1	93.5	98.0	98.4	78.2	88.4	38.4	55.2
Eating, bathing, toiletry								
% limited a lot	2.3	1.5	0.6	0.5	3.4	2.1	14.6	9.9
% limited a little	4.0	2.5	0.8	0.8	7.9	4.8	22.7	14.8
% not limited	93.7	96.0	98.7	98.7	88.6	93.1	62.7	75.3
Covariates, (1) If Age								
14–19	.19	.22	.28	.29				
20–24	.14	.14	.19	.18				
25–29	.12	.12	.16	.15				
30–34	.10	.10	.13	.13				
35–39	.08	.07	.10	.09				
40–44	.05	.06	.07	.08				
45–49	.05	.06	.07	.07				
50–54	.05	.05			.29	.28		
55–59	.04	.04			.24	.27		
60–64	.05	.05			.26	.23		
65–69	.04	.04			.21	.22		
70–74	.03	.03					.37	.39
75 Plus	.06	.05					.63	.61

Education (years)	8.4	8.4	9.1	9.0	6.5	6.5	6.2	6.0
	(2.6)	(2.6)	(2.3)	(2.3)	(2.4)	(2.6)	(2.3)	(2.5)
% 0–6 years	.27	.25	.14	.15	.59	.56	.66	.66
% 7–9 years	.39	.41	.40	.43	.37	.39	.32	.31
% 10 years plus	.34	.33	.45	.43	.03	.05	.02	.03
Log household	8.44	8.52	8.44	8.51	8.47	8.60	8.41	8.48
Per capita expenditure	(0.78)	(0.81)	(0.78)	(0.81)	(0.78)	(0.83)	(0.76)	(0.78)
(1) If Urban	.45	.41	.48	.43	.39	.38	.33	.28
(1) If partner in house	.35	.35	.32	.28	.49	.61	.28	.55
Partner's age	46.7	42.2	38.1	32.2	61.5	52.9	74.3	67.6
	(16.4)	(15.9)	(10.6)	(8.8)	(9.6)	(9.9)	(12.5)	(9.9)
Partner's education	7.6	7.9	8.1	8.7	6.5	6.9	6.1	6.5
	(2.7)	(2.6)	(2.6)	(2.5)	(2.5)	(2.5)	(2.6)	(2.1)
(1) If senior female exists	.94	.73	.93	.77	.98	.65	.95	.58
Education of senior female	7.6	7.5	7.9	7.7	6.6	7.0	6.5	6.7
	(2.7)	(2.4)	(2.4)	(2.4)	(2.4)	(2.4)	(2.3)	(2.2)
Age of senior female	48.1	47.3	42.4	44.8	58.4	53.3	72.7	65.8
	(16.0)	(15.0)	(13.6)	(14.6)	(8.0)	(11.0)	(12.9)	(12.1)
(1) If senior male exists	.58	.81	.61	.76	.53	.96	.39	.96
Education of senior male	7.3	7.4	7.6	7.8	6.5	6.5	6.6	6.1
	(2.6)	(2.6)	(2.5)	(2.5)	(2.5)	(2.6)	(2.5)	(2.5)
Age of senior male	50.2	49.7	46.6	44.2	61.0	58.7	66.6	74.8
	(15.2)	(16.2)	(14.1)	(14.7)	(10.3)	(6.8)	(15.7)	(8.6)

8 Quality of Medical Care and Choice of Medical Treatment in Kenya
An Empirical Analysis

Germano Mwabu
Martha Ainsworth
Andrew Nyamete

Germano Mwabu is a professor of economics at Kenyatta University, Nairobi, Kenya; Martha Ainsworth and Andrew Nyamete are researchers in the Africa Technical Department, The World Bank. This study was sponsored by the Africa Regional Study on Health Finance, managed by the Population, Health, and Nutrition Division of the Africa Technical Department of the World Bank. The authors greatly appreciate the comments on earlier drafts made by Charles Griffin, Raylynn Oliver, Mark Rosenzweig, T. Paul Schultz, Robert Willis, and participants in seminars at the World Bank and at the Rockefeller Foundation Conference on Women's Human Capital and Development. Khadija Bah, Karol Brown, and Jim Shafer provided valued assistance in preparation of the current draft. This chapter would never have been completed were it not for the kind and diligent assistance of Mrs. Annie Kihara, who was the critical "link" between the Nairobi and Washington researchers. The opinions expressed in this chapter are those of the authors and do not reflect official positions of the World Bank or its members.

I. Introduction

Assessment of medical care quality is problematic both to consumers and health care providers. Because of biomedical and technical aspects of health care, patients are normally unable to determine the quality of service they can get from medical care facilities. However, patients can assess the quality of medical service on the basis of experience and/or attributes of medical facilities. These are factors that providers may also use to assess medical care quality.

The quality of medical care is now well recognized as a key factor in determining the success of health care financing reforms in African countries (see for example, Barnum and Kutzin 1993; Bitran et al. 1986; Creese 1991; Denton et al. 1990; Dor, Gertler, and van der Gaag 1987; Ellis and Mwabu 1991; Gertler et al. 1987; Gertler and van der Gaag 1990; Lavy and Quigley 1993; Lavy et al. 1992; Reed 1990; World Bank 1990; Waddington and Enyimayew 1989). In many developing countries, the often stated objective of seeking additional resources for the health sector is to raise health care quality, particularly in peripheral facilities. However, empirical information is lacking as to the effect of quality improvements on health care demand or, for that matter, on health status.[1] A given improvement in service quality might increase demand for medical care by attracting new users or by increasing the intensity of service use by existing users. However, demand may move in the opposite direction if the improved service is more effective in dealing with patients' problems or with the underlying illness patterns. There is no a priori basis for predicting the demand effects of service improvement. In spite of the broad consensus among health care workers and policymakers about the importance of service quality in health care demand, in-depth empirical investigation of this issue has been rare because of data limitations.[2] Consequently, improvements in service quality such as staff redeployment or investments in facilities have either not been undertaken or have been implemented without the necessary information about their impact on the demand for health care. In an attempt to remedy this situation, we conduct an empirical analysis of the relationship between medical care quality and medical care demand using detailed household and facility data sets from a Kenyan rural district. Our analysis differs in two respects from recent work in this area (Denton et al. 1990; Ellis and Mwabu 1991; Lavy and Quigley 1993; Litvak and Bodart 1992). First, in contrast to previous research, we include various types of drugs and diagnostic equipment among measures of facility quality. Second, we separate out demand effects of specific quality measures, thereby enlarging policymakers' menu of health facility attributes that can be changed to improve service quality. This is in contrast to Ellis and Mwabu (1991), who use the principal component method to collapse different measures of facility quality into a composite quality index, and then estimate demand effect of that single variable. Our approach also differs from that of Lavy and Quigley who use facility "types" as proxies for medical care quality. It further differs from that of Denton and colleagues, who use broad drug availability as the crucial indicator of health facility quality. Our study deepens previous research on demand effects of medical care quality in Sub-Saharan Africa.

---

1. Thomas et al. (1992) and Lavy et al. (1992) have recently examined the relationship between disaggregated measures of health care quality and health status of adults and children in Côte d'Ivoire and Ghana, respectively.

2. The results of a natural experiment in Cameroon show that a combination of increased fees and improved quality *can* result in a net increase in demand for government health care, with the greatest proportionate increase among the poor (Litvack and Bodart 1992). However, the study results do not make it possible to disaggregate the size of the price and quality effects or, specifically, to determine which components of quality might have an effect on demand. Further, it is unclear the extent to which the increase in demand arose from shifts among care alternatives, as opposed to generation of new demand for health care.

The remainder of the paper is organized as follows. Section II reviews health care demand literature in developing countries, with a focus on Africa, and presents the basic model of health care demand, linking it to past studies. Section III describes the data collection methods, specifies and describes the variables to be used in model estimation, and outlines the estimation strategy. Empirical results are presented and discussed in Section IV. Simulation results are in Section V. Section VI concludes the paper.

II. Health Care Demand Modeling

A. Previous Literature

Health care demand modeling has undergone a major evolution since the early 1960s, when economists first became interested in estimating the demand for health services. Early health care demand models were simple reduced-form equations derived from the assumption of utility maximization. The demand for a particular health service, as measured by number of visits to a health facility, was hypothesized to depend on the price of that service, prices of alternative services, household income, and tastes. This formulation excluded from the demand equation variables that measured time costs associated with using the services and demographic characteristics of patients, such as age and education, even though these variables have since been shown to be important determinants of health care use. Acton (1975), Christianson (1976), and Grossman (1972) altered the above formulation substantially to allow for inclusion of demographic and time variables in the demand equation. An additional contribution by Acton and Christianson was the recognition of the discrete nature of health care decisions in health care demand. The quality of medical care was not an important issue in the specification of the earlier models, however. Akin et al. (1986), Heller (1982), and others studied medical care demand patterns in developing countries using discrete choice formulations of health care decisions originally employed by Acton and Christianson. Quality differences were often invoked in the interpretation of the estimation results, but were infrequently used in the specification of the estimating equations. Results from some of these studies, especially the research done by Akin et al. (1986) in the Philippines, showed that, contrary to predictions of the theory of consumer behavior, economic variables such as prices and household income had little or no impact on medical care use. These findings stimulated new efforts in health care demand modeling in developing countries. Gertler et al. (1987) argued that since observed health care demands are based on the postulate of utility maximization, demand parameter estimates must depend on the structure, or specification, of the utility function from which they are derived. Dor et al. (1987) and Gertler and van der Gaag (1990), using a conditional utility function, demonstrated analytically using data from rural Peru and Côte d'Ivoire that economic variables such as household income and prices *do* have an influence on health care decisions. Bitran (1991) has provided a comprehensive exposition of past studies on health care demand in developing countries. An excellent review of how findings of these studies have been applied in the analysis and implementation of health care financing policies, especially in Africa, is in Creese (1991).

A version of the demand model first proposed by Gertler, Locay, and Sanderson (1987), and refined and popularized by Gertler and van der Gaag (1990) has recently been used to study health care demand behavior in Ghana and Kenya (Lavy and Quigley 1993; Ellis and Mwabu 1991). A restatement of this model, a modification of which is adapted for this study, is presented below.

B. The Model

In the event of an illness, a patient is assumed to seek help from a health care system characterized by many providers. The patient or his relative is further assumed to choose the health care alternative that yields the maximum expected utility. Conditional on seeking treatment, the direct utility derived by individual i from treatment alternative j can be expressed as

(1) $u_{ij} = u_{ij}(h_{ij}, c_{ij})$

where u_{ij} is the direct conditional utility that individual i expects from health care provider j; h_{ij} is the expected improvement in health status for individual i after receiving treatment from provider j, and c_{ij} is the consumption of nonhealth care goods, the amount of which depends on choice j, because of the monetary and nonmonetary costs of treatment from provider j.

To facilitate empirical work, the unobservable variables, h_{ij} and c_{ij}, can be expressed as:

(2) $h_{ij} = h(x_i, z_{ij})$

(3) $c_{ij} = y_i - e_{ij}$

where x_i is a vector of observable socioeconomic attributes of individual i, such as age and education; z_{ij} is a vector of medical and physical attributes faced by individual i in facility j, such as availability of drugs and medical equipment and sanitary conditions of the facility; c_{ij} is the monetary value of nonhealth care goods that individual i can consume after paying for medical care in facility j; y_i is annual income of household i; e_{ij} is the value of resources that individual i devotes to medical care received from facility j. The level of e_{ij} is determined by such factors as the treatment fees, waiting time, and access variables such as distance and travel time. The observed medical care expenditure, e_{ij}, that determines the level of c_{ij} for a given level of y_i, can be written out in full as follows:

(4) $e_{ij} = D_{ij} + wT_{ij}$

where, D_{ij}, is the total monetary cost of seeking treatment from health facility j for individual i; T_{ij} is the travel time to health facility j for individual i, including the time spent to wait for treatment there; and w is the shadow wage rate. Notice that expressions (3) and (4) are merely accounting identities, which permit identification of c_{ij}, a variable for which information is normally not collected in health care demand surveys. Equation (2) extends previous empirical studies on health care demand (see for example, Gertler and van der Gaag 1990, p. 72; Ellis and

Mwabu 1991) by allowing, in an empirical specification, disaggregated treatment-related attributes of health facilities, z_{ij}, to influence health status.

Together, Equations (1)–(4) represent a general structural specification of a behavioral model of health care demand. The next stage in the implementation of this model is the choice of the functional form for the utility function in Equation (1). As is well known, there are many functional forms to choose from. Ideally we want a mathematical form for the utility function that is consistent both with actual demand behavior and with rules of rational choice, as regards for example, transitivity of consumer preferences. Gertler and van der Gaag (1990), in a remarkable attempt to deal with this problem, show that if the utility function in Equation (1) is linear in health status and quadratic in consumption, it is consistent with well-ordered preferences. Furthermore, such a functional form generates typically observed demand patterns. In the same vein, Gertler and van der Gaag demonstrate that a utility function that is linear both in health status and income, but in which income interacts with provider-specific attributes, is also consistent with empirical health care demand patterns. However, the latter utility function has the undesirable feature that the marginal utility of income can vary across health care providers, even when providers are assumed to produce the same improvement in health status at some constant price. Because of this feature, the utility function just described is inconsistent with the behavioral axiom of preference maximization, which underlies our study. It should however be stated that both of these utility functions deliver the same empirical information about demand behavior. In each of the specifications, for example, economic variables such as income and prices turn out to be important determinants of health care demand (Gertler and van der Gaag 1990, pp. 98–100). If the aim is to construct a prediction model, it may matter very little which of the two specifications is used. Under such circumstances the unstable utility function may even be preferred over other forms for ease of modeling.

The crucial property of the stable utility function is the nonconstancy of the marginal rate of substitution of commodities in consumption. Following Gertler and van der Gaag (1990), it is easy to show that this property exists in many simple forms of well behaved utility functions. For example, the property is maintained in a utility function that is log-linear in health status and consumption, or in a utility function that is linear in health status, but log-linear in consumption. In these specifications, as in others in the literature, it is the variation in monetary or time prices across health care providers that ensures identification of behavioral parameters. Given this role of prices, and a further assumption that consumer preferences over the entire range of consumption goods are well defined, empirical health care demands can be shown to be consistent with the assumption that ill individuals maximize an indirect conditional utility function, v_{ij}, as shown in Equation (5) below.

(5) $v_{ij} = v_{ij}(x_i, z_j, y_i, r_{ij}, a_i)$

where x_i, z_j, and y_i are as previously defined; r_{ij} is the price of health care received by individual i from health facility j; a_i is the price of nonhealth care good consumed by individual i.

The general functional form for the indirect utility function in (5) differs from that used by Gertler and van der Gaag (1990, p. 64)[3] in three important respects. First, by solving (5) one gets health care consumption bundles, rather than health status improvements or health outcomes, as in Gertler and van der Gaag. Second, consumption of nonhealth goods and services is constant for different levels of medical services. The constancy is achieved by assuming that the direct utility function that underlies (5) is separable in medical care goods and other consumption bundles. Third, apart from other prices, the indirect utility function in (5) is dependent on "medical care" prices and not on prices of "improvements in health status." The undesirable feature of (5) is that, in the underlying direct utility function, people's welfare depends on medical care services, rather than on health outcomes. This disadvantage is mitigated by the fact that in the event of illness, people restore health status by consuming medical care services. The attractiveness of Equation (5) lies in the fact that it permits an investigation of direct demand effects of prices and incomes.

Equation (5) is the standard expression for the indirect utility function in consumer demand theory (see Varian 1984). In the present context, it shows the maximum utility that individual i can achieve, conditional on seeking treatment for an illness, controlling for income y_i, health care prices r_{ij}, prices of other goods a_i, personal attributes x_i, and facility specific characteristics z_j. To ease econometric work, a_i may be normalized to unity. Normalization of this variable in our case is desirable because its variation in the sample is small. Notice further that all the elements of the indirect conditional utility function in Equation (5) are directly observable and are the variables of interest to policymakers.

The final step in econometric implementation of the model requires the standard assumption that the utility function in Equation (5) is stochastic, and is of the form

(6) $v_{ij} = v_{ij}^* + u_i$

where v_{ij}^* is the systematic component of utility and u_i is an additive disturbance term.

In a semi-log linear form, the systematic part of utility may be expressed as in Equation (7) below

(7) $v_{ij}^* = \beta' Q_{ij} + \alpha'_j S_i$

where Q_{ij} is a vector of generic attributes (in log form) that individual i faces in facility j; S_i is a vector of characteristics (in log form) specific to individual i, including income-facility interaction terms; α and β are vectors of parameters to be estimated. Assuming that u_i is distributed as Weibull, Equation (6) leads to a well known variety of logit specifications of individual choice of medical treatments (see for example, Gertler and van der Gaag 1990, Akin et al. 1986, Denton et al. 1990). Following these specifications, and others in the more general econometric literature (for example, Domencich and McFadden 1975; Maddala 1983;

---

3. The conditional indirect utility function they specify is as follows: $U = U(H_j, Y - P_j)$ where Y is income; H_j is an individual's improvement in health status after seeking medical treatment from facility j; and P_j is the monetary price of seeking medical care, including opportunity cost of time.

Greene 1990; Goldberger 1981; Manski and McFadden 1981; Amemiya 1981, 1984; Robertson and Symons 1990; Boskin 1974; Gertler and Glewwe 1989), the probability P_{ij} that individual i will seek treatment from health facility j can be expressed as

(8) $P_{ij} = \exp(\beta'Q_{ij} + \alpha'_j S_i)/\Sigma \exp(\beta'Q_{ik} + \alpha'_k S_i)$

Estimation of Equation (8) requires use of numerical methods to find values of parameter vectors α and β that maximize the likelihood (or the log-likelihood) of observing the sample data on Q and S. The log-likelihood function that needs to be maximized in order to estimate values of the parameter vectors α and β is simply

(9) $L = \Sigma_i \Sigma_j G_{ij} \log P_{ij}$

where L is the logarithm of the likelihood function; $G_{ij} = 1$ if individual i chose health facility j; otherwise G_{ij} takes a value of zero.

The estimated values for α and β show the marginal effects of social and provider characteristics on conditional utility from a medical care provision alternative, as shown for example, in Equation (7). Expression (9) can be used to estimate multinomial logit functions as well as the nested multinomial logit functions, the most commonly used formulations in empirical studies on health care decisions. In estimating the behavioral parameters, we assume that each household member faces four distinct health care provision alternatives, namely: the nearest government clinic, G, the nearest mission health facility, M, the nearest private health clinic, P, and a residual self-treatment alternative, S. S includes traditional healers as well as retail shops, where patients often buy drugs when they are not available in modern health facilities, especially in government clinics. An individual or his relative is presumed to pick and choose treatment from these four treatment options. Further, since there is no a priori way of determining the correct decision structure of patients, we assume that health care decisions are not nested. This means that perceived benefits from treatment options are not correlated. This paper explores empirically the household demand for medical care under this simple assumption. The analysis is motivated by a desire to generate information that can be used to inform health service management decisions.

III. Data and Variable Definitions

A. Data

The data for this study are from Meru District, a rural district in Eastern Kenya.[4] The data were collected over a fourteen-month period, between January 1980 and April 1981, using a stratified randomized survey procedure. The survey procedure used to collect the data is described in detail in Mwabu (1986, 1989). Two types of datasets are used: (1) data from a population-based survey on use of

---

4. The Meru data are representative of low-income areas in rural Kenya. Since the data were collected, the boundaries of the district have changed. The survey area covers four present-day districts: Meru; Tharaka-Nithi; Kitui; and parts of Embu.

health services; and (2) data obtained from a survey of health facilities on avail-ability of drugs, types of health personnel, conditions of medical equipment, and fees charged for medical services. These datasets are adequate for the purpose of the paper because they link household and individual characteristics with the attributes of available health facilities. They are comparable to the more recent medical care data collected by the Living Standards Measurement Study of the World Bank in Ghana and Côte d'Ivoire. Descriptions of sample sizes and specific characteristics of the surveyed units follow.

The probability sample consists of 315 households with 1,721 individuals. Mor-bidity data and data on treatment strategies were collected for 479 individuals who reported a recent illness.[5] For each of these individuals, information was obtained for up to four attempts to cure an illness. For example, for an individual who had made five attempts to cure an illness, information was obtained only for the first four such attempts. However, we use information on first visits only for the 251 household members aged 15 and older because the focus of the study is on a one-period analysis of health care demand by the adult population.[6] In addition to illness-related information, data were collected about demographic and socioeconomic characteristics of household members. Information on health facility attributes, such as distance to the nearest health facility of each type, the price of services, and travel time to the nearest facility, was also obtained from providers independently of the information reported by household members.

The dataset for health facilities consists of 15 facilities, of which eight are government health centers or dispensaries, two are mission clinics, and five are private clinics. These included virtually all the modern facilities closest to the households that were surveyed. For each of these facilities, information was collected about availability of drugs, types of medical equipment (and whether or not the equipment was in good working order), types of health personnel, prices charged for outpatient and inpatient services, physical condition of the facility, among many others.[7] The household dataset is linked to the facility data-set to create an enriched database containing information about facility attributes as well as those of individuals.

From the perspective of patients, the facility information in the enriched data-set, such as the charges for medical care, is exogenous. That is, each individual is linked to the characteristics of available services, not the services that were actually used. Thus, the endogeneity problem that arises when this information is collected from respondents is avoided. For an example, see Lavy and Quigley

---

5. All persons ill at the time of the survey were interviewed. For households in which no one was currently ill, the household member most recently ill was interviewed. Among the 251 adults in this study, 80 percent were ill at the time of the survey and 20 percent had been previously ill. Like many other health demand studies, this sample is conditioned on reporting an illness. Unfortunately, informa-tion was not collected on persons who were not ill. Thus, it will not be possible to correct for sample selection bias associated the endogenous reporting of an illness.

6. The 228 remaining individuals were children under the age of 15. Analysis of the impact of quality on provider choice among children is being performed separately.

7. A similar type of dataset was collected from 52 traditional healers but has not been fully incorporated into the present analysis.

(1993) for a detailed exposition and treatment of the endogeneity problem in survey data.

B. Variable Definitions

The dependent and explanatory variables used in the analysis are described in Table 1. There are four *dependent variables* indicating the type of provider selected for the patient's first consultation—government, mission, private, or self-treatment. The self-treatment option includes persons who purchased drugs in the market to treat themselves as well as those who consulted the traditional medical sector. The self-treatment option is the comparison group in this study.

There are three groups of *explanatory variables*. The first group, *access variables*, includes the distance to the nearest facility of each type and the exogenous adult outpatient charge at the nearest facility of each type. The second group includes measures of various aspects of the *quality of services* at the nearest health facility of each type. To construct the access and quality variables, each individual in the sample had to be linked to the nearest facility of each type and to that facility's exogenous quality characteristics. The third group of explanatory variables includes *individual and household characteristics*. Since these characteristics do not vary across providers, they have been interacted with dummy variables for each provider so that they will not drop out of the model. In addition, in several specifications the sex of the household member has been interacted with the distance, user fee, and quality at the nearest facility of each type to assess the differential impact on the demand for health care of these factors according to the gender of the patient.

C. A Priori Expectations on Behavioral Parameters

To facilitate interpretation of the demand effects of empirical values of the coefficients of the variables in Table 1, we discuss in this subsection their expected signs, drawing upon consumer theory and past health care demand studies. We expect that the demand effect of user charges and distance (both of which are "price" variables) is negative. This is the well known, nonpositive own-price effect in the case of non-Giffen goods and services. Past demand studies generally report this negative relationship (see Section II).

The "quality" of care (efficacy of treatment) has multiple attributes (Wouters 1991). The impact of improvement in medical care quality on demand is ambiguous. For example, improvement in medical care quality from the perspective of health practitioners will have no effect on demand if it is not perceived as a quality improvement by patients. On the other hand, if the improvement is perceived as efficacious in dealing with health problems—a "benefit in treatment"—it would increase demand. But to the extent that the improvement reduces population morbidity, its effect would be to reduce medical care demand in the longer run. The observed demand effect of improved medical care quality is thus a *net* effect that depends on which of these two factors is dominant.

Past research has found a positive demand effect of availability of drugs in a health facility (Denton et al. 1990). As the drug variety increases in a health

Table 1
Description of Variables

Dependent variables

$CHOICE\_G$ = 1 if the sick person sought treatment from government health facility; else $CHOICE\_G$ = 0.

$CHOICE\_M$ = 1 if the sick person sought treatment from a mission health facility; else $CHOICE\_M$ = 0.

$CHOICE\_P$ = 1 if the sick person sought treatment from a private clinic; else $CHOICE\_P$ = 0.

$CHOICE\_S$ = 1 if the sick person chose self-treatment; else $CHOICE\_S$ = 0; this option also includes traditional healers and retail shops.

Explanatory variables

Access variables

$USERFEE\_G$ Adult outpatient charges in the nearest government health facility.

$USERFEE\_M$ Adult outpatient charges in the nearest mission health facility.

$USERFEE\_P$ Adult outpatient charges in the nearest private health facility.

$USERFEE\_S$ Adult charges for self-treatment (values have been normalized to zero).

$DISTANCE\_G$ Distance to the nearest government health facility, in miles.

$DISTANCE\_M$ Distance to the nearest mission health facility.

$DISTANCE\_P$ Distance to the nearest private health facility.

$DISTANCE\_S$ Distance to "self-treatment facility" (normalized to zero).

Facility-specific quality variables

$DRUGS\_G$ Number of different types of drugs available in a government health facility. $DRUGS\_M$ and $DRUGS\_P$ are defined similarly.

$NOMALARIALS\_G$ Logarithm of the number of days in the last 180 days that a government health facility did not have anti-malarial drugs; and similarly for $NOMALARIALS\_M$ and $NOMALARIALS\_P$.

Table 1 (*continued*)

Facility-specific quality variables

NOASPIRIN_G Logarithm of the number of days in the last 180 days that a government health facility did not have aspirin drugs; similarly for *NOASPIRIN_M* and *NOASPIRIN_P*.

MEDSTAFF_G Number of health workers in a government health facility; and similarly for *MEDSTAFF_M* and *MEDSTAFF_P*

Individual and household-level variables

EDUCATION*G Education of a household member interacted with a government health facility. *EDUCATION*M* and *EDUCA-TON*P* are defined similarly.

INCOME*G Annual cash income of the household (in natural logarithm) interacted with a government health facility. *IN-COME*M* and *INCOME*P* are defined similarly.

SEX*G Sex of household member interacted with government health facility (male = 1, female = 0). *SEX*M* is sex of the household member interacted with mission facility and *SEX*P* interacted with a private facility.

SEX*DISTANCE_G Sex of household member interacted with distance to a health facility.

SEX*USERFEE_G Sex of household member interacted with outpatient charges at a health facility.

SEX*MEDSTAFF_G Sex of household member interacted with *MEDSTAFF_G* (etc.).

SEX*DRUGS_G Sex of household member interacted with *DRUGS_G* (etc.).

SEX*NOMALAR.'S_G Sex of household member interacted with *NOMALARIALS_G* (etc.).

SEX*NOASPIRIN_G Sex of household member interacted with *NOASPIRIN_G* (etc.).

facility, we expect to find an increase in the utilization of health facilities. This is because as the variety of drugs increases, people can expect to find medicines for their ailments at health facilities. It may, however, also be the case that, over a given period, availability of drugs may contribute to a reduction in morbidity in a community and hence reduce demand for medical services for any given individual in the community because that individual is less likely to contract an illness. The coefficient for drug availability can thus bear a negative or a positive sign. The same applies to the coefficients of other quality-related variables.

No firm expectations can be made on signs of the coefficients of the individual and household level variables. The signs of the income coefficients, for example, may be positive if health care services are perceived by the households to be normal goods. The coefficients would bear negative signs if households consider health services to be inferior goods. The signs of coefficients on education and sex are also ambiguous a priori.

IV. Empirical Results

A. Descriptive Statistics

Among the 251 adult patients in the study, 35.5 percent sought medical care from government health facilities, 5.6 percent from missionary health facilities, 19.5 percent from private clinics, and 39.4 percent self-treated or sought help from the informal health care sector. Table 2 reports the mean characteristics for the 15 facilities in the sample, by type of provider. Patients faced the highest monetary cost of treatment in private clinics—14.2 Kenyan shillings (Ksh).[8] All government facilities were nominally free, while the two mission clinics charged a mean adult outpatient fee of only 2.5 Ksh. Shortages in supplies of antimalarial drugs and antibiotics were most acute in government clinics. Aspirin was in better supply in all three types of facility, but less available in mission facilities than in the other two types. Overall, private providers had the most different types of drugs in stock (10.4); government and mission facilities did not differ much in this measure of quality (8.0 versus 8.5 types in government and mission, respectively). The government facilities were better equipped than mission and private providers in terms of stethoscopes, and less equipped than other facilities in microscopes. Finally, government facilities had many more medical staff—14.4, on average—than did mission or private providers (with 4.0 and 1.4 medical staff, respectively).

Among the 99 persons (39.4 percent of the sample) who selected the "self-treatment" option, many consulted a traditional healer. It was not possible to include traditional healer as a treatment option in this study because of the absence of comparable quality and price variables for the healers and modern facilities. Nevertheless, 52 healers were interviewed in the course of the Meru survey. Almost all of the healers were men (94 percent); they were 59 years old, on

---

8. The exchange rate at the time of the survey (1981) was 10.44 Ksh per dollar; in early 1993, the rate had risen to 50 Ksh per dollar.

Table 2

Mean Prices and Quality Indicators for Three Types of Medical Providers (Standard deviations in parentheses.)

| | Type of Provider | | |
Variable	Government (n = 8)	Mission (n = 2)	Private (n = 5)
USERFEE (for adults)	0.000	2.500	14.200
	(0.0)	(3.536)	(18.130)
NO MALARIA DRUGS	3.828	2.250	0.666
(log of days without)	(0.888)	(3.182)	(1.143)
NO ANTIBIOTICS	3.660	2.250	0.666
(log of days without)	(0.853)	(3.182)	(1.143)
NO ASPIRIN (log of	0.451	1.700	0.139
days without)	(1.277)	(2.405)	(0.310)
DRUGS (types)	8.000	8.500	10.400
	(2.204)	(4.950)	(1.817)
MEDICAL STAFF	14.375	4.000	1.400
(number of staff)	(27.614)	(2.828)	(1.140)

average, and had 29 years of experience as healers. They estimated that they spent an average of 418 Ksh in out-of-pocket cash costs to obtain healer training. The average patient treatment cost per visit (in cash) reported by the healers was 46 Ksh, far more than mean charges even in the private health facilities. In terms of the availability of drugs, 74 percent of the healers had malaria drugs available and 56 percent had traditional medicines. On average, the healers had treated 70 patients over the past three months, of which three could not be treated for lack of medicine. Some 85 percent of the healers refer patients to modern clinics for treatment, when necessary.

Other notable characteristics of the sample include the following. The average age of the patients was about 38 years and they had slightly more than one year of primary education. About two-thirds (68.5 percent) of the adult patients were females. Interestingly, among the sample of 228 children who reported an illness, roughly half were female. There are several possible reasons why female adults were more likely to be in the sample: (a) there may be more women than men in the rural population; (b) women may be more prone to illness (they have obstetrical care needs not relevant to men, for example); and (c) women may be more likely to accompany children to health care, and thus report and seek treatment for their own conditions at the same time. These hypotheses cannot be confirmed with the Meru data. However, another more recent study of health care demand in South Nyanza district, Kenya, found that 54 percent of the adult population was female and that women were more likely to report illness than men (41 percent versus 30 percent, respectively) (Ellis and Mwabu 1991). Conditional on reporting an illness, men and women were equally likely to seek treatment. The patients in our Meru data set lived an average of about six miles from a government facility, ten miles from a mission facility, and eight miles from a private provider. About 96 percent of the sample lived within ten miles of a government health facility, while only 40 percent and 61 percent of the sample lived within ten miles of a mission or private facility, respectively. Statistics on the mean values of all variables at the nearest facilities of each type to the patients are presented in Appendix Table 1.

B. *Maximum Likelihood Estimation Results*

Maximum likelihood estimates of the demand parameters in three specifications of the model are presented in Table 3. The first specification includes individual variables and two "access" or "price" variables—distance to the facility and the adult outpatient fee. The second and third specifications include two different combinations of quality variables. In both, the number of medical staff is introduced as a control for the size of the facility.

In all three specifications, income exerts a strong positive effect on the probability of seeking medical care from a mission or private provider, relative to self-treatment. In addition, patients with more schooling are more likely to consult a government health facility than to self-treat. The sign on the coefficients for user fees and distance is negative as expected in all specifications, but statistically significant in none. Distance is probably the most important "price" factor from the perspective of households, since it is directly related to the magnitude of the out-of-pocket costs and time costs for traveling to a facility to obtain medical care. In the case of government facilities, where user fees were not charged, travel costs are clearly the most important costs facing households. The same may also be true for mission and private providers.

There were many indicators of service quality collected by the Meru survey, including the availability of several different types of specific drugs, the qualification of medical staff, and the availability of equipment, such as microscopes and stethoscopes. Unfortunately, due to the small sample of facilities (15) multicollinearity across characteristics and sometimes perfect correlations between a characteristic and a service type, prevented us from examining the independent impact of each characteristic.

The second specification includes as a measure of quality the number of different drugs available. The positive sign—indicating higher demand when a greater number of drugs is available—is as expected, but not statistically significant. In the third specification, we replace the number of drugs with two variables indicating the logarithm of the number of days in the last six months in which the facility was out of stock. The two drugs selected represent both nonprescription (aspirin) and prescription drugs (antimalarials). Our expectation was that drug scarcities would reduce demand. Thus, the result that the coefficients on aspirin and antimalarials are significant but of opposite sign is unexpected.

A possible explanation for these counterintuitive results lies with the endogeneity of supply side variables affected by demand. The drug variables measure the availability of recurrent, consumable inputs into health. The availability of a drug

Table 3

Empirical Results: Access and Quality Variables, n = 251

	(1)		(2)		(3)	
	β	T	β	T	β	T
Individual variables						
EDUCATION*G	0.124	(1.974)	0.124	(1.955)	0.121	(1.907)
EDUCATION*M	−0.115	(−0.638)	−0.113	(−0.625)	−0.124	(−0.672)
EDUCATION*P	0.0774	(1.008)	0.0790	(1.027)	0.0830	(1.078)
INCOME*G	0.0511	(1.012)	0.0534	(1.052)	0.0699	(1.356)
INCOME*M	0.171	(1.786)	0.173	(1.798)	0.183	(1.886)
INCOME*P	0.167	(2.719)	0.169	(2.748)	0.183	(2.962)
Access variables						
DISTANCE	−0.0334	(−1.248)	−0.0276	(−0.990)	−0.0143	(−0.511)
USER FEE	−0.0357	(−1.457)	−0.0381	(−1.497)	−0.0288	(−1.185)
Quality variables						
MEDICAL STAFF			−0.0115	(−0.346)	−0.0835	(1.425)
DRUGS			0.0293	(0.513)		
NO ASPIRIN					−0.253	(−1.794)
NO MALARIALS					0.385	(2.364)
Intercepts						
Government	−0.199	(−0.763)	−0.344	(−0.560)	−1.088	(−1.435)
Mission	−1.988	(−3.674)	−2.217	(−3.075)	−2.061	(−3.431)
Private	−0.752	(−1.934)	−1.063	(−1.548)	−0.0873	(−0.117)
Log likelihood	−294.6		−294.3		−291.2	
χ^2 (r)	106.8		107.4		113.5	

on a particular day is thus indicative of the interaction of *both* supply and demand factors: if a drug is available there is excess supply, while if not available there was possibly excess demand. Thus, if a certain drug (like antimalarials) is out of supply, it might be due to very high demand. This would produce a correlation between the lack of a drug and higher demand. Drugs for which there is ample supply due to low demand would show the same effect. Because of the possible endogeneity of the availability of specific drugs, the signs might then be the *reverse* of our expectations for exogenous measures of quality that are less likely to be affected by demand, such as the availability of equipment or personnel.

This explanation seems plausible for the results on aspirin and antimalarial medicine. Demand is lower for facilities that don't have aspirin. However, aspirin is easily obtained in the market place. If a patient suspected that he/she needed aspirin, there would be no reason to go to a health facility. The negative coefficient on *NO ASPIRIN* might well be measuring this latter effect, rather than a perception by patients that a facility without aspirin is of lower quality. Antimalarials can also be bought on the market, but not of sufficient dosage to counter a major malaria attack. Obtaining treatment for a major bout of malaria would require going to a health facility. If malaria is common, as it is in Meru district, then this would lead to a very high demand for health services, and possibly shortages of antimalarials in the most popular health facilities. Thus, because of supply-demand interactions, the significant *positive* coefficient on lack of antimalarials may be evidence that they are in greater demand in health facilities than is aspirin, with a negative sign.

C. Gender and the Choice of Treatment

An important issue of policy relevance is whether service access and quality characteristics affect women more than men in seeking medical care. Table 4 presents results for the three specifications in Table 3 with the addition of interactions between gender and the access and quality variables.

The signs on the coefficients on distance and user fees indicate that both factors reduce the demand for health care, but that men are less constrained by distance and user fees than are women. With only one exception, none of the gender interaction terms are individually significant, and in none of the three models are gender terms jointly significant. The exception is the coefficient on the interaction of gender and the days with no antimalarial drugs. The absence of antimalarials is associated with higher demand (probably for reasons due to endogeneity) and if the patient is male the demand for facilities without antimalarials is even higher. None of the gender interactions with the type of facility achieve statistical significance. However, the signs on the intercepts indicate that, controlling for all other factors, women are more likely to consult all three types of provider of modern care compared to self-treatment than are men.[9]

D. Elasticities of Demand

Table 5 compares the own-price elasticities of medical care demand at government, mission, and private health facilities—that is, the sensitivity of demand for each type of facility to a change in the facility's own prices. The elasticity of medical care demand with respect to own user charges is smallest for government health facilities. A 10 percent increase in user charges in government health facilities would, for instance, reduce demand for medical care there by only 1.0 percent. In contrast, medical care demand in mission and private clinics is quite price elastic. A 10 percent increase in own user charges, for example, would reduce demand by about 15.7 percent in mission facilities, and by about 19.4 percent in private clinics. The demand elasticity with respect to own distance is also substantially lower for government health facilities.

Table 5 further shows that the probability of a visit to a government health facility is most sensitive to measures that reflect broad availability of drugs. A 1 percent increase in the number of drugs in government health facilities would increase medical care demand at government health facilities by 0.118 percent and demand in other facilities by 0.137 percent.[10] The cross-demand effects are

---

9. In other specifications (not shown), gender was interacted with education and income. However, in none of these specifications were the gender interactions individually or jointly significant.

10. Recall that the cross-price elasticities with respect to facility characteristics are confined to be the same across alternatives by the model's assumptions.

Table 4

Gender Effects (n = 251)

	(1)		(2)		(3)	
	β	T	β	T	β	T
Individual variables						
EDUCATION * G	0.138	(2.086)	0.135	(2.029)	0.134	(2.006)
EDUCATION * M	−0.124	(−0.663)	−0.122	(−0.652)	−0.154	(−0.803)
EDUCATION * P	0.0792	(0.991)	0.079	(0.988)	0.085	(1.054)
INCOME * G	0.0513	(1.012)	0.054	(1.048)	0.076	(1.452)
INCOME * M	0.170	(1.770)	0.169	(1.764)	0.184	(1.873)
INCOME * P	0.167	(2.716)	0.164	(2.679)	0.181	(2.908)
SEX * G	−0.639	(−1.379)	−0.400	(−0.360)	−1.025	(−0.501)
SEX * M	−0.794	(−0.915)	−0.173	(−0.139)	0.090	(0.084)
SEX * P	−0.885	(−1.235)	0.038	(0.029)	3.640	(1.279)
Access variables						
DISTANCE	−0.0597	(−1.807)	−0.050	(−1.480)	−0.042	(−1.229)
SEX * DISTANCE	0.0730	(1.297)	0.050	(0.838)	0.072	(1.191)
USER FEE	−0.040	(−1.477)	−0.050	(−1.522)	−0.043	(−1.379)
SEX * USER FEE	0.0302	(0.599)	0.036	(0.699)	0.071	(1.362)
Quality Variables						
MEDICAL STAFF			−0.026	(−0.668)	0.044	(0.661)
SEX * MEDICAL STAFF			0.058	(0.770)	0.202	(1.252)
DRUGS			0.058	(0.839)		
SEX * DRUGS			−0.086	(−0.704)		
NO ASPIRIN					−0.239	(−1.438)
SEX * NO ASPIRIN					−0.113	(−0.301)
NO MALARIALS					0.218	(1.170)
SEX * NO MALARIALS					1.099	(1.910)
Intercepts						
Government	0.0186	(0.062)	−0.221	(−0.303)	−0.737	(−0.871)
Mission	−1.694	(−2.843)	−2.108	(−2.561)	−1.898	(−2.793)
Private	−0.457	(−1.034)	−1.042	(−1.301)	−0.437	(0.536)
Log likelihood	−293.24		−292.09		−285.97	
χ² (r)	109.4		111.73		123.98	
Joint tests χ² (r)						
DISTANCE, SEX * DISTANCE	2.320	(p = .314)	2.191	(p = .334)	1.911	(p = .384)
FEE, SEX * FEE	3.373	(p = .185)	2.411	(p = .300)	2.367	(p = .306)
MEDICAL STAFF, SEX * MEDICAL STAFF			0.689	(p = .708)	3.021	(p = .221)
DRUGS, SEX * DRUGS			0.784	(p = .676)		
NO ASPIRIN, SEX * NO ASPIRIN					2.716	(p = .257)
NO MALARIALS, SEX * NO MALARIALS					6.168	(p = .046)
All gender interactions	2.618	(p = .759)	4.301	(p = .745)	8.917	(p = .414)

Table 5
Own and Cross-Elasticities of Demand

With respect to	Elasticity of demand*		
	Government	Mission	Private
Government fee	−0.100**	0.023	0.023
Own fee	−0.100	−1.571	−1.937
Distance to government facility	−0.079	0.090	0.090
Distance to own facility	−0.079	−0.300	−0.204
Number of drugs in government facility	0.118	−0.137	−0.137
Income	−.0063	0.293	0.319

* The income elasticity of demand for self treatment is −0.177.
** The own-price elasticity of demand for government services was computed at Ksh 5, which is the midpoint of the before and after prices (Ksh 0 and Ksh 10) of the previous table.

also strongest for drugs. Income elasticities are strongest for nongovernment health facilities. A 10 percent increase in household incomes would lead to a 3 percent increase in medical care demand in mission and private clinics. In contrast, the same percentage rise in incomes would reduce demand for self-care, and for government health services by relatively small percentages of about 1.8 and 0.06 respectively.

V. Simulation Results

We use a version of model 2 (Table 3), to simulate the ceteris paribus effects of various public policies on medical care demand in government and nongovernment health care facilities in rural Kenya. We examine system-wide effects of the following policies:

(1) increasing user charges in government health facilities from Ksh 0.0 to Ksh 10.00 (in other words, from US $0.0 to US $0.20 at the current exchange rate);[11]

(2) reducing mean distance to government health facilities by 20 percent (from 6.4 to 5.3 km);

(3) increasing the number of types of drugs in government health facilities by two;

11. Note, however, that because of inflation a Ksh 10 user fee applied at the time of the survey (1980–81) would now be approximately equivalent to Ksh 25.

(4) increasing household incomes by 20 percent;

(5) simultaneously implementing policies 1, 2, and 3.

Except for the fourth policy measure, raising household incomes by 20 percent, all of the others are achievable in the short-run. Between April and September 1992, for example, the government reintroduced user charges for outpatient services in government hospitals, ranging from Ksh 20.00 to 50.00 (US $0.40 to $1.00). In early 1993 the government plans to introduce user charges for outpatient care of about Ksh 10.00 (US $0.20) in rural hospitals and health centers, the types of facilities for which the results of the current study are most relevant. The simulation results we present are therefore timely, given the expressed need of the policymakers to know probable demand effects of current and planned health care financing reforms.

Table 6 shows new selection probabilities and changes in base probabilities consequent upon implementation of each of the policy measures. The sample proportions are the proportion of the sample that actually selected each treatment option. The base probabilities are the proportion of the sample *predicted* to select each treatment option. Our model has not been able to predict perfectly the selection of each option, so the sample proportions and base probabilities differ. In particular, our model overpredicts selection of government facilities and underpredicts the use of other sources of care, including self-treatment. Reading across the rows for the first policy simulated, raising user charges in government health facilities from zero to Ksh 10.00 reduces the selection probability for government health facilities from .536 to .438 or by .097. That is, the share of persons selecting government facilities would decline, from 53.6 percent of all patients to 43.8 percent, an absolute decline of 9.7 percentage points. Other things equal, this means that these modest user fees lower demand in government health facilities in a relative sense by about 18 percent. Simultaneously, health care demand in each nongovernment health facility (including the self-treatment option) increases relatively by about 20 percent. The constancy of the proportional cross-price effects in Table 6 arises from "the independence of irrelevant alternatives" restriction in the computation of selection probabilities.

As can be seen from Table 6, user charges in public clinics have two important functions in a pluralistic health care system. The first is to divert demand for modern medical care from government health facilities to nongovernment facilities (missionary and private clinics here). The second is to reduce demand for modern medical care altogether, by forcing a section of those who previously used government health facilities to rely on the informal medical care, such as traditional medicine and home remedies. It is the "demand reduction effect" of user fees, rather than the "demand diversion effect," that is the source of much concern about user fees in low-income countries. The best way to see this, is first to convert the absolute drop in the selection probability for government health facilities into the number of people who would likely stop using government health services after the increase in user charges, and then to determine how many people can be expected to drop off from the modern health care system altogether. Before the change in policy, assume that 1,000 people were sick, of which 536 were using government services, 40 were using missionary health ser-

Table 6
Policy Simulations

	Probability of selecting . . .			
	Government	Mission	Private	Self
Sample proportions	0.355	0.056	0.195	0.394
Base probability	0.536	0.040	0.135	0.290
Policy				
1) Increase in user fees in government facilities from 0–10 Ksh				
New probability of selecting . . .	0.438	0.048	0.163	0.351
Absolute change	-0.097	0.008	0.028	0.061
Relative change	-18.2%	20.9%	20.9%	20.9%
2) Reduce distance to government facilities by 20 percent				
New probability of selecting . . .	0.544	0.039	0.132	0.285
Absolute change	0.009	-0.001	-0.003	-0.005
Relative change	1.6%	-1.8%	-1.8%	-1.8%
3) Increase the number of drugs in government facilities by two				
New probability of selecting . . .	0.555	0.038	0.129	0.278
Absolute change	0.019	-0.002	-0.006	-0.012
Relative change	3.6%	-4.1%	-4.1%	-4.1%
4) Increase income by 20 percent				
New probability of selecting	0.535	0.042	0.143	0.280
Absolute change	-0.001	0.002	0.009	-0.010
Relative change	0.1%	5.9%	6.4%	-3.5%
5) Combination of policies 1, 2, and 3 above				
New probability of selecting . . .	0.466	0.048	0.165	0.321
Absolute change	-0.070	0.009	0.030	0.031
Relative change	-13.1%	21.7%	22.3%	10.8%

vices, 135 were using private care, and 290 did not seek modern treatment. As a result of the increase in user fees, about 97 people can be expected to abandon government health services after the fee increase. Further, eight of those leaving government facilities would seek treatment from missionary health facilities, 28 would shift to private clinics, and 61 people would self-treat. In this case 61 people (not 97) drop out from the modern health care system following the introduction of user fees. This discussion shows that the negative demand effect of user charges is overstated when diversion effects are not considered. Similarly, the positive consequence of user charges (in terms of revenue generation) is exaggerated when "demand reduction effects" are ignored.

The demand effects of the other policies in Table 6 are similar to those of the user fees. A reduction in distance to government health facilities increases the rate at which these facilities are utilized. Specifically, a 20 percent reduction in distance to government facilities increases the absolute selection probability for these facilities by about one percentage point, for a relative increase of 1.6 percent. In a community of 1,000 sick people, this implies that nine additional people would seek medical care from government health facilities. As can be seen from Table 6, four of the new users would be drawn from nongovernmental health facilities (due to the "demand diversion effect" of improved access to medical care in government clinics) while the other five would come from the informal health care system (due to the "demand creation effect" of the new policy). Notice that the demand creation effect is much stronger than the demand diversion effect. This is also observed with regard to policy 3. However, in the case of the composite policy in the last row, the demand reduction effect of policy 1 outweighs the demand creation effects of policies 2 and 3, so that the net effect is to increase the number of people outside the formal medical care system. Policy 1 makes it possible to pursue the other policies by enhancing the financial capacity of the government, however.

VI. Summary and Conclusion

This paper has empirically examined the effect of the quality of medical care on utilization of medical facilities in rural Kenya. We find that shortages in particular types of drugs may be either negatively or positively related to medical care demand. This is perhaps because shortages of these consumable inputs occur whenever demand is high relative to stocks. The general availability of drugs is positively related to demand, but the lack of significance of this result is likely related to the conflicting relation between availability of specific drugs and demand. Growth in income shifts demand from the informal health care sector to the modern sector, with much of this demand ending up in private and mission clinics. Although not significant in most specifications, access factors (user fees and distance) consistently reduce demand. The elasticity of medical care demand with respect to user fees and distance is greater in mission and private clinics than in government health facilities. In spite of the very low elasticity of demand, modest charges of Ksh 10.00 lead to a relatively large (18.0 percent) decline in demand in government facilities. The absolute decline in utilization, from 54 to 44 percent, is not as severe, particularly when only 6 percentage points of those dropping out will self-treat.

No significant differences in the demand for health care was found by gender, although the signs on the coefficients indicated that women may be more disadvantaged by distance and user fees than men. Additional research is warranted on this issue, however. The sample size for this study was small. Further, due to data limitations, we were unable to examine why women seem more likely to report an illness, and what role access and quality of services may play in illness reporting.

The results for quality variables reflecting drug scarcity show that they are significant determinants of demand. However, these variables as commonly measured are also subject to endogeneity, since drug availability reflects both the supply and demand for drugs. Demand may deplete supplies of these recurrent inputs. Researchers will have great difficulty measuring the potential demand effects of quality improvements of this nature using nonexperimental cross-sectional data because of the endogeneity issues noted above. Measuring the impact of service quality may require an experimental design, in which the inputs are exogenously varied by the researchers.

There are two definite policy implications of our findings. First, reducing the distance to government health facilities will likely raise demand, as will increasing the number of drugs available. Second, our results indicate unambiguously that private and mission health providers are important sources of medical care for high-income households in rural Kenya. This implies that improvements in public health facilities would benefit the poor proportionately more than the rich, since the rich have a greater propensity to seek private medical care. Thus, as income grows over time, increasingly Kenyans will seek medical attention from the private sector. However, given the small estimated demand effects of income in this rural area, very large increases in income are needed to substantially shift demand from the public and informal health care facilities to the private sector. Significant shifts in demand to private care are therefore only likely in the long run. In the short run, most Kenyans can be expected to seek medical treatment from the public and informal health facilities. Thus, even as the government creates incentives for long term growth of the private health care sector, it must also strengthen public health institutions to enable them to meet health care needs of the majority of the population in the short run.

Appendix Table 1

Descriptive Statistics: Sample Means (n = 251)

CHOICES	CHOICE-G	CHOICE-M	CHOICE-P	CHOICE-S
Sample Proportions	.3546	.0558	.1952	.3944
INCOME*G	2.8469	.0000	.0000	.0000
INCOME*M	.0000	2.8469	.0000	.0000
INCOME*P	.0000	.0000	2.8469	.0000
EDUCATION*G	1.3267	.0000	.0000	.0000
EDUCATION*M	.0000	1.3267	.0000	.0000
EDUCATION*P	.0000	.0000	1.3267	.0000
USERFEE	.0000	1.4542	8.7888	.0000
DISTANCE	5.9761	10.4701	8.0040	.0000
MEDSTAFF	7.9442	3.1633	1.0637	.0000
NOMALARIALS	3.8279	3.1911	.4204	5.1930
NOASPIRIN	1.3523	2.4120	.3783	3.6109
DRUGS (TYPES)	6.5737	7.0359	9.9044	.0000
SEX*G	.3147	.0000	.0000	.0000
SEX*M	.0000	.3147	.0000	.0000
SEX*P	.0000	.0000	.3147	.0000
SEX*DISTANCE	1.6414	3.3068	2.4980	.0000
SEX*USERFEE	.0000	.4382	2.6215	.0000
SEX*MEDSTAFF	2.3386	.9801	.3267	.3147
SEX*DRUGS	2.1394	2.1873	3.1116	.3147
SEX*NOASPIRIN	.3309	.7724	.1215	1.1365
SEX*NOMALARIALS	1.2387	1.0219	.1320	1.6344

IV   Education

9 Daughters, Education, and Family Budgets
Taiwan Experiences

William L. Parish
Robert J. Willis

William L. Parish is a professor of sociology and Robert J. Willis is a professor of education and public policy at the University of Chicago. Both are researchers at NORC. This research benefitted enormously by collaboration with Professors Ching-hsi Chang and Ying-chuan Liu, Economics Department, National Taiwan University, and Ching-lung Tsay, Economics Institute, Academia Sinica, Taipei. Woody Carter, NORC, Chicago, provided skillful survey guidance. In Chicago, Suk Chung Han, Ling-xin Hao, Alfred Ke-wei Hu, Nidhi Mehrotra, and Fang-lu Wang provided careful data analysis. The authors are also grateful to Angus Deaton, Claudia Goldin, Susan Greenhalgh, and an anonymous referee for extensive comments on earlier versions of this chapter. Funding was from NICHD, R01 HD23322-01; the National Science Council, Republic of China; the Chiang Ching Kuo Foundation, Taipei; and the Social Statistics Office, Ministry of Interior, Republic of China. Errors in this report remain the responsibility of its two authors. This paper was written for the Conference on Women's Human Capital and Development, Bellagio, Italy, May 18–22, 1992.

I. Hypotheses

Growth in the education of the labor force is commonly identified as one of the most important determinants of economic growth, and the distribution of education by sex is frequently argued to be a key determinant of gender inequality. In this paper, we examine how parents choose to invest in their children's education and, in particular, how they choose to invest in sons' versus daughters' education and the consequences of these choices for women's life chances. When these choices are made in societies that were historically patriar-

239

chal and where world market penetration has been rapid, there are several theses pointing in different directions. In this paper, we explore these questions using retrospective data on the life cycle and family behavior of Taiwanese individuals who came of age from the 1940s onward. Since the lives of these cohorts encompass one of the most rapid economic and demographic transitions in history, evidence from their experience may be of particular value in sorting out alternative hypotheses.

A. Altruism

Becker (1974, 1981) and other economists have developed theories of family behavior based on the assumption that parents are altruistic in the sense that they care about the welfare of their children in addition to caring about their own consumption. It should be emphasized that the altruism hypothesis does not require that parents care equally about all children. In particular, it is compatible with greater concern for the welfare of sons than of daughters.

Assuming perfect credit, insurance, and annuity markets, decisions by altruistic parents concerning investment in their children can be broken into two stages: (1) investments in each child are made efficiently (in other words, so as to maximize the expected wealth of the entire family) and (2) the family's (maximized) wealth is distributed among family members in a manner reflecting the parents' relative altruism toward each member (Becker and Tomes 1976). For example, if parents are more altruistic toward sons than daughters, total transfers (in other words, human capital plus money) to sons will be larger. Efficiency implies that marginal rates of return to investments are equalized across family members. Equalization of rates of return leads to equalization of the educational investment received by different children within the family only if the productivity of investment is the same for all children. Thus, altruistic parents will invest more heavily in the education of their "brighter" children and may seek to equalize the welfare of their children by making compensatory monetary transfers to their "slower" children.

Viewed from the perspective of the efficiency aspects of this theory, the fact that girls received far less education than boys in Taiwan during the 1940s and 1950s suggests that the returns to educating females were smaller in the predominantly agrarian economy of the period. Similarly, the relative and absolute growth of female educational attainment in the following 40 years suggests that the rapid growth of the Taiwanese economy led to a shift in the pattern of labor demand toward more skill-intensive occupations in which males had a smaller comparative advantage. In response to increased skill requirements in the labor market, altruistic parents increase investments in the human capital of children of both sexes to the point at which the present value of each child's lifetime earnings is maximized. Without further adjustments, pursuit of this policy would impose a considerable sacrifice on parents who must finance the increased investments. The theory suggests that parents will tend to reduce fertility in response to higher costs per child and, at the same time, partially offset the increased costs of children's human capital by reducing monetary bequests and transfers to children or seeking increased old age transfers from them (Willis 1982). The rapid decline of Taiwanese fertility since the late 1960s together with the persistence of coresidence between elderly parents and their children and the pattern of intergenerational transfers within families are broadly consistent with this theory.[1]

B. Lingering Patriarchy

There is an alternative literature that suggests a much more selfish, quid pro quo approach by parents. In this literature patriarchal traditions and the growth of market forces provide a deadly combination that often worsens women's economic and social position (Boserup 1970, Nash and Fernandez-Kelley 1983, Hartmann 1976). In the initial stages of economic development at least, males often capture the newer, higher-paid jobs while women remain behind in agriculture and urban informal jobs. Continuing high fertility often exacerbates the process by confining women to the home in the critical early career years where men begin to leap ahead. Poorer long-term job prospects then reduce incentives for women to get educated, thereby starting a vicious cycle of employers not hiring women because of poor education and parents not wanting to educate women because of poor prospects, all of which is difficult to break.

The process may be particularly pervasive in East Asia, some suggest (Greenhalgh 1985, Tang 1981, Salaff 1981, Brinton 1988). Even while female work and education expands rapidly, parents continue to control their daughters', and to a lesser extent sons', education and early work, diverting women into types of training and early work experiences that fail to evolve into long-term, high-paid careers. In the most cynical interpretations, parents give daughters an education only because parents subconsciously realize they can now reap a quick return on their investment as educated daughters continue to remit wages from well-paid jobs.

This much is very similar to the altruism account above. What is added is the suggestion that this occurs on a rigid quid pro quo basis that demands daughters go into jobs that have quick returns. Daughters must more than repay their investment before marriage, and hence are not allowed to experiment with the variety of early jobs that would build a strong foundation for later advancement (Greenhalgh 1985). The exploitation of daughters for family advantage is particularly strong when there are more sons in the family needing education in order to have the well-paid jobs that will allow them to support the parents well in old age. Older daughters suffer the most, being forced to quit school, go to work, and delay their marriages in order to support younger brothers through school (Salaff 1985). Conversely, one of the best things that can happen to a male, besides being born to rich, well-educated parents, is to have an older sister (Tang 1981).

1. The proportion of Taiwanese elderly living with children remained roughly constant at 80 percent *t* until the mid-1980s, after which it fell until reaching 65 percent in 1989 (Chen 1992). The recent fall may result both from the declining availability of children (especially sons) stemming from the earlier fertility decline and from increased health and affluence of elderly parents. Lee, Parish, and Willis (1992) find that integenerational transfers in Taiwan are predominantly in an upward direction, from children to the elderly. The magnitude of these transfers are directly related to the income of the children, inversely related to the income of the parents and directly related to the number of children, especially sons.

C. Resource Dilution

A third perspective suggests that regardless of altruism, parents' goals are often smothered by lack of resources and any child's education is heavily shaped by the nature of siblings who must share these resources (Blau and Duncan 1967, Leibowitz 1974, Blake 1989, Steelman and Powell 1989, 1991. For controversies, see Technical Appendix). Large numbers of brothers and sisters dilute family resources, leading to lower education for all children. Although there is considerable noise in observed patterns, middle siblings—or, more precisely, second, third, and fourth siblings—do the worst. Reaching working ages when family resources are stretched by so many children at home, they are forced out of school and into the work force. Later-born children who reach higher school ages when more older sisters have already left for work or marriage do much better in school (Blake 1989). Thus, due to family budget constraints, number of siblings and birth order may influence a child's educational opportunity even in the seeming absence of much self-interested manipulation by parents.[2]

D. Credit Constraints and Conditional Altruism

It is important to distinguish the adverse effects of sibship size which operate via resource dilution—or quality-quantity tradeoffs, using the terminology of economists—from the effects of birth order on the investment received by a given child. One possible explanation for birth order effects, holding sibship size constant, arises because family investment decisions may be credit-constrained. For example, suppose that the first child of five is sufficiently bright to make it optimal, based on a rate-of-return criterion, to send him to college. However, because the parents are at an early stage of their own careers and there are many mouths to feed, they may need to borrow to finance the first child's college education. Since human capital (in the form of the future earnings of the parents and of the child) is poor collateral, it may not be possible to borrow and the first child may not go to college. In contrast, it may be possible to finance the college education of an equally bright fifth child because his older siblings have left the home, the parents have had time to accumulate savings, and their current earnings are higher.

More broadly, the inability of individuals to borrow against their future income and the resulting crucial role for parental finance of investment in education is one of the main reasons that educational decisions are so heavily influenced by the interests of the family, as distinct from the interests of the child in whom the investment is embodied. Even if parents are altruistic, their interests and the child's interests tend to coincide fully only if the net transfers the parent wishes to make to the child exceeds the optimal educational investment in the child. In this case, parents will wish to make a monetary transfer to the child (for example,

---

2. Some lingering patriarchy accounts include the effects of resource constraints and sibling position (for example, Greenhalgh 1985, pp. 278, 282–84). Our account differs in emphasizing how these conditions are universal across cultures and, thus, require no appeal to special East Asian traditions of patriarchal manipulation.

a bequest or inter-vivos gifts) in addition to financing the child's education. However, the optimal investment may exceed the desired net transfer because the parent is poor, insufficiently altruistic, or the optimal investment is very large. In this case, the parents may be willing to finance the excess cost of the optimal level of schooling as an (implicit or explicit) loan, but only if they have reasonable assurance that the child will repay the loan. Otherwise investment in the child's schooling will fall short of the optimal level.

Obviously, this analysis provides a rationale for gender discrimination by parents in educational investments in their children that is highly compatible with Greenhalgh's hypothesis that was discussed earlier. That is, given the assumption that sons retain loyalty to their family of origin throughout their lives while daughters leave the family of origin upon marriage, daughters present a larger default risk than sons and should receive either less education or, alternatively, should invest in types of education with a quick pay-off so that they may repay implicit loans before marriage. However, by an emphasis on the credit-constraint origin of gender discrimination, we provide a less static image of gender investment patterns that includes several additional testable hypotheses. In particular, this emphasis suggests that factors increasing the parents' desire to make net monetary transfers to their children (in other words, factors that increase the total transfer to a child or reduce optimal educational expenditures on him or her) will tend to reduce gender differences in educational attainment within a given sibset. For example, we would expect that gender differentials would be smaller the higher the parents' income, the smaller the size of the sibset, and the greater the degree of public funding of education. In addition, growth of publicly funded pensions that reduce the parents' need for old age saving should increase the size of net transfers to children and thus reduce gender differentials in educational investment.

As our discussion illustrates, whether family behavior is motivated at the margin by altruism or by quid pro quo exchange is conditional upon the particular circumstances of the family. Given the rapidity of change in Taiwan, it is important to be alert to the implications of changing circumstances for the way in which parents realize their preferences. For example, even during the very first part of this century when Taiwanese daughters died more frequently than sons, it may be that parents always wanted to do well by their daughters. When confronted by scarce resources, however, they were forced to favor sons, who provided the family's long-term security. With increasing prosperity, fewer of those tough choices are necessary.

Although all these models of family practice overlap somewhat, they present three broad contrasting emphases: (a) conditional altruism, which emphasizes with greater prosperity and more old age security a change toward greater resource flows to children and potentially greater equality in these flows; (b) a closely related literature on current budget constraints, which suggests that the oldest children in large families are squeezed out of school into the work force in order to support younger siblings; and (c) lingering patriarchy, which suggests that cultural traditions favoring male descent continue to cause parents to manipulate their daughters for the benefit of their sons and themselves.

II. Previous Empirical Work

A. Non-Western Societies

To some extent, despite rapid development and a move into cities and mostly nonagricultural employment, one might expect family investment patterns in Taiwan to continue to approximate those in other patrilineal societies at lower levels of development. Although family size had shrunk dramatically by the 1980s, government and private pension programs were available to only a very small minority. The vast majority of old people continued to reside with a son, to rely mostly on sons for old age support, and to bequeath any available property to sons instead of daughters. Many adult daughters sent modest amounts of financial support to parents, but daughters usually provided major financial support only when there was no son (see Lee, Parish, and Willis 1992). Thus, in a policy environment providing few public welfare benefits, reliance on the male-based extended family remained strong.

In these kinds of environments in other societies, a large number of children in the family can lead not to universal resource dilution but to improved opportunities for the late born. Once they begin to work, early born children continue to send or bring resources back to the family. Thus, instead of the usual negative relationship between sibsize and education, one can find a positive or neutral relationship (Caldwell 1976, Mueller 1975), though Lillard and Willis (1993) find evidence of negative effects of number of siblings of one's own sex in Malaysia. In the Taiwan context, Hermalin et al. (1982) report a positive relationship among some subgroups of Taiwan women in earlier decades. These types of findings suggest that when family obligations are strong, credit-constraints help produce large inter-temporal transfers among siblings.

A less happy result of some of these environments can also be that daughters become the siblings from whom resources are drained. Illustrations of the problem include the higher death and malnutrition rates for women in South Asia (Chen et al. 1981, Levine 1987) and higher death rates for young women in Taiwan during the first half of this century (Barclay 1954, Zimmerman 1984).

B. Western Societies

Some of the resource use patterns among siblings may be quite general, depending not on extraordinary extended family obligations and patrilineal preferences but on credit constraints common to midlife-course families in many settings. For example, evidence from sibling studies surveyed by Griliches (1979) provide some hints that family investments in education tend to attenuate differences in innate ability among children by compensating to some extent for handicaps of less able children, a finding which is consistent with behavior predicted by the Becker-Tomes (1976) model when parents are credit-constrained. Despite many contradictory findings, linked in part to sampling and method issues, some more recent studies suggest resource dilution and credit constraint patterns among Western families (see the Technical Appendix for controversies). In large, general samples using sibling data, while early and late-born American children get considerable education, the early-middle born (siblings 2–3–4) do more poorly. They compete for family resources at a time when many siblings remain at home competing for a piece of the still-modest family income pie (Blake 1989, Steelman and Powell 1991, Blau and Duncan 1967). In this competition, daughters lose more education than sons (Powell and Steelman 1989, Blake 1989, figure 5.21). Investment in daughters is discretionary (Leibowitz 1974). Other findings from 19th Century Philadelphia suggest that sibling order effects for early market work were much as today, and that, as suggested in popular magazines, ". . . a girl was exepcted to work 'to relieve her hard-working father of the burden of her support, to supply [her] home with comforts and refinements, [and] to educate a younger brother' " (Goldin 1979, p. 127). Similar expectations extended well into the twentieth century according to oral histories of immigrant working class families in Pennsylvania (Bodnar 1982). All these patterns suggest more commonality in family behavior than might be expected from theories that emphasize the strong role of extreme patriarchal values.

III. Data

Our analysis uses data from the 1989 Taiwan Women and Family Survey, an island-wide probability survey of women age 25–60 years of age from all marital statuses and all walks of life.[3] These female respondents provide information on three subgroups: (a) themselves, both for a cross-sectional and person-year analysis, (b) all brothers and sisters of the respondent, including herself, and (c) respondent's children who are in the critical 15–32 age range when the question of how rapidly they leave school, work, and marry are paramount. Averages for the respondent and her children by decade illustrate variables use throughout the analysis (Table 1, also see Appendix Tables A, B). The respondent and children's data are not completely comparable. Respondents from large families are necessarily over-represented, thus inflating averages for sibsize, birth order, older brothers, etc. while at the same time deflating education and occupation (see Preston 1976a). The children's data are free of these distortions, and hence will show higher education, smaller sibsizes, etc. Nevertheless, the two sets of data still give some impression of trends in the larger population.

We seek to explain years of education, work, marriage, and marriage finance. Education is measured in years of education, ranging from a low of 0 for no education to 18 for graduate school. Education has risen rapidly over the last five decades in Taiwan, from a time in the 1940s when many females didn't even make it to the sixth grade to today when twelve years of education is rapidly becoming the norm for everyone (Row 1). The trend continues from the respondent's generation on into her children's generation, and for her younger children in the last column (who have not yet finished school) the levels will eventually

3. This survey was designed by the authors and collected in a collaborative project between NORC and National Taiwan University with support from NICHD, the National Science Council, Republic of China, and the Chiang Ching Kuo Foundation.

Table 1
Characteristics by Decade[a]

	Respondent				Children		Row Number
	1940–49	1950–59	1960–69	1970–75	1970–79	1980–85	
Education, years							
Females	3.8	5.5	8.6	10.4	11.0	10.9	(1)
Males[b]	6.0	7.8	9.7	11.1	11.4	11.1	(2)
Transitions (median age)							
Last schooling[c]	11	12	13	18			(3)
First job	15	15	17	19			(4)
Marriage	21	22	23	23			(5)
Marriage Finance							
Brideprice received (%)	54	60	54	48			(6)
Dowry given (%)	41	53	56	57			(7)
Excess brideprice (log)	2.17	1.06	.05	–.86			(8)
Sibling Characteristics							
Total							
Sibsize	5.9	6.2	5.7	5.2	4.0	3.5	(9)
Birth order	3.0	3.3	3.2	3.3	2.4	2.0	(10)

Gender/age specific:						
Older						
Sisters	1.0	1.1	1.1	1.2	.5	(11)
Brothers	1.0	1.1	1.1	1.1	.5	(12)
Younger						
Sisters	1.4	1.5	1.2	.9	.8	(13)
Brothers	1.4	1.5	1.3	1.0	.7	(14)
Parent status						
Mother's education	0.9	1.3	2.2	3.0	5.8	(15)
Father's						
Education	3.0	3.5	4.5	5.6	8.0	(16)
Occupation	2.7	3.1	3.7	4.4	5.1	(17)
Income	1.6	1.6	1.7	1.9	—	(18)
Individual background						
Urban[d]	.36	.36	.51	.61	.61	(19)
Maximum *n*	547	907	1,608	741	2,153	(20)

a. Means unless otherwise noted. Decade = year respondent reached age 12.

b. Males = respondent's brothers, sons.

c. Last schooling = age of schooling before break of three or more years.

d. Urban = when respondent age 15, child age 12.

be even higher.[4] Besides the rapid rise in education for both males and females, there was a rapid narrowing of the gap between male and female education (Rows 1 and 2). Indeed, in society-wide statistics, female years of education had caught up with male education by the last half of the 1980s.

For the respondent, increasing education was accompanied by changes in other life events. In rising, school leaving ages also began to delay the time one could take a full-time job and to help delay marriage (Rows 3–5). Although not fully obvious here, an increasing number of women began to work before marriage. Even in the earliest decade, half of all women were working by age fifteen—often with little or no pay—on the family farm or in the family store. Increasingly, in later decades, they began to move into paid work outside the home (Thornton et. al. 1984). The issue we must deal with is how parents and daughters related to these new income-earning opportunities.

The nature of marriage finance also changed. The brideprice includes cash and other items given by the groom's family to the bride's family. The dowry includes furniture, bedding, clothing, and other items brought with the bride to help endow the new couple. Over time dowry increased in frequency while brideprice decreased (Rows 6,7), and partly reflecting this change the inflation adjusted value of dowry began to exceed brideprice (Row 8). With a surplus of demobilized military men bidding up brideprices, it was initially more expensive to marry off sons. But as more and more working women bid up dowries, it eventually became more expensive to marry off daughters. While being sensitive to these trends, we will emphasize how sibling structure shapes marriage finance. Is it extra brothers (lingering patriarchy) or more sisters as well as brothers (credit constraint) that make a bride demand more money from her husband's family?

We use two measures of sibling characteristics. The total number of siblings and the birth order of a person provide measures comparable with Western studies (Rows 9–10). The total numbers of younger and older siblings of each sex provide a more detailed check on possible special East Asian patterns that require more sacrifice from older sisters (Rows 11–14). If present, older sisters should improve, or at least not harm, one's education prospects. Other siblings should harm prospects. The harmful effects should be particularly strong for the respondent and her sisters, and particularly harmful when the respondent or her sisters have many younger brothers for whom parents desire extra years of education.

Sibsize remained large through the early 1970s, and then began to taper off as the family planning revolution of the 1960s began to take hold. As noted earlier, sampling biases overstate the rate of decline. And the number appears somewhat smaller in the children's generation because we excluded children adopted after the child's education was completed and children who died while still in school. Nevertheless, the overall downward trend is real.

Birth order in our data set is not completely consistent with societal trends. In our data, the respondent is a bit too early in the initial three decades and too late in the last decade. Although we can't explain why, this is not of great moment

---

4. Note that in the children's data, a person who had not yet finished school was scored one year lower than the expected degree level.

in most tables where we analyze not only the respondent but all her siblings up and down the full range of birth orders. Among children, we necessarily have more of the early-born, for many of their younger siblings are too young to be included in this subsample of 15–32 years-old.

Besides siblings characteristics, we have data on several background measures that serve as controls (Rows 15–19). Although in somewhat more muted form, these also increased steadily over time. Occupation is measured on a scale of 1–10, where 10 is professional and technical occupations while 1 is farmer.[5] For the respondent, this is her father's longest occupation. For children, this is their father's occupation when they were age 12. Income is the respondent's assessment of whether in the prime of his work life, her father's income was inadequate, adequate, or generous. Urban status is where the respondent lived at age 15 and her children at age 12. The sharp upward trends on all these dimensions suggest that the family calculus should have been quite different in recent decades than it was in the past. Higher parental status, as measured by respondent's mother's education and respondent's father's education, occupation, and estimated income group, should allow higher education for all children (Panel B). Similarly, women who were in a city by age 15 and who came of age (reached age 12) in a more recent decade, when more schools were available and community norms supported more universal education, are likely to have done better (Panel C).

IV. Model Specification

In this paper, our chief goal is to explain the completed educational attainment of each child in a family. Specifically, we estimate equations of the form

(1) $ED_{ij} = \beta_0 + \beta_1 X_i + \beta_2 Z_{ij} + \delta_i + u_{ij}$

where ED_{ij} is the education of child j in family i, X_i is a vector of variables which are common to all family members (for example, mother's and father's education and occupation, number of siblings), and Z_{ij} is a vector of variables which vary across members of the sibset (for example, sex, cohort, birth order). Likewise, the error term is assumed to be composed of one component which is common to all siblings, δ_i, and another idiosyncratic component, u_{ij}, which varies independently across sibs. To control for rapid growth in educational attainment across cohorts, differences in trends by gender, and changes in national educational policy, we include single year cohort dummies interacted with sex in the vector Z_{ij}. To probe further into the meaning of our results for Equation (1), we also estimate several other equations involving job and marriage transitions by sons and daughters. Because of a lack of relevant information about siblings, these latter models are estimated using data on respondents only.

---

5. We also made these runs with a set of dummy variables for each occupation with similar results. For simplicity we present the combined scale.

Two econometric issues arise in estimating (1). First, the errors in the equations for siblings are not independent because of the common unmeasured family effect, δ_i. Failure to account for the clustered sampling scheme inherent in sibling data tends to cause an understatement of standard errors of the regression coefficients estimated by OLS. We deal with this issue by estimating robust standard errors using Huber's method (Huber 1967; also see White 1980) in all equations which use sibling data.

Second, the quality-quantity trade-offs emphasized in economic theories of fertility behavior (Willis 1973, Becker and Lewis 1973) suggest that high fertility families may choose to invest less in the education of each child, leading to a negative correlation between δ_i and the number of siblings and to correlations with related variables such as birth order. Although we are unable to use standard simultaneous equations methods to deal with potential bias caused by endogenous fertility because of the absence of valid instruments in our data, we can treat some aspects of the problem by exploiting the fact that we have sibling data. In particular, "within family estimates" obtained by differencing between sibling pairs may be used to eliminate the influence of δ_i on β_2, the coefficients of variables that vary across individuals within a family. As Griliches (1979) emphasizes, however, the within estimates are not necessarily closer to the "truth" because differencing may exacerbate the effects of other potential econometric problems such as measurement errors in explanatory variables or endogeneity involving the individual error component (Griliches 1979). An additional limitation of the within estimator, of course, is that we cannot estimate β_1, the coefficients of variables common to all siblings using the within estimator. Although the main results presented in this paper rely on direct estimates of the model in (1), we report some results from some experiments using within estimates in the next section.

V. Results

A. Education

The determinants of education among the respondent and her siblings provides an initial view of how children's life chances were shaped by their family situation (Table 2). An individual's background was important—in education, people who were advantaged were males (by almost two years), those who grew up in cities, had mainland origin parents, and went through school in recent years rather than earlier (Panel C). People were similarly advantaged if their parents were of higher status in education, occupation, and income (Panel D). However, the advantages provided by parental status declined over time. Much as in the United States, movement towards more universal education and towards higher levels of education weakened the impact of parents on educational achievement (see Mare 1979, 1980; Blake 1989).

Siblings also affected educational achievement (Panel A). Birth order effects were persistent (Rows 2 and 4). Even after controlling for time period, parental status, etc., children born early got less education. Those born late got more education.[6] We will delve more deeply into why later, but let us note for now that what is surprising is the considerable constancy of this pattern from decade to decade and its strength relative to places such as the United States where the pattern also appears, but at a much weaker level (see Technical Appendix).

Then, there was a surprising increase in the role of sibsize (Rows 1 and 3). As we saw earlier, the average number of children per family declined over these decades, and the average income per family to support the remaining children increased sharply. But instead of declining, the negative effect of each extra sibling increased. At first blush, this poses a paradox. But before going on to discuss solutions to the apparent paradox, let us ask more about the effect of different kinds of siblings.

The number of older and younger siblings of each gender helps reveal the source of these trends (Table 3). Here we repeat the same analysis as before, changing only the measures of sibling characteristics. Two findings emerge: First, older sisters were helpful to everyone (Rows 1 and 5). In the final two decades, regardless of whether one was male or female, adding an older sister provided an additional one-tenth to one-fourth year's education. Thus the view that older sisters were more helpful than older brothers is supported. What is not supported is the idea that older sisters benefitted males alone. Both males and females benefitted, which suggests the need for a more subtle interpretation of what creates the pattern.

Second, except for older sisters, siblings of the same sex were increasingly a threat to education. Males in the family were threatened by both older and younger brothers (Rows 6 and 8). Females were threatened by their younger sisters (Row 3). This is consistent with the previous table that found more siblings an increasing threat to one's education. What is inconsistent, however, is that cross-sex siblings were not a threat (Rows 2, 4, 7). This inconsistency is particularly damaging to explanations that assumed older sisters helped only their younger brothers. If females were sacrificing for younger brothers and not younger sisters, the pattern of results for younger brothers and sisters should be just reversed (Rows 3 and 4). Again, the pattern of mixed results suggests the need for more subtle interpretation.

For the moment we are left with the three broad conclusions—older sisters always help, most same-sex siblings hurt, and most cross-sex siblings are neutral to one's education attainment. The increasingly negative effect of same-sex siblings is consistent with the increasing negative effect of sibsize in general. The positive effect of older sisters is consistent with the advantages of being late-born in the family. Thus, we have in part disentangled the grosser effects noted earlier, though in doing so also revealed several additional complexities that require explanation.

---

6. We also compared between and within family estimates of the birth order effects within a somewhat simpler model in which the birth order coefficient was constrained to be constant across decades. The coefficient was .18 ($t = 11.4$) when estimated in levels and .47 ($t = 3.1$) when estimated from sibling differences. The relatively large magnitude of the within estimate is consistent with the hypothesis discussed earlier that families with high demands for number of children have low demands for investments per child. It should be noted, however, that the estimate from the level equation falls within the 95 percent confidence interval for the within estimate (0.17 to 0.77).

Table 2
Education by Family Situation, Respondent, and Siblings[a] *(regression coefficients)*

	Decade				All Years	First/Last Decade Change
	1940–49	1950–59	1960–69	1970–79		
A. Sibling Effects						
Effect on females of						
sibsize	−.03	−.10*	−.17*	−.21		*
birth order	.16*	.20*	.23*	.24*		
Effect on males of						
sibsize	.08	−.12*	−.23*	−.19*		*
birth order	.03	.19*	.24*	.18*		+[b]
B. Family Background						
Mother's education	.21	.22*	.20*	.13*		*
Father's						
Education	.38*	.31*	.26*	.22*		*
Occuaption	.25*	.28*	.20*	.12*		*
Income	.99*	.72*	.67*	.63*		*

Urban youth	.42*	.51*	.50*	.31*	*
Origin					
Mainland	.02	5.06*	7.41*	10.11*	
Taiwan	c	4.89*	7.12*	9.82	
C. Individual background					
Male			1.76* d		
Year12 * male					
D. Missing data controls					
Mother's education			−.68*		
Father's					
Education			−.55*		
Occupation			−.27		
Constant			−2.57		
R^2 (adjusted)			.51		
n, raw			(19,781)		

a. Results from a single regression equation for respondent and her siblings, using Huber standard errors to correct for multiple observations per family. The final column gives the significance of the difference in first/last decade coefficients.

b. First/third decade difference significant at .05.

c. Comparison group for mainland/Taiwan origin-decade comparisons.

d. Separate male/female dummies for each year when person age 12.

* p < .05 † p < .10.

Table 3

Education by Sibling Gender, Respondent, and Siblings[a] (regression coefficients)

	Decade				First/ Last Decade Change	Row Number
	1940–19	1950–59	1960–69	1970–79		
Effect on females of one more						
Older						
Sister	.23*	.02	.18*	.26*		(1)
Brother	.02	.20*	.03	−.02		(2)
Younger						
Sister	−.05	−.04	−.19*	−.19*	b	(3)
Brother	−.00	−.14*	−.05	−.01		(4)
Effect on males of one more						
Older						
Sister	.08	.11	.26*	.13*		(5)
Brother	.15	−.03	−.22*	−.19*	*	(6)
Younger						
Sister	.06	−.16*	−.09	.02		(7)
Brother	.09	.00	−.25*	−.16*	*	(8)

a. Single equation for respondent and her siblings, using Huber standard errors. Separately for male and female, each row asks, "What is the consequence of adding one more sibling." The underlying regression equation and sample is the same as in Table 2 only that now a different combination of sibling characteristics have been substituted. The rest of the items in the equation remain as before.
b. First/third decade p = .06, first/last decade p = .11.
* p < .05

B. Work and Marriage

One puzzle requiring explanation is why older sisters consistently help one's education. Is it (a) that they quit school and go to work, thereby earning additional income to help put their younger brothers and sisters through school, or (b) that they marry early and thereby reduce the number of people who need family support? Results for the work and marriage of the female respondent suggest that both may occur, though marriage seems the stronger pattern. Table 4 reports results for four separate regression Equations (A–D), each using the same set of background controls as before but varying the dependent variable and sibling characteristics.

The results for gross sibling characteristics are the clearest (A, C). For female respondents, being born into a large family with many siblings was increasingly disadvantageous. By the last decade, each extra sibling forced one to go to work and marry one-fifth to one-fourth year earlier (Rows 1, 7). Conversely, being late-born was increasingly advantageous, allowing one to postpone work and marriage while studying longer (Rows 2, 8). Being early-born, of course, had just the opposite effect, accelerating both work and marriage. Or, to summarize the results from Panels A and C, the best situation for a woman was to be born into a small family. If born into a large family, however, the best was to be born not early but late. Indeed, because by the last decade both sets of effects were almost equal, being born last in a large family was almost as good as being born into a small family.

The results for the precise age and gender of siblings are much less clear (B, D). Indeed, the only consistent effect is that increasingly in recent decades a woman accelerated her work and marriage when she had more younger sisters. Thus, again, it was not younger brothers that elicited female sacrifices but younger sisters. If female, one wanted to avoid being early born into a large family, particularly if the later born children were girls.

In the simple regression equations of Table 4, sibling competition for resources had a somewhat stronger effect on marriage than on work—the regression coefficients (shown) and additional explained variance (not shown) for sibsize and birth order were somewhat larger for marriage age. An analysis of transition to work versus marriage gives further evidence that marriage is the more important mechanism for relieving excess population pressure in the household. Here the unit of analysis is the person-year, with us following women from age 14 until they either begin work or get married. In any one year, the woman can remain in school or idle (we don't distinguish the two) or begin work or get married. These three competing alternatives enter a multinomial logit equation. The resulting coefficients give the likelihood of choosing the alternative of work or marriage over the education/idle alternative. We examine women who came to maturity in the last two decades, for in earlier tables it was among this group that sibling effects were strongest.

Structured this way, the answer is that while marriage was shaped by sibling pressures, work was not (Table 5). In the parts of the equation not shown, much else behaved as expected. Women were less likely to go to work early if they were born of higher status parents, for example. Although sibling pressure had no significant effect on speed of going to work, it did accelerate marriage. As in earlier results, women married early when they had many siblings and when they were among the early-born in the family (Panel A). And, again as in the previous table, it was not younger brothers but younger sisters who sped one's time of marriage (Panel B).

C. Marriage Arrangements

Data on marriage finance and husband characteristics provide additional clues about the consequences of different sibling combinations. Brideprice involves gifts and cash payments from the groom's to the bride's family. Dowry includes gifts (bedding, furniture, clothing, and other goods) and sometimes cash brought with the bride to help endow the new couple's married life. The inflation-adjusted value of each has increased—the median value in our sample for a brideprice in any year is over three times a male's average monthly income, while a dowry is about six times monthly income. Thus, daughters were potentially much more

Table 4

First Job and Marriage Age by Siblings, Respondent[a] (regression coefficients)

	Decade				First/ Last Decade Change	Row Number
	1940–49	1950–59	1960–69	1970–79		
I. First Job Age						
A. Sibling effects						
Sibsize	.04	.04	−.07	−.19†	†	(1)
Birth order	−.09	−.01	.19*	.16†	†b	(2)
B. Effect of one more						
Older						
Sister	−.18	.09	.18*	.08	b	(3)
Brother	.11	−.03	.07	−.14		(4)
Younger						
Sister	.00	−.02	−.12	−.37*	*	(5)
Brother	.09	.10	−.02	.06		(6)
II. First Marriage Age						
C. Sibling effects						
Sibsize	−.03	−.07	−.14†	−.29*	*	(7)
Birth order	.10	.17*	.22*	.20*		(8)
D. Effect of one more						
Older						
Sister	.18	.17†	.10	.01		(9)
Brother	−.04	.02	.06	−.24†		(10)
Younger:						
Sister	−.08	−.14	−.20*	−.39*	*	(11)
Brother	.03	.00	−.06	−.21		(12)

a. For female respondents alone, from four regression equations, A–D, using the same background controls as in Table 2. Sample sizes average 3,537 and R^2 values average .13 for job and .15 for marriage equations. The next-to-last column gives the significance of the difference in coefficients between the first and last decade.
b. First versus third decade differences in coefficient significant at .05.
* $p < .05$ † $p < .10$.

expensive to marry off than sons. Female respondents were less likely to get a brideprice when they came from higher status families, cities, or mainland origin families. These are all reasonable results and, hence, simply controlled without being shown below.

One's siblings influenced marriage payments as well. Families of women with more siblings were more likely to demand a brideprice (Table 6, Column 1). And when the value of brideprice is compared with the value of items her family returned as dowry, women with more siblings got somewhat more than they gave (Column 2). There was also a small birth order effect, with later born women less

Table 5

First Job and Marriage by Sibling Characteristics, Respondent[a]
(multinomial logit)

	Likelihood of ceasing school or idleness for	
	Work	Marriage
A. Sibling effects		
Sibsize	.01	.18*
Birth order	− .03	− .19*
B. Effect of one more		
Older		
Sister	− .04	− .01
Brother	− .01	− .01
Younger		
Sister	− .05	.22*
Brother	− .04	.12

a. For female respondents who reached age 12 after 1959. Based on two logit equations (A and B) with controls in each for parents' education and occupation plus respondent's urban origin, mainland origin, age, age squared, time since age 14, and this time squared. The unit of analysis is the person-year, with respondents dropping out of the sample once they switch from being in school or idle to work or marriage. Fewer than five respondents failed to begin work or marriage, 1,402 began work first, and 233 married first. Total person years = 10,214 for both equations.
* $p < .05$

pressured to get a brideprice from their new husband (Column 1). This is all as we would expect from the credit constraint hypothesis. Women with more siblings competing for resources were likely to need higher cash payments from their new husbands as were early-born women who had many siblings at home still clamoring for support. Or, as later results will suggest, they were more likely to have to accept a less desirable mate—older, less educated, less desirable occupation—in return for a higher cash exchange.[7]

Statistics separated by the age and gender of one's siblings help clarify the pattern (Panel B). More extra siblings caused one to receive a brideprice. Older sisters, however, freed one from that obligation (Column 1). The second column shows why. For most siblings, even if one received a brideprice, most of it

7. The tradeoff between desirable mate and brideprice illustrates the two-sex nature of the financial arrangements at marriage. Less desirable men have to provide more financial incentives in marriage. More desirable men provide less. Also, since the 1950s, as the number of women have become more nearly equal to the number of men, women's dowry payments have had to increase relative to men's brideprice payments. This secular trend is captured in a year-by-year time variable that was used as a control in these equations.

Table 6
Marriage Arrangements by Sibling Characteristics, Respondent[a]

	Bride Price Received	Excess Brideprice Value	Husband's			
			Age	Education	Occupation	Pay
A. Sibling effects						
Sibsize	.06*	.11†	.06	-.01	.02	-.00
Birth order	-.04*	-.07	-.10*	.15*	.07*	.02
B. Effect of one more						
Older						
Brother	.05*	.10	-.01	.18*	.14*	.00
Sister	.00	-.02	-.07	.12*	.05	.02
Younger						
Brother	.06*	.02	.03	.02	.07†	.01
Sister	.07*	.21*	.08	-.03	-.02	-.02
R^2 (adjusted)			.79	.36	.23	.07
n			3,300	3,289	3,290	2,678

a. First column contains probit coefficients. Remaining columns contain regression coefficients. Sample of first marriages. Adjusted R^2 and sample sizes (*n*) for Panel A.

* p < .05 † p < .10.

seemed to be returned to the new bride and groom through the dowry—the number of older and younger siblings had little or no influence on the excess value of brideprice over dowry.

However, if the respondent had a younger sister—who herself needed resources to arrange a good marriage—then the full value of the brideprice was not returned as dowry. Brideprice exceeded dowry, and more was left behind for possible use by the younger sister. Thus, among females one of the reasons for not getting a brideprice when one had an older sister (Column 1) was that the older sister had already provided part of one's dowry through the excess brideprice retained from that sister's marriage (Column 2). In turn, all of this may have contributed to the negative effect of younger sisters observed in earlier tables. That is, among females, younger sisters may have provided not only an extra mouth to feed but also the need for older sisters to get out of the way by marrying early and bringing in excess brideprice to help provide for the younger sister's own marriage.

The amount of money received was related to the kind of husband a woman married, with the strongest effects being through birth order. Although husband's pay was unaffected, early-born women were forced to take men who were on average older, less educated, and in lower status occupations. Late-born women, in contrast, married younger men with more education and higher status jobs (Table 6, last four columns). The remaining coefficients in the right hand corner of Table 6 only reinforce the conclusions about birth order. Having more older brothers or sisters means that one was later born, and thus under less pressure to leave the family quickly. The most general conclusion from these findings is that early-birth and the subsequent pressure for early marriage reduced not only a woman's education but also the desirability of her marriage mate.

D. Leaving Home

Data on the respondent's maturing children provide additional clues as to how older sisters help their family. For children age 15–32, we know whether that child is currently enrolled in school, idle, working, or gone. Our coding of working attempts to include all children who make a significant economic contribution to the family—in other words, we include all working children who have not married (since unmarried children tend to send significant parts of their income back home) and married children who remain at home, which for males is a large proportion. The "gone" category is for those who no longer make a significant economic contribution. These children were distributed:

	Sons	Daughters
Enrolled	30%	32%
Idle	16	6
Working	42	29
Gone	11	33
	100%	100%

In these static comparisons, daughters' earlier marriage ages and their tendency to leave home after marriage meant that more daughters were "gone." Sons were more likely to be home working for the family.

Of more interest is how these distributions change when the family is pressed by few resources and surplus siblings. Using much the same controls as in other tables, we examined the effect of extra siblings of different ages and gender (for controls, see Table B). A multinomial logit analysis gave the log odds of being idle, at work, or gone rather than enrolled. To make the results more easily interpretable we translated the logit coefficients back into change probabilities (Table 7). In an average family with one sibling of each type, these probabilities show what would happen if one added one more older sister, one more brother, or someone else.

Although small, all but a few are statistically significant. More importantly, the first row is statistically nonsignificant. Adding an extra older sister was neutral (Row 1). The older sister didn't help, but unlike all the other siblings she didn't hurt. All the other siblings drove one out of school and away from idleness into work and marriage. So, in part, the results here just repeat what we have seen earlier. Older sisters were better than other siblings if one wanted to avoid early work and marriage so as to remain in school.

Of even greater interest to us was the contrast between the consequences for males and the consequences for females. Additional siblings drove both males and females out of school. However, when so pressed, the female solution was to leave the family through marriage. The male solution was to go to work. Actually there was a little wrinkle that we can't capture in these statistics— around age 20, 21, for a period of two years when men typically performed their universal military service ("idle" in the table above), more daughters went to work. But except for this two-year period, caused more by the government than by conniving parents, marriage rather than work was the more common solution for economically pressured daughters.

Table 7
Life Transitions by Sibling Characteristics, Children (proportional changes)[a]

	Enrolled		Idle		Work		Gone	
	Female	Male	Female	Male	Female	Male	Female	Male
Effect of one more								
Older								
Sister	−.00	−.00	.01	−.01	−.01	.01	−.00	.00
Brother	−.03	−.02	−.01	−.02	−.01	.04	.05	.00
Younger								
Sister	−.03	−.03	.01	−.00	−.03	.03	.05	.00
Brother	−.06	−.04	−.01	−.02	.00	.04	.07	.01

a. Change in proportion enrolled, idle, working, gone as derived from a single multinomial logit equation for children age 15–32 with controls as in Table B. Except for older sisters and the effect of older brothers on idleness, all the original logit coefficients were significant at .05.

E. Children and Economic Security

The education of the respondent's children was also shaped by a combination of sibling composition and family economic security. The most important influence was economic security, indexed by the father's income as predicted by his education, occupation, and urban-rural residence, age, and age squared, and then split into three approximately equal subgroups of low, medium, and high "security." Besides the coefficients shown here we also included a set of background controls that parallel those for respondents (see appendix Table B). The results suggest that children's educational outcomes were highly dependent on economic security (Table 8). Families with low incomes chose more carefully who in the home got educated (Column 1). On average, girls in poor families suffered a loss of one-half year for each extra sibling. Although, conversely, those girls gained an additional one-fifth year's education for each step later they were in the birth order. These gains and losses did not quite fit the classic East Asian pattern that some would expect, for both male and female children suffered from the pressure of extra siblings.

To the extent that the classic East Asian pattern appeared it was in the effect of different types of siblings (Panel B, Column 1). Brothers were more damaging than sisters. The least damaging were older sisters. The most damaging were younger brothers, and this was particularly true when one was female, suggesting older-sister to younger-brother resource transfers. The dominant pattern, however, was in many ways parallel for male and female children, with both suffering more from brothers than from sisters. Thus, as in earlier results, we need more subtle interpretations of family resource flows. Results for the economically least secure families approach the classic model but are not completely consistent with it.

Among the most secure families, things were radically different. In this group, siblings essentially had no effect on educational opportunity (Column 3). Whether one was male or female, whether one had more older sisters or younger brothers, were all irrelevant to educational opportunity. All children from these blessed families had the same set of opportunities. The hard choices common in other families had disappeared. Moreover, in contrast to some accounts, this blessed group was not restricted to a narrow elite, but to about one-third of all families, and even to some extent to the broader middle class (see Greenhalgh 1985, p. 278, n. 20).

VI. Discussion

A. Time Trends

We are, thus, much closer to an answer than before. Yet, several puzzles remain to be explained. Premier among them is the puzzle about long-term trends. From the fall in number of siblings competing for resources (Table 1), the sharp increase in real incomes, and the modest increase in public old age support and welfare benefits, we would expect sibling competition for resources to be less critical today than in the past. That is, we would expect the longitudinal trends to parallel

Table 8

Education by Siblings' Characteristics and Parent's Economic Security,
Children[a] (regression coefficients)

	Economic Security			Significance of First/Last Column Differences
	Low	Medium	High	
A. Total				
Effect on females of				
Sibsize	− .49*	− .24*	− .03	*
Birth order	.20*	.15*	.02	†
Effect on males of				
Sibsize	− .31*	− .06	.05	*
Birth order	.03	− .01	− .06	
B. By sibling gender				
Effect on females of one more				
Older				
Sister	− .14†	− .20*	.01	
Brother	− .55	.04	− .06	*
Younger				
Sister	− .40*	− .27*	− .05	*
Brother	− .74*	− .22	− .03	*
Effect on males of one more				
Older				
Sister	− .20*	.03	− .02	†
Brother	− .46*	− .13	.04	*
Younger				
Sister	− .22*	.12	.10	*
Brother	− .46*	− .22†	.01	*

a. Regression with Huber standard errors to correct for multiple observations per family. Sample of children age 15–32, with one-year subtracted from education for those who have not yet graduated. Two equations, A and B, each with the unshown background conditions of mother's ecucation; father's education, occupation (eight dummy variables), and predicted income (the "security" dummy variables); city/town residence; and the child's gender and individual years of age.
* $p < .05$ † $p < .10$ Sample size = 4,234

the cross-sectional comparisons among more and less dependent families in Table 8. Just the opposite occurs, however. As in the United States, sibling competition has become more, not less limiting (Tables 2–4). Why?

It is not increasing variability in education. Measured in years of education, the standard deviation in education went down steadily for the respondent's brothers. For the respondent and her sisters, variability first went up as female education shifted from being bunched near 0 and 6 years of education to the middle years of education. But, then, by the 1970s education began to bunch towards twelve years of education and the standard deviation of female education declined. More women were getting similar levels of education. And this kind of pattern held not only across families but also among siblings in the same family. Thus, there is no statistical artifact driving these results.

What happened instead is that opportunity costs increased. With increasing educational levels children and their parents were increasingly confronted with conflicts among education, work, and marriage. Female trends in median age of last schooling, work, and marriage illustrate the pattern (Table 1). For women who matured in the 1940s, education was long finished before one ever entertained the idea of work or marriage. As a result, there was little or no conflict among school, work, and marriage. If everyone was leaving school by the sixth grade or age 12, then the chances of school conflicting with considerable work around the home or outside were small. By the 1970s, however, this situation had changed considerably. With schooling continuing on average into the late teens, youths and their parents were forced to make a choice between increasingly lucrative work not only around the family business but also increasingly outside the home. For females, at least, the possibility of early marriage also beckoned.

We see the results of these increasingly contradictory choices in the linkages among schooling, work, and marriage (Table 9). The pattern is clearest for work (Row 1). In the first two decades, when a woman finished school made little difference in when she began work. By the last decade, however, it made a great deal of difference. School leaving was followed almost immediately by work (for the narrowing gap between finishing school and beginning work, see Table 1, Rows 3 and 4). Thus, for women, and we suspect also for men, in the late teen and early adult years, work began to compete with education.

Although more muted, there was a similar tendency for marriage (Table 9, Row 2). Even though marriage ages rose slightly, average years of education began to catch up with average marriage ages (see Table 1, Rows 3, 5). For the first time, a few women began to marry before leaving school (not shown). And age of leaving school became more tightly linked to marriage age. Again, we suggest, women and their parents were confronted with a choice between education and marriage. A few women combined the two, but given the tendency to have children immediately upon marriage, this was a rare combination.

In short, we believe the increasing link among sibsize, birth order, and education can be explained. Furthermore, we believe that this explanation holds not only for Taiwan but also for the United States, where it was first discovered (Blake 1989, p. 55). With increasing education levels, and, for women, more pervasive opportunities for work outside the home, education, work, and marriage came to be competing alternatives. When pressured inside the parental home by too many siblings competing for the same resources, women and men were more likely to choose work or marriage over continuing enrollment in school. Thus, both in the United States and in Taiwan a credit constraint explanation seems sufficient to account for observed trends. Even while average family incomes have increased tremendously, the opportunities for productive work and marriage have increased at the same pace or more. The net result is that even with more family resources, the pull of alternatives outside school have become ever more attractive for those with few resources to go around.

Table 9
Last Schooling, Work, and Marriage, Respondents[a] (correlation coefficients)

	Decade			
	1940–49	1950–59	1960–69	1970–79
Last schooling and				
Work	.14	−.02	.30	.60
Marriage	.23	.34	.46	.46
n	(546)	(907)	(1,608)	(740)

a. Last schooling = age at which break of three or more years in schooling begun. Work = age at first job after beginning of break in schooling. Marriage = age at first marriage.

B. Marriage versus Work

Even if we can explain the apparent paradox of increasing sibling influence amidst increasing prosperity, can we explain who quits school? The classical patriarchal model of East Asian family behavior would lead one to believe that older daughters are prematurely forced into the work force by conniving parents who then expropriate the daughter's income to support younger sons. This is, at best, only part of the story.

Some parts of the story fit. While other siblings hurt one's educational prospects, older daughters are at least neutral and often help. The way they help, however, is not so much through early work as it is through early marriage. This early marriage not only brings in more brideprice for some but also permanently relieves the family of supporting an extra member.

The cynic who sees conniving parents everywhere will respond that this is but a small detail. Even if through marriage rather than work, daughters are being sacrificed for the sake of sons. This could be, but again it may not be so simple. For reasons beyond the control of parents, marriage may simply be more available to daughters than to sons. First, with most eligible women expecting to marry slightly older men, a young man may find few eligible mates in the appropriate age range. The problem is exacerbated because all young men still face two years of obligatory military service. Second, while poverty accelerates women's marriages it decelerates men's marriages. By marrying early, a poor woman with many siblings sitting around the same dinner table can help her family. In contrast, not only do women (and the women's parents) avoid poor men as husbands, poor families are less able to support a new wife and soon-to-arrive grandchildren. Thus, while poor women marry early, poor men marry later (results not shown). In short, older daughters help because they can marry away. Older brothers hurt because they cannot. Again, we suspect that this explanation applies almost as well to the United States as it does to Taiwan (for example, see Powell and

Steelman 1989). And, more importantly, these tendencies imply that, again, credit constraints rather than manipulative parents may be the more proper explanation of older daughters' assistance.

Two additional details further weaken the manipulative, patriarchal parent argument. First, except for older sisters, sacrifices and benefits were about equally distributed between males and females. Males were just as threatened by extra siblings as females were (Tables 2, 3, 7, 8). On average, females benefitted just as much from an older sister as males did (Tables 3, 7, 8). Second, for the respondent's generation, both males and females were more threatened by same-sex than cross-sex siblings. This was particularly true for older females who had to quit school, work, marry more quickly, and demand a higher brideprice when pressures by younger sisters. This was, in part, a cultural artifact. The norm was that both sons and daughters marry by birth order. By tradition, younger sisters could not marry until older sisters had found a mate. This alone, then, helped make one's younger sister a greater threat to continuing education. The need to provide the sister with a dowry further increased the threat (Tables 4, 5, 6). To be sure, parents were the guardian of this norm, but it is not clear whether they or the younger sisters captured its benefits.

In short, it appears that it is primarily through marriage rather than work that older sisters benefitted their families, and that for the respondent's generation it was the younger sisters as much as the brothers who often captured the benefits. Rather than manipulative parents, it is stories about credit constraints, marriage markets, and cultural norms about marrying in sibling order that seem to tell more about why all this happened.

C. Long-Term Consequences

As so forcefully argued by Greenhalgh, the negative consequences of daughter sacrifice include not only education. In the classic account, education for sons and daughters is becoming more equal as parents learn that they can get a quick return on daughter's education. They can get that quick return because they can subtly induce their daughters to engage in steady, dead-end jobs before marriage while sons are allowed to experiment with different, irregular jobs, often involving low-paying apprentice positions that provide a better base for building a rewarding career.

Several features contaminate any examination of this issue. With compulsory miltary service imposed between the time of leaving school and marrying, males are often forced to take temporary, make-do positions that increase the number of jobs they hold early in their career. With societal, marriage-market imposed later ages at marriage, males almost inevitably have more years of work before marriage, and more chance to experiment. Parents have little to do with this. Nor do parents necessarily have much to do with whether a woman is offered an apprenticeship position with long-term career mobility prospects. Around the world, fearing that women will leave to raise children, employers offer their best jobs with intake training and long term career prospects to men instead of women. Even with the best of intentions, parents could do little about this. Parents do influence whether young women remain at home—in towns and cities (not villages) daughters aged 19–21 are 10–20 percentage points more likely to be at home than males this age. However, more benign concerns about safety in urban areas that are increasingly perceived as a dangerous environment for young women seems as appealing an explanation as more exploitive income-expropriation motives.

Finally, in preliminary analysis we found little evidence that a woman's long-term income prospects were hurt by brothers. Leaving the respondent's education out of the equation, but including the same set of background controls as in Table 2, respondents with many brothers were just as likely to work today as women who were not so pressured and just as likely to get high incomes when they did work. This suggests that any negative effects must be transitory. The conclusion of all this, we believe, is that though women's situation in Taiwan is far from ideal, one should avoid temptations to blame too much of the situation on parents.

VII. Conclusion

In its crudest form, the patriarchal, East Asian family model does poorly. The solution to tight family budgets is more often marriage than work. When older sisters do marry early, the beneficiaries are as much younger daughters as sons. Parents themselves seem to reap few additional benefits. Many of the forces that shape the early marriage process seem out of the hands of parents. Although older daughters suffer in the short run—losing education, taking less desirable mates—their long-run income earning potential and the income of their mates seems little affected. So, yes, older sisters do suffer, but the process and its consequences fit no crude model of parental manipulation and involve no special East Asian model of family behavior.

In its simplest form the *conditional altruism* model has some problems as well. Instead of becoming less important over time, other siblings became more of a threat to educational achievement. Yet, the overall model seems to work well. Once families have the prospect of more income, and with this more saving for old age and occasionally greater social benefits at the place of work, sons and daughters begin to get more equal education. One sibling no longer needs to sacrifice for the other. This pattern suggests that concerns about resource dilution shape parental investments in children. What may be more important to altruism may be not the will to treat sons and daughters equally but the means to do so.

Finally, the model that performs perhaps best of all is that of *current credit constraints*. Early born children in large families do poorly, and particular poorly if they are female and can, hence, marry early. This is a model which seems to fit observed patterns both in Taiwan and abroad, where concerns about old age support are less severe. Thus, what we have inadvertently discovered by examining what once seemed like an extreme case is a very general case which may apply broadly around the developed world.

Technical Appendix

Two Matters Deserve Additional Explanation:

A. Variables

First job and marriage	Age of first full-time job after, or during, a major break in schooling is sharply skewed towards the higher ages. To reduce the skew, we recode later marriages to age 25, by which point more than four-fifths of everyone who will go to work before marriage has gone to work. Those who never work before marriage are also recoded at age 25 (see Table B). We treat age at marriage in the same way, using age 34 as the end point to which all late and nonmarriages are recoded. In the multinomial person-year analysis we impose no such restraints.
Decade	Female respondents reached age 12 from as early as 1935 to as late as 1982, but all but a few are concentrated in the 1940–75 period. Siblings were included only if at least age 20, and fall in a similar set of decades.
Mainland origin	These are people whose parents or grandparents came to Taiwan from China proper, mostly in 1945–49. They have some educational advantage because their mother-tongue is Mandarin, which is the official language of school.
Missing data controls	In order to maintain sample size we have included dummy (0, 1) variables for missing parent data. Missing parent's education and occupation was coded at their mean values and then separate dummy variables created to control for this additon.
Age of sibling	For the respondent's siblings, the current age and the year each sibling reached age 12 is estimated. Using an interval between births of 2.5 years, which is close to the average in Taiwan, we add this many years for each successive younger sibling and subtract this many years for each successive older sibling. This estimation provides a control for the educational opportunities at different points of time.
Economic security	For children, this is father's predicted pay from a regression equation including the father's education, occupation, urban-rural residence, age, and age squared. This continuous measure is then trichotimized from low security (1) to high security (3).

B. Birth Order Effects

There is some controversy in the literature about whether birth order effects really exist, and if they exist whether they are positive, negative, or parabolic in form (for example, Hauser and Sewell 1985; Hauser 1989; Behrman and Taubman 1986; Taubman and Behrman 1986; Blake 1989; Ernst and Angst 1983; Hermalin et al. 1982). Blake and Ernst and Angst provide extensive reviews and critiques of the literature on the consequences of birth order and sibset size for both intelligence and educational achievement. A particular caution in this literature is that one should examine birth order effects within sibsize groups, including controls for family background characteristics and the time period when each sibling went through school. All the text tables include controls for family background and time period. They also include a control for sibsize, but still do not examine birth order effects within sibsize groups.

An attempt to do that here suggests that the birth order effect, though not overwhelming, does indeed exist (Table C). It is parabolic in form. That is, except at smaller sibsizes, the first sibling does slightly better than the early-middle siblings. In Table C, Equation 2, when the birth order effects are graphed, they begin to decline initially (the simple term) followed by an upturn in education (the squared term) for fourth, fifth, and higher order kids. The upturn is so extreme that in large families, the late-born siblings do the best of all. In short, though inconsistent with patterns in data sets examined by Hauser and Sewell (1985), Hauser (1989), Taubman and Behrman (1986), and Behrman and Taubman (1986), the Taiwan data are consistent with U.S. data examined by Blake (1989), Steelman and Powell (1991), and Blau and Duncan (1967). Part of the reason for the strong birth order effects in Taiwan have to do with a greater prevalence of large families with late birth orders. Part of the reason for the failure to find birth order effects or a consistent decline in education with birth order may have to do with selectivity in the Hauser and Sewell and Taubman and Behrman samples that produces fewer larger families and few late birth order children (see Blake 1989, p. 174). In larger samples from a greater variety of respondents, the parabolic pattern within sibsizes appears.

There are some differences between the Taiwan patterns and the U.S. patterns discussed by Blake, however. In the respondent's generation, Taiwan sibsize effects are smaller and birth order effects larger than in the United States. One consequence is that in the Taiwan data, including sibsize in a regression without birth order produce not the expected negative but instead positive coefficients even with controls for cohort, all because the late-born in large families do so well. In Taiwan, the effect of extra siblings on education is more highly related to whether one is born early or late among all siblings.

Despite the mild parabolic pattern, our text tables use only the simpler straight line representation of birth order (Table C, Equation 1). Our plea is simplicity, and the fact that the parabolic form of Equation 2 yields only slightly improved explained variance (R^2s) over the first formulation.

One additional check was to run separate regressions within each family. The results for the mean of the birth order effects (not shown) are very similar to those for Equation 1 in Table C. Much as in Table C the slopes are steeper for small than large sibsize and absolute values are close—for example, for sibsize six Table C shows .198, while the mean of the separate slopes within households is .24.

There were also two checks on possible reporting error when the respondent

Appendix Table A
Characteristics of Respondent

	Mean	Standard Deviation	Minimum	Maximum
I. Dependent Variables				
Education, years	7.5	4.4	0	18
Transitions				
First job, age	18.20	3.6	15	25
Marriage, age	23.07	3.5	14	34
First event				
Job	.14		0	1
Marriage	.02		0	1
Marriage finance				
Brideprice received	.54	.4	0	1
Excess brideprice (log)	.41	5.6	− 15	15
II. Independent Variables				
A. Sibling characteristics				
Total				
Sibsize	5.74	2.1	1	15
Birth order	3.22	2.1	1	12
Gender/age specific				
Older				
Brothers	1.10	1.3	0	8
Sisters	1.11	1.3	0	8
Younger				
Brothers	1.30	1.2	0	6
Sisters	1.22	1.3	0	8
B. Family background				
Mother's education	1.9	3.1	0	16
Father's				
Education	4.3	3.9	0	18
Occupation	3.57	3.1	1	10
Income	1.74	.6	1	3
C. Individual background				
Urban	.47	.5	0	1
Mainland origin	.13	.3	0	1
Age 12 year	1961	9.1	1935	1982
D. Missing data controls				
Mother's education	.10	0.3	0	1
Father's				
Education	.10	0.3	0	1
Occupation	.07	.3	0	1

Sample sizes: Maximum 3,803 for all but marriage finance with 3,271 and life transitions analysis with 10,204 person-years.

Appendix Table B

Characteristics of Respondent's Children, Age 15–32[a]

	Mean	Standard Deviation	Minimum	Maximum
I. Dependent Variables				
Education, years	10.9	2.5	0	18
Life Cycle Status				
Enrolled in school	30.7		0	1
Idle	11.6		0	1
Working	35.7		0	1
Gone	22.1		0	1
Total	100.0%			
II. Independent Variables				
A. Sibling characteristics				
Total				
Sibsize	3.8	1.3	1	10
Birth order	2.2	1.3	1	10
Gender/age specific				
Older				
Brothers	.6	.8	0	6
Sisters	.6	.9	0	7
Younger				
Brothers	.8	.9	0	6
Sisters	.8	.9	0	7
B. Family background				
Mother's education	5.08	3.88	0	16
Father's				
Education	7.59	4.21	0	18
Occupation				
Professional and technical	.07	.26	0	1
Administrative and managerial	.06	.24	0	1
Clerical workers	.11	.31	0	1
Sales workers	.13	.33	0	1
Service workers	.07	.26	0	1
Manual workers	.28	.45	0	1
Casual labor	.02	.15	0	1
Farmers (comparison)				
Missing control	.05	.22	0	1
C. Individual Background				
Age	20.85	4.84	15	32
Male	.52	.50	0	1

a. Weighted by inverse of number of children analyzed per family.
Sample sizes: raw = 4,234. weighted = 1,443.

Appendix Table C
Birth Order Effects Within Sibsize, Respondent, and Siblings[a]

	Equation 1			Equation 2					
	Birth			Birth Order					
Sibsize	Order	Constant	R²	Simple	Squared	Significance[b]	Constant	R²	n
2	.295	−.646	−.002	—	—	—	—	—	229
3	.361†	−.685	.009	−.860	.306	—	.329	.010	752
4	.189†	−.367	.005	.204	−.003	†	−.382	.005	2,066
5	.191†	−.659	.008	−.125	.053*	†	−.291	.008	3,512
6	.198†	−.627	.011	−.185	.055†	†	−.116	.013	4,183
7	.154†	−.554	.009	−.061	.027*	†	−.233	.010	3,266
8	.118†	−.646	.006	−.366†	.054†	†	−.646	.012	2,700
9	.135†	−.802	.013	−.170	.031†	†	−.250	.016	1,547
10	.091*	−.523	.005	−.072	.015	*	−.199	.005	885
11	.064	−.141	.004	−.099	.014	—	.210	.001	435

a. Dependent variable is residual of years of education taken from the same equation as in Table 2, only without sibsize or birth order. Boths sets report significance levels calculated with Huber procedures to correct for multiple observations per family. n is raw n. R^2 is adjusted R^2.

b. Joint significance of birth order and birth order squared.

* $p < .05$

† $p < .01$

provides information on her siblings. One check on this was to rerun the sibling tables with data on the respondent alone. The results were very similar. Another implicit check was to use the respondent's children as the unit of analysis (Tables 7–8). One would expect uniform reporting on different age children. The results for the respondent's children again replicated the patterns found among the respondent's siblings. These separate checks suggest that reporting error can not explain away the results.

10 Gender Differences in the Returns to Schooling and in School Enrollment Rates in Indonesia

Anil B. Deolalikar

Anil B. Deolalikar is a professor of economics at the University of Washington. An earlier version of this chapter was presented at the Conference on Women's Human Capital and Development, Bellagio Italy, May 18–22, 1992. The author is grateful to Angus Deaton, Claudia Goldin, T. Paul Schultz, and other conference participants, and to two anonymous referees for their useful comments and suggestions on an earlier draft.

I. Introduction

In most developing countries, women have significantly less schooling than men. For instance, the average female literacy rate for the low-income group of countries (as characterized by the World Bank) was 42 percent in 1988, as compared to 70 percent for males. For the same group of countries, primary enrollment rates were 95 percent for females and 115 percent for males. The disparity in secondary enrollment rates was even greater—29 percent for females and 45 percent for males (World Bank 1991b).

Before jumping to the conclusion that such disparities reflect gender discrimination, it is important to know how the financial rewards from schooling differ across males and females. If males have higher pecuniary returns to schooling than females, the greater schooling attainment among males may reflect an efficient (although inequitable) household allocative response to scarce resources. On the other hand, if the reverse is true, the greater schooling of males relative to females would represent a serious misallocation of resources and loss of efficiency.

Recently, a few studies have attempted to estimate differential returns to schooling for males and females in developing countries.[1] With the exception of

---

1. These include Behrman and Wolfe (1990) for Nicaragua; and Birdsall and Behrman for Brazil (1990); Gannicott (1986) for Taiwan; Gindling (1988) for Brazil; Khandker (1990) for Peru; Behrman and Deolalikar (1990b) for Indonesia; and Vijverberg (1993) for Côte d'Ivoire.

Behrman and Deolalikar (1990b), these studies have found that although there are significant differences in male-female earnings even after controlling for schooling and experience, the returns to schooling do not differ significantly by gender. However, the study by Behrman and Deolalikar (1990b) for Indonesia found higher returns to schooling, especially at higher levels, for females than for males.

Generally, fewer studies have analyzed the intrahousehold distribution of schooling.[2] This is surprising in view of the growing number of studies that have analyzed the intrahousehold distribution of consumption expenditure, nutrition, health, mortality, and labor supply in developing countries.[3] This paper seeks to analyze the determinants of school enrollment using sample survey data from Indonesia. In particular, I test to see if the schooling of male and female children responds differentially to household socioeconomic variables and community intrastructure. In addition, using the same data set (but limiting myself to the sample of wage-earning adults), I test whether the pecuniary returns to schooling do indeed differ significantly across gender.

II. Analytical Issues

The focus of this paper is on the reduced-form demand relations for child school enrollment as dependent on prices, income, other child, and household and community characteristics. Such relations are consistent with constrained maximization of a unified preference function or with the bargaining framework emphasized by Folbre (1984a, 1984b, 1986a), Manser and Brown (1980), and McElroy and Horney (1981). In either case, preferences are defined over the schooling attainment of children, and the constraints typically include a budget constraint and schooling production functions for each child that characterize educational outcomes from schooling and (child and parental) time inputs, conditional on parental education and on various community influences.

The intrahousehold allocation process results in a system of reduced-form demand equations for child schooling, which have as their arguments the price of schooling inputs (including the opportunity cost of time of children and parents), household nonlabor income, parental schooling, and other household- and location-specific environmental variables. In its most general form, the model would yield separate schooling demand equations for each child because of age and gender differences in preferences, educational production functions, and genetic endowments.

In the absence of much structure and restrictions on preferences or schooling technology, a generic model of this type will generally yield few testable predictions. However, given that child schooling is typically a normal good, the effect

---

2. These include, among others, Rosenzweig and Evenson (1977) for India; King et al. (1985) for Malaysia: King and Lillard (1987) for Malaysia and the Philippines; and King and Bellew (1990) for Peru. See Schultz (1988) for a survey of the literature.

3. See, for example, Rosenzweig and Schultz (1982), Dasgupta (1987), Behrman (1988a, 1988b), Deaton (1989), Behrman and Deolalikar (1990a, 1991), Schultz (1990b), Thomas (1990), and Deolalikar (1991).

of household nonlabor income on schooling demand is likely to be positive. Likewise, the impact of prices of schooling inputs, including child and parental wage rates, on schooling demand will be negative. To the extent that educational infrastructure and proximity to schools serve to reduce the total cost (cash price plus the opportunity cost of time) of obtaining schooling, these variables will most likely be associated with higher levels of schooling inputs and enrollment.

An additional concern of the paper is the estimation of returns to schooling for adult men and women. It is well known that the earnings function has many interpretations depending on what factors generate the relationship between earnings and schooling. If hours worked are determined exogenously, the earnings function can be viewed as a generalization of the equilibrium relation between schooling and earnings derived by Mincer (1974), in which the partial derivative of log earnings with respect to schooling is the estimate of the private rate of return to the time spent in school instead of in the labor market. Alternatively, the earnings function can also be interpreted as an hedonic index yielding weights on characteristics that affect the price of a unit of the individual's time, as suggested by Tinbergen (1951) and Rosen (1974).

Gender differences in the returns to schooling may arise for several reasons: differential opportunity costs of schooling for males and females; gender differences in traits, such as manual dexterity, stamina, or strength, that are valued by the market; gender specialization in jobs and relative scarcity of one gender; and sex discrimination in the labor market. A priori none of these factors suggest a higher rate of return to schooling for males or females. For example, while the opportunity cost of schooling in terms of the market wage foregone is typically greater for males than for females, the opportunity cost in terms of home production may be greater for women, since school-age girls are generally more valuable in providing child care for siblings and in helping with cooking and other housework.[4]

Even if women have traits that are less rewarded by labor markets, gender differentials in paid labor force participation may result in those (few) women who do participate in the paid labor force being more capable on average than the larger numbers of participating men. This may occur particularly if women with the marketable traits are more likely to participate in the labor market, but because of household responsibilities or cultural norms many fewer women than men actually participate in the paid labor market. Thus, there is little guidance from theory as to whether women face lower or higher pecuniary returns to schooling relative to men; the question is largely an empirical issue.

III. Background, Data, and Empirical Model

A. Background

With a total population estimated at 175 million in mid-1988, Indonesia is the fifth most populous country in the world (World Bank 1991b). Although the World

---

4. For example, Pitt and Rosenzweig (1990) present estimates that indicate that in Indonesia older sisters stay home from school to care for sick younger siblings.

Bank ranks Indonesia as a low-income economy with a per capita income of $500 in 1989, the Indonesian economy has enjoyed rapid economic growth during the last two decades. Between 1965 and 1989, Indonesia achieved an annual growth rate of per-capita GNP of 4.4 percent—a rate that few developing countries could match. Available estimates also suggest an impressive growth in education over time; the adult literacy rate increased from 54 percent in 1970 to 74 percent in 1985 (UNDP 1990), while primary school enrollment went up from 72 percent in 1965 to 119 percent in 1988. Secondary school enrollments increased even more rapidly during the same period—from 12 percent to 48 percent (World Bank 1991b). While the adult literacy rate in Indonesia still lags behind other Southeast Asian countries such as Thailand and the Philippines, its enrollment rates are comparable to countries such as Malaysia that enjoy significantly higher income levels.

Indonesia has also been successful in narrowing gender disparities in adult literacy and school enrollment rates. The female literacy rate went up from 64 to 78 percent of the male literacy rate between 1970 and 1985 (UNDP 1990). The primary enrollment rate for females, which was 82 percent of the male primary enrollment rate in 1965, achieved virtual parity with the male primary enrollment rate by 1988. The secondary school enrollment rate for females, which was only 41 percent of the corresponding rate for males in 1965, virtually doubled to become 81 percent of the rate for males by 1988 (World Bank 1991b).

B. Data

The data for this study come from the 1987 round of the National Socioeconomic Survey (SUSENAS), which is a nationally representative survey of Indonesia that is undertaken periodically. The 1987 round, conducted in January, covered roughly 250,000 individuals residing in 50,000 households. While focusing on the health status of individuals and the choice of health providers for curative care, the 1987 SUSENAS survey also obtained information on (i) the gender, age, and current school enrollment of children; (ii) completed schooling level for all adults (recorded in the following categories: subprimary, primary, vocational lower secondary, general lower secondary, vocational higher secondary, general higher secondary, post-secondary diploma, and university); and (iii) the sources of household income, including monthly wages earned by salaried individuals.

The other data source used is the Village Potential (*Potensi Desa*) module of the Economic Census 1986—a census of all the villages in Indonesia. The Economic Census reports extensive information on the social and economic infrastructure of villages. Although, in principle, it is possible to merge the SUSENAS household data with the village-level information from the Economic Census, the SUSENAS data tapes identify only the district (*kabupaten*)—not the village—of residence of households to protect their confidentiality. Therefore, the facilities' data from the Economic Census can only be used at the (more aggregated) district level.

Although the SUSENAS data are rich in some areas—particularly, consumption expenditures and health care demand—they contain almost no information on household ownership of assets, time allocation, and the type of occupations held by individuals (other than the head of the household). This affects the nature of the empirical analysis undertaken in this paper.

C. School Enrollment Model

This paper focuses on the demand for schooling of children 6 to 23 years of age. Separate relations are estimated for four age groups: 6–11, 12–14, 15–17, and 18–23 years. These groups roughly correspond to the four levels of schooling, specifically, primary, lower secondary, higher secondary, and tertiary, respectively. Since an important objective of this paper is to test for differences in the determinants of male and female school enrollment, all the coefficients of each relation are allowed to differ by gender.[5] The equations to be estimated are:

$$(1) \quad \Pr(S_i = 1) = F(a^{jk} + b^{jk}A_i + c^{jk}H_i + d^{jk}C_i + \mu_i^{jk}),$$
$$j = m, f,$$

where

i	indexes the individual child,
j	indexes gender (m = males, f = females),
k	indexes the age group ($k = 1,4$)
$F(\cdot)$	= cumulative logistic distribution,
$Pr(S_i)$	= the probability of child i being enrolled in school,
A	= vector of single-year age dummies,
H	= vector of household characteristics, such as nonlabor income and schooling of the household head and spouse,
C	= vector of community-level characteristics, including schooling infrastructure,[6] and
μ	= i.i.d. disturbance term.

Since the school enrollment variable, S_i, is a dichotomous variable assuming the value one if the child was in school at the time of the survey and zero otherwise, Equation (1) is estimated by the maximum likelihood logit estimation method. Single-year age dummies are included in the enrollment equation to control for the possibly nonlinear relationship between schooling progression and child age. The vector of household characteristics (H_i) includes the natural log of household nonlabor income,[7] age and schooling of the household head, age and schooling of the head's spouse, and urban/rural residence. Unfortunately, the SUSENAS survey design does not permit identification of the parents of children residing in a household. As such, I use characteristics of the household

---

5. This is achieved by interacting all of the explanatory variables with a dichotomous variable for gender.
6. Of course, if the supply of schools, particularly private schools, responds to demand, it would not be proper to include schooling infrastructure as an explanatory variable in the enrollment equations. However, most, if not all, of the schooling infrastructure considered here is publicly provided, and is influenced little, if at all, by the local demand for schools.
7. In many survey data sets, a large majority of households report zero nonlabor income, which limits the usefulness of this measure. However, this is not the case with the 1987 SUSENAS sample, in which fewer than 5 percent of the sample reported zero nonlabor income.

head, who is typically the most senior decision-maker in a household, and his/her spouse. Insofar as there are some female household heads (in about 8 percent of the sample households), the age and schooling variables for the head and spouse are defined as being sex-specific, for example, age and schooling of the male head, female head, male head's wife, and female head's husband.

Since the generic model sketched in Section II treats the time allocation of children and parents (to schooling and other, including wage, activities) as choices made jointly with schooling decisions, the wage or labor income of the household cannot be included as an exogenous explanatory variable in Relation (1). Nonlabor income of the household is used instead. The age of the household head's spouse was not included because of its high collinearity with the head's age.

The vector of community characteristics, data on which are obtained from the 1986 Economic Census, includes the proportion of villages in the household's district of residence: (i) having a lower secondary school, a higher secondary school, and a college or academy;[8] (ii) accessible by an all-weather road; and (iii) accessible by water only.[9] The last variable is relevant since a number of villages in Indonesia, especially in the outer islands, can only be accessed by water; the isolation of such villages may reduce access to schools and colleges, among other things. All of the community-level variables are intended to capture the travel costs of schooling. In a situation where schooling is provided largely free of charge, as in Indonesia, distance and access to schools reflect the cost of schooling for households.

D. Returns to Schooling Model

In addition, the paper estimates the pecuniary returns to schooling for adult men and women who have completed their schooling, using the SUSENAS survey data. Note that the samples used to estimate the school enrollment equation and the earnings function are nonoverlapping. A semilog earnings (E) function is estimated in which the right-side variables are dichotomous variables for the time different schooling categories recorded in the survey (D_{id}), quadratics in age (A), and an i.i.d. disturbance term (ε):

$$(2) \quad \ln E_i = \alpha^j + \sum_d \beta_d^j(A_i)D_{id} + \gamma^j A_i + \lambda^j A_i^2 + \varepsilon_i^j,$$

where i indexes the individual and j indexes gender. The use of the nine dichotomous variables for the different schooling categories permits considerable nonlinearities in the schooling impact, as well as different effects for vocational than for general secondary schooling and for diploma than for university post-secondary schooling.[10] As in the case of the enrollment equation, each of the parameters of the earnings function is permitted to differ across females and males, since the basic question of interest in this study is whether there are gender differences

8. Since virtually all the villages in the sample have primary schools, it was not possible to include the availability of primary schools as a community characteristic affecting school enrollment.

9. That is, the proportion of villages in a district that are water-locked.

10. The excluded category is no schooling.

in the returns to schooling. Finally, since the sample of wage earners includes individuals belonging to very different age cohorts and since it is presumably the younger cohort's experiences in the labor market that should be most relevant for schooling decisions in the present, I permit all the schooling coefficients of the earnings function in (2) to vary (continuously) by age. This is done by interacting each of the nine dichotomous variables for the different schooling categories for males and females by age.

The major estimation issue in the context of the earnings function is sample selectivity bias. Sample selectivity may occur because earnings are observed only for individuals participating in the paid labor force—a nonrandom sample of individuals. While one could use the Heckman (1974, 1976) model of selectivity correction to control for sample selectivity, there is an analytical complication in the present context. Typically in the literature, selectivity in, say, female wage rate equations is identified by variables such as the number of children younger than age five or household nonlabor income, since these variables influence a woman's participation in the wage labor market but presumably not her market wage rate. However, when the observed market performance variable is annual earnings—as it is in the SUSENAS data (which do not report the annual days or hours worked by individuals)—there is an identification problem. Since earnings are the product of an hourly wage rate and the number of hours worked, the earnings function should, in principle, include all the regressors in the market wage and labor supply equations, including variables like nonlabor income and the number of children. Indeed, it is difficult to think of a single identifying instrument that would influence an individual's labor supply but not his/her participation in the wage market.[11]

For illustrative purposes, I still estimate a "traditional" earnings function with the Heckman selectivity correction being identified by marital status, household nonlabor income and spouse's age. This earnings function is valid only under the assumption that hours worked are exogenously set. However, given that much of the employment in Indonesia is in nonformal labor markets, where hours worked are highly variable and choice-based, especially for women, the traditional earnings function with its strict identifying restrictions for sample selectivity is untenable. Therefore, I also estimate (using ordinary least squares) an expanded earnings function that includes marital status, nonlabor income and spouse's age but that does not control for sample selectivity.

IV. Gender Differences in Labor Market Outcomes and in School Enrollments

The lower panel of Table 1, which reports the sample means and standard deviations for the sample of individuals in the paid labor force, shows that male labor force participants are somewhat older (by about four years) and

---

11. Of course, the Mills' ratio in the Heckman procedure will still work because of the normality assumption and the associated nonlinearity in the model, but nonlinearity is a weak basis for identifying nonlinearity.

Table 1
Means and Standard Deviations for Earnings Equation Sample, Indonesia, 1987

Variable	Both Sexes		Females		Males	
	Mean	Standard Deviation	Mean	Standard Deviation	Mean	Standard Deviation
	Sample of all Individuals Older than 15 Not Currently in School					
Age	36.070	14.853	35.019	14.656	37.150	14.978
Whether completed						
Some primary schooling	0.298	0.457	0.300	0.458	0.295	0.456
Primary schooling	0.289	0.453	0.272	0.445	0.307	0.461
General lower secondary schooling	0.080	0.271	0.069	0.253	0.092	0.289
Vocational lower secondary schooling	0.017	0.128	0.015	0.120	0.019	0.137
General higher secondary schooling	0.054	0.227	0.039	0.194	0.070	0.255
Vocational higher seconary schooling	0.050	0.218	0.039	0.194	0.061	0.239
Diploma 1 or 2	0.003	0.053	0.002	0.047	0.003	0.058
Diploma 3	0.007	0.082	0.004	0.063	0.010	0.097
University	0.006	0.077	0.003	0.051	0.009	0.096
% wage earners	0.232	0.422	0.111	0.314	0.357	0.479
Number of observations	123,282		62,483		60,799	

Sample of wage earners only

	Mean	SD	Mean	SD	Mean	SD
Age	37.033	12.334	33.980	11.880	38.007	12.317
Spouse's age	38.876	12.880	44.902	12.901	36.956	12.266
Spouse's schooling (years)	5.124	4.117	5.744	4.700	4.927	3.892
Monthly salary (Rp.)	78,484	88,322	45,940	48,445	88,859	95,364
Whether household head	0.654	0.476	0.001	0.034	0.862	0.345
Whether married	0.860	0.347	0.776	0.417	0.887	0.317
Household nonlabor income (Rp.)	25,099	78,520	30,591	118,046	23,349	60,634
Whether completed						
Some primary schooling	0.271	0.444	0.276	0.447	0.269	0.443
Primary schooling	0.249	0.433	0.186	0.389	0.270	0.444
General lower secondary schooling	0.083	0.277	0.047	0.212	0.095	0.293
Vocational lower secondary schooling	0.023	0.149	0.012	0.111	0.026	0.159
General higher secondary schooling	0.081	0.274	0.060	0.237	0.088	0.284
Vocational higher secondary schooling	0.116	0.320	0.145	0.352	0.106	0.308
Diploma 1 or 2	0.008	0.091	0.011	0.104	0.008	0.087
Diploma 3	0.019	0.136	0.014	0.119	0.020	0.141
University	0.019	0.136	0.011	0.106	0.021	0.144
Number of observations	28,624		6,919		21,705	

receive monthly wages that are almost two times as much as what females receive. Thus, a part of the male-female salary differential may be due to the average age difference, although the age difference is small enough that it would not seem to account for a large part of the differential.

Table 1 also indicates generally higher levels of schooling for men than women. For instance, 9.7 percent of the men in the sample, but as many as 23.8 percent of the women, had no schooling. While 36.6 percent of the men had not completed primary school, the corresponding number of women was 51.4 percent. A significantly larger proportion of males (18.3 percent) than females (10.7 percent) had completed general secondary school. Of individuals who had progressed beyond lower secondary school, the proportion who completed higher secondary vocational school is higher for females (60.2 percent) than for males (43.6 percent). Therefore, part of the male-female difference in earnings may also be due to the lower levels of schooling and greater concentration in vocational schooling by women.[12]

Figure 1, which plots mean monthly earnings of males and females by their level of schooling, reveals that males earn significantly more than females at all levels, with the disparity being greatest at the tertiary level (86.6 percent) and smallest at the secondary level (36.3 percent). However, since the data in Figure 1 represent averages over widely different age-cohorts, they may not accurately represent gender disparities in labor market returns to schooling for younger cohorts. It is the experience of the younger cohorts that is most relevant for current and future schooling decisions. Figure 2 shows mean monthly earnings by gender, schooling level, and age-cohort. The most interesting observation from Figure 2 is that, while gender differences in the earnings of secondary and tertiary-educated individuals are much smaller for the younger cohorts than for the older cohorts, exactly the opposite is true for individuals with no or little schooling. Among the youngest cohort (aged 23 and below), males with tertiary schooling earn only 11 percent more on average than their female counterparts, while males with secondary schooling earn 18.8 percent more than females with the same schooling level. In contrast, for the oldest cohort (aged 55 and over), men with tertiary schooling earn as much as 214.1 percent, and men with secondary schooling earn 52.8 percent, more than women with equivalent levels of schooling. Thus, if the differences across cohorts are indicative of what has been happening over time in Indonesia, the results suggest that there has been a remarkable increase in the relative (to men) labor market returns to female secondary and tertiary schooling.[13] This in turn may reflect that the rapid economic growth and diversification of economic activity that has been taking place in Indonesia during the last two or three decades has increased the demand for educated female labor relative to male labor.

---

12. Some researchers have suggested that vocational senior high school is of lower quality than general senior high school, though there is considerable controversy over the relative rates of return to general, vocational, and diversified schooling at the junior and senior secondary level. Psacharopoulos and Loxley (1985) review this controversy.

13. Note that both men and women with tertiary schooling in the youngest cohort earn significantly less in absolute terms than their counterparts in the oldest cohort (aged 55 and over).

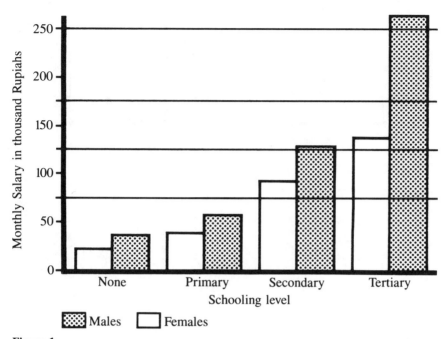

Figure 1
Mean Monthly Earnings of Men and Women of All Ages, by Schooling Level

Figure 3 shows average paid labor force participation rates for men and women with different levels of schooling, while Figure 4 presents the same information by age cohort. While male rates of participation in the paid labor force are greater than female participation rates at all schooling levels, the relative difference is smallest at the tertiary level (51.2 percent) and largest at the primary level (190.6 percent). Interestingly, the cohort-specific participation patterns shown in Figure 4 are similar to the cohort-specific earnings patterns observed in Figure 2. The gender disparity in paid labor force participation rates is smallest for the youngest cohort of individuals with tertiary education (10.3 percent) and greatest for the oldest cohort of tertiary-educated individuals (111.1 percent).

The results thus show that, among the youngest cohort of individuals aged 23 and below, almost as many women with tertiary schooling as men participate in the paid labor force. Furthermore, on average, these women earn only slightly less than their male counterparts. Thus, the Indonesian labor market seems to be remarkably even-handed in its treatment of males and females aged 23 and below with tertiary schooling. This may explain why women have been obtaining secondary and tertiary schooling in large numbers in recent decades; the tertiary enrollment rate (for women aged 18–23 years) jumped from merely one percent in 1960 to about 6 percent in 1980 and to 16 percent by 1987 (see Table 2 below). The secondary enrollment rate for women increased from 17.3 percent in 1960 to 73.6 percent in 1987, thereby reducing the gender disparity in secondary enroll-

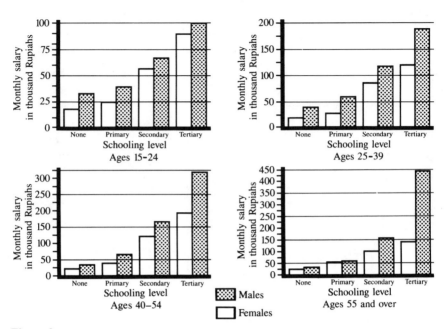

Figure 2
Mean Monthly Earnings of Men and Women, By Age Cohort, Indonesia, 1987

ments to merely 5.4 percent. These are impressive achievements to have accomplished within a span of 27 years.

Figure 5 plots the single-year age-specific school enrollment rates for the sample of males and females between the ages of 6 and 23 years. The plot echoes the results presented earlier; through age 11, school enrollment rates are very similar for boys and girls.[14] Beginning with age 12 (corresponding roughly to the start of secondary school), boys tend to have increasingly higher enrollment rates. Beyond age 17 (corresponding roughly to the completion of secondary school), the gender disparity in enrollment rates widens considerably.[15]

V. Empirical Results

A. *Returns to Schooling*

Table 3 reports three set of estimates of the log earnings function. The first two columns of the table contain the selectivity-corrected and -uncorrected estimates

---

14. Indeed, at ages 6 and 7, the school enrollment rate is somewhat higher for girls than for boys.

15. Note that the enrollment rates presented here are not biased due to the problem, common to many household surveys in developing countries, of nonenumeration of children living outside their parents' home. The SUSENAS survey enumerated all children in a household, irrespective of their relation to the household head. Since the SUSENAS is a nationally representative sample of *individuals*, children not residing at their parents' home are, in principle, enumerated at their new residences.

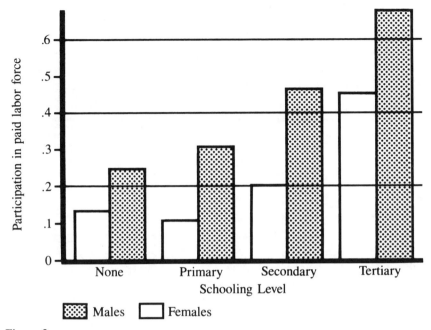

Figure 3
Paid Labor Force Participation Rates for Men and Women of All Ages, by Schooling Level, Indonesia, 1987

of the "traditional" earnings function, with its assumption of exogenous (or fixed) hours worked. The third column reports estimates of the "expanded" earnings function, which includes, in addition to the variables in the "traditional" earnings function, spouse's age, household nonlabor income, and marital status. Due to the inclusion of the these variables, no (theoretically plausible) correction for selectivity can be made.

In each of the three specifications, the coefficients on the male slope dummies are jointly significant at less than the 1 percent level, implying significant gender differences in the determinants of earnings. In addition, for all three specifications, the null hypothesis that the schooling coefficients do not vary by age is soundly rejected. However, in all three specifications, the coefficients on the schooling terms interacted with *both* the male dummy and age are not jointly significant even at the 10 percent level. Thus, the finding that age-cohort effects do matter in the earnings function but that they do not differ across gender is robust across all specifications.

In the first equation, the selectivity term (λ) is highly significant, indicating the importance of sample selectivity in influencing log earnings. The signs and significance of schooling coefficients are broadly similar across the selectivity-corrected and the expanded earnings specifications, reflecting the fact that both include (directly in the latter and indirectly via the Mills' ratio in the former)

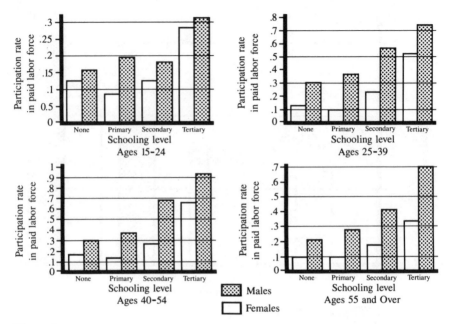

Figure 4
Paid Labor Force Participation Rates for Men and Women, By Age Cohort, Indonesia, 1987

Table 2
Enrollment Rates in Indonesia, 1960–87

Age group (years)	1960		1980		1987	
	Males	Females	Males	Females	Males	Females
6–11	55.0	43.1	89.4	76.3	78.2	79.0
12–17	30.7	17.3	58.6	43.9	77.6	73.6
18–23	3.4	1.0	13.4	5.9	27.3	16.0

Source: The 1960 and 1980 figures are from UNESCO 1989, "Trends and Projections of Enrollments by Level of Education and by Age, 1960–2025," November, mimeo. The 1987 figures are calculated from SUSENAS data files.

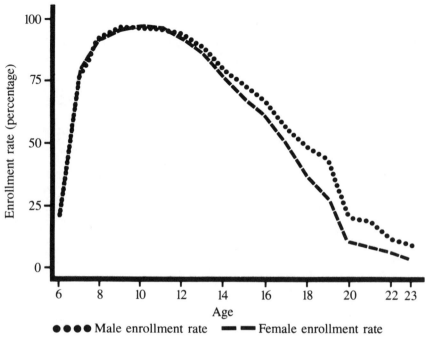

Figure 5
Age-specific schooling enrollment rates, ages 6–23, Indonesia, 1987

spouse's age, household nonlabor income, and marital status. However, the magnitude of the (uninteracted) schooling coefficients appears to be larger in the
selectivity-corrected specification than in the expanded specification. Another
important difference between the two specifications is that the expanded specification shows a significant gender difference in the coefficient on primary schooling while the selectivity-corrected specification does not. However, as cautioned
earlier, the analytical basis for identifying sample selectivity is weak, given that
the observed labor market performance variable in the SUSENAS data is earnings, and not the wage rate. Consequently, the coefficients of the selectivity-
corrected earnings function should be interpreted with caution.

Since the hypothesis that the age-cohort effects are identical for men and
women cannot be rejected, I impose a common (for men and women) set of
coefficients on the age-schooling interacted variables to reestimate the expanded
earnings function. Table 4 presents these estimates. The most interesting observation from Table 4 is that the schooling coefficients for men are significantly smaller
than those for women for all schooling levels above lower secondary. The magnitude of the gender difference increases from lower secondary to the Diploma 1/2
level and declines thereafter. Another finding is that the age-cohort effects are
highy significant for all schooling levels, with the magnitude of the age-schooling
interaction coefficients increasing with the level of schooling.

Table 3
Log Earnings Equations for Individuals Over 15 Not Currently in School, Indonesia, 1987

Independent Variable	Traditional Earnings Function								Expanded Earnings Function with no selectivity control			
	Selectivity control				No selectivity control							
			Variable interacted with male dummy				Variable interacted with male dummy				Variable interacted with male dummy	
	Parameter Estimate	T ratio	Parameter Estimate	T ratio	Parameter Estimate	T ratio	Parameter Estimate	T ratio	Parameter Estimate	T ratio	Parameter Estimate	T ratio
Intercept	10.344	85.9	−0.040	−0.3	9.517	85.6	−0.243	−1.8	9.597	69.8	0.133	0.8
Age (years)	−0.007	−1.5	0.028	4.8	0.002	0.5	0.045	7.8	−0.001	−0.1	0.033	5.2
Age squared ($\times 10^3$)	0.180	3.2	−0.412	−6.5	0.039	0.7	−0.571	−8.9	0.009	0.1	−0.365	−4.4
Household nonlabor income ($\times 10^6$)									0.630	2.4	1.218	2.8
Whether married									−0.092	−1.3	0.461	4.8
Spouse's age									−0.001	−0.5	−0.012	−4.0
Whether completed:												
Some primary schooling	0.116	1.4	0.044	0.4	0.064	0.8	0.226	2.1	0.073	0.9	0.166	1.6
Primary schooling	0.134	1.5	0.005	0.0	0.022	0.2	0.212	1.9	0.011	0.1	0.199	1.8
General lower secondary schooling	0.657	4.8	−0.209	−1.3	0.424	3.0	0.063	0.4	0.431	3.1	0.016	0.1
Vocational lower secondary schooling	0.721	2.6	−0.242	−0.8	0.521	1.8	0.130	0.4	0.521	1.8	0.022	0.1
General higher secondary	0.820	5.1	−0.199	−1.1	0.765	4.7	−0.126	−0.7	0.770	4.7	−0.177	−1.0
Vocational higher secondary	0.711	6.2	−0.301	−2.1	0.767	6.6	−0.170	−1.2	0.789	6.8	−0.312	−2.2
Diploma 1, 2	0.798	2.4	−0.845	−2.0	0.898	2.7	−0.587	−1.4	0.914	2.8	−0.707	−1.7
Diploma 3	1.406	3.6	−0.747	−1.7	1.378	3.5	−0.492	−1.1	1.323	3.4	−0.635	−1.5
University	0.913	2.1	−0.413	−0.9	0.975	2.3	−0.289	−0.6	0.982	2.3	−0.458	−1.0

Age interacted with (see cohort effects)

Variable	(1) Coef.	(1) T-ratio	(1) Age-int. coef.	(1) Age-int. T-ratio	(2) Coef.	(2) T-ratio	(2) Age-int. coef.	(2) Age-int. T-ratio	(3) Coef.	(3) T-ratio	(3) Age-int. coef.	(3) Age-int. T-ratio
Household nonlabor income ($\times 10^6$)									-0.006	-0.9	-0.014	-1.3
Whether married									0.004	1.7	-0.012	-4.0
Spouse's age									0.000	0.6	0.000	1.6
Some primary schooling	0.005	2.3	-0.003	-1.2	0.006	2.5	-0.006	-2.1	0.005	2.4	-0.004	-1.6
Primary schooling	0.014	6.0	-0.002	-0.7	0.015	6.1	-0.004	-1.4	0.015	6.2	-0.004	-1.4
General lower secondary schooling	0.018	4.5	-0.003	-0.5	0.023	5.6	-0.005	-1.1	0.022	5.5	-0.004	-0.8
Vocational lower secondary schooling	0.016	2.2	-0.002	-0.4	0.021	2.7	-0.008	-0.9	0.021	2.7	-0.005	-0.7
General higher secondary	0.021	4.1	0.000	-0.1	0.025	4.8	-0.001	-0.2	0.024	4.7	0.000	0.0
Vocational higher education	0.021	6.2	0.012	1.0	0.028	8.5	-0.005	-1.4	0.027	8.1	-0.002	-0.5
Diploma 1, 2	0.020	2.1	0.017	1.4	0.029	3.1	0.003	0.3	0.028	3.0	0.006	0.6
Diploma 3	0.006	0.5	0.006	0.4	0.016	1.3	0.010	0.8	0.016	1.4	0.013	1.1
University	0.026	2.0			0.035	2.7	0.001	0.1	0.034	2.6	0.005	0.4
λ (selectivity term)	-0.409	-15.6										
Number of observations	28,624				28,624				28,624			
R-squared	0.464				0.459				0.471			
F ratio	588.4				592.0				480.6			

F test for:

	(1)	(1)	(2)	(2)	(3)	(3)
No male-female differences in schooling coefficients	129.2	0.000	10.905	0.000	12.147	0.000
Zero cohort (age) effects in schooling coefficients	358.0	0.000	31.452	0.000	29.790	0.000
No male-female differences in cohort effects on schooling	5.684	0.770	1.430		1.260	

Notes: The selectivity term is obtained from the estimates reported in Table 6. Figures in "T-ratio" column for Wald/F tests are significance levels.

Table 4

Expanded Log Earnings Equation Without Selectivity Control and With No Gender Differences in Cohort Effects on Schooling Returns, Individuals Not Currently in School, Indonesia, 1987

Independent Variable	Parameter Estimate	T ratio	Variable interacted with male dummy Parameter Estimate	T ratio
Intercept	9.503	79.6	0.281	2.1
Age (years)	0.003	0.6	0.028	5.2
Age squared ($\times$ 10^3)	−0.018	−0.3	−0.332	−4.1
Household nonlabor income ($\times$ 10^6)	0.624	2.4	1.200	2.8
Whether married	−0.090	−1.3	0.458	4.8
Spouse's age	−0.001	−0.5	−0.011	−4.0
Whether completed				
Some primary schooling	0.184	3.7	0.000	0.0
Primary schooling	0.113	2.1	0.047	1.3
General lower secondary schooling	0.532	7.2	−0.134	−2.6
Vocational lower secondary schooling	0.675	5.0	−0.190	−2.1
General higher secondary	0.770	10.2	−0.208	−4.1
Vocational higher secondary	0.844	12.5	−0.404	−10.1
Diploma 1, 2	0.775	3.8	−0.502	−4.7
Diploma 3	0.936	6.2	−0.224	−2.5
University	0.825	5.2	−0.312	−3.2
Age interacted with (viz. cohort effects)				
Household nonlabor income ($\times$ 10^6)	−0.006	−0.9	−0.013	−1.3
Whether married	0.004	1.7	−0.012	−4.0
Spouse's age	0.000	0.6	0.000	1.6
Some primary schooling	0.002	2.0		
Primary schooling	0.012	9.9		
General lower secondary schooling	0.019	11.3		
Vocational lower secondary schooling	0.016	5.5		
General higher secondary	0.025	12.6		
Vocational higher secondary	0.026	14.6		
Diploma 1, 2	0.032	6.0		
Diploma 3	0.029	7.3		
University	0.039	9.6		
Number of observations	28,624			
R-squared	0.471			
F ratio	578.85			

The implied rates of return to various level of schooling for five age-cohorts, under the assumption that each level requires a certain number of years to complete, are presented in Table 5. Two important findings emerge from Table 5. First, the age-cohort differences in the returns to schooling are much greater for higher levels of schooling than lower levels. For instance, while the rate of return to a Diploma 1/2 is 7.1 percent for 20-year-old males, the corresponding rate of return for a 60-year-old male is 17.1 percent. The corresponding rates for females are 10.9 percent and 20.9 percent, respectively. The cohort disparity in the returns to higher education most likely reflects the facts that (a) the wage premium on work experience (proxied here by age) is greater in high-skill jobs (that attract individuals with secondary and tertiary schooling) than in low-skill jobs (attracting individuals with primary schooling or less), and (b) wage premiums on secondary and tertiary schooling have declined over time (and over age-cohorts) because of an enormous increase in the number of secondary- and tertiary-educated individuals in Indonesia.

Second, males have significantly lower returns to schooling than females at the secondary and tertiary levels. These differences are greatest at the level of Diploma 1 and vocational secondary education, but are still appreciable for nonvocational secondary schooling and university education. For instance, the return to university education is 25 percent higher for females than for males. (In contrast, the return to Diploma 1 is 53.5 percent higher for females.)

These results are broadly similar to those obtained by Behrman and Deolalikar (1990b) for 1986 using a different data set from Indonesia (see in particular, SAKERNAS or the Labor Force Survey). Behrman and Deolalikar, too, found significant gender differences in the returns to schooling at all levels. But the magnitude of returns estimated here considerably exceed those reported by Behrman and Deolalikar for both males and females. The differences between their estimates and the ones presented here may be attributed in part to differing methodologies (for example, there was no control for cohort effects in Behrman and Deolalikar), different samples (for example, individuals above 10 years of age in Behrman and Deolalikar, as opposed to individuals above 15 years and not currently in school in this paper), distinct data sets (SAKERNAS as opposed to SUSENAS), and disparate survey years (1986 as opposed to 1987).

The coefficients on age and age-squared in the earnings function reported in Table 4 also differ significantly across gender. Both coefficients are not significantly different from zero for females, indicating that age does not have an additional effect on earnings beyond increasing the returns to schooling. For males, the coefficient on age is significantly positive, while that on age-squared is significantly negative. This implies that pure (schooling-independent) earnings growth for men is positive and large early in the life-cycle (about 2 percent annually at age 15), but falls off rapidly with age (being only 0.3 percent at age 40 and -0.4 at age 50). The same result is observed in a plot of the age-earnings profiles, by schooling level, for men and women (Figures 6 and 7). The plots show a distinct tendency for male earnings growth to drop off faster than female earnings growth, particularly for individuals with secondary schooling.

What could account for the large gender differences in the returns to secondary and tertiary schooling? Unfortunately, an examination of the occupational distri-

Table 5

Implied Gender- and Cohort-Specific Rates of Return to Schooling, Indonesia, 1987

Schooling Level	Age					Assumed years of schooling
	20	30	40	50	60	
Females						
Some primary schooling	7.7	8.5	9.2	10.0	10.8	3
Primary schooling	6.0	8.0	10.1	12.2	14.2	6
General lower secondary schooling	10.2	12.4	14.6	16.7	18.9	9
Vocational lower secondary schooling	11.1	13.0	14.8	16.6	18.4	9
General higher secondary	10.5	12.6	14.7	16.7	18.8	12
Vocational higher secondary	11.3	13.5	15.7	17.8	20.0	12
Diploma 1, 2	10.9	13.4	15.9	18.4	20.9	13
Diploma 3	10.1	12.0	13.9	15.8	17.7	15
University	10.0	12.4	14.8	17.2	19.7	16
Males						
Some primary schooling	7.7	8.5	9.2	10.0	10.8	3
Primary schooling	6.8	8.8	10.9	12.9	15.0	6
General lower secondary schooling	8.8	10.9	13.1	15.3	17.4	9
Vocational lower secondary schooling	9.0	10.9	12.7	14.5	16.3	9
General higher secondary	8.8	10.9	12.9	15.0	17.1	12
Vocational higher secondary	8.0	10.1	12.3	14.4	16.6	12
Diploma 1, 2	7.1	9.6	12.1	14.6	17.1	13
Diploma 3	8.6	10.5	12.4	14.3	16.3	15
University	8.0	10.5	12.9	15.3	17.7	16

Notes: Parameter estimates reported in Table 3 are used in calculating the rates of return. Figures in bold indicate significant (at 5 percent level) gender differences. All age interactions were significant at the 5 percent level. The expanded earnings function includes marital status, spouse's age and household nonlabor income as explanatory variables.

bution of working males and females, which might have shed more light on the mystery, is not possible with the SUSENAS data because of the unavailability of information on occupations and tasks performed by labor market participants. However, it is possible to speculate on the reasons for the greater returns to higher education for women. If most salaried men are in manufacturing occupations and if the manufacturing technology is such that physical strength is important, the wage premium for men in unskilled factory positions (and with low schooling) would be considerable. The estimated returns to higher education would then be higher for females than for males. The data provide some evidence

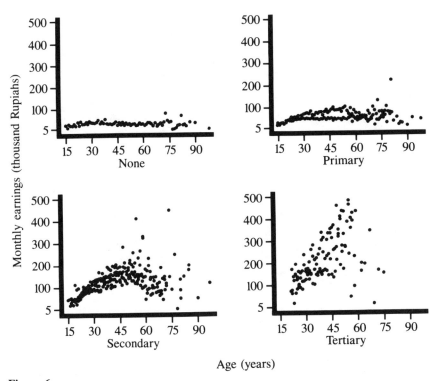

Figure 6
Age-earnings profiles for men, by schooling level, Indonesia, 1987

for this conjecture. For example, the finding that earnings growth, although larger in magnitude for men early in the life cycle, falls off more rapidly with age for men than for women, suggests that physical strength matters more for men.[16] Schooling is often the only vehicle by which women can move out of low-paid, physically demanding jobs. This is what happened in the United States from about 1880 to 1920, when women acquired secondary schooling and moved into clerical occupations in large numbers (Goldin 1992). As noted earlier, this trend appears to be already underway in Indonesia. While secondary school enrollment for males more than doubled (from about 31 percent to 78 percent) between 1960 and 1987, the secondary enrollment rate for females increased more than four-fold (from 17 percent to 74 percent) (Table 2). Thus, many more women than men entered secondary school over this period.

Not only has the relative rate of expansion of secondary schooling been greater among Indonesian females than males, but secondary-educated women are over-represented in the pool of wage earners (relative to the general population) to a

---

16. I am grateful to Claudia Goldin for suggesting this point.

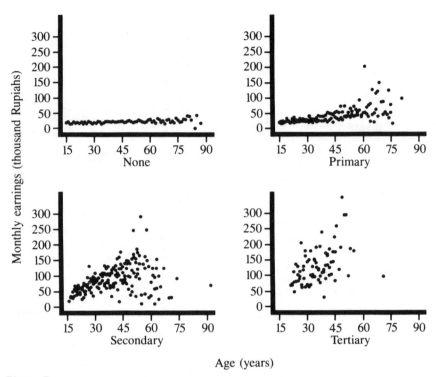

Figure 7
Age-earnings profiles for women, by schooling level, Indonesia, 1987

much greater extent than secondary-schooled men. For example, the data in Table 1 indicate that while only 0.9 percent of women in the SUSENAS sample had completed diplomas or university, as many as 3.6 percent of female wage earners had that level of schooling. This in itself is not surprising, since one would expect individuals with higher schooling to be overrepresented in the paid labor force. However, the degree of overrepresentation in the paid labor force for men with higher education is much smaller. While 2.2 percent of all men in the sample had diploma- or university-level schooling, 4.9 percent of male wage earners had the same level of schooling. Thus, while men with diploma or university education are overrepresented among the pool of wage earners (relative to the general population) by a factor of 2.2, the degree of overrepresentation for women with diploma/university education is 4.0.

Another explanation for the higher observed returns to schooling for females may have to do with selection. The rate at which women are selected out of the paid labor force means that, at higher education levels, earners are more heavily selected towards the more talented. Unfortunately, given the weak basis for identifying selectivity, it is difficult to test this conjecture. However, the probit participation results (see below) do show that while women's participation in the paid

Table 6

Maximum Likelihood Probit Estimates of the Probability of Wage Labor Participation Individuals Over 15 Currently in School, Indonesia, 1987

Independent Variable	Parameter Estimate	T ratio	Variable interacted with male dummy	
			Parameter Estimate	T ratio
Intercept	−1.1786	−11.7	0.1681	1.2
Age (years)	0.0234	5.9	0.0109	2.2
Age squared ($\times$ 10^3)	−0.6676	−13.0	0.0415	0.7
Household nonlabor income ($\times 10^6$)	0.3348	1.4	−0.0331	−0.1
Whether married	−0.4782	−9.2	0.8196	11.5
Spouse's age	−0.0085	−5.1	−0.0143	−6.6
Whether completed				
Some primary schooling	−0.1363	−2.2	0.4641	5.3
Primary schooling	−0.3865	−5.8	0.6018	6.6
General lower secondary schooling	−0.7294	−7.0	0.6988	5.4
Vocational lower secondary schooling	−0.6164	−3.2	0.8940	3.8
General higher secondary	−0.2493	−2.1	0.1251	0.8
Vocational higher secondary	0.0992	0.9	0.1972	1.4
Diploma 1, 2	0.1720	0.4	0.8891	1.6
Diploma 3	−0.2540	−0.7	0.6325	1.5
University	−0.0445	−0.1	−0.1482	−0.3
Age interacted with (see cohort effects)				
Household nonlabor income ($\times 10^6$)	−0.0105	−1.6	−0.0327	−3.1
Whether married	0.0130	8.7	−0.0074	−3.5
Spouse's age	0.0003	6.2	0.0001	1.1
Some primary schooling	0.0012	0.8	−0.0053	−2.6
Primary schooling	0.0041	2.2	−0.0050	−2.2
General lower secondary schooling	0.0155	5.0	−0.0026	−0.7
Vocational lower secondary schooling	0.0140	2.6	−0.0051	−0.8
General higher secondary	0.0151	4.0	0.0113	2.5
Vocational higher secondary	0.0276	8.4	−0.0050	−1.2
Diploma 1, 2	0.0348	2.7	−0.0205	−1.3
Diploma 3	0.0368	3.4	−0.0076	−0.6
University	0.0358	2.6	0.0149	0.9
Number of observations	123,282			
Log likelihood ratio	−55,177			
Chi squared	23,260			

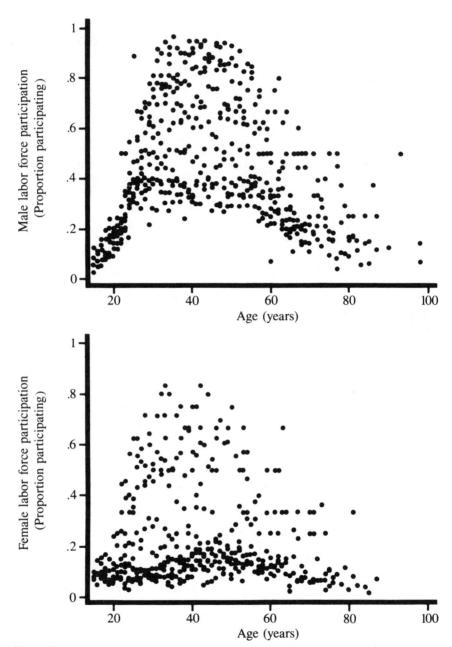

Figure 8
Age Profile of Paid Labor Force Participation

labor force increases more rapidly (relative to male participation) with age early in the life-cycle, they also drop out of the paid labor force at a faster rate at older ages. This is an indication that the self-selection (into the paid labor force) process is much more discriminating at older ages and higher education levels for women.

A brief discussion of the probit model of wage labor participation used to correct for sample selectivity may be instructive (Table 6). The estimates indicate a nonlinear effect of schooling on female labor force participation. Up to the lower secondary level, schooling reduces paid labor force participation among women, but completion of higher secondary and tertiary schooling increases the probability of participation. Men with lower secondary schooling and below have a significantly higher probability of participating in the paid labor force relative to women, but beyond the lower secondary level there are few significant gender differences. The age-schooling interaction terms are generally significant in the probit model, indicating that age-cohort effects are important. However, with the exception of primary and general higher secondary schooling, the cohort effects do not differ significantly by gender.

The U-shaped (with respect to schooling) labor force participation curve for women suggests that the income effect associated with greater schooling (and wages) outweighs the substitution effect at low levels of schooling and wages, but that the female labor supply curve becomes forward-sloping at higher levels of schooling and wages. Again, this phenomenon is strikingly similar to what happened in the United States earlier in this century (Goldin 1992).

Other effects differ across males and females. The coefficient on age is significantly larger for males than for females, indicating that the age-profile of participation in the paid labor force is steeper for males than for females. This is also observed in Figure 8 which plots the age profile of labor force participation rates for males and females.

Finally, while household nonlabor income has no significant effect on female wage labor participation, it has a significant and large negative effect on male wage labor participation when interacted with age. The latter result could mean either that households value the leisure of older males more than that of (older or younger) females or that an increase in nonlabor income induces older males— but not females—to participate more in own firm/farm enterprises (and proportionately less in market wage activities).

B. Determinants of School Enrollment

Table 7 reports the means and standard deviations of variables used in the estimation of schooling demand equations, while Table 8 reports the logit estimates of the probability of an individual being enrolled in school for the age groups (6–11 (corresponding to primary school), 12–14 (lower secondary), 15–17 (higher secondary), and 18–23 (tertiary). Note that the enrollment rates for older children are not biased by the selectivity problem of older children leaving home. The SUSENAS survey enumerated all children in a household, irrespective of their relation to the household head. Since the SUSENAS is a nationally representative sample of *individuals,* children not residing at their parents' home are enumerated

Table 7

Means and Standard Deviations, Persons Aged 6–23 Years, Indonesia, 1987

Variable	Mean	Standard Deviation
Age (years)	13.73	5.32
Whether male	0.50	0.50
Whether currently enrolled in school	0.61	0.49
Monthly household nonlabor income (Rp.)	27,802	70,742
Age of household head	43.70	11.34
Schooling years of household head	5.57	3.93
Schooling years of household head's spouse	4.31	3.52
Whether urban resident	0.33	0.47
Proportion of villages in district of residence having		
Access by water only	0.07	0.15
All-weather road	0.79	0.22
Lower secondary school	0.37	0.25
Higher secondary school	0.19	0.22
College or academy	0.09	0.29
Number of observations	89,089	

at their new residence. For this reason, I have estimated enrollment equations at the individual—not the household—level.

For the two youngest age groups, the coefficients of the logit equation were not significantly different for boys and girls even at the 10 percent level. Therefore, a single model for both sexes was estimated for these age groups.

A number of household characteristics are observed to influence enrollment. For all age groups, household nonlabor income increases enrollment probabilities significantly, with a 10 percent increase in nonlabor income increasing the probability of enrollment by 0.03, 0.06, 0.11, and 0.08, respectively, for the age groups 6–11, 12–14, 15–17, and 18–23.

Interestingly, schooling of the household head and his spouse have some of the strongest effects on enrollment probabilities, but only if the household head is male (which occurs in the vast majority—some 92 percent—of the sample households). The characteristics of the female household head and her spouse do not have any significant effects. The fact that there is a strong transmission of schooling across generations in male-headed but not in female-headed households points to an intrinsic difference in the way child schooling decisions are made in these two types of households. Among male-headed households, schooling of the household head has a larger effect on the probability of secondary and tertiary enrollment than schooling of the head's wife. However, for primary-aged children, the wife's schooling has a somewhat larger effect on the enrollment probability than the head's schooling. The age of the male head and his wife are also generally associated with a higher probability of enrollment among all age groups of children.

Community characteristics have relatively few significant effects on school enrollment. The one community variable that is ubiquitously significant in all the estimated equations is urban residence, which, as expected, is associated with higher rates of enrollment for all four age groups. The presence of an all-weather road also has large and significant effects on school enrollment, but only for children aged 6–11 and 18–23. For children aged 12–14, road access has a puzzling negative effect on enrollment. Perhaps the most surprising result is that local availability of schools has few significant effects on enrollment for any age group. A possible reason for the lack of significance of school availability on enrollment may be the limited sample variability in the school facility data. As mentioned in Section III, the individual and household data from the SUSENAS survey can be merged with the PODES village facility data only at the level of the district. A large portion of the inter-village variation in school availability may be lost due to this aggregation. Another reason for the lack of significance of school availability may be due to a high degree of collinearity between included variables, like urban residence and road access, and school availability.

The bottom panel of Table 8 reports the interaction effects of the explanatory variables with the male dummy variable. As noted earlier, a Wald test could not reject the hypothesis that the male slope dummies were jointly significant for the two youngest age groups. The following inferences can be drawn from the male interaction effects. First, the coefficient on the male intercept dummy, as well as most of the coefficients on the age-gender interaction variables (which are not reported in the table), are significantly positive for the age groups 12–14, 15–17, and 18–23, indicating that, after controlling for all household characteristics and locational variables, male children have a significantly higher probability of school enrollment at the secondary and tertiary levels. In contrast, among children aged 6–11, females have a significantly higher probability of being enrolled in school than males. Second, the effect of household nonlabor income on the probability of school enrollment does not differ significantly across gender for any age group of children. Third, the age of a male head and the schooling of his wife have significantly smaller effects on the enrollment probability of tertiary school-aged boys relative to girls aged 18–23. This suggests that older male heads and better-schooled head's wives tend to provide relatively more schooling opportunities at the tertiary levels of female children relative to male children. The fact that an increase in the wife's schooling increases female relative to male tertiary enrollment is consistent with the aggregate (district-level) results obtained by Rosenzweig and Evenson (1977) from India showing an increase in female relative to male child (age 5–14) enrollments with an increase in adult female literacy. If one interprets the male-female differences in school enrollment as evidence of parental bias, the Indonesian results hint at mothers favoring the tertiary schooling of their daughters.

Fourth, only two of the community-level variables are significant in their interactions with the male dummy variable. The isolation of a community on account of being surrounded by water lowers the probability of enrollment for male but

Table 8

Maximum Likelihood Logit Estimates of the Probability of Being Enrolled in School, Ages 6–23, Indonesia, 1987

Independent Variable	Ages 6–11 Coefficient	Ages 6–11 Asymptotic T Ratio	Ages 12–14 Coefficient	Ages 12–14 Asymptotic T Ratio	Ages 15–17 Coefficient	Ages 15–17 Asymptotic T Ratio	Ages 18–23 Coefficient	Ages 18–23 Asymptotic T Ratio
Intercept	-0.678	-28.8	0.079	3.5	-0.600	-11.8	-1.030	-25.5
Ln hh nonlabor income	0.003	2.9	0.006	5.2	0.011	5.1	0.008	5.4
Whether urban resident	0.023	2.6	0.064	7.1	0.209	11.9	0.128	10.3
If hh head male,								
His schooling (years)	0.015	12.1	0.019	14.8	0.033	12.6	0.023	11.8
His age (years)	0.001	2.4	0.001	2.3	0.002	2.0	0.005	5.1
His wife's schooling (years)	0.017	11.7	0.010	6.9	0.017	6.0	0.018	8.6
His wife's age	0.002	2.3	0.001	1.4	0.008	6.3	0.007	7.3
If hh head female,								
Her schooling (years)	-0.028	-0.6	-0.477	0.0	-2.123	0.0	1.510	0.0
Her age (years)	0.009	0.9	-0.330	0.0	-0.314	0.0	0.060	0.0
Her husband's schooling (years)	0.032	0.9	5.382	0.0	3.611	0.0	3.102	0.0
Her husband's age	-0.003	-0.3	0.018	0.0	0.092	0.0	-1.214	0.0
Proportion of villages in district of residence having								
All-weather road	0.171	9.9	-0.051	-3.1	-0.064	-1.6	0.118	3.3
Access by water only	-0.008	-0.4	-0.029	-1.4	0.028	0.5	0.057	1.3
Lower secondary school	0.077	2.3	-0.026	-0.8	0.060	0.9	-0.022	-0.4
Higher secondary school	-0.170	-4.1	0.046	1.1	-0.106	-1.3	0.038	0.6
College or academy	0.009	0.8	-0.008	-0.6	-0.052	-1.7	-0.005	-0.2

Male dummy interacted with

	(1) coef.	(1) t	(2) coef.	(2) t	(3) coef.	(3) t	(4) coef.	(4) t
Intercept	−0.016	−2.5	0.026	4.6	0.200	2.7	0.298	5.5
Ln hh nonlabor income					0.000	0.1	0.003	1.6
Whether urban resident					−0.033	−1.3	−0.025	−1.5
Schooling of hh head, if male					0.003	0.8	0.001	0.2
Age of hh head, if male					−0.002	−1.2	−0.003	−2.4
Schooling of head's wife, if head male					−0.002	−1.0	−0.003	−2.1
Age of head's wife, if head male					0.003	0.8	−0.003	−1.0
Schooling of hh head, if female					−0.359	0.0	−1.471	0.0
Age of hh head, if female					1.169	0.0	−0.110	0.0
Schooling of head's husband, if head female					−0.993	0.0	1.274	0.0
Age of head's husband, if head female					−0.543	0.0	−3.169	0.0
All-weather road					0.025	0.5	0.036	0.8
Access by water only					−0.060	−0.9	−0.121	−2.0
Lower secondary school					−0.086	−0.9	0.062	0.8
Higher secondary school					0.323	2.6	−0.078	−1.0
College or academy					0.036	0.9	0.037	1.3
Log likelihood	−10,371		−5,641		−7,660		−7,872	
Wald test for no gender differences in coefficients	22.848	0.296*	24.457	0.108*	52.008	0.000*	90.792	0.000*
Number of observations	36,690		16,517		13,800		22,082	
Proportion attending school	0.786		0.866		0.626		0.211	

Note: The age groups 6–11, 12–14, 15–17, and 18–23 correspond roughly to primary, lower, secondary, higher secondary, and tertiary levels of schooling, respectively. All equations included single-year age dummies, the coefficients of which are not reported due to space considerations. All reported coefficients are normalized (in other words, multiplied by P.(1 − P), where P is the proportion of children in school) to reflect marginal effects on probabilities.
* Significance level of the corresponding chi-squared statistic.

not for female children (but only for the age group 18–23 years). On the other hand, the presence of a higher secondary school in a community sharply increases the enrollment probability of secondary school-aged boys but not of girls.

VI. Concluding Remarks

Earnings data on a nationally representative sample of Indonesian adults show that males have significantly lower returns to schooling than females at the secondary and tertiary levels. These differences are greatest at the level of Diploma 1 and vocational secondary education, but are still substantial for nonvocational secondary schooling and university education. For instance, the return to university education is 25 percent higher for females than for males. (In contrast, the return to Diploma 1 is 53.5 percent higher for females.) The earnings function estimates also indicate important age-cohort differences in the returns to schooling, with older cohorts obtaining significantly higher returns to schooling, especially at the secondary and tertiary levels, than younger cohorts. However, the estimated models do not indicate that the cohort effects on the returns to schooling differ by gender. There are two possible explanations for the disparity in the returns to higher education among young and old cohorts. First, the higher returns enjoyed by older cohorts may reflect the fact that the wage premium on work experience (proxied here by age) is greater in high-skill jobs (that attract individuals with secondary and tertiary schooling) than in low-skill jobs (attracting individuals with primary schooling or less). Second, the lower returns to higher education enjoyed by younger cohorts may indicate that wage premiums on secondary and tertiary schooling have declined over time (and over age-cohorts) because of an enormous increase in the number of secondary- and tertiary-educated individuals in Indonesia. Both of these phenomena are likely to have occurred.

It is more difficult to explain the gender differences in the returns to schooling. One conjecture is that the gender difference in returns is the result of the manufacturing technology in Indonesia. If factories are structured in such a way that physical strength is important to productivity, the wage premium for men in unskilled factory positions (and with low schooling) would be considerable. The estimated returns to schooling beyond the primary level would then be higher for females than for males. The Indonesian data provide some evidence for this argument. Earnings growth over the life-cycle is observed to be higher for men than for women at early ages, but it falls off more rapidly at later ages for men. Another reason for the higher returns to secondary and tertiary schooling among women may have to do with selectivity. The rate at which women are selected out of the paid labor force means that, at higher education levels, earners are more heavily selected towards the more talented. Unfortunately, the available data do not permit a test of these competing hypotheses.

Despite the higher returns to secondary and tertiary schooling for females, the data on school enrollment show lower enrollment rates for females, particularly at the secondary and above levels. Indeed, the gap between male and female enrollment rates, which is nonexistent at early ages, starts manifesting itself around secondary school age (about 12 years), and increases progressively through age 23.

The analysis in this paper does not show many strong and systematic gender differences in the effects of household and community characteristics on school enrollments. Some evidence suggests that older household heads and better-schooled head's wives provide relatively more schooling opportunities, especially at the tertiary level, for their female relative to male children. In addition, the presence of a higher secondary school in a community sharply increases the enrollment probability of higher secondary school-aged boys but not of girls.

How can one reconcile the findings that schooling attainment, especially at the secondary and tertiary levels, is lower for female than for male children in Indonesia even though women have higher returns to secondary and tertiary schooling than men? The answer may have to do with lags in household and individual responses to perceived returns to schooling. Indeed, all the evidence shows that Indonesian women have been acquiring secondary and tertiary education in relatively larger numbers than men in recent years, probably in response to the greater relative returns to female higher education. Gender differences in enrollment rates in Indonesia have closed dramatically during the last two decades. Between 1965 and 1987, the secondary enrollment rate for females increased more than four-fold to achieve virtual parity with the male secondary enrollment rate. Interestingly, a similar trend occurred in the United States from about 1880 to 1920, when women began acquiring secondary schooling and moving into clerical occupations in large numbers, in part because schooling was the primary skill that allowed women to move out of low-paid manual occupations (Goldin 1992).

Not only has the relative rate of expansion of secondary schooling been greater among Indonesian females, but women with secondary schooling are over-represented in the pool of wage earners (relative to the general population) to a much greater extent than men with secondary schooling. For example, while men with diploma or university education are overrepresented among the pool of wage earners (relative to the general population) by a factor of slightly more than two, the degree of overrepresentation for women with diploma/university education is four. Again, the greater representation of secondary- and tertiary-educated women in the paid labor force probably represents a behavioral response to the higher returns to secondary and tertiary schooling that women enjoy. Since the investigation in this paper is based on a single cross-section of individuals, the analysis of school enrollments does not capture the dynamic process by which households and individuals have been taking advantage of the higher returns to female schooling.

At the same time, it is important to recognize that households may underinvest in their female children's higher schooling, even when the market returns to secondary and tertiary schooling are greater for females, because the opportunity cost of schooling in terms of home production may be higher for older girls. This may be the case because older daughters are generally responsible for housework, cooking, and care of younger siblings. If so, it may be important to experiment with new and innovative ways of encouraging women to attend and stay in school, such as offering evening or night schools and providing monetary incentives (for example, scholarships) to female students.

11 Educational Investments and Returns for Women and Men in Côte d'Ivoire

Wim P. M. Vijverberg

Wim P. M. Vijverberg is an associate professor of economics and political economy at the School of Sciences, the University of Texas at Dallas. This is a revised version of the paper presented at the Conference on Women's Human Capital and Development, Bellagio, Italy, May 18–22, 1992. This chapter has benefitted from comments of Angus Deaton, Claudia Goldin, participants of the Conference and of seminars at Tilburg University, the University of Amsterdam, and the University of Texas at Dallas, and an anonymous referee. The World Bank does not accept responsibility for the views expressed herein, which are those of the author and should not be attributed to the World Bank or its affiliated organizations.

I. Introduction

Do women in the labor market enjoy the same returns to their human capital investments as men do? Is the different treatment of women in the labor market a cause for the lower educational attainment so often observed among women in the Third World? These questions are well worth asking. There are reasons to expect that women's education has an impact on family health and nutrition, on fertility behavior and population growth, on child quality, on poverty and income distribution. If labor market conditions are such that they provide incentives to investments in schooling for women, focused labor market policy can assist in bringing about changes in family behavior and raise levels of schooling attainment.

This paper focuses on Côte d'Ivoire. Schooling levels there have long been low. In 1985, literacy rates were 63 percent for men over 14 years of age and 34 percent for women. While low, they are a substantial improvement over the 18 percent population-wide figure in 1970 (UNDP 1991, Tables 4 and 5), a reflection of intensive efforts to upgrade education over the previous decades. In 1973, Côte d'Ivoire spent 33 percent of its total recurrent public revenue on education, the highest percentage in the world (Den Tuinder 1978, p. 281), and even in 1985 about 22.6 percent of public expenditure went to education, more than all but a few Third World countries (UNDP 1991, Table 15). At the same time, the statistics on literacy illustrate the discrepancy between men and women. Côte d'Ivoire should therefore present an interesting case study for the questions raised above.

Estimation results indicate that, in the late 1980s, private rates of return to education and other forms of technical training were exceptionally high in comparison to other countries. Both directly, through increased earnings in a given mode of employment, and indirectly, through improved access to high-paying wage employment and migration to urban markets, education raises earnings for men and women. However, men's wages exceed women's by a substantial margin for all but the most educated groups of the population, and women have fewer chances to obtain the wage jobs to which they undoubtedly aspire. Labor market conditions do indeed favor the education of men, although women in Côte d'Ivoire should have plenty of incentive to acquire all the schooling they can get.

The number of nonfarm self-employed individuals in the Ivorian labor force is roughly the same as the number of wage employees but two-thirds of them are female. Generally, estimated returns to education are not as high, but they appear to be positive. Among women, returns to elementary schooling are substantial, similar to those estimated among female wage employees.

Côte d'Ivoire does have certain characteristics that prevent one from generalizing these conclusions too broadly. Long a country with a labor shortage, its labor force contains both substantial numbers of unskilled non-Ivorian Africans and highly skilled foreigners, especially from France and Lebanon, who almost certainly have an impact on the distribution of wages. The official public policy has been for a long time to replace them with Ivorian workers, a process called Ivorianization. When this process is completed, one should expect a compression of the wage distribution and smaller returns to education.

Section II elaborates on the regional and sexual differences in human capital acquisitions in Côte d'Ivoire, as they are observed in the sample used for this study, the Côte d'Ivoire Living Standards Survey (CILSS). Section III opens with a discussion of the Ivorian labor market and proceeds with laying out the econometric model. With this model, we study the sorting mechanism in the labor market as well as earnings in wage and nonfarm self-employment (applying the appropriate correction for selectivity). Section IV discusses the sample. Section V presents the empirical results which, following the econometric model, come in three parts. Section VI concludes the paper with a summary and final remarks.

II. Differences in Human Capital Acquisitions

Before delving into the details of the estimation procedure of the returns to human capital, we ought to elaborate on the differences in accumulated human capital between Ivorian males and females. In Côte d'Ivoire, formal schooling plays a significant role in today's skill accumulation. A high proportion of governmental expenditures is devoted to education (see Section I). Until the most recent cohorts started attending school in large numbers, most people in Côte d'Ivoire completed few years of education or remained illiterate. Table 1,

Table 1

Human Capital Among Men and Women in Côte d'Ivoire

	Males			Females		
	Abidjan	Other Urban	Rural	Abidjan	Other Urban	Rural
A. Average years of completed schooling by age						
20 ≤ age < 30	8.20	6.98	3.72	5.65	4.15	1.19
30 ≤ age < 40	8.81	6.63	2.56	4.73	1.78	0.47
40 ≤ age < 50	5.38	3.42	0.92	1.50	0.48	0.06
50 ≤ age ≤ 60	3.06	1.56	0.31	0.65	0.18	0.00
Overall	7.32	5.52	2.03	4.42	2.40	0.52
All Côte d'Ivoire		4.19			1.69	
B. Distribution by schooling levels (%)[a]						
No education (Educ = 0)	24.54	37.77	68.01	48.31	66.25	89.81
Elementary (1 ≤ Educ ≤ 6)	22.39	21.96	21.36	19.32	19.20	8.95
Junior high (7 ≤ Educ ≤ 10)	27.24	21.89	7.48	22.02	10.97	1.15
Senior high (11 ≤ Educ ≤ 13)	16.52	14.39	3.05	6.28	2.90	0.09
Post-secondary (Educ ≥ 14)	9.31	3.99	0.10	4.07	0.68	0.00
	100.00	100.00	100.00	100.00	100.00	100.00
C. Average years of completed schooling by employment status						
Wage earners	7.81	7.67	5.25	9.40	8.06	3.38
Nonfarm self-employed	3.85	2.37	1.67	1.65	1.33	0.84
Farm self-employed	—	2.51	1.61	—	1.11	0.40
Nonemployed	7.89	7.10	5.32	4.13	3.18	1.19
D. Technical training and apprenticeships						
No technical training (%)	71.03	80.27	96.85	78.45	93.13	99.59
Average years if positive	2.71	2.31	2.14	2.47	2.23	2.06
No apprenticeship training (%)	74.81	71.28	82.68	92.82	92.27	97.94
Average years if positive	4.01	3.89	3.90	2.49	2.51	2.00

a. Completion rates are well over a half in elementary school, roughly half in junior high, and about a third in senior high. Completion rates are somewhat lower among females and in rural areas.

part A, illustrates this by means of statistics on basis of the sample used for this study:[1] younger cohorts have received substantially more education. Clearly, also, it is the Ivorian male who has benefitted the most. Education among women still lags behind.[2] Moreover, the impact of education is spread unevenly: whether by individual choice (migration of the educated) or by government-provided opportunities (urban schools), it favors the urban population.

Part B of Table 1 illustrates the variation of educational attainment among the Ivorian population. In every region, many people never attended school. The

1. The data source is described in Section IV.
2. The sample contains only African households. Non-Ivorian Africans are overrepresented among the less educated. While non-Ivorians make up 14.8 percent of the sample, they constitute 24.1 percent of those without an education, and 42.4 percent of all wage earners without an education.

schooling system itself is distinguished into four levels (Michel and Cintrón 1988, Alessie et al. 1992). The system, which was inherited from the former French colonial rulers, starts with a primary school of six grades. At the end, students take a national exam to earn a diploma (the *Certificat d'Études Primaires*). This allows entry into the secondary school, distinguished into a lower secondary or "junior high" (four grades) with the *Brevet d'Études du Premier Cycle* as a diploma and an upper secondary or "senior high" (three grades) with the *Baccalauréat* as a diploma. Students can enroll into vocational training programs after completing primary school and into technical training after either junior or senior high school. Post-secondary education is a mixture of university education and other advanced programs.

Repeat rates are high. In the academic year 1973–74, 26 percent of total student enrollment ended up repeating their class (Den Tuinder 1978, p. 280). This is in part because of the restricted entry into secondary school. Only 24 percent of the sixth grade enrollment of the previous year is admitted into junior high. Many students repeat the last two years of primary school to get better grades on the entrance exam: in sixth grade, the last year of primary school, repeat rates are 50 percent. Many enroll into a private secondary school, to transfer to public school after one year.[3]

In urban areas, the proportion of men and women with some elementary schooling is roughly equal (Table 1), and in Abidjan the proportion with some junior high school is also quite close. Other than that, education of women is at a deficit in every aspect. School completion rates[4] among urban men decline from 68 percent for elementary schooling to 37 percent for senior high. Among urban women, these percentages decline from 57 to 27. School completion rates in rural areas are about equal between men and women and, at about 45 percent at both elementary and junior high levels, below the urban rates.

Schooling is correlated with employment status (part C). In all regions, wage earners are the most educated. The nonemployed group shows a surprisingly high average. This group is dominated by individuals aged between 20 and 30 years and thus may include full-time students. Yet, it has been found elsewhere that educated youngsters stay out of the work force for lengthy periods of time in search for a suitable wage job (Newman 1987), and that wage employees are more likely to switch to the nonemployed status than to self-employment (Vijverberg 1990b).

As mentioned above, technical training programs are available. Part D of Table 1 shows the degree to which they contribute to human capital accumulation. Fewer women enroll in such programs, but if they do, they stay in it as long as

---

3. As a result, Clignet and Foster (1971) reported that each student who finally gained the *Baccalauréat* cost $14,000, and each *BEPC* holder cost $5,000. As their discussion seems to suggest, these amounts include the costs of educating those who drop out before completing the degree. The recurrent cost of secondary education per student in 1972–73 was $430. In 1974, income per capita was $450 (Den Tuinder 1978). It is worth noting that little changed over the next decade: UNDP (1991, Table 15) reports repeat rates of 28 percent of primary enrollment and 19 percent of secondary enrollment in 1986–88.

4. In other words, the proportion of people at a certain schooling level who have completed the highest grade at that level.

men do. Another feature of especially West-African economies is the prevalence of apprenticeships.[5] Women use such opportunities less frequently and their apprenticeships have a shorter duration.

III. Research Methodology

A. Motivation

When measuring market returns to education, one should consider how the labor market operates. In industrial societies, the vast majority of labor market participants draw their labor income in the form of wages and salaries earned in the service of an employer.[6] Liquidity constraints might be a substantial enough barrier to self-employment that for many the only option to wage employment is nonemployment (Evans and Jovanovic 1989). Econometric research has therefore focused primarily on correcting estimates of the wage equation for the effect of the worker's labor force participation decision. In many Third World countries, family enterprises are prevalent and employ large numbers of labor force participants. The concept of market returns to education applies to a larger variety of earned incomes than just wages and salaries.

In a competitive labor market, returns to education are equalized across the various income-earning activities: the premium that employers pay to a worker with an additional year of schooling needs to be no greater than the earnings gain that such a worker can obtain in his own family enterprise. There is then no need to look at earning patterns in other activities. Suppose, however, that labor markets are not fully competitive. Reasons may include barriers of entry to wage employment, pervasive regulation of wages, a large public sector with wage scales that are not guided by productivity considerations, a colonial or multinational influence on wages of skilled nationals. All of these could cause different returns across various modes of employment, most likely raising returns in wage employment above those earned elsewhere.[7] Returns in other segments of the labor market should therefore be estimated separately as part of a self-selection model

5. See Peil (1981), Oyeneye (1981), Wilcock and Chuta (1982), Liedholm and Mead (1987).
6. Steinmetz and Wright (1989) reports statistics on the extent of self-employment (in other words, worker on own account or unpaid family worker), for both the United States and Western Europe. In 1985, 12.6 percent of the European labor force in industry and services was self-employed (with Italy as an outlier at 24.7 percent). Of the overall labor force, including agriculture, the average percentage was 16.7. U.S. percentages were similar.
7. Even in a competitive labor market, the fact that family enterprises provide potential returns to family savings may raise returns to education in wage employment above those in self-employment. In the ideal case, a person could be drawn out of self-employment into wage employment as easily as he could change wage jobs: savings utilized in the family enterprise would be converted into liquid assets and lent out in the capital market. In imperfect capital markets, enterprise capital could well be illiquid or would earn lower rates of return when lent out, because of risk, information cost and the like. To draw a person out of self-employment would necessitate a compensation for lost returns on family savings. Thus, to the extent that (i) capital markets are imperfect, and (ii) education is correlated with savings, this compensation causes a gap between measured returns to education in wage employment and those in self-employment.

that allows one to determine the effect of choices and barriers among the various modes of employment.

At the time of its gaining independence in 1960, Côte d'Ivoire was a labor-scarce, skill-scarce, and capital-scarce country with a strong agricultural base. Through its agricultural wage policy, it drew in large numbers of Africans from neighboring countries; the Sahelian droughts sent even more people southward. Many of these were unskilled (footnote 2). Most administrative positions within government were still filled by French expatriates (Clignet and Foster 1971). Furthermore, foreign investment was encouraged through generous investment incentives and convertability of the CFA franc (Campbell 1978, Den Tuinder 1978, Alschuler 1988). Foreign investors, many from France, brought in skilled personnel. The push for increased education implied a great need for teachers, many of whom came from France (Den Tuinder 1978). As a result, the number of skilled Europeans grew dramatically.[8] By historic precedent, wages of skilled Ivorians were tied to those of expatriate civil servants.[9] It would therefore not be surprising if the returns to education in the wage sector differ from those in among the self-employed.

A related consideration is self-selection through migration.[10] Because Third World economies are in the early stages of industrialization, the market for educated, skilled labor is regionally more concentrated. To obtain the highest returns from one's education, a rural person may need to migrate. More generally, earnings opportunities across the regions of the economy—whether in wage employment or in self-employment—are expected to have an impact on migration patterns. The sample of workers in any region is not a random sample of the population at large.

B. Econometric Modeling

The self-selection model contains two decision variables:[11] where to live, denoted by region R with outcomes $r = 1, 2, \ldots, r'$; and whether to work in region r,

---

8. Campbell (1978, p. 103) reported that the number of skilled Europeans grew from 10,000 in 1956 to 50,000 in 1975. Den Tuinder (1978, p. 296) stated that in 1974 there were 9,480 Europeans in the private and semi-private sector and 2,900 in the public sector, a 15 percent growth since 1971. Of the 2,900, some 2,100 were teachers; in secondary schools, 80 percent were French expatriates.

9. Before independence, Africans in French territories were permitted to elect officials to local and colonial governments. These officials were sensitive to African civil servants' demands for higher salaries, equal to those of the Europeans. While base salaries were equal for a long time already, Europeans received travel and family allowances which roughly doubled their salaries. Africans pressed successfully for passage of the Second Lamine Guèye Law in 1950, granting equality in fringes as well as salary for all civil servants. This law was not immediately implemented, however: the Europeans viewed polygamy and the corresponding large families as a fraudulent use of the system. Further pressure by African politicians and unions led to the law's implementation in the mid-1950s. For more information, see Thompson and Adloff (1968, pp. 504–6) and Manning (1988, p. 126). Although in 1984 Ivorians earned less than non-Africans in the same occupational category (Benie 1989), with the large numbers of Europeans still in Côte d'Ivoire, the law still affects the Ivorian wage structure.

10. For example, Kuznets and Thomas (1957), Nakosteen and Zimmer (1980), Schultz (1988), Williamson (1988).

11. The model and estimation stategy are an extension of Vijverberg (1992b). Other studies of earnings of wage and self-employed workers, controlling for selectivity, include Hill (1983), Blau (1985), Rees

denoted by labor force status S_r with outcomes $s = h, a, n, w$ denoting, respectively, nonemployment (or home), agricultural self-employment, nonagricultural self-employment and wage employment. The model is based on utility comparisons. Utility experienced in state (r, s) equals:

$$(1) \quad U_{rs} = V_{rs} + \varepsilon_{rs}$$
$$= Z_r \gamma_r + Y_{rs} \delta_{rs} + \varepsilon_{rs}$$

where Z_r represents variables affecting the desirability of region r apart from the outcome of the labor force status choice; Y_{rs} has a bearing on the choice of activity; and ε_{rs} is a random disturbance.[12] As δ_{rs} differs between regions, the employment decision is conditional upon the location. Figure 1 illustrates the (R, S_r) choice set, where the work choice branches below the nodes are region-specific.[13] Note, though, that the (R, S_r) choice is *not* viewed as a sequential choice. It is rather plausible that the R- and S_r-decisions are interwoven: a person may prefer a wage job in one region over the next-best alternative of farming or nonfarm self-employment in another.

By assumption, a person chooses region $R = r$ and labor force status $S_r = s$ such that the utility experienced in that state is highest:

$$(2) \quad (R, S_r) = (r, s) \quad \text{iff } U_{rs} \geq U_{qt}$$
$$\text{for all } q \neq r \text{ and/or } t \neq s.$$

Note that this model assumes perfect information about all regions and work states and ignores dynamic considerations of the migration decision such as repeat and return migration.

The empirical analysis will focus on earnings in wage and nonfarm self-employment. For each of these labor force states, a separate earnings function is posited for each region:

$$(3) \quad \ln(W_{rs}) = X_{rs} \beta_{rs} + u_{rs} \quad \text{for } s = n, w.$$

Sample selectivity produces biased estimates of the earnings equation when the disturbance terms in the earnings equation (u_{rs}) and the selection rule (combinations of ε_{rs}) are correlated.

To estimate Equations (1)–(3), a distributional assumption is needed. Given that there are a total of $4r'$ alternative (r, s) states, a normality assumption for ε_{rs} is impractical. Instead, we assume a Gumbel distribution, so that the choice model (1)–(2) takes a logit form. Furthermore, we assume that u_{rs} has a normal

and Shah (1986), Vijverberg (1986), Gill (1988), Borjas and Bronars (1989), Evans and Jovanovic (1989), Evans and Leighton (1989). None of them address the selection for migration nor the association of several family members with some of the household enterprises. Tunali (1986) uses a two-by-two selection model of employment and migration choices to correct for selectivity among wage earners.

12. Earnings in state (r, s) should affect U_{rs} and be one of the variables in Y_{rs} in a structural model. In a reduced-form model, the observable determinants of earnings are part of Y_{rs} and the disturbance term of the earnings equation [u_{rs} in Equation (3)] is part of ε_{rs}.

13. When the labor force participation decision is not region-specific, we have $\delta_{rs} = \delta_s$, and the (R, S_r) decision as modeled in Equations (1) and (2) is empirically indistinguishable from separate R and S decision models. In that case, locational choice is independent of work choice.

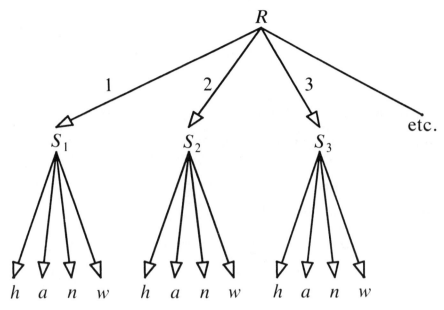

Figure 1
Decision Tree of the (R, S$_r$) *Choice*

distribution.[14] The correlation between ε_{rs} for all (r, s) and u_{rs} is not easily parameterized; instead, additional distributional assumptions will be made below.

To account for selectivity, one could estimate Equation (3) along the lines of Lee (1983): let p_{rs} be the probability that $R = r$ and $S_r = s$. The overall selection is summarized as $\eta_{rs} \leq \Phi^{-1}[p_{rs}]$, where Φ^{-1} is the inverse of the normal cdf. Assuming a joint normal distribution for (u_{rs}, η_{rs}) is then sufficient for estimation of (3). But note that the covariance of u_{rs} and η_{rs} reflects the comovement between unobserved wage factors on the one hand and unobserved migration *and* labor market status choice factors on the other. If the latter two are separately correlated with u_{rs} in opposite ways, the combined correlation with u_{rs} would likely be small and no selectivity effect would be detected.

The dual-λ method (Vijverberg 1992b) circumvents this objection and yields information on the nature of selectivity by migration as well as labor force status choice. Consider a person choosing $R = r$ and $S_r = s$. The choice of s, given r, implies:

(4) $U_{rs} \geq \max_{t \neq s} U_{rt} = V'_{rs} + \varepsilon'_{rs}.$

14. In the reduced form interpretation of Equation (1), u_{rs} is part of ε_{rs}. The distributional assumptions made in regard to ε_{rs} and u_{rs} should therefore be consistent with each other. The assumptions of a Gumbel distribution for ε_{rs} and a normal distribution for u_{rs} are somewhat but not fully consistent (Vijverberg 1992b), but must be made to render the model estimable.

The maximum of U_{rt} for $t \neq s$ has a Gumbel distribution with location parameter V'_{rs}, defined as:

$$(5) \quad V'_{rs} = \ln\left(\sum_{t \neq s} e^{V_{rt}}\right)$$

such that ε'_{rs} has regular Gumbel distribution. The choice of s, given r, can thus be written as $\eta_{s|r} = \varepsilon'_{rs} - \varepsilon_{rs} \leq V_{rs} - V'_{rs}$. Let $p_{s|r}$ be the probability that s is the best choice in region r: $p_{s|r} = p_{rs}/\Sigma_s p_{rs} = F(V_{rs} - V'_{rs})$, where $F(x) = 1/(1 + e^{-x})$ is the logit cdf. Then the condition on the choice of s, given r, can also be written in normal-distribution-equivalent form as $\eta^n_{s|r} \leq \Phi^{-1}[p_{s|r}] = A^n_{s|r}$.

The person chooses region r if:

$$(6) \quad \max_s U_{rs} \geq \max_{q \neq r}\left\{\max_s U_{qs}\right\}.$$

The left-hand side has a Gumbel distribution with location parameter

$$(7) \quad V_r = \ln\left(\sum_s e^{V_{rs}}\right)$$

whereas the right-hand side also follows a Gumbel distribution but with location parameter

$$(8) \quad V'_r = \ln\left(\sum_{q \neq r} \sum_s e^{V_{qs}}\right).$$

Thus if the left-hand side of (6) equals $V_r + \theta_r$ and the right-hand side of (6) equals $V'_r + \theta'_r$ (thus defining θ_r and θ'_r), condition (6) is restated as $V_r + \theta_r \geq V'_r + \theta'_r$, or as $\eta_r = \theta'_r - \theta_r \leq V_r - V'_r$, or, stated in its normal distribution equivalent, $\eta^n_r \leq \Phi^{-1}[p_r] = A^n_r$, where p_r is the probability that region r is the best alternative: $p_r = \Sigma_s p_{rs} = F(V_r - V'_r)$.

The choice of r and s is now described in terms of conditions on normal random variables η^n_r and $\eta^n_{s|r}$. Parameterizing the aforementioned correlation between u_{rs} and the ε_{rs}'s, let us assume a joint trivariate normal distribution for $(\eta^n_{s|r}, \eta^n_r, u_{rs})$ with covariance matrix Ξ:

$$(9) \quad \Xi = \mathrm{Var}\begin{pmatrix} \eta^n_{s|r} \\ \eta^n_r \\ u_{rs} \end{pmatrix} = \begin{pmatrix} 1 & \rho_{rs} & \sigma_{1u,rs} \\ \rho_{rs} & 1 & \sigma_{2u,rs} \\ \sigma_{1u,rs} & \sigma_{2u,rs} & \sigma_{uu,rs} \end{pmatrix}.$$

We calculate the expected earnings of a worker in region r and labor force status s as:[15]

---

15. See Fishe, Trost, and Lurie (1981), Catsiapis and Robinson (1982), Maddala (1983), Tunali (1986). Formulas needed to calculate the correct standard errors of the estimates of β_1, $\sigma_{1u,rs}$, and $\sigma_{2u,rs}$ are given in Appendix 1.

(10) $E[\ln(W_{rs})|\eta^n_{s|r} \le A^n_{s|r}, \eta^n_r \le A^n_r] = X_{rs}\beta_{rs} + \sigma_{1u,rs}\lambda_{s|r} + \sigma_{2u,rs}\lambda_r$

where

(11) $\lambda_{s|r} = \dfrac{-\phi(A^n_{s|r})\Phi[(1 - \rho^2_{rs})^{-1/2}(A^n_r - \rho_{rs}A^n_{s|r})]}{p_{rs}}$

$\lambda_r = \dfrac{-\phi(A^n_r)\Phi[(1 - \rho^2_{rs})^{-1/2}(A^n_{s|r} - \rho_{rs}A^n_r)]}{p_{rs}}$

and where Φ and ϕ are the standard normal cdf and pdf. $\sigma_{1u,rs}$ is the covariance between u_{rs} and $\eta^n_{s|r}$ and measures the effect of selectivity by work status: a negative value of $\sigma_{1u,rs}$ implies positive selectivity, where the individuals in region r with a higher-than-average earnings potential in activity s indeed choose activity s. Similarly, $\sigma_{2u,rs}$ is the covariance between u_{rs} and η^n_r and measures the effect of selectivity by migration choice: a negative value of $\sigma_{2u,rs}$ implies positive selectivity, where people in the overall population who seek out region r have a higher than average earnings potential in activity s. Furthermore, ρ_{rs} is the correlation coefficient between $\eta^n_{s|r}$ and η^n_r. Both of these variables are transformations of underlying logit variables: for example, $\eta^n_r = \Phi^{-1}[F(\eta_r)]$. In principle, then, ρ_{rs} would be calculated from the following equation:

(12) $\rho_{rs} = \int_{-\infty}^{\infty}\int_{-\infty}^{\infty} \Phi^{-1}[F(\eta_{s|r})]\Phi^{-1}[F(\eta_r)]g(\eta_{s|r}, \eta_r)d\eta_{s|r}d\eta_r$

where $g(\eta_{s|r}, \eta_r)$ is the joint distribution of $\eta_{s|r}$ and η_r, derived from the joint i.i.d. Gumbel distribution of ε_{rs}. However, for lack of closed-form integrals, there exists no analytical expression for g, nor for $\Phi^{-1}[F(\cdot)]$ for that matter. Numerical integration (third order, over ε_{rs}, ε'_{rs} and θ'_r) is at least tedious. The following algorithm yields an estimate of ρ_{rs} in a fairly speedy fashion:

(1) Generate m random numbers from the Gumbel distribution for each ε_{rs} $(r = 1, \ldots, r'; s = h, a, n, w)$.

(2) From these, calculate for each person m values of $\eta_{s|r}$ and η_r, given his estimated values of each V_{rs}.

(3) Derive the normal distribution equivalents $\eta^n_{s|r}$ and η^n_r.

(4) Compute the correlation ρ_{rs} between $\eta^n_{s|r}$ and η^n_r.

Unlike with commonly used forms of the normal distribution, ρ_{rs} is not constant but rather varies between people. For someone choosing region r, $\partial\rho_{rs}/\partial V_{rs} = -\Sigma_{t \ne s}(\partial\rho_{rs}/\partial V_{rt})$, and $\partial\rho_{rs}/\partial V_{qt} = 0$ for $q \ne r$ and any t. (Proof is given in Appendix 2.) According to the first of these properties, a large value of V_{rs} relative to all other V_{rt} in the region leads to a positive value of ρ_{rs}.[16] The second property

---

16. Accordingly, a change in Z_r, which affects all V_{rs} equally, has no effect on ρ_{rs}. A change in Y_{rs}, a determinant in the choice of labor market status s, does change ρ_{rs}. If V_{rs} is large relative to all other V_{rt}, variation in ε_{rs} will have more impact on $\eta_{s|r}$ and θ_r, because U_{rs} is more likely to be the highest in region r. Therefore, the correlation between $\eta^n_{s|r}$ and η^n_r is more likely positive.

derives from the fact that the utility of any state (q, s) for $q \neq r$ affects only one variable (η_r) involved in the correlation. The correlation coefficient ranges from about -0.5 to 0.5 for the different values of V_{rs}. The simulation approach that yields an estimate of ρ_{rs} also implies some variability in the estimate: in the empirical analysis, we use $m = 2{,}000$, for which the standard deviation of repeated estimates of ρ_{rs} for the same set of V_{rs}-values appears to be less than 0.028. For the estimator to be consistent, this variability must disappear asymptotically, so m must rise to ∞ together with the sample size (Vijverberg 1992b).

C. Special Considerations about Nonagricultural Self-Employment Earnings

The analysis of self-employment earnings presents additional econometric challenges. The econometric model above describes choices of an individual and their effect on his earnings equation. It is an individual-focused model and, in that way, follows the mainstream literature. If the individual chooses the nonagricultural self-employment model (or, for that matter, farming), he operates his own enterprise, by nature of the activity. Yet, it is not unusual for family enterprises to employ several family members. This already suggests that family enterprises represent an outcome of a household time allocation choice involving several family members. Indeed, individual time allocation choices in general could be interactive (Newman and Gertler 1992). This paper is not striving to address that weakness of the customary time allocation model but rather adheres to the individual-focused model.

Moreover, the model focuses on *hourly* earnings. Ideally, one would like to measure earnings over a relevant production period, so that one can estimate diminishing returns and economies of scale of the production process. Such a relevant production period is unknown and probably varies among enterprises in different industries. Without such information, attempting to estimate the characteristics of self-employment production processes is hazardous (Appendix 3), so the empirical analysis will use a relatively simple specification of an hourly enterprise earnings function.

Let us return now to the problem that some enterprises employ several family members. If the enterprise sample consisted only of single-person enterprises, we could estimate the earnings function by Equation (10) with $s = n$, using OLS. As it is, the hourly earnings of a multi-worker enterprise is a weighted average of the hourly earnings of the individual members, indexed by i:

$$(13) \quad W_{rn} = \frac{\Pi_{rn}}{\sum_i L_{rn,i}} = \frac{\sum_i \Pi_{rn,i}}{\sum_i L_{rn,i}} = \sum_i \left(\frac{L_{rn,i}}{\sum_i L_{rn,i}} \right) \frac{\Pi_{rn,i}}{L_{rn,i}} = \sum_i \alpha_{rn,i} W_{rn,i}$$

where Π_{rn} is enterprise earnings, and $L_{rn,i}$ is hours worked in the enterprise by household member i. By using a Taylor expansion around a common value W_0, we arrive at an estimable form of the earnings equation for the nonfarm self-employed:

$$(14) \quad \ln(W_{rn}) = \ln(W_0) + \frac{1}{W_0}(W_{rn} - W_0)$$

$$= \sum_i \alpha_{i,rn} \ln(W_0) + \frac{1}{W_0}\left(\sum_i \alpha_{rn,i}(W_{rn,i} - W_0)\right)$$

$$= \sum_i \alpha_{rn,i} \ln(W_{rn,i})$$

and so:

$$(15) \quad \ln(W_{rn}) = \left(\sum_i \alpha_{rn,i}X_{rn,i}\right)\beta_{rn} + \sigma_{1u,rn}\left(\sum_i \alpha_{rn,i}\lambda_{n|r,i}\right)$$

$$+ \sigma_{2u,rn}\left(\sum_i \alpha_{rn,i}\lambda_{r,i}\right) + v_{rn}$$

where $v_{rn} = \Sigma_i \alpha_{rn,i}v_{rn,i}$, with $v_{rn,i}$ being the disturbance for each family worker separately. OLS estimation of Equation (10) would proceed by assuming a constant variance σ_v^2 for $v_{rn,i}$. Thus, $\text{Var}(v_{rn}) = (\Sigma_i \alpha_{rn,i}^2)\sigma_v^2$. Since $\Sigma_i \alpha_{rn,i}^2$ varies between enterprises, v_{rn} is heteroskedastic. This has further implications for the computation of the correct standard errors; see Appendix 1.

One troublesome aspect of this manipulation is the potential endogeneity of $\alpha_{rn,i}$, the proportion of total hours of labor contributed by family worker i. Fortunately, multi-worker enterprises are not all that common. In the enterprise sample used later on, 124 of 522 employ more than one family member. Moreover, as explained later, more than half of them (69) are aggregates of smaller separate family enterprises, for reasons of questionnaire design, so that those workers did act individually.

Finally, whereas earnings functions for wage earners are estimated separately for men and women, in multi-worker enterprises, men and women sometimes work together, so that Equation (15) cannot be estimated separately. Rather, a single equation combines both men and women with different parameters on crucial variables such as years of education. Given that the (R, S_r) choice model is estimated separately, the selectivity effects ($\sigma_{1u,rn}$ and $\sigma_{2u,rn}$) are distinguished between the sexes. Furthermore, since the sample of enterprises is rather small, all regions are combined in one equation, allowing for a different intercept, a differential in the return to human capital, and different selectivity effects in each region.

IV. Data

The data for the empirical analysis are derived from the Côte d'Ivoire Living Standards Survey (CILSS), held in 1985–87 (Ainsworth and Muñoz 1986). The CILSS is an overlapping panel where randomly selected

African households are interviewed in two consecutive years.[17] The three waves are pooled for the purpose of this study to maximize the number of observations: in particular, the sample of female wage employees is small in any given year. The sample of family enterprises, however, refers to 1986 only. The 1985 questionnaire suffered from a design flaw in the enterprise module such that the responses on sales revenue and net earnings may have been confused with one another; and the 1987 data could not be included for lack of access.[18]

Data used for this study includes all individuals between 20 and 60 years of age with complete information on all variables. Thus, schooling choices and the effects of aging are largely avoided. Earnings of wage employees include cash earnings and the monetary value of non-cash benefits (for example, housing, food) as far as could be monetized. A number of wage employees reported not receiving anything for their work. They are most likely apprentices and are dropped from the wage worker samples, as they are in the process of learning skills, like others in the formal schooling system. Earnings of family enterprises are computed as the sum of the reported value that "is left over at the end of the day after all expenses are paid" and the value of home consumption of commodities produced by the enterprise (Vijverberg 1992a). Eleven family enterprises that reported zero earnings were omitted.[19]

General enterprise information derives from the enterprise module of the survey; information on family workers is extracted from the time allocation module. This questionnaire design generated ambiguous information in the case that a household reported more than one enterprise in a given industry: one cannot link workers to their enterprise anymore. In such a case, the enterprises are lumped

---

17. Each year 1,600 households were interviewed as a representative sample of the population of Côte d'Ivoire. For the second year, a randomly selected group of 800 households interviewed in 1985 were revisited, and 800 new households were added. The latter were interviewed again in 1987, the third year, together with another group of 800 households. This means, therefore, that about one third of the pooled sample refers to individuals measured once; two thirds of the observations in the pooled sample refer to people measured twice. As such, the i.i.d. assumption underlying our analysis may be incorrect, since the disturbances of different observations of the same person may be correlated. Thus, estimates may be less than efficient, and their standard errors may also be incorrect. To examine this, I randomly dropped for each panel household either the first or second year of observation. This yields a proper cross-sectional sample with N^* rather than N observations; $N^* < N$. Selectivity-corrected wage equations were estimated for the three largest subsamples and standard errors were multiplied with $(N^*/N)^{0.5}$ to account for the decreased sample size. In the three subsamples, the average ratio of these "adjusted cross-sectional" standard errors to the standard errors reported in this paper were 1.021 (*Abidjan males*), 0.993 (*Other Urban males*) and 0.993 (*Abidjan females*). The pooling of the three waves does not appear to present an estimation problem.

18. The CILSS contains a module on family farms from which a measure of earnings might be derived. There appear to be ambiguities in the relationship between sharecroppers and landlords that, in the 1985 CILSS survey, affected some 27 percent of the sample, and about ownership of land: 64 percent claimed that they own the land on which they farm but also stated that they could not sell it if they wanted to (Kozel 1990). An analysis of farm earnings would promise to yield uninterpretable results.

19. Other omissions on suspicion of measurement error include 11 wage workers whose earnings information seemed highly questionable, and one enterprise with monthly earnings 81 times as high as the average of the sample used here and 4.5 times as much as the next highest. All of these generated large residuals and, being far removed from the main body of the scatter diagram, were very influential on parameter estimates.

into one unit, employing all family workers reporting to be self-employed in that industry. This affected 69 (13.2 percent) of the 522 enterprises in our sample.

Table 2 provides a guide to the variables used for the present analysis. Where appropriate, the statistics describe the subsamples separately. Among the personal characteristics, it is worth noting that wage employees in general and females in particular have an urban origin. Detailed tabulations show that 59.5 (49.9) percent of the male (female) wage earners were born in locations that are more rural than the place where they are currently living, and those with such rural birthplace tend to have less education.[20] Female wage employees tend to be younger and are not married as often. Among wage workers, the male-female difference in hourly wages is only two percent. Human capital, urban residence, and nationality all differ and could cause the wage gap to go either way. For women, rural wage employment opportunities are virtually nil: out of 4,424 rural women, only 13 (0.29 percent) reported to work for someone else.

Hourly earnings in nonfarm self-employment are substantially lower than in wage employment: the log-difference is about 1.08. Self-employed men work with significantly more capital and inventory than their women counterparts.[21] This corresponds also with the divergence in industry: women engage in food commerce, while men manufacture, trade nonfood items or perform a variety of services. Food commerce is the least capital intensive form of self-employment (Vijverberg 1990a). Men have a slight edge in prior human capital acquisitions, in particular in the form of apprenticeship training. Note also that fully one-half of the men are non-Ivorian.[22]

Age and location of the business are used as explanatory variables of enterprise performance. The age dummies are chosen such that each (including the omitted category) covers about a third of the sample. Enterprises operating from a fixed location may be steadier and consequently more profitable than others; however, the survey information does not state whether that fixed location is a shack in the backyard or a formal-sector shop elsewhere.

---

20. Respondents were queried about their birthplace only if it differed from their current place of residence. If so, the respondent could call his birthplace a (1) city, (2) town, (3) large village, (4) small village, (5) camp, or (6) other. I have chosen to equate "city" with Abidjan, "town" with other urban areas, and all other categories with rural areas. This may entail some misclassification, but trends are reasonably indicative. With almost half of the urban residents of rural descent, the sample exhibits the urban-bound migration that characterizes African populations in general (for example, Roussel 1975, Zachariah and Condé 1981, Scott 1985).

21. Capital and inventory are measured in thousands CFA before taking the logarithm. Capital is the value of equipment, tools, buildings, and land. Inventory measures stocks of both inputs and unsold outputs. Among the enterprises, 26.4 percent did not report using capital, and 47.7 percent reported no inventory. An arbitrary value of .01 was added to all capital and inventory values before taking the logarithm, as the log of 0 is not defined.

22. Cohen (1974, p. 40) reports that in 26 towns with public commercial registry for all persons involved in business activity, only 53 percent of the businesses started between 1962 and 1969 were owned by Ivorians. Of the foreign owned, 14 percent were French, 12 percent were Lebanese, and the rest (76 percent) were non-Ivorian Africans. In Abidjan, Ivorians owned barely a quarter. In the CILSS sample, 58 percent of the nonfarm self-employed males in Abidjan are non-Ivorian. Ivorianization is proceeding, slowly.

Table 2
Descriptive Statistics, by Sex and Labor Force Status[a]

	Males			Females			
	All Population (N = 6,011)	Wage Worker (N = 1,453)	Nonagricultural Self-Employed (N = 240)	All Population (N = 7,633)	Wage Worker (N = 356)	Nonagricultural Self-Employed (N = 453)	Nonfarm Enterprises (N = 522)
Born in							
Abidjan/city	0.13 (0.3)	0.20 (0.4)	0.19 (0.4)	0.12 (0.3)	0.33 (0.5)	0.15 (0.4)	—
Other urban/town	0.16 (0.4)	0.19 (0.4)	0.19 (0.4)	0.16 (0.4)	0.32 (0.5)	0.19 (0.4)	—
Childhood years[b] lived in:							
Abidjan/city	1.53 (4.3)	2.20 (5.0)	2.24 (5.1)	1.37 (4.1)	3.65 (6.1)	1.97 (4.9)	—
Other urban/town	2.02 (4.9)	2.27 (5.1)	2.54 (5.5)	2.13 (5.1)	3.37 (5.7)	2.57 (5.5)	—
Rural areas	9.49 (6.6)	7.36 (6.6)	8.40 (7.0)	9.93 (6.7)	3.52 (5.6)	8.60 (6.9)	—
Years of schooling							
Elementary	2.77 (2.9)	4.36 (2.6)	1.90 (2.6)	1.26 (2.3)	5.15 (2.0)	1.00 (2.1)	1.38 (2.3)
Junior high	1.01 (1.7)	1.97 (1.9)	0.29 (1.0)	0.33 (1.0)	2.44 (1.8)	0.11 (0.6)	0.18 (0.7)
Senior high	0.29 (0.8)	0.68 (1.2)	0.04 (0.3)	0.07 (0.4)	0.68 (1.2)	0.01 (0.2)	0.02 (0.2)
University	0.12 (0.7)	0.39 (1.3)	0.00 (0.0)	0.03 (0.4)	0.52 (1.6)	0.00 (0.0)	0.00 (0.0)
Years technical training	0.34 (1.0)	0.98 (1.5)	0.16 (0.8)	0.14 (0.6)	1.60 (1.6)	0.03 (0.3)	0.09 (0.6)
Years apprentice	0.87 (2.2)	0.84 (1.9)	1.95 (2.5)	0.10 (0.6)	0.14 (0.6)	0.25 (1.3)	0.86 (2.0)
Occupational experience	—	9.80 (8.1)	10.24 (9.7)	—	7.41 (7.0)	6.47 (7.9)	7.75 (8.2)
Prior experience	—	11.70 (9.3)	18.27 (11.9)	—	9.29 (8.2)	23.29 (11.7)	22.19 (11.2)

Age	36.05 (12.1)	35.70 (8.9)	37.84 (12.0)	35.50 (11.4)	32.22 (7.5)	36.11 (8.8)	37.44 (10.5)
Married	0.63 (0.5)	0.78 (0.4)	0.72 (0.5)	0.75 (0.4)	0.62 (0.5)	0.73 (0.4)	0.75 (0.4)
Non-Ivorian	0.17 (0.4)	0.18 (0.4)	0.50 (0.5)	0.13 (0.3)	0.08 (0.3)	0.21 (0.4)	0.28 (0.4)
Female	—	—	—	1.00	1.00	1.00	0.63 (0.5)
Year 1986	0.34 (0.5)	0.32 (0.5)	1.00	0.35 (0.5)	0.33 (0.5)	1.00	1.00 (0.0)
Year 1987	0.30 (0.5)	0.34 (0.5)	—	0.30 (0.5)	0.33 (0.5)	—	—
λ_{slr}	—	-0.60 (0.4)	-1.00 (0.3)	—	-0.67 (0.4)	-1.08 (0.3)	-1.06 (0.3)
λ_r	—	-1.00 (0.5)	-0.81 (0.4)	—	-0.56 (0.4)	-0.87 (0.4)	-0.85 (0.4)
Ln(*Capital*)[c]	—	—	2.65 (4.2)	—	—	0.56 (3.4)	0.97 (3.7)
Ln(*Inventory*)[c]	—	—	0.06 (4.6)	—	—	-0.97 (3.5)	-0.82 (3.9)
Fixed location	—	—	0.79 (0.4)	—	—	0.90 (0.3)	0.86 (0.3)
Business age ≤ 3	—	—	0.21 (0.4)	—	—	0.44 (0.5)	0.39 (0.5)
Business age ≥ 10	—	—	0.60 (0.5)	—	—	0.32 (0.4)	0.39 (0.5)
Dependent variables							
Residence							
Abidjan	0.25 (0.4)	0.50 (0.5)	0.19 (0.4)	0.19 (0.4)	0.66 (0.5)	0.22 (0.4)	0.22 (0.4)
Other Urban	0.25 (0.4)	0.38 (0.5)	0.42 (0.5)	0.23 (0.4)	0.30 (0.5)	0.40 (0.5)	0.38 (0.5)
Activity							
Wage employed	0.24 (0.4)	1.00	—	0.05 (0.2)	1.00	—	—
Nonagricultural self-employed	0.13 (0.3)	—	1.00	0.18 (0.4)	—	1.00	—
Agricultural self-employed	0.45 (0.5)	—	—	0.52 (0.5)	—	—	—
Nonemployed	0.18 (0.4)	—	—	0.25 (0.4)	—	—	—
Ln(hourly earnings)	—	6.11 (1.2)	—	—	6.09 (1.1)	—	4.92 (1.3)

a. Standard deviation in parentheses.

b. Years of residence at the place of birth until the household moved away or until, at most, age 15.

c. In thousands CFA before taking logs.

V. Estimates

As described in Section III, the estimates of the returns to human capital are arrived at via a two-stage estimation procedure. In the first stage, we estimate a logit model of migration choice and labor force status. These estimates allow us in the second stage to obtain selectivity-corrected estimates of the returns to human capital. As mentioned, we will obtain separate estimates for wage employees and nonfarm self-employment workers.

A. First-Stage Estimates: The (R, S_r) Model

The (R, S_r) model describes an individual's choice of the region to live in and the activity with which to earn a living. The parameter estimates of the (R, S_r) model may be found in Appendix 4, along with comments on specification and identification issues. Table 3 highlights the impact of years of schooling on the choice of location R and labor market status S_r, illustrated by p_r and $p_{s|r}$. These probabilities depend on other personal characteristics as well, here chosen to be the grand mean of men and women (in other words, the weighted average of Columns 1 and 4 of Table 2). Since education and age are interacted in the specification of the (R, S_r) model, the impact of education is shown for two age levels, 25 and 45 years.

The more educated Ivorians live in urban areas, particularly in Abidjan. Cohen (1974, p. 48) mentions that secondary education was mostly an urban affair in the late 1960s and, together with jobs, an important reason for the rural exodus of people. The geographical variation in school enrollment rates is prompting the government to stimulate rural education (Den Tuinder 1978). The migration equation of the (R, S_r) model measures more than mere past differences in educational opportunities, as the variables measuring a person's "rural roots," while lowering the likelihood of urban residence, are not all-important.[23] Urban dwellers with a rural birthplace have acquired substantial education, though less than native urbanites. Table 3 also points out that few of the educated Ivorians return to rural areas, electing to stay and work in the urban environment that they migrated to. As this is even more true for the older cohort, one may speculate that secondary education is indeed spreading into more rural areas.

Having an education raises the chances of wage employment quite dramatically, and in every case more so for the older cohort. Only for the 25-year-old male in Abidjan, the probability $p_{w|r}$ declines up to the ninth year of schooling. These estimates cannot tell whether this reflects unemployment among young educated males (Newman 1987) or a decision to continue schooling. It does happen for various regions and age cohorts that the estimated probability of nonemployment rises with the education level. The likelihood of nonagricultural self-employment generally declines with the person's education level, with the exception of rural females.

---

23. Even if people migrated to urban areas for their education in their youth, employment and location decisions as an adult are subsequent choices. Being part of a recursive model, the (R, S_r) model can treat educational attainment as predetermined.

Table 3

Effect of Education on Choice of Region R and Labor Market Status S_r, by Sex and Age[a]

| | Male | | | | | | Female | | | | | |
| | Age = 25 | | | Age = 45 | | | Age = 25 | | | Age = 45 | | |

A: Probability of Choosing Region *R*

Years of Schooling	P_{Abid}	P_{OthU}	P_{Rurl}	P_{Abid}	P_{OthU}	P_{Rurl}	P_{Abid}	P_{OthU}	P_{Rurl}	P_{Abid}	P_{OthU}	P_{Rurl}
0	0.08	0.13	0.79	0.13	0.18	0.69	0.17	0.24	0.59	0.17	0.24	0.59
6	0.17	0.22	0.61	0.40	0.31	0.29	0.29	0.36	0.34	0.54	0.27	0.19
10	0.35	0.33	0.32	0.60	0.34	0.07	0.51	0.39	0.10	0.80	0.18	0.02
15	0.53	0.35	0.12	0.73	0.26	0.01	0.71	0.28	0.01	0.90	0.08	0.02

B: Probability of Choosing Mode of Employment S_r[b]

Years of Schooling	$P_{a\mid r}$	$P_{n\mid r}$	$P_{w\mid r}$	$P_{a\mid r}$	$P_{n\mid r}$	$P_{w\mid r}$	$P_{a\mid r}$	$P_{n\mid r}$	$P_{w\mid r}$	$P_{a\mid r}$	$P_{n\mid r}$	$P_{w\mid r}$
(i) R = Abidjan[c]												
0	—	0.15	0.58	—	0.17	0.66	—	0.27	0.03	—	0.43	0.04
6	—	0.08	0.50	—	0.12	0.70	—	0.14	0.09	—	0.26	0.48
10	—	0.06	0.49	—	0.10	0.76	—	0.07	0.17	—	0.05	0.89
15	—	0.05	0.54	—	0.08	0.84	—	0.02	0.33	—	0.00	0.99
(ii) R = Other Urban Areas												
0	0.30	0.31	0.22	0.40	0.25	0.29	0.23	0.36	0.01	0.30	0.44	0.01
6	0.16	0.26	0.37	0.17	0.14	0.64	0.16	0.24	0.06	0.11	0.41	0.33
10	0.09	0.14	0.53	0.06	0.04	0.86	0.06	0.14	0.19	0.01	0.08	0.88
15	0.03	0.03	0.70	0.01	0.00	0.97	0.01	0.03	0.50	0.00	0.00	0.99
(iii) R = Rural Areas												
0	0.89	0.06	0.04	0.89	0.07	0.02	0.77	0.13	0.01	0.79	0.15	0.00
6	0.78	0.09	0.09	0.77	0.10	0.12	0.58	0.21	0.01	0.36	0.49	0.02
10[d]	0.57	0.07	0.26	0.47	0.06	0.44	0.35	0.22	0.04	0.06	0.34	0.50

a. Measures refer to an average person, defined by the mean of the independent variables across the male and female samples in all modes of employment combined.

b. The subscripts "*a*," "*n*," and "*w*" refer to agricultural self-employment, nonagricultural self-employment, and wage employment, respectively. An alternative choice is nonemployment: the probability of choosing it equals $1 - P_{a\mid r} - P_{n\mid r} - P_{w\mid r}$.

c. Agriculture is not an option in Abidjan.

d. Few individuals in rural areas have more than 10 years of schooling. The row for 15 years of schooling is omitted as it would extrapolate outside the range of the data.

Another significant human capital variable is apprenticeship training, which in Côte d'Ivoire is an informal form of schooling. Although a substantial number of wage employees have completed some apprenticeship training, we find that, after controlling for other factors, apprenticeship training raises the likelihood of nonagricultural self-employment, and more so for men than for women. Given that women's apprenticeships are of a shorter duration (Section II), this may indicate that men use apprenticeships specifically to prepare for small-scale business opportunities in the future (Peil 1981, p. 104; Wilcock and Chuta 1982). The survey data also contain information on years of technical training, but this variable may well be endogenously related to the choice of wage employment, in the sense that employers provide or require technical training. Thus, years of technical training is not included in the logit model. For further discussion of the logit estimates of the (R, S_r) model, see Appendix 4.

All together, the sample of wage and nonfarm self-employed workers is clearly self-selected according to human capital characteristics. If the random components in this selection mechanism correlate with the unobserved determinants of productivity, the estimates of the returns to human capital could be substantially biased. We now turn to those estimates.

B. Second-Stage Estimates: The Wage Earnings Function

Table 4 shows for both males and females in each region the OLS and Dual-λ estimates of the hourly wage earnings function. The selectivity variables $\lambda_{w|r}$ and λ_r are significant sometimes, in which case the OLS estimates are biased. In the three largest samples (males and females in Abidjan and males in other urban areas), the selectivity variables are jointly significant ($p = 0.025$).

Years of schooling enter in a splined fashion into the estimated specification, in order to capture nonlinearities. Such nonlinear effects appear to exist in every region for every sample, and usually the rate of return increases with the level of schooling. Generally, the increase in men's hourly wages per year of elementary schooling is around 11 percent and per year of post-primary schooling 20 percent, ranging from 12 to 31 percent. In particular, the post-primary return is high in comparison to other developing countries (Psacharopoulos 1985). The interpretation is open to debate. The high returns may derive from a pattern of institutionalized wage setting, still as a consequence of the Second Lamine Guèye Law of 1950. (This may also explain why returns in other urban areas are higher than in Abidjan: highly educated workers operate in a narrower market with a standardized pay scale, whereas workers with elementary schooling only face regional diversity with lower wages in other urban areas.) On the other hand, one might argue that the large numbers of students repeating grades and failing the final *BEPC* and *Baccalauréat* exams (Cohen 1974) is evidence of high educational standards, and that secondary school graduates are of high quality, warranting the large premia.

Women earn similar returns to education compared to men. The returns to elementary schooling in Abidjan are lower (not significantly so: $t = 1.58$) but offset by the higher returns at the junior high level. Overall, the education parameter estimates are statistically different ($p = 0.009$). In other urban areas, the estimates are statistically similar ($p = 0.87$), but the point estimates are actually substantially higher for women. Note that the OLS estimates are similar but more precise: for the *Other Urban* sample of female wage earners, the selectivity variables introduce substantial multicollinearity. But even the OLS estimates of the education parameters are statistically similar ($p = 0.63$). In rural areas, no comparison is possible due to the small number of female wage earners.

Technical training pays off as well. Per year of training, Ivorian men can expect a raise of between 12 and 18 percent; women receive less, between 8 and 10 percent. Apprenticeship training does little to wage rates. Only for men in *Other*

Table 4

Estimates of the Hourly Earnings Function, Wage Employees, by Region and Sex,[a] *Dependent Variable = ln(Hourly Earnings) in Wage Employment)*

Parameter	Male		Female	
	OLS	Dual-λ	OLS	Dual-λ
Abidjan				
Intercept	4.078 (26.27)	4.495 (16.67)	4.182 (13.39)	3.651 (8.95)
Years elementary school	0.107 (7.22)	0.099 (5.94)	0.041 (1.02)	0.020 (0.42)
Years junior high	0.128 (5.37)	0.121 (4.81)	0.253 (6.43)	0.286 (6.63)
Years senior high	0.178 (5.51)	0.162 (4.88)	0.185 (3.78)	0.230 (4.52)
Years university	0.213 (11.04)	0.196 (9.53)	0.212 (6.72)	0.246 (7.04)
Years technical training	0.122 (7.27)	0.116 (6.89)	0.069 (2.32)	0.076 (2.61)
Years apprenticeship	0.006 (0.37)	0.005 (0.33)	-0.077 (0.92)	-0.079 (0.93)
Occupational experience	0.099 (9.71)	0.083 (7.31)	0.085 (4.73)	0.102 (5.35)
(Occupational experience)^2/100	-0.169 (4.81)	-0.121 (3.27)	-0.148 (2.26)	-0.158 (2.54)
Prior experience	0.033 (3.30)	0.026 (2.63)	0.030 (1.70)	0.049 (2.50)
(Prior experience)^2/100	-0.016 (0.59)	-0.005 (0.20)	-0.033 (0.72)	-0.057 (1.13)
Non-Ivorian	-0.180 (2.72)	-0.110 (1.51)	0.212 (1.37)	0.080 (0.51)
Year 1986	0.041 (0.67)	0.035 (0.57)	0.120 (1.15)	0.141 (1.37)
Year 1987	0.013 (0.21)	-0.012 (0.19)	0.065 (0.61)	0.087 (0.82)
$\lambda_{w|r}$	—	0.346 (3.09)	—	-0.518 (2.65)
λ_r	—	0.018 (0.23)	—	0.218 (1.13)
S_{uu}, R^2	0.437, 0.634	0.468, 0.639	0.421, 0.648	0.483, 0.660

Table 4 (*continued*)

Parameter	Male		Female	
	OLS	Dual-λ	OLS	Dual-λ
Other Urban				
Intercept	3.745 (21.42)	4.462 (14.67)	3.613 (8.21)	3.528 (6.54)
Years elementary school	0.117 (6.51)	0.083 (4.02)	0.141 (2.75)	0.115 (0.63)
Years junior high	0.186 (7.02)	0.129 (4.12)	0.192 (3.75)	0.176 (1.11)
Years senior high	0.284 (7.35)	0.264 (6.81)	0.379 (3.57)	0.363 (1.00)
Years university	0.244 (6.47)	0.205 (5.16)	0.305 (2.60)	0.300 (0.31)
Years technical training	0.184 (6.74)	0.175 (6.37)	0.114 (2.07)	0.107 (1.28)
Years apprenticeship	0.030 (1.67)	0.034 (1.89)	0.063 (0.58)	0.064 (0.55)
Occupational experience	0.101 (9.15)	0.078 (6.47)	0.115 (3.40)	0.112 (2.57)
(Occupational experience)^2/100	−0.148 (4.05)	−0.101 (2.64)	−0.200 (1.52)	−0.194 (1.52)
Prior experience	0.021 (1.87)	0.007 (0.55)	0.016 (0.53)	0.015 (0.28)
(Prior experience)^2/100	0.020 (0.70)	0.042 (1.42)	0.040 (0.48)	0.035 (0.35)
Non-Ivorian	−0.230 (2.37)	−0.216 (1.91)	−0.052 (0.16)	0.042 (0.05)
Year 1986	0.053 (0.71)	0.049 (0.66)	−0.231 (1.34)	−0.251 (1.21)
Year 1987	−0.105 (1.48)	−0.095 (1.33)	−0.229 (1.40)	−0.245 (1.17)
$\lambda_{w|r}$	—	0.519 (3.20)	—	−0.110 (0.42)
λ_r	—	−0.117 (1.36)	—	−0.259 (0.11)
S_{uu}, R^2	0.463, 0.665	0.525, 0.676	0.454, 0.672	0.390, 0.677

Rural Areas

	(1)		(2)		(3)		(4)	
Intercept	3.985	(10.01)	3.354	(5.62)	6.900	(2.29)	5.880	(1.51)[d]
Years elementary school	0.114	(2.85)	0.133	(3.09)	0.152[b]	(2.22)	0.090[b]	(0.95)[d]
Years junior high	0.200	(3.05)	0.221	(3.00)	—		—	
Years senior high	0.273	(3.06)	0.306	(2.87)				
Years technical training	0.183	(2.33)	0.179	(2.53)	—		—	
Years apprenticeship	-0.033	(0.75)	-0.010	(0.21)				
Occupational experience	0.103	(3.96)	0.099	(3.75)	-0.313[c]	(1.07)	-0.198[c]	(0.56)[d]
(Occupational experience)^2/100	-0.207	(2.23)	-0.188	(2.05)	0.859[c]	(1.28)	0.629[c]	(0.79)[d]
Prior experience	0.020	(0.77)	0.023	(0.86)				
(Prior experience)^2/100	0.006	(0.11)	0.001	(0.02)				
Non-Ivorian	-0.709	(3.91)	-0.576	(2.78)	—		—	
Year 1986	-0.155	(0.98)	-0.154	(1.02)	—		—	
Year 1987	0.015	(0.10)	0.016	(0.11)	—		—	
$\lambda_{w|r}$	—		-0.373	(1.47)	—		1.548	(0.96)[d]
λ_r	—		-0.084	(0.43)	—		-2.819	(0.80)[d]
S_{uu}, R^2	0.759, 0.583		0.634, 0.589		0.486, 0.719		0.467, 0.755	

a. Asymptotic t-statistics, corrected for selectivity, in parentheses.

b. Total years of completed schooling.

c. Experience (defined as the sum of occupational and general experience) and Experience squared/100, respectively.

d. t-statistics are not corrected for selectivity: the selectivity-corrected asymptotic covariance matrix was not positive definite, and the sample is too small anyway ($N = 13$) to attach much credence to asymptotic t-statistics.

Urban areas is there a significant positive effect of 3.4 percent per year of apprenticeship.

The parameter estimates for experience, both occupational and prior, are very similar for men and women.[24] The effect of occupational experience starts out at about 8 percent per year[25] and flattens out at around 30 years of experience. Prior experience pays little, except for a slight 3 or 4 percent per year in Abidjan.

Finally, non-Ivorian men earn sharply lower wages than Ivorian men, especially in rural areas where they have long worked as cheap labor on plantations (Cohen 1974). Non-Ivorian women in urban areas do not seem to be at such disadvantage. The time dummy variables do not show a particular business cycle trend: the recession after 1985 did little to wage rates.

C. Second-Stage Estimates: Nonagricultural Self-Employment Earnings

The earnings function for the self-employed is estimated for men and women together, pooled across regions, allowing for different selectivity effects in each region for each sex. The estimates are found in Table 5. We shall focus on the dual-λ estimates; the WLS estimates are provided for comparison. To arrive at the reported specification, we retained only those human capital/sex interactions that were statistically significant.[26]

Let us turn first to the human capital variables. Given the low level of education among the self-employed, all post-primary schooling is lumped into one variable. Education parameters indicate higher returns for women than for men ($p = 0.10$). For women, the elementary schooling estimate is comparable to that in wage employment. Technical and apprenticeship training does not lead to higher earnings. From a human capital perspective, one would theorize that apprentices learn from their supervisors, such that with those skills they are able to start up their own business. The first- and second-stage results together suggest, however, that the social function of apprenticeships may be one of licensing more than of transmitting skills. (It should be noted that years of apprenticeship training was an important variable in the instrumental variable equations predicting ln($Capital$) and ln($Inventory$); see below.)

Occupational experience does help, but for men only (difference with women's parameters; $p = 0.075$). For men, the effect is only slightly smaller than that

---

24. Occupational experience measures the number of years spent in the same occupation on the last three jobs, if these three jobs were not interrupted by a spell of unemployment. Prior experience measures all time not covered by schooling, technical or apprenticeship training, occupational experience, or childhood (five years).

25. This percentage is quite high in comparison to other studies. It is also consistent with Benie's (1989) observation that seniority is important in the wage system of Côte d'Ivoire and that salaries of public officials move up a step *automatically* every two years unless the employee had been sanctioned during the period.

26. Differences in the effect of general experience were insignificant ($p = 0.26$); similar for years of apprenticeship training ($p = 0.85$). The difference in the effect of years of technical training was marginally significant ($p = 0.091$), but while the effect was slightly positive for men (0.0378, $t = 0.25$), it was strongly negative for women (-0.4799, $t = 1.82$). Such an estimate is clearly unrealistic and probably results from the fact that the 453 women in nonfarm self-employment have a total of 16 years of technical training among them, in other words, too little variation in the explanatory variable.

among wage earners (Table 4). Starting with an increase in earnings of 6.9 percent per year of experience, the effect peaks out at 22 years. Prior experience appears to be irrelevant to enterprise earnings.

Self-employed non-Ivorian Africans achieve the same earnings as Ivorians. This is significant in view of the earnings gap in wage employment and the large number of non-Ivorians that have owned businesses in Côte d'Ivoire ever since the days of independence (for example, Cohen 1974, p. 40): non-Ivorians have a greater incentive to make a living through self-employment and indeed do so: see Tables 3 and A.1.

If the success of the enterprise leads the entrepreneur to invest some of his profits, and if enterprise earnings are correlated over time, the capital and inventory variables could be correlated with the disturbance term and cause estimation bias. Thus, we enter predicted values of ln(*Capital*) and ln(*Inventory*). Earnings increase with capital and inventory. To put the estimated parameters in perspective, adding CFA 1,000 worth of capital to an (arithmetic-) average enterprise raises its annual income by CFA 582; adding CFA 1,000 of inventory increase annual income by CFA 3,738. These estimates are large but comparable to other findings (Vijverberg 1991a, 1991b). There may well be diminishing returns as stocks increase, but the instrumental variable equations were not strong enough to include higher-order terms and detect diminishing returns.

Businesses operating from a fixed location have lower earnings. Given the controls for the entrepreneur's experience, the age of the enterprise has no impact on its earnings.

Self-employed workers do not work in isolation from the household to which they belong, even if they operate the enterprise themselves. Other household members have a financial incentive to interact at least casually with the general affairs of the enterprise and could well have an impact on its performance.[27] In particular, the schooling of other household members could compensate for the entrepreneur's own lack of it. As it turns out in the present Ivorian case, educational attainment among household members beyond that completed by the entrepreneur has a slight positive effect for women only, but the estimate is imprecise and therefore omitted from the current specification. Yet, the hypothesis is interesting and should be further investigated with a larger sample of enterprises.

Negative parameter estimates on the selectivity variables denote positive selectivity, such that these self-employed earn higher incomes than a person randomly drawn from the population at large would. The statistical significance level of the selectivity variables as a group equals $p = 0.073$. Individually, five parameter estimates approach significance, four negative and one positive (on a region effect). These estimates in combination with the negative (if significant) selectivity among wage earners support the notion that labor markets are characterized by asymmetric information about the productivity of workers (Weiss 1980, Foster and Rosenzweig 1993): because of lack of information, employers underpay the

---

27. These would be part of the gain from marriage (Becker 1974a, Benham 1974, Scully 1979, Wong 1986), but there is no reason to restrict such interactions to people within the band of marriage (Vijverberg 1991b). Every household member has an interest in the productive performance of all breadwinners of the household.

Table 5

Estimates of the Hourly Earnings Function, Nonagricultural Self-Employment,[a] dependent variable = ln(Enterprise Earnings per Hour of Family Labor)

Parameter	WLS		Dual-λ	
(i) Constant across Region and Sex				
$\ln(Capital)$[b]	0.099	(1.74)	0.129	(2.14)
$\ln(Inventory)$[b]	0.234	(3.24)	0.262	(3.31)
Fixed location	-1.177	(4.19)	-1.333	(4.37)
Business age ≤ 3	-0.091	(0.46)	-0.136	(0.68)
Business age ≥ 10	-0.219	(1.02)	-0.094	(0.43)
Non-Ivorian	-0.078	(0.48)	0.151	(0.87)
Years technical training	-0.104	(0.82)	-0.091	(0.72)
Years apprenticeship	0.014	(0.30)	0.016	(0.31)
Prior experience	0.030	(1.05)	0.019	(0.67)
$(Prior\ experience)^2/100$	-0.050	(0.97)	-0.038	(0.73)
(ii) Differing by Region				
Intercept for Abidjan	5.270	(9.13)	5.035	(7.34)
Intercept for Other Urban	5.146	(8.78)	5.150	(8.12)
Intercept for Rural Areas	5.097	(8.76)	4.739	(7.71)

(iii) Differing by Sex	Male		Female		Male		Female	
Female	—		0.490	(1.35)	—		0.389	(0.86)
Years elementary school	-0.012	(0.23)	0.133	(2.58)	-0.023	(0.42)	0.130	(2.33)
Years post-elementary school	0.039	(0.29)	0.065	(0.43)	0.039	(0.27)	0.036	(0.22)
Occupational experience	0.080	(1.82)	-0.009	(0.21)	0.069	(1.55)	-0.030	(0.70)
(Occupational experience)^2/100	-0.160	(1.30)	0.013	(0.10)	-0.154	(1.24)	0.048	(0.38)
(iv) Selectivity Variables								
Abidjan								
$\lambda_{n|r}$	—		—		0.094	(0.12)	-0.243	(0.44)
λ_r	—		—		-0.310	(0.37)	-0.797	(1.86)
Other Urban								
$\lambda_{n|r}$	—		—		-1.009	(1.93)	-0.619	(1.34)
λ_r	—		—		0.698	(1.81)	0.006	(0.02)
Rural Areas								
$\lambda_{n|r}$	—		—		-0.673	(1.77)	-0.691	(2.18)
λ_r	—		—		0.300	(0.48)	-0.305	(0.58)
S_{uu}, pseudo-R^2 [c]	2.673, 0.055				2.659, 0.066			

a. Asymptotic *t*-statistics, corrected for selectivity, in parentheses.

b. Treated as an instrumental variable; instruments are characteristics of the entrepreneur(s) and of the enterprise and household nonlabor income, including linear and higher-order terms. The instrumental variable equations explain 30 percent of the variation in ln(*Capital*) and 21 percent of the variation in ln(*Inventory*).

c. The pseudo-R^2 is defined as the squared Pearson correlation coefficient between the actual and the predicted value of the dependent variable.

most productive workers, who then, knowing their own productivity, have an incentive to withdraw from the wage labor market and engage in self-employment activities.

VI. Conclusion

This paper has set out to estimate the returns to human capital for men and women in Côte d'Ivoire. For both formal schooling and technical training, the returns in wage employment are considerable, and possibly higher for women than for men. The latter finding is not uncommon (Schultz 1993, Deolalikar 1993). Among the self-employed, returns to formal schooling are not as high but the estimates are not precise either. For women, there are measurable returns; for men there are not. Self-employed workers do not appear to gain much, if anything, from technical training, maybe because such training teaches different skills. Apprenticeship training raises neither wage earnings nor nonfarm self-employment earnings. Its function seems to be to allow the apprentice entry into certain occupations (crafts).

An individual obtains benefits from human capital through increased earnings *as well as* through access to different employment opportunities, possibly located in a different region. Do women obtain benefits similar to men? We may evaluate this question by calculating the expected earnings (or more appropriate: value of time), denoted as ln W, averaged over all opportunities:

$$(16) \quad \ln W = \sum_r \sum_s \text{Prob}[R = r, S_r = s] E[\ln W_{rs} | R = r, S_r = s]$$

$$= \sum_r \sum_s p_r p_{s|r} E[\ln W_{rs} | \eta_{s|r}^n \le A_{s|r}^n, \eta_r^n \le A_r^n].$$

Thus, the effect of changes in a variable X on ln W can be decomposed into three components, a regional choice effect, an activity choice effect, and an activity-specific earnings effect:

$$(17) \quad \frac{\partial \ln W}{\partial X} = \Delta_r + \Delta_{s|r} + \Delta_w$$

where

$$\Delta_r = \sum_r \sum_s \frac{\partial p_r}{\partial X} p_{s|r} E[\ln W_{rs} | \eta_{s|r}^n \le A_{s|r}, \eta_r^n \le A_r^n]$$

$$\Delta_{s|r} = \sum_r \sum_s p_r \frac{\partial p_{s|r}}{\partial X} E[\ln W_{rs} | \eta_{s|r}^n \le A_{s|r}^n, \eta_r^n \le A_r^n]$$

$$\Delta_w = \sum_r \sum_s p_r p_{s|r} \frac{\partial E[\ln W_{rs} | \eta_{s|r}^n \le A_{s|r}^n, \eta_r^n \le A_r^n]}{\partial X}.$$

To operationalize this decomposition, we need estimates of earnings equations in each alternative (r, s). For agricultural $(s = a)$ and home $(s = h)$ activities, we have not estimated such equations and need to rely on assumptions. Since the focus is on the effect of years of schooling, we specify values of $\ln W_{ra}$ and $\ln W_{rh}$ for an unschooled individual, their increase with years of schooling and experience, and the nature of selectivity (in other words, the value of the parameters of the selectivity variables). Thus, for an average person (see Table 6) without schooling, we assume that earnings in nonfarm self-employment equal the earnings in farming and value of time in home activities: $\ln W_{ra} = \ln W_{rh} = \ln W_{rn}$. Moreover, $\ln W_{ra}$ changes with years of schooling and experience in the same way as $\ln W_{rn}$ and also has the same nature of selectivity, whereas $\ln W_{rh}$ rises by 0.05 for each year of schooling and, for lack of a better a priori guess, is not affected by selectivity variables. One more assumption is made: since the estimates of rural female wage equation are not reliable, predictions of women's $\ln W_{3w}$ are generated with the equation $\ln W_{3w} = 3.5 + 0.08\,YRSCH + 0.05\,EXP - 0.000714\,EXP^2$, with an 8 percent return to schooling and an experience profile peaking at 35 years of experience. Since p_{3w} is very small, this assumption will not affect the decomposition much.

Table 6 reports the results of such decomposition, for men and women of age 25 and 45. These men and women are "typical" in that they have the same personal characteristics but, if self-employed, operate an enterprise described by sex-specific averages. Under these assumptions, the first two columns illustrate what is widely known: women's earnings are substantially lower than men's, except for the older well-educated women. The third and seventh columns show the marginal increase of the value of time $(\Delta \ln W)$ as a result of one more year of schooling. For example, the value of time rises by 13.2 percent for a 25-year-old woman in response to the first year of schooling. Note that, by definition, an increase in schooling is accompanied by a reduction in general experience.

Among 25-year-old men, elementary schooling hardly affects the value of time. The majority of men are self-employed and experience little benefit from schooling (Table 5). Only at higher levels of education does one benefit from the raised earnings in each employment alternative and from the opportunities to move toward better paying activities and regions: almost half (0.047/0.098) of the marginal benefit of the seventh year of schooling derives from migration (Δ_r), and one seventh (0.014/0.098) derives from changed employment choices $(\Delta_{s|r})$. At the end of senior high school, one fourth of the marginal gain of 19.8 percent derives from changes of employment. For 45-year-old men, both secondary effects $(\Delta_r$ and $\Delta_{s|r})$ tend to be even stronger.

Women reap benefits from elementary schooling in self-employment (Table 5) and so experience substantial increases in the overall value of their time at that level. Gains from changing regions are smaller for 25-year-old women than men but almost equivalent for 45-year-old individuals. For 25-year-old women, education also leads to smaller gains from changing employment; however, this type of gain helps 45-year-old women as much as equivalent men. Generally, more educated men and women enter into wage jobs (Table 3), which, relative to self-employment, pay much better. For example, for a 45-year-old average

Table 6
Predicted Effect of Education on the Log-Value of Time, By Age and Sex, 1986

Years of Schooling	E[ln(W)] Male	E[ln(W)] Female	Male Δ ln W	Male Δ_r	Male Δ_{s|r}	Male Δ_w	Female Δ ln W	Female Δ_r	Female Δ_{s|r}	Female Δ_w
A: Age = 25										
Elementary										
1	4.81	4.03	−0.013	0.003	0.004	−0.021	0.132	0.004	0.006	0.122
6	4.79	4.63	0.020	0.034	0.010	−0.031	0.110	0.016	0.000	0.098
Junior high										
7	4.89	4.71	0.098	0.047	0.014	0.030	0.079	0.016	−0.003	0.057
10	5.34	5.06	0.172	0.066	0.041	0.062	0.140	0.043	0.000	0.087
Senior high										
11	5.55	5.24	0.215	0.056	0.049	0.108	0.179	0.045	0.003	0.120
13	5.97	5.63	0.198	0.020	0.053	0.125	0.194	0.033	0.015	0.136
B: Age = 45										
Elementary										
1	4.85	4.18	0.055	0.024	0.007	0.022	0.169	0.032	0.014	0.124
6	5.38	5.01	0.149	0.096	0.018	0.023	0.151	0.069	0.016	0.071
Junior high										
7	5.59	5.22	0.217	0.100	0.023	0.088	0.214	0.062	0.015	0.120
10	6.18	5.94	0.182	0.038	0.036	0.113	0.245	0.041	0.030	0.169
Senior high										
11	6.39	6.20	0.211	0.018	0.033	0.161	0.264	0.028	0.028	0.200
13	6.77	6.71	0.186	−0.002	0.029	0.160	0.252	0.008	0.036	0.205

Based on an average person defined as the grand mean across the samples of men and women in all modes of employment combined, however, with sex-specific averages for the enterprise characteristics. Predictions apply to the year 1986, since the self-employment earnings data apply only to that year. Occupational experience is set at five years; general experience equals age (25 or 45) − 5 years of schooling, technical training, apprenticeship, and occupational experience. For assumptions on the value of time in agricultural self-employment, home activities and, for women, rural wage employment, see text.

woman, earning opportunities in nonfarm self-employment (in log form) in Abidjan rise from 4.21 to 5.15 (for a man: 5.06 to 5.32) as years of schooling rise from 0 to 13; log-wage offers rise from 5.11 to 7.04 (for a man: 5.57 to 7.16).

Two notes are still in order. First, the strategy to compute the statistics of Table 6 with sex-specific enterprise characteristics is not innocuous. With the overall mean enterprise characteristics, the earnings gap is much narrower: ln W rises among 25-year-olds from 4.16 to 5.69 (women) or from 4.32 to 5.72 (men), and among 45-year-olds from 4.30 to 6.73 (women) or from 4.40 to 6.69 (men), as years of schooling rises from 0 to 13. In Côte d'Ivoire, women tend to operate enterprises with less capital and inventory from a fixed location (Table 2), each of which lowers enterprise earnings significantly. Second, Table 6 presents point estimates. The statistical variance of the estimates has not been computed, but, given that crucial parameters in this computation are statistically imprecisely estimated, the point estimates should be treated with caution.

In summary, therefore, overall labor market returns to education are generally higher for women. At all levels of education, women's earnings are substantially below men's, but the difference narrows (and vanishes for older women, of whom there are few) at higher levels of education. This corresponds to a greater increase in the likelihood of obtaining wage employment. Still, women are less likely to hold wage jobs than men. Therefore, if the cause for lower education among women lies in the labor market, the reason cannot be found in a lower rate of return; instead, sex discrimination may be to blame.[28,29] Future research may shed light on this by examining occupational structure as well as determinants of children's schooling (for example, Deolalikar 1993). Such research may also lead to insights as to why women get to use less capital in their enterprises, a fact that, in this paper, explains much of the male-female earnings gap.

Does the future hold out a promise of improvement? School enrollment rates at all levels are increasing. The process of Ivorianization at the high end of the occupational ladder, replacing expatriates at their skilled positions, is not complete but may become harder. As long as expatriates hold jobs that Ivorians can take over, school leavers should not face excessive unemployment. The expatri-

---

28. Peil (1981) came to the conclusion that sex discrimination existed in the eight towns in Ghana, Nigeria, and The Gambia in the late 1970s. Women had difficulty obtaining clerical jobs. Relatively speaking, educated women held more professional and administrative jobs. Both findings are consistent with the Ivorian wage employment patterns.

29. Thompson and Adloff (1969, pp. 528–29) write: "The conservative attitude of West African parents towards women's education has a number of causes. Most of them see no use in it and even regard schooling for girls as an economic handicap, mostly because it delays their marriage or makes it more difficult. . . . The hard work that women perform in the home and in the fields has an economic value that accounts for the very high bride-price prevailing in contemporary West Africa. . . . As the number of educated African men increases, it is becoming ever more difficult for them to find wives of comparable cultural background, and to some extent this situation is breaking down their long-standing indifference or hostility to the education of girls." On the other hand, an indirect benefit of education is the improved likelihood of marrying a better educated spouse (Goldin 1992). In CILSS sample, counting each panel household once, the correlation in years of schooling of spouses is 0.71. It is not merely a generational phenomenon that younger couples belong to a more educated younger generation: for couples over (under) age 40, the correlation coefficient equals 0.61 (0.72). This makes the shortfall of education among women all the more fascinating.

ates holding public sector jobs, especially as teachers, will be more easily replaced—and will soon be—than those in the private sector holding managerial positions. If there is discrimination against women now, it will not be easy to overcome that in the future. Predicting a labor shortage developing in the near future that would lead to more equal opportunities for women would be optimistic. Whether the wage gap could be narrowed may depend on the willingness of multinationals to hire women.

Furthermore, if expatriates are all replaced, one can only expect a narrowing of the wage differentials across educational levels. In both Ghana and Côte d'Ivoire, large rates of returns were measured in the early 1970s (Hinchliffe 1974, Monson 1979). Ghana pursued its Africanization policy more vigorously than Côte d'Ivoire, relying less also on foreign investment (Rimmer 1984, p. 97). After a decade of intense economic difficulties, rates of return to education in Ghana are small, both in wage employment and in nonfarm self-employment (Glewwe 1990, Vijverberg 1991b). Although the Ivorian wage scale is stretched at the bottom by unskilled non-Ivorian African workers, returns to education will decline, since the Ivorian government cannot continue paying expatriate-level salaries to its civil servants, nor will the private sector pay them to its skilled employees, when the large cohorts of young educated workers enter the labor market. If sex discrimination exists at present, it is doubtful that an excess supply situation would benefit women and reduce the wage gap.

On the other hand, to let it come that far may not be in the interest of the Ivorian bureaucracy, which, for that matter, oversees the educational process. Campbell (1978) and Alschuler (1988) depict the Ivorian ruling elite as one quite capable of looking after its own gains. Many have questioned the wisdom of maintaining an educational system with such high repeat rates and tight restrictions on entrance rates into secondary schooling.[30] Goreux (1977) projected the need for manpower in the future, assuming a completion to the Ivorianization process by 1990, and concluded that secondary school enrollment rates would need to drop drastically to avoid large-scale unemployment. That rationalizes a policy of limiting current school enrollment. If school enrollment policies are sex-neutral, the artificial shortage of educated personnel may indeed help women in Côte d'Ivoire.

Appendix 1

Adjusting the Standard Errors of the Dual-λ Earnings Equation

Section III outlined the estimation strategy by which one can correct for the selectivity bias resulting from dual selection criteria with multiple alternatives. This appendix sketches the formulae needed to adjust the standard errors of the earnings equation for the use of the two-stage estimation technique.

First, define the disturbance term in the selectivity corrected earnings equation as v_{rs} [in other words, as in Equation (15)]:

---

30. For example, Clignet and Foster (1971), Cohen (1974, pp. 50–51), Den Tuinder (1978, Appendix D).

(A.1) $v_{rs} = \ln(W_{rs}) - E[\ln(W_{rs})|\eta^n_{s|r} \le A^n_{s|r}, \eta^n_r \le A^n_r]$.

We will need an estimate of $\sigma_{uu,rs}$, which can be derived from $\text{Var}(v_{rs})$. Define $b(A^n_{s|r}, A^n_r, \rho_{rs})$ as the standardized bivariate normal density function with arguments $A^n_{s|r}$ and A^n_r and correlation coefficient ρ_{rs}. It can be shown that

$$(A.2)\quad \text{Var}(v_{rs}) = \sigma^2_{1u,rs}A^n_{s|r}\lambda_{s|r} + \sigma^2_{2u,rs}A^n_r\lambda_r - (\sigma_{1u,rs}\lambda_{s|r} + \sigma_{2u,rs}\lambda_r)^2 + \sigma_{uu,rs}$$

$$+ \frac{b(A^n_{s|r}, A^n_r, \rho_{rs})}{\rho_{rs}}(-\rho_{rs}\sigma^2_{1u,rs} + 2\sigma_{1u,rs}\sigma_{2u,rs} - \rho_{rs}\sigma^2_{2u,rs}).$$

OLS estimation of Equation (9) yields, through (A.1), residuals $\hat{v}_{rs}$ which are inserted into (A.2) to yield an estimate of $\sigma_{uu,rs}$.

With standard statistical manipulations, one finds the correct standard errors of the OLS estimates as:

$$(A.3)\quad \text{Var}\begin{pmatrix} \hat{\beta}_{rs} \\ \hat{\sigma}_{1u,rs} \\ \hat{\sigma}_{2u,rs} \end{pmatrix} = (G'G)^{-1}G'(\text{Var}(v_{rs}) + H\,\text{Var}(\hat{\Gamma})H')G(G'G)^{-1}$$

where:

(A.4) $G = [X_{rs}\,\hat{\lambda}_{s|r}\,\hat{\lambda}_r]$

$$(A.5)\quad H = \frac{\partial(\sigma_{1u,rs}\lambda_{s|r} + \sigma_{2u,rs}\lambda_r)}{\partial\Gamma'}$$

and where Γ represents all the parameters of the first-stage selection model, estimated by $\hat{\Gamma}$. For notational convenience, let κ_1 and κ_2 denote the numerators of $\lambda_{s|r}$ and λ_r. Let $\xi = (1 - \rho^2_{rs})^{-1/2}$. Also, let $\pi_1 = \xi(A^n_r - \rho A^n_{s|r})$ and let $\pi_2 = \xi(A^n_{s|r} - \rho A^n_r)$. Then $\kappa_1 = \phi(A^n_{s|r})\Phi(\pi_1)$ and $\kappa_2 = \phi(A^n_r)\Phi(\pi_2)$, and

$$(A.6)\quad \frac{\partial\kappa_1}{\partial p_{s|r}} = -A^n_{s|r}\Phi[\pi_1] - \rho_{rs}\xi\phi(\pi_1)$$

$$(A.7)\quad \frac{\partial\kappa_1}{\partial p_r} = \frac{b(A^n_{s|r}, A^n_r, \rho_{rs})}{\phi(A^n_r)}$$

$$(A.8)\quad \frac{\partial\kappa_1}{\partial\rho_{rs}} = -\pi_2\xi b(A^n_{s|r}, A^n_r, \rho_{rs})$$

$$(A.9)\quad \frac{\partial\kappa_2}{\partial p_{s|r}} = \frac{b(A^n_{s|r}, A^n_r, \rho_{rs})}{\phi(A^n_{s|r})}$$

$$(A.10)\quad \frac{\partial\kappa_2}{\partial p_r} = -A^n_r\Phi[\pi_2] - \rho_{rs}\xi\phi(\pi_2)$$

$$(A.11)\quad \frac{\partial\kappa_2}{\partial\rho_{rs}} = -\pi_1\xi b(A^n_{s|r}, A^n_r, \rho_{rs}).$$

Note that $p_{s|r}$ and p_r are logit probabilities, straightforwardly differentiated with respect to Γ. The denominator of $\lambda_{s|r}$ and λ_r can in fact be written as p_{rs} and is also straightforwardly differentiated with respect to Γ.

Next, consider the case of the family enterprises, some of which employ more than one family worker. For each person, the variance of the disturbance $v_{rn,i}$ is given in (A.2), but let us simplify the expression by defining $c_{rn,i}$ as everything in (A.2) except for $\sigma_{uu,rn}$: $\text{Var}(v_{rn,i}) = \sigma_{uu,rn} + c_{rn,i}$. We already defined v_{rn} as $\Sigma_i \alpha_{rn,i} v_{rn,i}$. To account for the heteroskedasticity correction applied in estimating Equation (16), define $v_{rn}^* = v_{rn}/\Sigma_i \alpha_{rn,i}^2$. Its variance equals

$$(A.12) \quad \text{Var}(v_{rn}^*) = \sigma_{uu,rn} + \frac{\displaystyle\sum_i \alpha_{rn,i}^2 c_{rn,i}}{\displaystyle\sum_i \alpha_{rn,i}^2}.$$

By pooling the male and female observations across regions, the selectivity term becomes a complicated expression. We must add a subscript g to indicate gender. The selectivity term can then be written as:

$$(A.13) \quad \sum_r \sum_g \left[\sigma_{1u,rng}\left(\sum_i D_{ig}\alpha_{rn,ig}\lambda_{n|r,ig} \right) + \sigma_{2u,rng}\left(\sum_i D_{ig}\alpha_{rn,ig}\lambda_{r,ig} \right) \right]$$

where $D_{ig} = 1$ if individual i has gender g. This makes the formulation of the matrix H as in (A.5) a tedious exercise; it is a combination of the expressions created for each region separately. In terms of (A.3), since the selection model is separately estimated for men and women, there are three terms inside the parentheses in the middle, rather than two.

Appendix 2

The Effect of V_{rs} on ρ_{1w}

This appendix shows the effect of V_{rs} on the correlation coefficient ρ_{1w}. First, note that the effect of V_{rs} on ρ_{1w} is:

$$(B.1) \quad \frac{\partial \rho_{1w}}{\partial V_{rs}} = \frac{1}{m}\left(\Sigma\, \eta_1^n \frac{\partial \eta_{w|1}^n}{\partial V_{rs}} + \Sigma\, \eta_{w|1} \frac{\partial \eta_1^n}{\partial V_{rs}} \right)$$

$$= \frac{1}{m}\left(\Sigma\, \eta_1^n \frac{\partial \Phi^{-1}[F(\eta_{w|1})]}{\partial \eta_{w|1}} \frac{\partial \eta_{w|1}}{\partial V_{rs}} + \Sigma\, \eta_{w|1} \frac{\partial \Phi^{-1}[F(\eta_1)]}{\partial \eta_1} \frac{\partial \eta_1}{\partial V_{rs}} \right)$$

where $\partial \Phi^{-1}[F(x)] = F(x)(1 - F(x))/\phi(\Phi^{-1}[F(x)])$. Recall that $\eta_{w|1} = \varepsilon_{1w}' - \varepsilon_{1w}$, with

$$(B.2) \quad \varepsilon_{1w}' = \max_{s \neq w} (V_{1s} + \varepsilon_{1s}) - \ln\left(\sum_{s \neq w} e^{V_{1s}} \right)$$

and $\varepsilon_{1w} = U_{1w} - V_{1w}$. Similarly, recall that $\eta_1 = \theta_1' - \theta_1$, where

(B.3) $\theta_1' = \max\limits_{r \neq 1} \max\limits_{s} (V_{rs} + \varepsilon_{rs}) - \ln\left(\sum\limits_{r \neq 1} \sum\limits_{s} e^{V_{rs}}\right)$

and

(B.4) $\theta_1 = \max\limits_{s} (V_{1s} + \varepsilon_{1s}) - \ln\left(\sum\limits_{s} e^{V_{1s}}\right)$

Suppose V_{1w} rises. Then since $\partial\varepsilon_{1w}'/\partial V_{1w} = \partial\varepsilon_{1w}/\partial V_{1w} = 0$, the first term of (B.1) vanishes. Moreover, $\partial\theta_1'/\partial V_{1w} = 0$, and

(B.5) $\dfrac{\partial\theta_1}{\partial V_{1w}} = 1 - p_{w|1}$ if $U_{1w} \gtreqqless \max\limits_{s \neq 1} U_{1s}$

$\qquad = -p_{w|1}$ if $U_{1w} < \max\limits_{s \neq 1} U_{1s}$.

This insight helps us to solve the next question: let all V_{1s} rise by the same amount. We easily establish that $\partial\varepsilon_{1w}/\partial V_{1s} = \partial\theta_1'/\partial V_{1s} = 0$, because V_{1s} is not part of those expressions. Also:

(B.6) $\sum\limits_{s} \dfrac{\partial\varepsilon_{1w}'}{\partial V_{1s}} = 1 - \sum\limits_{s \neq w} \dfrac{e^{V_{1s}}}{\sum\limits_{s \neq w} e^{V_{1s}}} = 0$

and

(B.7) $\sum\limits_{s} \dfrac{\partial\theta_1}{\partial V_{1s}} = 1 - \sum\limits_{s} \dfrac{e^{V_{1s}}}{\sum\limits_{s} e^{V_{1s}}} = 0.$

This proves that

(B.8) $\dfrac{\partial\rho_{1w}}{\partial V_{1w}} = -\sum\limits_{s \neq w} \dfrac{\partial\rho_{1w}}{\partial V_{1s}}.$

Now consider a change in V_{rs} for $r \neq 1$ and any s. We have $\partial\varepsilon_{1w}'/\partial V_{rs} = \partial\varepsilon_{1w}/\partial V_{rs} = \partial\theta_1/\partial V_{rs} = 0$. Define

(B.9) $p_{rs}^c = \dfrac{e^{V_{rs}}}{\sum\limits_{r \neq 1} \sum\limits_{s} e^{V_{rs}}}$

which is the conditional probability of choosing (r, s) if $r = 1$ is unavailable. Then:

(B.10) $\dfrac{\partial\theta_1'}{\partial V_{rs}'} = 1 - p_{rs}^c$ if $U_{rs} = \max\limits_{q,t;\,q \neq 1} U_{qt}$, with probability p_{rs}^c

$\qquad = -p_{rs}^c$ if $U_{rs} < \max\limits_{q,t;\,q \neq 1} U_{qt}$, with probability $(1 - p_{rs}^c)$.

Thus, in an expected value sense, $\partial\theta'_r/\partial V_{rs} = 0$. In the context of Equation (B.1), the changes in η''_1 are generated by θ'_1, which in turn depend on ε_{rs} for $r \neq 1$ and all s. However, $\eta''_{w|1}$ depends on all ε_{1s}. The i.i.d. assumption of the distribution of ε_{rs} for all (r, s) implies independence between $\eta_{w|1}$ and $\partial\theta'_1/\partial V_{rs}$ for $r \neq 1$. Therefore, $\partial\rho_{1w}/\partial V_{rs} = 0$ for $r \neq 1$.

Appendix 3

Aggregation and the Nonfarm Self-Employment Earnings Equation

What can be learned from an analysis of hourly self-employment earnings about the nature of the family enterprise production process? Suppose one posits a production function $Q = Q(L, K, M)$ to describe the production process. Q measures output, L is family labor, K stands for the entrepreneur's own capital, and M represents inputs purchased in the market. This process has a time dimension, which could range from several hours (for example, street vending) to a full season or longer (for example, farming or wood processing). Profit maximization during the length of this period yields an earnings (restricted profit) function $\Pi = \Pi(L, K, p_Q, p_M)$, which inherits its properties from the production function Q. In particular, the first and second order derivatives of Π with respect to L and K are the same as those of Q. In empirical research, one measures enterprise earnings over a given period (month, hour). Let τ represent the ratio of the measurement period over the production period: τ measures how many times the production process can be repeated over the length of the measurement period. During the measurement period, the enterprise uses τL labor. The capital stock is still K but yields τ times as the quantity of capital services as during the proper production period. To see the effect on the estimated parameters, let us examine the Taylor expansion of $\tau\Pi$ around (L_0, K_0), ignoring other variables:

$$(C.1) \quad \tau\Pi \approx \tau\Pi(L_0, K_0) + \frac{\partial\Pi}{\partial L}(\tau L - \tau L_0) + \tau\frac{\partial\Pi}{\partial K}(K - K_0)$$

$$+ \frac{1}{\tau}\frac{\partial^2\Pi}{\partial L^2}(\tau L - \tau L_0)^2 + \frac{\partial^2\Pi}{\partial L\partial K}(\tau L - \tau L_0)(K - K_0) + \tau\frac{\partial^2\Pi}{\partial K^2}(K - K_0)^2$$

with the right-hand side written as a function of $(\tau L, K)$. On the other hand, $\tau\Pi$ may be viewed as a function of $(\tau L, K)$ and then has a Taylor expansion around $(\tau L_0, K_0)$ equal to:

$$(C.2) \quad \tau\Pi = \Pi^*(\tau L, K)$$

$$\approx \Pi^*(\tau L_0, K_0) + \frac{\partial\Pi^*}{\partial(\tau L)}(\tau L - \tau L_0)$$

$$+ \frac{\partial\Pi^*}{\partial K}(K - K_0) + \frac{\partial^2\Pi^*}{\partial(\tau L)^2}(\tau L - \tau L_0)^2$$

$$+ \frac{\partial^2\Pi^*}{\partial(\tau L)\partial K}(\tau L - \tau L_0)(K - K_0) + \frac{\partial^2\pi^*}{\partial K^2}(K - K_0)^2.$$

Equation (C.1) contains the parameters of the true production process. Equation (C.2) interprets the production process within the context of the measurement period. The marginal returns of L and K, as well as the cross-partial, are estimated correctly. However, if $\tau < 1$, the diminishing returns to labor are overstated by a factor of $1/\tau$; the diminishing returns to capital are understated by a factor of τ. Therefore, given that different kinds of enterprises are represented in the sample and that we have no a priori knowledge of the length of the production process, there appears to be little benefit from trying to estimate diminishing returns and scale economies in self-employment production processes.[31] In our empirical analysis, we use the log of hourly enterprise earnings as the dependent variable.

Appendix 4

The Parameter Estimates of the (R, S_r) Model

Table A1 presents the parameter estimates of the model of locational choice and labor market status, for both males and females on the left and right half of the table, respectively. Determinants of the choice of R include information about the person's background, in other words, where he or she was born and how long he or she lived there as a child (until age 15, or less if the household moved away before the fifteenth birthday). In each case, one's roots have an impact where one is found at the time of the survey; it is worth emphasizing that it was left to the respondent to characterize the place of birth as a city, town or village. For men, years of schooling is not much of a factor except in interaction with age. Age is an important determinant for women: the probability of choosing Abidjan and *Other Urban* areas reaches its maximum at age 35 and 33, respectively. It may signify that women have become more mobile in the last few decades. Non-Ivorian males are less likely to reside in rural areas.

Labor market status depends on human capital, age, marital status, ethnic background and a time trend. The omitted category within each region is nonemployment. In each region, years of completed schooling is an important determinant, both directly and in interaction with age, as is years of apprenticeship training. Their effect is discussed in detail in Section V. Another strong effect comes from marital status for males into anything but nonemployment. Ethnic background is also a strong determinant: non-Ivorians are more likely found in nonfarm self-employment, which correlates appropriately with the report by Cohen (1974) that in the late 1960s Ivorians owned about a half of the urban businesses and commercial licenses. Rural male non-Ivorians are also found in wage employment, as cheap wage labor on plantations. Finally, even though Côte d'Ivoire fell into a recession after 1985, the estimates give little consistent evidence that people went unemployed.

---

31. The issue may be stated as a special case within the framework of aggregation of economic relationships (for example, Van Daal and Merkies 1984). Data are gathered within a measurement period as simple sums over production periods. Consistent aggregation is a quite hopeless endeavor. To estimate diminishing returns, data relevant to the production period proper are needed.

Table A1

Estimates of (R, S_r) Logit Model for both Males and Females[a]

Parameter	Male				Female			
	R = Abidjan		R = Other Urban		R = Abidjan		R = Other Urban	
Intercept	0.858	(0.60)	3.109	(1.98)	-2.198	(2.54)	-.623	(.71)
Birthplace:								
Abidjan/city	0.875	(2.40)	0.556	(1.52)	-0.288	(0.88)	-0.164	(0.50)
Other Urban/town	0.917	(2.19)	0.142	(0.34)	1.377	(3.37)	0.731	(1.81)
Childhood years[b] lived in:								
Abidjan/city	0.080	(3.17)	0.007	(0.25)	0.124	(5.61)	0.036	(1.57)
Other Urban/town	0.062	(2.12)	0.171	(5.96)	-0.045	(1.65)	0.099	(3.71)
Rural areas	-0.067	(4.66)	-0.095	(6.94)	-0.119	(8.98)	-0.103	(8.25)
Years schooling	-0.112	(0.89)	-0.077	(0.58)	-0.150	(0.93)	0.083	(0.50)
Years schooling squared/100	-0.743	(1.37)	-0.756	(1.30)	2.106	(2.27)	1.246	(1.32)
Years schooling * age/100	1.164	(3.31)	0.797	(2.05)	0.351	(0.72)	-0.357	(0.70)
Age	-0.025	(0.31)	-0.128	(1.45)	0.228	(4.85)	0.112	(2.34)
Age squared/100	0.027	(0.28)	0.121	(1.09)	-0.318	(5.29)	-0.168	(2.75)
Non-Ivorian	1.265	(3.64)	0.840	(2.22)	0.100	(0.59)	0.089	(0.50)
Year 1986	0.523	(2.20)	0.507	(2.00)	0.165	(1.01)	0.044	(0.26)
Year 1987	-0.011	(0.50)	0.069	(0.29)	0.230	(1.39)	0.275	(1.62)

Parameter	S_r = Agricultural	S_r = Nonagricultural self-employed		S_r = Wage		S_r = Agricultural	S_r = Nonagricultural self-employed		S_r = Wage	
R = Abidjan										
Intercept	—	-9.002	(6.57)	-9.696	(9.70)	—	-4.618	(4.85)	-9.696	(5.33)
Years schooling	—	-0.340	(3.63)	-0.263	(4.04)	—	-0.293	(2.45)	-0.296	(2.19)
Years schooling squared/100	—	0.693	(1.83)	0.720	(2.87)	—	-0.614	(0.96)	-0.056	(0.15)
Years schooling * age/100	—	0.516	(2.58)	0.489	(3.46)	—	0.830	(2.66)	1.877	(5.53)
Years apprentice	—	0.126	(4.34)	0.022	(0.78)	—	-0.002	(0.02)	-0.010	(0.09)

	(1)	(2)	(3)	(4)	(5)
Age	0.420 (5.70)	0.559 (10.48)	—	0.223 (4.25)	0.411 (4.27)
Age squared/100	-0.554 (6.19)	-0.754 (11.46)	—	-0.267 (3.92)	-0.547 (4.36)
Married	1.559 (6.16)	1.655 (10.81)	—	0.070 (0.46)	-0.132 (0.70)
Non-Ivorian	1.626 (7.65)	0.207 (1.18)	—	-0.157 (0.95)	-1.263 (4.03)
Year 1986	-0.130 (0.60)	-0.065 (0.44)	—	-0.275 (1.75)	0.036 (0.17)
Year 1987	0.120 (0.55)	0.080 (0.51)	—	-0.525 (3.20)	-0.196 (0.90)
R = Other Urban Areas					
Intercept	-8.104 (6.31)	-12.404 (9.38)	-3.786 (4.30)	-4.178 (5.25)	-7.866 (3.67)
Years schooling	-0.020 (0.17)	-0.121 (1.32)	-0.049 (0.31)	-0.307 (2.49)	-0.303 (1.77)
Years schooling squared/100	-1.216 (1.95)	0.074 (0.20)	-1.632 (1.73)	-0.701 (1.00)	0.122 (0.21)
Years schooling * age/100	0.070 (0.25)	0.635 (2.66)	0.153 (0.34)	0.945 (2.71)	2.092 (4.75)
Years apprentice	0.116 (4.43)	0.003 (0.08)	-0.050 (0.57)	0.141 (2.76)	0.062 (0.59)
Age	0.422 (5.75)	0.661 (9.06)	0.184 (3.81)	0.223 (5.07)	0.299 (2.60)
Age squared/100	-0.542 (5.89)	-0.849 (9.33)	-0.211 (3.45)	-0.272 (4.81)	-0.398 (2.66)
Married	1.796 (8.55)	2.179 (12.78)	0.196 (1.41)	0.019 (0.16)	-0.446 (1.93)
Non-Ivorian	1.470 (6.07)	0.211 (0.83)	-1.544 (6.37)	-0.100 (0.66)	-1.455 (2.91)
Year 1986	0.041 (0.20)	-0.096 (0.51)	0.283 (1.81)	0.193 (1.32)	-0.179 (0.65)
Year 1987	0.214 (1.03)	-0.006 (0.03)	-0.166 (1.03)	0.210 (1.49)	-0.247 (0.92)
R = Rural Areas					
Intercept	-4.797 (3.08)	-7.302 (3.99)	-1.788 (2.62)	-4.407 (5.07)	-5.136 (1.12)
Years schooling	0.066 (0.38)	-0.192 (1.29)	-0.046 (0.27)	-0.191 (0.96)	-1.020 (2.95)
Years schooling squared/100	-3.470 (3.50)	-1.015 (1.61)	-0.932 (0.87)	-0.721 (0.54)	2.770 (1.70)
Years schooling * age/100	0.521 (1.21)	1.226 (3.04)	-0.343 (0.67)	0.674 (1.17)	3.243 (2.98)
Years apprentice	0.063 (2.26)	-0.098 (1.92)	-0.732 (7.50)	0.069 (0.99)	—
Age	0.271 (3.18)	0.418 (4.11)	0.252 (6.68)	0.297 (6.19)	0.208 (0.68)
Age squared/100	-0.388 (3.73)	-0.645 (5.00)	-0.334 (7.05)	-0.391 (6.43)	-0.483 (0.98)
Married	2.053 (9.01)	2.346 (9.59)	0.478 (5.63)	-0.078 (0.60)	0.956 (1.19)
Non-Ivorian	1.532 (4.46)	1.369 (3.71)	-1.752 (11.59)	-0.256 (1.45)	-1.859 (1.74)
Year 1986	0.473 (1.82)	0.222 (0.80)	0.067 (0.48)	0.116 (0.70)	-0.079 (0.13)
Year 1987	-0.482 (1.92)	-0.387 (1.47)	-0.179 (1.26)	-0.460 (2.56)	-1.008 (1.21)
Log-likelihood	-8,621.18			-10,748.73	
Number of observations	6,011			7,633	
χ^2-test on slopes (p-value)	6,471.38 (0.00)			5,981.32 (0.00)	
Pseudo-R^2	0.2729			0.2177	

a. Asymptotic t-statistics in parentheses.

b. Years of residence at the place of birth until the household moved away or until, at most, age 15.

In terms of specification, note that there is no agriculture in Abidjan, or actually that the eight persons in Abidjan who report time spent on agricultural activities are lumped into the nonemployed category, since Abidjan is a nonagricultural environment. The 13 rural female wage employees did not have apprenticeship training.

The coefficients of the selectivity variables $\lambda_{s|r}$ and λ_r in the second-stage earnings functions are identified on the basis of birthplace and childhood residence, marital status, and the schooling/age interaction, as well as, of course, the nonlinearity inherent in the expressions for $\lambda_{s|r}$ and λ_r. Only in one subsample, female wage earners in *Other Urban* areas, did the selectivity variables introduce excessive multicollinearity into the regression. As for other possible identifying variables, unearned income and value of durable household assets, no convincing case could be made that these are truly exogenous to the choice of employment mode: high past earnings could lead to an accumulation of assets *and* at the same time be correlated with the present level of earnings.

V   Household Structure and Labor Markets in Brazil

12 Poverty among Female-Headed Households in Brazil

Ricardo Barros
Louise Fox
Rosane Mendonça

Ricardo Barros is assistant professor of economics at Yale University and senior research economist at the Instituto de Pesquisa Economica Aplicada, in Rio de Janeiro, Brazil. Barros has written extensively on issues of the measurement and alleviation of poverty in Brazil. Louise Fox is senior staff economist at the World Bank. Rosane Mendonça works at the Instituto de Pesquisa Economica Aplicada, in Rio de Janeiro, Brazil, and has written on issues of children and youth in Brazil.

Female-headed households (FHHs) have been of increasing concern around the world, in particular, in Brazil. This concern stems from five facts about FHHs. First, the prevalence of FHHs has been increasing since 1950 (Barros and Fox 1990; Goldani 1989). Second, FHHs tend to be overrepresented among the poor (Merrick and Schmink 1983). Third, the overrepresentation of FHHs among the poor tends to increase as the level of poverty declines, indicating that poverty among FHHs may be harder to eradicate. Fourth, the well-being and development of children tend to be adversely affected by living in FHHs. Finally, the consequences of poverty on child development and human capital accumulation seem to be more severe among those living in FHHs.

The first section of this chapter documents the extent to which FHHs are in fact overrepresented among the poor. Then the proximate determinants of the relatively greater poverty among FHHs are investigated. Finally, the consequences of living in FHHs upon children's labor force participation and school attendance are examined. The analyses were conducted separately for three Brazilian metropolitan areas using the 1984 Brazilian annual household survey called Pesquisa Nacional por Amostra de Domicílios (PNAD).

I. The Extent of Poverty among Female-Headed Households

Most studies concerned with FHHs and poverty agree that FHHs are overrepresented among the poor. Studies for Brazil about this relationship (Merrick and Schmink 1983; Pastore, Zylberstajn, and Pagotto 1983) are not exceptions. These studies have all confirmed that in Brazil, as in most other countries, FHHs are overrepresented among the poor.[1]

This section of the study first describes the extent to which FHHs and children living in FHHs are overrepresented among the poor in Brazil. The limited results available in the literature are reviewed, and new findings are presented. The prevalence of poverty among children living in FHHs and the age structure of these children, which are investigated at length, have never been analyzed before for Brazil. This section also introduces some basic concepts and methodological issues, which will be used throughout the paper.

A. Basic Data

The 1984 PNAD, from which the basic data for this study were obtained, had a series of special questions for women aged 15 to 54.[2] PNAD-84 contains information on almost 150,000 Brazilian households (see Table 1). Due to large, but not precisely known, regional disparities in the cost of living and to the fact that FHHs are expected to be quite distinct with respect to their composition, structure, and forms of economic support depending on their regional location, the analysis was limited to three metropolitan areas: São Paulo, Recife, and Porto Alegre. Basic differences among these three areas are briefly described below. Table 1 presents the sample screening process as well as the final sample size for each metropolitan area.

B. The Concept of Household Resources

To investigate the extent to which FHHs and children in FHHs are overrepresented among the poor, it is necessary to specify a definition of household resources in order to rank households. In this study, households are ranked according to a slight modification of the traditional concept of household per capita income. Specifically, the income from all sources of all adult members of the household[3] is divided by the total number of members in the household. This is referred to as the *household per capita adult income*.[4]

Removing from the household income that part contributed by non-adult members prevents households from upgrading their ranking by using their children in

---

1. Surprisingly, the study by Dvorak (1989) does not reveal FHHs as being overrepresented among the poor.
2. See Goldani (1989) for extensive analyses of the special questions on women contained in this survey.
3. Adult members are the head of the household, his (her) spouse, and all other members at least 18 years old.
4. A similar concept has been used by Masters (1969).

Table 1
Brazil: Sample Screening: PNAD-84

Strata	Screening	Sample Size
Brazil		142,227
Urban Brazil	Sampled	110,625
	Interviewed	92,397
	Private households	91,900
	Report household income	91,361
Metropolitan		51,637
Recife		4,839
São Paulo		8,506
Porto Alegre		6,361

Source: PNAD-84 Public Tapes: authors' tabulations.

the labor market.[5] One of the goals of this study is to assess how outcomes for children, such as their labor force participation and school attendance, depend on the rank of their households (see section III). Hence, it is absolutely essential to measure the household resources without the contribution of non-adult members. It would confound the analysis to permit children's time allocation (that is, their labor force participation and school attendance) to affect the ranking of households.[6] Ideally, households would be ranked based on the resources they would have if all children were attending school and out of the labor force. The income measure used in this study, the adult total income, will equal this ideal measure whenever the labor supply of the household adult members is not influenced by how non-adult members allocate their time.

C. The Income Classes

The overrepresentation of FHHs among the poor is investigated by verifying whether the prevalence of FHHs declines as one moves from poor households

---

5. To what extent does the exclusion of the income of the non-adult members have an impact on the ranking of households? To answer this question households were ranked and classified first by their per capita adult income and second by their per capita total income (this analysis was carried out only for the Metropolitan Area of São Paulo). The concordance between these two rankings revealed that 94 percent of all households were classified in the same relative income group whether they were ranked by per capita adult income or per capita total income. Among those classified as extremely poor based on the ranking by per capita adult income, only 88.3 percent were also extremely poor according to the ranking by per capita total income. However, among those classified as nonpoor according to the per capita adult income, 98.6 percent were also classified as nonpoor according to per capita total income. This proportionally larger number of changes in classification among poor households is a consequence (1) of non-adult income being more important for relatively poorer households, and (2) of the income classes being more disaggregated among the poor and, therefore, more sensitive to how income is defined.

6. See Barros and Mendonça (1990a) for further discussion and evidence on this issue.

to non-poor households. To operationalize this movement from poor to non-poor households, households were grouped into five income classes according to their per capita adult income.

Given the focus of this study on poverty, the grouping scheme was designed to be more disaggregated among poor households. To define the classes precisely, let Q_α be the α-percentile of the distribution of households according to the household per capita adult income. In other words, Q_α was defined as the smallest number such that at least α percent of all households have per capita adult income lower than Q_α. Five income classes were constructed based on Q_5, Q_{10}, Q_{25}, and Q_{50}. Specifically, households were grouped according to their per capita adult income into five groups as follows: (1) below Q_5, the extreme poor; (2) between Q_5 and Q_{10}, the very poor; (3) between Q_{10} and Q_{25}, the poor; (4) between Q_{25} and Q_{50}, the quasi-poor; and (5) above Q_{50}, the non-poor. By construction the first and second groups each have 5 percent of all households; the third group 15 percent; the fourth group 25 percent; and, finally, the last group has 50 percent of all households.

D. Regional Disaggregation

Given the large regional variations in the cost of living that exist across Brazil, it would be unwise to conduct a detailed investigation of poverty without a concomitant regional disaggregation. Accordingly, the analysis was conducted separately for three Brazilian Metropolitan Areas: Recife, São Paulo, and Porto Alegre. São Paulo is the largest metropolitan area in the country; it has the highest average per capita income, and it is the most industrialized area. Recife and Porto Alegre are similar in size, both being considerably smaller than São Paulo. Recife is the largest metropolitan area in Northeast Brazil, which is a poor and densely populated region. Porto Alegre is the largest metropolitan area in South Brazil; it has a relatively homogeneous population and an average level of income close to that of São Paulo.

As the overall income levels vary significantly across these regions, so do the percentiles of the distribution of households according to their per capita adult income and consequently the income brackets used to group households. To clarify the analysis that follows, Table 2 presents, for each metropolitan area, the values for the selected percentiles that were used to define the five income groups. As Table 2 reveals, there is virtually no difference between São Paulo and Porto Alegre with respect to these percentiles. The percentiles for Recife, however, tend to be considerably lower: close to one-half of those for São Paulo and Porto Alegre. Notice that all these comparisons are in nominal terms; no attempt has been made to adjust for differences in cost of living between metropolitan areas. Hence, although it is likely that households in the same income class are poorer in Recife than in São Paulo and Porto Alegre, there are no guarantees that this is in fact the case.

E. Previous Studies of Poverty among FHHs

The strong relationship between poverty and FHHs in Brazil was first formally documented by Merrick and Schmink (1983) (see Table A1.1 in Appendix 1).

Table 2

Brazil: Selected Percentiles of the Distribution of Households According to Their Per Capita Adult Income[a] by Metropolitan Area, 1984

Percentile[b]	Recife[c]	São Paulo[c]	Porto Alegre[c]
Q_5	0.12	0.28	0.29
Q_{10}	0.18	0.42	0.41
Q_{25}	0.32	0.75	0.72
Q_{50}	0.60	1.36	1.35

Source: PNAD-84 Public Tapes: authors' tabulations.

a. Income refers to the sum of the income from all sources of all *adult* members of the household. Members considered as adults are the household head, his or her spouse, and all other members age 18 or more.

b. Q_α denotes the α percentile. So, for instance, Q_{25} is the first quartile and Q_{50} is the median.

c. Multiples of the national minimum wage.

They divided the universe of households into three income classes: Poor (bottom 30 percent), Low (middle 46 percent), and Middle/High (top 24 percent). The prevalence of FHHs in these classes was estimated as varying from 11 percent for the Middle/High class households to 25 percent among Poor households. Overall, the prevalence of FHHs was estimated as 17 percent.[7]

Pastore, Zylberstajn, and Pagotto (1983) and Dvorak (1989) studied the evolution of poverty in Brazil from 1970 to 1980 by dividing the universe of families into two income classes according to their per capita income: a family was considered poor if the per capita income was lower than one-fourth of the minimum wage and non-poor otherwise. The findings of Pastore et al. reveal, perhaps surprisingly, only a slightly higher prevalence of FHHs among the poor than among the non-poor (see Table A1.2 in Appendix 1). Even more surprising is Dvorak's finding that in 1980 the prevalence of FHHs was higher among non-poor than among poor households. The fact that these two studies encountered a weaker sensitivity of the prevalence of FHHs to income levels than both Merrick and Schmink (1983) and this study (see Table 3) should be related to the fact that they included urban and rural areas in their studies, whereas the Merrick and Schmink study as well as this one only considered metropolitan areas. Nevertheless, these discrepancies certainly deserve further investigation.

---

7. In their study, single-person households were excluded. As noted elsewhere (Barros and Mendonça 1990a, Part 3, Table 10), this exclusion tends to bias the estimates for the prevalence of FHHs downward by approximately 3 percent.

F. Basic Results

Table 3 presents estimates for the prevalence of FHHs by income class. Three categories of FHHs are considered: (1) all FHHs, (2) FHHs with children, and (3) FHHs with children and no other adults besides the head.[8] The results agree perfectly with those obtained by Merrick and Schmink (1983). Independent of the category of FHH or of metropolitan area, the prevalence of FHHs diminishes drastically as one moves from low-income to high-income classes. This strong sensitivity of the prevalence of FHHs to income levels demonstrates the existence of a close connection between metropolitan poverty and female-headed households.

The sensitivity of the prevalence of FHHs to income levels varies across metropolitan areas and types of FHH. These variations were investigated further by computing, based on the data in Table 3, two types of summary statistics for each metropolitan area and category of FHH: (1) the logit variation, Δ_L, between the extremely poor and the non-poor, and (2) the percentage of FHHs that are extremely poor, Δ_p. These statistics are reported in Table 4 and were obtained as follows:

(1) $\quad \Delta_L = \ln[p_5/(1 - p_5)] - \ln[p_{50}/(1 - p_{50})]$

(2) $\quad \Delta_p = 5(p_5/p)$,

where p_5, p_{50}, and p are the prevalence of FHHs among extremely poor households, non-poor households, and all households, respectively. Computing statistics like Δ_L and Δ_p is more desirable than simply computing $p_5 - p_{50}$ because p_5 and p_{50} are proportions and, therefore, bounded between zero and one.[9] Boundedness turns comparison of variations into a difficult problem.[10]

Table 4 presents the proportion of FHHs for each category and metropolitan area that are extremely poor, Δ_p. Recall that, by construction, 5 percent of all households are extremely poor. Hence, proportions above 5 percent would indicate that FHHs are overrepresented among the poor. The higher the proportion, the stronger the association between female-headship and poverty. The results are somehow easier to interpret than those for Δ_L.

With respect to regional variations, the sensitivity is higher in Recife and lower in Porto Alegre, with São Paulo occupying an intermediate position. While 9 percent of the FHHs in Recife are extremely poor, in Porto Alegre only 7 percent of the FHHs are extremely poor. With respect to variations by category of FHH, FHHs with children and no other adult besides the head are more likely to be poor than the average FHH with children, which in turn is more likely to be poor

---

8. For this study FHHs will refer to households which *report* a female, *without a husband present,* as the head.

9. If p_5 is close to zero or p_{50} is close to one, then p_5-p_{50} would be necessarily small.

10. When does a proportion vary more, when it varies (1) from 0.1 to 0.2, (2) from 0.4 to 0.5, or (3) from 0.8 to 0.9? A reasonable answer would be to consider that variations 1 and 3 are of the same magnitude and that they are larger than 2. That is exactly the answer obtained by using logit variations, Δ_L. The logit-transformation eliminates boundedness. Due to this property it is commonly used to compare the sensitivity of proportions. The differences in logit Δ_L are presented in Table 4.

Table 3

Brazil: Proportion of Female-Headed Households by Metropolitan Area and Per Capita Income[a] Class, 1984

Income Class[b]	Recife Categories			São Paulo Categories			Porto Alegre Categories		
	(1)	(2)	(3)	(1)	(2)	(3)	(1)	(2)	(3)
$<Q_5$	40.9	35.5	21.0	27.0	19.3	11.2	26.7	19.9	13.2
Q_5-Q_{10}	32.2	27.7	9.9	19.7	16.7	9.7	21.6	15.9	8.4
$Q_{10}-Q_{25}$	24.1	15.8	5.9	19.5	11.2	4.1	21.8	11.3	4.5
$Q_{25}-Q_{50}$	21.8	12.1	2.7	14.0	5.3	1.6	16.3	6.0	1.7
$>Q_{50}$	18.1	6.0	1.2	15.6	2.8	1.1	17.5	3.5	1.9
All	21.8	11.6	3.7	16.5	6.2	2.6	18.5	6.7	3.1

Source: PNAD-84 Public Tapes: authors' tabulations.

a. Income refers to the sum of the income from all sources of all *adult* members of the household. Members considered as adults are the household head, his or her spouse, and all other members age 18 or more.

b. Q_α denotes the α percentile. So, for instance, Q_{25} is the first quartile and Q_{50} is the median.

(1) All FHHs; (2) FHHs with children; (3) FHHs with children and no other adults besides the head.

Table 4

Brazil: Income Sensitivity of the Prevalence of Female-Headed Households and Proportion of Extremely Poor by Type of Household and Metropolitan Area, 1984

Type of Household	Recife		São Paulo		Porto Alegre	
	Δ_L	Δ_p	Δ_L	Δ_p	Δ_L	Δ_p
Female-headed	1.1	9	0.7	8	0.5	7
Female-headed with children	2.2	15	2.1	16	1.9	15
Female-headed with children and no adult besides the head	3.1	30	2.4	22	2.1	21

Source: PNAD-84 Public Tapes: authors' tabulations.

than the average FHH. For instance, in Recife 30 percent of the FHHs with children and no other adult besides the head are extremely poor while the corresponding percentages for FHHs with children and for all FHHs are 15 percent and 9 percent, respectively.

The fact that the category of FHH with the strongest association with poverty is the class of FHHs with minors and no other adults besides the head confirms the generalized belief that this is the class of FHH that deserves the greatest attention in fighting poverty.

G. Poverty among Children

To study poverty among households, households were divided into five income classes based on the per capita adult income of the household. To keep the analysis about children consistent with the analysis of households, the universe of children was also divided into five income classes, which were determined by the corresponding household income classes. In other words, children inherit the income class of their respective households.

This procedure has important implications for the analysis that follows. While the proportion of households in each of the five income classes was constructed to be 5 percent, 5 percent, 15 percent, 25 percent, and 50 percent, respectively, the proportion of children in each income class will be variable and unknown a priori. The proportion of children in each income class will depend on how the average number of children per household varies across income classes.

Table 5 presents the distribution of children across income classes for each metropolitan area. This table reveals that the distribution of children by income class varies somewhat across metropolitan areas and is approximately 10 percent, 10 percent, 23 percent, 27 percent, and 30 percent. Hence, the proportion of children classified as extremely poor, 10 percent, is twice as large as the proportion of households classified as extremely poor, 5 percent. These results indicate that the number of children per household should be strongly and inversely related to the household income level. This hypothesis is confirmed in the table, which shows that the number of children per household among extremely and very poor households is close to twice the average number of children per household among all households.

This inverse relationship between the number of children per household and the level of income is clearly sensitive to which income concept is being used. If, instead of income per capita, income per adult equivalent were used, and if children were equivalent to less than one adult, then the inverse relationship revealed by Table 5 would be much weaker, and consequently the proportion of children classified as extremely poor would be much smaller.

H. Children in FHHs

Since one of the main concerns about poverty is its consequences on the welfare of children, perhaps the extent to which *children* living in FHHs are overrepre-

Table 5

*Brazil: Distribution and Average Number of Children Per Household by
Per Capita Income[a] Class and Metropolitan Area, 1984*

	Recife		São Paulo		Porto Alegre	
Income Class[b]	Dist.	Average Number	Dist.	Average Number	Dist.	Average Number
$<Q_5$	9	2.9	10	2.5	11	2.4
Q_5-Q_{10}	10	3.5	10	2.6	10	2.2
$Q_{10}-Q_{25}$	23	2.6	23	2.0	22	1.6
$Q_{25}-Q_{50}$	28	1.9	27	1.4	26	1.1
$>Q_{50}$	30	1.0	30	0.8	32	0.7
All	100	1.7	100	1.3	100	1.1

Source: PNAD-84 Public Tapes: authors' tabulations.
a. Income refers to the sum of the income from all sources of all *adult* members of the household. Members considered as adults are the household head, his or her spouse, and all other members age 18 or more.
b. Q_α denotes the α percentile. So, for instance, Q_{25} is the first quartile and Q_{50} is the median.

sented among poor *children* should be more important than is the extent to which female-headed *households* are overrepresented among poor *households*.

Table 6 presents estimates of the prevalence of children in FHHs by metropolitan area. This table reveals that the proportion of children living in FHHs is considerably smaller than the proportion of households that are female-headed (Table 3). In fact, the prevalence of FHHs overestimates the prevalence of children in FHHs by approximately seven percentage points. The prevalence of children living in FHHs is slightly higher than the prevalence of FHHs with children (see Tables 3 and 6).

Moreover, children in FHHs tend to be more overrepresented among the poor than are FHHs. This can be observed in Table 7A. This table presents the logit differences for the prevalence of FHHs and for the prevalence of children in FHHs between the extremely poor and non-poor. The table reveals differences in logit that are much higher for the prevalence of children in FHHs than for the prevalence of FHHs.

Table 7B presents the proportion of children in FHHs that are classified as extremely poor. This table reveals that from 9 to 11 percent of all children are classified as extremely poor, while the proportion of children in FHHs that are classified as extremely poor varies from 19 to 22 percent. However, by construction 5 percent of all households are classified as extremely poor, while as shown in Table 4 only 7 to 9 percent of the FHHs are extremely poor. Consequently, together, these tables reveal that children in FHHs are more overrepresented among the extremely poor than are FHHs themselves.

Table 6

Proportion of Children in Female-Headed Households by Metropolitan Area and Relative Per Capita Income,[a] 1984

Relative Income[b]	Recife	São Paulo	Porto Alegre
$<Q_5$	37.2	18.6	22.1
Q_5-Q_{10}	23.2	15.2	14.5
$Q_{10}-Q_{25}$	14.4	12.5	12.2
$Q_{25}-Q_{50}$	12.1	6.3	8.6
$>Q_{50}$	9.0	5.0	6.6
All	15.0	9.5	10.8

Source: PNAD-84 Public Tapes: authors' tabulations.
a. Income refers to the sum of the income from all sources of all *adult* members of the household. Members considered as adults are the household head, his or her spouse, and all other members age 18 or more.
b. Q_α denotes the α percentile. So, for instance, Q_{25} is the first quartile and Q_{50} is the median.

Table 7A

Brazil: Income Sensitivity of the Prevalence of Female-Headed Households and of the Prevalence of Minors in Female-Headed Households by Age Group and Metropolitan Area, 1984: Difference in Logits

Type of Unit	Recife	São Paulo	Porto Alegre
FHH	1.1	0.7	0.5
Children in FHHs	1.8	1.5	1.4
Children aged 0–6 in FHHs	1.9	1.7	1.2
Children aged 7–9 in FHHs	1.7	1.4	1.1
Children aged 10–14 in FHHs	1.6	1.3	1.7

Source: PNAD-84 Public Tapes: authors' tabulations.

Table 7B

Brazil: Proportion of Extremely Poor Children by Type of Household and Metropolitan Area, 1984

Type of Households	Recife	São Paulo	Porto Alegre
All households	9	10	11
Female-headed with children	21	19	22
Female-headed with children and no other adult	33	26	32

Source: PNAD-84 Public Tapes: authors' tabulations.

I. Children in FHH by Age Group

The age structure of children in FHHs is very different from that of all children. Children in FHHs tend to be much older. Consequently, the prevalence of children in FHHs increases with the age of children (Table 8). The sensitivity of the prevalence of children in FHHs to household income levels also varies by the children's age. This sensitivity is decreasing in age. Hence, children aged 0–6 in FHHs tend to be more overrepresented among the poor than are children aged 7–14.

II. The Determinants of Poverty among Female-Headed Households

In this section the proximate determinants of poverty among FHHs and among FHHs with children are discussed. Specifically, we investigate the extent to which the relative poverty of FHHs is a consequence of (1) smaller earnings capacity among FHHs than among non-FHHs, (2) less intensive use of the available earnings capacity by FHHs (that is, lower participation rates in the labor force) compared to other households, or (3) higher dependency ratios (that is, number of children to adults) among FHHs. The determinants of earnings capacity will also be examined. The objective is to identify whether smaller earnings capacity among FHHs is due to the composition of earners in FHHs or due to differences in the earnings capacity of each demographic group in FHHs compared to those in non-FHHs.

A. Measuring Relative Poverty

Since the objective is to investigate why FHHs are relatively poorer than other households, a measure of relative poverty is required. To define this measure, let z denote per capita adult total household income, $\mathcal{F}$ a class of households, $\mathcal{H}$ the set of all households, and $\mathcal{C} = \mathcal{H} - \mathcal{F}$ the class of all households that are not in $\mathcal{F}$. Let F_F be the cumulative distribution of z in the class $\mathcal{F}$, F_H be the cumulative distribution of z among all households, and F_C the cumulative distribution of z in the class $\mathcal{C}$. The poverty measure G can be obtained from the triplet (F_F, F_H, F_C). To specify how it can be obtained, let $E_F[z]$ be the expected value of z in $\mathcal{F}$, with $E_H[z]$ and $E_C[z]$ defined similarly.

The average poverty gap, G, is defined as the relative difference between the average per capita adult income among households in $\mathcal{C}$ and the average per capita adult income among households in $\mathcal{F}$, that is,

$$(3) \quad G = f(F_F, F_C) = \frac{E_C[z] - E_F[z]}{E_C[z]}.$$

Hence, positive values for G imply that households in $\mathcal{F}$ are poorer than other households.

Table 9 presents the average per capita adult income, $E[z]$, and estimates for

Table 8

Proportion of Children in Female-Headed Households by Metropolitan Area and Relative Per Capita Income,[a] 1984

Relative Income[b]	Recife			São Paulo			Porto Alegre		
	0–6	7–9	10–14	0–6	7–9	10–14	0–6	7–9	10–14
$<Q_5$	35.3	38.3	39.3	14.6	20.5	24.6	16.6	20.1	31.8
Q_5-Q_{10}	21.9	25.1	23.8	10.8	19.6	19.8	12.3	15.7	17.6
$Q_{10}-Q_{25}$	10.9	14.1	19.7	10.3	10.9	17.5	9.3	12.2	17.5
$Q_{25}-Q_{50}$	11.1	11.6	13.7	4.8	5.9	9.5	6.4	9.9	11.9
$>Q_{50}$	7.3	10.5	11.1	3.0	6.2	8.2	5.4	7.9	8.1
All	12.9	15.6	17.6	7.0	10.2	13.6	8.8	11.5	15.0

Source: PNAD-84 Public Tapes: authors' tabulations.
a. Income refers to the sum of the income from all sources of all *adult* members of the household. Members considered as adults are the household head, his or her spouse, and all other members age 18 or more.
b. Q_α denotes the α percentile. So, for instance, Q_{25} is the first quartile and Q_{50} is the median.

Table 9

Brazil: Selected Metropolitan Areas Average Per Capita Adult Income (E[z]) and Average Poverty Gap (G) by Class of Household and Metropolitan Area, 1984

Metropolitan Area	Class of Household	Average Per Capita Adult Income ($E[z]$)	Average Poverty Gap (G)
Recife	All	1.27	—
	FHHs	1.04	0.22
	FHHs with children	0.58	0.57
São Paulo	All	2.52	—
	FHHs	2.39	0.06
	FHHs with children	1.14	0.56
Porto Alegre	All	2.54	—
	FHHs	2.56	−0.01
	FHHs with children	1.26	0.52

Source: PNAD-84: authors' tabulations.

the average poverty gap, G, for FHHs and FHHs with children for the three Brazilian Metropolitan Areas used above.

The principal results of this table, which forms the basis for the analysis in this section, are the following.

Poverty in FHHs: Relative poverty among FHHs varies considerably across regions. In Recife, FHHs are much poorer than other households; in São Paulo, they are only slightly poorer; in Porto Alegre, FHHs exhibit similar levels of poverty to other households.

Poverty in FHHs with children: FHHs with children are considerably poorer than other FHHs. Indeed, the average per capita total income in FHHs with children is less than half of the average for all FHHs. Consequently, FHHs with children are much poorer than the average household in the population.

B. Earnings Capacity, Capacity Utilization, and Dependency Ratio

There are three stages in the investigation of the determinants of relative poverty among FHHs and FHHs with children. First, three proximate determinants, earnings capacity, capacity utilization, and dependency ratio, are defined and analyzed. Then the determinants of the earnings capacity are considered. Finally, the impacts of these determinants on poverty are evaluated.

First, z can be written as

(4) $z = \mathcal{z}(y, p, d) = y \cdot p/(1 + d),$

where y is the average income among adults in the household with positive labor or nonlabor income;[11] p is the proportion of adults in the household who have positive income; and d is the ratio of the number of non-adult members (members who are less than 18 years old) to the number of adult members in the household.

Holding constant household age composition and the labor supply of each adult, increments in the earnings capacity of a household will increase y but keep p and d constant. In this sense, y is a measure of the earnings capacity of households. It should be emphasized, however, that differences across households in y may not be due to differences in the earnings capacity among these households, but rather they could be due to differences in the number of hours worked by household members. In the analysis that follows, this possibility is ignored and y is taken as a measure of the earnings capacity of households.

Under the assumption that the earnings capacity of members who currently have positive income is similar to the earnings capacity of those who currently have no income, p measures the extent to which the household is actually using its earnings capacity or participating in the labor force. In general, the earnings capacity of members who do not currently receive any income is smaller than that of members with positive income. In this case, p would underestimate the extent to which the household is currently using its earnings capacity. Finally, d is the dependency ratio; it measures how many non-adult members each adult has to support.

---

11. Note that y is defined taking averages *within* households.

Expression 4, therefore, illustrates the three proximate reasons why a class of households would be overrepresented among the poor. These three factors are: (1) a smaller earnings capacity, (2) less intensive use of the available earnings capacity, and (3) higher dependency ratio.

Determinants of the Earnings Capacity. The second step is to investigate the proximate determinants of the earnings capacity, y. With this objective in mind and assuming that earnings capacities among males tend to be higher than among females and that earnings capacities among heads tend to be higher than among non-heads, it was reasonable to divide household earners into two groups: (1) males versus females, and (2) heads versus non-heads. Relative to any grouping of household earners, the earnings capacity of a household can be written as a weighted average of the group-specific earnings capacities, the weights reflecting the composition of earners in the household.

Let y_m, y_f, y_h, y_a denote the average earnings capacity in the household of male earners, female earners, head earners, and non-head earners (all adult earners except the head), respectively.[12] Further, let α and β denote, respectively, the proportion of earners who are females and the proportion of earners who are non-heads. Hence the overall household earnings capacity can be written as

$$(5) \quad y = \psi_1 (y_m, y_f, \alpha) \equiv (1 - \alpha) \cdot y_m + \alpha \cdot y_f = y_m - \alpha \cdot (y_m - y_f)$$

or, alternatively, as

$$(6) \quad y \equiv \psi_2 (y_h, y_a, \beta) \equiv (1 - \beta) \cdot y_h + \beta \cdot y_a = y_h - \beta(y_h - y_a).$$

Expressions (5) and (6) indicate six reasons why the earnings capacity can be smaller in a given class of household. The reasons are: (1) smaller earnings capacity among males, (2) smaller earnings capacity among female earners, (3) larger fraction of earners who are female, (4) smaller earnings capacity of the head, (5) smaller earnings capacity among other adult earners, and, (6) larger fraction of earners who are non-heads. These reasons will be discussed in more detail below.

Contrasting Means. Expression (4) indicates that z is an increasing function of earnings capacity, y, and capacity utilization, p. Moreover, z is a decreasing function of the dependency ratio, d.

Expressions (5) and (6) indicate that y, and therefore z, is an increasing function of each group's earnings capacity—y_m, y_f, y_h, y_a—and a decreasing function of the fraction of female earners, α, and of the fraction of non-head earners, β.

Hence, a natural first step in investigating the causes of relative poverty in a given class of households is to compare the mean value of these proximate determinants of per capita adult total income for this class to the mean of these determinants for the overall population. For the classes of FHHs and FHHs with children these means are reported in Tables 10, 12, and 13. These tables will be analyzed in detail.

---

12. Notice that like y all these group averages (y_m, y_f, y_h, y_a) are averages *within* households. If the household has no one in a given group, the average for the group is set equal to zero.

It should be noticed, however, that expressions (4), (5), and (6) are nonlinear. Hence, the extent of relative poverty, measured by G, will depend not only on the means but also on higher moments and the correlation among the several variables involved in these expressions.

Even if the expressions were linear, contrasting the means would be, at most, informative about the signs but not conclusive about the relative strength of the effects of the variables. A series of counterfactual simulations are performed to obtain a clearer view of the direction and magnitude of the contribution of each of the determinants.

Counterfactual Simulations. The simulation procedure will first consider the impact of higher dependency ratios on poverty. The objective is to estimate how the average poverty gap would change if the average dependency ratio in a household class $\mathcal{F}$ were equalized to the average in its complement, $\mathcal{C}$. This goal was accomplished as follows: first, the dependency ratio for each household in $\mathcal{F}$ was proportionally changed such that, after the transformation, the average dependency ratios in $\mathcal{F}$ and $\mathcal{C}$ were equal. This could be accomplished by changing, for each household in $\mathcal{F}$, d to d^* where

(7) $d^* = \dfrac{E_C[d]}{E_F[d]} \cdot d.$

Notice that $E_F[d^*] = E_C[d]$. Based on these new values of the dependency ratio, d^*, for households in $\mathcal{F}$ the corresponding new values for the per capita adult total income, z^d, can be computed. This can be done using Expression 4, that is,

(8) $z^d = z(y, p, d^*) = y \cdot p/(1 + d^*).$

The value for z^d generates a new distribution of per capita adult income in $\mathcal{F}$ that is denoted by F_F^d. Next, there is a new average poverty gap, G^d, based on the pair (F_F^d, F_C), that is,

(9) $G^d = f(F_F^d, F_C) = \dfrac{E_C[z] - E_F[z^d]}{E_C[z]}.$

This new average poverty gap, G^d, is the gap that would be obtained if the average dependency ratio in $\mathcal{F}$ and in $\mathcal{C}$ were the same. Hence,

(10) $\Delta^d = G - G^d$

measures the reduction in the average poverty gap that would be obtained if the average dependency ratios in $\mathcal{F}$ and $\mathcal{C}$ were equalized.

Following identical procedures it is possible to estimate the reduction in the average poverty gap that would be obtained if either the average earnings capacity or the average capacity utilization in $\mathcal{F}$ and $\mathcal{C}$ were made equal.[13] The reduction in G that would be obtained by equalizing earnings capacity in $\mathcal{F}$ and $\mathcal{C}$ is denoted by Δ^y. The result of equalizing capacity utilization is denoted by Δ^p. Values for

---

13. The complete simulation procedure is described in detail in Appendix 2.

Δ^y, Δ^p, and Δ^d, relative to the classes of all FHHs and FHHs with children, are reported in Table 11.

The contribution of the determinants of the earnings capacity (y_m, y_f, y_h, y_a, α, β) to the relative poverty of a given class of households, $\mathscr{F}$, can also be investigated via a similar simulation procedure (Appendix 2).

C. Proximate Determinants of Relative Poverty

Contrasting the Means. Table 10 presents for all households, all FHHs, and FHHs with children average values for earnings capacity, y, capacity utilization, p, and dependency ratio, d. This table reveals that a smaller earnings capacity is the only reason why FHHs are relatively poorer than other households. In fact, on average, households in this class use their earnings capacity more intensively and have smaller average dependency ratios than other households. Their average earnings capacity is 30–40 percent smaller than the average for all households, whereas their average capacity utilization is 20 percent higher and their dependency ratio is 10 percent lower.

Table 10 reveals two reasons why FHHs with children are relatively poorer than all FHHs and, consequently, much poorer than non-FHHs. First, they have smaller earnings capacities and higher dependency ratios. In fact, their average earnings capacity is around half of the average for all households and 10–15 percent smaller than the average for all FHHs. Second, their average dependency ratio is twice the average for all households. Since the average dependency ratio for all FHHs is very similar to the overall average, the average dependency ratio for FHHs with children is also twice as high as the average for all FHHs. As was the case for all FHHs, FHHs with children have an average capacity utilization 10–20 percent higher than the average for all households. Hence, poverty among FHHs with children is partially offset by their more intensive use of their earnings capacity.

Counterfactual Simulations. The results of these simulations for the three factors that determine the per capita adult income (earnings capacity, capacity utilization, and dependency ratio) are presented in Table 11. This table confirms previous findings and reveals several new ones.

The simulations for earnings capacity are the ones that lead to the highest reduction of the average poverty gap. This confirms that the lack of earnings capacity is the main reason FHHs and FHHs with children are overrepresented among the poor. The simulation results in Table 11 indicate that a smaller earnings capacity is so important in explaining poverty among FHHs that if the average earnings capacity for FHHs were equalized to the average for all households, FHHs would no longer be overrepresented among the poor but would become *underrepresented* among them. For FHHs with children, the same equalizing procedure would eliminate two-thirds of the average poverty gap. The poverty gap would change from 0.6 to 0.2.

The simulations relative to capacity utilization indicate that the poverty gap for both FHHs and FHHs with children would be increased if, by a proportional change, their capacity utilization was equalized with that of all other households.

Table 10

Brazil: Selected Metropolitan Areas, Proximate Determinants of Relative Poverty among Female-Headed Households by Class of Household and Metropolitan Area: Average Values, 1984

Metropolitan Area	Class of Household	Earnings Capacity (y)	Capacity Utilization (p)	Dependency Ratio (d)
Recife	All	3.02	0.67	0.90
	FHHs	1.85 (0.61)	0.79 (1.18)	0.87 (0.97)
	FHHs with children	1.66 (0.55)	0.75 (1.12)	1.53 (1.70)
São Paulo	All	5.08	0.73	0.67
	FHHs	3.26 (0.64)	0.88 (1.21)	0.58 (0.87)
	FHHs with children	2.81 (0.55)	0.86 (1.18)	1.42 (2.12)
Porto Alegre	All	4.78	0.76	0.61
	FHHs	3.42 (0.72)	0.91 (1.20)	0.57 (0.93)
	FHHs with children	2.96 (0.62)	0.89 (1.17)	1.42 (2.33)

Source: PNAD-84: authors' tabulations.
Note: Values in parentheses are the ratio between the average value for a given class of households and the corresponding average value for all households.

Table 11

Brazil: Selected Metropolitan Areas, Proximate Determinants of Relative Poverty by Class of Household and Metropolitan Area: Variations in G (Δ^y, Δ^p, Δ^d), 1984

Metropolitan Area	Class of Household	Earnings Capacity (Δ^y)	Capacity Utilization (Δ^p)	Dependency Ratio (Δ^d)
Recife	FHHs	0.62	−0.14	−0.01
	FHHs with children	0.39	−0.06	0.12
São Paulo	FHHs	0.63	−0.20	−0.01
	FHHs with children	0.37	−0.08	0.16
Porto Alegre	FHHs	0.49	−0.20	−0.01
	FHHs with children	0.32	−0.07	0.21

Source: PNAD-84: authors' tabulations.

Because FHHs and FHHs with children use their earning capacity more intensively than other households, their poverty gap is actually smaller than it would be if they used their earning capacity as intensively as other households. In sum, FHHs and FHHs with children alleviate their poverty by using their relatively smaller earnings capacity more intensively. The average poverty gap would be 0.15 to 0.20 higher for FHHs and 0.05 to 0.10 higher for FHHs with children if they decided to use their earnings capacity as intensively as non-FHHs do.

The simulations relative to the dependency ratio reveal heterogeneity among

FHHs. The class of FHHs as a whole have an average dependency ratio slightly below the overall average. Hence, proportionally increasing their dependency ratios to equate their average with the average for other types of households actually leads to a small increase, 0.01, in the average poverty gap relative to this class of households. FHHs tend to alleviate their poverty slightly by having smaller dependency ratios. The results for FHHs with children are very different. Since this class of FHHs tends to have dependency ratios well above average, by proportionally reducing their dependency ratio to equate it with the average among all other types of households, the average poverty gap associated with this class of households can be dramatically reduced. This reduction, although large, between 0.1 to 0.2, is still only half of that obtained by equating their average earnings capacity with that of all other households. In sum, among FHHs with children, a higher dependency ratio is the second major reason why this class is overrepresented among the poor.

Since a smaller earnings capacity is the main reason FHHs and FHHs with children are overrepresented among the poor, it is important to investigate the determinants of earnings capacity in more detail.

D. Determinants of Earnings Capacity

As discussed previously, earnings capacities can be smaller in FHHs due to either smaller group-specific earnings capacities or due to a composition of earners that gives more weight to groups with a smaller earnings capacity. Two groupings of earners, males versus females and heads versus non-heads, will be considered sequentially in order to investigate the six reasons that were presented above as to why the earnings capacity can be smaller in a given class of households.

Grouping by Gender. Table 12 presents, by metropolitan area, averages for male earnings capacity, y_m, female earnings capacity, y_f, and the fraction of earners who are female, α. These averages were computed for all households, FHHs, and FHHs with children. This table reveals three important facts that hold for all metropolitan areas. First, the average earnings capacity among male earners in FHHs and FHHs with children represents 35 to 50 percent of the average earnings capacity of male earners in all households. Second, the earnings capacity of female earners in FHHs and FHHs with children is very similar to the overall earnings capacity of female earners. Third, as expected, the fraction of earners who are females is more than twice as high in FHHs and FHHs with children than among all households.

In summary, the smaller earnings capacity of FHHs and FHHs with children is related to (1) the smaller proportion of earners who are males, and (2) the smaller earnings capacity of their male earners. It is important to emphasize that it is incorrect to associate the smaller earnings capacity of FHHs and FHHs with children to a smaller earnings capacity of female earners in these types of households. As Table 12 shows, the earnings capacity of female earners in FHHs and FHHs with children is as high as the earnings capacity of female earners in non-FHHs.

To investigate the magnitude of each of these effects the simulations described

Table 12

Brazil: Selected Metropolitan Areas Proximate Determinants of Earnings Capacity by Class of Household and Metropolitan Area: Average Values, 1984

Metropolitan Area	Class of Household	Male Earnings Capacity (y_m)	Female Earnings Capacity (y_f)	Fraction of Earners Who Are Female (α)
Recife	All	3.66	1.87	0.34
	FHHs	1.89 (0.52)	1.81 (0.97)	0.83 (2.44)
	FHHs with children	1.64 (0.45)	1.63 (0.87)	0.81 (2.38)
São Paulo	All	6.00	2.90	0.32
	FHHs	2.89 (0.48)	3.22 (1.11)	0.83 (2.59)
	FHHs with children	2.07 (0.35)	2.84 (0.98)	0.83 (2.59)
Porto Alegre	All	5.87	2.87	0.36
	FHHs	2.67 (0.45)	3.37 (1.17)	0.88 (2.44)
	FHHs with children	2.27 (0.39)	2.92 (1.02)	0.86 (2.39)

Source: PNAD-84: authors' tabulations.
Note: Values in parentheses are the ratio between the average value for a given class of households and the corresponding average value for all households.

previously were performed. The results of these simulations[14] reveal that 20 to 30 percent of the poverty gap generated by the smaller earnings capacity among FHHs could be eliminated by equating the earnings capacity of male earners in this class of households to that among all households. Also, although FHHs have a higher proportion of female earners than other households, reducing this proportion would have no impact on their poverty levels. The reason for this is that in FHHs male and female earners have approximately the same earnings capacity. Finally, equating female earnings in FHHs to those in the overall population may have no impact or may even increase poverty in FHHs. This is a consequence of female earners in FHHs having an earnings capacity in most cases as high and, in some cases, even higher than in the overall population.

In summary, poverty among FHHs is not due to smaller earnings capacity among female earners. Poverty is due to smaller earnings capacity of male earners and a smaller fraction of earners who are males. But an increase in the fraction of male earners per se will bring no reduction in poverty if the earnings capacity of male earners in FHHs is not simultaneously increased. These results are very similar for the three metropolitan areas investigated and for the two classes of FHHs.

Heads versus Non-Heads. The final points to investigate are the extent to which the earnings capacity of heads and non-heads is smaller in FHHs than in all households and the extent to which the fraction of earnings that comes from non-head earners is larger.

---

14. The results of these simulations are presented in Table A2.1 in Appendix 2.

Table 13

Brazil: Selected Metropolitan Areas, Proximate Determinants of Earnings Capacity by Class of Household and Metropolitan Area: Average Values, 1984

Metropolitan Area	Class of Household	Head Earnings Capacity (y_h)	Other Adults Earnings Capacity (y_a)	Fraction of Earners Who Are Not the Head (β)
Recife	All	3.34	1.86	0.71
	FHHs	1.65 (0.49)	1.75 (0.94)	0.67 (0.94)
	FHHs with children	1.42 (0.43)	1.49 (0.80)	0.63 (0.89)
São Paulo	All	5.72	2.91	0.69
	FHHs	3.00 (0.52)	2.76 (0.95)	0.66 (0.96)
	FHHs with children	2.62 (0.46)	2.12 (0.73)	0.66 (0.96)
Porto Alegre	All	5.65	2.63	0.69
	FHHs	3.45 (0.61)	2.44 (0.93)	0.75 (1.09)
	FHHs with children	2.96 (0.52)	2.08 (0.79)	0.72 (1.04)

Source: PNAD-84: authors' tabulations.
Note: Values in parentheses are the ratio between the average value for a given class of households and the corresponding average value for all households.

Table 13 presents, for all households, FHHs, and FHHs with children, the average earnings capacity of heads and non-heads and the fraction of earners who are not heads. This table reveals that the earnings capacity of heads in FHHs is around half of the earnings capacity of heads in other households. Non-head earnings capacity is approximately the same, although it is a little smaller (80 percent) in FHHs with children. The proportion of earners who are not the head is also very similar in FHHs and in all households.

This table reveals that FHHs have smaller earnings capacity because their heads have a smaller earnings capacity. Non-heads in FHHs have a similar earnings capacity than elsewhere, and FHHs do not rely more on non-head earners than other households.

Again the same counterfactual simulation described earlier was performed.[15] The results corroborate previous findings. Equating the earnings capacity of heads in FHHs to that of other heads will fully explain the lack of earnings capacity among FHHs. Equating earnings capacity of non-heads or the fraction of earners who are non-heads has no impact.

III. Consequences of Living in Female-Headed Households on Children

One of the main reasons for concern about the rapid growth of female-headed households is the potential negative consequences this has on

---

15. The results are in Table A2.2 in Appendix 2.

the welfare of children. In this section, evidence related to three aspects of the relationship between children's welfare and female headship will be presented.

The first and fundamental question is whether the welfare of children in FHHs tends to be below the average for all children. This question will be investigated by comparing school attendance and labor force participation rates for children in FHHs with the corresponding levels for all children.

A second important question is to what extent lower outcomes for children in FHHs can be explained by FHHs being overrepresented among the poor. The answer to this question depends on two factors: (1) how much poorer are children in FHHs compared to all children, and (2) how sensitive to family resources are the outcomes of these children?

Factor 1 has been investigated at length in the first section of this paper but will be reconsidered very briefly here. Factor 2 is a crucial parameter to any society. It is a measure of how much society deviates from the ideal of equal opportunity. It entails, however, the estimation of a causal relationship and hence is an estimation from nonexperimental data that are always based on nontestable assumptions and also always surrounded by controversy.

The third major question considered in this section is whether or not the consequences of poverty on children are particularly more severe among those living in FHHs. To shed some light on this question, the sensitivity of school attendance and labor force participation rates of children to family resources for FHHs is compared with the sensitivity for all households. Finding greater sensitivity for FHHs would be evidence in favor of the hypothesis that the consequences of poverty are more severe for children in FHHs than for all children.

A. Children's Outcomes

Outcomes and Subpopulations Investigated. Two types of outcomes for children were considered: school attendance and labor force participation. These outcomes were investigated separately for three subpopulations: children aged 7 to 9 years, children aged 10 to 14 years, and children aged 10 to 14 years who are in the labor force. Only four of the six possible outcome-population combinations were used. Labor force participation of 10- to 14-year-olds who are in the labor force was excluded because it was redundant, and labor force participation for the 7- to 9-year-old group could not be studied since the household survey that was used asked labor market–related questions only to persons 10 years or older. The inability of children 10 to 14 in the labor force to attend school will be used as an indicator of their welfare loss in working because of the conflict between study and work activities.

B. Are Children in FHHs Worse Off?

Table 14 presents estimates of the average outcome for all children and for children living in FHHs, for three selected metropolitan areas, and for the four outcome-population combinations. The main findings are the following:

School Attendance. The results for school attendance differ by age group and metropolitan area. On the one hand, among 7- to 9-year-olds in São Paulo and

Table 14

Brazil: Outcomes for Children by Type of Household and Metropolitan Area, 1984

Outcome	Recife			São Paulo			Porto Alegre		
	FHH	All	T-st[a]	FHH	All	T-st[a]	FHH	All	T-st[a]
Children aged 7–9									
not in school	23	14	3.6	8	8	0.0	12	10	1.1
Children aged 10–14									
not in school	22	14	5.1	12	8	2.9	18	12	3.1
in the labor force	10	7	2.9	13	8	3.1	16	9	3.9
Children aged 10–14 in the labor force									
not in school	69	56	2.2	42	36	0.9	69	67	0.2

Source: PNAD-84 Public Tapes: authors' tabulations.

a. T-st refers to the T-statistics for testing whether the difference between FHHs and all households is zero.

Porto Alegre, children living in FHHs have school attendance rates very *similar* to those of all children in the same metropolitan area and age group. On the other hand, for both age groups in Recife and for 10- to 14-year-olds in São Paulo and Porto Alegre, children living in FHHs have *lower* school attendance rates than all children in the same age group and metropolitan area.

The differences across age groups in São Paulo and Porto Alegre are derived from the fact that only for children in FHHs in these areas do school attendance rates decrease significantly with age. Overall attendance rates do not vary with age and are higher in São Paulo and lower in Recife.

Labor-Force Participation. In each metropolitan area, the labor force participation rate of children 10 to 14 years old living in FHHs is *higher* than that of all children in the same area. The surprising fact about labor force participation in Table 14 is that higher participation rates are found in São Paulo and Porto Alegre than in Recife. This fact is investigated further by Barros and Mendonça (1990b, 1991) and Levison (1991).

Conflict between Study and Work Activities. Table 14 reveals that, among children in the labor force, the proportion not attending school is *higher* among those living in FHHs. The magnitude of the difference in attendance rate by type of household varies by metropolitan area. The difference is more than 10 percentage points and statistically significant in Recife but very small and statistically insignificant in Porto Alegre. Hence, at least in Recife, it seems more difficult for children in FHHs to combine work and study activities than for those living in other types of households.

C. Isolating the Poverty Effect

As was demonstrated in the first section of this study, children in FHHs are much poorer than children living in non-FHHs. Moreover, there exists a large literature supporting the notion that the level of household resources is an important determinant of children's outcomes in Brazil (see Calsing and Schmidt 1986; IBGE 1987–1990; Barros and Mendonça 1990a, 1991; Levison 1991). Given these two facts, it can be argued that differences in outcomes between children in FHHs and all children, such as those reported above, are simply a consequence of the greater poverty among children in FHHs. As a matter of fact, there is a great debate about whether or not the absence of the father really has any independent impact on children's school attendance and labor force participation. More generally, it is still debatable whether variations in children's outcomes across households with different structures is really due to differences in the structures of the households per se, or is entirely due to other differences across households, such as household income, which just happen to be correlated with differences in household structure.

In this section differences in outcomes between children in FHHs and all children are decomposed into two parts: one due to the gap in outcomes between children in FHHs and all children within income classes, and one due to the fact that children in FHHs are overrepresented in poorer income classes. This second component is referred to as the *poverty effect*. The first component would account for the impact of differences between FHHs and all other households in all dimensions other than income.

The magnitude of the poverty effect depends on two factors: (1) how overrepresentative children in FHHs are among the poor, and (2) how sensitive each outcome is to household resources. Hence, before estimating the poverty effect itself, some evidence about the size of each of these two factors will be presented.

Poverty among Children in FHHs. To investigate the poverty of children in FHHs relative to all children, let q be the first quartile and m the median of the distribution of households according to the per capita adult income. Each given population of children is then divided into three income classes. The first class consists of all children in this given population who are living in households with per capita adult total income smaller than q. A child belongs to the second class if and only if he or she lives in a household with per capita adult total income between q and m. All children in the population who are living in households with per capita adult total income above the median form the third class. The relative poverty of three categories of children in FHHs is investigated, namely: (1) children aged 7 to 9 years old, (2) children aged 10 to 14 years old, and (3) children aged 10 to 14 years old who are in the labor market.

Let f_i^F and f_i denote, respectively, the fraction of children in FHHs in income class i and the fraction of all children in income class i, $i = 1, 2, 3$. Of particular interest are the ratios

(11) $r_i = \dfrac{f_i^F}{f_i}$ $i = 1, 2, 3.$

If children in FHHs are overrepresented among the poor, the sequence r_1, r_2, r_3 will be decreasing with $r_1 > 1$ and $r_3 < 1$. Table 15 reports values for r_1, r_2, r_3 for each subpopulation and metropolitan area. In all but one case, r_1, r_2, r_3 is a decreasing sequence with $r_1 > 1$ and $r_3 < 1$. Hence, this table confirms that children in FHHs are indeed overrepresented among the poor.

Sensitivity to Household Resources. The second factor that influences the magnitude of the poverty effect indicates how sensitive each outcome is to household resources. Each outcome is estimated by income class in order to evaluate its sensitivity. To summarize the steepness of the relationship, the index of dissimilarity, *ID*, is computed. To define the index of dissimilarity, let O_i denote the average outcomes for children in income class i. Hence, the overall outcome among all children, O, can be written as

(12) $O = \displaystyle\sum_i O_i \cdot f_i$

and the index of dissimilarity can be defined as

(13) $ID = \dfrac{\displaystyle\sum_i |O_i - O| \cdot f_i}{2 \cdot O} \cdot 100.$

Table 15

Brazil: Proportion of Children in Female-Headed Households to the Proportion in All Households by Income Quartile, Age Group, Labor Force Participation Status, and Metropolitan Area, 1984

Subpopulation	Recife			São Paulo			Porto Alegre		
	r_1	r_2	r_3	r_1	r_2	r_3	r_1	r_2	r_3
Children aged 7–9	1.4	0.7	0.7	1.5	0.6	0.6	1.3	0.9	0.7
Children aged 10–14	1.4	0.8	0.6	1.4	0.7	0.6	1.4	0.8	0.5
Children aged 10–14 in the labor force	1.3	0.5	0.2	1.1	1.1	0.5	1.1	0.6	1.0

Source: PNAD-84 Public Tapes: authors' tabulations.

The dissimilarity index has a simple and intuitive interpretation. If O represents the proportion of children not currently in school, then ID represents the minimum proportion of children not in school that must be reassigned to different income classes to make the proportion of children not in school in every income class equal to O. Table 16 presents estimates of the average outcome by income class $\{O_i\}$ and the corresponding indices of dissimilarity, ID.[16]

School Attendance. Table 16 confirms the well-established fact that school attendance increases with household resources. Specifically, this table reveals that school attendance rates among children in poor households (bottom 25 percent) are 10 to 18 percentage points lower than those among children in non-poor households (top 50 percent). The index of dissimilarity indicates that between 20 and 30 percent of all children not in school need to be reallocated to higher income classes in order that the percentage of children not in school be uniform across all income classes.

Labor Force Participation. Perhaps surprisingly, all estimates available for Brazil of the relationship between the labor force participation of children and their per capita family income are systematically nonmonotonic.[17] All these estimates have an inverted-U shape. As demonstrated in Barros and Mendonça (1990a), previous studies have found a nonmonotonic relationship because they have included in the income of the household the income of children. Barros and

---

16. The estimates of ID in Table 16 as well as in Table 18 were computed using a division of the population into five income classes instead of the division into the three classes presented in Table 16. The disaggregation into five classes entails a disaggregation of the poor class (bottom 25 percent) in Table 16 into three classes.

17. See Calsing and Schmidt (1986); IBGE (1987–1990).

Table 16
Brazil: Outcomes for Children by Income Class and Metropolitan Area, 1984

Outcome	Recife				São Paulo				Porto Alegre			
	Income Class				Income Class				Income Class			
	$<q$	$q-m$	$>m$	ID	$<q$	$q-m$	$>m$	ID	$<q$	$q-m$	$>m$	ID
Children aged 7–9 not in school	22	12	4	24	14	6	2	31	17	6	3	31
Children aged 10–14 not in school	21	14	4	22	12	7	3	21	18	10	4	23
in the labor force	10	6	2	23	11	8	4	17	13	8	3	24
Children aged 10–14 in the labor force not in school	61	47	42	7	40	32	23	13	69	65	56	4

Source: PNAD-84 Public Tapes: authors' tabulations.

Mendonça also showed that, once the incomes of children are excluded, the relationship becomes monotonically decreasing.

Since this study used only the income of adults as a measure of household resources, the labor force participation rates obtained are monotonically decreasing with household resources (see Table 16). Specifically, this table reveals that children in poor households have labor force participation rates from 7 to 10 percentage points higher than those living in non-poor households. The dissimilarity index indicates that from 15 to 25 percent of working children must be reallocated to higher income classes to equalize the labor force participation rates across income classes.

Conflict Between Study and Work Activities. Finally, Table 16 reveals that the proportion of children in the labor force who are not attending school is 10 to 20 percentage points higher among children in poor households than among children in non-poor households. The index of dissimilarity indicates a lower degree of steepness, since at most 13 percent of children not in school need to be reallocated to ensure identical school attendance rates across income classes.

D. The Poverty Effect

In order to obtain the poverty effect, the first step is to estimate what the outcome for children would have been if the distribution of household resources among children in FHHs were the same as the distribution among all children. This standardized outcome is denoted by O^*.

To describe how O^* is actually estimated, f_i^F and f_i are defined as before, and O_i^F and O_i denote the average outcome for children in FHHs in income class i and the average outcome for all children in income class i, respectively. Hence, the overall average outcome among all children, O, and the overall average outcome among all children in FHHs, O^F, can be written as

$$(14) \quad O = \sum_i O_i \cdot f_i$$

and

$$(15) \quad O^F = \sum_i O_i^F \cdot f_i^F.$$

The income standardized outcome for children in FHHs, O^*, is therefore defined by

$$(16) \quad O^* = \sum_i O_i^F \cdot f_i$$

and the poverty effect, PE, by

$$(17) \quad PE = \frac{O^* - O^F}{O - O^F}.$$

Alternatively, PE can be written as

$$(18) \quad PE = \frac{1}{O - O^F} \cdot \sum_i O_i^F (f_i - f_i^F).$$

Table 17 presents, for each metropolitan area, population, and outcome considered in this study, estimates for (1) the outcome among all children, O, (2) the outcome among children in FHHs, O^F, (3) the outcome among children in FHHs that would be observed if the distribution of household resources among children in FHHs were the same as that among all children, O^*, and (4) the poverty effect, PE.

The results for school attendance vary substantially by metropolitan area and age group. Among children 7 to 9 years old in São Paulo and Porto Alegre there are no differences to be explained in school attendance between children in FHHs and all children. However, for São Paulo and Porto Alegre Table 17 reveals a significant difference in school attendance between children in FHHs and all children for those 10 to 14 years old. However, only 20 to 40 percent of these differences can be explained by children in FHHs being overrepresented among the poor. Recife is, among all the three areas, the one with the largest gap between the school attendance rate of children in FHHs and all children. In addition, Recife is also the area in which poverty has the largest explanatory power. The poverty effect in Recife varies from 0.4 to 0.7.

Table 17 reveals that in São Paulo and in Porto Alegre the contribution of poverty to the higher labor force participation rates of children in FHHs is very small. The poverty effect is between 20 and 30 percent. In these metropolitan areas, poverty among FHHs could explain at most a gap of 2 percentage points in the labor force participation rate, whereas the participation rate among children in FHHs is from 5 to 7 percentage points above average. Consequently, in these two metropolitan areas the income standardized labor force participation rate for children in FHHs is still between 3 and 5 percentage points above average. For Recife the findings are quite distinct. First, the nonstandardized difference is already smaller, 3 percentage points. Second, the fact that children in FHHs are overrepresented among the poor can explain the majority of this difference, $PE = 0.8$.

E. Are the Consequences of Poverty More Severe among Children in FHHs?

If the consequences of poverty were more severe among children in FHHs, then not only the proportion of these children in the labor force and out of school would be larger but also these proportions would be more sensitive to family resources (see Figure 1).

Therefore, to evaluate this hypothesis it must be shown that the steepness of the relationship between labor force participation (or school attendance) and per capita adult income is greater for children in FHHs than for all children. To measure the steepness of these relationships, their corresponding indices of dissimilarity were estimated. Estimates of these indices are presented in Table 18.

Table 17
Brazil: Poverty Effects and Outcomes for Children by Household Types and Metropolitan Area, 1984

Outcome	Recife				São Paulo				Porto Alegre			
	O	O^F	O*	PE	O	O^F	O*	PE	O	O^F	O*	PE
Children aged 7–9 not in school	14	23	19	0.5	8	8	7	*	10	12	11	0.6
Children aged 10–14 not in school	14	22	17	0.7	8	12	11	0.2	12	18	16	0.4
in the labor force	7	10	7	0.8	8	12	11	0.3	9	16	14	0.2
Children aged 10–14 in the labor force not in school	56	69	65	0.3	36	42	40	0.2	66	67	70	*

Source: PNAD-84 Public Tapes: authors' tabulations.

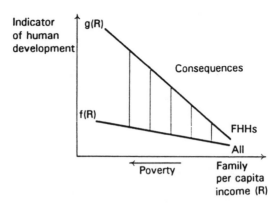

Figure 1
Consequences of Higher Levels of Poverty in Female-Headed Households Compared To All Households

The results in this table present no evidence whatsoever that the relationships for children in FHHs are steeper, as portrayed in Figure 1.

IV. Conclusions

One of the primary issues investigated in this study is whether the welfare of children in female-headed households (FHHs) is below the average of that for all children in metropolitan Brazil. This question was analyzed by comparing the school attendance and labor force participation rates for children in FHHs with the corresponding levels for all children. The rates indicate that children in FHHs are more likely to be out of school, to be in the labor force, and to have greater difficulties in solving the conflict between work and study activities; that is, among children in the labor force, the proportion not attending school is higher for those living in FHHs.

There are several reasons that could lower the welfare of children living in FHHs. If policies are going to be implemented to improve the welfare of children in FHHs, the factors that cause the welfare of children to be lower in FHHs must be identified. One of these factors, the greater poverty of FHHs, is investigated in detail. An analysis of the extent of poverty in FHHs demonstrates that in metropolitan Brazil, as in other areas in the world, FHHs are over-represented among the poor, and children in FHHs are over-represented among poor children.

Three proximate determinants of poverty in FHHs are investigated: (1) the earnings capacity of the adult members, (2) the extent to which this capacity is actually being used, and (3) the dependency ratio. The data indicate that dependency ratios in FHHs are not greater than they are in other households and that the degree of participation of adults in the labor force is as high in FHHs as in other households. As a result, the main proximate determinant of poverty in FHHs is the lower earnings capacity of adults in this type of household. Further

Table 18

Brazil: Dissimilarity Index for Children's Outcomes by Type of Household and Metropolitan Area, 1984

Outcome	Recife		São Paulo		Porto Alegre	
	FHH	All	FHH	All	FHH	All
Children aged 7–9						
not in school	19	24	30	31	30	31
Children aged 10–14						
not in school	26	22	14	21	15	23
in the labor force	32	23	20	17	17	24
Children aged 10–14 in the labor force						
not in school	11	7	9	13	12	4

Source: PNAD-84 Public Tapes; authors' tabulations.

investigation indicates that the main cause of the lower earnings capacity of adults in these households is gender differences in earnings. As is shown, if men and women earn identical income levels on average, the average per capita income in FHHs would not be below the average for all households.

In summary, the welfare of children in FHHs is below average, and children in FHHs are overrepresented among the poor. To some extent the greater poverty of children in FHHs is the cause of their lower welfare level. An investigation of the causes of the greater level of poverty of FHHs indicates that gender differences in wages are a major factor. As a consequence, policies devoted to reducing the gender gap in wages will be central to reducing poverty in FHHs and, in turn, to increasing levels of welfare for children living in this type of household.

Nevertheless, it should be emphasized that greater poverty can explain only part of the gap in welfare between children in FHHs and all households. Other social policies, in particular those designed to provide public services that can be good substitutes for parental time, also have a great potential for improving the welfare of children in FHHs.

Appendix 1

Table A1.1
Brazil, Belo Horizonte: Prevalence of Female-Headed Households by Income Class, 1972

Income Class	Proportion of Households in the Income Class	Prevalence of FHHs in the Income Class
Poor	30.3	24.6
Low	46.2	14.2
Middle/High	23.5	11.0
All	100.0	16.6

Source: Merrick and Schmink (1983), Table 12.3.

Table A1.2
Brazil: Prevalence of Female-Headed Families by Income Class, 1970–1980

Year	Income Class	Proportion of Households in the Income Class		Prevalence of FHHs in the Income Class	
		Pastore et al.	Dvorak	Pastore et al.	Dvorak
1970	All	100	100	10	13
	Poor	44	42	12	14
	Non-Poor	56	58	9	12
1980	All	100	100	12	14
	Poor	18	17	16	13
	Non-Poor	72	73	11	14

Sources: (1) Pastore, Zylberstajn, and Pagotto (1983), Tables I.8, I.14, and II.7. (2) Dvorak (1989), Table 1.

Appendix 2

Following identical procedures as the example in the section on counterfactual simulations, it is possible to estimate the reduction in the average poverty gap that would be obtained if either the average earnings capacity or the average capacity utilization in $\mathcal{F}$ and $\mathcal{C}$ were made equal. The reduction in G that would be obtained by equalizing earnings capacity in $\mathcal{F}$ and $\mathcal{C}$ is denoted by Δ^y. The result of equalizing capacity utilization is denoted by Δ^p. For instance, Δ^y can be obtained as follows. Let

$$(1) \quad y^* = \frac{E_C[y]}{E_F[y]} \cdot y.$$

Notice that $E_F[y^*] = E_C[y]$. Next, obtain z^y via

$$(2) \quad z^y = \mathcal{z}(y^*, p, d) = y^* \cdot p/(1 + d).$$

z^y generates a new distribution of per capita adult income in $\mathcal{F}$ that is denoted by F_F^y. Next, a new average poverty gap, G^y, is computed based on the pair (F_F^y, F_C), that is,

$$(3) \quad G^y = \frac{E_C[z] - E_F[z^y]}{E_C[z]}.$$

This new average gap, G^y, is the gap that would be obtained if the average earnings capacity were the same in $\mathcal{F}$ and in $\mathcal{C}$. Therefore,

$$(4) \quad \Delta^y = G - G^y.$$

In this case, Δ^y can be rewritten as

(5) $\Delta^y = \dfrac{E_C[y] - E_F[y]}{E_F[y]} \cdot \dfrac{E_F[z]}{E_C[z]}.$

This expression reveals the connection between contrasting means ($E_C[y]$ versus $E_F[y]$) and performing counterfactual simulations, i.e., estimating Δ^y.

The contribution of the determinants of earnings capacity (y_m, y_f, y_h, y_a, α, β) to the relative poverty of a given class of households, $\mathcal{F}$, can also be investigated via a similar simulation procedure. Consider the case of assessing the contribution of smaller earnings capacity among male earners, y_m, to relative poverty. The analysis of all other determinants can be done using exactly the same procedure. First, the earnings capacity of male earners in FHHs is changed proportionally such that, after the change, the average among FHHs is identical to the average among all households, that is, y_m is substituted for y_m^* for households in $\mathcal{F}$, where

(6) $y_m^* = \dfrac{E_C[y_m]}{E_F[y_m]} \cdot y_m.$

Notice that $E_F[y_m^*] = E_C[y_m]$. Next, using expression 3, the earnings capacity of households in $\mathcal{F}$ is computed using y_m^* instead of y_m, that is,

(7) $y^m = \psi_1(y_m^*, y_f, \alpha) = (1 - \alpha) \cdot y_m^* + \alpha \cdot y_f.$

Finally, the per capita adult total income for all households in $\mathcal{F}$ is computed using y^m instead of y, that is,

(8) $z^m = \gamma(y^m, p, d) = y^m \cdot p/(1 + d).$

z^m generates a new distribution in $\mathcal{F}$ which is denoted by F_F^m. Then the average poverty gap is computed based on the pair (F_F^m, F_G), G^m:

(9) $G^m = \dfrac{E_C[z] - E_F[z^m]}{E_C[z]}.$

G^m is the relative poverty gap that would be obtained if the average earnings capacity of male earners in $\mathcal{F}$ were identical to the average in $\mathcal{C}$. Hence,

(10) $\Delta^m = G - G^m$

is the contribution of smaller earnings capacity among male earners to relative poverty among households in $\mathcal{F}$. As it would be more interesting to assess the contribution of smaller earnings capacity among male earners *relative* to the overall contribution of smaller earnings capacity, the following is computed:

(11) $R\Delta^m = \dfrac{\Delta^m}{\Delta^y} = \dfrac{G - G^m}{G - G^y}.$

Identical simulations can be done for y_f, y_h, y_a, α, and β to obtain values for $R\Delta^f$, $R\Delta^h$, $R\Delta^a$, $R\Delta^\alpha$, and $R\Delta^\beta$. Tables A2.1 and A2.2 present these results.

Table A2.1

Brazil: Selected Metropolitan Areas, Proximate Determinants of Earnings Capacity by Class of Household and Metropolitan Area: Relative Variations in G ($R\Delta^m$, $R\Delta^f$, $R\Delta^\alpha$), 1984

Metropolitan Area	Class of Household	Male Earnings Capacity ($R\Delta^m$)	Female Earnings Capacity ($R\Delta^f$)	Fraction of Earners Who Are Female ($R\Delta^\alpha$)
Recife	FHHs	0.21	0.05	0.03
	FHHs with children	0.26	0.15	0.03
São Paulo	FHHs	0.25	−0.17	0.03
	FHHs with children	0.32	0	−0.03
Porto Alegre	FHHs	0.22	−0.41	0.02
	FHHs with children	0.31	−0.03	0.03

Source: PNAD-84: Authors' tabulations.

Table A2.2

Brazil: Selected Metropolitan Areas, Proximate Determinants of Earnings Capacity by Class of Household and Metropolitan Area: Relative Variations in G ($R\Delta^h$, $R\Delta^a$, $R\Delta^\beta$), 1984

Metropolitan Area	Class of Household	Head Earnings Capacity ($R\Delta^h$)	Other Adults Earnings Capacity ($R\Delta^a$)	Fraction of Earners Who Are Not the Head ($R\Delta^\beta$)
Recife	FHHs	1.11	0.03	0
	FHHs with children	1.00	0.13	−0.03
São Paulo	FHHs	1.17	0.03	0
	FHHs with children	1.03	0.14	0
Porto Alegre	FHHs	1.33	0.04	0
	FHHs with children	1.09	0.09	0

Source: PNAD-84: Authors' tabulations.

13 Gender Differences in Brazilian Labor Markets

Ricardo Barros,
Lauro Ramos,
Eleonora Santos

Ricardo Barros is assistant professor of economics at Yale University and senior research economist at the Instituto de Pesquisa Economica Aplicada, in Rio de Janeiro, Brazil. Barros has written extensively on issues of the measurement and alleviation of poverty in Brazil. Lauro Ramos is senior economist at the Instituto de Pesquisa Economica Aplicada, in Rio de Janeiro, Brazil. Eleonora Santos is from the Universidade Federal de Minas Gerais, at Belo Horizonte, Brazil, and is currently working at Banco da Bahia.

I. Introduction

Discrimination is the unequal treatment of individuals with equal merit based on the group, class, or category to which they belong. As it represents a major deviation from the ideal of equal opportunity, any kind of discrimination is a source of social distress.

Wage discrimination occurs whenever equally productive workers receive different wages based on some of their nonproductive attributes, such as gender or race. Usually discrimination translates into undesirable increments in inequality and poverty, to the extent that it operates against the groups that would receive lower wages even in the absence of discrimination.[1] However, if for instance, women were more productive than men, then wage discrimination favoring men could contribute to reducing inequality and poverty. But, in general, the groups who are discriminated against tend to be those with lower average productivity.

The questions of social justice, equality, and poverty, although relevant per se, are not the only negative aspects of discrimination. Discrimination may also

---

1. Chapter 12, for instance, showed that the major reason for poverty among female-headed households in Brazil is the existence of a large gender gap in wages.

lead to the inefficient allocation of labor and capital and, therefore, to reductions in total output. In fact, discrimination implies that equally productive workers are receiving different wages and thus are facing different incentives to work. Therefore, as long as labor supply is not perfectly inelastic, groups that are discriminated against through lower wages may reduce their labor supply below the social optimum, leading to an underutilization of human resources. On the firm side, the greater the taste for discrimination the higher will be the cost of labor. As a consequence, *ceteris paribus,* the size of firms will be inversely related to their taste for discrimination. This implies that capital in firms with a greater taste for discrimination will be underutilized with the inverse occurring in firms that do not discriminate. In summary, discrimination may lead to the inefficient utilization of capital and, therefore, to reductions in total output.[2]

The inefficiency brought about by discrimination is particularly important in a country like Brazil, where around one-third of the population is below the poverty line, and there are no clear prospects for economic recovery or improvements in the distribution of income, at least in the short run. Under these circumstances, the waste of economic and human resources due to discrimination is particularly harmful to social welfare.

The contribution of women to the economy is, in principle, no different than that of men. The possibility that gender discrimination in wages may be discouraging women from participation in economic activities in Brazil is an issue of particular concern. The incentives to greater participation of women in the labor market as well as the benefits of this greater engagement in market activities to their families will be larger the greater are their labor market opportunities. Hence, gender discrimination in the labor market will deter women's participation and will reduce the impact of their participation on the reduction of poverty. The main purpose of this chapter is to investigate gender differences in the Brazilian labor market.

The existence of wage differentials by gender does not constitute definitive evidence of wage discrimination, as men and women may not be equally productive or employed in the same occupation. Differences in human capital and in access to occupations are among possible reasons for differences in wage levels. Thus, it is fundamental to estimate how much of the overall wage gap remains when the comparison is restricted to men and women with the same level of schooling and age working in the same occupation.

Overall, the objective of this study is to organize and analyze the extensive information on gender differences related to *wages, educational attainment,* and *occupational distribution* contained in a set of National Household Surveys (PNADs) collected annually by the Brazilian Census Bureau (IBGE). The analysis will focus on the behavior of the urban labor markets from 1981 to 1989.

More specifically, the goal is to answer the following five questions related to gender differences in urban Brazil.

1. What is the overall level of the gender gap in wages?

---

2. As Arrow (1972) has emphasized, this argument relies on a certain degree of immobility of capital.

2. To what extent do men and women differ with respect to educational attainment and occupational distribution?

3. How have these gender differences evolved over the 1980s, and how do they vary across regions?

4. To what extent can gender differences in educational attainment and occupational structure explain gender differences in wages?

5. To what extent can temporal and regional variations in the gender gap in educational attainment and occupational structure explain the concomitant temporal and regional variations in the gender gap in wages?

The second section of this paper will describe the dataset, the unit and universe of analysis, and will define the variables. The third section contains a discussion of the gender gap in wages. In the next five sections a series of decomposition procedures are described and empirically implemented. A final section presents conclusions.

II. Empirical Preliminaries

This study is based on nine annual household surveys, covering the period from 1981 to 1989. These surveys, which are called PNADs (*Pesquisa Nacional por Amostra de Domicílios*), are part of a larger set of household surveys collected by IBGE (*Instituto Brasileiro de Geografia e Estatística*).[3]

The PNAD is an annual national survey based on a probabilistic sample of households.[4] The sampling scheme is based on a three-stage stratified sample of households, with sampling rates varying across geographical areas from 1/400 to 1/50. Given the size of the Brazilian population, these sampling rates generate very large samples. Each year, PNAD interviews around 0.5 percent of Brazilian households, which corresponds to more than 50,000 households.

In this study the unit of analysis is the individual. The universe consists of working men and women, 25 to 50 years old, living in urban areas and working in nonagricultural occupations. Additionally, the sample does not include workers who either work 20 hours or less per week in their main occupation, receive no income, or are currently attending school. The sample screening and the final sample sizes by year are presented in Tables 1 and 2. The overall sample entails close to 500,000 observations, ranging from 35,000 to 65,000 observations each year.

---

3. Besides the PNADs, IBGE also collects (1) a monthly employment survey called PME (*Pesquisa Mensal de Emprego*) covering the six larger Brazilian Metropolitan Areas which contains information on labor income and (2) the Demographic Censuses which are collected each ten years and have information on income since 1960.

4. Only the rural areas of Northern Brazil are not included in the sample.

Table 1
Sample Screening

Criteria	Reduction (%)
Urban	21.6
25 ≤ Age ≤ 50	57.8
Labor force	30.9
Not in school	
Known education	5.0
Known income	
Positive income	1.6
Known hours worked	
Hours worked > 20	6.0
Known occupation	
Nonagriculture	18.0
Known position in occupation	0.0

Source: Computed from the PNADs, 1981–89.

Table 2
Sample Size

Year	Sample
1981	54,744
1982	59,626
1983	60,346
1984	61,976
1985	65,628
1986	36,599
1987	38,564
1988	38,308
1989	40,065
Total	455,856

Source: Computed from the PNADs, 1981–89.

In 1988 this universe represented 15 percent of the overall Brazilian population, 35 percent of the employed labor force, and 48 percent of the employed labor force in urban areas. In this segment of the Brazilian workforce, the degree of feminization—the fraction of the labor force formed by women—is close to one-third and has varied from 30 percent in 1981 to 35 percent in 1989 (see Table 3).

Regional disparities in Brazil are very important. Therefore, the data were disaggregated into six regions: Northeast, East, state of Rio de Janeiro, state of São Paulo, South, and Frontier.[5] The distribution of the labor force among these six regions is presented in Table 4. This table reveals that 32 percent of the labor force is in the state of São Paulo, the largest regional labor market. The state of Rio de Janeiro, the South, the East, and the Northeast have labor markets of similar size (approximately one-half of the size of the labor force in São Paulo). The Frontier is the smallest market, displaying a labor force equivalent to one-fourth of São Paulo's labor force.

In addition to region of residence, six other variables were used in this study: wages, education, age, position in the family, occupation, and type of job or occupation. Wages were defined as the income received in the main occupation in the month prior to the interview, standardized by the number of hours worked in the week before the interview.[6]

Education is measured by the number of completed years of schooling, a statistic that is not readily available from the questionnaire, but can be constructed from four other basic questions on education using an algorithm described in Barros and Ramos (1992). Age is measured by the number of completed years at the date of the interview. Position in the family indicates the relationship of each person to the head of the family. There are four possibilities: (1) head, (2) spouse, (3) other relatives, and (4) nonrelative. The analysis of this variable is based on 1989 data.

In order to investigate gender differences in the occupational structure, the occupational spectrum was divided into seven groups: Technical (9.7 percent), Managerial (19.6 percent), Blue Collars (28.2 percent), Services (10.4 percent), Transportation (7.4 percent), Trade (11.4 percent), and Others (13.3 percent).[7] Tables 5 and 6 present the average income level and the average education level for men and women in each occupational group. The values in these tables are averages of corresponding values by region (weighted) and year (unweighted). According to these tables, the group of Technical occupations has the highest levels of average income and average education. Managerial occupations come in second. An intermediate group is formed by occupations in Trade and Trans-

---

5. The Northeast region includes the states of Maranhão, Piauí, Ceará, Rio Grande do Norte, Paraíba, Pernambuco, Sergipe, Alagoas, and Bahia. The states of Minas Gerais, Espírito Santo, and the Federal District make up the East. The South region is formed by the states of Paraná, Santa Catarina, and Rio Grande do Sul. The Frontier includes the states of Acre, Amapá, Amazonas, Goiás, Mato Grosso, Mato Grosso do Sul, Pará, Rondônia, Roraima, and Tocantins.

6. That is, wages were defined as the ratio between monthly labor income and hours worked per week. Since differences in log-wages will be used, it makes no difference whether or not the number of hours worked per week is multiplied by a standard (constant) number of weeks worked per month.

7. These percentages are unweighted averages over the 1981 to 1989 period.

Table 3
Degree of Feminization of the Labor Force

Year	Degree (%)
1981	29.8
1982	31.2
1983	31.6
1984	32.4
1985	32.6
1986	33.8
1987	34.0
1988	35.0
1989	35.0

Source: Computed from the PNADs, 1981–89.

Table 4
Regional Distribution of the Labor Force

Region	Proportion
Rio de Janeiro	0.140
São Paulo	0.318
South	0.151
East	0.135
Northeast	0.173
Frontier	0.084

Source: Computed from the PNADs, 1981–89.
Note: These proportions were computed by first evaluating the regional distributions of the labor force for every year between 1981 and 1989. The final figures are the unweighted average of them.

portation. The occupational groups with the lowest levels of income and education are Services, Blue Collars, and Others.

To investigate gender differences according to type of employment, workers were divided into five groups: Public Servants (14.8 percent), Nongovernment Employees with formal labor contracts (47.3 percent), Nongovernment Employees without formal labor contracts (11.9 percent), Self-employed workers (20.7 percent), and Employers (5.3 percent).

Tables 7 and 8 present, for men and women, the average income level and the

Table 5
Log-Wage Differentials by Occupational Group

Group	Men	Women
Technical	0.00	0.00
Managerial	0.28	−0.01
Trade	0.98	0.79
Transportation	1.07	0.38
Blue collars	1.21	1.11
Services	1.44	1.57
Others	1.34	1.10

Source: Computed from the PNADs, 1981–89.
Note: All figures are differences between the average log-wages in Technical occupations and the average log-wage in each occupational group. These differentials are computed first for each year, region, and gender. The figures in the table are averages by gender across all regions (weighted) and years (unweighted).

Table 6
Educational Levels by Occupational Group

Group	Men	Women
Technical	12.4	11.9
Managerial	9.3	10.6
Trade	6.3	6.4
Transportation	4.9	7.9
Blue collars	4.3	4.6
Services	4.6	3.4
Others	4.8	4.3

Source: Computed from the PNADs, 1981–89.
Note: These averages are computed first for each year, region, and gender. The figures in the table are averages by gender across all regions (weighted) and years (unweighted).

average educational level by their types of employment. Again, the values in these tables are averages of the corresponding values by region (weighted) and year (unweighted). These tables reveal a clear hierarchy among types of employment. Employers have the highest income level and, jointly with Public Servants, also the highest educational level. Public Servants rank first in education and second in income. They are followed by Nongovernmental Formal Employees; next in line appear Self-employed workers. Finally, Nongovernmental Informal Employees have the lowest income and educational levels.

Table 7
Log-Wage Differentials by Position in Occupation

Group	Men	Women
Employers	0.00	0.00
Public servants	0.58	0.49
Formal employees	0.79	0.99
Self-employed	0.90	1.35
Informal employees	1.35	1.91

Source: Computed from the PNADs, 1981–89.
Note: All figures are differences between the average log-wage among employers
and the average log-wages in each position in occupation. These differentials are
computed first for each year, region, and gender. The figures in the table are
weighted averages by gender across all regions (weighted) and years (unweighted).

Table 8
Educational Levels by Position in Occupation

Group	Men	Women
Employers	8.3	9.3
Public servants	8.1	10.4
Formal employees	6.3	7.1
Self-employed	5.1	4.9
Informal employees	4.6	3.8

Source: Computed from the PNADs, 1981–89.
Note: These averages are computed first for each year, region, and gender. The
figures in the tables are weighted averages by gender across all regions (weighted)
and years (unweighted).

III. The Gender Gap in Wages

A. The Overall Gap

Table 9 presents the temporal evolution of the gender gap in wages over the 1980s
for each of the six regions.[8] These estimates reveal very large gender gaps in
wages. In most cases, the gap lies between 0.45 and 0.65, indicating that the
(geometric) mean wage for men is from 55 to 90 percent higher than the corresponding mean for women.

---

8. The gender gap in wages is defined as the difference between the average log-wage of men and the
average log-wage of women.

Table 9
Gender Wage Differentials—Temporal Evolution: Brazil, 1981–1989

Region	1981	1982	1983	1984	1985	1986	1987	1988	1989	Average[a]
Rio de Janeiro	0.53	0.53	0.53	0.49	0.53	0.51	0.55	0.47	0.44	0.51
São Paulo	0.57	0.55	0.58	0.59	0.56	0.53	0.50	0.54	0.51	0.54
South	0.47	0.45	0.48	0.52	0.55	0.53	0.53	0.51	0.51	0.51
East	0.53	0.59	0.54	0.56	0.58	0.55	0.50	0.51	0.53	0.54
Northeast	0.64	0.64	0.63	0.63	0.63	0.57	0.57	0.56	0.59	0.60
Frontier	0.54	0.58	0.54	0.57	0.56	0.51	0.51	0.49	0.53	0.54
Average[b]	0.55	0.55	0.56	0.57	0.57	0.53	0.53	0.52	0.52	0.54
STD[b]	0.05	0.06	0.05	0.05	0.03	0.02	0.03	0.03	0.04	0.03
Range	0.17	0.19	0.15	0.14	0.10	0.06	0.07	0.09	0.15	0.09

a. Unweighted average.
b. Weighted average and standard deviation, with the weights being time-invariant. The weights are given by the average distributions of the labor force across regions as shown in Table 4.

For all regions, except the South, there is a decline in the gender gap in wages over this period. Considering the average for all regions, the decline from 1981 to 1989 is equal to 0.03, which should be considered very modest. All of this small decline occurs from 1985 to 1986. From 1981 to 1985, and from 1986 to 1989, the wage gap was stable or even slightly increasing at times (see Table 10).

Both the level and the temporal evolution of the gender gap in wages are very different across regions. With respect to levels, the gap is the smallest in Rio de Janeiro and in the South—around 0.5—and the largest in the Northeast—above 0.6. In the remaining three areas (São Paulo, the East, and the Frontier), the gap stays between 0.5 and 0.6, with averages close to 0.55.

With respect to the temporal evolution, Table 9 reveals decreasing wage gaps in Rio, São Paulo, and the Northeast. In the East and the Frontier the gap remained at the same levels in the end years, despite some fluctuation over time. Surprisingly, it increased in the South, especially from 1981 to 1985. As a consequence, this region, which had displayed the lowest gender gap in 1981, had the third highest differential by 1987! There exists, however, an important behavior shared by all the six areas: a substantial decline in the gender gap in wages between 1985 and 1986.

Table 9 also indicates that regional differences, as measured by the standard deviation of the wage gaps across regions, decreased from 1981 to 1986 and have increased since 1986. In fact, while in 1981 the wage gap had a range of 0.17 (from 0.47 in the South to 0.64 in the Northeast) and of 0.15 in 1989 (from 0.44 in Rio de Janeiro to 0.59 in the Northeast), its range was reduced to only 0.06 in 1986 (0.51 in Rio de Janeiro and 0.57 in the Northeast).

B. Gender Gap in Wages by Position in the Family

Table 11 presents estimates by region of the gender gap in wages by position in the family. Three comparisons are made: (1) wages of male heads to female heads, (2) wages of male heads to female spouses, and (3) wages of males and females who are relatives of the heads (other than the spouse).[9] The table also presents the overall gap from Table 9. All estimates are for 1989. This table reveals three facts. First, the gender gap in wages for those who are neither head nor spouse is considerably smaller. Since this group is younger, this fact indicates that the gender gap in wages tends to increase with age. Second, the gender gap in wages among heads tends to be greater than between male heads and female spouses revealing that, on average, working female heads earn less than working female spouses. Finally, Table 11 reveals that the ranking of regions according to the gender gap varies considerably depending on which comparison is used. For instance, São Paulo has the smallest gender gap among other relatives, whereas Rio has the smallest gap according to all other comparisons. Similarly, the Northeast has the greatest gaps according to all comparisons except that for other relatives.

---

9. Note that there is a group that is not included in any of these three comparisons: household members who are not relatives of the head.

Table 10
Gender Wage Differentials—Temporal Evolution: Brazil, 1981–1989

Region	1981–1985	1986–1989	Average[a]	Decline
Rio de Janeiro	0.53	0.49	0.51	0.03
São Paulo	0.57	0.52	0.54	0.05
South	0.49	0.52	0.51	−0.03
East	0.56	0.52	0.54	0.04
Northeast	0.63	0.57	0.60	0.06
Frontier	0.56	0.51	0.54	0.05
Average[b]	0.56	0.52	0.54	0.04
STD[b]	0.04	0.02	0.03	—
Range	0.14	0.08	0.11	—

a. Unweighted average.
b. Weighted average and standard deviation, with the weights being time-invariant. The weights are given by the average distributions of the labor force across regions as shown in Table 4.

Table 11
Gender Gap in Wages by Position in the Family: Brazil, 1989

Region	All/All	Head/Head	Head/Spouse	Others/Others
Rio de Janeiro	0.44	0.51	0.41	0.23
São Paulo	0.51	0.58	0.58	0.12
South	0.51	0.57	0.51	0.24
East	0.53	0.70	0.48	0.21
Northeast	0.59	0.78	0.54	0.20
Frontier	0.53	0.74	0.48	0.15
Average	0.52	0.63	0.52	0.18

It is clear from Tables 9–11 that there are four major questions to be addressed in this study: (1) Why is the gender gap in wages so large in Brazil? (2) Why was the decline from 1985 to 1986 so pronounced? (3) Why is the gap so much higher in the Northeast than in Rio de Janeiro (or in the South)? and (4) Why is the wage gap so much higher for heads and spouses than for other relatives? A series of decompositions of the gender gap was undertaken to investigate these questions.

IV. Gender Differences in Education and Age and the Gender Gap in Wages

The previous section showed that the gender gap in wages in Brazil is large. In this section an attempt will be made to determine what fraction of this gap is due to gender differences in education and age. If men were better educated and had greater labor market experience than women, there would be a positive gender gap in wages without any wage differential between equally productive men and women.

A procedure aimed at eliminating the contribution of gender differences in age and education to the overall gap compares the wages of men and women with the same education and age. This procedure will succeed to the extent that age and education are unrelated to other productive characteristics. In this case, the remaining gap will result from discrimination.

To describe the decomposition methodology used, let W, G, E, and A be random variables representing (log)wage, gender, education, and age, respectively. Assume first that[10]

(1) $\quad E[W|G = g, E = e, A = a] = \alpha_g + \beta_g \cdot e + \delta_g \cdot a + \gamma_g \cdot a^2.$

Using the Law of Iterated Expectations gives

(2) $\quad E[W|G = g] = \alpha_g + \beta_g \cdot E[E|G = g] +$

$\qquad \delta_g \cdot E[A|G = g] + \gamma_g \cdot E[A^2|G = g].$

Hence, the overall gap, $\Delta \equiv E[W|G = m] - E[W|G = f]$, can be written as

(3) $\quad \Delta = \Delta_d + \Delta_e$

where

(4) $\quad \Delta_d \equiv (\alpha_m - \alpha_f) + (\beta_m - \beta_f) \cdot E[E|G = f] + (\delta_m - \delta_f) \cdot E[A|G = f]$

$\qquad + (\gamma_m - \gamma_f) \cdot E[A^2|G = f];$

and

(5) $\quad \Delta_e \equiv \beta_m \cdot (E[E|G = m] - E[E|G = f]) + \delta_m \cdot (E[A|G = m] - E[A|G = f])$

$\qquad + \gamma_m \cdot (E[A^2|G = m] - E[A^2|G = f]).$

Note that Δ_d is the weighted average of the gender gap in wages within each educational and age group, where the weights are given by the distribution of women by educational level and age group. Hence, if education and age capture the relevant productive characteristics, Δ_d is in fact the wage differential between equally productive men and women. For simplicity, this is referred to as the "discrimination component."

Note that Δ_e is a weighted sum of gender differences in education and age.

---

10. Note that in this equation it is assumed that (log)wage is quadratic in age.

Hence, $\Delta_e = 0$ whenever there exists no gender differences in education or age. Thus, Δ_e is the "explainable component."

Tables 12 and 13 present estimates for Δ_d and Δ_e by region and year. These tables reveal two facts. First, the "explainable component" is *negative* in all but one case.[11] This is a consequence of the fact that women are actually better educated than men. Hence, the gender gap in wages for men and women equally educated and of the same age is greater than the overall differential, that is, $\Delta_d > \Delta$. Gender differences in age and education do not help in explaining the gender gap in wages. On the contrary, these differences offset part of the gap in the sense that the wage gap between men and women with the same age and education is greater than the overall gap.

Second, controlling for age and education does not help at all in explaining either why the Northeast has a greater gender gap in wages than Rio or why the gender gap in wages experienced a sharp decline from 1985 to 1986. In fact, both the difference between Rio and the Northeast and the decline from 1985 to 1986 are greater when we compare men and women of equal education and age than when these two characteristics are not controlled for.

In summary, gender differences in education and age do not explain the large gender gap in wages, the large difference between the Northeast and Rio, or the sharp decline from 1985 to 1986. Controlling for age and education actually increases all three differentials. The overall gender gap in wages increases from 0.54 to 0.62. The average differential between the Northeast and Rio increases from 0.09 to 0.15. Finally, the decline from 1985 to 1986 increases from 0.04 to 0.05. Given the fact that education and age do not explain these differentials, our next step will be to investigate the role played by gender differences in occupational structure in explaining them.

V. Gender Differences in Occupation

The gender gap in wages can be viewed as being formed by two components. First, men have a higher average wage due to a possible over-representation in high-paying occupations. Second, even if men and women were evenly represented in all occupations, a gender gap could arise if they received, on average, different wages in the same occupation. The objective of this section is to decompose the overall gender gap in wages into these two components using the following methodology. Let O be a random variable representing occupation. Then, by the Law of Iterated Expectations,

(6) $E[W|G = g] = \displaystyle\sum_{o=1}^{7} E[W|G = g, O = o] \cdot P[O = o|G = g]$

and the gender gap in wages can be written as

(7) $E[W|G = m] - E[W|G = f] = \Delta_i + \Delta_o$

---

11. The only exception is Rio de Janeiro, 1987.

Table 12
Discrimination Component (Δ_d): Brazil, 1981–1989

Region	1981	1982	1983	1984	1985	1986	1987	1988	1989	Average[a]
Rio de Janeiro	0.56	0.54	0.54	0.51	0.54	0.52	0.53	0.50	0.48	0.52
São Paulo	0.61	0.58	0.60	0.61	0.61	0.56	0.54	0.59	0.57	0.59
South	0.57	0.56	0.56	0.59	0.62	0.58	0.58	0.57	0.57	0.58
East	0.66	0.70	0.64	0.67	0.70	0.64	0.61	0.63	0.66	0.65
Northeast	0.77	0.76	0.75	0.76	0.78	0.71	0.71	0.71	0.76	0.74
Frontier	0.63	0.66	0.62	0.66	0.66	0.62	0.60	0.60	0.64	0.63
Average[b]	0.63	0.62	0.62	0.63	0.65	0.60	0.59	0.60	0.61	0.62
Range	0.21	0.22	0.21	0.25	0.24	0.19	0.18	0.21	0.26	0.15

a. Unweighted average.
b. Weighted average with the weights being time-invariant. The weights are given by the average distributions of the labor force across regions as shown in Table 4.

Table 13
Explainable Component (Δ_e): Brazil, 1981–1989

Region	1981	1982	1983	1984	1985	1986	1987	1988	1989	Average[a]
Rio de Janeiro	−0.03	−0.01	−0.02	−0.02	−0.01	−0.01	−0.02	−0.03	−0.04	−0.02
São Paulo	−0.04	−0.03	−0.02	−0.03	−0.05	−0.03	−0.04	−0.06	−0.06	−0.04
South	−0.09	−0.11	−0.08	−0.07	−0.07	−0.05	−0.05	−0.07	−0.06	−0.07
East	−0.13	−0.11	−0.10	−0.11	−0.12	−0.10	−0.10	−0.12	−0.13	−0.11
Northeast	−0.13	−0.12	−0.11	−0.12	−0.15	−0.14	−0.14	−0.15	−0.17	−0.14
Frontier	−0.09	−0.08	−0.07	−0.08	−0.11	−0.11	−0.09	−0.11	−0.10	−0.09
Average[b]	−0.08	−0.07	−0.06	−0.06	−0.08	−0.06	−0.06	−0.08	−0.09	−0.07

a. Unweighted average.
b. Weighted average with the weights being time-invariant. The weights are given by the average distributions of the labor force across regions as shown in Table 4.

where

$$(8) \quad \Delta_i = \sum_{o=1}^{7} \{E[W|G = m, O = o] - E[W|G = f, O = o]\} \cdot P[O = o|G = f]$$

$$(9) \quad \Delta_o = \sum_{o=1}^{7} E[W|G = m, O = o] \{P[O = o|G = m] - P[O = o|G = f]\}.$$

We can refer to Δ_o as the degree of occupational discrimination, and Δ_i can be referred to as either the degree of wage discrimination or the intra-occupational gender gap in wages. These two components (Δ_o and Δ_i) have useful interpretations. On the one hand, Δ_i measures by how much the gender gap in wages would decrease if all intra-occupational gaps in wages were eliminated, holding constant men's and women's occupational structure. So, the contribution of the occupational group "o" to Δ_i is denoted by $\delta(o)$ and given by

$$(10) \quad \delta(o) \equiv \{E[W|G = m, O = o] - E[W|G = f, O = o]\} \cdot P[O = o|G = f].$$

This makes it possible to investigate which occupational group contributes the most to the overall degree of wage discrimination.

On the other hand, Δ_o is the contribution of gender differences in occupational structure to the gender gap in wages. More precisely, it measures by how much the gender gap in wages would decrease if men had the same occupational structure as women, holding constant both men's and women's average wages in each occupation. As already mentioned, it is referred to as the degree of occupational discrimination.

These two components (Δ_o and Δ_i) of the decomposition described above reveal that the gender gap in wages, Δ, is a function of four elements:

1. The intra-occupational gender gap, which is donated by $\lambda(o)$ and given, for $0 = 1, \ldots, 7$, by

$$(11) \quad \lambda(o) \equiv E[W|G = m, O = o] - E[W|G = f, O = o];$$

2. The extent to which men are overrepresented in each occupation, which is denoted by $\pi(o)$ and given, for $o = 1, \ldots, 7$, by

$$(12) \quad \pi(o) \equiv P[O = o|G = m] - P[O = o|G = f];$$

3. The occupational distribution for women,

$$(13) \quad \{P[O = o|G = f]:o = 1, \ldots, 7\};$$

and

4. The average wage of men in each occupational group,

$$(14) \quad \{E[W|G = m, O = o]:o = 1, \ldots, 7\}.$$

As a function of these four elements, the gender gap in wages, Δ, and its two components, Δ_i and Δ_o, can be written as

$$(15) \quad \Delta = \Delta_i + \Delta_o,$$

$$(16) \quad \Delta_i \equiv \sum_{o=1}^{7} \lambda(o) \cdot P[O = o | G = f] = \sum_{o=1}^{7} \delta(o)$$

and

$$(17) \quad \Delta_o \equiv \sum_{o=1}^{7} E[W | G = m, O = o] \cdot \pi(o).$$

Therefore, differences in the gender gap in wages, Δ, occur if and only if at least one of these four components varies.

The limitation associated with this decomposition is precisely the clause "holding constant both men's and women's average wages in each occupation." In this decomposition the counterfactual experiment of changing the occupational structure of the men to mirror the women's occupational structure was performed. In the counterfactual experiment it was assumed that, as the occupation structure of the men was changed, the wage structure by occupation of men and women would remain unchanged.

If one wants to consider, as it seems plausible, situations where changes in the distribution of workers by occupation is motivated mainly by changes in the wage structure or situations where changes in the distribution of workers by occupation induce changes in the occupational structure of wages, then this decomposition could be of dubious interest. However, given that the main goal here is simply to identify the main sources of wage differences by gender, this procedure is particularly useful since it provides a simple estimate of the contribution of gender differences in occupational structure to gender differences in wages.

A. The Occupation Structure by Gender

Table 14 presents the occupational structure by gender. The figures in this table are averages of the occupational structure estimated for each year (unweighted) and region (weighted). This table reveals the following: (1) in the group with the highest average income level (Technical occupations), women are overrepresented; (2) in the group with the second highest income level (Managerial), men and women are equally represented; (3) in the groups with intermediate levels of wages (Trade and Transportation), men are overrepresented; and (4) in the two low-income groups (Blue-Collars and workers in Services), taken as a whole, women are slightly overrepresented. Nevertheless, the distribution by gender in these two groups is very segregated: men represent most of the Blue-Collar workers and women most of the workers in Services.

Overall, this table reveals, quite surprisingly, absolutely no evidence of occupational discrimination against women; in other words, there is no indication of women being overrepresented in low-paying occupations. As a matter of fact, this table indicates that, on the contrary, women tend to be overrepresented in high-paying occupations. Therefore, if there is any occupational discrimination by gender it seems to be against men!

Table 14
Occupational Structure by Gender

Group	Men	Women	Feminization	Male Wages
Technical	6.5	16.3	0.55	0.00
Managerial	19.5	19.7	0.33	0.28
Trade	12.0	10.2	0.29	0.98
Transportation	10.5	1.0	0.05	1.07
Blue Collars	34.6	15.3	0.18	1.21
Services	2.3	26.8	0.85	1.44
Others	14.6	10.7	0.26	1.34
All	100.0	100.0	0.33	—

Note: All estimates were computed first for each year and region. The estimates in the table are averages for all regions (weighted) and years (unweighted). Feminization refers to the proportion of women in the occupation. Male wages are differences between the average log-wage in Technical occupations and the average log-wage in each occupational group. Hence, the higher the value, the lower the average male wage in the occupation.

B. Intra-Occupational Gender Gaps in Wages and the Degree of Wage Discrimination

Table 14 indicates that gender differences in occupational structure lead the overall gender gap in wages, Δ, to underestimate the (weighted) average of the intra-occupational gaps in wages, Δ_i. Table 15 confirms this prediction. This table presents estimates for the average intra-occupational gender gap, Δ_i, also referred to as the degree of wage discrimination. As predicted from Table 14, the degree of wage discrimination, Δ_i, is, in most cases, greater than the overall gap, Δ (compare Tables 15 and 9). In particular, the regional and temporal average degree of wage discrimination is 0.05 greater than the corresponding average for the overall gap in wages. On average, $\Delta_i = 0.59$ and $\Delta = 0.54$.

Table 16 presents the gender gap in wages disaggregated for each occupational group. This table reveals that the average intra-occupational gender gap, Δ_i, is greater than the average overall gender gap, Δ, despite the fact that in only three (Technical, Services, and Blue Collars) out of the seven occupational groups is the intra-occupational gap greater than the overall gap, Δ. The fact that Δ_i tends to be greater than Δ holds because women are overrepresented in the two occupational groups in which the gender gap is the greatest (Technical and Services).

Indeed, as Table 16 reveals, the average value of the degree of occupational discrimination, Δ_o, is -0.05.[12] A negative figure reveals that men would obtain a wage gain (not loss!) if men had the occupational structure of women.

---

12. The average is taken over regions (weighted) and over time (unweighted).

Table 15

Intra-Occupational Gender Gap in Wages or Degree of Wage Discrimination (Δ_j): Brazil, 1981–1989

Region	1981	1982	1983	1984	1985	1986	1987	1988	1989	Average[a]
Rio de Janeiro	0.55	0.50	0.46	0.46	0.48	0.51	0.49	0.44	0.52	0.49
São Paulo	0.53	0.53	0.57	0.57	0.56	0.57	0.54	0.63	0.62	0.57
South	0.56	0.53	0.57	0.62	0.61	0.67	0.63	0.54	0.57	0.59
East	0.62	0.61	0.57	0.61	0.65	0.62	0.54	0.59	0.61	0.60
Northeast	0.75	0.67	0.74	0.73	0.74	0.66	0.69	0.71	0.73	0.71
Frontier	0.62	0.60	0.61	0.62	0.61	0.56	0.55	0.59	0.59	0.59
Average[b]	0.59	0.57	0.59	0.60	0.61	0.60	0.58	0.59	0.61	0.59
Range	0.22	0.17	0.28	0.27	0.26	0.15	0.20	0.27	0.21	0.22

a. Unweighted average.
b. Weighted average with the weights being time-invariant. The weights are given by the average distributions of the labor force across regions as shown in Table 4.

Table 16
*Intra-Occupational Gender Gap in Wages by
Occupational Group*

Group	Wage Gap
Technical	0.68
Managerial	0.39
Trade	0.50
Transportation	−0.01
Blue collars	0.58
Services	0.82
Others	0.44
Average[a] (Δ_i)	0.59
Overall gap	0.54
Difference (Δ_o)	−0.05

Note: These figures are computed first for each year and region. The figures in the
table are averages of all regions (weighted) and years (unweighted).
a. Average taken using women's occupational structure as weights.

Table 16 reveals three additional facts. First, the gender gap in wages varies
considerably across occupational groups. The gap varies from approximately zero
in Transportation to 0.82 in Services.[13] Second, the gap is greater in occupational
groups where women are overrepresented: Technical and Services. Third, there
is no indication that the gap in wages is either lower or higher in high-paying
occupations. In fact, it is greatest in Services, which is one of the low-paying
occupations, followed by Technical occupations, which is the group with the
highest average income level.

C. Occupational Structure and the Degree of Occupational Discrimination

Table 17 presents estimates for Δ_o, the contribution of gender differences in
occupational structure to the overall gap in wages. This table reveals that, except
for Rio de Janeiro (1982–88) and for São Paulo (1981–85), the contribution of
gender differences in occupation is negative. Therefore, for the majority of regions and time periods, the occupational structure favors women instead of men,
in other words, holding all intra-occupational average wages constant, if men had
the occupational structure of women their average wage would be higher.

One could imagine that this counterintuitive result is a consequence of the very
aggregated treatment of the occupational spectrum used here. However, Mello
(1982, pp. 28, 32), using a disaggregation of the economy into 42 sectors, also
found that the occupational discrimination explained less than 5 percent of the
gender gap in wages.

13. It is actually slightly negative in transportation, therefore favoring women.

Table 17
Occupational Discrimination (Δ_o): Brazil, 1981–1989

Region	1981	1982	1983	1984	1985	1986	1987	1988	1989	Average[a]
Rio de Janeiro	-0.02	0.03	0.07	0.03	0.05	0.00	0.05	0.02	-0.08	0.02
São Paulo	0.04	0.02	0.01	0.02	-0.01	-0.04	-0.04	-0.09	-0.10	-0.02
South	-0.09	-0.08	-0.09	-0.10	-0.06	-0.14	-0.09	-0.04	-0.06	-0.09
East	-0.09	-0.02	-0.04	-0.05	-0.08	-0.08	-0.04	-0.08	-0.09	-0.06
Northeast	-0.11	-0.03	-0.11	-0.10	-0.11	-0.09	-0.12	-0.15	-0.14	-0.11
Frontier	-0.08	-0.02	-0.06	-0.04	-0.05	-0.05	-0.04	-0.09	-0.06	-0.06
Average[b]	-0.04	-0.01	-0.03	-0.03	-0.04	-0.06	-0.05	-0.08	-0.09	-0.05
Range	-0.15	-0.11	-0.18	-0.13	-0.16	-0.14	-0.17	-0.17	-0.08	-0.13

a. Unweighted average.
b. Weighted average with the weights being time-invariant. The weights are given by the average distributions of the labor force across regions as shown in Table 4.

D. The Contribution of Each Occupational Group to the Degree of Wage Discrimination

Table 18 presents estimates of the contributions of each occupational group, $\delta(o)$, to wage discrimination by region. The estimates in this table are temporal averages covering the period 1981–89. The major finding of this table is that Services is the occupational group making the largest contribution. Services contributes, on average, 37 percent of the total degree of wage discrimination. Since there are seven occupations, if all had equal contributions, each would contribute approximately 14 percent. Hence, the contribution of Services is greater than 2.5 times the average contribution. Only one other occupation has a contribution significantly above average: Technical, with a contribution of 19 percent. Blue Collars (15 percent) and Managerial (13 percent) have contributions close to average. Among the remaining groups, Trade (9 percent) and Others (8 percent) have contributions close to 60 percent of the average, whereas Transportation has an insignificant contribution.

E. Regional Differences in Gender Gap in Wages

Table 9 showed that, considering the temporal averages, the gender gap in wages ranged from 0.51 in Rio de Janeiro to 0.60 in the Northeast. It has been demonstrated that these regional disparities are not explained by regional differences in the gender gap in education and age. In fact, the range of the gender gap in wages almost doubles after controlling for age and education (compare Tables 9 and 12). This question will now be considered in the context of the decomposition of the gender gap in wages into occupation discrimination and wage discrimination. As previously explained, occupation and wage discrimination are functions of four elements: the intra-occupational gender gap in wages, the extent to which men are overrepresented in each occupation, the occupational distribution for women, and the average wage of men in each occupational group.

Table 17 revealed that Δ_o is smaller for the Northeast than for Rio. Therefore, regional differences in occupational discrimination do not explain regional differences in the overall gender gap in wages. As a consequence, regional disparities in the two elements from which Δ_o can be obtained cannot explain regional disparities in Δ. So, it can be concluded that regional disparities in gender differences in occupational structure, $\{\pi(o): o = 1, \ldots, 7\}$, are not one of the reasons the gender gap in wage is much greater in the Northeast than in Rio de Janeiro.

Since regional disparities in Δ_o do not explain regional variations in Δ, it must be the case that regional variations in Δ are explained by regional differences in the degree of wage discrimination, Δ_i. Table 15 confirms this prediction. We must still, however, identify which of the two components of Δ_i is responsible for the regional disparities.

To identify which of the two elements is responsible for the regional variations, Δ_i was recomputed for all regions and years standardizing the values of $\lambda(o)$. More specifically, for each region and year, Δ_i was recalculated using as values for $\lambda(o)$, $o = 1, \ldots, 7$, the values for Rio relative to the year in consideration. The results of this simulation are presented in Table 19. This table reveals that

Table 18

Contribution of Each Occupation Group to the Degree of Wage Discrimination: Brazil, 1981–1989

Region	Technical	Managerial	Trade	Transport	Blue Collars	Services	Others
Rio de Janeiro	0.10	0.06	0.05	0.00	0.06	0.18	0.04
São Paulo	0.10	0.09	0.04	-0.00	0.11	0.19	0.05
South	0.11	0.07	0.06	-0.00	0.08	0.22	0.06
East	0.14	0.07	0.04	0.00	0.07	0.24	0.05
Northeast	0.13	0.08	0.08	0.00	0.13	0.26	0.04
Frontier	0.11	0.09	0.05	0.00	0.05	0.24	0.04
Average (1)	0.11	0.08	0.05	-0.00	0.09	0.22	0.05
Percentage of row total	19%	13%	9%	-0%	15%	37%	8%
NE-RJ (2)[a]	0.03	0.01	0.03	0.00	0.07	0.09	-0.00
Percentage of row total	12%	6%	13%	0%	30%	39%	-0%
(2)/(1)	25%	17%	58%	-33%	75%	40%	-2%

a. Difference between the Northeast and Rio.

Table 19
Wage Discrimination with Standardized Intra-Occupational Gender Gaps

Region	1981	1982	1983	1984	1985	1986	1987	1988	1989	Average[a]
Rio de Janeiro	0.55	0.50	0.46	0.46	0.48	0.51	0.49	0.44	0.52	0.49
São Paulo	0.55	0.50	0.47	0.47	0.48	0.50	0.51	0.43	0.51	0.49
South	0.57	0.51	0.48	0.48	0.50	0.52	0.52	0.43	0.51	0.50
East	0.58	0.52	0.48	0.49	0.50	0.52	0.51	0.44	0.54	0.51
Northeast	0.57	0.51	0.48	0.47	0.50	0.53	0.52	0.44	0.52	0.50
Frontier	0.57	0.51	0.48	0.48	0.49	0.52	0.51	0.44	0.52	0.50
Average[b]	0.56	0.51	0.47	0.47	0.49	0.51	0.51	0.43	0.52	0.50
Range	0.03	0.02	0.02	0.03	0.02	0.03	0.03	0.01	0.03	0.02

a. Unweighted average.
b. Weighted average with the weights being time-invariant. The weights are given by the average distributions of the labor force across regions as shown in Table 4.

after having controlled for regional disparities in the intra-occupational gender gaps, $\{\lambda(o):o = 1, \ldots, 7\}$, almost all regional disparities in Δ_i disappear. Therefore, greater values for $\{\lambda(o):o = 1, \ldots, 7\}$ in the Northeast are the main cause for the greater overall gender gap in that region, with the converse being true for Rio. In fact, if the Northeast had the intra-occupational gender gap of Rio, the degree of wage discrimination would be 0.50 which is very close to the level for Rio, 0.49, and much smaller than the nonstandardized value, 0.71.

Although Table 19 clearly indicates that regional disparities in intra-occupational gaps in wages are the main source of regional variation in the overall gap, it does not identify which occupation is the most responsible for all regional disparities. Table 18 presents some evidence on this question. This table reports the gap between Rio and the Northeast along with the relative contribution of each occupational group to the degree of wage discrimination. It reveals that Services (39 percent) and Blue Collars (30 percent) are the two occupations which contribute the most to the differences between the Northeast and Rio. The fact that Services is the group with the largest contribution to the NE-RJ difference in the wage gap is expected since this is the group with the largest contribution to the overall gap. To measure the relative capacity of each occupational group to explain the NE-RJ gap difference, the contribution to the NE-RJ gap difference is expressed as a percentage of the contribution to the overall gap. To interpret this estimate, note that the NE-RJ gap itself is 38 percent of the degree of wage discrimination. In this relative sense, Blue Collars (75 percent) and Trade (58 percent) are the occupational groups which contribute the most to explain the NE-RJ gap. Services comes in third place with 40 percent. All other occupational groups have contributions below average, that is, lower than 38 percent.

It can be concluded that most of the regional differences in Δ are explained by concomitant regional differences in the intra-occupational gender gaps in wages, $\{\lambda(o):o = 1, \ldots, 7\}$. Moreover, the contributions of the occupational groups are quite diverse. Services, Blue Collars, and Trade are the groups with the largest absolute and relative contribution. Jointly, these three groups explain more than 80 percent of the regional difference in wage discrimination between the Northeast and Rio de Janeiro.

VI. Intra-Occupational Gender Differences in Educational Attainment and the Degree of Wage Discrimination

The results of the previous section showed, rather surprisingly, that gender differences in occupational structure favor women rather than men. As a consequence, the average intra-occupational gender gap in wages is larger than the overall gap. Therefore, the task of identifying the determinants of such large intra-occupational gaps in wages still remains. In principle, they can be partially explained by intra-occupational gender differences in educational attainment. In other words, intra-occupational differences in wages by gender could be the result of men being, on average, better educated than women in the same occupation.

Table 20

Intra-Occupational Gender Gap in Education and the Degree of Proper Wage Discrimination

Group	Educational Gap[a]	Overall Wage Discrimination	Proper Wage Discrimination[c]	
			$b = 0.1$	$b = 0.2$
Technical	0.5	0.68	0.63	0.58
Managerial	-1.3	0.39	0.52	0.65
Trade	-0.1	0.50	0.51	0.52
Transportation	-3.0	-0.01	0.29	0.59
Blue collars	-0.3	0.58	0.62	0.65
Services	1.2	0.82	0.70	0.58
Others	0.5	0.44	0.39	0.34
Average[b]	0.1	0.59	0.58	0.57
Overall	-0.6	0.54	0.54	0.54
Range	4.2	0.83	0.41	0.31

a. These intra-occupational averages are computed first for each year, region, and gender. The figures in the table are averages across all regions (weighted) and years (unweighted).
b. Average evaluated using women's occupational structure as weights.
c. Assuming different rates of return on schooling.

Estimating the magnitude of the contribution of intra-occupational gender differences in education to intra-occupational gender gaps in wages is the object of this section. Given that differences in wages due to differences in educational attainment may be considered ethically more acceptable than those attributed strictly to gender, estimating the magnitude of the contribution of education is fundamental for any evaluation of gender gap in wages.

A. Intra-Occupational Gender Gap in Education

Overall, working women are better educated than working men. In fact, working women are, on average, 0.6 years more educated than working men (see Table 20). This fact, however, does not necessarily imply that the average gender differential in education within occupations must favor women. As a matter of fact, Table 20 reveals that women are more educated than men in four occupational groups and less educated in three groups. Since women are less educated precisely in the occupational groups in which they are overrepresented (Technical and Services), when the weighted average of the intra-occupational gender gaps in education are computed using women's occupational structure as weights, the average turns out to be positive, that is, among men and women in the same occupation group men tend to be more educated. Thus, gender differences in education within occupation groups must be responsible for at least a fraction of the intra-occupational gender gaps in wages.

B. Degree of Proper Wage Discrimination: A Simplified Approach

In this section and the following an attempt will be made to remove from the degree of wage discrimination, Δ_i, the component due to intra-occupational gender differences in education. The wage gap obtained by removing the contribution of education will be referred to as the degree of "proper" wage discrimination.

This section will use a simplified methodology based on the assumption that

(18) $E[W|G = g, S = s, O = o] = a_{go} + b \cdot s.$

There are two implicit hypotheses behind this expression. First, the regression is linear in the number of completed years of schooling. Second, the coefficient on years of schooling (or the often referred to rate of return on schooling) b, is invariant across genders and occupational groups. Under these assumptions

(19) $E[W|G = g, O = o] = a_{go} + b \cdot E[S|G = g, O = o]$

and the intra-occupational gender gap in wages, $\lambda(o)$, can be decomposed as follows:

(20) $\lambda(o) \equiv E[W|G = m, O = o] - E[W|G = f, O = o] = \Delta_e(o) + \Delta_d(o),$

where

(21) $\Delta_e(o) = b \cdot \{E[S|G = m, O = o] - E[S|G = f, O = o]\}$

and

(22) $\Delta_d(o) = a_{mo} - a_{fo}.$

In this decomposition, $\Delta_e(o)$ is the component of the intra-occupational gender gap in wages that would be eliminated if men and women had the same level of education. On the other hand, $\Delta_d(o)$ is the average gap in wages between men and women with the same educational attainment and occupation. In short, $\Delta_d(o)$ is referred to as the degree of proper wage discrimination.

Table 20 presents estimates for the average value of $\Delta_d(o)$ using two alternative values for b.[14] The results in Table 20 reveal that educational differences by gender explain, on average, very little of the intra-occupational gender gap in wages. In fact, using the larger value for b ($b = 0.2$) the gap in wages is reduced only from 0.59 to 0.57 when the component due to gender differences in education within occupations is removed.

Table 20 also reveals that, despite the small overall impact, the effect on each individual intra-occupational gap in wages for most occupational groups is large. This apparent paradox is a consequence of sizeable gender differences in education for some occupational groups (for instance, 3.0 years in favor of women in Transportation and 1.2 years in favor of men in Services). Finally, it is worth noting that the range across occupations of the intra-occupational gender gap in wages is reduced substantially after the educational gap in education is taken into account: the range declines from 0.83 to 0.31, using $b = 0.2$, and to 0.41, using $b = 0.1$.

---

14. The average is taken over all years in the period 1981–89 and across all regions.

In summary, eliminating the component due to intra-occupational gender differences in education from the intra-occupational gender gap in wages has two consequences: first, it reduces by an insignificant margin the average intra-occupational gender gap in wages. Second, it reduces substantially the variability of the intra-occupational gender gaps across occupations.

C. Degree of Proper Wage Discrimination: A More General Approach

Two modifications are now made to the methodology used above: (1) age is introduced as an additional variable, and (2) the coefficients on all variables are allowed to vary freely by gender and occupation. Specifically, it is assumed that

$$(23) \quad E[W|G = g, A = a, S = s, O = o] = \alpha_{go} + \beta_{go} \cdot s + \delta_{go} \cdot a + \gamma_{go} \cdot a^2.$$

As in the previous section it is still assumed that (log)wages are linear in years of schooling, but now the slope may vary freely by gender and occupation. It is also assumed that (log)wages are quadratic in age. Under these assumptions

$$(24) \quad E[W|G = g, O = o] = \alpha_{go} + \beta_{go}E[S|G = g, O = o] + \delta_{go}E[A|G = g, O = o]$$
$$+ \gamma_{go}E[A^2|G = g, O = o],$$

and similar to what was done in the previous section, the intra-occupational gender gap in wages, $\lambda(o)$, can be decomposed as follows:

$$(25) \quad \lambda(o) \equiv E[W|G = m, O = o] - E[W|G = f, O = o] = \Delta_e(o) + \Delta_d(o),$$

where

$$(26) \quad \Delta_e(o) = \beta_{mo} \cdot (E[S|G = m, O = o] - E[S|G = f, O = o])$$
$$+ \delta_{mo} \cdot (E[A|G = m, O = o] - E[A|G = f, O = o)]$$
$$+ \gamma_{mo} \cdot (E[A^2|G = m, O = o] - E[A^2|G = f, O = o])$$

and

$$(27) \quad \Delta_d(o) = (\alpha_{mo} - \alpha_{fo}) + (\beta_{mo} - \beta_{fo}) \cdot E[S|G = f, O = o]$$
$$+ (\delta_{mo} - \delta_{fo}) \cdot E[A|G = f, O = o]$$
$$+ (\gamma_{mo} - \gamma_{fo}) \cdot E[A^2|G = f, O = o].$$

The interpretation of this decomposition is parallel to the one offered in the last section. On the one hand, $\Delta_e(o)$ is the part of the intra-occupational gap in wages that could be eliminated by giving men the distribution by age and education of women in the same occupation. On the other hand, $\Delta_d(o)$ is the gender gap in wages between men and women with the same age and education working in the same occupation.

Table 21 presents estimates for the average value for the intra-occupational gender gap in wages, $\lambda(o)$, and for its two components $\Delta_e(o)$ and $\Delta_d(o)$. This table reveals that most of the intra-occupational gender gap in wages remains after controlling for gender differences in education and age.

Table 21

Intra-Occupational Gender Gap in Wages and Its Components

Group	$\lambda(o)$	$\Delta_e(o)$	$\Delta_d(o)$
Technical	0.68	0.08	0.60
Managerial	0.39	−0.07	0.46
Trade	0.50	0.02	0.48
Transportation	−0.01	−0.21	0.20
Blue collars	0.58	−0.04	0.62
Services	0.82	0.14	0.68
Others	0.44	0.07	0.37
Averages[a]	0.59	0.03	0.56

Note: Estimates are computed first for each year and region. The figures in the table are averages across all years (unweighted) and regions (weighted).

a. Averages evaluated using women's occupational structure as weights.

Finally, notice that

(28) $\Delta_i = \Delta_e + \Delta_d$

where

(29) $\Delta_e = \sum_{o=1}^{7} \Delta_e(o) \cdot P[O = o | G = f]$

and

(30) $\Delta_d = \sum_{o=1}^{7} \Delta_d(o) \cdot P[O = o | G = f].$

These two components are referred to respectively as the degree of apparent discrimination and the degree of "proper" wage discrimination. Tables 22 and 23 present estimates for these two components.

The results shown in Tables 20 to 23 are impressive. They indicate that more than 90 percent of the intra-occupational gender gap in wages remains unexplained after removing the intra-occupational gender differences in education and age. In other words, in Brazil women receive, on average, a wage 60 percent lower than men in the same occupation, with the same eduational level and the same age.

D. Differences in the Gender Gap by Position in the Family

In this section the gender gap in wages is decomposed into its three components (occupational discrimination, and "proper" and apparent wage discrimination) for (1) male and female heads, (2) male heads and female spouses, and (3) male

Table 22
Degree of "Proper" Wage Discrimination

Region	1981	1982	1983	1984	1985	1986	1987	1988	1989	Average[a]
Rio de Janeiro	0.49	0.47	0.45	0.46	0.44	0.49	0.44	0.40	0.47	0.46
São Paulo	0.51	0.50	0.53	0.54	0.52	0.48	0.51	0.55	0.51	0.52
South	0.53	0.51	0.54	0.56	0.56	0.61	0.58	0.51	0.52	0.55
East	0.58	0.59	0.53	0.58	0.59	0.59	0.52	0.57	0.61	0.57
Northeast	0.73	0.68	0.71	0.73	0.75	0.66	0.70	0.70	0.74	0.71
Frontier	0.62	0.57	0.56	0.58	0.59	0.57	0.52	0.55	0.60	0.57
Average[b]	0.57	0.55	0.55	0.57	0.57	0.56	0.55	0.55	0.57	0.56
Range	0.23	0.21	0.26	0.27	0.30	0.16	0.26	0.30	0.27	0.25

a. Unweighted average.
b. Weighted average with the weights being time-invariant. The weights are given by the average distributions of the labor force across regions as shown in Table 4.

Table 23
Degree of Apparent Wage Discrimination

Region	1981	1982	1983	1984	1985	1986	1987	1988	1989	Average[a]
Rio de Janeiro	0.05	0.03	0.01	0.00	0.04	0.01	0.05	0.05	0.04	0.03
São Paulo	0.02	0.03	0.04	0.03	0.05	0.09	0.04	0.08	0.10	0.05
South	0.03	0.02	0.04	0.06	0.05	0.06	0.05	0.03	0.05	0.04
East	0.03	0.02	0.05	0.03	0.07	0.04	0.02	0.02	0.00	0.03
Northeast	0.02	−0.01	0.03	−0.00	−0.00	−0.00	−0.01	0.02	−0.01	0.00
Frontier	−0.01	0.03	0.05	0.04	0.02	−0.01	0.03	0.03	−0.00	0.02
Average[b]	0.02	0.02	0.04	0.03	0.04	0.04	0.03	0.04	0.04	0.03
Range	−0.03	−0.03	0.02	−0.01	−0.05	−0.01	−0.06	−0.03	−0.06	−0.03

a. Unweighted average.
b. Weighted average with the weights being time-invariant. The weights are given by the average distributions of the labor force across regions as shown in Table 4.

and female non-heads or spouses. The main goal is to investigate why the gap in wages between males and females who are neither heads or spouses is so much smaller than among male and female heads or male heads and female spouses.

Tables 24–27 present estimates for all components in 1989. These tables reveal that although the overall gender gap in wages is much smaller among non-heads or spouses than between male and female heads and spouses, the gender gap among persons with the same level of education and age and working in the same occupation is similar for both groups. In fact, whereas the difference in the overall gap in wages between these two groups is 0.45 (see Table 24), the gap in the degree of "proper" wage discrimination is 0.19 (see Table 25). The reduction in the differential is due to the fact that among non-heads or spouses the overall gender gap underestimates significantly the degree of wage discrimination. As a

Table 24
Overall Gender Gap in Wages: Brazil, 1989

Region	All/All (1)	Head/Head (2)	Head/Spouse (3)	Others/Others (4)	(3)–(4)	(3)–(2)	(2)–(4)
Rio de Janeiro	0.44	0.41	0.51	0.23	0.27	0.09	0.18
São Paulo	0.51	0.58	0.58	0.12	0.46	−0.00	0.46
South	0.51	0.51	0.57	0.24	0.32	0.06	0.26
East	0.53	0.48	0.70	0.21	0.50	0.22	0.27
Northeast	0.59	0.54	0.78	0.20	0.58	0.24	0.35
Frontier	0.53	0.48	0.74	0.15	0.59	0.26	0.34
Average	0.52	0.52	0.63	0.18	0.45	0.11	0.33

Table 25
Degree of "Proper" Wage Discrimination: Brazil, 1989

Region	All/All (1)	Head/Head (2)	Head/Spouse (3)	Others/Others (4)	(3)–(4)	(3)–(2)	(2)–(4)
Rio de Janeiro	0.47	0.45	0.46	0.47	−0.00	0.02	−0.02
São Paulo	0.51	0.54	0.48	0.41	0.07	−0.05	0.12
South	0.52	0.52	0.60	0.40	0.21	0.08	0.12
East	0.65	0.61	0.63	0.44	0.18	0.02	0.16
Northeast	0.74	0.76	0.78	0.50	0.28	0.01	0.26
Frontier	0.60	—	—	—	—	—	—
Average	0.57				0.19	0.01	0.18

— data on Frontier omitted.

Table 26
Degree of Apparent Wage Discrimination: Brazil, 1989

Region	All/ All (1)	Head/ Head (2)	Head/ Spouse (3)	Others/ Others (4)	(3)–(4)	(3)–(2)	(2)–(4)
Rio de Janeiro	0.04	0.05	0.09	−0.09	0.19	0.04	0.15
São Paulo	0.10	0.11	0.13	−0.02	0.15	0.02	0.13
South	0.05	0.07	0.03	−0.07	0.10	−0.04	0.14
East	0.00	−0.01	0.04	−0.06	0.10	0.04	0.05
Northeast	−0.01	−0.02	0.05	−0.12	0.17	0.07	0.10
Frontier	−0.00	—	—	—	—	—	—
Average	0.04				0.10	0.03	0.07

— data on Frontier omitted.

Table 27
Degree of Occupational Discrimination: Brazil, 1989

Region	All/ All (1)	Head/ Head (2)	Head/ Spouse (3)	Others/ Others (4)	(3)–(4)	(3)–(2)	(2)–(4)
Rio de Janeiro	−0.08	−0.08	−0.05	−0.14	0.09	0.04	0.05
São Paulo	−0.10	−0.06	−0.04	−0.27	0.23	0.03	0.21
South	−0.06	−0.08	−0.07	−0.08	0.02	0.02	−0.00
East	−0.09	−0.12	0.04	−0.18	0.21	0.16	0.06
Northeast	−0.14	−0.20	−0.05	−0.18	0.13	0.15	−0.02
Frontier	−0.06	—	—	—	—	—	—
Average	−0.09				0.16	0.08	0.09

— data on Frontier omitted.

matter of fact, while the overall gap among non-head or spouse is 0.18, the degree of "proper" discrimination is 0.43.

VII. Gender Differences in the Type of Employment Structure

As was discussed earlier, the overall gender gap in wages can be regarded as being the result of two factors: (1) men are overrepresented in the

Table 28

Type of Employment Structure by Gender

Group	Men	Women	Feminization	Male Wages
Employers	6.8	2.2	0.14	0.00
Public servants	11.7	20.9	0.47	0.58
Formal employees	51.1	39.7	0.28	0.79
Self-employed	20.9	20.3	0.32	0.90
Informal employees	9.5	16.7	0.46	1.35
All	100.0	100.0	0.33	—

Note: These averages are computed first for each year, region, and gender. The figures in table are averages by gender across all regions (weighted) and years (unweighted). Feminization refers to the proportion of women in the employment group. Male wages are differences between the average log-wage of employers and the average log-wage in each employment group.

high-paying groups, and (2) men receive higher wages within the same occupational group. The first component, which was referred to as Δ_o, can be understood as the contribution of gender differences in the group structure to the overall gap, and the second, Δ_i, as the contribution of intragroup wage gaps.

The expressions for Δ_i and Δ_o (see equations (16) and (17)) have been modified so that now the random variable O represents the type of employment, and the summation is over the following five groups: Employers, Public Servants, Formal Employees, Self-employed, and Informal Employees. Of course, the caveats mentioned earlier are still valid.

A. The Type of Employment Structure by Gender

Table 28 shows the type of employment structure by gender. The figures in this table are averages of the type of employment distributions estimated by year (unweighted) and region (weighted). The table reveals that women are underrepresented in the highest income group (Employers). They are about even in the intermediate groups (Self-employed and Formal Employees), and overrepresented in a low-income position (Informal Employees) and in a high-income position (Public Servants). This combination of overrepresentation in the low-income categories and in the high-income groups is an indication that, as for occupational groups, only a small part of the wage gender gap may be a consequence of the differences in the distribution by type of employment of men and women.

B. Intra-Type of Employment Gender Gaps in Wages and the Degree of Wage Discrimination

Tables 29 and 30 reveal that, in fact, only a small part of the wage differences between males and females is due to differences in their distribution according

Table 29

Intra-Type of Employment Gap in Wages or Degree of Wage Discrimination (Δ_i): Brazil, 1981–1989

Region	1981	1982	1983	1984	1985	1986	1987	1988	1989	Average[a]
Rio de Janeiro	0.46	0.47	0.45	0.41	0.45	0.44	0.47	0.41	0.39	0.44
São Paulo	0.49	0.47	0.49	0.49	0.48	0.47	0.44	0.46	0.44	0.47
South	0.44	0.41	0.45	0.47	0.50	0.48	0.47	0.46	0.45	0.46
East	0.50	0.53	0.49	0.48	0.53	0.49	0.46	0.46	0.50	0.49
Northeast	0.61	0.60	0.59	0.59	0.60	0.53	0.47	0.53	0.54	0.56
Frontier	0.51	0.36	0.49	0.50	0.51	0.44	0.46	0.44	0.46	0.46
Average[b]	0.50	0.49	0.49	0.49	0.51	0.48	0.46	0.46	0.46	0.48
Range	0.17	0.23	0.14	0.17	0.15	0.09	0.04	0.12	0.15	0.12

a. Unweighted average.
b. Weighted average with the weights being time-invariant. The weights are given by the average distributions of the labor force across regions as shown in Table 4.

Table 30
Type of Employment Discrimination (Δ_o): Brazil, 1981–1989

Region	1981	1982	1983	1984	1985	1986	1987	1988	1989	Average[a]
Rio de Janeiro	0.07	0.06	0.08	0.08	0.08	0.07	0.08	0.06	0.05	0.07
São Paulo	0.08	0.08	0.09	0.10	0.08	0.06	0.06	0.08	0.07	0.07
South	0.03	0.04	0.03	0.05	0.05	0.05	0.06	0.05	0.06	0.05
East	0.03	0.06	0.05	0.08	0.05	0.06	0.04	0.05	0.03	0.05
Northeast	0.03	0.04	0.04	0.04	0.03	0.04	0.10	0.03	0.05	0.04
Frontier	0.03	0.22	0.05	0.07	0.05	0.07	0.05	0.05	0.07	0.08
Average[b]	0.05	0.06	0.07	0.08	0.06	0.05	0.07	0.06	0.06	0.06
Range	0.05	0.18	0.06	0.06	0.05	0.03	0.06	0.05	0.04	0.04

a. Unweighted average.
b. Weighted average with the weights being time-invariant. The weights are given by the average distributions of the labor force across regions as shown in Table 4.

Table 31
Intra-Job Type Gender Gap in Wages

Group	Wage Gap
Employers	0.23
Public servants	0.14
Formal employees	0.42
Self-employed	0.68
Informal employees	0.79
Average[a] (Δ_i)	0.48
Overall gap	0.54
Difference (Δ_o)	0.06

Note: These averages are computed first for each year, region, and gender. The figures in the table are averages by gender across all regions (weighted) and years (unweighted).
a. Average taken using women's occupational structure as weights.

to type of employment. In Table 29 one can find the temporal evolution by region of what would be the gender gap were men and women equally distributed among type of employment group (Δ_i). Table 30 displays the part of the overall gender gap in wages that can be attributed to disparities between their distributions according to type of employment, in other words, the job-type discrimination (Δ_o).

As had been observed above, the average intra-job-type gap (0.48) is lower than the overall gap in wages (0.54), implying a positive job-type discrimination component (0.06). In other words, if women were distributed across type of employment as men are, the overall gender gap in wages would be reduced by close to 11 percent. It is worth noticing that the job-type discrimination is of lesser importance for the Northeast (6%), with the Frontier and the richer states of Rio and São Paulo standing on the other edge (15, 14, and 13 percent, respectively).

Table 31 presents the intra-job-type gender gaps for each type of employment as well as a summary of the decomposition of the overall difference into the intra-job-type gap (Δ_i) and the part due to differences in the gender distribution by type of employment (Δ_o). As was the case for occupational groups, the gap varies substantially among the categories of type of employment—from a minimum of 0.14 for Public Servants to a maximum of 0.79 for Informal Employees. Two facts are noteworthy: (1) there is no relation between the magnitude of the gender gap in wages and the degree of feminization for each group, as women are overrepresented both among Public Servants and Informal Employees, and (2) the intra-job-type gap tends to display an inverse relationship with the group average wages—it is small for the high-paying categories (Employers and Public Servants) and large for low-paying ones (Self-employed and Informal Employees). In both situations the behavior is just the opposite of what was found for occupational groups.

Table 32

Contribution of Each Type of Employment to the Degree of
Wage Discrimination

Region	Employers	Public Servants	Self-Employed	Employees Informal	Employees Formal
Rio de Janeiro	0.00	0.03	0.13	0.12	0.16
São Paulo	0.01	0.01	0.08	0.12	0.24
South	0.01	0.03	0.11	0.12	0.20
East	0.00	0.03	0.15	0.15	0.15
Northeast	0.00	0.06	0.25	0.17	0.09
Frontier	0.00	0.06	0.16	0.14	0.09
Average[a]	0.00	0.03	0.14	0.13	0.17
Percentage of row total	1	6	30	27	35
NE-RJ[b]	0.00	0.02	0.12	0.04	−0.07
Percentage of row total	0	20	99	35	−55

Notes: Estimates are computed first for each year and region. The figures in the table are averages across all years (unweighted) and regions (weighted).
a. Averages evaluated using women's job types as weights.
b. Difference between the Northeast and Rio.

C. The Contribution of Each Type of Employment to the Degree of Wage Discrimination

Estimates for the contribution of each type of employment, $\delta(o)$, to the degree of wage discrimination are shown in Table 32. It is transparent from the table that two out of the five groups have an almost irrelevant contribution: Employers, which account for only 1 percent of the degree of wage discrimination, and Public Servants, which are responsible for no more than 6 percent. The other three groups have contributions around 30 percent, the highest one coming from Formal Employees (35 percent). Even though the gender differences within Formal Employers, Informal Employees, and the Self-employed have similar impacts on the average degree of wage discrimination, their effects are quite distinct in regard to regional disparities, an issue that is analyzed in the next section.

D. Regional Differences in the Gender Gap in Wages

The analysis of regional differences in the gender gap in wages according to type of employment indicates that, as was the case for occupational groups, type of employment discrimination does not play an important role. As revealed by Tables 29 and 30, besides being clearly overshadowed by wage discrimination in all regions and years, the job-type discrimination reaches its lowest level in the

Northeast, the region that exhibits the largest wage differentials by gender. Hence, if one wants to develop an understanding of the factors behind regional disparities, attention should be focused on wage discrimination.

Table 33 shows the results of wage discrimination by year and region obtained by imposing Rio's intra-job-type gender gaps on all the other regions. In other words, the estimates of wage discrimination by region were standardized using the vector $\{\lambda(o):o = 1, \ldots, 5\}$ observed for Rio for each year under consideration, in an attempt to assess the importance of gender differences in the job-type structure vis-à-vis intra-job-type wage gaps for understanding regional disparities.

The results show that differences in the vector $\{\lambda(o):o = 1, \ldots, 5\}$ are the main source of regional variation, as it is greatly reduced after the standardization, especially in the most recent years. The difference between wages in Rio and the Northeast is virtually eliminated when the job-type gaps in wages in the Northeast are equal to those prevailing in Rio.

In spite of offering indisputable evidence of the relevance of intra-job-type gaps in wages in explaining regional variation, the previous exercise does not provide any insight into the type(s) of employment most responsible for such disparities. The last two rows of Table 32 constitute a first step in this direction. The difference in wage discrimination between Rio and the Northeast is calculated as if there were no wage differences by gender within the job-type group under question. This new difference is then compared to the original one (0.12, as shown in Table 29). It is shown that the main cause of the differences between Rio and the Northeast are the differences associated with the class of Self-employed workers: when the contribution of this category to the overall gap is eliminated, the divergence between the two regions is eliminated, and the wage discrimination in the Northeast drops below the average!

VIII. Gender Differences in Educational Attainment by Type of Employment and the Degree of Wage Discrimination

Table 34 reports the difference between the average number of completed years of schooling for men and women in each type of employment (see Table 8 for reference), as well as the overall wage discrimination and the "proper" wage discrimination evaluated via the simplified approach of assuming different returns to schooling, b, outlined in section VI(b). It shows that women are better educated than men (by one year of schooling, on average) in the highest-paying job type, Employers, a group where they are underrepresented. They are also better educated in the intermediate-ranked groups, Public Servants and Formal Employees, particularly in the former, where their advantage over men reaches 2.4 years of schooling. Concerning the lowest-ranked categories in terms of wages, Self-employed and Informal Employees, the picture is reversed, and women are less educated there by 0.2 and 0.8 years of schooling, respectively. Using the women's distribution according to type of employment as weights it was found that the intra-job-type educational gender gap is equal to 0.7 years of

Table 33
Wage Discrimination with Standardized Intra-Job-Type Gender Gaps: Brazil, 1981–1989

Region	1981	1982	1983	1984	1985	1986	1987	1988	1989	Average[a]
Rio de Janeiro	0.46	0.47	0.45	0.41	0.45	0.44	0.47	0.41	0.39	0.44
São Paulo	0.46	0.46	0.44	0.41	0.42	0.41	0.47	0.39	0.37	0.43
South	0.42	0.44	0.42	0.39	0.42	0.40	0.46	0.39	0.37	0.41
East	0.45	0.47	0.43	0.40	0.43	0.41	0.43	0.39	0.37	0.42
Northeast	0.49	0.51	0.46	0.42	0.45	0.45	0.40	0.42	0.39	0.44
Frontier	0.47	0.48	0.44	0.41	0.43	0.41	0.44	0.41	0.38	0.43
Average[b]	0.46	0.47	0.44	0.41	0.43	0.42	0.45	0.40	0.38	0.43
Range	0.07	0.07	0.03	0.03	0.03	0.04	0.08	0.03	0.02	0.03

a. Unweighted average.
b. Weighted average with the weights being time-invariant. The weights are given by the average distributions of the labor force across regions as shown in Table 4.

Table 34

Intra-Job-Type Gender Gap in Education

Group	Educational Gap	Overall Wage Discrimination	Proper Wage Discrimination[b]	
			$b = 0.1$	$b = 0.2$
Employers	−1.0	0.23	0.33	0.43
Public servants	−2.4	0.14	0.38	0.61
Formal employees	−0.9	0.42	0.51	0.59
Self-employed	0.2	0.68	0.66	0.63
Informal employees	0.8	0.79	0.71	0.64
Average[a]	−0.7	0.48	0.54	0.61
Overall	−0.6	0.54	0.54	0.54
Range	3.3	0.65	0.38	0.21

Note: Estimates are computed first for each year and region. The figures in the table are averages by gender across all regions (weighted) and years (unweighted).
a. Average taken using women's job type as weights.
b. Assuming different rates of return on schooling.

schooling in favor of women. This is an indication that differences in educational attainment cannot be viewed as an explanation for the intra-job-type gender gaps in wages. In fact, wage discrimination is higher when differences in education are taken into account: it goes up from 0.48 to 0.54 for $b = 0.1$, and to 0.61 for $b = 0.2$. It follows that the apparent wage discrimination is equal to −0.06 with the first hypothesis, and −0.13 with the second.

It is interesting to note that, contrary to what happened with occupational groups, there are no great changes in the rank of the intra-job-type wage gaps according to type of employment after differences in average schooling at group level are accounted for (the only exception being Public Servants). However, the decrease in the dispersion of these gaps is remarkable: the standard deviation falls from 0.22 to 0.03 when educational differences by gender are accounted for, as shown in Table 35. A quick look at this table makes it easy to understand the reasons for such a significant decrease: the proper wage discrimination is bigger than the crude wage gaps (reflecting the fact that women are better educated than men) exactly in those groups that display the lowest gaps, and it is lower than the overall gap in the groups where the gender differences in wages are the highest, Self-employed and Informal Workers. Thus, accounting for differences in education moves all the groups toward the mean and reduces the standard deviation.

Using the more general approach to estimating the degree of "proper" wage discrimination, it is possible to arrive at a better estimate of the effect of intra-job-type gender differences in age and education on the intra-job-type gender gap in wages. The results of this exercise for the case of type of employment are shown in Tables 36, 37, and 38. From these tables one can see that the contribution of differences in education and age in explaining the gender gap in wages is highly negative. In other words, had women the same educational level and age as men, the intra-job-type wage differential would be 0.09 higher than it actually is: it goes from 0.48 to 0.57, an increase of around 20 percent! It should be noticed that this increase takes place among Employers, Public Servants, and Formal Employees, that is, in the highest paying and most educated categories.

It is worth noting that accounting for differences in education and age profiles ends up widening the regional disparities in wage discrimination. The difference between the highest degree of wage discrimination (Northeast) and the lowest degree (Rio) goes up from 0.12 (Table 29) to 0.21 (Table 36), merely reflecting the fact that differences in age and education are more important for the Northeast, where the apparent discrimination averages -0.14, than for Rio (-0.05) (see Table 37).

IX. Final Remarks

From this study it can be concluded that the gender gap in wages in metropolitan Brazil is substantial, reaching values of around 70 percent. There has been a slow trend toward diminishing this gap: from 1981 to 1989 the reduction was equivalent to 5 percentage points. Given the extremely high differences, one can safely say that this improvement is rather modest.

From a regional perspective, there are clear indications that the gender gap in wages in urban areas is systematically higher in the Northeast, where it was 90 percent in 1981, dropping to 80 percent in 1989. At the same time, the gap in Rio de Janeiro dropped from 70 percent in 1981 to 55 percent in 1989. São Paulo, the largest center in Brazil, also displayed a decrease of 10 percentage points in the period, with differentials widening between those of Northeast and Rio de Ja-

Table 35
Intra-Job-Type Gender Gaps in Wages (by Type of Employment)

Group	Overall Wage Gap	Proper Wage Discrimination (b = 0.2)
Employers	0.23 (4)	0.43 (5)
Public servants	0.14 (5)	0.61 (3)
Formal employees	0.42 (3)	0.59 (4)
Self-employed	0.68 (2)	0.63 (2)
Informal employees	0.79 (1)	0.64 (1)
STD	0.22	0.03

Note: Numbers in parentheses are column ranks.

Table 36

Degree of "Proper" Wage Discrimination (Δ_d): Brazil, 1981–1989

Region	1981	1982	1983	1984	1985	1986	1987	1988	1989	Average[a]
Rio de Janeiro	0.53	0.51	0.49	0.47	0.50	0.48	0.50	0.47	0.45	0.49
São Paulo	0.54	0.51	0.53	0.53	0.54	0.51	0.48	0.52	0.49	0.52
South	0.53	0.51	0.53	0.54	0.57	0.55	0.54	0.53	0.52	0.54
East	0.62	0.61	0.61	0.62	0.66	0.61	0.58	0.59	0.62	0.60
Northeast	0.74	0.72	0.68	0.72	0.75	0.68	0.68	0.67	0.70	0.70
Frontier	0.59	0.60	0.56	0.59	0.60	0.55	0.54	0.54	0.54	0.57
Average[b]	0.59	0.56	0.56	0.57	0.60	0.56	0.55	0.55	0.55	0.57
Range	0.26	0.21	0.19	0.25	0.25	0.20	0.20	0.20	0.25	0.21

a. Unweighted average.
b. Weighted average with the weights being time-invariant. The weights are given by the average distributions of the labor force across regions as shown in Table 4.

Table 37
Degree of Apparent Wage Discrimination (Δ_e): Brazil, 1981–1989

Region	1981	1982	1983	1984	1985	1986	1987	1988	1989	Average[a]
Rio de Janeiro	−0.07	−0.04	−0.04	−0.06	−0.05	−0.04	−0.03	−0.06	−0.06	−0.05
São Paulo	−0.05	−0.04	−0.04	−0.04	−0.06	−0.04	−0.04	−0.06	−0.05	−0.05
South	−0.09	−0.10	−0.08	−0.07	−0.07	−0.07	−0.07	−0.07	−0.07	−0.08
East	−0.12	−0.08	−0.12	−0.14	−0.13	−0.12	−0.12	−0.13	−0.12	−0.11
Northeast	−0.07	−0.12	−0.09	−0.13	−0.15	−0.15	−0.21	−0.14	−0.16	−0.14
Frontier	−0.08	−0.24	−0.07	−0.10	−0.10	−0.07	−0.08	−0.10	−0.08	−0.09
Average[b]	−0.09	−0.07	−0.07	−0.08	−0.09	−0.08	−0.09	−0.09	−0.09	−0.09
Range	−0.07	0.20	0.08	0.10	0.10	0.11	0.17	0.08	0.07	0.09

a. Unweighted average.
b. Weighted average with the weights being time-invariant. The weights are given by the average distributions of the labor force across regions as shown in Table 4.

Table 38

Decomposition of the Wage Discrimination by Type of Employment

Group	Wage Discrimination	"Proper" Wage Discrimination	Apparent Discrimination
Employers	0.23	−0.07	0.30
Public servants	0.14	−0.29	0.44
Formal employees	0.42	−0.10	0.52
Self-employed	0.68	0.03	0.65
Informal employees	0.79	0.08	0.70
Averages	0.48	−0.09	0.57
STD	0.22		

Note: These averages are computed first for each year and region. The figures in the table are weighted averages across all years (unweighted) and regions (weighted).

neiro. The gap remained essentially unchanged in the East and in the Frontier: close to 70 percent. The South is the only region where the earnings of men increased relative to those of women: from a gap equal to 60 percent in 1981, the smallest for the entire country, there was an increase to 66 percent in 1989, a level similar to that of São Paulo and above that of Rio de Janeiro.

The results of the decomposition regarding groups of occupations revealed that, in general, the differences in earnings between men and women cannot be attributed to differences in the access to good (high-paying) occupations. As a matter of fact, women are overrepresented in these occupations, and, accordingly, the contribution of differences in the occupational structure to the overall gender gap in wages is negative! On the other hand, differences in educational attainment by gender, as well as in the respective age profiles, seem to affect earnings differentials only marginally: an equalization of education and age distribution across gender and occupations would reduce the overall gap in wages by just 5 percentage points.

The combination of these two findings leads to a striking conclusion: if one takes into account gender differences in the occupational structure, educational attainment, and age distribution, the wage gap between genders increases. In other words, the discrimination by gender, as far as wages go, is even more pronounced than what one would find through a simple comparison between male and female wages.

Regarding the decomposition according to type of employment, the results are also surprising. In this case, over 10 percent of the gender gap in wages can be related to the differences in the type of employment by gender. The contribution of education and age, however, works in an offsetting way, as the contribution of these attributes to the explanation of the wage gap is negative and significant (around 15 percent). As in the previous case, the results seem to indicate that the effective degree of discrimination is even higher than what one would find by simply comparing average earnings of men and women.

References

Acton, J. 1975. "Nonmonetary Factors in the Demand for Medical Services: Some Empirical Evidence." *Journal of Political Economy* 83(3):595–614.

Aigner, D. J., and G. G. Cain. 1977. "Statistical Theories of Discrimination in the Labor Market." *Industrial and Labor Relations Review* 30(2):175–87.

Ainsworth, M., and J. Muñoz. 1986. "The Côte d'Ivoire Living Standards Survey." Living Standard Measurement Study Working Paper no. 26. World Bank, Washington, D.C.

Akin, J., C. Griffin, D. Guilkey, and B. Popkin. 1986. "The Demand for Primary Health Care Services in the Bicol Region of the Philippines." *Economic Development and Cultural Change* 34(4):755–82.

Alessie, R., P. Baker, R. Blundell, C. Heady, and C. Meghir. 1992. "The Working Behavior of Young People in Rural Côte d'Ivoire." *World Bank Economic Review* 6(1):139–54.

Almeida dos Reis, J. G., and R. Barros. 1991. "Wage Inequality and the Distribution of Education." *Journal of Development Economics* 36(1):117–43.

Alschuler, L. R. 1988. *Multinational and Maldevelopment, Alternative Development Strategies in Argentina, the Ivory Coast and Korea.* New York: St. Martin's Press.

Altonji, J., F. Hayashi, and L. Kotlikoff. 1992. "Is the Extended Family Altruistically Linked? Direct Tests Using Micro Data." *American Economic Review* 82(4):1177–98.

Amemiya, T. 1981. "Qualitative Response Models: A Survey." *Journal of Economic Literature* 19(4):1483–1536.

———. 1984. "Tobit Models: A Survey." *Journal of Econometrics* 24(1/2):3–61.

Anderson, K., and R. Burkhauser. 1984. "The Importance of the Measure of Health in Empirical Estimates of the Labor Supply of Older Men." *Economics Letters* 16(4):375–80.

———. 1985. "The Retirement-Health Nexus: A New Measure of an Old Puzzle." *Journal of Human Resources* 20(3):315–30.

Andrews, G., A. Esterman, A. Braunack-Mayer, and C. Rungie. 1986. *Aging in the Western Pacific.* World Health Organization Regional Office for the Western Pacific, Manila.

Angrist, J., and A. Krueger. 1991a. "Does Compulsory Schooling Affect Schooling and Earnings?" *Quarterly Journal of Economics* 106(4):979–1014.

———. 1991b. "Estimating the Payoff to Schooling Using the Vietnam-Era Draft Lottery." Industrial Relations Section, Princeton University. Processed.

Antoine, P., and J. Nanitelamie. 1990. "La montée du célibat féminin dans les villes Africaines, trois cas: Abidjan, Brazzaville et Pikine." *Dossiers du CEPED* no. 12. Paris.

Arispe, L. 1977. "Women in the Informal Labor Sector: The Case of Mexico City." *Signs* 3(1):25–37.

Arrow, K. J. 1972. "Some Mathematical Models of Racial Discrimination in the Labor Market." Pp. 83–102 in *Racial Discrimination in Economic Life,* ed. Anthony H. Pascal. Lexington, Mass.: Heath.

Barclay, G. W. 1954. *Colonial Development and Population in Taiwan.* Princeton: Princeton University Press.

Barnum, H., and J. Kutzin. 1993. *Public Hospitals in Developing Countries: Resource Use, Cost.* Baltimore: Johns Hopkins University Press.

Barro, R., and J.-W. Lee. 1993. "International Comparisons of Educational Attainment." National Bureau of Economic Research Working Paper no. 4349. Cambridge, Mass.

Barros, R., and L. Fox. 1990. "Female Headed Households, Poverty and the Welfare of Children in Urban Brazil." World Bank, Washington, D.C. Processed (December).

Barros, R., L. Fox, and R. Mendonça. 1992. "Poverty among Female-Headed Households in Brazil." Paper presented at Conference on Women's Human Capital and Development, Bellagio, Italy (May). This book.

Barros, R. and R. Mendonça. 1990a. "Taxa de Participacão no Mercado de Trabalho e Frequência à Escola de Crianças e Adolecentes no Brasil." IPEA, Rio de Janeiro. Processed.

————. 1990b. "Determinantes da participação de menores na força de trabalho." Discussion Paper No. 200. IPEA, Rio de Janeiro (November).

————. 1991. Infãncia e adolescência no Brasil: as consequências de pobreza diferenciadas por gênero, faixa etária e região de reisdência. *Pesquisa e Planejamento Econômico* 21(2):355–76.

————. 1992. "A Research Note on Family and Income Distribution: The Equalizing Impact of Married Women's Earnings in Metropolitan Brazil." *Sociological Inquiry* 62(2):208–19.

Barros, R., and L. Ramos. 1992. *A Note on the Temporal Evolution of the Relationship between Wages and Education among Brazilian Prime-Age Males: 1976–1989.* Seminar on Labor Market Roots of Poverty and Inequality in Brazil. Rio de Janeiro.

Barros, R., L. Ramos, and E. Santos. 1992. "Gender Differences in Brazilian Labor Markets. Paper presented at Conference on Women's Human Capital and Development, Bellagio, Italy (May). This book.

Bassett, T. 1991. "Migration et féminization en l'agriculture dan le nord de la Côte d'Ivoire." Pp. 219–45 in *Les Spectres de Malthus*, ed. F. Gendreau et al. Paris: EDI.

Basta, S. S., M. S. Soekirman, D. Karyadi, and N. S. Scrimshaw. 1979. "Iron Deficiency Anemia and the Productivity of Adult Males in Indonesia." *American Journal of Clinical Nutrition* 35(1):127–34.

Beaudry, P., N. K. Sowa. 1990. "Labour Markets in an Era of Adjustment: A Case Study of Ghana." University of Montreal and University of Ghana. Processed.

Becker, G. S. 1964. *Human Capital.* New York: Columbia University Press.

————. 1965. "A Theory of the Allocation of Time." *Economic Journal* 70:493–517.

————. 1974a. "A Theory of Marriage." Pp. 299–344 in *Economics of the Family, Marriage and Children*, ed. T. W. Schultz. Chicago: University of Chicago Press.

————. 1974b. "A Theory of Social Interactions." *Journal of Political Economy* 82(6):1063–93.

————. 1981. *A Treatise on the Family.* Cambridge: Harvard University Press.

Becker, G. S., and H. Gregg Lewis. 1973. "On the Interaction between the Quantity and Quality of Children." *Journal of Political Economy* 82(2, Part 2):S279–88.

Becker, G. S., and N. Tomes. 1976. "Child Endowments and the Quality and Quantity of Children." *Journal of Political Economy* 84(4, Part 2):159–79.

————. 1979. "An Equilibrium Theory of the Distribution of Income and Intergenerational Mobility." *Journal of Political Economy* 87(6):1153–89.

Beets, G. 1991. "Wordt Zweden Traditioneler?" (Is Sweden Turning More Traditional?) *Demos* 7(4):28–39.

Behrman, J. R. 1988a. "Intrahousehold Allocation of Nutrients in Rural India: Are Boys Favored? Do Parents Exhibit Inequality Aversion?" *Oxford Economic Papers* 40(1):32–54.

———. 1988b. "Nutrition, Health, Birth Order and Seasonality: Intrahousehold Allocation among Children in Rural India." *Journal of Development Economics* 28(1):43–62.

Behrman, J. R., and A. B. Deolalikar. 1987. "Interhousehold Transfers in Rural India: Altruism or Exchange?" University of Pennsylvania, Philadelphia. Processed.

———. 1990a. "The Intrahousehold Demand for Nutrients in Rural South India: Individual Estimates, Fixed Effects and Permanent Income." *Journal of Human Resources* 25(4):665–96.

———. 1990b. "Are there Differential Returns to Schooling by Gender? The Case of Indonesian Labor Markets." University of Pennsylvania, Phildelphia. Processed.

———. 1991. "Are Households Averse to Inequality of Market Labor Supply among Their Members? Econometric Estimates for Rural South India." University of Washington, Seattle. Processed.

Behrman, J. R., and P. Taubman. 1986. "Birth Order, Schooling, and Earnings." *Journal of Labor Economics* 4(3, Part 2)S121–45. See also comment in same issue by Z. Griliches, 4(3):S146–50.

Behrman, J. R., and B. Wolfe. 1989. "Does More Schooling Make Women Better Nourished and Healthier? Adult Sibling Random and Fixed Effects Estimates for Nicaragua." *Journal of Human Resources* 24(4):644–63.

———. 1990. "Earnings and Labor Force Participation Functions in a Developing Country: Are There Sexual Differentials?" Pp. 95–119 in *Labor Market Discrimination in Developing Economies,* ed. N. Birdsall and R. Sabot. Washington, D.C.: World Bank.

Benham, L. 1974. "Benefits of Women's Education within Marriage." Pp. 375–89 in *Economics of the Family, Marriage and Children,* ed. T. W. Schultz. Chicago: University of Chicago Press.

Benie, M. K. 1989. "Wage Policy in Côte d'Ivoire." Pp. 3–13 in *Government Wage Policy Formulation in Developing Countries: Seven Country Studies.* International Labour Office, Geneva.

Ben-Porath, Y. 1986. "Self Employment and Wage Earners in Israel." In *Studies in the Population of Israel,* vol. 30, ed. U. O. Schmelz and G. Nathan. Jerusalem: Hebrew University, Magnes Press.

Bernheim, D., A. Scheiffer, and L. Summers. 1985. "The Strategic Bequest Motive." *Journal of Political Economy* 93(6):901–18.

Bielicki, T. 1986. "Physical Growth as a Measure of the Economic Well-Being of Populations: The Twentieth Century." Pp. 283–305 in *Human Growth,* vol. 3, ed. F. Falkner and J. M. Tanner. New York: Plenum Press.

Binswanger, H. P., S. Khandker, and M. R. Rosenzweig. 1993. "How Infrastructure and Financial Institutions Affect Agricultural Output and Investment in India." *Journal of Development Economics* 41:337–66.

Binswanger, H. P., and M. R. Rosenzweig. 1986. "Behavioral and Material Determinants of Production Relations in Agriculture." *Journal of Development Studies* 21(2):503–39.

Birdsall, N. 1991. "Birth Order Effects and Time Allocation." Pp. 191–214 in

Research in Population Economics, vol. 7, ed. T. P. Schultz. Greenwich, Conn.: JAI Press.

Birdsall, N., and J. R. Behrman. 1990. "Why Do Women Earn Less than Men in Urban Brazil? Earnings Discrimination? Job Discrimination?" Pp. 147–69 in *Labor Market Discrimination in Developing Economies,* ed. N. Birdsall and R. Sabot. World Bank, Washington, D.C.

Bitran, R. 1991. "Health Care Demand in Developing Countries: A Model of Household and a Market Simulation Model of Health Care Financing." Ph.D. dissertation. Department of Economics, Boston University.

Bitran, R., M. Mpese, S. Bavugabgose, M. Kasonga, N. Nsuka, T. Vian, and K. Wambenge. 1986. "Zaire Health Zones." Resources for Child Health, USAID, Arlington, Va. Processed.

Blake, J. 1989. *Family Size and Achievement.* Berkeley: University of California Press.

Blau, D. 1985. "Self-Employment and Self-Selection in Developing Country Labor Markets." *Southern Economic Journal* 52(2):351–63.

Blau, P. M., and O. D. Duncan. 1967. *The American Occupational Structure.* New York: Wiley.

Bodnar, J. 1982. *Worker's World: Kinship, Community, and Protest in an Industrial Society, 1900–1940.* Baltimore: Johns Hopkins University Press.

Boggild, L. 1983. "The Influence of Socialization and Formal Education on the Position of Turkish Women." In *Women in Islamic Societies: Social Attitudes and Historical Perspectives,* ed. B. Utas. London: Curson Press.

Bohman, K. 1984. *Women of the Barrio: Class and Gender in a Colombian City,* Stockholm Studies in Social Anthropology. University of Stockholm.

Borjas, G. J., and S. G. Bronars. 1989. "Consumer Discrimination and Self-Employment." *Journal of Political Economy* 97(3):581–605.

Boserup, E. 1970. *Women's Role in Economic Development.* New York: St. Martin's Press.

———. 1990a [1975]. "Women in the Labour Market." Pp. 154–60 in *Economic and Demographic Relationships in Development,* ed. T. Paul Schultz. Baltimore: Johns Hopkins University Press.

———. 1990b. "Economic Change and the Roles of Women." Pp. 133–43 in *Economic and Demographic Relationships in Development,* ed. T. Paul Schultz. Baltimore: Johns Hopkins University Press.

Boskin, M. 1974. "A Conditional Logit Model of Occupational Choice." *Journal of Political Economy* 82(2, Part 1):389–98.

Bouis, H. E., and L. J. Haddad. 1990. *Agricultural Commercialization, Nutrition, and the Rural Poor: A Study of Philippine Farm Households.* Boulder: Lynne Rienner Publishers.

Bound, J. 1991. "Self-Reported Objective Measures of Health in Retirement Models." *Journal of Human Resources* 26(1):106–38.

Bowen, W. G., and T. A. Finegan. 1969. *The Economics of Labor Force Participation.* Princeton: Princeton University Press.

Breckinridge, S. 1933. *Women in the Twentieth Century.* New York: McGraw-Hill.

Brinton, M. 1988. "The Social-Institutional Bases of Gender Stratification: Japan as an Illustrative Case." *American Journal of Sociology* 94(2):300–334.

Brown, R. S., M. Moon, and B. S. Zoloth. 1980. "Incorporating Occupational Attainment in Studies of Male-Female Earnings Differentials." *The Journal of Human Resources* 15(1):3–28.

Browning, M., A. Deaton, and M. Irish. 1985. "A Profitable Approach to Labor

Supply and Commodity Demands over the Life-Cycle." *Econometrica* 53(3):503–44.

Bustillo, Ines. 1993. "Latin America and the Caribbean." Pp. 175–210 in *Women's Education in Developing Countries: Barriers, Benefits, and Policies*, ed. E. M. King and M. A. Hill. Baltimore: Johns Hopkins University Press.

Caldwell, J. C. 1976. *The Socio-Economic Explanation of High Fertility: Papers on the Yoruba Society of Nigeria*. Changing African Family Project Series. Department of Demography, Australian National University, Canberra.

Caldwell, J. C., I. O. Orubuloye, and P. Caldwell. 1991. "The Destabilization of the Traditional Yoruba Sexual System." *Population and Development Review* 17(2):229–62.

Caldwell, J. C., P. H. Reddy, and P. Caldwell. 1986. "Periodic High Risk as a Cause of Fertility Decline in a Changing Rural Environment: Survival Strategies in the 1980–83 South Indian Drought." *Economic Development and Cultural Change* 34(4):677–701.

Calsing, E. F., and B. V. Schmidt. 1986. "Situação Sócio-Econômica e Demográfica dos Menores no Brasil e no Nordeste." Pp. 15–121 in *O Menor e a Pobreza*. Brasília: IPLAN/IPEA/UNICEF.

Campbell, B. 1978. "Ivory Coast." Pp. 66–116 in *West African States: Failure and Promise, A Study in Comparative Politics*, ed. John Dunn. Cambridge: Cambridge University Press.

Card, D., and A. B. Krueger. 1992. Does School Quality Matter?" *Journal of Political Economy* 100(1):1–40.

Carney, J., and M. Watts. 1991. "Disciplining Women? Rice Mechanization and the Evolution of Mandinke Gender Relations in Senegambia." *Signs* 16(4):651–81.

Castro, E., and K. Mokate. 1988. "Malaria and Its Socioeconomic Meanings: The Study of Cunday in Colombia." In *Economics, Health and Tropical Disease*, ed. A. Herrin and P. Rosenfield. Manila: University of the Philippines, School of Economics.

Catsiapis, G., and C. Robinson. 1982. "Sample Selection Bias with Multiple Selection Rules." *Journal of Econometrics* 18(3):351–68.

Chamberlain, G. 1980. "Analysis of Covariance with Qualitative Data." *Review of Economic Studies* 47(4):225–38.

———. 1984. Panel Data. Pp. 1247–1318 in *Handbook of Econometrics*, vol. 2, ed. Z. Griliches and M. Intrilligator. Amsterdam: North-Holland.

Chen, C. 1992. "Living Apart from Children in Later Life—The Case of Taiwan." Paper prepared for Conference on Family Formation and Dissolution: East and West Perspectives, Academica Sinica, Taipei, Taiwan, May 21–23.

Chen, L., E. Huq, and S. D'Souza. 1981. "Sex Bias in the Family Allocation of Food and Health Care in Rural Bangladesh." *Population and Development Review* 7(1):55–70.

Chiappori, D. A. 1988a. "Rational Household Labor Supply." *Econometrica* 56(1):63–89.

———. 1988b. "Nash-Bargained Household Decisions." *International Economic Review* 29(4):791–96.

Chipande, G. 1988. "The Impact of Demographic Changes on Rural Development in Malawi." Pp. 162–74 in *Population, Food and Rural Development*, ed. R. D. Lee, W. B. Arthur, A. C. Kelley, G. Rodgers, and T. N. Srinivasan. London: Clarendon Press.

Chiswick, C. U. 1979. "The Determinants of Earnings in Thailand." *Research Project No. 671-36*. World Bank, Washington, D.C.

Choi, K. S. 1991. "Changes in Wage Profiles in Korea During the 1980s." Yale University. Processed.

Christianson, J. B. 1976. "Evaluating Location for Outpatient Medical Care Facilities." *Land Economics* (University of Wisconsin) 52(3):298–313.

Cigno, A. 1991. *Economics of the Family.* Oxford: Oxford University Press.

Clignet, R., and P. Foster. 1971. "Convergence and Divergence in Educational Development in Ghana and the Ivory Coast." Pp. 265–91 in *Ghana and The Ivory Coast, Perspectives on Modernization,* ed. P. Foster and A. R. Zolberg. Chicago: University of Chicago Press.

Coate, S., and M. Ravallion. 1993. "Reciprocity without Commitment: Characterization and Performance of Informal Insurance Arrangements." *Journal of Development Economics* 40(1):1–24.

Cochrane, S. H., J. Leslie, and D. J. O'Hara. 1980. "The Effects of Education on Health." World Bank Staff Working Paper No. 405. World Bank, Washington, D.C.

Cohen, M. 1974. *Urban Policy and Political Conflict in Africa: A Study of the Ivory Coast.* Chicago: University of Chicago Press.

Coltrane, S. 1990. "Birth Timing and the Division of Labor in Dual-Earner Families: Exploratory Findings and Suggestions for Future Research." *Journal of Family Issues* (University of California, Riverside) (June): 157–81.

Cornia, G. A. 1984a. "A Summary and Interpretation of the Evidence." *World Development* (UNICEF) 12(3):381–91.

————. 1984b "A Survey of Cross-Sectional and Time-Series Literature on Factors Affecting Child Welfare." *World Development* (UNICEF) 12(3):187–202.

Costa, D. 1993. "Height, Weight, Wartime Stress and Old Age Mortality: Evidence from the Union Army Records." *Explorations in Economic History* 30(4):424–29.

Cox, D. 1987. "Motives for Private Income Transfers." *Journal of Political Economy* 95(3):508–46.

————. 1990. "Intergenerational Transfers and Liquidity Constraints." *Quarterly Journal of Economics* 105(1):187–218.

Cox, D., and E. Jiminez. 1989. "Private Transfers and Public Policy in Developing Countries: A Case Study for Peru." Working Paper WPS 345. Country Economics Department, World Bank, Washington, D.C. (December).

Creese, A. 1991. "User Fees for Health Care: A Review of Recent Experience." *Health Policy and Planning* 6(4):309–19.

Dasgupta, M. 1987. "Selective Discrimination againt Female Children in Rural Punjab, India." *Population and Development Review* 13(1):77–100.

Deaton, A. 1989. "Looking for Boy-Girl Discrimination in Household Expenditure Data." *World Bank Economic Review* 3(1):1–15.

Denton, H., J. Akin, D. Guilkey, R. Vogel, and A. Wouters. 1990. "Federal Republic of Nigeria: Health Care Cost, Financing and Utilization." Western Africa Department, Population, and Human Resources Operations Division. World Bank, Washington, D.C. Processed.

Den Tuinder, B. A. 1978. *Ivory Coast, the Challenge of Success.* Baltimore: Johns Hopkins University Press.

Deolalikar, A. 1988. "Nutrition and Labor Productivity in Agriculture: Estimates for Rural South India." *Review of Economics and Statistics* 70(3):406–13.

————. 1991. "Intrahousehold Allocation of Health Inputs and Distribution of Health Outcomes among Indonesian Children." Tenth Anniversary Publication of the Robert S. McNamara Fellowships Program. World Bank, Washington, D.C.

————. 1993. "Gender Differences in the Returns to Schooling and in School Enrollment Rates in Indonesia." *Journal of Human Resources* 28(4):899–932. This book.

Desai, S. 1991. "Children at Risk: The Role of Family Structure in Latin America and Africa." Abstract prepared for Demographic and Health Surveys World Conference, session on Determinants of Feeding Practice and Nutritional Status.

Diaz, A., and J. Stewart. 1989. "Occupational Status and Female Headed Households in Santiago Maior do Iguape, Brazil 1835." Preliminary version of a paper presented at the Social Science History Association Annual Meeting (November).

Domencich, T. D., and D. McFadden. 1975. *Urban Travel Demand.* Amsterdam: North-Holland.

Dooley, M. D. 1989. "The Demography of Child Poverty in Canada: 1973–1986." QSEP Research Report No. 251. McMaster University.

Dor, A., P. Gertler, and J. van der Gaag. 1987. "Non-Price Rationing and the Choice of Medical Provider in Rural Côte d'Ivoire." *Journal of Health Economics* 6(4):291–304.

Dougherty, C. R. S., and E. Jimenez. 1991. "The Specification of Earnings Functions: Tests and Specifications." *Economics of Education Review* 10(2):85–98.

Duraisamy, M. 1993. "Women's Choice of Work and Fertility in Urban Tamil Nadu, India." Economic Growth Center Discussion Paper No. 695. Yale University.

Durand, J. 1975. *The Labor Force in Economic Development: A Comparison of International Census Data, 1946–66.* Princeton: Princeton University Press.

Dvorak, S. 1989. "Female Headed Household in an Industrializing Society: Brazil, 1970–1980." Ph.D. dissertation. University of Wisconsin, Madison.

ECIEL. 1982. *Determinantes de la Oferta de Trabajo en America Latina.* Programa de Estudios Conjunctos sobre Integracion Economica Latinoamerica. Rio de Janeiro, Brazil.

El-Badry, M. A. 1969. "Higher Female Than Male Mortality in Some Countries of South Asia." *Journal of American Statistical Association* 64(328):1234–44.

Ellis, R. P., and G. M. Mwabu. 1991. "The Demand for Outpatient Medical Care in Rural Kenya." Department of Economics, Boston University. Processed.

Eltis, D. 1982. "Nutritional Trends in Africa and The Americas." *Journal of Interdisciplinary History* 12(4):453–75.

Epstein, A., P. Gertler, and K. Thorpe. 1990. "Medicaid Payment Mechanisms and Nursing Home Patient Health Outcomes." Rand Corporation, Santa Monica. Processed.

Ernst, C., and J. Angst. 1983. *Birth Order and Its Influence on Personality.* Berlin: Springer-Verlag.

Evans, D. S., and B. Jovanovic. 1989. "An Estimated Model of Entrepreneurial Choice under Liquidity Constraints." *Journal of Political Economy* 97(4):808–27.

Evans, D. S., and L. S. Leighton. 1989. "Some Empirical Aspects of Entrepreneurship." *American Economic Review* 79(3):519–35.

Eveleth, P. B., and J. M. Tanner. 1976. *Worldwide Variation in Human Growth.* Cambridge: Cambridge University Press.

Falkner, F., and J. M. Tanner, eds. 1986. *Human Growth: A Comprehensive Treatise,* vol. 3. 2d edition. New York: Plenum Press.

Feachem, R., T. Kjellstrom, C. Murray, M. Over, and M. Phillips. 1992. *The Health of Adults in the Developing World.* Oxford: Oxford University Press.

Fernandez, R., and D. Sawyer. 1988. "Socioeconomic and Environmental Factors Affecting Malaria in an Amazon Frontier Area." In *Economics, Health and Tropical Disease,* ed. A. Herrin and P. Rosenfield. School of Economics, University of the Philippines.

Fields, G., and T. P. Schultz. 1982. "Income Generating Functions in a Low
Income Country: Colombia." *Review of Income and Wealth* 28(1):71–87.

Fishe, R. P. H., R. P. Trost, and P. Lurie. 1981. "Selectivity Bias and Comparative
Advantage: A Generalized Approach." *Economics of Education Review*
1:169–91.

Floud, R., K. Wachter, and A. Gregory. 1990. *Height, Health and History.*
Cambridge: Cambridge University Press.

Fogel, R. W. 1986. "Growth and Economic Wellbeing: 18th and 19th Centuries."
Pp. 263–81 in *Human Growth,* vol. 3, ed. F. Falkner and J. M. Tanner. New
York: Plenum Press.

———. 1990. "The Conquest of High Mortality and Hunger in Europe and
America." NBER Working Paper No. 16. Cambridge, Mass. (September).

———. 1991. "New Sources and New Techniques for the Study of Secular Trends
in Nutritional Status, Health Mortality and the Process of Aging." NBER
Working Paper No. 26. Cambridge, Mass. (May).

———. 1993. "The Relevance of Malthus for the Study of Mortality Today."
Working Paper, University of Chicago, Department of Economics.

Folbre, N. n.d. "Mothers on Their Own: Policy Issues for Developing Countries."
New York: Population Council. Processed.

———. 1984a. "Comment on 'Market Opportunities, Genetic Endowments, and
Intrafamily Resource Distribution.'" *American Economic Review* 74(3):518–20.

———. 1984b. "Household Production in the Philippines: A Non-Neoclassical
Approach." *Economic Development and Cultural Change* 32(2):303–30.

———. 1986a. "Cleaning House: New Perspectives on Households and Economic
Development." *Journal of Development Economics* 22(1):5–40.

———. 1986b. "Hearts and Spades: Paradigms of Household Economics." *World
Development* 14(2):245–55.

———. 1991. "Women on Their Own: Global Patterns of Female Headship." Pp.
89–126 in *The Women and International Development Annual,* vol. 2, ed. R. S.
Gallin and A. Ferguson. Boulder: Westview Press.

Foster, A. D. 1988. "Why Things Fall Apart: A Strategic Analysis of Repeated
Interaction in Rural Financial Markets." University of California, Berkeley.
Processed.

Foster, A. D., and M. R. Rosenzweig. 1991. "Unequal Pay for Unequal Work:
Asymmetric Information, Sex Discrimination, and the Efficiency of Casual Labor
Markets." Manuscript.

———. 1992. "A Test for Moral Hazard in the Labor Market: Effort, Health and
Calorie Consumption." Manuscript.

———. 1993. "Information, Learning and Wage Rates in Low-Income Rural
Areas." *Journal of Human Resources* 28(4):759–90. This book.

Fox, L. 1982. "Income Distribution in Brazil: Better Numbers and New Findings."
Ph.D. dissertation. Vanderbilt University.

———. 1990. "Poverty Alleviation in Brazil, 1970–87." World Bank Staff Working
Paper No. 072. World Bank, Washington, D.C.

Franz, W. 1985, "An Economic Analysis of Female Work Participation, Education
and Fertility: Theory and Empirical Evidence in the Federal Republic of
Germany." *Journal of Labor Economics* 3:S218–34.

Friedman, G. C. 1982. "The Heights of Slaves in Trinidad." *Social Science History*
6(4):482–515.

Fuchs, V. R. 1968. *The Service Economy.* New York: Columbia University Press
for NBER.

Gannicott, K. 1986. "Women, Wages and Discrimination: Some Evidence from Taiwan." *Economic Development and Cultural Change* 39(4):721–30.

Garfinkel, I., and S. S. McLanahan. 1985. "The Feminization of Poverty: Nature, Causes and a Partial Cure." University of Wisconsin, Madison. Processed.

———. 1986. *Single Mothers and Their Children: A New American Dilemma.* Washington, D.C.: Urban Institute Press.

Gertler, P. 1988. "A Latent-Variable Model of Quality Determination." *Journal of Business and Economic Statistics* 6(1):97–104.

Gertler, P., and H. Alderman. 1989. "Family Resources and Gender Differences in Human Capital Investments." Paper presented at a conference on The Family, Gender Differences and Development. Yale University, Economic Growth Center.

Gertler, P., and P. Glewwe. 1989. "The Willingness to Pay for Education in Developing Countries: Evidence from Rural Peru." Living Standards Measurement Study Working Paper No. 54. World Bank, Washington, D.C.

Gertler, P., L. Locay, and W. Sanderson. 1987. "Are User Fees Regressive? The Welfare Implications of Health Care Financing Proposals in Peru." *Journal of Econometrics* 36(1/2):67–80.

Gertler, P., and J. van der Gaag. 1990. *The Willingness to Pay for Medical Care: Evidence from Two Developing Countries.* Baltimore: Johns Hopkins University Press.

Gill, A. M. 1988. "Choice of Employment Status and the Wages of Employees and the Self-Employed: Some Further Evidence." *Journal of Applied Econometrics* 3(3):229–34.

Gindling, T. H. 1988. "An Investigation into the Existence of Labor Market Segmentation: The Case of San Jose, Costa Rica." University of Maryland, Baltimore. Processed.

Glaeser, E. L. 1991. "Who Knows What about Whom: An Empirical Analysis of Heterogeneous Information in the Labor Market." University of Chicago. Processed.

Glewwe, P. 1990. "Schooling, Skills and the Returns to Education: An Econometric Exploration Using Data from Ghana." Welfare and Human Resources Division, Living Standards Measurement Study Working Paper No. 84. World Bank, Washington, D.C.

Goldani, A. M. 1989. "Women's Transitions: The Intersection of Female Life Course, Family and Demographic Transition in Twentieth Century Brazil." Ph.D. dissertation. University of Texas at Austin.

Goldberger, A. 1981. "Linear Regression after Selection." *Journal of Econometrics* 15(3):357–66.

Goldin, C. 1979. "Household and Market Production of Families in a Late Nineteenth Century American City." *Explorations in Economic History* 16(2):111–31.

———. 1984. "The Historical Evolution of Female Earnings Functions and Occupations." *Explorations in Economic History* 21(1):1–27.

———. 1986a. "Monitoring Costs and Occupational Segregation by Sex: A Historical Analysis." *Journal of Labor Economics* 4(1):1–27.

———. 1986b. "The Economic Status of Women in the Early Republic: Quantitative Evidence." *Journal of Interdisciplinary History* 16(2):375–404.

———. 1989. "Life-Cycle Labor Force Participation of Married Women: Historical Evidence and Implications." *Journal of Labor Economics* 7(1):20–47.

———. 1990. *Understanding the Gender Gap: An Economic History of American Women.* New York: Oxford University Press.

————. 1991. "Marriage Bars: Discrimination against Married Women Workers, 1920 to 1950." In *Favorites of Fortune: Technology, Growth, and Economic Development since the Industrial Revolution,* ed. H. Rosovsky, D. Landes, and P. Higgonet. Cambridge: Harvard University Press.

————. 1992. "The Meaning of College in the Lives of American Women: The Past One-Hundred Years." Paper presented at Conference on Women's Human Capital and Development, Bellagio, Italy (May).

————. 1994. "How America Graduated from High School: 1910 to 1960." National Bureau of Economic Research Working Paper no. 4762. Cambridge, Mass.

Goldman, N. 1993. "Marriage Selection and Mortality Patterns: Inferences and Fallacies." *Demography* 30(2):189–208.

Goreux, L. M. 1977. *Interdependence in Planning: Multilevel Programming Studies of the Ivory Coast.* Baltimore: Johns Hopkins University Press.

Greene, W. H. 1990. *Econometric Analysis.* New York: Macmillan.

Greenhalgh, S. 1985. "Sexual Stratification in East Asia: The Other Side of 'Growth with Equity' in East Asia." *Population and Development Review* 11(2):265–314.

Griliches, Z. 1969. "Capital-Skill Complementarity." *Review of Economics and Statistics* 51(4):465–68.

————. 1977. "Estimating the Returns to Schooling." *Econometrica* 45(13):1–22.

————. 1979. "Sibling Models and Data in Economics: Beginnings of a Survey." *Journal of Political Economy* 87(5, Part 2):S37–65.

Gronau, R. 1977. "Leisure, Home Production and Work: The Theory of the Allocation of Time Revisited." *Journal of Political Economy* 85(6):1099–1123.

Grossman, M. 1972. "On the Concept of Health Capital and the Demand for Health." *Journal of Political Economy* 80(2):223–55.

Gruber, J. 1991. "The Incidence of a Group-Specific Mandated Benefit: Evidence from Health Insurance Benefits for Maternity." Harvard University. Processed.

Guralnik, J., L. Branch, S. Cummings, and J. D. Curb. 1989. "Physical Performance Measures in Aging Research." *Journal of Gerontology* 44(5):M141–46.

Gustafsson, S. 1991. "Single Mothers in Sweden; Why is Poverty Less Severe? A Policy Analysis." Paper presented at the International Conference on Poverty and Public Policy. Washington, D.C. (September).

————. 1992. "Separate Taxation and Married Women's Labor Supply, A Comparison of West Germany and Sweden." *Journal of Population Economics* 5(1):61–85.

————. 1994a. "Single Mothers in Sweden: Why is Poverty Less Severe?" In *Poverty, Inequality, and the Future of Social Policy: Western States in the New World Order,* ed. K. McFate. New York: Russell Sage Foundation.

————. 1994b. "Childcare and Types of Welfare States." In *Gendering Welfare States,* ed. D. Sainsbury. London: Sage Publications.

Gustafsson, S., and M. Bruyn-Hundt. 1991. "Incentives for Women to Work: A Comparison between the Netherlands, Sweden and West Germany." *Journal of Economic Studies* 18(1):30–65.

Gustafsson, S., and R. Jacobsson. 1985. Trends in Female Labor Force Participation in Sweden. *Journal of Labor Economics* 3(1, part 1):S256–74.

Gustafsson, S., and F. Stafford. 1992. "Daycare Subsidies and Labor Supply in Sweden." *Journal of Human Resources* 27(1):204–30.

Gustafsson, S., and R. J. Willis. 1990. "Interrelations Between the Labor Market and Demographic Change." Pp. 125–44 in *Demographic Impact of Political Action,* ed. H. Birg and R. Mackensen. Documentation from the International

Conference 1986 by the German Demographic Association and the European Association for Population Studies, Campus, Frankfurt, and New York.

Haaga, J., C. Peterson, J. DaVanzo, and S. Lee. 1990. "Health Status and Family Support of Older Malaysians." Paper presented at Population Association of America Annual Meeting, 1991.

Hartmann, H. 1976. "Capitalism, Patriarchy, and Job Segregation by Sex." Pp. 137–69 in *Women and the Workplace,* ed. M. Blaxall and B. Reagan. Chicago: University of Chicago Press.

Hartog, J., and J. Theeuwes. 1985. "The Emergence of the Working Wife in Holland." *Journal of Labor Economics* 3:S235–55.

Hauser, R. M. 1989. "Review of Blake, Family Size and Achievement." *Population and Development Review* 15(1):561–67.

Hauser, R. M., and W. H. Sewell. 1985. "Birth Order and Educational Attainment in Full Sibships." *American Educational Research Journal* 22(3):1–23.

Haveman, R., and B. Wolfe. 1984. "Education and Well Being: The Role of Nonmarket Effects." *Journal of Human Resources* 19:377–407.

Heckman, J. J. 1974. "Shadow Prices, Market Wages, and Labor Supply." *Econometrica* 42(4):679–94.

———. 1976. "The Common Structure of Statistical Models of Truncation, Sample Selection, and Limited Dependent Variables and a Simple Estimator for Such Models." *Annals of Economic and Social Measurement* 5:475–92.

———. 1979. "Sample Bias as a Specification Error." *Econometrica* 47(1):153–62.

———. 1980. "Sample Selection Bias as a Specification Error." Pp. 206–48 in *Female Labor Supply: Theory and Estimation,* ed. J. P. Smith. Princeton: Princeton University Press.

———. 1987. "Selection Bias and Self Selection." Pp. 206–48 in *The New Palgrave: A Dictionary of Economics,* vol. 4, ed J. Eatwell, M. Milgate, and P. Newman. London: Macmillan.

———. 1988. "Time Constraints and Household Demand Functions." Pp. 3–14 in *Research in Population Economics,* vol. 6, ed. T. P. Schultz. Greenwich, Conn.: JAI Press.

Heckman, J. J., and G. Sedlacek. 1985. "Heterogeneity, Aggregation, and Market Wage Functions." *Journal of Political Economy* 93(6):1077–1125.

Hein, C. 1986. "The Feminisation of Industrial Employment in Mauritius: A Case of Sex Segregation." In *Sex Inequalities in Urban Employment in the Third World,* ed. R. Anker and C. Hein. New York: St. Martin's Press.

Heller, P. 1982. "A Model of the Demand for Medical and Health Services in Peninsular Malaysia." *Social Science and Medicine* 16(3):267–84.

Hermalin, A. I., J. A. Seltzer, and C. Lin. 1982. "Transitions in the Effect of Family Size on Female Educational Attainment: The Case of Taiwan." *Comparative Education Review* 26(2):254–70.

Hill, M. A. 1983. "Female Labor Force Participation in Developing and Developed Countries: Consideration of the Informal Sector." *Review of Economics and Statistics* 65(3):459–68.

Hill, M. A., and E. M. King. 1993. "Women's Education in Developing Countries: An Overview." Pp. 1–50 in *Women's Education in Developing Countries: Barriers, Benefits, and Policies,* ed. E. M. King and M. A. Hill. Baltimore: Johns Hopkins University Press.

Hill, M. A., and M. Mamdani. 1989. *Operational Guidelines for Measuring Health through Household Surveys.* Centre for Population Studies, School of Hygiene and Tropical Medicine, University of London.

Hinchliffe, K. 1974–75. "Education, Individual Earnings and Earnings Distribution." *Journal of Development Studies* 11:149–61.

Hout, M. 1988. "More Universalism, Less Structural Mobility: The American Occupational Structure in the 1980s." *American Journal of Sociology* 93(6):1358–1400.

Hu, Y., and N. Goldman. 1990. "Mortality Differentials by Marital Status: An International Comparison." *Demography* 27(2):233–49.

Huber, P. J. 1967. "The Behavior of Maximum Likelihood Estimates Under Non-Standard Conditions." Proceedings of the Fifth Berkeley Symposium on Mathematical Statistics and Probability 1(1):221–33.

Imhasly, B. 1991. "Angst vor Kolonialismus aus dem All: BBC-TV unterläuft staatliches Rundfunkmonopol in Indien." *Neue Zürcher Zeitung,* November 15.

Instituto Brasileiro de Georgrafia e Estatística (IBGE). 1987–1990. *Indicadores Sociais: Crianças e Adolescentes,* vols. 1–4. Rio de Janeiro.

International Center for Research on Women (ICRW). 1988. "Women-Headed Households: Issues for Discussion." Paper prepared for joint Population Council/ International Center for Research on Women.

International Labour Office. 1986. *Economically Active Population—Estimates, 1950–1980, Projections, 1985–2025.* 6 vols. ILO, Geneva.

Jain, B. 1991. "Returns to Education: Further Analysis of Cross Country Data." *Economics of Education Review* 10(3):253–58.

Jamison, D. T., and L. T. Lau. 1982. *Farmer Education and Farm Efficiency.* Baltimore: Johns Hopkins University Press.

John, A. M. 1984. "The Demography of Slavery in 19th Century Trinidad." Ph.D. dissertation. Princeton University.

Jolly, R., and G. A. Cornia. 1984. "Editor's Introduction." *World Development* 12(3):171–76.

Jorgenson, D. W., F. M. Gollop, and B. M. Fraumeni. 1987. *Productivity and U.S. Economic Growth.* Cambridge: Harvard University Press.

Ju, A., and G. Jones. 1989. *Aging in ASEAN and its Socio-Economic Consequences.* Institute of Southeast Asian Studies, Singapore.

Khandker, S. R. 1989. "Returns to Schooling and Male-Female Wage Differences in Peru." Paper presented at a Conference on the Family, Gender Differences and Development. Yale University (September).

———. 1990. "Labor Market Participation, Returns to Education, and Male-Female Wage Differences in Peru." World Bank, Washington, D.C. Processed.

Killingsworth, M. R., and J. J. Heckman. 1986. "Female Labor Supply: A Survey." Pp. 103–204 in *Handbook of Labor Economics,* vol. 1, ed. O. Ashenfelter and R. Layard. Amsterdam: North-Holland.

King, E. M., and R. Bellew. 1990. "Gains in the Education of Peruvian Women, 1940 to 1980," Working Paper No. 472, Population and Human Resources Department, World Bank, Washington, D.C.

King, E. M., and M. A. Hill, eds. 1993. *Women's Education in Developing Countries: Barriers, Benefits, and Policies.* Baltimore: Johns Hopkins University Press.

King, E. M., and L. A. Lillard. 1987. "Education Policy and Schooling Attainment in Malaysia and the Philippines." *Economics of Education Review* 6(2):167–81.

King, E. M., L. A. Lillard, and D. De Tray. 1985. "Gender and Ethnic Differences in Schooling Levels in Malaysia." Santa Monica, Rand Corporation. Processed.

Kinsella, K. 1988. *Aging in the Third World.* U.S. Bureau of the Census, International Population Reports Series P-95, No. 79. Washington, D.C.

Knight, J. B., and R. H. Sabot. 1987. "The Rate of Return on Educational Expansion." *Economics of Education Review* 6(3):255–62.

Korenman, S., and D. Neumark. 1991. "Does Marriage Really Make Men More Productive?" *Journal of Human Resources* 26(2):282–307.

———. 1992. "Marriage, Motherhood and Wages." *Journal of Human Resources* 27(2):233–55.

Kossoudji, S., and E. Mueller. 1983. "The Economic and Demographic Status of Female-Headed Households in Rural Botswana." *Economic Development and Cultural Change* 31(4):831–59.

Kozel, V. 1990. "The Composition and Distribution of Income in Côte d'Ivoire." Welfare and Human Resources Division. Living Standards Measurement Study Working Paper No. 68. World Bank, Washington, D.C.

Kung, L. 1983. *Factory Women in Taiwan.* Ann Arbor: UMI Research Press.

Kuznets, S., and D. S. Thomas. 1957. "Introduction." Pp. 1–7 in *Population Distribution and Economic Growth, United States, 1870–1950,* vol. 1, ed. E. S. Lee, A. R. Miller, C. P. Brainerd, and R. A. Easterlin. Philadelphia: American Philosophical Society.

Lam, D., and D. Levison. 1992. "Declining Inequality in Schooling in Brazil and Its Effect on Inequality in Earning." *Journal of Development Economics* 37(1/2):199–225.

Lam, D., and R. F. Schoeni. 1993. "Effects of Family Background on Earnings and Returns to Schooling in Brazil." *Journal of Political Economy* 101(4):710–40.

Lavy, V. 1992. "Supply Constraints and Investment in Human Capital: Schooling in Rural Ghana." Department of Population and Human Resources. World Bank, Washington, D.C.

Lavy, V., and J. M. Quigley. 1991. "On the Economics of Medical Care: The Choice of Quality and Intensity of Medical Care in Ghana." World Bank, Washington, D.C. Processed.

———. 1993. "Willingness to Pay for the Quality and Intensity of Medical Care: Low-Income Households in Ghana." Living Standards Measurement Study, Working Paper no. 94. World Bank, Washington, D.C.

Lavy, V., J. Strauss, D. Thomas, and P. de Vreyer. 1992. "Quality of Health Care and Survival and Health Outcomes in Ghana." World Bank, Human Resources Department, Poverty Analysis Division. Processed.

Law and the Status of Women. 1977. *Columbia Human Rights Review* 8(1).

Layard, R., and J. Mincer, eds. 1985. "Trends in Women's Work, Education and Family Building." *Journal of Labor Economics* 3(1, part 1) (January supplement).

Layard, P. R. G., and A. A. Walters. 1978. *Micro-economic Theory.* New York: McGraw Hill.

Lazear, E. P. 1986. "Salaries and Piece Rates." *Journal of Business* 59(3):405–31.

Lee, L. F. 1983. "Generalized Econometric Models with Selectivity." *Econometrica* 51(2):507–12.

Lee, Y., W. Parish, and R. Willis. 1992. "Sons, Daughters, and Intergenerational Support in Taiwan." Population Association of America, Annual Meeting Paper. Revised 1993.

Leibowitz, A. 1974. "Home Investments in Children." Pp. 432–52 in *Economics of the Family,* ed. T. W. Schultz. Chicago: University of Chicago Press.

Levine, N. E. 1987. "Differential Child Care in Three Tibetan Communities." *Population and Development Review* 13(2):281–304.

Levison, D. 1991. "Children's Labor Force Participation and Schooling in Brazil."

Ph.D. dissertation. Department of Economics, University of Michigan, Ann Arbor.

Lewis, M. 1988. *Financing Health Care in Jamaica.* Report No. 3714-04, Urban Institute, Washington, D.C.

Lewis, W. A. 1955. *The Theory of Economic Growth.* London: Allen and Unwin.

Liedholm, C., and D. C. Mead. 1987. "Small-Scale Industry." Pp. 308–30 in *Strategies for African Development,* ed. R. J. Berg and J. S. Whitaker. Berkeley: University of California Press.

Lillard, L. A., and R. J. Willis. 1993. "Intergenerational Educational Mobility: Effects of Family and State in Malaysia." *Journal of Human Resources.* Forthcoming.

Litvack, J., and C. Bodart. 1992. *User Fees and Quality of Health Care in Cameroon: Policy Implications of a Field Experiment.* World Bank, Washington, D.C. Processed.

Lloyd, C., and A. Brandon. 1991. *Women's Role in Maintaining Households: Poverty and Gender Inequality in Ghana.* Population Council Working Paper no. 25. New York.

Londoño de la Cuesta, J. L. 1990. "Income Distribution during the Structural Transformation: Colombia 1938–88." Ph.D dissertation. Harvard University.

Lucas, R. E. B., and O. Stark. 1985. "Motivations to Remit: Evidence from Botswana." *Journal of Political Economy* 93(5):701–18.

Lundberg, S. J., and R. Starz. 1983. "Private Discrimination and Social Intervention in Competitive Labor Markets." *American Economic Review* 73(3):340–47.

Lututtala, M. 1991. "Modernization et Déséquilibres Démographiques en Zaire." Seminar on nuptiality in sub-Saharan Africa, current changes and impacts on fertility. INED, Paris.

Maassen van den Brink, H. 1991. "Arbeidsdeelname tegen elke prijs? Keuzen van ouders en de zorg voor kinderen" (Labor force participation at what price? Parent's choices and the care of children). Pp. 9–27 in *Wetenschappers over kinderopvang in Nederland, Uit en Thuis* (Social Research about childcare in the Netherlands, Out and at Home), ed. E. Singer and K. Tijdens. Utrecht: Jan van Arkel.

———. 1994. "Female Labor Supply, Childcare and Marital Conflict." Amsterdam: Amsterdam University Press.

MaCurdy, T. 1981. "An Empirical Model of Labor Supply in a Life-Cycle Setting." *Journal of Political Economy* 89(6):1059–85.

Maddala, G. S. 1983. *Limited-Dependent and Qualitative Variables in Econometrics.* New York: Cambridge University Press.

Malathy, R. 1989. "Labor Supply Behavior of Married Women in Urban India." Economic Growth Center Discussion Paper no. 585. Yale University.

Manning, P. 1988. *Francophone Sub-Saharan Africa 1880–1985.* Cambridge: Cambridge University Press.

Manning, W., J. Newhouse, N. Duan, E. Keeler, A. Leibowitz, and M. Marquis. 1987. "Health Insurance and the Demand for Medical Care: Evidence from a Randomized Experiment." *American Economic Review* 77(3):251–77.

Manser, M. E., and M. Brown. 1980. "Marriage and Household Decision-Making: A Bargaining Analysis." *International Economic Review* 21(1):31–44.

Manski, C., and D. McFadden, eds. 1981. *Structural Analysis of Discrete Data: With Economic Application.* Cambridge: MIT Press.

Manton, K., M. Woodbury, and E. Stallard. 1991. "Statistical and Measurement

Issues in Assessing the Welfare Status of Aged Individuals and Populations.'' *Journal of Econometrics* 50(1/2):151–81.

Mare, R. D. 1979. ''Social Background Composition and Educational Growth.'' *Demography* 16(1):55–72.

———. 1980. ''Social Background and School Continuation Decisions.'' *Journal of the American Statistical Association* 75(370):295–305.

Martin, L. 1989a. ''Emerging Issues in Cross-National Survey Research on Aging in Asia.'' *Proceedings of the International Conference on the International Union for the Scientific Study of Population*, vol. 3, 69–80. New Delhi: International Union.

———. 1989b. ''Living Arrangements of the Elderly in Fiji, Korea, Malaysia and the Philippines.'' *Demography* 26(4):627–43.

Masters, S. H. 1969. ''The Effect of Family Income on Children's Education: Some Findings on Inequality of Opportunity.'' *Journal of Human Resources* 4(2):158–75 (Spring).

McElroy, M. B. 1990. ''The Empirical Content of Nash Bargained Household Behavior.'' *Journal of Human Resources* 25(4):559–83.

McElroy, M. B., and M. J. Horney. 1981. ''Nash-Bargained Household Decisions: Toward a Generalization of the Theory of Demand.'' *International Economic Review* 22(2):333–50.

McKeown, T., and R. G. Record. 1962. ''Reasons for the Decline of Mortality in England and Wales during the 19th Century.'' *Population Studies* 16(2):94–122.

Meekers, D. 1988. ''Consequences of Marriage and Premarital Childbearing in Côte d'Ivoire.'' Seminar on nuptiality in sub-Saharan Africa, current changes and impact on fertility. INED, Paris.

Mello, M. F. 1982. *Uma Análise da Participação Feminia no Mercado de Trabalho no Brasil.* M.Sc. dissertation. Pontificia Universidade Catolica, Rio de Janeiro.

Mencher, J. P. n.d. ''Female-Headed/Female-Supported Households in India: Who Are They and What Survival Strategies Are Possible for Them?'' Paper prepared for Joint Population Council/International Center for Research on Women. Lehman College and CUNY Graduate Center, New York.

Menchik, P. 1993. ''Economic Status as a Determinant of Mortality among Black and White Older Males.'' *Population Studies.* Forthcoming.

Merrick, T. W., and M. Schmink. 1983. ''Households Headed by Women and Urban Poverty in Brazil.'' Pp. 244–71 in *Women and Poverty in the Third World,* ed. M. Buvinic, M. A. Lycette, and W. P. McGreevey. Baltimore: Johns Hopkins University Press.

Michael, R. T. 1982. ''Measuring Non-Monetary Benefits of Education: A Survey.'' In *Financing Education,* ed. W. W. McMahon and T. G. Geske. Urbana: University of Illinois Press.

Michel, C., and J. Cintrón. 1988. ''Ivory Coast.'' Pp. 667–79 in *World Education Encyclopedia*, vol. 2, ed. G. T. Kurian. New York: Facts On File.

Miller, B. D. 1982. ''Female Labor Participation and Female Seclusion in Rural India: A Regional View.'' *Economic Development and Cultural Change* 30(4):777–794.

Miller, J., J. Trussell, A. Pebley, and B. Vaughan. 1992. ''Birth Spacing and Mortality in Bangladesh and the Philippines.'' *Demography* 29(2):305–18.

Mincer, J. 1962. ''Labor Force Participation of Married Women: A Study of Labor Supply.'' In *Aspects of Labor Economics,* ed. H. G. Lewis. Universities National Bureau Committee for Economic Research. Princeton: Princeton University Press.

———. 1963. "Opportunity Costs and Income Effects." Pp. 67–82 in *Measurement in Economics,* ed. C. Christ et al. Stanford: Stanford University Press.

———. 1974. *Schooling Experience and Earnings.* New York: Columbia University Press for National Bureau of Economic Research.

———. 1978. "Family Migration Decisions," *Journal of Political Economy* 86(5):749–73.

———. 1985. "Inter-Country Comparisons of Labor Force Trends and of Related Developments." *Journal of Labor Economics* 3(1, part 1):S1–32.

Mincer, J., and S. Polachek. 1974. "Family Investments in Human Capital: Earnings of Women." *Journal of Political Economy* 82(2):S76–108.

Monson, T. D. 1979. "Educational Returns in the Ivory Coast." *Journal of Developing Areas* 13:415–30.

Moock, P., and J. Leslie. 1986. "Childhood Malnutrition and Schooling in the Terai Region of Nepal." *Journal of Development Economics* 120(1):33–52.

Mueller, E. 1975. "The Impact of Agricultural Change on Demographic Development in the Third World." Pp. 307–44 in *Population Growth and Economic Development in the Third World,* vol. 1, ed. L. Tabah. Dolhain: Ordina Editions.

Mukhopadhyay, S. K., 1991. "Adapting Household Behavior to Agricultural Technology in West Bengal, India: Wage Labor, Fertility and Child Schooling Determinants." Economic Growth Center Discussion Paper No. 631. Yale University.

Murphy, K. M., and F. Welch. 1990. "Empirical Age-Earnings Profiles." *Journal of Labor Economics* 8(2):202–29.

Mwabu, G. M. 1986. "Health Care Decisions at the Household Level: Results of a Rural Health Survey in Kenya." *Social Science and Medicine* 22(3):315–19.

———. 1989. "Nonmonetary Factors in the Household Choice of Medical Facilities." *Economic Development and Cultural Change* 37(2):383–92.

Nakosteen, R. A., and M. Zimmer. 1980. "Migration and Income: The Question of Self-Selection." *Southern Economic Journal* 46(3):840–51.

Nash, J., and M. P. Fernandez-Kelley, eds. 1983. *Women, Men, and the International Division of Labor.* Albany: State University of New York Press.

Newman, J. L. 1987. "Labor Market Activity in Côte d'Ivoire." Welfare and Human Resources Division, Living Standards Measurement Study Working Paper no. 36. World Bank, Washington, D.C.

Newman, J. L., and P. J. Gertler. 1992. "Family Productivity, Labor Supply and Welfare in a Low Income Country." Paper presented at the Conference on Women's Human Capital and Development, Bellagio, Italy (May).

Ngondo, P. 1988. "Les législations sur le mariage en Afrique sud de Sahara." Seminar on nuptiality in sub-Saharan Africa, current changes and impact on fertility. INED, Paris.

Norris, M. E. 1992. "The Impact of Development on Women: A Specific-Factors Analysis." *Journal of Development Economics* 38(January):183–201.

Okojie, C. 1991. "Fertility Response to Child Survival in Nigeria." Pp. 93–112 in *Research in Population Economics,* vol. 7, ed. T. P. Schultz. Greenwich, Conn.: JAI Press.

Over, M., R. Ellis, J. Huber, and O. Solon. 1992. "The Consequences of Adult Ill-Health," Pp. 161–207 in *The Health of Adults in the Developing World,* ed. R. Feachem, T. Kjellstrom, C. Murray, M. Over, and M. Phillips. Oxford: Oxford University Press.

Oyeneye, O. 1981. "Factors Influencing Entry into the Informal Sector Apprenticeship System: The Nigerian Case." *African Social Research* 31:1–27.

Papanek, H. 1990. "To Each Less than She Needs, To Each More than She Can Do: Allocations, Entitlement and Value." Pp. 162–81 in *Persistent Inequalities: Women and World Development,* ed. I. Tinker. New York: Oxford University Press.

Parish, W. L., and R. J. Willis. 1993. "Daughters, Education, and Family Budgets: Taiwan Experiences." *Journal of Human Resources* 28(4):863–98. This book.

Parsons, D. O. 1984. "On the Economics of Intergenerational Control." *Population and Development Review* 10(1):41–54.

Pastore, José, H. Zylberstajn, and C. S. Pagotto. 1983. "Mudanca Social e Pobreza no Brasil: 1970–1980 (O que Ocorreu com a Familia Brasileira?)." Estudos Econômicos, FIPE/PIONEIRA, São Paulo, Brazil.

Pebley, A., and J. DaVanzo. 1988. "Maternal Depletion and Child Survival in Guatemala and Malaysia." Rand Corporation, Santa Monica. Processed.

Peil, M. 1981. *Cities and Suburbs: Urban Life in West Africa.* New York: Africana Publishing Co.

Pilon, M. 1988. "Nuptialité et système matrimoniale chez les Moba-Gourma du nord Togo." Seminar on nuptiality in sub-Saharan Africa, current changes and impact on fertility. INED, Paris.

Pitt, M., and M. R. Rosenzweig. 1985. "Health and Nutrition Consumption across and within Farm Households." *Review of Economics and Statistics* 47(2):212–23.

———. 1986. "Agricultural Prices, Food Consumption, and the Health and Productivity of Indonesian Farmers." Pp. 153–82 in *Agricultural Household Models: Extensions, Applications, and Policy,* ed. I. Singh, L. Squire, and J. Strauss. Baltimore: Johns Hopkins University Press.

———. 1990. "Estimating the Intrafamily Incidence of Health: Child Illness and Gender-Inequality in Indonesian Households." University of Minnesota. Processed.

Pitt, M. M., M. R. Rosenzweig, and M. D. N. Hassan. 1990. "Productivity, Health, and Inequality in the Intrahousehold Distribution of Food in Low Income Countries." *American Economic Review* 80(5):1139–56.

Pope, C. L. 1992. "Adult Mortality in America Before 1900." In *Strategic Factors in Nineteenth Century American Economic History,* ed. C. Goldin and H. Rockoff. Chicago: University of Chicago Press.

Pott-Buter, H. 1993. "Facts and Fairy Tails about Female Labor, Family and Fertility: A Seven Country Comparison 1850–1990." Amsterdam: Amsterdam University Press (dissertation).

Powell, B., and L. C. Steelman. 1989. "The Liability of Having Brothers: Paying for College and the Sex Composition of the Family." *Sociology of Education* 62(2):134–47.

Preston, S. H. 1976a. "Family Sizes of Children and Family Sizes of Women." *Demography* 13(1):105–14.

———. 1976b. *Mortality Patterns in National Populations.* New York: Academic Press.

Preston, S. H., and M. Haines. 1991. *The Fatal Years.* Princeton: Princeton University Press.

Preston, S. H., and J. A. Weed. 1976. "Causes of Death Responsible for International and Intertemporal Variation in Sex Mortality Differentials." World Health Organization Report, Geneva.

Psacharopoulos, G. 1985. "Returns to Education: A Further International Update and Implications." *Journal of Human Resources* 20(4):583–97.

———. 1989. "Time Trends in the Returns to Education." *Economics of Education Review* 8(3):225–331.

Psacharopoulos, G., and A. M. Arriagada. 1989. "The Determinants of Early Age Human Capital Formation Evidence from Brazil." *Economic Development and Cultural Change* 37(4):683–708.

Psacharopoulos, G., and W. Loxley. 1985. *Diversified Secondary Education and Development: Evidence from Colombia and Tanzania.* Baltimore: Johns Hopkins University Press.

Psacharopoulos, G., and Z. Tzannatos. 1989. "Female Labor Force Participation: An International Perspective." *World Bank Research Observer* 4(2):187–202.

Psacharopoulos, G., and M. Woodhall. 1985. *Education for Development.* New York: Oxford University Press.

Rahman, O., A. Foster, and J. Menken. 1992. "Older Widow Mortality in Rural Bangladesh." *Social Science and Medicine* 34(1):89–96.

Ram, R., and T. W. Schultz. 1979. "Life Span, Health, Savings and Productivity." *Economic Development and Cultural Change* 27(3):399–422.

Reed, S. 1990. "Characteristics of Health Facilities in Nigeria." World Bank, Washington, D.C. Processed.

Rees, H., and A. Shah. 1986. "An Empirical Analysis of Self-Employment in the U.K." *Journal of Applied Econometrics* 1:95–108.

Republic of Kenya. 1989. *Development Plan, 1989–1993.* Government Printer, Nairobi.

Rimmer, D. 1984. *The Economies of West Africa.* New York: St. Martin's Press.

Rivers, D., and Q. Vuong. 1988. "Limited Information Estimators and Exogeneity Tests for Simultaneous Probit Models." *Journal of Econometrics* 39(3):347–66.

Robertson, D., and J. Symons. 1990. "The Occupational Choice of British Children." *Economic Journal* 100(402):828–41.

Rosen, S. 1974. "Hedonic Functions and Implicit Markets." *Journal of Political Economy* 82(1):34–55.

Rosenhouse, S. 1988. "Identifying The Poor: Is Headship a Useful Concept?" Population Council, New York. Processed.

Rosenzweig, M. R. 1982. "Wage Structure and Sex-Based Wage Inequality: The Family as Intermediary." *Population and Development Review* 8(Supplement):S192–206.

———. 1986. "Program Interventions, Intrahousehold Distribution and the Welfare of Individuals: Modeling Household Behavior." *World Development* 14(2):232–43.

———. 1988. "Risk, Implicit Contracts and the Family in Rural Areas of Low-Income Countries." *Economic Journal* 98(4):1148–70.

Rosenzweig, M. R., and H. P. Binswanger. 1993. "Wealth, Weather Risk and the Composition of Agricultural Investments." *Economic Journal* 103(416):56–78.

Rosenzweig, M. R., and R. E. Evenson. 1977. "Fertility, Schooling, and the Economic Contribution of Children in Rural India: An Econometric Analysis." *Econometrica* 45(5):1065–80.

Rosenzweig, M. R., and T. P. Schultz. 1982. "Market Opportunities, Genetic Endowments and Intrafamily Resource Distribution: Child Survival in Rural India." *American Economic Review* 72(4):803–15.

———. 1983. "Estimating a Household Production Function." *Journal of Political Economy* 91(5):723–46.

Rosenzweig, M. R., and O. Stark. 1989. "Consumption Smoothing, Migration, and Marriage: Evidence from Rural India." *Journal of Political Economy* 94(4):905–26.

Rosenzweig, M. R., and K. I. Wolpin. 1985. "Specific Experience, Household Structure and Intergenerational Transfers: Farm Family Land and Labor

Arrangements in Developing Countries." *Quarterly Journal of Economics* 100(Supplement):461–87.

———. 1993a. "Intergenerational Support and the Life-Cycle Incomes of Young Men and Their Parents." *Journal of Labor Economics* 11(1):84–112.

———. 1993b. "Credit Market Constraints and the Accumulation of Durable Production Assets in Low-Income Countries: Investments in Bullocks." *Journal of Political Economy* 101(2):223–43.

Roumasset, J., and M. Uy. 1980. "Piece Rates, Time Rates, and Teams: Explaining Patterns in the Employment Relation." *Journal of Economic Behavior and Organization* 1(4):343–60.

Roussel, L. 1975. "Ivory Coast." Pp. 657–78 in *Population Growth and Socioeconomic Change in West Africa,* ed. John C. Caldwell. New York: Columbia University Press.

Sahelton, B. A. 1990. "The Distribution of Household Tasks: Does Wife's Employment Status Make a Difference?" *Journal of Family Issues* 11(2):115–35.

Sahn, D. E., and H. Alderman. 1988. "The Effect of Human Capital on Wages and the Determinants of Labor Supply in a Developing Country." *Journal of Development Economics* 29(2):157–83.

Salaff, J. W. 1981. *Working Daughters of Hong Kong.* Cambridge: Cambridge University Press.

Schultz, T. P. 1980. "Estimating Labor Supply Functions for Married Women." Pp. 25–89 in *Female Labor Supply: Theory and Estimation,* ed. J. Smith. Princeton: Princeton University Press.

———. 1981. *Economics of Population.* Reading, Mass.: Addison-Wesley.

———. 1987. "School Expenditures and Enrollments, 1960–1980." In *National Academy of Sciences Background Papers,* ed. D. G. Johnson and R. Lee, Population Growth and Economic Development. Madison: University of Wisconsin Press.

———. 1988. "Education Investment and Returns." Pp. 543–630 in *Handbook of Development Economics,* vol. 1, ed. H. Chenery and T. N. Srinivasan. Amsterdam: Elsevier Science Publishers.

———. 1989a. "Women and Development. Objectives, Framework, and Policy Interventions." Population and Human Resources Department, Working Paper WPS 200. World Bank, Washington, D.C.

———. 1989b. "Accounting for Public Expenditures on Education." Paper presented at a conference on Human Capital and Economic Growth, Buffalo, N.Y. (May).

———. 1990a. "Women's Changing Participation in the Labor Force: A World Perspective." *Economic Development and Cultural Change* 38(3):457–88.

———. 1990b. "Testing the Neoclassical Model of Family Labor Supply and Fertility." *Journal of Human Resources* 25(4):599–634.

———. 1991. "International Differences in Labor Force Participation in Families and Firms." Yale University Working Paper (July). Paper presented at the American Association for the Advancement of Science Meetings, Washington, D.C. (February 1991).

———. 1993. "Investments in the Schooling and Health of Women and Men: Quantities and Returns." *Journal of Human Resources* 28(4):694–734. This book.

———. 1994a. "Marriage and Fertility in the United States: The Role of Welfare and Labor Markets." *Journal of Human Resources* 29(2):637–69.

———. 1994b. "Human Capital, Family Planning and Their Effects on Population Growth." *American Economic Review* 83(3):255–60.

Schultz, T. P., and A. Tansel. 1992. "Measurement of Returns to Adult Health:

Morbidity Effects on Wage Rates in Côte d'Ivoire and Ghana." Economic Growth Center Discussion Paper no. 663. Yale University.

Schultz, T. W., 1961. "Investments in Human Capital." *American Economic Review* 51(1):1–17.

———. 1975. "The Ability to Deal with Disequilibria." *Journal of Economic Literature* 13(3):827–46.

Schultz, T. W., ed. 1974. *Economics of the Family, Marriage, Children and Human Capital.* Chicago: University of Chicago Press.

Scott, E. P. 1985. "Lusaka's Informal Sector in National Economic Development." *Journal of Developing Areas* 20:71–100.

Scully, G. W. 1979. "Mullahs, Muslims and Marital Sorting." *Journal of Political Economy* 87(5, Part 1):1139–43.

Sen, A. 1990. "Gender and Cooperative Conflicts." Pp. 123–49 in *Persistent Inequalities,* ed. I. Tinker. New York: Oxford University Press.

Shinn, M. 1978. "Father Absence and Children's Cognitive Development." *Psychological Bulletin* (University of Michigan) 85(2):295–324.

Sindelar, J. 1982. "Differential Use of Medical Care by Sex." *Journal of Political Economy* 90(5):1003–19.

Smith, J. P., ed. 1980. *Female Labor Supply: Theory and Estimation.* Princeton: Princeton University Press.

Smith, J. P., D. Thomas, and L. Karoly. 1992. "On the Road: Marriage and Mobility in Malaysia." Paper presented at the Conference on Women's Human Capital and Development, Bellagio, Italy (May).

Smith, J. P., and M. P. Ward. 1984. *Women's Wages and Work in the Twentieth Century.* Rand Corporation, Santa Monica.

Smith, R. J., and R. W. Blundell. 1986. "An Exogeneity Test for a Simultaneous Equation Tobit Model with an Application to Labor Supply." *Econometrica* 54(3):679–85.

Smolensky, E., S. Danziger, and P. Gottschalk. 1987. "The Declining Significance of Age in the United States: Trends in the Well-Being of Children and the Elderly since 1939." Institute for Research on Poverty Discussion Paper no. 839-87. Madison: University of Wisconsin.

Statistical Institute of Jamaica. 1990. *Demographic Statistics.* Kingston, Jamaica.

Steelman, L. C., and B. Powell. 1989. "Acquiring Capital for College." *American Sociological Review* 54(5):844–55.

———. 1991. "Parental Willingness to Pay for Higher Education." *American Journal of Sociology* 96(6):1505–29.

Steinmetz, G., and E. O. Wright. 1989. "The Fall and Rise of the Petty Bourgoisie: Changing Patterns of Self-Employment in the Postwar United States." *American Journal of Sociology* 94(5):973–1018.

Stern, S. 1989. "Measuring the Effect of Disability on Labor Force Participation." *Journal of Human Resources* 24(3):361–95.

Stewart, A., R. Hays, and J. Ware. 1988. "The MOS Short-Form General Health Survey: Reliability and Validity in a Patient Population." *Medical Care* 26(7):724–35.

Stewart, A., J. Ware, R. Brook, and A. Davies-Avery. 1978. *Conceptualization and Measurement of Health Status for Adults in the Health Insurance Study,* vol. 6, *Physical Health in Terms of Functioning.* R-1987/2-HEW. Rand Corporation, Santa Monica.

Stolnitz, G. 1955, 1956. "A Century of International Mortality Trends." Part I, *Population Studies* 9(1):24–55; Part II, *Population Studies* 10(1):17–42.

Strauss, J. 1986. "Does Better Nutrition Raise Farm Productivity?" *Journal of Political Economy* 94(2):297–320.

———. 1993. "The Impact of Improved Nutrition on Labor Productivity and Human Resource Development." Pp. 149–70 in *Political Economy of Food and Nutrition Policies,* ed. P. Pinstrup-Andersen. Baltimore: Johns Hopkins University Press.

Strauss, J., P. Gertler, O. Rahman, and K. Fox. 1993. "Gender and Life-Cycle Differentials in the Patterns and Determinants of Adult Health." *Journal of Human Resources* 28(4):791–837. This book.

Strauss, J., and D. Thomas. 1991. "Wages, Schooling and Background Investments in Men and Women in Urban Brazil." Economic Growth Center Discussion Paper No. 649. Yale University.

Summers, R., and A. Heston. 1991. "The Penn World Tables (Mark 5): An Expanded Set of International Comparisons, 1950–1988." *Quarterly Journal of Economics* 106:327–68; computer diskette supplement.

Sun, T. H., H. S. Lin, and R. Freedman. 1978. "Trends in Fertility, Family Size Preferences, and Family Planning Practice: Taiwan, 1961–76." *Studies in Family Planning* 9(4):54–70.

Sundström, M. 1991. "Sweden: Supporting Work, Family and Gender Equality." In *Child-Care, Parental Leave and the Under 3s: Policy Innovation in Europe,* ed. S. B. Kamerman, and A. J. Kahn. New York: Auburn House.

Sundström, M., and F. Stafford. 1991. "Female Labor Force Participation, Fertility, and Public Policy." Stockholm Research Reports in Demography no. 63. Stockholm, Sweden.

———. 1992. "Parental Leaves? Female Labor Force Participation and Public Policy in Sweden." *European Journal of Population* 8:199–215.

Tang, S. L. W. 1981. "The Differential Educational Attainment of Children: An Empirical Study of Hong Kong." Ph.D. dissertation. University of Chicago.

Tanner, J. M. 1981. *A History of the Study of Human Growth.* Cambridge: Cambridge University Press.

Tansel, A. 1993. "School Attainment, Parental Education and Gender in Côte d'Ivoire and Ghana." Economic Growth Center Discussion Paper no. 692. Yale University.

Taubman, P., and J. R. Behrman. 1986. "Effect of Number and Position of Siblings on Child and Adult Outcomes." *Social Biology* 33(1/2):22–34.

Thomas, D. 1990. "Intra-Household Resource Allocation: An Inferential Approach." *Journal of Human Resources* 25(4):635–64.

———. 1991. "Like Father, Like Son: Gender Differences in Household Resource Allocations." Economic Growth Center Discussion Paper no. 619. Yale University.

Thomas, D., V. Lavy, and J. Strauss. 1992. "Public Policy and Anthropometric Outcomes in Côte d'Ivoire." Living Standards Measurement Survey Working Paper no. 89. World Bank, Washington, D.C.

Thomas, D., and J. Strauss. 1992. "Health, Wealth and Wages of Men and Women in Urban Brazil." Paper presented at the Conference on Women's Human Capital and Development, Bellagio, Italy (May).

Thomas, D., J. Strauss, and M. Henriques. 1990. "Child Survival, Height for Age and Household Characteristics in Brazil." *Journal of Development Economics* 33(1):197–234.

Thompson, V., and R. Adloff. 1968. *French West Africa.* New York: Greenwood Press.

Thornton, A., M. C. Chang, and T. H. Sun. 1984. "Social and Economic Change, Intergenerational Relationships, and Family Formation in Taiwan." *Demography* 21(4):475–99.

Tinbergen, J. 1951. "Remarks on the Distribution of Labor Incomes." *International Economics Papers* 1:195–207.

Tinker, I. 1987. "Street Food: Testing Assumptions about Informal Sector Activity by Women and Men." *Current Sociology* 35(3).

———. 1990. *Persistent Inequalities: Women and World Development.* New York: Oxford University Press.

Townsend, R. 1989. "Risk and Insurance in Village India." University of Chicago. Processed.

Tunali, I. 1986. "A General Structure for Models of Double Selection and an Application to a Joint Migration-Earnings Process with Remigration." Pp. 235–82 in *Research in Labor Economics,* vol. 8, Part B, ed. R. G. Ehrenberg. Greenwich, Conn.: JAI Press.

United Nations. 1982. *Levels and Trends of Mortality Since 1950.* Department of International Economic and Social Affairs, ST/ESA/SER.A/74. New York.

———. 1990. *Statistical Yearbook.* United Nations, Paris.

———. 1992. *WISTAT: Women's Indicators and Statistics Spreadsheet Database for Microcomputers (Version 2): Users Guide and Reference Manual.* United Nations, New York.

United Nations, Department of International Economics and Social Affairs. 1987. *Fertility Behavior in the Context of Development,* Population Studies 100. United Nations, New York.

United Nations Development Programme (UNDP). 1990. *Human Development Report 1990.* New York: Oxford University Press.

———. 1991. *Human Development Report 1991.* New York: Oxford University Press.

United Nations Educational Scientific and Cultural Organization (UNESCO). Various years. *UNESCO Statistical Yearbook.* Paris.

United States Bureau of the Census. Various years. Current Population Reports, Series P-20, various numbers, *Educational Attainment in the United States.* Washington, D.C.: U.S. Government Printing Office.

———. Various years. Current Population Reports, Series P-20, various numbers, *Fertility of American Women.* Washington, D.C.: U.S. Government Printing Office.

———. 1991. *Statistical Abstracts of the United States.* Washington, D.C.: U.S. Government Printing Office.

United States Commissioner of Education. Various years. *Biennial Reports of the Commissioner of Education.* Washington, D.C.: U.S. Government Printing Office.

United States National Center for Health Statistics. 1991. *Vital Statistics of the United States.* Washington, D.C.: U.S. Government Printing Office.

Vallin, J. 1983. "Sex Patterns of Mortality: A Comparative Study of Model Life Tables and Actual Situations with Special Reference to the Cases of Algeria and France." Pp. 443–76 in *Sex Differentials in Mortality: Trends, Determinants, and Consequences,* ed. A. D. Lopez and L. T. Ruzicka. Department of Demography, Australian National University, Canberra.

Van Daal, J., and A. H. Q. M. Merkies. 1984. *Aggregation in Economic Research.* Dordrecht: Reidel.

van der Gaag, J., and W. Vijverberg. 1987. *Wage Determinants in Côte d'Ivoire.* Living Standards Measurement Study Working Paper no. 33. World Bank, Washington, D.C.

van Wieringen, J. C. 1986. "Secular Growth Change." Pp. 307–31 in *Human Growth,* vol. 3, ed. F. Falkner and J. C. Tanner. New York: Plenum Press.

Varian, H. R. 1984. *Microeconomic Analysis.* New York: Norton.

Verbrugge, L. M. 1976. "Sex Differentials in Morbidity and Mortality in the United States." *Social Biology* 23(4):275–96.

———. 1980. "Sex Differences in Complaints and Diagnoses." *Journal of Behavioral Medicine* 3(4):327–55.

———. 1985. "Gender and Health: An Update on Hypotheses and Evidence." *Journal of Health and Social Behavior* 26(3):156–82.

———. 1989. "The Twain Meet: Empirical Explanations of Sex Differences in Health and Mortality." *Journal of Health and Social Behavior* 30(3):282–304.

Vickery, C. 1977. "The Time-Poor: A New Look at Poverty." *Journal of Human Resources* 12(1):28–48.

Vijverberg, W. P. M. 1986. "Consistent Estimates of the Wage Equation when Individuals Choose among Income-Earning Activities." *Southern Economic Journal* 52(4):1028–41.

———. 1990a. "Non-Farm Self-Employment and the Informal Sector in Côte d'Ivoire: A Test of Categorical Identity." *Journal of Developing Areas* 24(4):523–42.

———. 1990b. "Labor Market Dynamics in a Developing Country: Microeconomic Evidence." University of Texas at Dallas. Manuscript.

———. 1991a. "Profits from Self-Employment: The Case of Côte d'Ivoire." *World Development* 19(6):683–96.

———. 1991b. "Returns to Schooling in Non-Farm Self-Employment: An Econometric Case Study of Ghana." University of Texas at Dallas. Manuscript.

———. 1992a. "Measuring Income from Family Enterprises with Household Surveys." *Small Business Economics* 4:287–305.

———. 1992b. "Dual Selection Criteria with Multiple Alternatives: Migration, Work Status, and Wages." Welfare and Human Resources Division, Living Standards Measurement Study Working Paper 78. World Bank, Washington, D.C.

———. 1993. "Educational Investments and Returns for Women and Men in Côte d'Ivoire." *Journal of Human Resources* 28(4):933–74. This book.

Visaria, P. M. n.d. *The Sex Ratio of the Population of India, Census of India 1961,* vol. 1, Monograph 10. New Delhi: Office of the Registrar General.

VNG (Vereniging Nederlandse Gemeenten). 1991. Kinderopvang in gemeenten. Stand van zaken per 31 december 1989, 's-Gravenhage (Childcare in communities: Facts, 31 December 1989). Confederation of Dutch Communities, The Hague.

Waddington, C. J., and K. A. Enyimayew. 1989. "A Price to Pay: The Impact of User Charges in Ashanti-Akim District, Ghana." *International Journal of Health Planning and Management* 4(1):417–47.

Waldron, I. 1983a. "Sex Differences in Human Mortality: The Role of Genetic Factors." *Social Science and Medicine* 17(6):321–33.

———. 1983b. "Sex Differences in Illness Incidence, Prognosis and Mortality." *Social Science and Medicine* 17(16):1107–23.

———. 1986. "What Do We Know about Causes of Sex Differences in Mortality?" *Population Bulletin of the United Nations,* no. 18. United Nations, New York.

Walker, T. S., and J. G. Ryan. 1990. *Village and Household Economics in India's Semi-Arid Tropics.* Baltimore: Johns Hopkins University Press.

Ware, J., R. Brook, A. Davies-Avery, K. Williams, A. Stewart, W. Rogers, C. Donald, and S. Johnston. 1980. *Conceptualization and Measurement of Health Status for Adults in the Health Insurance Study,* vol. 1, *Model of Health and Methodology.* R-1987/1-HEW. Rand Corporation, Santa Monica.

Ware, J., A. Davies-Avery, and R. Brook. 1980. *Conceptualization and*

Measurement of Health Status for Adults in the Health Insurance Study, vol. 6,
Analysis of Relationships among Health Status Measures. R-1987/6-HEW. Rand
Corporation, Santa Monica.

Waterlow, J. C., ed. 1988. *Linear Growth Retardation in Less Developed Countries,*
Nestle Nutrition Workshop Series, vol. 14. New York: Raven Press.

Weiss, A. 1980. "Job Queues and Layoffs in Labor Markets with Flexible Wages."
Journal of Political Economy 88(3):526–38.

———. 1990. *Efficiency Wages: Models of Unemployment, Layoffs and Wage
Dispersion.* Princeton: Princeton University Press.

White, H. 1980. "A Heteroskedasticity-Consistent Covariance Matrix Estimator and
a Direct Test for Heteroskedasticity." *Econometrica* 48(4): 817–30.

Wilcock, D., and E. Chuta. 1982. "Employment in Rural Industries in Eastern
Upper Volta." *International Labour Review* 121(4):455–68.

Williamson, J. G. 1988. "Migration and Urbanization." Pp. 424–65 in *Handbook of
Development Economics,* vol. 1, ed. H. Chenery and T. N. Srinivasan. New
York: Elsevier.

Williamson, N. E. 1976. *Sons or Daughters: A Cross-Cultural Survey of Parental
Preferences.* Beverly Hills: Sage.

Willis, R. J. 1973. "A New Approach to the Economic Theory of Fertility
Behavior." *Journal of Political Economy* 81(2, Part 2):S14–64.

———. 1980. "The Old Age Security Hypothesis and Population Growth." In
Demographic Behavior: Interdisciplinary Perspectives on Decision-Making, ed. T.
Burch. Boulder: Westview.

———. 1982. "The Direction of Intergenerational Transfers and Demographic
Transition: The Caldwell Hypothesis Reexamined." *Population and Development
Review* 8(Supplement):S207–34.

Wingard, D. 1984. "The Sex Differential in Morbidity, Mortality and Lifestyle." In
Annual Review of Public Health, ed. L. Breslow, J. Fielding, and L. Lave. Palo
Alto: Annual Reviews.

Wolf, M. 1975. "Women and Suicide in China." Pp. 111–42 in *Women in Chinese
Society,* ed. M. Wolf and R. Witke. Stanford: Stanford University Press.

Wolfe, B., and J. Behrman. 1984. "Determinants of Women's Health Status and
Health Care Utilization in a Developing Country: A Latent Variable Approach."
Review of Economics and Statistics 56(4):696–703.

Wong, Y. C. 1986. "Entrepreneurship, Marriage, and Earnings." *Review of
Economics and Statistics* 68(4):693–99.

Wood, C. H. 1989. "Women Headed Households and Child Mortality in Brazil,
1960–1980." Department of Sociology. University of Florida, Gainesville.
Processed.

Wood, C. H., and J. Carvalho. 1988. *The Demography of Inequality in Brazil.*
Cambridge: Cambridge University Press.

World Bank. 1981. *World Development Report 1981.* New York: Oxford University
Press.

———. 1990. *Kenya: Human Resources—Improving Quality and Access.* Country
Operations Division, Eastern Africa Department, Washington, D.C.

———. 1991a. *Social Indicators of Development 1990.* Baltimore: Johns Hopkins
University Press.

———. 1991b. *World Development Report 1991.* New York: Oxford University
Press.

———. 1992. *World Development Report 1992.* New York: Oxford University
Press. (Supplementary Data, IV.B.)

Wouters, A. 1991. "Essential National Health Research: Health Care Financing and Quality of Health Care." *International Journal of Health Planning and Management* 6(4):253–71.

Zachariah, K. C., and J. Condé. 1981. *Migration in West-Africa: Demographic Aspects.* New York: Oxford University Press.

Zimmerman, F. E. 1984. "Fertility Measures of Sex Preference in China." M.A. Thesis. Department of Anthropology, Hunter College, City University of New York.

Index

Activity of daily living (ADL) measures, 174–75
Adult health
determinants, 207–8
in developing countries, 171–73
effect of age and socioeconomic factors, 186–207
gender differences, 177–86
per capita household expenditure to explain, 197, 200–205
Adverse selection
in casual labor market, 156–57
efficiency costs, 141–45
in labor markets, 139–40, 14
Age
and division of labor, 52, 54
effect on health, 186–207
reported adult health by, 177–80, 182–85ff
Brazil: as factor in gender gap in wages, 391–92
Aigner, D. J., 146
Ainsworth, M., 41, 315
Akin, J., 216, 219
Alderman, H., 32, 34
Alessie, R., 307
Almeida dos Reis, J. G., 25, 38
Alschuler, L. R., 309, 334
Altonji, J., 115
Altruism, 240–43
Amemiya, T., 220
Andrews, G., 173, 175

Antoine, P., 60
Apprenticeships, Côte d'Ivoire, 308, 326, 330
ARIS-NCAER (Additional Rural Income Survey-National Council of Applied Economic Research), India, 119–21
Arispe, L., 53
ASEAN health surveys, 175

Barclay, G. W., 244
Barnum, H., 215
Barro, R. J., 64
Barros, R., 3, 25, 38, 345, 367, 369, 384
Bassett, T., 59
Basta, S. S., 150
Becker, G. S., 2, 16, 93, 102, 240, 244, 250
Behrman, J. R., 274, 291
Benefits
education, 31
risk pooling, 117
Ben Porath, Y., 33
Bias in sample selection, 33–34, 38–46, 334–36
Bielicki, T., 30
Binswanger, H. P., 131
Birth order effects, 267–72
Bitran, R., 215, 216
Blake, J., 242, 245, 250, 263
Blau, D., 242
Blundell, R. W., 131
Bodart, C., 215
Bodnar, J., 245

The letter *t* following a page number stands for *table;* the letter *f* stands for *figure.*

Body-mass-index, 3
Boggild, L., 58
Bohman, K., 53
Boserup, E., 5, 9, 38, 53, 58, 67, 73, 74, 241
Boskin, M. J., 220
Bouis, H. E., 34, 151
Bowen, W. G., 84
Brandon, A., 54
Breckinridge, S., 84
Brinton, M., 241
Brook, R., 174, 175, 176
Brown, M., 274

Cain, G. G., 146
Caldwell, J. C., 60, 115, 244
Calsing, E. F., 367
Campbell, B., 309, 334
Capacity utilization, Brazil
    as determinant of relative poverty, 357
    female-headed households, 360–62
    in reduction of poverty gap, 377–79
Card, D., 40
Carney, J., 54
Chamberlain, Gary, 122
Chen, L., 244
Child care subsidies
    effect on women's labor force
        participation, 96, 97
    estimates using labor supply model of
        married women, 110–12
Children
    consumption and management, women's
        role in, 35
    Brazil: ages in female-headed
        households, 355–56; in female-headed
        households, 352–56, 360, 364–74; in
        household income classes, 352; labor
        force participation, 367; school
        attendance, 365–67
Chipande, G., 54
Chiswick, C. U., 33
Choi, K. S., 38
Christianson, J. B., 216
Chuta, E., 321
CILSS. See Côte d'Ivoire Living
    Standards Survey (CILSS)
Cintrán, J., 307
Clignet, R., 309
Coate, S., 118
Cochrane, S. H., 31
Cohen, M., 320, 322, 326, 327, 339

Costs
    of education, 31
    efficiency, 141–45
    of information in labor market, 146–48
    of monitoring worker output, 141–42
Côte d'Ivoire Living Standards Survey
    (CILSS), 315–16, 321
Cox, D., 115, 122
Creese, A., 215, 217

Data sources
    adult health status analysis, 176–77,
        209–10
    Côte d'Ivoire employment earnings
        model, 315–16, 318–19, 321
    determinants of adult ill-health, 172–73
    health care demand model, 220–21
    incomplete information and employer
        bias analysis, 151–53, 156, 160–61,
        163–64
    investment in education analysis, 245–49
    poverty in female-headed households,
        345–46
    rural risk pooling and technological
        change analysis, 119–20
    school enrollment model, 276–77
    school enrollment rates, 17, 20, 23
    U-shaped female labor force
        participation, 64–66, 86
    wage rates in area of in-migration,
        162–63
    worker productivity information, 150–53
Davies-Avery, A., 174, 175, 176
Denton, H., 215, 219, 222
Den Tuinder, B. A., 304, 307, 309, 320
Deolalikar, A., 26, 34, 46, 149, 274, 291,
    330, 333
Dependency ratio, Brazil
    as determinant of relative poverty, 357
    female-headed households, 360–62
    impact of higher, 359
Discrimination
    against women in developing countries,
        58–60
    in job-matching and worker rewards, 138
    statistical and taste, 145–46
    tests for statistical and taste, 157–60
    Brazil: wage and occupational, 380–424
    India: caste, 157–60
    Taiwan: by gender, 240–43
    See also Social stigma; Statistical
        discrimination; Taste discrimination

Division of labor, developing country rural
    areas, 52–54
Domencich, T. D., 219
Dor, A., 215, 216
Duncan, O. D., 242
Durand, J., 6, 63, 79
Dvorak, S., 349

Earnings
    life-cycle inequality, 146–48
    Côte d'Ivoire: relation to education, 307
    Indonesia: estimates of returns to
        education, 278–302
Earnings, self-employment, Côte d'Ivoire
    model, 309–15
    model estimates, 326–30
Earnings capacity, Brazil
    as determinant of relative poverty, 357
    determinants of, 358, 362–64
    female-headed households, 360–63
    in reduction of poverty gap, 377–79
ECIEL, 48
Economic Census, Village Potential
    module, Indonesia, 276
Economic development
    changes in education with, 87–88
    effect of, 51
    female education with, 78
    gender equality with, 61–62
    levels of country, 52
    U-shaped female participation rate with,
        63–78, 88
    women's labor force participation with,
        63–78
Education
    altruism theory related to, 240–43
    benefits, 31
    changes with economic development,
        87–88
    effect on health, 189–91, 194, 198t, 207,
        209–10
    factors in lack of, 241–42
    gender differences in returns to, 38–46
    impact of, 58–60
    inverse correlation with fertility, 35–37
    link to health, 34n.11
    patriarchal theory related to, 241
    returns within a level of schooling,
        36–38
    social externalities, 50
    measurement of returns to, 33–34

Brazil: factor in gender gap in wages,
    391–92, 404; intra-occupational gender
    differences, 312–99, 404–8
    Côte d'Ivoire: predicted effect, 331–33;
        private wage returns to, 41, 43–44
    Taiwan: choices, 240–43; determinants
        of women's, 245–66
    See also Expenditures, education;
        Investment in education; School
        enrollment
Education, female
    effect on young women, 57
    in developing countries, 273
    relation to economic development, 78
    Indonesia: secondary, 293–94
    United States, 83
Educational attainment model, Taiwan
    estimates, 250–61
    specification, 249–50
Education levels
    increase with development, 67–68
    women's labor force participation with
        higher, 68, 72–78
    Côte d'Ivoire, 304–7
    Germany, Sweden, the Netherlands:
        relation to women's hours of work,
        107–9
    Indonesia: labor force participation by,
        279–302
Efficiency
    of altruistic investment, 240
    costs of incomplete labor market
        information, 141–44
    See also Nutrition efficiency wage
        theory
Efficiency-wage model, 139
Ellis, R. P., 215, 217–18, 226
Employers
    discrimination with incomplete
        information, 145–46
    job tenure information, 163–64
    learning behavior, 146–48
    worker productivity information, 150–65
Employment
    white-collar, 85–87
    Brazil: gender differences in different
        structures of, 412–18
    United States: marriage bars for
        females, 86
    See also Self-employment, Côte d'Ivoire
Employment earnings model, Côte
    d'Ivoire, 315–16, 318–19, 321

Enyimayew, K. A., 215
Evans, D. S., 308
Evenson, R. E., 299
Expected years of school enrollment, global regions, 17–20, 23–25
Expenditures, education
Côte d'Ivoire, 305
ratio of female-to-male, 24
regions of world, 22–26

Falkner, F., 3, 29
Family enterprises, 53–57
Feachem, R., 173
Female-headed households, Brazil, 376–77
Females. See Education, female; Women; Women, married
Fernandez-Kelly, M. P., 241
Fertility
and human capital, 35–36
related to women's health, 201, 206–7
and women's education, 36–37
Germany, Sweden, Netherlands: relation to labor force participation, 96–101, 102f
Taiwan, 240–41
Fertility and labor force participation model, 92–96
Fertility rates
Germany, Sweden, Netherlands (1940–90), 100
plotted against women's labor force participation, 100, 102f
Fields, G., 33
Finegan, T. A., 84
Fogel, R. W., 3, 15, 27, 29
Folbre, N., 274
Foster, A. D., 118, 142, 146, 151, 157, 166, 174, 327
Foster, P., 309
Fox, L., 3, 345
Franz, W., 99, 100, 104
Fuchs, V. R., 24, 38

Gender
mortality of adults by, 180–81
reported adult health by, 177–80, 182–85ff, 186
India: discrimination, 157–60
Taiwan: discrimination, 240–43
Gender differences
developing-country division of labor, 52
in adult health, 177–86

in returns to schooling, 38–46, 274–75
Brazil: in education, age, and occupation, 391–404; employment structure by, 412–13; factors in wage gap, 391–404; related to position in family constellation, 389–90; in wages, 381, 387–89
Côte d'Ivoire: education, 305–8; in human capital, 305–6
Indonesia: labor market and school enrollment, 279–302; in returns to schooling, 302–3
Thailand: in education, 41
See also Discrimination; Education levels; Men; Women
Gender equality
relation to economic development, 61–62
of U.S. education, 83
Gender preference, 133–36
Gertler, P. J., 32, 215–20, 314
Glaeser, E. L., 147, 160
Glewwe, P., 220, 334
Goldani, A. M., 345
Goldberger, A., 220
Goldin, C., 5, 6, 20, 79, 83, 84, 86, 87, 104, 107, 112, 142, 245, 293, 297, 303
Goreux, L. M., 334
Greene, W. H., 220
Greenhalgh, S., 241
Green revolution, India, 116, 119
Griliches, Z., 33, 38, 244, 250
Gronau, R., 93
Grossman, M., 187, 216
Gruber, J., 111
Guralnik, J., 175
Gustafsson, S., 92, 96, 97, 100, 103, 109–12

Haddad, L. J., 34, 151
Haines, M., 49
Hartmann, H., 241
Hartog, J., 100, 103
Haveman, R., 16
Hays, R., 175
Health
differences over life cycle, 193f, 194–95
effect of education on, 189–91, 194, 196, 198t, 207, 209–10
effect of location on, 207–8
link to education, 34n.11
measurement of returns to, 33–34

as stock of human capital, 187
See also Adult health
Health care demand model
    specification, 217–20
    utility function, 218–19
    variables, 222
Health measures, self-reported, 174–75
Health services
    determinants of demand, 216
    health care demand model, 217–31
    health care demand model policy
        simulations, 231–34
Heckman, J. J., 4, 16, 33, 100, 101, 279
Height
    male-female differences in adult, 29–30
    as measure of nutritional status, 3
Heller, P., 216
Henriques, M., 197
Hermalin, A. I., 244
Heston, A., 64
HIE. *See* RAND Health Insurance
    Experiment (HIE)
Hill, M. A., 66, 174
Hinchcliffe, K., 334
Horney, M. J., 2, 274
Household production
    model, 186–88
    women's role, 52–53, 62
Households
    relation of technological change and
        gender preference, 133–36
    risk pooling and consumption smoothing
        model, 117–19
    Brazil: income, 346–48, 350, 352,
        355–57; resources, 346
    India: estimates of transfers and
        borrowing, 123–29; resource
        allocation, 115–16
Huber, P. J., 250
Human capital
    health as stock of, 187
    investment in, 167–68
    returns to, 136–37
    India: as insurance premium, 117–18
Human capital formation
    Côte d'Ivoire, 305–8
    labor market information effect on,
        138–39
    shift in gender composition, 48–50, 91

IADP. *See* Intensive Agricultural District
    program (IADP), India

ICDDR-B. *See* International Center for
    Diarrheal Disease Research
    (ICDDR-B)
ICRISAT. *See* International Crops
    Research Institute for the Semi-Arid
    Tropics (ICRISAT)
IFPRI. *See* International Food Policy
    Research Institute (IFPRI)
Imhasly, B., 59
Income, household, Brazil
    adult per capita, 346–48
    averages of per capita income and
        poverty gap, 355–57
    children in five classes, 352
    female-headed households, 350
Income distribution, 138
Income effect
    on education and supply of workers, 73
    related to technological change and
        gender preference, 135–36
    on women's labor force participation,
        62–78, 80–81, 84, 88
    Germany, Sweden, Netherlands: relation
        to educational level, 107
Informal sector, developing countries,
    52–53
Information
    casual labor markets, 148
    costs with lack of, 146–48
    efficiency costs of, 141–45
    employer, 163–64
    in job-matching and worker rewards, 138
Information, incomplete
    costs of, 141–42
    employer's statistical and taste
        discrimination with, 145–46
    labor market inefficiency with, 141
    returns to investment with, 143
    unemployment as outcome of, 142–43
    worker allocation with, 141
Insurance arrangements, rural India,
    117–18
Insurance capital
    effect of economic development on, 118
    intrahousehold East Indian, 115–16
    in married women's human capital,
        117–18, 136
    of unmarried women, 118
Intensive Agricultural District Program
    (IADP), India, 121, 131
International Center for Diarrheal Disease
    Research (ICDDR-B), 176

International Crops Research Institute for the Semi-Arid Tropics (ICRISAT), 152–65
International Food Policy Research Institute (IFPRI), 151–65
Investment in education
  levels of returns to, 36–38
  measures of, 17–27
  parents' altruistic, 240–43
  returns to, 36–38
  Western and non-Western societies, 244–45
  Taiwan: determinants, 245–61
  See also Expected years of school enrollment, global regions
Ivorianization, 305, 333

Jacobsson, R., 100, 103
Jain, B., 37
Jamison, D. T., 38
Jimenez, E., 122
Jones, G., 172, 175
Jorgenson, D. W., 16
Jovanovic, B., 308
Ju, A., 172, 175

Khandker, S. R., 46, 131
Killingsworth, M. R., 100
King, E. M., 66
Kinsella, K., 171, 173
Knight, J. B., 25, 38
Knowledge, imperfect, 145
Krueger, A. B., 40
Kutzin, J., 215

Labor force participation
  women: in Asian NECs, 88; with education, 48, 68; effect of economic development, 87–88; effect of tax system and child care subsidies, 92, 94–96; historical U-shaped rate, 62–63, 88; income and substitution effects, 62–78, 80–81, 84, 88; tax system effect, 92, 94–96; U-shaped rate related to economic development, 63–78
  Africa: women, 59–60
  Brazil: children, 367
  Côte d'Ivoire: skilled foreigners, 305, 309, 333–34
  Germany, Sweden: married women with differences in taxation, 109–19

Germany, Sweden, the Netherlands: relation to fertility, 96–100, 102f; men and women, 98–99
  Indonesia: male and female, 279–302; U-shaped curve in, 297; women, 273–75
  United States: married women, 85–88; origins of women's, 78–87
Labor force participation and fertility model, 92–96
Labor markets
  adverse selection, 139–40, 143, 156–57
  casual, 148, 151–65
  casual market job tenure, 163–64
  costs of information in, 146–48
  effect of changes in demand, 240
  efficiency levels with incomplete information, 141–44
  employer's statistical and taste discrimination, 145–46
  information, 138–39, 146–48
  skill hierarchy, 54–55
  with technological change, 54
  women's role in modern, 56–57
  Côte d'Ivoire: Ivorianization policy, 305
  Germany, Sweden, Netherlands: supply with child care subsidies, 110–12
  India: village, 152–53
  Indonesia: demand for educated females, 282; gender outcomes, 279–302
  Philippines, 151
Labor supply model, married women, Germany, Sweden, Netherlands
  wages and income, 100–104
  wages and income with day care subsidy, 110–12
  wages and income with income tax, 104–7
Lam, D., 25, 33
Lau, L. T., 38
Lavy, V., 26, 215, 217, 221–22
Law and the Status of Women, 52
Layard, R., 80, 91, 92
Lazear, Edward, 142
Lee, J.-W., 64
Lee, L. F., 311
Lee, Y., 244
Legal position
  rights of husbands, 53–54
  women in Africa, 60
  of women in India, 60

Legislation
  limiting power of family head, 58
  to prevent change in women's position,
    58
  See also Public policy
Leibowitz, A., 242, 245
Levine, N. E., 244
Levison, D., 25, 367
Lewis, H. Gregg, 250
Lewis, W. Arthur, 61
Lillard, L. A., 244
Literacy, 273, 276
Litvak, J., 215
Lloyd, C., 54
Locay, L., 217
Londoño de la Cuesta, J. L., 25, 38
Lucas, R. E. B., 115
Lundberg, S. J., 144
Lututtala, M., 60

Maasen van den Brink, H., 111
McElroy, M. B., 2, 274
McFadden, D., 219, 220
McKeown, T., 49
Maddala, G. S., 103, 219
Malaysian Family Life Survey (MFLS-2),
    176
Mamdani, M., 174
Manser, M. E., 274
Manski, C., 220
Mare, R. D., 250
Martin, L., 172
Medical care quality
  health care demand model policy
    simulations, 231–34
  health care demand model specification
    and estimates, 217–31
  relation to health, 214–15
Meekers, D., 60
Men
  control of wives in developing countries,
    58–60
  education with reduced resource
    constraints, 72–73
  expected years of enrollment in
    education, 17–20, 23–24
  expected years of school enrollment by
    regions, 17–20
  investment in schooling across regions,
    17–27
  life expectancy, 27–30
  mortality, 27–30
  private wage returns to education, 40–47
  role in developing country family
    business, 53–54
  schooling completed in selected
    countries, 20–22
  years of schooling completed, 21–22
  Brazil: earnings capacity, 362–64;
    education of working men, 404–5
  Côte d'Ivoire: earnings and returns to
    education, 333
  Germany, Sweden, the Netherlands:
    labor force participation, 98–99
  Indonesia: returns to schooling, 302;
    secondary school enrollment, 293
Mendonça, R., 3, 367, 369
Menken, J., 174
Merrick, T. W., 345, 346, 348, 349, 350
MFLS-2. *See* Malaysian Family Life
    Survey (MFLS-2)
Michael, R. T., 16
Michel, C., 307
Mincer, J., 2, 3, 5, 6, 7, 34, 48, 49, 80, 91,
    92, 101, 104, 146, 275
Mincer earnings function, 101
Modernization, 56–57
Monson, T. D., 334
Mortality
  of adults in developing countries,
    173–75, 180–81
  male and female differences, 27–30
Mueller, E., 244
Muñoz, J., 41, 315
Murphy, K., 40
Mwabu, G. M., 215, 217–18, 220, 226

Nanitelamie, J., 60
Nash, J., 241
National Socioeconomic Survey
    (SUSENAS), Indonesia, 276
Newman, J. L., 307, 314, 320
Ngondo, P., 52
Norris, M. E., 62
Nutritional status
  calorie intake, 164–66
  effect of adequate diet, 29–30
  food consumption, 148–50
  as measure of human capital, 3
  relation to health, 27–30
Nutrition efficiency wage theory, 148–50,
    164–65

Occupations, Brazil
factor in gender gap in wages, 392–404
intra-occupational gender gap in wages, 404–12
Over, M., 171, 174

Pagotto, C. S., 346, 349
Papenek, H., 59
Parish, W., 244
Pastore, José, 346, 349
Peil, M., 321
Pilon, M., 60
Pitt, M. M., 30, 34, 149
PNADs (Pesquisas Nacional por Amostra de Domicílios), Brazil
in gender differences analysis, 381–87
poverty in female-headed household analysis, 345
Pope, C. L., 27
Pott-Buter, H., 112
Poverty, Brazil
among households, 352
of children in female-headed households, 352–54, 357, 367–68, 372–74
determinants in female-headed households, 355–64
in female-headed households, 348–52, 357, 376–77, 379
measurement of relative female-headed household, 355–57
Poverty effect, Brazil
components in estimation of, 368–71
measurement, 371–73
Poverty gap, Brazil, 377–79
Powell, B., 242, 245, 264–65
Preston, S. H., 27, 28–29, 49, 245
Psacharopoulos, G., 24, 31, 36, 37, 38, 63, 322
Public policy
health care demand model simulations, 231–34
Ivorianization in Côte d'Ivoire, 305, 333
See also Legislation

Quigley, J. M., 215, 217, 221–22

Rahman, O., 174
Ramos, L., 383
RAND Health Insurance Experiment (HIE), 175, 176
RAND Medical Outcomes study, 175
Ravallion, M., 118

Record, R. G., 49
Reed, S., 215
Resource allocation
effect of technical change on intrahousehold, 118–19
intrahousehold East Indian, 117–18
relation to marriage-based risk pooling, 116
in returns to human capital, 136–37
Returns to education
gender differences, 38–46
measurement, 33–34
social and private, 31–33, 36–38
Côte d'Ivoire: estimates of self-employment earnings, 326–30; model estimates of wage earnings, 322–26
Indonesia: males and females, 274–75, 294–95, 302
Thailand: for men and women, 41–42
United States, 44–46
See also Earnings; Income effect; Income, household; Returns to schooling model, Indonesia; Wages
Returns to health measurement, 33–34
Returns to human capital, 136–37
Returns to schooling. See Returns to education
Returns to schooling model, Indonesia
paid labor force participation by gender, 284–97
specifications, 278–79
Rimmer, D., 334
Risk pooling, rural India, 116–17
Risk pooling and consumption smoothing model
estimation procedure, 119–23
framework, 117–19
Rivers, D., 197
Robertson, D., 220
Rosen, S., 275
Rosenzweig, M. R., 27, 30, 115, 117, 118, 121, 131, 134, 142, 146, 151, 157, 160, 166, 299, 327
Roumasset, J., 142
Ryan, J. G., 150, 152

Sabot, R. H., 25, 38
Sahn, D. E., 34
Salaff, J. W., 241
Sample selection bias, 33–34, 38–46
Sanderson, W., 217

Schmidt, B. V., 367
Schmink, M., 345, 346, 348, 349, 350
Schoeni, R. F., 33
School attendance, Brazil, 365–67
School enrollment
    expected years and public expenditures,
        22–25
    expected years by regions of world,
        17–20
    increased rates of, 26
    ratio of male to female and years of
        male education, 73–74
    Côte d'Ivoire: rates, 333
    Indonesia: determinants, 297–302;
        gender differences, 279–303; increases
        in, 276
    United States: increase in secondary,
        81–83, 87
School enrollment model, Indonesia,
    277–78
Schooling completed, 20–22
Schultz, T. P., 2, 6, 16, 17, 20, 24, 26, 27,
    30, 31, 33–35, 37, 38, 40, 41, 44, 46,
    48, 58, 63, 66, 102, 115, 134, 174, 330
Schultz, T. W., 2
Sedlacek, G., 4
Selection. See Sample selection bias
Self-employment, Côte d'Ivoire, 305,
    309–15, 326–30
Sen, A., 59
Sex preference. See Gender preference
Skills
    with education in developing countries,
        54–57
    effect of increased requirements for, 240
    hierarchy in modern labor market, 54–55
    traditional, 54
SLC. See Survey of Living Conditions
    (SLC), Jamaica
Smith, J. P., 100, 104
Smith, R. J., 131
Social stigma
    of wife's working, 70–72, 74, 78, 84
    against women's work outside home,
        70–72
Stafford, F., 92, 96, 100, 110
Stark, O., 115, 117, 121
Starz, R., 144
Statistical discrimination, 145–46, 167
Steelman, L. C., 242, 245, 264–65
Stewart, A., 175
Stolnitz, G., 28

Strauss, J., 3, 27, 31, 33, 34, 46, 48, 49,
    149, 164, 197
Substitution effect, 62–78, 80–81, 84, 88
Summers, R., 64
Sundström, M., 100, 111
Survey of Living Conditions (SLC),
    Jamaica, 172
SUSENAS. See National Socioeconomic
    Survey (SUSENAS), Indonesia
Symons, J., 220

Taiwan Women and Family Survey (1989),
    245–49
Tang, S. L. W., 241
Tanner, J. M., 29
Tansel, A., 26, 31, 34, 174
Taste discrimination, 145–46, 167
Tax system
    effect on women's achievements, 7
    effect on women's labor force
        participation, 92, 94–96
    Germany, Sweden, the Netherlands:
        wages and incomes model, 104–9
Technical training, Côte d'Ivoire, 307–8,
    321, 326
Technological change
    effect on labor market organization, 54
    effect on rural risk-sharing and marriage
        insurance premium, 118–19
    gender preference in India with, 133–36
    green revolution in India, 116, 119
    risk pooling and technology adoption in
        India, 129–33
Theeuwes, J., 100, 103
Thomas, D., 2, 33, 35, 46, 48, 49, 63, 115,
    136, 197
Thornton, A., 248
Tinbergen, J., 275
Tinker, I., 48, 52, 53
Tomes, N., 240, 244
Townsend, R., 116
Tzannatos, Z., 63

United Nations, 27, 64
United Nations Development Programme
    (UNDP), 276, 304, 305
U.S. Bureau of the Census, 173
Urbanization, Africa, 60
Uy, M., 142

Van der Gaag, J., 44, 215–19
van Wieringen, J. C., 30

Varian, H., 219
Verbrugge, L. M., 186
Vijverberg, W., 44, 46, 48, 307, 311, 314, 316, 317, 327, 334
Visaria, P. M., 28
VNG, 111
Vuong, Q., 197

Waddington, C. J., 215
Wage discrimination, Brazil, 413–16
Wage returns to education. *See* Returns to education
Wages
  differences related to expected productivity, 167
  relation to food consumption and calorie intake, 148–50, 164
  with employer's taste discrimination, 145
  Brazil: differences in, 381–82; with discrimination, 391–401, 412–18; gender gap related to position in family, 389–90
  Côte d'Ivoire: non-Ivorian men and women, 326–27
  Germany, Sweden, the Netherlands: labor supply model, 100–107, 110–12
  Indonesia: women, 293–94
  See also Nutrition efficiency wage theory
Wage-setting models, 148–50
Waldron, I., 30
Walker, T. S., 150, 152
Ward, M. P., 104
Ware, J., 174, 175, 176
Watts, M., 54
Weed, J. A., 29
Weiss, A., 142, 327
Welch, L., 40
White, H., 250
Wilcock, D., 321
Willis, R. J., 92, 94, 240, 244, 250
Wingard, D., 181
Wolfe, B., 16
Wolpin, K. I., 115, 118
Women
  authority in developing countries, 52–54
  developing-country legislation related to, 58–60
  education/fertility relationship, 35–37
  education in developing countries, 273
  effect of modernization, 56–57
  expected years of enrollment in education, 17–20, 23–24
  impact of education and legal change, 58–60
  in developing-country informal sector, 53
  influences of education on, 31, 35–36
  investment in schooling across regions, 17–27
  labor force participation with education, 72–78
  legal rights of husbands, 53–54
  life expectancy, 27–30
  mortality rates, 27–30
  private wage returns to education, 40–47
  relation of fertility to education, 36–37
  role in children's consumption and management, 35
  role in developing country family business, 52–54, 56–57
  role in modern labor market, 56–57
  schooling completed in selected countries, 20–22
  social stigma against work outside home, 70–72, 74, 78, 84
  sources of handicaps, 51–52
  U-shaped labor force participation, 63–78
  years of schooling completed, 21–22
  discrimination in developing countries, 58–59
  Africa: role in family and business, 59–60; social stratification, 59–60
  Brazil: earnings capacity, 362–64; education of working women, 404–5
  Côte d'Ivoire: earnings and returns to education, 307, 333
  Germany, Sweden, the Netherlands: labor force participation, 98–99, 103; relation of educational levels to work hours, 107–9
  India: discrimination against, 58–60; inferiority of, 58–59
  Indonesia: returns to schooling, 302; secondary school enrollment, 293; as wage earners, 293–94
  Taiwan: education, 245–66
  United States: historical labor force participation, 78–87; secondary school attendance, 83–84; white-collar employment, 85–87

Women, married
  Germany, Sweden, the Netherlands:
    labor supply model, 100–107, 110–12
  India: insurance capital of, 115–18, 136
  United States: white-collar employment,
    85–87
  wages and incomes model of labor
    supply, 100–112
Women, unmarried, 118
Woodhall, M., 24, 31, 36, 38
Worker misallocation, 141–44
Worker productivity
  casual labor market data, 150–53
  known and unknown to employer,
    153–65
  relation to calorie intake, 164
  relation to food consumption, 148–50

World Bank, 20, 24, 41, 171, 215, 273, 275,
  276
World Health Organization (WHO) health
  surveys, 175
Wouters, A., 222

Years of schooling completed
  estimates of men's and women's, 17
  as measure of human capital, 3
  secondary school graduation in United
    States, 81–82
  selected countries, 21–22

Zilberstajn, H., 346, 349
Zimmerman, F. E., 244